LEARNING AND COGNITION IN EDUCATION

LEARNING AND COGNITION IN EDUCATION

EDITOR

VIBEKE GRØVER AUKRUST
Faculty of Education
University of Oslo
Norway

AMSTERDAM • BOSTON • HEIDELBERG • LONDON • NEW YORK • OXFORD
PARIS • SAN DIEGO • SAN FRANCISCO • SINGAPORE • SYDNEY • TOKYO
Academic Press is an imprint of Elsevier

ELSEVIER

ACADEMIC
PRESS

Academic Press is an imprint of Elsevier
The Boulevard Langford Lane, Kidlington, Oxford OX5 1GB, UK

British Library Cataloguing in Publication Data
A catalogue record for this book is available from the British Library

Library of Congress Catalog Number
A catalogue record for this book is available from the Library of Congress

ISBN: 9780123814388

For information on all Elsevier publications
visit our website at books.elsevier.com

Printed in the United States of America
Transferred to Digital Printing, 2012

PREFACE

The 3rd edition of The International Encyclopedia of Education appeared recently, with articles having a comprehensive view of up-to-date knowledge and a global perspective, relevant to anyone who is concerned about education. While the Encyclopedia is primarily meant for libraries, we do believe that research overviews written by distinguished scholars in their areas of specialization should be made available to larger groups of readers. This volume presents a selection of articles on learning and cognition from the Encyclopedia. Leading researchers have been asked to review critically and present in an easily understandable manner the current state of knowledge in their fields of expertise and have put much effort into drafting, writing, and revising thorough and balanced overview articles intended for a broad readership, spanning parents, policy makers, students, teachers, and researchers who want to be updated on areas outside their particular realm of specialization. The result of their work is a comprehensive overview of the major research in learning and cognition, offering a source of reference for readers who want to obtain an introduction that is authoritative without reducing or understating the complexities and uncertainties that characterize most of the available knowledge.

In the last few decades, there has been a growing interest in learning and cognition. There is an increasing understanding among teachers as well as policy makers that to improve educational outcomes a major focus should be on learning and transforming, and what makes students change, learn, and acquire knowledge. Obviously, this is an enormously challenging task involving perspectives from brain research and neuroscience as well as from research addressing the individual, social, technological, institutional, and cultural aspects of learning and cognition. The authors of this volume come from a variety of academic disciplines from several universities around the world, but they share an interest in how issues of learning and cognition can be made relevant to and useful for education.

As editor of the Learning and Cognition section in the Encyclopedia, I identified the key domains and concepts in the field of learning and cognition that had both a strong research base and high relevance to education and recruited notable researchers to cover them. Many of the articles in this volume have been chosen from the Encyclopedia's section on learning and cognition (while there are also a few articles from other sections), addressing issues ranging from neuroscience bases of learning to cross-cultural perspectives; from self-regulated learning to learning as inquiry and cooperation; from problem solving and knowledge domains to learning in specific contexts and throughout the ages; and from attention, memory, and intelligence to relationships between cognition and emotion. Language (reading and writing) is essential to cognitive processes and to learning in and outside schools and is covered from a variety of perspectives. While this handbook offers a broad spectrum, clearly not every educationally relevant topic in the field of learning and cognition is included. For example, readers who are interested in learning and knowledge building in particular areas such as the learning of history, math, or music are referred to the Encyclopedia.

The scholars contributing to this volume present a diversity of research approaches to learning and cognition. A sincere 'thank you' to all the authors who, within the format and guidelines they were offered, have put much effort into presenting in a thorough and readable way the knowledge base of their research area. In doing this, they have also demonstrated why research on learning and cognition, which acknowledges the complexities of these processes, is so crucial to the field of education and to student outcomes.

Vibeke Grøver Aukrust

CONTENTS

CONTRIBUTORS

T W Acee
Texas State University – San Marcos, San Marcos, TX, USA

P A Alexander
University of Maryland, College Park, MD, USA

R Andrews
University of London, London, UK

J S Arnfast
University of Copenhagen, Copenhagen S, Denmark

V G Aukrust
University of Oslo, Oslo, Norway

L Baker
University of Maryland, Baltimore County, Baltimore, MD, USA

T Brennen
University of Oslo, Oslo, Norway

I Bråten
University of Oslo, Oslo, Norway

M S Burns
George Mason University, Fairfax, VA, USA

M T H Chi
Arizona State University, Tempe, AZ, USA

A Collins
Northwestern University, Evanston, IL, USA

F Cuisinier
University of Paris Ouest, Nanterre, France

M de Rosnay
University of Sydney, Sydney, NSW, Australia

P-E Ellström
Linköping University, Linköping, Sweden

J Field
University of Stirling, Stirling, UK

K W Fischer
Harvard University Graduate School of Education, Cambridge, MA, USA

S R Goldman
University of Illinois, Chicago, IL, USA

U Goswami
University of Cambridge, Cambridge, UK

J G Greeno
University of Pittsburgh, Pittsburgh, PA, USA

A F Hadwin
University of Victoria, Victoria, BC, Canada

B E Hagtvet
University of Oslo, Oslo, Norway

M Heimann
Linköping University, Linköping, Sweden; The Swedish Institute for Disability Research, Linköping, Sweden; The Norwegian Network for Infant Mental Health, Oslo, Norway

L Hemphill
Wheelock College, Boston, MA, USA

A Holmen
Aarhus University, Copenhagen NV, Denmark

M H Immordino-Yang
University of Southern California, Los Angeles, CA, USA

B D Jee
Northwestern University, Evanston, IL, USA

J N Jørgensen
University of Copenhagen, Copenhagen S, Denmark

J Jung
The University of Texas at Austin, Austin, TX, USA

J K Kidd
George Mason University, Fairfax, VA, USA

S R Ludvigsen
University of Oslo, Oslo, Norway

L Maggioni
University of Maryland, College Park, MD, USA

S Magnussen
University of Oslo, Oslo, Norway

R E Mayer
University of California, Santa Barbara, CA, USA

J McLeod
The University of Melbourne, Melbourne, VIC, Australia

B Means
SRI International, Menlo Park, CA, USA

D L Medin
Northwestern University, Evanston, IL, USA

A I Mørch
University of Oslo, Oslo, Norway

T J Nokes
University of Pittsburgh, Pittsburgh, PA, USA

T Nunes
University of Oxford, Oxford, UK

J M Parisi
University of Illinois at Urbana–Champaign, Champaign, IL, USA

F Pons
University of Oslo, Oslo, Norway

J Radinsky
University of Illinois, Chicago, IL, USA

N B Ratner
University of Maryland, College Park, MD, USA

J Roschelle
SRI International, Menlo Park, CA, USA

R Säljö
Göteborg University, Göteborg, Sweden

C D Schunn
University of Pittsburgh, Pittsburgh, PA, USA

T R Shultz
McGill University, Montreal, QC, Canada

R E Slavin
Johns Hopkins University, Baltimore, MD, USA

C E Snow
Harvard Graduate School of Education, Cambridge, MA, USA

R J Sternberg
Tufts University, Boston, MA, USA

E A L Stine-Morrow
University of Illinois at Urbana–Champaign, Champaign, IL, USA

K Strid
University of Gothenburg, Gothenburg, Sweden

T Tjus
University of Gothenburg, Gothenburg, Sweden

S Tozer
University of Illinois, Chicago, IL, USA

S J Unsworth
San Diego State University, San Diego, CA, USA

C E Weinstein
The University of Texas at Austin, Austin, TX, USA

J V Wertsch
Washington University in St. Louis, St. Louis, MO, USA

J Wiley
University of Illinois at Chicago, Chicago, IL, USA

D Wink
University of Illinois, Chicago, IL, USA

P H Winne
Simon Fraser University, Burnaby, BC, Canada

L Yates
The University of Melbourne, Melbourne, VIC, Australia

L-F Zhang
The University of Hong Kong, Hong Kong

LEARNING AND COGNITION: INTRODUCTION

Cognition: Overview and Recent Trends

J Wiley, University of Illinois at Chicago, Chicago, IL, USA
B D Jee, Northwestern University, Evanston, IL, USA

All processes of thought, conscious and unconscious, fall into the realm of cognition. These processes operate by manipulating information-laden mental representations, which are either retrieved from memory or constructed from sensory information. In this way, the mind can be understood as an information processor, continuously adding to its repertoire of mental representations as well as producing overt physical behaviors. The study of human cognition thus becomes the study of the information-processing characteristics of the mind: What is the nature of the representations? How are they manipulated? How much information can be active at once? Cognitive researchers are concerned with discovering such facts about cognition, with the overarching goal of explaining human behavior in its various forms.

The study of human cognition is relevant to many fields, and researchers from several disciplines have contributed to our understanding of the mind. These disciplines include psychology, philosophy, linguistics, artificial intelligence, anthropology, education, and neuroscience. In fact, many cognitive researchers are multidisciplinary, simultaneously working in a variety of fields, and interdisciplinary, integrating aspects of the different disciplines.

The growing field of cognitive science was born out of the perspective that cognitive research must span multiple disciplines. However, less than 50 years ago, the study of cognition was largely considered unscientific, at least among many psychologists in North America. To understand the current approach to the study of cognition, it is important to consider its origins, as well as its obstacles. It is not the goal of this article to provide a detailed historical review of inquiries into human cognition (for such a review, see Gardner, 1985). Rather, we focus on the relatively recent emergence of the information processing framework that permeates contemporary cognitive science, and consider various major areas of cognitive research.

The Cognitive Revolution

The modern approach to the study of human cognition was forged by a series of events in the mid-twentieth century, known as the cognitive revolution. While scholars continue to debate whether the cognitive revolution truly qualifies as a scientific revolution, the era certainly marks an important shift in psychological theory and methodology, especially for psychology in North America. In the first half of the twentieth century, experimental psychology in North America was dominated by behaviorism, which generally disavows the use of mentalistic explanations of behavior. Mentalistic terms, such as belief and desire, were branded as superfluous and unscientific, and removed from accepted terminology. Behaviorism came in a variety of forms, including theoretical behaviorism and methodological behaviorism. The methodological behaviorist did not necessarily dismiss the existence of mental constructs, but would argue that psychological science should not include such unobservable entities. Theoretical behaviorism went further, holding that mentalistic constructs could be reduced to overt behaviors. Under this view, remembering a certain stimulus, like a sugar cube or a foul-tasting liquid, amounts to producing a specific learned behavior in response to it. Rather than building explanatory theories, behaviorism had the goal of describing relationships between reinforcements and observable behavior. Such descriptions were, according behaviorism's founding father, Watson, as far as experimental psychology could and should progress.

The apparent scientific rigor of behaviorism played a large role in its rise to prominence in psychology. However, to many American psychologists of the mid-twentieth century, it became increasingly apparent that limiting psychology to a science of behavior would be inadequate for explaining learning and higher-order processes of problem solving, reasoning, and decision making. Evidence for this inadequacy came from various sources, including a central research area in behaviorism, animal learning. For example, studies finding that rats could quickly learn an association between ingesting salty water and illness or an association between a certain noise and a shock, but had difficulty learning other pairings of the same elements (salt with shock or noise with illness), seemed to defeat the notion that learning is purely a result of experiential factors. The behaviorist approach could also not explain instances of creative cognition where novel responses are generated.

It would be incorrect to assert that the decline of behaviorism in American psychology was immediate, or due to any single set of events (Miller, 2003). Indeed, behaviorism was widely debated and defended throughout the 1960s and into the 1970s in various areas of psychology. In addition, the shift from behaviorism to cognitivism that marks the cognitive revolution in American psychology was influenced by developments outside of America. For example, the Swiss psychologist Jean Piaget argued that the organization of the human mind is shaped by biological factors, while Russian psychologist Lev Vygotsky stressed sociocultural influences. Besides advancing new theories of psychological development, these researchers provided examples that psychology could maintain its scientific rigor without the constraints of strict behaviorism.

The cognitive revolution was also fueled by developments outside of psychology, notably in the fields of linguistics and artificial intelligence (AI). The linguist Noam Chomsky's famous critique of B. F. Skinner's *Verbal Behavior* stands out to many as a critical event. Skinner, the leading behaviorist researcher of his era, attempted to provide an explanation of language strictly in terms of environmental input. Chomsky argued that behaviorist principles are inadequate to explain human verbal behavior, because language acquisition does not seem to develop as a function of the environmental conditions that are presented to the learner. Chomsky cited evidence of children's rapid language learning, and of people's ability to create and comprehend entirely novel expressions. Chomsky argued that the external conditions are too impoverished to support such learning, and posited universal, innate language abilities. While Chomsky's arguments did not settle the issue on language learning, they did, in the eyes of many, serve to defeat the purely behaviorist account.

Fueled by post-World War II interests in advancing science and technology, the field of AI flourished in the 1950s and 1960s, and played a crucial role in the rise of cognitivism. The birth of AI can be traced back to 1956, when an influential conference on AI was held at Dartmouth College (Miller, 2003). Attendees included John McCarthy, Marvin Minsky, Herbert Simon, and Allen Newell, each of whom became leading figures in AI and cognitive-science research for decades to come. AI labs around the United States began producing computer programs that were capable of carrying out tasks that were previously believed to require the highest human intellect, such as solving complex logic and math problems. The new synergy between computer science and psychology was apparent not only in the tasks that computers were programmed to perform, but also in how they carried these tasks out. For example, McCarthy's List Processing (LISP) possessed a unique memory organization for its time, which stored not only the contents of independent entries, but also their connectedness. These memory trees allowed the computer to store complex relational structures, a powerful new tool.

With advancing computer technology bringing promise of creating AI, the abstract notion of the computer served as a powerful metaphor for the human mind. Broadbent is widely credited with developing this computer metaphor into the information-processing model of the mind, which has become the dominant model for cognitive science.

The new idea was that the mind could be described in terms of input, internal representation, processing, and output. In this way, the mind was not only like a computer, it was a computer. Psychological theories could be legitimately instantiated in computer models, a view that more closely bound psychology to the field of AI.

The Birth of Cognitive Psychology

The emergence of new scientific fields outside psychology and the open consideration of alternative theoretical positions within psychology supported the birth of a new psychological field, one committed to the study of human cognition under the information-processing framework. The publication of Neisser's *Cognitive Psychology* in 1967 marked the emergence of this new field. Neisser defined cognition as all of the processes that transform, reduce, elaborate, store, recover, and use sensory input. For Neisser, the realm of cognitive psychology included how actions and experiences are affected by perceptions, memories, and beliefs. Like behaviorists, cognitive psychologists apply a strict scientific method to study the mind, but unlike behaviorists, they accept the existence of internal mental states within their science.

Armed with the information-processing framework, cognitive psychologists set out to explore many new questions about the mind. A primary concern was the mind's basic architecture: Is the mind comprised of distinct cognitive systems, and if so, how do these systems operate? Research on human memory was central in addressing these questions. Memory is not simply a storage system, but is thought to be actively engaged in all aspects of cognition. The memory system has three interrelated functions: encoding, storing, and retrieving information. Evidence from numerous studies suggested the existence of distinct, but interacting systems of memory, distinguished primarily by the duration that information is retained. First, there is sensory memory, which holds a large amount of incoming sensory information for only a few hundred milliseconds. There is thought to be a unique sensory store for each of the five senses, although visual sensory memory has received the most research attention. The next memory system is short-term memory, which receives input from sensory memory, and holds, by recent estimate (Cowan, 2001), about four chunks (i.e., meaningful units) of information for a few seconds. A more contemporary view, Baddeley's model of working memory (e.g., Baddeley, 2007), emphasizes not only short-term storage, but also how information is manipulated in immediate memory. The most recent incarnation of the working-memory model consists of three distinct short-term memory subsystems, commanded by a central executive. One subsystem processes and stores visuospatial information, a second deals with phonological information (including speech), and a third integrates different modalities of information and integrates temporal information into an episodic representation. A final major memory system is long-term memory, characterized by its near-unlimited capacity and duration. Information from working memory may be stored in long-term memory for later retrieval; however, the storage of information depends on many factors, including how it is processed during encoding. Long-term memory can also input information into working memory, affecting the interpretation and elaboration of its contents, and making information accessible for use in higher-order processes such as comprehension, problem solving, and reasoning.

The field of cognitive psychology, realizing the potential of information-processing theory and building on basic assumptions about the architecture of memory, flourished in the latter quarter of the twentieth century. New areas of research emerged, exploring a range of cognitive phenomena, from the most basic processes, such as perception and pattern recognition, to more complex, higher-order processes, like comprehension and problem solving. Traditionally, cognitive researchers aim to determine specific processes that underlie human performance using experiments that isolate the particular demands of any given task. Participants are usually presented with fine-grained variations of stimuli or tasks, and performance is typically measured in terms of response accuracy or reaction time. This approach is essentially reductionist in nature, but it allows for causal determinations to be made through adherence to the scientific principles of quantification and strict experimental control. Beyond the basic controlled experiment, cognitive scientists have a number of other approaches in their methodological arsenal. Cognitive modeling, the simulation of cognition through computer programs, is a popular tool for instantiating theories and pitting them against one another. Technology in neuroscience, particularly functional magnetic resonance imaging (fMRI), has made it possible to examine the online brain activity of normal adults. Similar recordings can be obtained in terms of event-related potentials (ERPs), eye movements, skin conductance, and pupil dilation. Verbal and video protocols also provide a rich source of data, including gestures and think-aloud reports, which may give insights into the behaviors that people engage in during cognitive tasks.

Overview of Research in Cognition

Given that one of the main goals of education is to train and inform students through instruction, research in cognition has direct application, especially with respect to issues of learning. There are several areas of cognitive research, including perception and attention, language acquisition and reading, memory, comprehension, problem solving

and reasoning, and metacognition, which can all inform educational practice.

Perception and Attention

One of the most basic areas of research within cognitive science concerns perceptual and attentional processes, which serve as gatekeepers for stimuli and determine what is available for further cognitive processing. The extent to which information must be explicitly processed, how attention is drawn to or away from stimuli, and how often information needs to be attended to during learning, are important and well-studied topics (Pashler, 1998). Repeated exposure or practice is a central mechanism in skill and knowledge acquisition, and can result in automaticity and proceduralization of cognitive processes over time. These principles can inform our understanding of successful acquisition of spoken language, reading skills, and various problem-solving skills. A related literature explores individual differences in the ability to control one's attention, or the ability to focus on a goal in the face of interference. Research has found that these abilities affect the amount of information that people can consider in immediate memory, which in turn impacts their performance on many cognitive tasks. As such, the ability to control one's attention has also been referred to as working-memory capacity (Conway et al., 2005).

Language Acquisition and Reading

First-language acquisition is perhaps the most impressive of all cognitive skills. Language develops universally in some form in all humans, and development typically proceeds in a remarkably rapid fashion. Present approaches emphasize both the biological predisposition to acquire language as well as the role of exposure to patterns in the environment (Gleitman and Newport, 1995). The differences between first-language acquisition occurring in infancy, and second-language acquisition that occurs afterward, are important issues, as are the questions of how bilinguals represent and process information in their second language (Kroll and Tokowicz, 2005). Additionally, recent research has highlighted several cognitive advantages among young bilingual students and aging bilingual adults, including superior executive functioning and facilitated acquisition of reading skills (Stock, 2001). A great deal of cognitive research has also explored reading behavior more generally. This research supports two important conclusions: that mastering the alphabetic principle (that written symbols correspond to sounds, or phonics) is essential to becoming proficient, and that methods that teach the alphabetic-decoding principles that underlie our written language are more effective than methods that do not, especially for children who are having difficulty learning to read (Rayner et al., 2001).

Memory

The relevance of cognitive research on memory is perhaps obvious if a main goal of education is the acquisition of knowledge. Memory research concerns the mechanisms that enable the encoding, storage, and retrieval of new information. A long tradition of research has demonstrated more durable learning and memory result from spaced practice (Cepeda *et al.*, 2006), and when information is presented in a context that allows for imagery, elaboration, or integration with prior knowledge (Baddeley, 2007). Other highly relevant lines of investigation examine how memory tests affect subsequent memory for information, in some cases by introducing false memory traces through distractors in multiple-choice tests (Roediger and Karpicke, 2006). Testing may also cause patterns of facilitation for the tested information, and interference for nonretrieved information.

Comprehension and Conceptual Understanding

Perhaps the most common medium for subject-matter transmission is through expository text, with lectures and discussion also being common forms of instruction. In these cases, learning depends on text and discourse processing which is another major area of cognitive research. As information is processed, multiple levels of representation are constructed, and as Kintsch (1998) has suggested, it is especially the deepest level of representation, called the situation model, that represents understanding or comprehension of phenomena. This area of research has explored the contexts and individual differences that support construction of better-situation models during learning, including encouraging the activation or use of prior knowledge and encouraging active processing through tasks such as question-asking or self-explanation (Graesser *et al.*, 1997; McNamara, 2007). A special case of learning occurs when new information or evidence in some way conflicts with prior understandings. In these cases, conceptual change or belief change may be required, especially for learning in science (Chi, 2000; Chinn and Malhotra, 2002).

Problem Solving and Reasoning

A great deal of research on problem solving has been informed by using a contrastive approach – comparing better or more expert problem solvers to less-effective, or less-expert, problem solvers. This work has shown that experts use their experience to see the deep (more explanatory) structure of a problem, while novices often process problems at a superficial level. This line of research has in fact spurred the research on self-explanation cited above (Chi, 2000). In a similar vein, instruction that emphasizes procedural elements of math problem solving can promote shallow understanding, while conceptual or mixed approaches can lead to better understanding as well

as improvement in procedural skill (Siegler, 2003). A third important area of problem-solving research has explored the effectiveness of scaffolded practice, worked examples, and feedback (Atkinson *et al.*, 2000).

Ill-structured problems represent a special class, where solutions, goals, and assumptions are less constrained. But even here, expertise in a domain gives the solver ways to constrain the problem space (Voss *et al.*, 1983) and turn the problem into a well-structured one. Solving this type of problem, where no single agreed-upon answer exists, requires argumentation or informal reasoning skills. In such cases, the reasoner must consider the evidence and arguments and whether they provide support for conclusions. Such skills underlie disciplinary thinking in both the humanities and the sciences, as well as reasoning in most everyday contexts. Thus, the development of scientific reasoning and argumentation skills in students has been an area of much recent interest.

As opposed to these skills of informal reasoning, formal reasoning relies on the application of the rules of logic or mathematics, with the goal of determining the validity of syllogistic or propositional arguments. Formal-reasoning performance often improves with more familiar or meaningful contexts, as well as when arguments are phrased in more intuitive language. Several forms of reasoning have been found to improve with training in statistics, but generally, people tend to be poor at all types of reasoning without training. Substantial individual differences in reasoning abilities have been attributed to thinking dispositions (Stanovich *et al.*, 2003) which have been found to correlate with the ability to learn and engage in many higher-order cognitive tasks. This in turn suggests a critical role for instruction in reasoning that is largely absent from our current curricula.

Metacognition

Metacognition is the act of monitoring cognitive performance, which serves as input to self-regulation of cognitive behaviors such as studying. Much research on this topic has used prediction paradigms for memory and comprehension tasks. Metamemory paradigms typically consist of the task of learning word pairs, such as a word in a foreign language and its English translation. When students are asked to predict their ability to recall a translation, metamemory accuracy has been found to be quite good, especially when judgments are made at a delay (Dunlosky *et al.*, 2007). Predictive accuracy for comprehension tests following the reading of expository texts is typically much lower, although recently some contexts that promote accurate metacomprehension have been found. When readers are asked to self-explain while reading, or to generate summaries or keywords at a delay before making their judgments, metacomprehension accuracy can be substantially improved (Thiede *et al.*, 2009). The ultimate value of supporting better predictive accuracy among students is that it then can help them to make effective decisions of what material to re-study as they attempt to learn material on their own.

Recent Trends

Transfer

The goal of instruction is ultimately to promote learning that transfers to new problems and situations, especially ones that are quite dissimilar from the initial learning context. When students are able to activate prior knowledge or learned-solution strategies and apply them by analogy in novel contexts, it is referred to as far transfer. However, a recurring theme in the cognitive literature is that students often fail to activate relevant prior knowledge as they process new information. Thus, little experimental evidence has supported the existence of far transfer (Barnett and Ceci, 2002). More often that not, people are unlikely to recall critical information in situations that are superficially dissimilar to the context of acquisition. Despite the elusiveness of findings of far transfer in cognitive laboratories, there is evidence from observational studies that people can and do apply analogies to solve novel problems in the real world. Scientists, for example, spontaneously construct analogies to help solve problems that they encounter in their research. One reason for the apparent void between laboratory and observational findings could be that experimental participants are not able to represent the analog at a level of abstraction that is sufficient to support transfer. The issue of whether initial instruction should be concrete and contextualized, versus abstract and symbolic, is currently receiving a great deal of attention, with some advantages being found for each mode of acquisition. When students are taught a principle through concrete examples that gradually become more abstract, they are better able to transfer the principle in some contexts (Goldstone *et al.*, 2008). However, in other contexts, starting with abstract or symbolic representations leads to better learning and transfer, as concrete representations may distract learners from recognizing the basic principles.

Spatial Thinking and Gesture

Spatial skills are thought to be important to many aspects of cognition, including thinking and problem solving in math and science domains. Individual differences in spatial ability have been well documented, and recent work is attempting to differentiate among distinct subtypes of spatial abilities (Hegarty and Waller, 2005). One important aspect of spatial thought is the ability to parse, mentally manipulate, and use symbolic representations, such as maps and diagrams. To the extent that spatial skills affect learning and understanding, it is particularly encouraging

that such skills do seem to improve with practice or input from the environment (Newcombe and Huttenlocher, 2000). Another important aspect of spatial cognition is the bodily gestures that people produce (Alibali, 2005). Gestures can be used to support spatial thinking and communication, but also may be used to express knowledge that is difficult to verbalize. Gestures may reveal a student's preparedness for learning a concept even when their verbal expressions suggest poor understanding. Interestingly, gestures seem to be used as much for the self as for others. Such findings suggest that cognitive processes may be tied to the body's interactions with the world, and an extreme version of this perspective, referred to as embodied cognition, is receiving a great deal of attention in the recent literature.

Culture and Cognition

Research in early science education and developmental psychology has demonstrated that most children need to overcome some of their intuitive ideas of the world around them in order to comprehend scientifically accurate explanation of phenomena. However, the vast majority of this work has involved children in mainstream, North American, urban, technologically dependent populations. Recent work by Medin and his colleagues has shown how intuitive concepts are shaped by society, and how children in specific cultures (such as Native American communities) differ in their understandings of biological concepts (Bang *et al.*, 2007). These differences are attributed to exposure to cultural values and beliefs transmitted through the discourse within the community. Interestingly, children in Native American communities were found to have more advanced understandings of living things and ecologies. Yet, disturbingly, they did less well than mainstream students in academic classroom performance. These results suggest conflicts between traditional science instruction and the ways of thinking instilled by different communities. Such findings highlight the need to recognize the differences in intuitive understandings that children from many different kinds of communities bring to the classroom, and represent one example of the recent research trend to better understand the interaction of culture and cognition.

Collaboration

A final trend in recent research explores the impact of social interaction on learning. The communication between the teacher and a class is essentially a social interaction, but because of the number of students, it is essentially one-sided. The teacher necessarily becomes the transmitter of information, and there is little role for either individualized discourse or interactive activity on the part of most students. Thus, it is not surprising that researchers have attempted to increase interactive communication for all students through the creation of small group exercises, peer-collaboration activities, or intelligent tutoring environments. Interacting with others can be particularly motivating, but there are also a number of pitfalls that can make collaborative learning less successful than individual work. Intelligent tutors can provide students with timely feedback and expert knowledge, but if systems provide too much scaffolding or help, then the students may never actually engage with the content (Anderson *et al.*, 1995). Alternatively, working with peers can be quite motivating and effective as a supplement to classroom instruction, but guidance for students on how to collaborate is critical, otherwise they may engage in superficial discussions that do not reach a high level of discourse (O'Donnell and King, 1999). The goal of current investigations is determining which contexts are most effective and in what ways, for different subject matters, and different kinds of students (VanLehn *et al.*, 2007), as well as the discovery of the mechanisms that are responsible for successful collaborative learning and transfer.

See also: Cognition and Emotion; Concept Learning; Memory; Metacognition; Neuroscience Bases of Learning; Problem Solving and Human Expertise; Problem Solving and Reasoning; The Adult Development of Cognition and Learning.

Bibliography

Alibali, M. W. (2005). Gesture in spatial cognition: Expressing, communicating and thinking about spatial information. *Spatial Cognition and Computation* **5**, 307–331.

Anderson, J. R., Corbett, A. T., Koedinger, K. R., and Pelletier, R. (1995). Cognitive tutors: Lessons learned. *Journal of the Learning Sciences* **4**(2), 167–207.

Atkinson, R. K., Derry, S. J., Renkl, A., and Wortham, D. (2000). Learning from examples: Instructional principles from the worked examples research. *Review of Educational Research* **70**(2), 181–214.

Baddeley, A. D. (2007). *Working Memory, Thought and Action.* Oxford, UK: Oxford University Press.

Bang, M., Medin, D., and Atran, S. (2007). Cultural mosaics and mental models of nature. *Proceedings of the National Academy of Sciences* **104**, 13868–13874.

Barnett, S. M. and Ceci, S. J. (2002). When and where do we apply what we learn? A taxonomy for far transfer. *Journal of Experimental Psychology: General* **128**, 612–637.

Bialystok, E. (2001). *Bilingualism in Development: Language, Literacy, and Cognition.* New York: Cambridge University Press.

Cepeda, N. J., Pashler, H., Vul, E., Wixted, J. T., and Rohrer, D. (2006). Distributed practice in verbal recall tasks: A review and quantitative synthesis. *Psychological Bulletin* **132**, 354–380.

Chi, M. T. H. (2000). Self-explaining expository texts: The dual processes of generating inferences and repairing mental models. In Glaser, R. (ed.) *Advances in Instructional Psychology*, pp 161–238. Mahwah, NJ: Erlbaum.

Chinn, C. A. and Malhotra, B. A. (2002). Children's responses to anomalous scientific data: How is conceptual change impeded? *Journal of Educational Psychology* **19**, 327–343.

Conway, A. R. A., Kane, M. J., Bunting, M. F., *et al.* (2005). Working memory span tasks: A methodological review and users guide. *Psychonomic Bulletin and Review* **2**(5), 769–786.

Cowan, N. (2001). The magical number 4 in short-term memory: A reconsideration of mental storage. *Behavioral and Brain Sciences* **24**(1), 87–185.

Dunlosky, J., Serra, M. J., and Baker, J. M. C. (2007). Metamemory applied. In Durso, F. (ed.) *Handbook of Applied Cognition,* 2nd edn., pp 137–161. Chichester, UK: Wiley.

Gardner, H. (1985). *The mind's New Science: A History of the Cognitive Revolution.* New York: Basic Books.

Gleitman, L. R. and Newport, E. L. (1995). The invention of language by children: Environmental and biological influences on the acquisition of language. In Gleitman, L. R. and Liberman, M. (eds.) *An Invitation to Cognitive Science, Vol. 1: Language,* 2nd edn. Cambridge: MIT Press.

Goldstone, R. L., Landy, D., and Son, J. (2008). A well-grounded education: The role of perception in science and mathematics. In Glenberg, A., DeVega, M., and Graesser, A. (eds.) *Proceedings of the Garachico Workshop on Symbols, Embodiment and Meaning,* Universidad de La Laguna, Tenerife.

Graesser, A. C., Millis, K., and Zwaan, R. A. (1997). Discourse comprehension. *Annual Review of Psychology* **48**, 163–189.

Hegarty, M. and Waller, D. (2005). Individual differences in spatial abilities. In Shah, P. and Miyake, A. (eds.) *Handbook of Higher-Level Visuospatial Thinking*, pp 121–169. New York: Cambridge University Press.

Kintsch, W. (1998). *Comprehension: A paradigm for Cognition.* New York: Cambridge University Press.

Kroll, J. F. and Tokowicz, N. (2005). Models of bilingual representation and processing: Looking back and to the future. In Kroll, J. F. and de Groot, A. M. B. (eds.) *Handbook of Bilingualism: Psycholinguistic Approaches*, pp 531–553. New York: Oxford University Press.

McNamara, D. S. (ed.) (2007). *Reading Comprehension Strategies: Theories, Interventions, and Technologies.* Mahwah, NJ: Erlbaum.

Miller, G. A. (2003). The cognitive revolution: A historical perspective. *Trends in Cognitive Sciences* **7**, 141–144.

Newcombe, N. S. and Huttenlocher, J. (2000). *Making Space: The Development of Spatial Representation and Reasoning.* Cambridge, MA: MIT Press.

O'Donnell, A. and King, A. (1999). *Cognitive Perspectives on Peer Learning.* Mahwah, NJ: Erlbaum.

Pashler, H. (1998). *The Psychology of Attention.* Cambridge, MA: MIT Press.

Rayner, K., Foorman, B. R., Perfetti, C. A., Pesetsky, D., and Seidenberg, M. S. (2001). How psychological science informs the teaching of reading. *Psychological Science in the Public Interest* **2**(2), 31–74.

Roediger, H. L. and Karpicke, J. D. (2006). Test-enhanced learning: Taking memory tests improves long-term retention. *Psychological Science* **17**, 249–255.

Siegler, R. S. (2003). Implications of cognitive science research for mathematics education. In Kilpatrick, J., Martin, W. G., and Schifter, D. E. (eds.) *A Research Companion to Principles and Standards for School Mathematics*, pp 119–233. Reston, VA: National Council of Teachers of Mathematics.

Stanovich, K. E., Sá, W. C., and West, R. F. (2003). Individual differences in thinking, reasoning, and decision making. In Leighton, J. P. and Sternberg, R. J. (eds.) *The Nature of Reasoning*, pp 375–409. New York: Cambridge University Press.

Thiede, K. W., Griffin, T. D., Wiley, J., and Redford, J. (2009). Metacognitive monitoring during and after reading. In Hacker, D. J., Dunlosky, J., and Graesser, A. C. (eds.) *Handbook of Metacognition in Education*, pp 85–106. New York: Routledge.

VanLehn, K., Graesser, A. C., Jackson, G. T., *et al.* (2007). When are tutorial dialogues more effective than reading? *Cognitive Science* **31**(1), 3–52.

Voss, J. F., Greene, T. R., Post, T. A., and Penner, B. C. (1983). Problem-solving skill in social sciences. *Psychology of Learning and Motivation* **17**, 165–213.

Neuroscience Bases of Learning

M H Immordino-Yang, University of Southern California, Los Angeles, CA, USA
K W Fischer, Harvard University Graduate School of Education, Cambridge, MA, USA

Glossary

Domain – A culturally constructed area of knowledge, such as language, math, music, or social interaction.
Neural network – A set of neurons that are structurally and functionally interconnected so that they activate in coherent patterns associated with mental functions.
Neuroimaging – A variety of research techniques, some invasive and some not, concerned with measuring and mapping the physiology and structure of the brain.
Neuromyth – A misguided, oversimplified, or incorrect tenet in education that concerns the brain or neuroscience.
Skill – An ability to behave or think in an organized way in a particular context.

Beyond Neuromyths: Mind, Brain, and Education Is a Cross-Disciplinary Field

All human behavior and learning, including feeling, thinking, creating, remembering, and deciding, originate in the brain. Rather than a hardwired biological system, the brain develops through an active, dynamic process in which a child's social, emotional, and cognitive experiences organize his or her brain over time, in accordance with biological constraints and principles. In the other direction, a child's particular neuropsychological strengths and weaknesses shape the way he or she perceives and interacts with the world. Like the weaving of an intricate and delicate web (Fischer and Bidell, 2006), physiological and cultural processes interact to produce learning and behavior in highly nuanced and complex patterns of human development.

People in the field of education often begin with a preconception that biology refers to traits that children are born with, that are fixed and unfold independent of experience, while children's social and cultural experiences, including schooling, are at the mercy of these biological predispositions, somehow riding on top of, but not influencing, biology. However, current research in neuroscience reinforces the notion that children's experiences shape their biology as much as biology shapes

children's development. The fields of neuroscience and more broadly biology are leading education toward analyzing the dynamic relationship between nurture and nature in development and schooling. A more nuanced understanding of how biology and experience interact is critically relevant to education. As neuroscientists learn about which aspects of experience are most likely to influence biology and vice versa, educators can develop increasingly tailored educational experiences, interventions, and assessments.

Due to this bi-directional relationship between a child's biological predispositions and social and cognitive experiences, the fields of neuroscience and education are coming increasingly into a research partnership. This relationship can be studied at many levels of analysis, from the workings of genes inside cells to the workings of communities inside cultures. However, in order for new information about the brain and learning to influence the design of learning environments, teachers and others involved in educational policy and design need to know about the newest principles about the brain and learning. Likewise, neuroscientists need to investigate phenomena that are relevant to real-world learning and development. To these ends, a new field has gradually taken shape over the last few years: mind, brain, and education (MBE). As a field, MBE encompasses educational neuroscience (a branch of neuroscience that deals with educationally relevant capacities in the brain), philosophy, linguistics, pedagogy, developmental psychology, and others.

In this interdisciplinary and applied climate, educators are in a particularly good position to help generate new questions and topics for research on learning and the brain, as they deal on a daily basis with the developmental issues and situations that affect real children and adults in their learning. For this reason, educators including teachers should have some familiarity with neuroscience and brain functioning, in order to become more informed consumers of educationally relevant findings as well as, ideally, contributors who help identify and shape new questions for neuroscience to pursue. For example, teachers can use information on the development of networks for numeric processing to design more effective curricula to teach math concepts, and educational assessments of students' math learning can help to shape new scientific questions about the development of math networks.

However, this does not mean that neuroscience is capable of contributing insights into all educational problems.

One of the challenges for the new field of MBE is for educators to learn about the applicability, implications, and limits of neuroscience research methods to various sorts of educational questions, and for neuroscientists at the same time to learn about the problems, issues, and processes of education, so that the two fields can collaborate as profitably as possible. For this to happen, educators and educational researchers need to know something about the tools, techniques, assumptions, and approaches that guide neuroscience research on learning, and need to develop a critical ability to consume and digest neuroscience findings and evaluate them for their potential applicability in the classroom. Toward this goal, teacher-training programs are beginning to incorporate information about the science of learning into their course offerings, and several new graduate programs in MBE have been launched at major universities in several countries in the last few years.

Before proceeding further, we felt the need to insert a strong cautionary note. As is typical during periods of rapid discovery, technological innovation, and theoretical advance, the field of MBE, as well as other related fields seeking to apply brain science to mainstream societal issues, are experiencing a lag between new technologies and findings on the one hand and the ability to interpret these findings on the other. In recent years, multiple examples of brain research misapplied have gone forward, including, for example, the overt labeling of elementary students as different categories of learners, from kinesthetic to auditory and beyond. Indeed, the scientific community agrees that much of what has been called brain-based education rests on very shaky ground. There is a proliferation of books written by nonscientists about the applications of neuroscience to learning, and while some of these books might present useful interpretations of neuroscience for educators, many of them suffer from a lack of basic understanding about the meaning and limitations of neuroscience research on learning and related processes. These books should be read with skepticism, as they often present models that are so oversimplified as to be misleading or even harmful or dangerous to children.

Overall, major changes in neuroscience research methods and theory are allowing better applicability of brain findings to educational issues and questions, and new insights into the processes that happen in schools. In this article, we focus on the prominent contribution of neuroimaging to the current view of learning as the construction of distributed neural networks that support skills, and how the development and recruitment of these neural networks is modulated and facilitated by domain-general processes in the brain, including emotion, attention, and mechanisms of social learning. We conclude with a call for further research that evaluates neuroscientific principles as they play out in classroom contexts.

New Neuroscience Methods Bring New Information and New Challenges for Interpretation

Educators' views of brain research have shifted in the past few years. While many educators continue to cling to so-called neuromyths, neuroscientists in the MBE field have been working to dispel these myths. In particular, the last decade has seen huge advances in *in vivo* neuroimaging technologies. Scientists are now able to study the workings of the human mind in healthy participants as they solve problems and perform other sorts of cognitive and emotional tasks in real time. Availability of these new research technologies is pushing the field forward at an unprecedented pace; hardly a week goes by, it seems, without a picture of the brain appearing on the cover of a major magazine or in a major newspaper article.

To make sense of the new findings, it is critical that educators understand the logic and constraints in the neuroscience research underlying these articles. While neuroimaging techniques differ in their specifics, there are three main approaches. The first approach involves measuring and localizing changes in the flow of blood in the brain as subjects think in different ways, under the assumption that changes in regional blood flow are indicative of changes in neural activity. The second approach involves measuring the electrical activity of the brain, generated by the firing of networks of neurons (brain cells). The third approach involves measuring changes in the anatomy and structure of the brain. In conjunction or separately, these techniques can be used to study the neurological correlates of a wide variety of tasks, such as reading, math, or social processing, as well as developmental changes (for reviews, see Katzir and Pare-Blagoev, 2006; Thatcher *et al.*, in press).

While these recent advances in neuroimaging have had a profound effect on the field of neuroscience and its potential relevance to education, it is important to remember that new technological capabilities inevitably come with limitations. For example, in functional magnetic resonance imaging (fMRI), the changes in regional blood flow in the brain associated with a particular task of interest are not absolute, but either implicitly or explicitly calculated from comparisons between a target and a control task. The design of the two tasks and the differences between them are critical to the findings and interpretation. When one brain area is reported to light up (i.e., to become more active) for a particular task, this does not mean that the lighted brain area is the only area actively processing. Instead, this means that this particular area was relatively more active for this task than for the control task. Many other areas are certainly actively involved, but are equivalently active in the two conditions. In reality, a network of neural areas always supports the skill being tested. As educators are concerned with supporting the development of coherent functional skills rather than isolated brain areas, it is essential that neuroimaging findings be correctly interpreted before any attempt can be made to apply them in the classroom.

Educational Skills are Supported by Specialized Neural Networks

Nonetheless, the advent of neuroimaging has precipitated major advances in neuroscientists' understanding of how the brain works. In the past, the neuroscientific localization tradition prevailed; that is, cognitive functions were mapped onto specific locations in the brain, as much as possible in one-to-one correspondence. However, neuroscientists now understand that learning involves the development of connections between networks of brain areas, spread across many regions of the brain. This means that while specific brain areas do carry out characteristic kinds of processing, skills for real-world and academic tasks are embodied in the networks they recruit, rather than in any one area of the brain. For example, there is no music, reading, or math area of the brain that is not also involved in processing many other skills and domains (culturally constructed areas of knowledge).

Instead of one brain area, learning involves actively constructing neural networks that functionally connect many brain areas. Due to the constructive nature of this process, different learners' networks may differ, in accordance with the person's neuropsychological strengths and predispositions, and with the cultural, physical, and social context in which the skills are built (Immordino-Yang, 2008). There are various routes to effective skill development, for example, in reading (Fischer et al., 2007) or math (Singer, 2007). The job of education is to provide support for children with different neuropsychological profiles to develop effective, yet flexible skills. Children use whatever capacities they have to learn the most important skills in their lives, and although there is often a modal way of learning a specific skill, people can adapt their capacities to learn skills in diverse ways. For example, Knight and Fischer (1992) found that young children followed one of three pathways in learning to read words. In a related vein, in studying two high-functioning adolescent boys who had recovered from the surgical removal of half of their brain, Immordino-Yang (2007) found that each boy had compensated for weaknesses by transforming important neuropsychological skills into new ones that suited the boys' remaining strengths.

Neural Networks for Mathematics

One area that has seen much advance in the past few years is the study of neurological networks underlying processing for mathematics and number representation. Overall, the findings suggest that networks for processing in math are built from networks for the representation of quantity that start in infancy – one for the approximate representation of numerosity (numeric quantity), and one for exact calculation using numbers (Dehaene et al., 2004). These networks are further organized and differentiated with development and training in math concepts (Singer, 2007). For example, preschoolers go beyond innate number systems to build a mental number line, gradually adding one digit at a time (Le Corre et al., 2006).

Interestingly, this math network shares many processing areas and features with language processing, including reading. Current research is exploring how math processing relates to other domains, such as spatial representation, as well as the development of math networks in atypically developing populations, such as children with learning disabilities.

Neural Networks for Reading

Another area of concentrated research interest is the study of reading development, both in typically developing and dyslexic children. Acquiring literacy skills impacts the functional organization of the brain, differentially recruiting networks for language, visual, and sound representation in both hemispheres, as well as increasing the amount of white-matter tissue connecting brain areas. Work on individual differences in the cognitive paths to reading has enriched the interpretation of the neurological research (e.g., Knight and Fischer, 1992), and helped to bridge the gap between the neuroscience findings and classroom practice (Katzir and Pare-Blagoev, 2006; Wolf and O'Brien, 2006). In dyslexic readers, progress is being made toward better understanding of the contributions of rapid phonological processing (Gaab et al., 2007), orthographic processing (Bitan et al., 2007), and visual processing to reading behaviors, as well as to thinking in other domains (Boets et al., 2008). For example, the visual field of dyslexics may show more sensitivity in the periphery and less in the fovea compared to nondyslexics, leading to special talents in some dyslexics for diffuse-pattern recognition (Schneps et al., 2007). Most recently, research looking at developmental differences in neurological networks for reading across cultures has begun to appear (e.g., Cao et al., 2009), which ultimately may contribute to knowledge about how different kinds of reading experiences shape the brain.

The neural networks for learning reading and math have important implications for education, as the most effective lessons implicitly scaffold the development of brain systems responsible for the various component skills. For example, successful math curricula help students to connect skills for calculation with those for the representation of quantity, through scaffolding the development of mental structures like the number line (Carey and Sarnecka, 2006; Griffin, 2004; Le Corre *et al.*, 2006). While different students will show different propensities for the component skills, all students will ultimately need to functionally connect the brain systems for quantity and calculation to be successful in math.

Domain-General and Emotion-Related Processes Enable Learning

The brain is a dynamic, plastic, experience-dependent, social, and affective organ. Due to this, the centuries-long debate over nature versus nurture is an unproductive and overly dichotomous approach to understanding the complexities of the dynamic interdependencies between biology and culture in development. New evidence highlights how humans are fundamentally social and symbolic beings (Herrmann *et al.*, 2007), and just as certain aspects of our biology, including our genetics and our brains, shape our social, emotional, and cognitive propensities, many aspects of our biology, including processes as fundamental as body growth, depend on adequate social, emotional, and cognitive nurturance. Learning is social, emotional, and shaped by culture!

For a stark example of this interdependence between biology, social interaction, and cognitive stimulation, in their work with Romanian orphans, Nelson *et al.* (2007) found that cognitive, social, and physical growth were delayed in institutionalized children, relative to their peers raised in foster or biological families. Although the institutionalized children's basic physical needs were met, the lack of high-quality social interaction and cognitive stimulation lead these children not to thrive.

Overall, while educators often focus on neural networks for domain-specific skills like reading and math, domain-general and emotion-related networks function as modulators and facilitators of memory and domain-specific learning. These networks include emotion, social processing, and attention.

Emotion and Social Processing

One cutting-edge area of research in neuroscience is the study of affective and social processing. All good teachers know that the way students feel, including their emotional states (e.g., stressed vs. relaxed, depressed vs. enthusiastic) and the state of their bodies (e.g., whether they are sick or well, whether they have slept enough, or whether they have eaten), are critical factors affecting learning. In addition, it is now becoming increasingly evident that emotion plays a fundamental role not only in background processes like motivation for learning, but in moment-to-moment problem solving and decision making as well (Adolphs and Damasio, 2000; Haidt, 2001). That is, emotion forms the

rudder that steers learners' thinking, in effect helping them to call up information and memories that are relevant to the topic or problem at hand. For example, as a student solves a math problem, she is emotionally evaluating whether each cognitive step is likely to bring her closer to a useful solution, or whether it seems to be leading her astray.

From a neurobiological perspective, emotional processing in the brain depends on somatosensory systems – the systems in the brain responsible for sensing the state of the viscera and body. These systems can reflect actual changes to the state of the body during emotions (i.e., increased heart rate during fearful states, or a feeling of having been kicked in the stomach when hearing bad news), or they can reflect simulated body states, conjuring how the viscera and body would feel, without actually imposing those physiological changes onto the body (see Figure 1 from Immordino-Yang and Damasio, 2007). Through regulating and inciting attention, motivation, and evaluation of simulated or actual outcomes, emotion serves to modulate the recruitment of neural networks for domain-specific skills, for example, for math or reading. In this way, cognition and emotion in the brain are two sides of the same coin, and most of the thought processes that educators care about, including memory, learning, and creativity among others, critically involve both cognitive and emotional aspects (**Figure 1**).

In addition, social processing in the brain is strongly interrelated with the processing of emotion. People's behavior is organized and influenced by cultural factors and the social context, which in turn reflect experience and learning. For example, many of the reasons the student above solves her math problem relate to the emotional aspects of her social relationships and cultural goals – the way her parents will feel about her behavior, or her desire to go to college. In turn, she feels the influences of these cultural constructs as emotional reactions that play out in her body and mind, and predispose her to think in particular ways.

But how does this student internalize or predict the emotional reactions of her parents? Interestingly, research over the past decade has revealed glimmers of the workings of a basic biological system for internalizing the actions, emotions, and goals of others, in order to learn from, empathize with, and influence others in social contexts (Immordino-Yang, 2008; Oberman *et al.*, 2007). Specifically, it appears that watching other people's actions and inferring their emotions and implicit goals recruits some of the same neural systems involved in planning and carrying out those actions in one's own self. This discovery was dubbed as mirroring by its discoverers (Gallese *et al.*, 1996; Umiltà *et al.*, 2001), and while neural systems for mirroring do not tell the whole story of the neurological system for social learning, current research suggests that they afford an important low-level mechanism on which social and cultural learning can build.

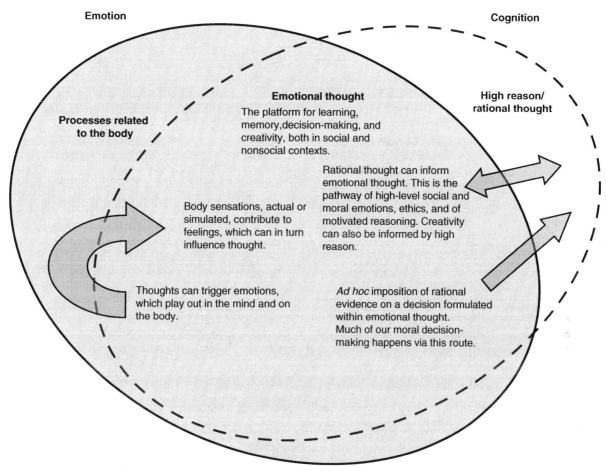

Figure 1 Emotion and cognition come together to produce the thought processes that educators care about, among them learning and memory. In the figure, the solid ellipse represents emotion and the dashed ellipse represents cognition. The extensive overlap between the two ellipses represents the domain of emotional thought. Note that emotional thought reflects a dynamic relationship between the brain and body. Reprinted from Immordino-Yang, M. H. and Damasio, A. R. (2007). We feel, therefore we learn: The relevance of affective and social neuroscience to education. *Mind, Brain and Education* 1(1), 3–10, with permission from Blackwell publishing.

Memory and Attention

To understand the current state of research on memory and attention, it is helpful to first discuss current views on how reality is constructed in the mind and brain, and the relationship of this process to perception. Work in various areas of neuroscience, for example, in vision or somatosensory perception and location of the body in space, has shown that unlike the often predominant intuitive view, we humans do not construct reality directly from our perception of the environment, as if we were equipped with some sort of internal video camera. Instead, our prior learning, our neuropsychological predispositions, and the current context heavily influence the reality that we construct and experience. That is, reality is never perceived directly from the environment. Instead, we construct reality based on our own best guesses, interpretations, and expectations. For a trite but illustrative example, imagine why visual illusions work: our visual system

uses context and prior experience with the world to construct images that incorporate our best guesses about the color, form, movement, and identity of what is actually in front of our eyes.

Related to this, our memories do not reflect the objective replaying of an actual occurrence, but our iterative mental reconstruction of an event, fact, or procedure, for example, the skills to solve a math problem, or a student's conversation with her teacher about her test grade. This means that the iterative reconstruction or mental conjuring of a remembered event will be very similar to the neural processes for imagining an event that never happened, or for simulating possible outcomes of future events. Notably, each of these processes is organized by our emotions, and reflects the subjective meaningfulness and relevance of the remembered, imagined, or simulated thought, as well as the social, physical, biological, and developmental contexts in which the person is operating.

Given all these factors, it is no wonder that different teachers and learners perceive, experience, and remember lessons and educational contexts in different ways!

Another process that is related to the study of memory and emotion, and that is an important prerequisite for the recruitment of neural networks, is attention. The last decade marks theoretical and methodological advances in the study of attention and its relationship to the development of academic skills (Corbetta and Shulman, 2002). In particular, Posner and colleagues have distinguished three different attentional networks important for learning, including networks for alerting, orienting, and executive attention (for a review, see Posner and Rothbart, 2007). They have also shown that individual differences in attention networks can be related to genetic and environmental factors, and that training in these aspects of outwardly directed attention, that is, the ability to regulate one's focus on different aspects of the environmental context, can improve preschooler's academic abilities in various areas such as reading skills and social interaction at school (Berger *et al.*, 2007). Future work should investigate how attention monitoring can be taught in schools, as a way to increase the efficiency with which neural networks are built and recruited.

Back to the Big Picture: Mind, Brain, and Education are Becoming Usefully Connected

Over a decade ago, John Bruer cautioned educators that given the current state of knowledge, directly connecting brain science and education was premature – a bridge too far (Bruer, 1997). But, much has happened since then to narrow the chasm between these two sources of knowledge about development and learning. A new field has been established whose aim is to further knowledge about children's learning by bringing together methods and evidence from various fields, among them neuroscience, psychology, cognitive science, and education.

In this stimulating climate, it is important that new neuroscience advances be carefully examined in light of psychological, developmental, and pedagogical theory and research, to ensure that the field proceeds with caution as well as optimism toward educational innovation. In the past, techniques and ideas from so-called brain-based education have led to the formation of neuromyths – oversimplified, misunderstood, or misapplied notions whose integration into educational contexts is unjustified and, in some cases, detrimental or even dangerous. Instead, findings from neuroscience must be carefully implemented and evaluated, starting in educational microcosms such as research schools, where students and faculty partner with cognitive neuroscientists in the design and assessment of research.

In conclusion, it is an exciting time for the field of MBE, and for studying the neuroscientific bases of learning. In the end, learning happens primarily in the brain; studying the neuroscientific bases of learning can therefore provide educationally relevant insights that, with careful implementation and evaluation, may improve schools and other learning environments for the generations to come.

See also: Attention in Cognition and Early Learning; Knowledge Domains and Domain Learning; Neuroscience of Reading.

Bibliography

Adolphs, R. and Damasio, A. R. (2000). The interaction of affect and cognition: A neurobiological perspective. In Forgas, J. P. (ed.) *Handbook of Affect and Social Cognition*, pp 27–49. Mahwah, NJ: Erlbaum.

Berger, A., Kofman, O., Livneh, U., and Flenik, A. (2007). Multidisciplinary perspectives on attention and the development of self-regulation. *Progress in Neurobiology* **82**(5), 256–286.

Bitan, T., Burman, D. D., Chou, T. L., *et al.* (2007). The interaction between orthographic and phonological information in children: An fMRI study. *Human Brain Mapping* **28**(9), 880–891.

Boets, B., Wouters, J., Wieringen, A. V., Smedt, B. D., and Ghesquière, P. (2008). Modelling relations between sensory processing, speech perception, orthographic and phonological ability, and literacy achievement. *Brain and Language* **106**(1), 29–40.

Bruer, J. (1997). Education and the brain: A bridge too far. *Educational Researcher* **26**(8), 4–16.

Cao, F., Peng, D., Liu, L., *et al.* (2009). Developmental differences of neurocognitive networks for phonological and semantic processing in Chinese word reading. *Human Brain Mapping* **30**(3), 797–809.

Carey, S. and Sarnecka, B. W (2006). The development of human conceptual representations: A case study. In Munakata, Y. and Johnson, M. H. (eds.) *Processes of Change in Brain and Cognitive Development*, pp 473–498. Oxford: Oxford University Press.

Corbetta, M. and Shulman, G. L. (2002). Control of goal-directed and stimulus-driven attention in the brain. *Nature Neuroscience Reviews* **3**, 210–215.

Dehaene, S., Molko, N., Cohen, L., and Wilson, A. (2004). Arithmetic and the brain. *Current Opinion in Neurobiology* **14**, 218–224.

Fischer, K. W., Bernstein, J. H., and Immordino-Yang, M. H. (eds.) (2007). *Mind, Brain and Education in Reading Disorders*. Cambridge: Cambridge University Press.

Fischer, K. W. and Bidell, T. (2006). Dynamic development of action and thought. In Damon, W. and Lerner, R. (eds.) *Handbook of Child Psychology: Volume 1. Theoretical Models of Human Development*, 6th edn, pp 313–399. Hoboken, NJ: Wiley.

Gaab, N., Gabrieli, J. D. E., Deutsch, G. K., Tallal, P., and Temple, E. (2007). Neural correlates of rapid auditory processing are disrupted in children with developmental dyslexia and ameliorated with training: An fMRI study. *Restorative Neurology and Neuroscience* **25**(3–4), 295–310.

Gallese, V., Fadiga, L., Fogassi, L., and Rizzolatti, G. (1996). Action recognition in the premotor cortex. *Brain* **119**, 593–609.

Griffin, S. (2004). Building number sense with number worlds: A mathematics program for young children. *Early Childhood Research Quarterly* **19**(1), 173–180.

Haidt, J. (2001). The emotional dog and its rational tail: A social intuitionist approach to moral judgment. *Psychological Review* **108**(4), 814–834.

Herrmann, E., Call, J., Hernandez-Lloreda, M. V., Hare, B., and Tomasello, M. (2007). Humans have evolved specialized skills of social cognition: The cultural intelligence hypothesis. *Science* **317**(5843), 1360–1366.

Immordino-Yang, M. H. (2007). A tale of two cases: Lessons for education from the study of two boys living with half their brains. *Mind, Brain and Education* **1**(2), 66–83.

Immordino-Yang, M. H. (2008). The smoke around mirror neurons: Goals as sociocultural and emotional organizers of perception and action in learning. *Mind, Brain, and Education* **2**(2), 67–73.

Immordino-Yang, M. H. and Damasio, A. R. (2007). We feel, therefore we learn: The relevance of affective and social neuroscience to education. *Mind, Brain and Education* **1**(1), 3–10.

Katzir, T. and Pare-Blagoev, J. (2006). Applying cognitive neuroscience research to education: The case of literacy. *Educational Psychologist* **41**(1), 53–74.

Knight, C. and Fischer, K. W. (1992). Learning to read words: Individual differences in developmental sequences. *Journal of Applied Developmental Psychology* **13**, 377–404.

Le Corre, M., Van de Walle, G., Brannon, E. M., and Carey, S. (2006). Re-visiting the competence/performance debate in the acquisition of counting as a representation of the positive integers. *Cognitive Psychology* **52**, 130–169.

Nelson, C. A., Zeanah, C. H., Fox, N. A., *et al.* (2007). Cognitive recovery in socially deprived young children: The Bucharest early intervention project. *Science* **318**, 1937–1940.

Oberman, L. M., Pineda, J. A., and Ramachandran, V. S. (2007). The human mirror neuron system: A link between action observation and social skills. *Social, Cognitive and Affective Neuroscience* **2**(1), 62–66.

Posner, M. I. and Rothbart, M. K. (2007). Research on attention networks as a model for the integration of psychological science. *Annual Review of Psychology* **58**, 1–23.

Schneps, M. H., Rose, T. L., and Fischer, K. W. (2007). Visual learning and the brain: Implications for dyslexia. *Mind, Brain, and Education* **1**(3), 128–139.

Singer, F. M. (2007). Beyond conceptual change: Using representations to integrate domain-specific structural models in learning mathematics. *Mind, Brain, and Education* **1**(2), 84–97.

Thatcher, R. W., North, D. M., and Biver, C. J. (2008). Development of cortical connections as measured by EEG coherence and phase delays. *Human Brain Mapping* **29**(12), 1400–1415.

Umiltà, M. A., Kohler, E., Gallese, V., *et al.* (2001). I know what you are doing: A neurophysiological study. *Neuron* **31**(1), 155–165.

Wolf, M. and O'Brien, B. (2006). From the Sumerians to images of the reading brain: Insights for reading theory and intervention. In Rosen, G. (ed.) *The Dyslexic Brain*, pp 5–10. Timonium, MD: York Press.

Further Reading

Damasio, A. R. (2003). *Looking for Spinoza: Joy, Sorrow and the Feeling Brain*. New York: Harcourt.

Goswami, U. (2006). Neuroscience and education: From research to practice? *Nature Reviews Neuroscience* **7**(5), 406–411.

Jossey-Bass Publisher (2008). *The Jossey-Bass Reader on the Brain and Learning*. San Francisco, CA: Wiley.

National Research Council (1999). *How People Learn: Brain, Mind, Experience, and School*, ch. 5. Washington, DC: National Academy Press.

Organization for Economic Co-Operation and Development (OECD) (2007). *Understanding the Brain: The Birth of a Learning Science*. Paris: OECD.

Powell, K. (2006). How does the teenage brain work? *Nature* **442**, 865–867.

Ramachandran, V. (1998). *Phantoms of the Brain: Probing the Mysteries of the Human Mind*. New York: William Morrow.

Rose, D. H. and Meyer, A. (eds.) (2006). *A Practical Reader in Universal Design for Learning*. Cambridge, MA: Harvard Education Press.

Relevant Websites

http://www.uknow.gse.harvard.edu – Harvard Graduate School of Education, Usable Knowledge forum.
http://www.imbes.org – International Mind, Brain and Education Society.
http://www.oecd.org – Organization for Economic Cooperation and Development, Centre for Educational Research and Innovation (CERI): Brain and Learning.
http://faculty.washington.edu – UW Faculty, Neuroscience for Kids.

Learning in a Cross-Cultural Perspective

L-F Zhang, The University of Hong Kong, Hong Kong
R J Sternberg, Tufts University, Boston, MA, USA

Glossary

Capital – In sociology, the word "capital" is a general term for four specific forms of capital: cultural, economic, human, and social capital. *Cultural capital* refers to the knowledge and experience that individuals gain chiefly through participating in cultural events. *Economic capital* essentially refers to wealth. *Human capital* refers to the knowledge and skills that individuals gain through education and experience. *Social capital* refers to the tangible benefits and resources that individuals build up because of their inclusion in social networks.

Field dependence/independence – This concept is also known as psychological differentiation and perceptual style. Individuals who are more *field-dependent* are less able to view objects separate from the overall environment. They are likely to be influenced by the prevailing context. Individuals who are more *field-independent* are good at identifying objects that have surroundings that might obscure their view. They tend to see things as discrete from their backgrounds.

Intellectual styles – This term is the general one for concepts such as cognitive styles, learning styles, teaching styles, and thinking styles. All these styles address people's preferred ways of processing information.

Learning approaches – Ways of learning a task that are contingent upon the student's intentions. Three common learning approaches are: *surface*, which involves meeting the minimum requirements by reproducing what is taught; *deep*, which involves a true understanding of what is learned; and *achieving*, which involves using a strategy that would maximize one's academic grades.

Self-construal – A specific dimension of self-definition. Broadly speaking, there are two types of self-construal: interdependent and independent. Individuals with an *interdependent self-construal* have a tendency to view themselves in terms of their close relationships with others. Individuals with an *independent self-construal* are likely to perceive themselves as being autonomous and separated from others.

Thinking styles – This refers to people's preferred ways of using the abilities that they have.

For nearly a century, researchers have sought alternative ways to account for learning gaps among various cultural groups. As a result of increasing globalization, understanding learning in a cross-cultural perspective has become more important than ever before. There is no such thing as a context-and/or meaning-free environment (LeVine *et al.*, 1988). We learn and make sense of our learning experiences within cultural contexts. Indeed, a substantial amount of literature concerning cross-cultural learning is converging on one conclusion – culture has a great impact on student learning. However, the major findings in this research have created several paradoxes. What could have happened? What are some of the major explanations regarding differential learning across cultures? What can scholars do to move the field forward?

This article aims at addressing the above questions in three parts. First, we describe important works concerning the learning process, focusing on intellectual styles. Second, we introduce the major works on learning outcome, centering on academic achievement. Finally, we draw some conclusions and suggest future research directions.

Intellectual Styles as Learning Processes

What are Intellectual Styles?

Intellectual styles, an encompassing term for such constructs as cognitive styles, learning styles, and thinking styles, refer to people's preferred ways of processing information and dealing with tasks (Zhang and Sternberg, 2006). The field of intellectual styles has a long history, dating back to Allport's (1937) study of personality types. One of the major reasons that theorists and researchers have maintained their interest in styles is that styles play an important role in the process of learning. They also account for individual differences in learning outcomes. Research suggests that intellectual styles are malleable to some degree, depending on many factors. One is culture. Sternberg (1997) proposed that culture is the foremost variable that helps shape people's styles and argued that some cultures are likely to be more rewarding of particular styles than of others.

Intellectual Styles and Culture

The impact of culture on intellectual styles is indisputable. However, very little concerted effort has been made to systematically investigate cross-cultural differences (or similarities) in intellectual styles. Most existing research examining intellectual styles in relation to culture has focused on testing the relationships between intellectual styles and academic achievement in different cultures, rather than on making direct comparisons of intellectual styles among students from different cultural settings. Direct comparisons may promote stereotypical views about certain cultural groups.

The studies documented in the literature have identified a certain degree of universality of intellectual styles across cultures as well as style differences based on culture (e.g., Berry, 1966). They have also presented challenges to some of the stereotypical views about particular cultural groups. These challenges pertain to claims that: (1) Black and Hispanic (including Mexicans, Puerto Ricans, Cubans, and people of other Hispanic origin) students have a higher preference for the surface approach to learning (see Watkins and Mboya, 1997); (2) Asian students are rote learners; (3) Black and Hispanic students are more field dependent than are Anglo-American students; (4) students from group-oriented societies tend to be more field dependent than students from individualistically oriented societies (see Bagley and Mallick, 1998); and (5) students from group-oriented cultures are more norm-conforming in their thinking styles (see Sternberg, 1997). The challenges to the first two claims (1 and 2) are the result of research based on Biggs' (1978) construct of learning approaches. The challenges to the next two claims (3 and 4) are derived from research grounded in Witkin's (1962) concept of field-dependence/independence. The challenge to the final claim (5) is manifested through research based on Sternberg's (1997) theory of thinking styles.

Learning approaches

One group of cross-cultural studies of students' intellectual styles has been based on Biggs' (1978) three approaches to learning: surface, which involves meeting the minimum requirements by reproducing what is taught; deep, which involves a real understanding of what is learned; and achieving, which involves using a strategy that will maximize one's grades.

However, with regard to the first two claims above (1 and 2), recent studies have found no evidence to support them. Comparative studies on the learning approaches of Black (and Hispanic) and White students in several cultures (e.g., Watkins and Mboya, 1997) have failed to reveal any significant differences in learning approaches. Similarly, the results from research comparing the learning approaches of Asian students with those of Caucasian students are at odds with the stereotypical view that Asian students are rote learners. Traditionally, Asian students' higher academic achievement has been attributed to the value they place on hard work mainly characterized by rote learning, among other factors.

However, such a view has not been supported. On the contrary, there is evidence indicating that White American students show a greater tendency to rely on the surface approach to learning than do their Asian peers.

Field dependence/independence

Field dependence/independence (FDI), alternatively known as psychological differentiation and perceptual style (Witkin, 1962), refers to the extent to which people are dependent on versus independent of the organization of the surrounding perceptual field. Field-independent individuals are thought to be better at cognitive restructuring because of their propensity for being free from external referents. Field-dependent individuals are considered to be more socially oriented as a result of their higher levels of sensitivity to external referents. Based on the definition of field dependence and of field independence, one would expect that students from individualistically oriented societies in which people enjoy social looseness (Pelto, 1968) would be more field independent and that students from group-oriented cultures would be more field dependent. Indeed, this hypothesis has been supported by numerous empirical studies.

At the same time, there is also evidence at variance with this hypothesis. For example, Buriel's (1978) comparative study found no difference in the level of field dependence/independence between Anglo-American and Mexican-American school children. In a review of the literature, Bagley and Mallick (1998) concluded that, compared with their Western counterparts (in this case, students from Canada, the UK, and the US), students from group-oriented cultures (in this case, Chinese and Japanese cultures) were more field independent.

Thinking styles

A relatively recent theory of intellectual styles, Sternberg's (1997) theory of mental self-government, states that there are 13 different ways in which people can use their abilities (i.e., thinking styles). Zhang and Sternberg (2005) classified these styles into three types. Type I thinking styles tend to be more creativity generating and denote higher levels of cognitive complexity (e.g., the global style – the tendency to focus on the holistic picture; the liberal style – the propensity for adopting a new approach to tasks). Type II thinking styles denote a norm-favoring tendency and tend to require lower levels of cognitive complexity (e.g., the local style – the preference for focusing on details; the executive style – the inclination to implement tasks with given guidelines). Type III styles may manifest the characteristics of styles from either Type I or Type II groups, depending on the stylistic demands of a specific task (e.g., internal style – preferring to work on one's own; external style – preferring to work in groups).

One might predict that the internal style and Type I styles would be more encouraged in individualistically oriented cultures and that the external and Type II styles would be more beneficial in group – or collectively oriented cultures. However, this appears to be true in some cases, but not in others. For example, Type I styles have been found to be related to higher academic achievement among American students (e.g., Grigorenko and Sternberg, 1997), whereas Type II styles have been strongly associated with better achievement in collectively oriented cultures such as Hong Kong and the Philippines. However, contrary to the prediction, better academic achievement has been found to be related to Type I styles among university students in Korea, a highly collectively oriented society, whereas better achievement has been associated with Type II styles in Spain, a more individualistic society. Finally, higher academic achievement has been found to be related to the internal style in all cultures investigated so far, be they individualistically oriented or group oriented.

Academic Achievement as Learning Outcome

The two major bodies of literature on academic achievement as learning outcomes concern Asian and African students.

Research Centered on Asian Students

In the earliest and most comprehensive study of cross-cultural learning among 625 000 students from six ethnic groups (Coleman, 1966), Asian Americans emerged as the only ethnic minority group that performed as well as or outperformed Caucasian students on many indicators of intellectual value, aspiration, and achievement. The superior achievement of Asian students in the international arena has been maintained to this day (Trends in International Mathematics and Science Study, 2008).

This finding is puzzling for several reasons. Traditional educational and psychological theories assume that better academic performance should be associated with higher levels of self-efficacy and with a stronger sense of individuality; yet, the Asian students who outperform their Western peers do so despite their expressed lower levels of self-efficacy (e.g., Eaton and Dembo, 1997). Likewise, although psychologists generally maintain that higher academic achievement tends to be positively correlated with attributions to ability, not effort, Asian students tend to attribute their academic success to effort. Anthropologists and sociologists believe that school performance has a great deal to do with wealth and socioeconomic status. However, Southeast Asian refugee students thrive academically despite their low socioeconomic status. Such paradoxes require alternative explanations of Asian students' high academic performance.

Consider three explanations of the paradoxes. The first is from the perspective of cultural values; the second uses Markus and Kitayama's (1991) concept of self-construal; and the third is based on Sue and Okazaki's (1990) notion of relative functionalism.

Cultural values

Asian students' superior achievement is believed to be largely the outcome of the strong influence of Confucian philosophy, which emphasizes authoritarian moralism, collectivism, effort, endurance, filial piety, modesty, passion for learning, and self-improvement. Many scholars have argued that, as a result of such traditional values, students of Asian origin tend to be more respectful of their elders. Asian parents have been/are known for having higher expectations of and making greater sacrifices for their children's learning. In return, Asian students feel a strong obligation to repay their parents' devotion and sacrifice with good academic performance, which is normally perceived to be one of the best forms of filial piety. Empirical evidence also suggests that Asian people often show greater passion for learning than Westerners, who usually put more emphasis on fun, self-esteem, and social development (e.g., Chao, 1996).

Cultural values have also been used to address the paradox that Asian students outperform their Western peers despite attributing their superior performance to effort rather than to ability (as would be expected by attribution theories), and while reporting lower levels of self-efficacy. Eaton and Dembo (1997) have suggested that modesty is deeply rooted in Confucianism. When Asian students do well academically, instead of boasting how naturally talented they are, they express their need to work harder and do better.

Modest people may tend to be more aware of their inadequacies and, as a result, feel the need for self-improvement through being engaged in their work more diligently. On a similar note, other researchers have proposed that Asian students may score lower on tests of self-efficacy because their Western counterparts overestimate their own abilities by evaluating themselves based on their underachieving peers or on their parents' lower expectations. Western students' higher levels of self-efficacy could also be attributed to the Western view that students need to feel good about themselves and about their achievements. For example, in both the United Kingdom and the United States, it is commonly accepted that having positive self-regard is critical for students to strive to achieve in all aspects of life.

Markus and Kitayama's concept of self-construal

Recently, several authors have borrowed Markus and Kitayama's (1991) concept of self-construal to resolve the paradox of high Asian achievement. According to Markus and Kitayama, the way in which achievement motivation drives goal-directed behavior is culture specific. Westerners tend to perceive goals as an expression of individual wishes. They consider themselves as independent selves, in contrast to Asians, who tend to view goals as an expression of their family or other communal objectives. Asians are more likely to consider themselves as interdependent selves. Moreover, Westerners tend to perceive individual action as the means of achieving personal goals, whereas Asians are likely to perceive the individual as being reflective of past and future generations. Such a strong sense of responsibility, not only for one's own success, but also for glorifying one's own family and community, has been found to be an important factor in Asian students' motivation to work harder and to find ways to fit their interests with the expectations of others.

Sue and Okazaki's relative functionalism

Sue and Okazaki (1990) have argued that in explaining the differential achievement between students of immigrant cultures and students in the host cultures, one should take into account the economic and social status of the immigrant groups in the host cultures, as well as the immigrant groups' traditional cultural values. The authors put forward their theory of relative functionalism to accommodate both cultural and social factors. They believe that immigrants make great efforts to take advantage of the opportunities (such as for education) not available in their motherlands, with the ultimate goal of upward social mobility via education. The authors have further argued that education can be the principal vehicle for upward social mobility when other means are impossible, which is often true for the Southeast Asian refugees in Western cultures. Consequently, superior academic achievement is a principal route to achieving higher social status.

Research Centered on Black and/or Hispanic Students

Most research on the academic achievement of minority students has used the cross-race comparative paradigm. Typically, Blacks and/or Hispanics are compared with their Caucasian counterparts and with their Asian peers studying in industrial countries. Such studies have usually obtained largely the same finding – Black and/or Hispanic students' academic performance lagged behind that of their Caucasian and Asian peers. Black and Hispanic students underperform on many indicators of academic achievement (DeBlassie and DeBlassie, 1996). In early research (especially between the 1960s and the early 1970s), scholars turned their attention to the notion of compensatory education, viewing minority students' academic failure as the result of some kind of culturally or racially related deficit, most noticeably, poor home preparation for school experience (Deutsch, 1964). The essence of this viewpoint is best illustrated by Crow *et al.*

(1966), who listed 60 alleged psycho-educational deficits of the culturally disadvantaged child.

Yet, this culturally/racially related deficit model cannot explain the academic success of some of the minority students and has given rise to several competing explanatory models. Below, we first discuss an explanatory model that is oriented toward racial/cultural differences – that of social class, wealth, and capital. We then discuss two alternative models that take within-culture differences into account, specifically, (1) types of minorities and (2) school structure.

Social class, wealth, and capital

Social class and wealth affect school achievement (e.g., Adler, 1968; Davis, 1948). Sociologists have integrated the concepts of social class and wealth with Bourdieu's theory of capital in explaining the achievement gap between Blacks/Hispanics and Whites. According to Bourdieu, there are four forms of capital: cultural, economic, human, and social. Although varying in their degrees of liquidity (or, the levels of ease by which they can be converted), the four forms of capital are convertible. Economic capital (i.e., wealth) is the most convertible and the most important for school achievement. Wealth, as economic capital, can enable parents to provide children with many important educational resources, such as books, computers, and access to school that is of higher quality.

Wealth can also be transformed into cultural capital – broadly defined as "instruments for the appropriation of symbolic wealth socially designated as worthy of being sought and possessed" (Bourdieu, 1977: 488). Cultural capital can be represented by activities such as attendance at art performances or exhibitions, symphony concerts, and other types of live shows. Activities such as these that require great financial expenses can enhance school achievement (e.g., Hattie *et al.*, 1997).

Wealth can also affect human capital, which in turn, affects children's school achievement. Wealthy parents may be more cognizant of the role of self-confidence in school achievement than are less wealthy parents. Such awareness may help wealthy parents to pay more attention to adopting strategies that boost their children's self-confidence.

Finally, wealth can also be transformed to social capital, which in turn affects academic achievement. Social capital is defined as the concrete benefits and resources that people build up by virtue of their inclusion in a social structure/network. Students from wealthy families have the opportunities to interact with people of greater social capital, who serve as role models for success. Seeing these role models can be very conducive to the positive development of learning motivation, and thus to the enhancement of academic achievement.

As Blacks/Hispanics are substantially less wealthy, on average, than are Whites, wealth, as manifested in different forms of capital, can be used to explain at least a portion of the racial-achievement gap. However, using social class, wealth, and capital to account for the racial-achievement gap can also be perceived as using a race-related-deficit approach, for it stresses the disadvantages associated with lack of wealth and capital commonly experienced by Blacks and Hispanics. Furthermore, it cannot explain the success of some Black and Hispanic students.

Ogbu's two types of minorities

Ogbu (1978) differentiated between two types of minorities in accordance with their initial terms of incorporation and treatment by the majority in the host culture: voluntary minorities and involuntary minorities. Voluntary minorities are those who choose to go to the host country because of perceived opportunities for economic advancement and political freedom. Involuntary minorities refer to those who were either originally brought to the host country in the form of human labor or were subdued through colonization.

A major difference between the two minority groups is what Ogbu called cultural frame of reference. Voluntary minorities tend to hold a positive frame of reference, interpreting various obstacles they are confronted with in their host countries as temporary problems that can be solved through hard work and education. In contrast, involuntary minorities tend to hold an oppositional cultural frame of reference, distrusting dominants and their institutions and perceiving them as the gatekeepers obstructing them from channels to success and social mobility.

Ogbu suggested that children from voluntary minority groups tend to achieve better than those from the involuntary groups because the parents of the voluntary minority children tend to adopt schooling strategies that are conducive to the social adjustment and academic success of their children. By contrast, the oppositional cultural frame of reference held by the involuntary minorities has promoted an anti-educational orientation that is counterproductive to academic success.

Ogbu's model accounts for some of the differences in achievement across minority groups. However, the model has been criticized on the grounds that it does not explain why some students fail whereas other students succeed even though they are from the same minority group, be it voluntary or involuntary.

Institutional practice

Explaining the achievement gap between Blacks/Hispanics and Whites from the perspective of institutional practice is a relatively recent endeavor in response to Ogbu's (1978) argument that involuntary minorities tend to take an oppositional stance toward school and that Black/Hispanic high achievers tended to act White. According to this alternative view, many institutional practices may affect the academic

engagement and achievement of Black/Hispanic minority students (e.g., Flores-Gonzalez, 2005). We highlight three such factors.

The first is known as the subtractive schooling process, in which minority culture is devalued by school teachers and administrators. Under such a school system, teachers and administrators select and reward students who possess mainstream cultural attributes and deprive minority students of important cultural and social resources, "leaving them progressively vulnerable to academic failure" (Valenzuela, 1999: 3).

The second school institutional practice that is thought to be responsible for Black/Hispanic students' low academic achievement is what is known as cultural tracking (see Flores-Gonzalez, 2005; Valenzuela, 1999). Cultural tracking is an institutional practice that puts students into particular programs based on their dominant-culture proficiency within schools. The result of such a practice is that students are divided into two main groups – those students who are believed to be equipped with dominant culture skills and those who are not. As minority culture is often devalued, the majority of minority students are sorted into the lower tracks. On the other hand, because White students have the advantage of possessing dominant culture skills, they (along with a very small number of minority students who demonstrate dominant-culture proficiency) are placed into more advanced programs. Not only does such an institutional practice shape opportunities for academic success, it also places students into different peer groups on the basis of their socially defined racial backgrounds (e.g., Lucas, 1999).

A final institutional practice believed to underlie the low achievement of Black/Hispanic students is what has been identified as Eurocentric curricula and pedagogy. Although the call for culturally responsive curricula and pedagogy was made more than two decades ago (e.g., Boykin, 1983), the curricula used in industrial countries (in particular, the United States where the minority groups being considered reside) are designed to address issues in the predominant White culture. The pedagogy used often does not take into account minority students' ways of learning. Such an institutional practice tends to discourage minority students from being active in their learning because they see little connection between their educational experiences in predominantly White schools and their own cultural values.

Conclusions and Future Directions

Convergent empirical evidence on students' learning processes and outcomes enables us to draw several conclusions. First, culture does have a significant impact on student learning. However, the influence of culture on student learning is rarely direct. Rather, the relationship between culture and student learning is often mediated by other factors of a sociological or psychological nature. Existing studies on both learning processes and learning outcomes cast doubt on some of the stereotypical views about particular cultural groups. To achieve a better understanding of learning in a cross-cultural perspective, further research is needed regarding both learning process (as represented by intellectual styles) and learning outcome (as represented by academic achievement).

On Intellectual Styles

Research on intellectual styles may help resolve some of the issues arising in this article. First, cross-cultural research on intellectual styles should be conducted among a wider range of populations. Second, we need to know more how culture interacts with intellectual styles. Third, we need better instruments to assess styles – ones that can be used in a variety of cultures.

On Academic Achievement

We also need to have a better understanding of academic achievement. First, cross-cultural research on academic achievement should involve more countries. At present, many countries in the world have been left out in existing cross-national studies. Furthermore, the bulk of the immigrant literature is about comparing the academic achievement of students from the so-called underdeveloped countries with that of students from Western industrial countries. Practically nothing is known about the differential (or similar) achievement among students across underdeveloped nations. Second, more attention should be given to the learning gaps between students from different regions or different ethnic groups within countries. Third, we need to examine more closely the impact of the interplay of culture, social class, family and school environment, psychological factors, and other student-developmental dimensions (e.g., cognitive development and psychosocial development) on student learning. Fourth, research comparing students' academic achievement should go beyond using results from tests of basic skills. Other intellectual skills such as higher-order cognitive skills, critical thinking, and creative problem solving should be examined. Finally, cross-cultural research on academic achievement should go beyond studying school achievement. Progress is being made, but there is a long way to go. Given the costs to nations of slow progress, there is little time to lose.

Bibliography

Adler, M. (1968). Intelligence testing of the culturally disadvantaged: Some pitfalls. *Journal of Negro Education* **37**(4), 364–369.

Allport, G. W. (1937). *Structure et développement de la personnalité.* Neuchatel: Delachaux-Niestlé.

Bagley, C. and Mallick, K. (1998). Field independence, cultural context and academic achievement: A commentary. *British Journal of Educational Psychology* **68**, 581–587.

Berry, J. W. (1966). Temne and Eskimo perceptual skills. *Journal of International Psychology* **1**, 207–299.

Biggs, J. B. (1978). Individual and group differences in study processes. *British Journal of Educational Psychology* **48**, 266–279.

Bourdieu, P. (1977). Cultural reproduction and social reproduction. In Karabel, J. and Halsey, A. H. (eds.) *Power and Ideology in Education,* pp 487–511. New York: Oxford University Press.

Boykin, W. (1983). On task performance and Afro-American children. In Spencer, U. R. (ed.) *Achievement and Achievement Motives,* pp 324–371. Boston, MA: Freeman.

Buriel, R. (1978). Relationship of the three field-dependence measures to the reading and math achievement of Anglo American and Mexican American children. *Journal of Educational Psychology* **70**(2), 167–174.

Chao, R. K. (1996). Chinese and European American mothers' beliefs about the role of parenting in children's school success. *Journal of Cross-Cultural Psychology* **27**, 403–422.

Coleman, J. S. (1966). *Equality of Educational Opportunity.* Washington, DC: U.S. Government Printing Office, US Department of Health, Education and Welfare, Office of Education.

Crow, L. D., Murray, W. I., and Smythe, H. H. (1966). *Educating the Culturally Disadvantaged Child.* New York: D. McKay.

Davis, A. (1948). *Social-Class Influences upon Learning.* Cambridge, MA: Harvard University Press.

DeBlassie, A. M. and DeBlassie, R. R. (1996). Education of Hispanic youth: A cultural lag. *Adolescence* **31**(121), 205–216.

Deutsch, M. P. (1964). The disadvantaged child and the learning process. In Reissman, F., Cohen, J., and Pearl, A. (eds.) *Mental Health of the Poor,* pp 172–187. New York: The Free Press.

Eaton, M. J. and Dembo, M. H. (1997). Differences in the motivational beliefs of Asian American and non-Asian students. *Journal of Educational Psychology* **89**(3), 433–440.

Flores-Gonzalez, N. (2005). Popularity versus respect: School structure, peer groups and Latino academic achievement. *International Journal of Qualitative Studies in Education* **18**(5), 625–642.

Grigorenko, E. L. and Sternberg, R. J. (1997). Styles of thinking, abilities, and academic performance. *Exceptional Children* **63**(3), 295–312.

Hattie, J., Marsh, H. W., Neill, J. T., and Richards, G. E. (1997). Adventure education and outward bound: Out-of-class experiences that make a lasting difference. *Review of Educational Research* **67**(1), 43–87.

LeVine, R., Miller, P., and West, M. (eds.) (1988). *Parental Behavior in Diverse Societies: Volume 40. New Directions for Child Development.* San Francisco, CA: Jossey-Bass.

Lucas, S. (1999). *Tracking Inequality: Stratification and Mobility in American Schools.* New York: Teachers College Press.

Markus, H. R. and Kitayama, S. (1991). Culture and the self: Implications for cognition, emotion and motivation. *Psychological Review* **98**, 224–253.

Ogbu, J. U. (1978). *Minority Education and Caste: The American System in Cross-Cultural Perspective.* New York: Academic Press.

Pelto, P. J. (1968). The difference between "tight" and "loose" societies. *Transaction* **April**, 37–40.

Sternberg, R. J. (1997). *Thinking Styles.* New York: Cambridge University Press.

Sue, S. and Okazaki, S. (1990). Asian–American educational achievements. *American Psychologist* **45**, 913–920.

Trends in International Mathematics and Science Study (2008). The International Association for the Evaluation of Educational Achievement, Amsterdam.

Valenzuela, A. (1999). *Subtractive Schooling: US–Mexican Youth and the Politics of Caring.* Albany, NY: SUNY Press.

Watkins, D. and Mboya, M. (1997). Assessing the learning processes of Black South African students. *Journal of Psychology* **131**, 623–640.

Witkin, H. A. (1962). *Psychological Differentiation; Studies of Development.* New York: Wiley.

Zhang, L. F. and Sternberg, R. J. (2005). A threefold model of intellectual styles. *Educational Psychology Review* **17**(1), 1–53.

Zhang, L. F. and Sternberg, R. J. (2006). *The Nature of Intellectual Styles.* Mahwah, NJ: Erlbaum.

Further Reading

Lew, J. (2006). *Asian Americans in Class: Charting the Achievement Gap among Korean American Youth.* New York: Teachers College Press, Columbia University.

Mandara, J. (2006). The impact of family functioning on African American males' academic achievement: A review and clarification of the empirical literature. *Teachers College Record* **108**(2), 206–223.

Zhang, L. F. and Sternberg, R. J. (eds.) (2009). *Perspectives on the Nature of Intellectual Styles.* New York: Springer.

COGNITION AND LEARNING: THEORY

Connectionism and Learning

Self-Regulated Learning and Socio-Cognitive Theory

Vygotsky and Recent Developments

Theoretical Bases of Computer Supported Learning

Personal Epistemology in Education

Learning in a Sociocultural Perspective

Situative View of Learning

Connectionism and Learning

T R Shultz, McGill University, Montreal, QC, Canada

Glossary

1-of-n coding – A method of activation coding such that only one of a group of units is active.

Algorithm – Explicit instructions for solving a problem.

Base 10 – Having any of ten values, for example, 0–9.

Binary – Having either of two values, for example, 0 or 1.

Composite number – An integer greater than 1 having more than two divisors; thus, it is not a prime number.

Connection weight – A link between units in a neural network, represented as a real number. It is roughly analogous to a brain synapse.

Connectionism – A style of computing inspired by how brains are thought to function, using networks of simple interconnected units.

Constructivism – The idea that knowledge is constructed by the learner, often by building on top of existing knowledge.

Context – Incidental cues that accompany a learning experience.

Course coding – A method of activation coding such that one unit is very active and its neighboring units are a bit active.

Disequilibrium – In Piaget's theory, it refers to a mismatch between mental representation and environmental outcome, indicating a misunderstanding.

Divisor – An integer that divides equally (i.e., with no remainder) into another integer.

Dyslexia – Impaired reading.

Error – A measure of how far off a network is from learning its training patterns, computed as the sum of squared differences between actual outputs and target outputs, summed over all training patterns.

Error function – A hypothetical function relating network error to the size of a connection weight, usually conceptualized as a parabola with arms opening upward.

Excitation – Increasing the activity of a unit.

Generalize – To perform correctly on problems that have not been trained. It is used to distinguish understanding from mere memorization.

Gradient descent – A learning method that changes network weights in proportion to the slope of the error function in order to reduce network error.

Hidden unit – A unit that mediates between input and output units, thus hiding from the environment and enabling the learning of nonlinear relations.

Hz – The abbreviation for hertz: unit of frequency in cycles per second.

Inhibition – Dampening the activity of a unit.

Input – A vector of activations supplied to a network's input units. The pattern of these activations describes a problem to the network.

Integer – A whole number.

Integer part – The part of a real number preceding the decimal.

KBCC – Knowledge-based cascade correlation, a learning algorithm that builds a network topology by recruiting previously learned networks and single hidden units as needed.

Learning rate – A proportion that multiplies the error slope and, thus, controls the size of weight changes and the speed of learning. A programmer sets this proportion at the start of a simulation so that a network's weights change enough to support quick learning, but not so much that error oscillates across an error minimum.

Modeling – Building and running a computer program to simulate scientific phenomena.

Multiplicand – A number to be multiplied by another.

Net input – The net amount of input entering a unit, computed as the sum of products of sending-unit activations and respective connection weights.

Nonlinear – A kind of function that cannot be represented as a simple linear combination of its inputs, for example, distinguishing the points inside a circle from those outside the circle. The degree of nonlinearity typically makes learning more difficult.

Output – A vector of activations computed by the output units of a network. The pattern of these activations describes the network's response to a particular input pattern.

Prime number – An integer greater than 1 having only two divisors, 1 and itself.

Real number – A decimal number, not having an imaginary part.

Simulate – To reproduce natural phenomena, usually by presenting a computer program with the similar inputs to those found in nature. The program (or model) usually abstracts and simplifies so as not to be overwhelmed by natural complexity.

Slope – The rate at which one variable changes as a function of changes in another variable.
Source network – In KBCC, it refers to a previously learned network that may be recruited to aid the current learning task.
Target network – In KBCC, it refers to a network learning the current problem.
Target vector – The activation values supplied by a teacher or by the environment, indicating correct output values for a particular input pattern.
Threshold – The region in which a unit is highly sensitive to changes in net input.
Topology – The way a network is laid out in terms of its organization and connectivity.
Unit – The basic processing element of an artificial neural network. A unit has a fluctuating level of activity, represented as a real number, corresponding to the average firing rate of a neuron.
Vector – An ordered list of numbers.

Introduction

Connectionism is a style of computing that partly mimics the properties and functions of brains. Incorporating ideas from computer science, artificial intelligence, mathematics, physics, neuroscience, and psychology, connectionists build working computational models of learning and other psychological processes. A few connectionist projects have modeled educational phenomena such as reading and arithmetic, and these applications are highlighted here. After reviewing the basics of modeling and connectionism and focusing on some models of particular relevance to education, the broader implications of connectionism for education are discussed.

Importance of Modeling

The value of building computer models of psychological processes may not be immediately apparent. A general justification is that modeling was consistently useful in a variety of scientific disciplines. A good scientific model typically:

- implements a theory in a precise, concrete, easy-to-manipulate way;
- covers (or generates) a variety of interesting phenomena;
- helps to explain the phenomena that it covers;
- links various observations together, making them easier to understand;
- predicts new phenomena that can be tested; and
- can be improved when evidence reveals new facts or contradicts model predictions.

Since the renaissance of connectionism in the mid-1980s, all of these advantages have been realized to some degree. Indeed, of all the available techniques for psychological modeling, none has produced as many valuable insights into learning as connectionism has.

Modern Connectionism

The central idea of connectionism is that mental processes can be modeled by interconnected networks of simple units. These artificial neural networks can largely be understood in terms of activity and connectivity. As noted in the first row of **Table 1**, neural networks are composed of two elements: units and connection weights. Units are analogous to brain neurons, while weights are analogous to synapses, the connection points between neurons. Unit activity corresponds to the average firing rate in neurons, that is, how often they send an electrical impulse from their cell body down their axon to other neurons. Connection weights correspond to the ability of neurons to excite or inhibit the activity of other neurons. Both units and weights can be implemented in neural networks as vectors of real numbers. In psychological terms, unit activity corresponds to active memory, a focus on particular ideas, while weights encode long-term memory for how ideas are related. Unit activity changes over seconds, whereas changes to connection weights can occur rather quickly or over a period of years, enabling networks to learn.

An artificial neural network is thus a set of units and weights organized in a particular topology. Most neural networks are programmer designed and static, meaning that their topology remains constant, but others build their own network topology automatically during learning.

As shown in **Figure 1**, each unit in a network runs a simple program in which it computes a weighted sum of

Table 1   Activity and connectivity in artificial neural networks

Feature	Elements	Brain analogy	Behavior	Implementation	Memory type	Time scale of change
Activity	Units	Neurons	Firing rate	Real numbers	Active	Seconds
Connectivity	Connection weights	Synapses	Excitation, inhibition	Real numbers	Long term	Seconds to years

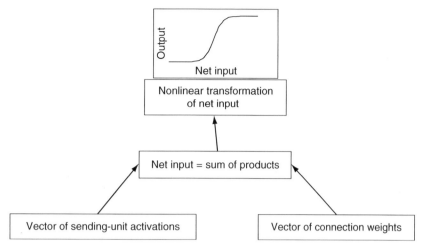

Figure 1 Update of unit activation in a neural network.

inputs coming from other units and then outputs a number, which is a nonlinear function of the weighted sum of inputs. This output is then sent to other units running this same simple program. Units are active at various levels and communicate their level of activity to other units in a way that modulates the activity of those other units.

As **Figure 1** shows, a receiving unit's level of activity changes in two steps. In the first step, a vector of sending-unit activations is multiplied by a vector of connection weights. Some of these products might be positive (with an excitatory influence on the receiving unit), while others are negative (having an inhibitory effect). The sum of these products constitutes the net input to the receiving unit.

In a second step, this net input is then passed through a nonlinear activation function like that shown in the top of **Figure 1**. Like real neurons, this function has a floor (corresponding to no activity), a ceiling (corresponding to the maximum firing rate of about 300 Hz in real neurons), and a continuous but sharp transition between them (a threshold). As net input increases below the threshold, there is little change in activity of the receiving unit. However, as net input further increases across the threshold, there is a sharp increase in the activity of the receiving unit. Well beyond the threshold, if net input continues to increase, activity of the receiving unit would again fail to change much because it would be nearing its maximal level. Nonlinear activation functions enable the learning of complex, nonlinear target functions, which are common in the real world. They also prevent networks from overheating through continual increases in activity.

The primary way that neural networks learn is by adjusting their connection weights to reduce error. In supervised learning, connection weights are typically trained by being presented with examples – pairs of input values and target output values. Since there are often multiple inputs and multiple outputs, the example

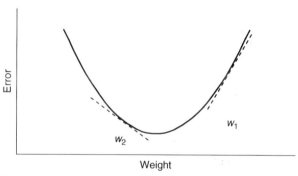

Figure 2 A hypothetical function relating network error to the value of a network weight. Slopes of the error function at two weight values (w_1 and w_2) are drawn with dashed lines.

values (represented by real numbers) are presented in the form of vector pairs. In each pair, one vector holds input values and the other holds target output values. By processing such examples, a network gradually learns to produce the correct output vector in response to a particular input vector. The vector pairs used in such training are called the training set; those used in testing generalization to untrained examples are known as the test set. Error at the output units is computed as the sum of squared differences between actual outputs and target outputs.

Imagine that the error contributed by a single connection weight is some unknown parabolic function of the value of that connection weight as shown in **Figure 2**. This makes sense on the assumption that there is some optimal value for each connection weight such that either increasing or decreasing the value of the weight from this optimum would increase error. If the precise shape of this error function was known, learning would be easy – simply adjust each connection weight to the value that minimizes error. Unfortunately, these error functions are unknown to the learner, and are unlikely to assume the simple, smooth parabola drawn in **Figure 2**. The neural network learner may know the size of the discrepancy between actual and target responses in the training set, but not the exact shape of the error function.

However, this meager information can be used to compute the slope of the error function at each connection-weight value that has been experienced. The slope (or gradient) is the first derivative of a function, evaluated at a particular point. Slope is a measure of how rapidly error changes as a function of changes in a connection weight. Two such hypothetical slopes are shown in **Figure 2** for two different weight values (w_1 and w_2). If the slope at a given weight value is known, then the direction in which the connection weight should change is also known. If the slope is negative (as at w_2), then the weight should increase; however, if the slope is positive (as at w_1), then the weight should decrease.

However, how much should a connection weight change? If a weight is changed too much, the floor of the error valley could be missed, perhaps creating an oscillation in weight adjustments than never settles near the minimum error. One could make only tiny steps of weight change to avoid passing over the minimum error, but this slows learning. A better solution is to make the amount of weight change proportional to slope. With a steep slope, as at w_1, a large change in weight is suggested, whereas with a shallow slope, as at w_2, weight change should be smaller because the error minimum may be close. This technique of using information on the slope of the error function is known as gradient descent because it attempts to slide downhill on the error surface to reach the point of minimum error in weight space. Thus, weight change is a negative proportion (known as learning rate) of the derivative of error with respect to weight.

Relations to the Old Connectionism

Modern connectionism differs from the older connectionism of Thorndike. Thorndike was a founder of behaviorism, emphasizing the idea that organisms learn associations between stimuli and responses. Responses become habitual by being rewarded and thus having their associations to stimuli strengthened. As in other versions of behaviorism, learning was explained without recourse to internal states.

As in this article, there were applications to educational issues such as reading and arithmetic.

Despite minor historical influence on, and superficial similarities with, modern connectionism, the differences are more profound than is sometimes recognized. Some important differences between old and new versions of connectionism are listed in **Table 2**, most of which are important for applications to education. Whereas behaviorists wrote about single associations between stimuli and responses, modern connectionists deal with large, multilevel, massively parallel networks. Moreover, some modern networks are designed with recurrent connectivity which allows for sequential processing and complex network dynamics, akin to the interesting behavior of differential equations. Following from these differences, the knowledge representations in behaviorist schemes were entirely local. In contrast, modern networks can as well employ distributed schemes in which each unit represents many different ideas and each idea is represented by many different units. Such distributed representations are more efficient and robust and account for many interesting psychological phenomena, along with being more biologically realistic. Behaviorism disavowed interest in mental states, emphasizing a direct association between stimulus and response. Modern connectionists instead invest considerable energy into determining what their networks know at various points in learning. Such knowledge-representation analyses often play an essential role in explaining psychological phenomena.

Thorndike's law of effect emphasized that habit formation was controlled by rewards. Contemporary connectionist models have clearly demonstrated the difficulty of learning from evaluative reward signals that tell the organism that it is doing well or badly, but fail to indicate what is needed for improvement. In contrast, supervised neural networks learn from fully specified target vectors that indicate the correct response to particular inputs, making learning faster and more accurate. All of the foregoing provide modern networks with vastly more learning power than habits. A habit can handle only a simple linear relation between a stimulus and a response, whereas there are now proofs that a network with a single layer of hidden units can learn any continuous function to any degree of accuracy if this layer has enough hidden units. There are also proofs that any function can be

Table 2   Some key differences between old and new connectionism

Characteristic	Topology	Knowledge representation	Emphasis	Feedback signal	Learning power	Method
Old connectionism	Single association	Local	Behavior	Evaluative	Linear	Vague speculation
Modern connectionism	Massive parallelism	Distributed	Knowledge representation	Informational	Nonlinear	Explicit modeling

learned by a network with two hidden layers, provided there are enough hidden units in each layer. Finally, most of the theoretical work in behaviorism was vague and speculative; however, the new connectionism is aided by working computational models that clearly indicate data coverage and predictions.

Models of Reading

Connectionism has been more concerned with establishing a theoretical basis for understanding learning than with developing applications in the field of education. So far, the area of education best modeled by connectionism is that of reading. Reading is an unnatural act for humans that typically requires several years of education. A debate about whether it is better to teach reading by the rules of letter-to-sound correspondence or by learning to visually recognize whole words stretches back to the 1960s. There are hundreds of such phonic rules, but because letter-to-sound correspondence is only somewhat regular, they are not that useful to learn. There is some regularity in reading aloud, as in the pronunciations of the words *lint*, *mint*, and *hint*, but plenty of exceptions, as in *pint*.

A theoretical framework for an influential series of connectionist simulations of reading is pictured in **Figure 3**. The rectangles represent groups of network units encoding information on spelling, sound, or meaning, or hidden units that effect nonlinear transformations between these three encodings. The bidirectional arrows indicate connection weights in both directions. By adjusting these connection weights, the system might learn to transform written words into meanings or pronunciations, meanings into pronunciations or written words, and pronunciations into meanings or written words. So far, research has concentrated on the mapping from written words to pronunciations, that is, reading aloud. These models learned to pronounce the words they were trained on, such as *gate* and *save*, and generalized successfully to novel words such as *rave*.

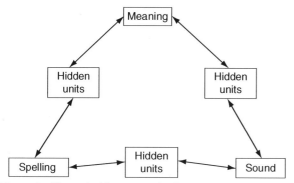

Figure 3 Theoretical framework for Seidenberg's connectionist models of reading.

Such connectionist models also captured a number of psychological phenomena such as frequency, similarity, and consistency effects. The frequency effect is that common words are read more quickly than rare words. The model correctly predicted that frequency effects are smaller for words with many similar neighbors (e.g., *save*) than for more isolated words such as *sieve*. The consistency effect is that words with regular neighbors are read more quickly than words with irregular neighbors. For example, the word gave has a regular pronunciation, but irregular neighbors such as *have*. So words like gave take longer to read aloud than words such as *must*, which do not have irregular neighbors. Consistency effects are larger for lower-frequency words and less-skilled readers.

Since all words share the same set of connection weights and neural learning tries to reduce as much error as possible, frequent words, words with high similarity to other words, and words with regular neighbors are read quickly and accurately. Frequency, similarity, and consistency can compensate for each other in that words at a disadvantage in one respect might benefit from another factor. For example, an infrequent word might be read quickly and accurately because of its similarity to other words.

A curiosity of these models is that the network has no explicit representation of lexical entries (words). Not only is it common for language researchers to assume and use a lexicon, but the frequency effect in reading is also customarily explained by storing frequencies within a lexicon. Remarkably, networks exhibit the frequency effect without a lexicon, which shows that a lexicon is not required for this effect.

The recent focus on the mapping from spelling to meaning has enabled connectionist models to address the issue of how to teach reading. In contrast to previous models emphasizing a conflict between visual and phonetic routes, these networks reveal collaboration between the two routes. Early in training, networks relied more on the spelling–sound route (see **Figure 3**); however, with more training, the spelling–meaning–sound route increased in importance, mimicking a psychological progression. As with humans, skilled reading of words involved convergent contributions of both routes from print to sound.

Dyslexia can be simulated in these models by damaging either the network or its training. Reducing the number of hidden units would be analogous to a child with fewer cognitive resources. Limiting the amount of training would correspond to inadequate educational opportunity. Ignoring training in the spelling–sound route would correspond to teaching without phonics. Letting each letter string activate more spelling units could implement a visual impairment. In all of these impaired cases, network learning focuses on the largest current source of error, namely that contributed by regular words, thus sacrificing exception words.

Other computational models using symbolic rules have relatively more difficulty accounting for these psychological phenomena. The main implication of connectionist models for reading instruction is to provide students with plenty of examples (not rules) of printed words and their meanings and pronunciations.

Models of Mathematics

Mathematics is another example of unnatural skills taught over several years of formal instruction that have been modeled with neural networks. The two examples considered here are learning of the single-digit multiplication table and prime-number detection.

Multiplication

Learning the 0–9 multiplication table requires 5–6 years of schooling and continues to generate errors even in adults. The most widely studied problem is the production task in which two single-digit multiplicands are presented and the person is asked to provide their product. Several regularities are evident in the psychological literature:

- Computational procedures such as repeated addition ($m \times n =$ adding m, n times) are gradually replaced by recall.
- Reaction time increases with the size of the multiplicands, except that the 5's table and tie problems (e.g., 4×4, 7×7) are quicker than expected.
- Adults under mild time pressure make about 8% errors.
- Errors are usually close to the correct product, and often substitute a close multiplicand (see **Figure 6** for a breakdown of error types).
- There is a strong positive correlation between errors and reaction time across problems.

Building on the successes and limitations of several earlier models, Dallaway designed a feed-forward network learning with multiplicands 2–9 that captured the last four of these psychological phenomena. The topology of his network is shown in **Figure 4**, and the nature of his course coding of multiplicands is shown in **Figure 5**. Target output vectors were designed by turning on one product unit and leaving the others off. The percentage of error types plotted in **Figure 6** for adults and Dallaway's model indicate a good fit, although the overall error rate was higher for the networks at 14%.

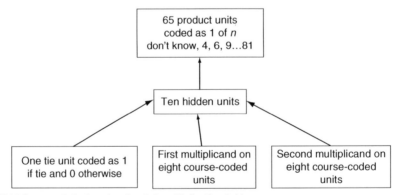

Figure 4   Dallaway's (1994) network for learning the 2–9 multiplication table.

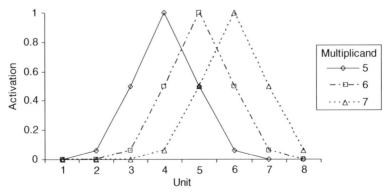

Figure 5   Course coding of the input multiplicands 5, 6, and 7 in Dallaway's (1994) network. Activation representing a given integer is maximal for the unit corresponding to that integer itself and drops off for neighboring values less than or greater than the integer. Only integers from 2 to 9 were included in this simulation; therefore, integer n centers on unit $n-1$.

As shown in **Table 3**, operand errors involve changing one of the operands, close-operand errors involve changing to a close operand, and frequent-product errors involve selecting a frequently occurring product. Table errors involve choosing a less-frequent product that is in the multiplication table and does not share any multiplicands with the problem being tested. Operation errors involve adding instead of multiplying. Networks reacted about as quickly to multiplication by 6 as 5, complicating explanation of the 5's speedup. The fit to human data was not as good when the 0 and 1 tables were also trained. Some psychologists believe that multiplication by 0 and 1 is rule governed, rather than being based on connectionist pattern matching; however, it seems possible that the greater regularity of 0 and 1 multiplications just makes them seem rule governed. The fit to human reaction time data worsened when the training sample was not biased in favor of smaller multiplicands.

Applications of this and related models to education remain tentative, but likely would be similar to those made for reading, namely to include many examples of correct multiplication that go just beyond the student's current ability. The role of addition in learning and understanding multiplication should be explored in future modeling because of its evident role in children's learning and its possible role in several multiplication errors.

Primality

Prime-number detection is a more advanced mathematical skill that has also been modeled with connectionist methods. The primality of an integer n can be determined by seeing if n is divisible by any integers between 2 and the integer part of $\sqrt{n}$. It is efficient to test in this order because the smaller the prime divisor, the more composites it detects in a fixed range of integers.

A connectionist system called knowledge-based cascade-correlation (KBCC) learned this algorithm from examples by recruiting previously learned knowledge of divisibility. KBCC is based on a simpler connectionist algorithm called cascade-correlation (CC) that learns from examples by recruiting single hidden units. CC and KBCC have simulated a large number of phenomena in learning and cognitive development. KBCC has the added advantage that it can recruit its existing network knowledge as well as single hidden units. Both CC and KBCC are constructive learners that build their new learning on top of existing knowledge.

For primality, the pool of source knowledge contained networks that had previously learned whether an integer could be divided by each of a range of divisors, for example, a divide-by-2 network, a divide-by-3 network, etc., up to a divisor of 20 (see **Figure 7**). These source networks were trained on integers from 2 to 360. Twenty KBCC target networks trained on 306 randomly selected integers from 21 to 360 only recruited source networks involving prime divisors below the square root of the largest number they were trained on (360). Moreover, they recruited these sources in order from small to large, and avoided recruiting single hidden units, source networks with composite divisors, any divisors greater than square root of 360 even if prime, and divisor networks with randomized connection weights.

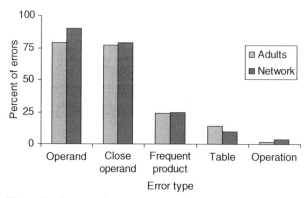

Figure 6 Percent of multiplication errors of different kinds in adults (Campbell and Graham, 1985) and neural networks (Dalloway, 1994). The values do not sum to 100 because error types are not exclusive.

Table 3 Multiplication table with three error types highlighted[a]

x	2	3	4	5	6	7	8	9
2	4	6	8	10	*12*	14	*16*	*18*
3	6	9	*12*	15	*18*	21	24	27
4	8	*12*	*16*	20	*24*	28	32	36
5	10	15	20	25	30	35	40	45
6	*12*	*18*	*24*	30	36	42	48	54
7	14	21	28	35	42	49	56	63
8	*16*	*24*	*32*	*40*	*48*	*56*	64	72
9	*18*	27	36	45	54	63	72	81

[a]Light-gray-shaded boxes indicate close operand errors for 5 × 4; dark-gray-shaded boxes indicate operand errors for 8 × 9; and frequent-product errors are given in italics.

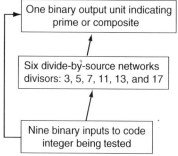

Figure 7 Topology of a KBCC network that learns prime-number detection (Egri and Shultz, 2006).

KBCC target networks never recruited a divide-by-2 source network; however, this was because they, instead, used the least significant digit of n, binary coded, to directly determine if n was odd or even. As with people who use the 1's digit of base-10 numbers to check for divisibility by 5 or 10, this is a shortcut to dividing by 2.

The KBCC target networks learned to classify their training integers 3 times faster than did knowledge-free networks, with fewer recruits on fewer network layers, and generalized almost perfectly to novel test integers. Networks without knowledge of divisibility did not generalize better than chance guessing.

As predicted by this simulation, university students testing the primality of integers also mainly used prime divisors below $\sqrt{n}$ and ordered their divisors from small to large. The recommendation for education is not only to use examples, but also to structure curricula so that later learning can build on existing knowledge.

Educational Relevance

As connectionist modeling of learning continues, potential applications to education could become more apparent. Some implications of connectionist models of reading and mathematics were already noted, namely the use of examples with fully specified feedback on what to do with these examples. Teaching with examples is compatible with the long-recognized notion of learning by doing. Since students may vary considerably in their skills, this can be challenging in a classroom, but could be accomplished with materials that vary enough in difficulty to continuously provide at least some examples just beyond the ability of each student.

Accompanying examples with full feedback is more informative than the evaluative feedback provided by rewards or equally vague cues to disequilibrium which were characteristic of the educational recommendations of classical behaviorist theory and Piagetian theory, respectively. Computational results make it clear that having to convert information about being wrong into a useful target vector makes learning both slower and more difficult.

Another educational suggestion stemming from connectionism is that repetition and patience are often required. This stems, in part, from the fact that connectionist learning can be quite slow. Some insight into this slowness has been gained from studying variation in learning-rate parameters. When learning rate is too high, networks may oscillate across error minima. To settle near such minima, it is often necessary to take small steps in connection-weight adjustments. This could also be true of brain networks, and if so, teachers should not rush through difficult material.

Of course, methods for increasing both the speed and accuracy of network learning are under active investigation. Networks learn faster and more accurately if they can recruit relevant existing knowledge. In the case of prime-number detection, successful generalization to untrained integers requires recruiting existing knowledge. This suggests curricula designed to ensure that lessons are optimally ordered. Network simulations might identify the most beneficial lesson sequences.

Another implication of neural modeling is that context is important and that it limits generalization. Connectionist learning algorithms naturally exhibit context effects whenever contextual cues aid learning. However, such contextual effects ensure that generalization may not be as universal as desired. Similar to network researchers, teachers might try to decontextualize learning by varying contextual cues in teaching. Again, exploratory network simulations could help.

Many of these educational suggestions emanating from connectionist research (practice, feedback, prior knowledge, and structured lessons) at first appear more consistent with teacher-centered, rather than child-centered, approaches to education. This seems paradoxical given that constructive connectionist approaches (CC and KBCC) are consistent with a Piagetian approach to knowledge acquisition that is the psychological basis for child-centered education.

Whereas teacher-centered education focuses on structured lesson plans, extensive practice, and feedback, child-centered education emphasizes curiosity, problem solving, and discovery learning. Although these approaches are often portrayed as being opposed, constructivist connectionist modeling suggests a possible rapprochement, with computational demonstrations that effective learning incorporates both methods. In connectionist learning, knowledge representations are constructed and abstracted, rather than memorized. Moreover, this learning is particularly effective when experience is well structured, building more complex ideas on top of earlier simpler ideas, and well practiced, with detailed feedback.

See also: Neuroscience Bases of Learning.

Bibliography

Campbell, J. I. D. and Graham, D. J. (1985). Mental multiplication skill: Structure, process, and acquisition. *Canadian Journal of Psychology* **39**, 338–366.

Chall, J. S. (2000). *The Academic Achievement Challenge: What Really Works in the Classroom?* New York: Guilford.

Dallaway, R. (1994). *Cognitive Science Research Papers 306: Dynamics of Arithmetic: A Connectionist View of Arithmetic Skills*. Brighton: University of Sussex.

Egri, L. and Shultz, T. R. (2006). A compositional neural-network solution to prime-number testing. In *Proceedings of the Twenty-Eighth Annual Conference of the Cognitive Science Society*, pp 1263–1268. Mahwah, NJ: Erlbaum.

Fodor, J. A. and Pylyshyn, Z. W. (1988). Connectionism and cognitive architecture: A critical analysis. *Cognition* **28**, 3–71.

Foorman, B. R. (1994). The relevance of a connectionist model of reading for "the great debate" *Educational Psychology Review* **6**, 25–47.

Hertz, J., Krogh, A., and Palmer, R. G. (1991). *Introduction to the Theory of Neural Computation*. Reading, MA: Addison-Wesley.

Lemaire, P. and Siegler, R. S. (1995). Four aspects of strategic change: Contributions to children's learning of multiplication. *Journal of Experimental Psychology:General* **124**, 83–97.

Seidenberg, M. S. (2005). Connectionist models of word reading. *Current Directions in Psychological Science* **14**, 238–242.

Shultz, T. R. (2003). Computational Developmental Psychology. Cambridge, MA: MIT Press.

Shultz, T. R. and Rivest, F. (2001). Knowledge-based cascade-correlation: Using knowledge to speed learning. *Connection Science* **13**, 1–30.

Sun, R. (ed.) (2008). *Cambridge Handbook of Computational Cognitive Modeling*. Cambridge: Cambridge University Press.

Thorndike, E. (1913). *Educational Psychology: The Psychology of Learning*. New York: Teachers College Press.

Thorndike, E. (1932). *The Fundamentals of Learning*. New York: Teachers College Press.

Further Reading

Anderson, J. A. (1995). *An Introduction to Neural Networks*. Cambridge, MA: MIT Press.

Arbib, M. A. (ed.) (1995). *The Handbook of Brain Theory and Neural Networks.* Cambridge, MA: MIT Press.

Dayan, P. and Abbott, L. F. (2001). *Theoretical Neuroscience: Computational and Mathematical Modeling of Neural Systems*. Cambridge, MA: MIT Press.

Elman, J. L., Bates, E. A., Johnson, M. H., *et al.* (1996). *Rethinking Innateness: A Connectionist Perspective on Development*. Cambridge, MA: MIT Press.

Harm, M. W. and Seidenberg, M. S. (1999). Phonology, reading acquisition, and dyslexia: Insights from connectionist models. *Psychological Review* **106**, 491–528.

Haykin, S. (1999). *Neural Networks: A Comprehensive Foundation*, 2nd edn. Upper Saddle River, NJ: Prentice-Hall.

Plaut, D. C. (1999). A connectionist approach to word reading and acquired dyslexia: Extension to sequential processing. *Cognitive Science* **23**, 543–568.

Plaut, D. C., McClelland, J. L., Seidenberg, M. S., and Patterson, K. E. (1996). Understanding normal and impaired word reading: Computational principles in quasi-regular domains. *Psychological Review* **103**, 56–115.

Rumelhart, D. E., Hinton, G. E., and McClelland, J. L. (1986). A general framework for parallel distributed processing. In Rumelhart, D. E. and McClelland, J. L. (eds.) *Parallel Distributed Processing: Explorations in the Microstructure of Cognition,* vol. 1, pp 45–76. Cambridge, MA: MIT Press.

Rumelhart, D. E., Hinton, G. E., and Williams, R. J. (1986). Learning internal representations by error propagation. In Rumelhart, D. E. and McClelland, J. L. (eds.) *Parallel Distributed Processing: Explorations in the Microstructure of Cognition,* vol. 1, pp 318–362. Cambridge, MA: MIT Press.

Relevant Website

http://www.psych.mcgill.ca/perpg/fac/shultz/personal/default.htm – LNSC Cascade-correlation Simulator Applet: Allows users to run constructive and static neural networks on canned and designed learning problems, without programming; Tutorial on cascade-correlation; Tutorial on knowledge-based cascade-correlation.

Self-Regulated Learning and Socio-Cognitive Theory

P H Winne, Simon Fraser University, Burnaby, BC, Canada
A F Hadwin, University of Victoria, Victoria, BC, Canada

Glossary

Agency – The human capacity to choose and act on choices.

Coregulation – The temporary sharing or distributing of self-regulated learning between a learner and a more capable other (peer or teacher) to help the learner advance toward more effective self-regulated practice.

Enactive learning – Learning by doing or practicing.

Metacognition – The thought about cognition and the products of cognition usually involving monitoring and choosing among tactics and strategies.

Scaffolding – The dynamic interaction between a learner and an other in which the kind and degree of support is carefully matched to the goal of learning and the learner's current level of mastery relative to that goal.

Self-regulated learning – The intentional and strategic adaptation of learning activities to change cognition, motivation, and behavior outcomes.

Sociocognitive theory – A theory that acknowledges the joint roles of cognitive factors, self-beliefs, and environmental factors in human learning; an extension of social-learning theory.

Sociocultural theory – A theory that emphasizes social interactions and participation as central in enculturating learners into the practices of their learning communities.

Strategy – A carefully selected set of tactics coordinated to achieve a learning goal.

Tactic – A basic technique for learning that is initiated under specific conditions and produces a well-defined result.

Vicarious learning – Learning by observing others.

What Is Self-Regulated Learning?

Self-regulated learning (SRL) refers to intentionally and strategically adapting learning activities to achieve goals of learning. Learners self-regulate by applying learning tactics they predict will be successful. They monitor how well tactics achieve goals and, when differences exceed a threshold, they make adjustments. Adjustments can be made to learning processes and strategies; to conditions, like motivation or factors in the learning environment, that affect learning activities or to learning outcomes and products.

For example, after writing a paragraph, I typically pause to read it. I check it against at least two standards; whether it is (1) clear and (2) presents content I intended it to. If the paragraph falls short of these standards, I adjust the words or phrasing (products), then reexamine the paragraph to judge whether these adjustments are sufficient to meet the standards I set.

I often write without making a written outline. However, when the topic is particularly complex or relatively new to me, past experience in producing less–than-satisfactory products leads me to adjust my writing process. In these cases, I begin by creating an outline, then writing to fill in its sections. I also add a third standard to be used when pausing and reviewing my writing, namely, examining the match between what I have written and the outline.

These examples of regulating my writing are instances of self-regulation because I, rather than some external person or source of feedback (e.g., a computer beep) initiated and performed the regulating activity. I determined the standards to use in monitoring whether adjustments were necessary, and I decided whether the product and processes met those standards. If instead, my coauthor read my draft and made changes to it, that is regulation by an external source or other-regulation. If my coauthor modeled the development of a concept map as a method for improving my writing, that adjustment to my typical writing process also is other-regulation. If my coauthor asked me questions that prompted me to reflect on and adjust my writing process or product, this would be considered coregulation because rather than doing the regulation or changes for me, she encouraged me to metacognitively reflect upon and regulate my own writing.

In sum, regulation occurs when learners adjust products they create or methods they use to create products. Adjustments are made in relation to standards that characterize ideal or sufficient products and processes. Regulation is metacognitive because the monitoring examines prior cognitive activities that were methods by which the person engaged in a task. When regulation is initiated and managed by one's self, that is self-regulation. When people regulate processes they use to acquire new knowledge – to learn – they engage in SRL.

Models of SRL

The number and scope of models of SRL make it impossible to address all of them here. We select models that are prevalent in the research literature and provide context for considering sociocognitive aspects of SRL.

Boekaert's Model of Adaptable Learning

Boekaerts' model of adaptable learning focuses on students in classrooms. A basic premise is that learners strive to balance two priorities: (1) extending knowledge and skills to enhance their personal resources – a mastery mode of learning – and (2) preserving what one knows and believes to avoid injuring the self – a coping or well-being mode of learning. Corresponding to these two modes, the learner draws on constellations of: (1) learning strategies that build resources and (2) coping strategies that protect resources. Thus, Boekaerts' model, like others, blends cognitive and motivational elements. Success in this depends on the learners' capacity to appraise the overall situation and, on that basis, control their approach to learning as well as elements in their task environment.

When learners participate in learning, they draw on three main sources of information. The first is their perception of the task environment. This is an amalgam of the task they are assigned, the teacher's (or textbook's) instructions, and features of the physical and social context in which the task is situated. The second source of information is a spectrum of knowledge and skills specific to the domain of the task that comprise an action plan. The plan includes: prior declarative and procedural knowledge, tactics and strategies they have successfully used before, plus metacognitive knowledge. The third source of information concerns the student's hierarchy of goals, motivations, and values.

Boekaerts' model emphasizes learners' goal setting and ways they apply control to deal with successes and failures. Productive self-regulating learners plan for how they can receive feedback about goals. When goals are not met, learners seek to balance goals relating to mastery and those of coping in ways that adapt to maintain a satisfactory balance and sense of self.

Winne and Hadwin's Model of Recursive Self-Regulation

Winne and Hadwin developed their model to describe occasions when learners study, as in doing homework or preparing for an oral presentation. They postulate that SRL unfolds over four flexibly ordered and recursive phases.

In phase one, learners identify what they perceive to be conditions that define the assigned task. Conditions fall into two main categories. Task conditions are features of the assigned task such as objectives the teacher (or textbook) set, time available, whether peers are involved, social structure (e.g., cooperative vs. competitive, or whether responsibility is individual or shared), resources available to start and then support work on the task, and guidance or scaffolding. Cognitive conditions are internal to the learner. They include the scope and relevance of prior knowledge, motivational orientation, epistemological beliefs, known study tactics, and other qualities that make the learner a unique individual.

In phase two of this model, learners construct a perception of what the task is and, on that basis, set their own goals. In phase three, learners begin engaging with the task, taking steps to reach goals. In phase four, large-scale changes to preceding phases may be made, including changing metacognitive knowledge, to enhance success in the present and for future tasks.

Within each phase, Winne and Hadwin hypothesize that learners engage in metacognitive monitoring. For example, in phase one, learners may reexamine external resources or what they know about the task to revise their description of the assignment. When metacognitive monitoring in later phases reveals gaps of the kinds the learner perceives to be too great, learners retreat to a prior phase to make adjustments – this is the recursive property of their model.

Zimmerman's Social–Cognitive Model

Zimmerman's model extends Bandura's social cognitive theory. It also is a phased model. In the forethought phase, learners undertake two main activities. One couples an analysis of the task the learner perceives to be assigned to planning that identifies what the learner forecasts are optimal techniques for succeeding at the task. The other facet of the forethought phase is where learners survey their self-motivational beliefs, specifically: self-efficacy, expectations they have for the outcome(s) of the task, their intrinsic interest in the task and its value to them, and goals they seek to achieve.

In the second phase, learners engage in the task and simultaneously apply control processes to stay on track toward goals. One key component is applying self-control, for which there are four main elements: (1) self-instruction, where learners overtly or covertly describe what they are to do; (2) imaging, where learners mentally picture their activities; (3) attention focusing, where learners change their external and cognitive environment to screen out distractions; and (4) applying strategies that decompose a complex task into parts that can be managed. The second key component, self-observation, sets the stage for applying control. Learners record mentally or materially (e.g., in a personal log) what they do and how well it works, and engage in cycles of self-experimenting to explore whether variations in their approach will lead to greater success.

In the third and final phase, learners self-reflect. This has two components: self-judgment, where learners determine the extent to which goals are achieved; and self-evaluation, where learners compare their achievements to standards. Standards have four forms: mastery, one's prior performance, normative expectations, and in collaborative task environments, whether one's expectations were successfully fulfilled.

Commonalities across Models of SRL

Task Environment

Whenever SRL occurs, it occurs in the context of a task the learner is pursuing. Tasks may be assigned by teachers, textbooks, or peers in a collaborative work group; or, tasks may be self-generated, as when a learner pursues knowledge and skills related to a hobby. Tasks are multifaceted and there is great variety among typologies for characterizing tasks. Common facets include time available, resources at hand, whether standards are explicit or implicit, and characteristics of feedback the learner can access (e.g., timing, topic, and guidance).

Agency

To have capacity to self-regulate learning, learners must be able to make choices and, within relatively wide limits, to act on their choices. Without such latitude of behavior, learning is other-regulated rather than self-regulated. Agency is the common term used to describe this capacity to choose and act on choices. Sociocognitive theory emphasizes the role of individual agency on human learning. Bandura proposed that human agency involves four core features including: intentionality, forethought, self-reactiveness, and self-reflectiveness. These features of agency are cornerstones in most models of SRL and account for the perception that self-regulation is a sociocognitive process. As such, every model of SRL rests on the assumption that learners can exercise agency although it is recognized that, for practical and other reasons, agency is not boundless. For example, expressions of agency are strongly prescribed by social conventions.

Goals

Making adjustments to products of learning or processes used in learning might sometimes be trial and error. Notwithstanding a universal assumption tacit in some models of SRL is that learners are purposeful and oriented to particular goals. Goals define standards for judging the adequacy or sufficiency of products and processes. Formally, a standard is a description of an observable

feature of a product or process that can be measured at least nominally, that is, present or absent. Goals also can have features that are measured at finer distinctions, such as ranks and intervals.

Goals have two characteristics. One is purely informational. In this sense, standards that constitute goals are just descriptions of products or processes. The other characteristic of goals is what they mean to people. In this sense, goals matter because they have *qualia* – feelings, emotions, motivation, and values. Some models of SRL give different prominence to the informational features and the *qualia* of goals.

Monitoring

Goals play roles in SRL across time. First, goals are information learners consider as they shape their approach to tasks, including whether the task is accepted as presented, accepted but modified, or rejected. Second, learners may consider goals in the midst of engaging in a task. Some tasks have explicit subgoals. Third, learners can examine products and processes used in learning at point of completion. In all three instances, standards inherent in the goals are compared to attributes of the products and processes at each point along the timeline. Monitoring is the cognitive process responsible for making this comparison and generating a description of the match between goals and events. In this sense, all models of SRL are metacognitive models because this monitoring is inherently metacognitive.

Memory and Reasoning

New situations are never exactly the same as prior experiences. Thus, learners interpret each new situation in relation to what they remember about previous situations they deem similar. In this way, all SRL is integrally dependent on what a learner can remember about previous situations, as well as what that knowledge permits them to perceive about new situations. In matching history to the present, learners interpolate or interpret.

When learners adjust a product or process, models of SRL assume learners do this with an intention that making that particular adjustment, as opposed to some other adjustment, will align the product or process with standards defined in goals. Having this intention entails that learners reason about the likelihood the adjustment will have intended effects.

Sociocognitive Accounts of SRL

When is Cognition Social?

From a sociocognitive perspective, learners are agents who can choose how they will behave. Bandura's triadic theory describes learners' choices as shaped by reciprocal interactions among: (1) past behaviors; (2) personal variables, such as interest in a task and beliefs about whether they have efficacy to complete a task; and (3) environmental variables, such as instructional supports they can draw on, material resources, and task contexts. The reciprocity involving environment, particularly peers and models, in learning represents cognition as fundamentally social. As learners work on tasks, they generate new information that updates any or all three factors. In addition to reciprocal influences between personal beliefs and behavior, social and environmental factors mediate learning. Environmental factors include things such as social modeling, feedback, and instructional conditions. Each can influence on personal variables and behavior before, during, or after a task. Each can, in turn, be shaped or regulated by behaviors and personal variables. For example, my coauthor, who initially thought he would easily complete his writing task, might revise that belief after several unsuccessful attempts to generate an outline. Personal beliefs about the writing task might be influenced by the fact that the deadline is approaching. Collectively, these beliefs about his person and the environment might lead him to adopt a different strategy for writing, such as abandoning the preliminary outline, writing an introductory section, and using that introduction as a vehicle for collaboratively generating an outline with his coauthor.

Sociocognitive theory recognizes that learners can learn in two ways. They can learn by doing, called enactive learning; and by observing, called vicarious learning. Both kinds of learning are social because the activities of learning are embedded in a task environment that is reciprocally influenced by: (1) others directly (e.g., modeling and feedback), (2) memories of others' behaviors (e.g., attention to what is observed), and (3) tools others created (e.g., instructions and examples).

Sociocognitive Learning and SRL

Vicarious learning is central to sociocognitive accounts of SRL because regulation is described as a developmental trajectory moving from observation, through emulation of others usually involving guided practice, to self-control, and finally to self-regulation. Observation is fundamentally social because it involves attending to actions of a proficient model, participating in guided practice, and learning in relation to instrumental feedback. Through these social processes, students develop competence with the task, content, and context; as well as their capabilities to self-regulate learning.

From this perspective, SRL is a developmental process assisted by observing models, trying out the behavior, and receiving feedback from others. There is a tacit assumption in most sociocognitive descriptions of SRL that social supports are prominent while SRL proficiency develops

and become less prominent afterward. In fact, however, environmental factors such as instructional sequence and classroom context continually exert a reciprocal influence on self-regulatory behaviors and beliefs.

The three models of SRL introduced earlier share two features with sociocognitive perspectives of learning. First, they emphasize the role of individual agency. Second, they acknowledge the role of task environment in shaping self-regulatory activity.

Alternatives to Sociocognitive Theories of SRL

More recent perspectives of learning reveal increased interest in explaining the role of social and contextual influences on SRL.

Sociocultural influences on SRL

Sociocognitive perspectives of SRL emphasize self-regulation as developing within the individual and assisted by external modeling and feedback. In contrast, sociocultural perspectives of SRL emphasize it as a fundamentally social process wherein students learn to internalize language, signs, and activities existing first in the sociocultural practices of their communities. This shift in perspective changes the emphasis from self- to coregulation.

From a sociocultural perspective, SRL is a stage occurring as children are socialized into speech patterns and practices. Coregulation is the temporary sharing or distributing of self-regulatory processes and thinking between a learner and more capable other (peer or teacher), while the learner transitions toward self-regulatory practice.

Three basic concepts characterize coregulatory aspects of self-regulation. First, rather than focusing on the individual learner, the focus is on the relationships among individuals, objects, and settings. Second, regulating learning involves coordinating and negotiating social contexts as well as self and social expectations and goals. Third, instructional supports afford opportunities for learners to experiment with and learn motivation as well as strategies and self-evaluations central to SRL.

Informed by Vygotsky's notion of internalization, regulation is seen as a social process because it appears first on the intrapsychological plane and then later becomes part of a child's understanding, appearing on the interpsychological plane. Borrowing from partners in learning and joint problem solving are considered core coregulatory processes in the social exchange between learners and more capable others. From this perspective, the mark of SRL is when the activity and practice appears in a learner's own performance, and when those activities are internalized and automated.

Coregulation

From the sociocultural perspective, coregulation is a central transitional process in a learner's development of more productive SRL. Coregulation is an interactive process whereby ownership of self-regulatory activity and thinking is first shared among participants, then gradually taken up or appropriated by the individual learner. During coregulation, student and teacher regulate together, sharing thinking and decision making and developing a shared or intersubjective task environment where each brings expertise and control to the task. Slowly, as knowledge and control are transferred to the learner, self-regulation emerges and students begin to develop realistic self-evaluations. Hence, this process is referred to as emergent interaction. Finally, the student independently engages behaviors, actions, and thinking associated with SRL.

In contrast to a sociocognitive perspective of SRL that emphasizes self-regulation developing within the individual in reciprocal interaction with external modeling and feedback, coregulation emphasizes a shifting in who shapes the regulation. Through scaffolding, cognitive demands arising from engaging in a task are eased by sharing the demands of metacognitively monitoring, evaluating, and regulating task processes. For example, rather than a mother modeling her own steps and thinking while tying a shoe lace, she takes on the regulation of her child's tying shoe laces by metacognitively monitoring and evaluating with the child. The mother might ask questions like: "What do you know about how to connect those two laces?" "How do you know when you have completed the first step properly?" "What do you need to do now?" In this way, the child focuses on task enactment while the mother supports metacognitive engagement and regulatory control of learning.

Research on SRL and Sociocognitive Models

Several core social components appear in theoretical and empirical accounts of SRL. We provide a snapshot of findings.

Feedback and SRL

Feedback provided by others is a social tool that exerts powerful effects. An important distinction about feedback is whether it is targeted at tactics and strategies, called process feedback, or at products, called knowledge of results. The distinction is somewhat artificial in the case of SRL because, when a learner is attempting to regulate processes, these are products of metacognition that are being affected by feedback describing how processes were carried out.

The small amount of research on how feedback affects SRL and products generated in tasks is quite consistent. When learners face challenging tasks for which their current tactics and strategies are not sufficient for success, performance in the long run can be improved by providing feedback about processes in the short run. What occurs in this case is that, while the learner is shaping up tactics and strategies, there is little success in meeting the goals of the task per se. Delaying gratification, in the sense of postponing progress toward task goals, often frustrate learners and their teachers but overcoming this pays off in the end.

Modeling and SRL

Modeling is considered an important antecedent of self-regulation. When students observe models, they acquire knowledge and strategies for successfully completing a task. Under productive conditions of modeling, they also develop beliefs regarding their efficacy for that task. Models can display mastery of the task or methods for coping with the challenges of a task not yet mastered. Research shows both kinds of models are beneficial under different circumstances. When children have experienced failure or challenges, coping models enhance self-efficacy and skills better than mastery models. Observing multiple peer models is more effective. Modeling has been shown to improve self-regulation of academic skills in domains such as mathematics and writing, motor skills, strategy knowledge, and metacognitive strategies.

Models are effective when observers perceive them as competent, regardless of model age. Children are more influenced by models they perceive as similar in ability to themselves.

Scaffolding and SRL

Scaffolding is a dynamic interaction between the learner and an other. The other provides support that is carefully calibrated to the goal of the task and the learner's current level of mastery relative to that goal. Through scaffolding, learners can achieve something that would not be possible by themselves. With effective scaffolding, the learner gradually assumes full regulatory control of cognition, metacognition, motivation, and behavior.

Research has yet to systematically examine the role of diagnosis, calibration, and fading on specific subprocesses of cognition, motivation, metacognition, and behavior associated with SRL. The picture that is beginning to emerge suggests that scaffolding takes time. It involves forms of coregulatory dialog. The teacher requests information, confirms the learner's results or interpretation, restates results, and models thinking or requests judgments about learning or performance. In coregulatory dialog, students request information, confirm interpretations of the teacher's activities, elaborate on features of the task and goals, and request evaluations of performance and learning. Furthermore, when scaffolding is adapted, timely and targets specific aspects of SRL such as planning, monitoring, and using strategies, students experience shifts in their mental models, use more strategies, and regulate their learning by planning, activating prior knowledge, and monitoring their progress toward goals.

See also: Metacognition.

Further Reading

Bandura, A. (1986). *Social Foundations of Thought and Action: A Social Cognitive Theory.* Englewood Cliffs, NJ: Prentice-Hall.

Bandura, A. (2001). Social cognitive theory: An agentic perspective. *Annual Review of Psychology* **52**, 1–26.

Boekaerts, M. (2006). Self-regulation and effort investment. In Sigel, E. and Renninger, K. A. (vol. eds.) *Handbook of Child Psychology: Volume 4. Child Psychology in Practice*, pp 345–377. Hoboken, NJ: Wiley.

Boekaerts, M., Pintrich, P. R., and Zeidner, M. (2000). *Handbook of Self-Regulation.* Academic PressSan Diego, CA.

Butler, D. L. and Winne, P. H. (1995). Feedback and self–regulated learning: A theoretical synthesis. *Review of Educational Research* **65**, 245–281.

Corno, L. and Mandinach, E. B. (2004). What we have learned about student engagement in the past twenty years. In McInerney, D. M. and Van Etten, S. (eds.) *Big Theories Revisited: Volume 4. Research on Sociocultural Influences on Motivation and Learning*, pp 299–328. Greenwich, CT: Information Age.

Gallimore, R. and Tharpe, R. (1990). Teaching mind in society: Teaching, schooling, and literate discourse. In Moll, L. C. (ed.) *Vygotsky and Education: Instructional Implications and Applications of Sociohistorical Psychology*, pp 175–205. New York: Cambridge University Press.

McCaslin, M. and Hickey, D. T. (2001). Self-regulated learning and achievement: A Vygotskian view. In Zimmerman, B. J. and Schunk, D. H. (eds.) *Self-Regulated Learning and Academic Achievement: Theoretical Perspectives,* 2nd edn., pp 227–252. Mahwah, NJ: Erlbaum.

McGivern, J. E., Levin, J. R., Ghatala, E. S., and Pressley, M. (1986). Can selection of an effective memory strategy be induced vicariously. *Contemporary Educational Psychology* **11**, 170–186.

Puustinen, M. and Pulkkinen, L. (2001). Models of self-regulated learning. *Scandinavian Journal of Educational Research* **45**, 269–286.

Rosenthal, T. L. and Zimmeman, B. J. (1978). *Social Learning and Cognition.* New York: Academic Press.

Schunk, D. H. (1987). Peer models and children's behavioural change. *Review of Educational Research* **57**, 149–174.

Schunk, D. H. (2001). Social cognitive theory and self-regulated learning. In Zimmerman, B. J. and Schunk, D. H. (eds.) *Self-Regulated Learning and Academic Achievement: Theoretical Perspectives,* 2nd edn., pp 125–151. Mahwah, NJ: Erlbaum.

Schunk, D. H. and Zimmerman, B. J. (1997). Social origins of self-regulatory competence. *Educational Psychologist* **32**, 195–208.

Winne, P. H. and Hadwin, A. F. (1998). Studying as self-regulated learning. In Hacker, D. J., Dunlosky, J., and Graesser, A. C. (eds.) *Metacognition in Educational Theory and Practice*, pp 277–304. Mahwah, NJ: Erlbaum.

Zimmerman, B. J. (2000). Attaining self-regulation: A social cognitive perspective. In Boekaerts, M., Pintrich, P., and Zeidner, M. (eds.) *Handbook of Self-Regulation*, pp 13–39. San Diego, CA: Academic Press.

Zimmerman, B. J. (2004). Socio-cultural influence and students' development of academic self-regulation: A socio-cognitive perspective. In McInerney, D. M. and Van Etten, S. (eds.) *Big Theories Revisited: Volume 4. Research on Sociocultural Influences on Motivation and Learning*, pp 139–164. Greenwich, CT: Information Age.

Zimmerman, B. J. and Schunk, D. H. (2001). *Self-Regulated Learning and Academic Achievement: Theoretical Perspectives,* 2nd edn. Mahwah, NJ: Erlbaum.

Vygotsky and Recent Developments

J V Wertsch, Washington University in St. Louis, St. Louis, MO, USA

The study of learning and cognition has been heavily influenced by the ideas of Lev Semënovich Vygotsky. Vygotsky was born in Byelorussia in 1896 and spent the most important period of his professional life working in research and educational institutes in Moscow, where he died of tuberculosis in 1934. During his short life, Vygotsky addressed a remarkable range of topics in philosophy, psychology, semiotics, pedagogy, and literary analysis.

Vygotsky's works fill more than ten volumes, most written during the final decade of his life. His ideas have spawned a new round of research in the post-Soviet years, including intellectual biographies and analyses of how his ideas are tied to those of other major figures of his time such as Gustav Gustavovich Shpet.

Vygotsky's contributions to contemporary psychology can be spelled out in terms of three general themes that run throughout his writings. To one degree or another, these themes also characterize much of the writing of contemporary researchers influenced by Vygotsky, researchers who have developed ideas about cultural–historical and sociocultural approaches to psychology, and they characterize much of the writing on activity theory as well. These themes can be stated as follows:

- Cognition must be understood developmentally (i.e., genetically) in terms of its origins and subsequent development at individual and cultural levels of analysis.
- Cognition is mediated by semiotic mechanisms, especially natural language.
- Higher (i.e., uniquely human) mental processes such as problem solving, voluntary memory, and voluntary attention have their origins in social activity.

All of these themes reflect the general idea that mental functioning in the individual is fundamentally shaped by the social and historical context. Instead of focusing on how individual mental processes are made manifest in social expression, Vygotsky focused on how social expressions become manifest in individual mental processes.

Although such an approach emphasizes the social world, social interaction, and what Vygotsky termed intermental functioning, it does not amount to some form of social reductionism. Individual agency is still a central part of the picture. Like Mead, Vygotsky postulated that the key to understanding higher mental processes is how individuals participate in, and appropriate, social processes. In a nutshell, the approach asserts that developmental or genetic analysis must be employed to study how processes that originate in social action shaped by semiotic mediation are transferred to the individual plane and shape higher mental processes.

Genetic Analysis

Vygotsky approached the early years of ontogenesis in terms of the interaction of two lines of development: the natural and the cultural, and he viewed the qualitative transformation of mental functioning that results from this interaction as key. He viewed any attempt to reduce all mental functions to amalgamations of lower order, biologically driven stimulus–response patterns as fundamentally misguided. The development of will or volition, for instance, is not to be seen as growing out of an iterative process of stimulus–response mechanisms, but as a qualitatively different type of phenomenon grounded in social processes. This was part of his effort to avoid the traps of the associationist and other reductionist approaches.

Like other major developmental theorists of his day, Vygotsky did not view developmental analysis as applying only to ontogenesis, and although much of his empirical study focused on children, he by no means assumed that developmental analysis could be equated with child psychology. Instead, it applies to several, qualitatively distinct genetic domains (Wertsch, 1985), namely phylogenesis, sociocultural history, ontogenesis, and microgenesis. As such, his notion of developmental psychology was much broader than what is often assumed in contemporary writings.

Vygotsky's approach to genetic analysis tends to interpret cultural differences in terms of developmental hierarchy, something that is no longer readily accepted by many cultural anthropologists. In their comparative studies of abstract reasoning in the 1930s, for example, Vygotsky and Luria interpreted differences between Uzbek and Russian performance as reflecting different stages in a grand developmental hierarchy. For them, this was what might be termed a cross-historical, rather than a cross-cultural study since they interpreted differences in the groups' performance as reflecting different stages in the evolution of a single general form of human civilization. The findings from these studies and the methods Luria used to generate them continue to provide inspiration for empirical research today. For example, a great deal of fruitful work over the last three decades on cross-cultural comparisons of the psychological effects of literacy and schooling stems from the ideas of Vygotsky and Luria.

Contemporary modes of interpreting empirical findings, however, are quite different from what Vygotsky and Luria used. While accepting genetic analysis as a valuable technique in domains such as sociocultural history and ontogenesis, investigators today are likely to reject Vygotsky's assumption that cross-cultural differences can somehow be reduced to cross-historical differences. At least since the work of Franz Boas (1966) and Edward Sapir (1921), this assumption has been highly suspect in disciplines such as cultural anthropology in the US and Europe. Specifically, any tendency to view cultural differences in terms of historical evolution is likely to lead to charges of Eurocentrism since it is virtually always the case that the perspective used to do the comparing turns out to be at the top of the developmental hierarchy. Even with this caveat, however, Vygotsky's ideas have had a powerful impact on cross-cultural comparisons of cognition and other forms of mental functioning (Cole, 1996).

Mediated Nature of Human Mental Functioning

For Vygotsky and sociocultural approaches to cognition in general, the key to development is that social interactions are mediated by semiotic systems, most importantly language. His emphasis was on how forms of language use that shape human communication are appropriated by children in the development of cognitive processes on the individual plane. Vygotsky made increasingly strong claims toward the end of his career to the effect that an understanding of language and other cultural tools provides the foundation for the rest of his approach. Under the general heading of psychological tools, he included "language; various systems for counting; mnemonic techniques; algebraic symbol systems; works of art; writing; schemes, diagrams, maps, and mechanical drawings; [and] all sorts of conventional signs" (Vygotsky, 1981a: 137). Researchers such as John-Steiner (1991) have explored the role of symbol systems including drawing, gesture, music, or diagrams in the development of cognition.

An essential aspect of Vygotsky's treatment of mediational means is that its incorporation into human action (including mental functioning) does not simply make this action easier or more efficient in some quantitative sense. Instead, its incorporation typically results in a qualitative transformation. In his view "by being included in the process of behavior, the psychological tool [sign] alters the entire flow and structure of mental functions. It does this by determining the structure of a new instrumental act, just as a technical tool alters the process of a natural adaptation by determining the form of labor operations" (Vygotsky, 1981a: 137).

Vygotsky's emphasis on language as a cultural tool is evident in the writings of his followers as well. For example, Luria (1982) argued that just as mastery of a physical tool transforms human physical activity, mastery of the symbolic tool transforms human mental activity:

Language, in the course of social history, became the decisive instrument which helped humans transcend the boundaries of sensory experience, to assign symbols, and to formulate certain generalizations or categories. Thus, if humans had not possessed the capacity for labor and had not had language, they would not have developed abstract, "categorical" thinking. (p. 27)

Such studies by Vygotsky and his colleagues reveal that they tended to view language and other cultural tools as always working in favor of more advanced human functioning, as inevitably leading to more sophisticated performance. Other analysts have challenged Vygotsky's relatively uncritical stance toward mediation and have explored ways in which cultural tools constrain as well as facilitate action. These critiques suggest that language and other cultural tools may restrict, as well as enable activity often because they emerge or are privileged for reasons other than to facilitate the action in which they are eventually embedded.

The study of forces that give rise to cultural tools has not usually been the main focus of analyses of mediated action, but there are a few general points to make nonetheless. Perhaps the most interesting of these is that many of the cultural tools employed in mediated action were not designed for the role they have come to play. An illustration of this can be found in the keyboards used to type in English. Almost all users of such keyboards use the so-called QWERTY version, named after the fact that these letters are located at the upper left-hand portion of the array. Unless otherwise informed, most users of this keyboard assume that it was designed to facilitate their typing. In actuality, however, just the opposite is the case from today's perspective. The QWERTY keyboard was designed in an era of mechanical typewriters when the biggest impediment to efficient typing was having two or more keys jam together. As a result, the designers of the QWERTY keyboard specifically devised it to slow typists down.

With the appearance of electric typewriters and word processors, there is obviously no such need to slow typists down. Nevertheless, the vast majority of individuals who type in English continue to use the QWERTY keyboard, something that is made all the more striking by the fact that there is a readily available alternative keyboard design that is superior for most typists in terms of speed and accuracy. For example, the Dvorak keyboard is relatively easy to master, and most computer keyboards can easily be converted to its configuration.

The fact that the vast majority of individuals typing in English continue to use the QWERTY keyboard speaks of the power of historical, economic, and other forces in shaping the cultural tools we employ. It also speaks of the tendency to use whatever psychological tools are handed to us in an uncritical way. This suggests that many of these tools may not be designed, or may not have evolved to facilitate the forms of mediated action in which they are currently employed. The particular case of the QWERTY keyboard is sometimes viewed as an isolated example of how technological and economic forces can go wrong. However, as authors such as Norman (1993) have argued, institutional, cultural, and historical forces often result in technology that is far from ideally designed from the perspective of the user, and this raises the question of whether similar issues might not be involved for all sorts of cultural tools.

The history of natural language presents an intriguing set of problems from this perspective. For the most part, language is not consciously planned or designed, a point that makes it somewhat different from the QWERTY keyboard example. However, many of the lessons of this illustration apply to language as well. For example, literacy and its impact on social and individual action raise several interesting questions. Literacy skills acquired in formal educational settings are associated with a specific set of cognitive skills, and the kind of language use required in formal literacy training is related to a willingness and ability to engage in tasks such as syllogistic reasoning.

However, it is generally accepted that literacy did not emerge in human history as part of an effort to facilitate skills such as those required in abstract reasoning tasks. Instead, literacy emerged in response to needs such as keeping records and conducting communication about commercial transactions. Furthermore, specific writing systems have often emerged when speakers of one language have borrowed the script used for another. Such facts serve to reinforce the claim that many cultural tools arise in response to forces that have little to do with the range of functions they are eventually required to serve.

In summary, cultural tools are often not simply neutral cognitive instruments. Instead, they may introduce historical and political dimensions into mental functioning and its socialization. Indeed, the distribution of psychological tools is often part of larger sociocultural debates and social differentiation. An example of this can be found in debates in the US surrounding the efficacy of Spanish or African-American vernacular as classroom instructional languages. These debates provide stark reminders that all mediational means are not equally valued in a society. Nor are they made equally available. This of course also applies to the distribution and use of tools such as computers in modern societies. The digital divide in the US means that computers may be widespread in many well-funded public and private schools, and all but absent in low-income urban or rural schools.

This suggests that cultural tools are implicated in the reproduction of social hierarchies. Many analysts of learning and cognition may consider these issues to be outside the boundaries of their area of inquiry, but to the extent that sociocultural psychology is concerned with the intersection of human mental functioning and the institutional, historical, and cultural contexts in which it occurs, it must take account of the social and political aspects of cultural tools. As scholars such as Duncan (1996) suggest, those working within a Vygotskyan tradition must critically appraise the function of cultural tools and pattern of access to social spheres that they afford.

Social Origins of Individual Mental Functioning

In his approach to human mental functioning, Vygotsky outlined an account that began with action, namely mediated action (Zinchenko, 1985). Furthermore, he argued that the origins of this action are social, and in this connection he sought the developmental precursors of individual mental functioning in social processes. Perhaps the most general statement of this theme in Vygotsky's writings can be found in his general genetic law of cultural development:

> Any function in children's development appears twice, or on two planes. First it appears on the social plane and then on the psychological plane. First it appears between people as an interpsychological category and then within the individual child as an intrapsychological category. . . .but it goes without saying that internalization transforms the process itself and changes its structure and function. Social relations or relations among people genetically [i.e., developmentally] underlie all higher functions and their relationships. (Vygotsky, 1981b: 163)

In this view, human mental functioning originates in inter-individual activities and only gradually develops into intramental processes. The very definition of mind is expanded such that its origins can be traced to activities between people, and the structural and functional organization of mind on the intermental plane provides the foundation for intramental functioning.

An essential part of Vygotsky's formulation of the intermental and intramental planes is that he viewed them as being inherently related. Indeed, the boundaries between social and individual functioning are quite permeable in his account, and his concern was with ongoing transformations between intermental and intramental processes rather than with any sharp distinctions that can be drawn. From this perspective, an element of sociality characterizes even the most private and internal forms of mental functioning:

[Higher mental functions'] composition, genetic structure, and means of action – in a word, their whole nature – is social. Even when we turn to [internal] mental processes, their nature remains quasi-social. In their own private sphere, human beings retain the functions of social interaction. (Vygotsky, 1981b: 164)

This statement does not assume that higher mental functioning in the individual is a direct and simple copy of socially organized processes; the point Vygotsky made in his formulation of the general genetic law of cultural development about transformations in internalization warns against any such view. Furthermore, it does not assume that nothing of interest goes on in the mind or brain of the individual when participating in intermental functioning. Instead, it simply posits a close connection, grounded in genetic transformations, between the specific strategies and processes of intermental and intramental functioning.

Vygotsky's general genetic law of cultural development underlies several aspects of his account of human mental functioning. For example, his research on what Piaget had called egocentric speech convinced him that the origins of children's problem solving and concept development lay not in interaction with the physical environment, but in their participation in social processes. By participating in social interaction, children appropriate certain linguistically mediated problem solving, thinking, and regulatory techniques first for external, social activity, then for individual cognitive activity as well. In Kozulin's (1990) words, "Development is therefore not an unfolding or maturation of pre-existing 'ideas'; on the contrary, it is the formation of such ideas – out of what originally was not an idea – in the course of socially meaningful activity" (p. 114).

The general genetic law of cultural development has received the most attention in the West in it incarnation as the zone of proximal development. The implications of this construct have been examined from perspectives such as general development and learning and psychoeducational assessment. In many cases, Vygotsky's comments about this zone are extracted from the more general context of his argument, and as a result it may be difficult to appreciate that it is just one way that he played out the implications of the general theme about the social origins of individual mental functioning. In fact, he developed the notion of the zone or proximal development fairly briefly on only a couple of occasions in his writings.

Vygotsky defined the zone of proximal development as distance between the performance level of an apprentice operating independently on the intramental plane and the level of intermental functioning involving an apprentice and an expert. It has provided the foundation for analyzing adult–child interaction and instruction; interaction and learning of children with disabilities; assessment; and other purposes.

Vygotsky's discussion of intermental processes has also played a role in the formulation of ideas about socially shared cognition, distributed cognition, and other topics. In several of these cases, the discussion does not posit a transition from the social to the individual plane that Vygotsky mentioned in the general genetic law of cultural development. Instead of speaking of social origins, with the assumption that the primary role of intermental functioning is to give rise to intramental functioning, investigators of socially shared cognition are often concerned with human cognitive activity that remains on the intermental plane. This is now widely recognized in studies of workplace activities, and it has taken on new importance in educational settings as well with the rise of interest in issues such as reciprocal teaching (Palincsar and Brown, 1984) and communities of learners (Lave and Wegner, 1991).

In analyzing these processes, investigators have raised questions about how to understand and assess intermental functioning in its own right, that is, independent of how it may give rise to intramental functioning. This brings with it some interesting new assumptions about how the expression cognitive development is to be used. In contrast to the usual assumptions grounded in methodological individualism (Lukes, 1977), the point is that intermental functioning itself may be examined from the perspective of development. From this perspective, it is appropriate to examine the development of cognition of a group and not just of the individuals in it.

Some dyads and larger groups such as institutions and even entire societies seem to function differently and perhaps at more advanced levels than others. Differences in how institutions think (Douglas, 1986) or societies remember (Connerton, 1989) have long been recognized by anthropologists, sociologists, and other scholars, but such expressions, let alone the conceptual framework behind them are quite alien to most studies of cognitive development.

This raises questions requiring conceptual frameworks that will be quite different from those we currently employ. What does it mean for a group – as a group – to develop cognitively? How can we formulate the processes involved such that they can be studied in some kind of a principled way? How would we go about assessing the relative levels of development of groups? Such issues need to be addressed without falling into the traps of strong versions of collective memory or cognition (Wertsch, 2002).

Returning to the issue of social origins of individual mental functioning as outlined by Vygotsky in his general genetic law of cultural development, it becomes crucial to consider how the transition from intermental to intramental functioning is envisioned. As suggested by Vygotsky, development should not to be understood as simply the internalizing for private uses of what were originally social forms of behavior. In fact, Cazden (1988) warns against a "mechanical conception of the process of internalization whereby overt social interaction (speaking and listening) becomes transformed into covert mental processes (thinking)" (p. 108).

Instead, during learning activity, a transfer of competence – or the transfer of strategic responsibility – from expert to novice occurs. In the process, both the learner and the activity are transformed. In order for this transfer and transformation to take place, both the learner (novice) and the teacher (expert) must be active partners in the dialog surrounding a task.

This focus on active participation on the part of the tutor as well as the apprentice has been a major theme in the writings of Rogoff (1990) on guided participation. From this perspective, it is as essential to recognize and understand the contributions made by the learner, or apprentice, as it is to recognize those made by the teacher. This amounts to a corrective to what some view as sort of cultural transmission model inherent in Vygotsky's view, a model in which the learner is taken to have little active role. Instead of being passive recipients of an input or a hypothesis-generating algorithm, children (or adult novices for that matter) are taken to be active participants in the co-construction of conversation and activity. Strategic responsibility for the task is gradually transferred to them, and through activity, they transfer strategies for organizing and monitoring problem solving from the intermental to the intramental plane. On the way, the practice itself undergoes qualitative changes.

Conclusion

This overview of Vygotsky's model of cognitive development has focused on three basic themes that run throughout his writings. The first of these is the supposition that genetic or developmental analysis provides the foundation for understanding human mental functioning. For Vygotsky, genetic analysis was not simply one among many modes of inquiry – it was the most important and fundamental one. Furthermore, this vision of developmental analysis did not apply only to ontogenesis, but to other genetic domains as well.

A second theme that runs throughout Vygotsky's writings concerns the mediated nature of human mental functioning. Instead of viewing cognition as a process that occurs within the skin, his approach posits that human mental functioning is typically distributed between active agents and cultural tools. His insights about cultural tools and the mediated action to which they give rise bring with them a range of conceptual implications that are still to be fully explored. Among other things, it leads us to introduce cultural and political questions into the study of cognition by asking where the cultural tools that shape cognition come from and whether they are accessed in equal or unequal ways in the contemporary world.

The third theme in Vygotsky's writings concerns the social origins of individual mental functioning. This constitutes a second sense, along with mediated action, in which Vygotsky viewed mind as extending beyond the skin and as being distributed. His claims about how higher mental processes appear first on the intermental, and then on the intramental planes of functioning underlie many other aspects of his thinking, including his claims about the zone of proximal development.

Although Vygotsky died in 1934, many of his ideas have come to have a powerful impact on discussions of cognitive development only over the past few decades in the West. This impact has grown drastically as contemporary researchers continue to employ his theoretical claims to formulate new empirical studies. There is every reason to expect this trend to continue as we focus on how cognitive development occurs in complex sociocultural settings.

See also: Language and Literacy in Educational Settings; Learning in a Sociocultural Perspective.

Bibliography

Boas, F. (1966). Introduction. In Boas, F. (ed.) *Handbook of American Indian Languages.* Lincoln: University of Nebraska Press.

Cazden, C. (1988). *Classroom Discourse: The Language of Teaching and Learning.* Portsmouth, NH: Heinemann.

Cole, M. (1996). *Cultural Psychology: A Once and Future Discipline.* Cambridge, MA: Harvard University Press.

Connerton, P. (1989). *How Societies Remember.* Cambridge: Cambridge University Press.

Douglas, M. (1986). *How Institutions Think.* Syracuse, NY: Syracuse University Press.

Duncan, G. (1996). Space, place, and the problem of race: Black adolescent discourse as mediated action. *Journal of Negro Education* 65(2), 133–150.

Lave, J. and Wegner, E. (1991). *Situated Learning: Legitimate Peripheral Participation.* Cambridge: Cambridge University Press.

Lukes, S. (1977). Methodological individualism reconsidered. In Lukes, S. (ed.) *Essays in Social Theory*, pp 177–186. New York: Columbia University Press.

Palincsar, A. S. and Brown, A. L. (1984). Reciprocal teaching of comprehension-fostering and comprehension-monitoring activities. *Cognition and Instruction* **1**, 117–175.

Rogoff, B. (1990). *Apprenticeship in Thinking: Cognitive Development in Social Context.* Cambridge: Cambridge University Press.

Salomon, G. (ed.) (1993). *Distributed Cognitions: Psychological and Educational Implications.* Cambridge: Cambridge University Press.

Sapir, E. (1921). *Language: An Introduction to the Study of Speech.* New York: Harcourt, Brace.

Vygotsky, L. S. (1981a). The instrumental method in psychology. In Wertsch, J. V. (ed.) *The Concept of Activity in Soviet Psychology*, pp 134–143. Armonk, NY: M.E. Sharpe.

Vygotsky, L. S. (1981b). The genesis of higher mental functions. In Wertsch, J. V. (ed.) *The Concept of Activity in Soviet Psychology*, pp 144–188. Armonk, NY: M.E. Sharpe.

Wertsch, J. V. (1985). *Culture, Communication and Cognition: Vygotskyan Perspectives.* New York: Cambridge University Press.

Further Reading

Brown, A. L. and Ferrara, R. A. (1985). Diagnosing zones of proximal development. In Wertsch, J. V. (ed.) *Culture, Communication, and Cognition: Vygotskian Perspectives*, pp 273–305. New York: Cambridge University Press.

Cole, M. and Engeström, Y. (1993). A cultural–historical interpretation of distributed cognition. In Salomon, G. (ed.) *Distributed Cognitions: Psychological and Educational Considerations*, pp 1–46. Cambridge: Cambridge University Press.

Daniels, H. (in press). Pedagogy. In Daniels, H., Cole, M., and Wertsch, J. V. (eds.) *The Cambridge Companion to Vygotsky*. Cambridge: Cambridge University Press.

Edwards, A. (in press). An interesting resemblance: Vygotsky, mead, and american pragmatism. In Daniels, H., Cole, M., and Wertsch, J. V. (eds.) *The Cambridge Companion to Vygotsky*. Cambridge: Cambridge University Press.

Engeström, Y. (in press). Putting Vygotsky to work: The change laboratory as an application of double stimulation. In Daniels, H., Cole, M., and Wertsch, J. V. (eds.) *The Cambridge Companion to Vygotsky*. Cambridge: Cambridge University Press.

Gee, J. P. (1999). *An Introduction to Discourse Analysis: Theory and Method*. New York: Routledge.

John-Steiner, V. (in press). Vygotsky on thinking and speech. In Daniels, H., Cole, M., and Wertsch, J. V. (eds.) *The Cambridge Companion to Vygotsky*. Cambridge: Cambridge University Press.

Kozol, J. (1991). *Savage Inequalities: Children in America's Schools*. New York: Crown Publishers.

Kozulin, A. (1990). *Vygotksy's Psychology: A Biography of Ideas*. Brighton, UK: Harvester Wheatsheaf.

Kozulin, A. and Gindis, B. (in press). Sociocultural theory and education of children with special needs. In Daniels, H., Cole, M., and Wertsch, J. V. (eds.) *The Cambridge Companion to Vygotsky*. Cambridge: Cambridge University Press.

Leont'ev, A. N. (1981). The problem of activity in psychology. In Wertsch, J. V. (ed.) *The Concept of Activity in Soviet Psychology*, pp 37–71. Armonk, NY: M.E. Sharpe.

Linell, P. (1998). *Approaching Dialogue: Talk, Interaction, and Contexts in Dialogical Perspectives*. Amsterdam: John Benjamins.

Luria, A. R. (1979). *The Making of Mind: A Personal Account of Soviet Psychology*. Cambridge, MA: Harvard University Press.

Luria, A. R. (1982). *Language and Cognition*. New York: Wiley.

Mead, G. H. (1955). In *Mind, Self & Society from the Stand-Point of a Social Behaviorist*. Morris, C. W. (ed.) Chicago, IL: University of Chicago Press.

Meshcheryakov, B. G. (in press). Terminology in L.S. Vygotsky's writings. In Daniels, H., Cole, M., and Wertsch, J. V. (eds.) *The Cambridge Companion to Vygotsky*. Cambridge: Cambridge University Press.

Middleton, D. and Edwards, D. (eds.) (1990). *Collective Remembering*. London: Sage.

Minick, N. (1987). Introduction. In Vygotsky, L. S. (ed.) *Thinking and Speech*. New York: Plenum.

Newman, F. and Holzman, L. (1993). *Lev Vygotsky: Revolutionary Scientist*. London: Routledge.

Norman, D. A. (1988). *The Psychology of Everyday Things*. New York: Basic Books.

Norman, D. A. (1993). *Things that Make Us Smart: Defending Human Attributes in the Age of the Machine*. Reading, MA: Addison-Wesley.

Olson, D. R. (1994). *The World on Paper: The Conceptual and Cognitive Implications of Writing and Reading*. Cambridge: Cambridge University Press.

Resnick, L. V., Levine, J. M., and Teasley, S. D. (eds.) (1991). *Perspectives on Socially Shared Cognition*. Washington, DC: American Psychological Association.

Rogoff, B. (1981). Schooling and the development of cognitive skills. In Triandis, H. C. and Heron, A. (eds.) *Handbook of Cross-Cultural Psychology*, vol. 4, pp 233–294. Boston, MA: Allyn and Bacon.

Rogoff, B. (1997). Evaluating development in the process of participation: Theory, methods, and practice building on each other. In Amsel, E. and Renninger, A. (eds.) *Change and Development*, pp 265–285. Hillsdale, NJ: Erlbaum.

Rogoff, B. and Wertsch, J. V. (1984). Children's learning in the "zone of proximal development." In Rogoff, B. and Wertsch, J. V. (eds.) *New Directions for Child Development*, vol. 23, pp 19–30. San Francisco, CA: Jossey-Bass.

Scollon, R. (1998). *Mediated Discourse as Social Interaction: A Study of News Discourse*. London: Longman.

Scribner, S. and Cole, M. (1981). *The Psychology of Literacy*. Cambridge, MA: Harvard University Press.

Shweder, R. A. (1990). Cultural psychology – What is it? In Stigler, J. W., Shweder, R. A., and Herdt, B. (eds.) *Cultural Psychology: Essays on Comparative Human Development*, pp 1–46. New York: Cambridge University Press.

Sternberg, R. J. and Grigorenko, E. L. (2002). *Dynamic Testing: The Nature and Measurement of Learning Potential*. New York: Cambridge University Press.

Taylor, C. (1985). *Human Agency and Language: Philosophical Papers I*. Cambridge: Cambridge University Press.

van der Veer, R. (in press). Vygotsky in context: 1900–1935. In Daniels, H., Cole, M. and Wertsch, J. V. (eds.) *The Cambridge Companion to Vygotsky*. Cambridge: Cambridge University Press.

van der Veer, R. and Valsiner, J. (1991). *Understanding Vygotsky: A Quest for Synthesis*. Oxford: Blackwell.

Vygodskaya, G. L. and Lifanova, T. M. (1996). *Lev Semënovich Vygotskii: Zhizn', deyatel'nost', shtrikhi, i portrety (Lev Semënovich Vygotskii: Life, Activity, Traits, and Portraits)*. Moscow: Smysl.

Vygotsky, L. S. (1978). *Mind in Society: The Development of Higher Psychological Processes*, In Cole, M., John-Steiner, V., Scribner, S., and Souberman, E. (eds.). Cambridge, MA: Harvard University Press.

Vygotsky, L. S. (1986). *Thought and Language*. Kozulin, A. (trans.) Cambridge, MA: MIT Press.

Werner, H. (1948). *Comparative Psychology of Mental Development*. New York: International Universities Press.

Wertsch, J. V. (1979). From social interaction to higher psychological processes: A clarification and application of Vygotsky's theory. *Human Development* **22**, 1–22.

Wertsch, J. V. (1991). *Voices of the Mind: A Sociocultural Approach to Mediated Action*. Cambridge, MA: Harvard University Press.

Wertsch, J. V. (1998). *Mind as Action*. New York: Oxford University Press.

Wertsch, J. V., del Rio, P., and Alvarez, A. (1995). Sociocultural studies: History, action, and mediation. In Wertsch, J. V., del Rio, P., and Alvarez, A. (eds.) *Sociocultural Studies of Mind*, pp 1–36. New York: Cambridge University Press.

Wertsch, J. V., Tulviste, P., and Hagstrom, F. (1993). A sociocultural approach to agency. In Forman, E. A., Minick, N., and Stone, C. A. (eds.) *Contexts for Learning: Sociocultural Dynamics in Children's Development*, pp 336–356. New York: Oxford University Press.

Zinchenko, V. P. (1985). Vygotsky's ideas about units for the analysis of mind. In Wertsch, J. V. (ed.) *Culture, Communication, and Cognition: Vygotskian Perspectives*, pp 94–118. New York: Cambridge University Press.

Zinchenko, V. P. (in press). Thought and word: The approaches of L.S. Vygotsky and G.G. Shpet. In Daniels, H., Cole, M., and Wertsch, J. V. (eds.) *The Cambridge Companion to Vygotsky*. Cambridge: Cambridge University Press.

Theoretical Bases of Computer Supported Learning

S R Ludvigsen and A I Mørch, University of Oslo, Oslo, Norway

Introduction

Computer-supported collaborative learning (CSCL) is the field concerned with how information and communication technology (ICT) might support learning in groups (co-located and distributed). It is also about understanding the actions and activities mediated by ICT. Its educational applications range from generic collaboration environments (e.g., forums) to tools for developing domain-specific knowledge. The research questions addressed by CSCL include how individuals learn with specific tools, how small groups interact and develop shared meanings over time, how institutions change and create new conditions for teaching and learning, and even how the opportunities for learning change as society adopts new models for education. Societies increasingly require new types of knowledge, new means of knowledge advancement and, consequently, new models of education.

To account for the multiple perspectives associated with CSCL without risking oversimplification, we adopt a sociocultural approach and present the main concepts and results. In particular, we make use of two overarching concepts – scaffolding and mediating artifact. Scaffolding is an instructional technique with which the teacher models the learning task, then gradually fades away and shifts responsibility to the students (Wood *et al.*, 1976). In collaborative learning, students might also take on this role. By a technological scaffold, we mean features built into educational software that perform similar functions (e.g., guidance in virtual collaboration).

Related to scaffolding is the concept of mediation, proposed by Vygotsky (1986). This implies that technology for teaching and learning is first of all a mediating and enhancing artifact. In the article we explore a special type of mediation, which is the relation between design-based research (DBR) and innovative CSCL tools (Collins *et al.*, 2004), on the one hand, and how this creates new opportunities for education on the other (Andriessen *et al.*, 2003).

CSCL emerged in response to skills that are important in a knowledge-based society. These are skills that were previously associated with deep learning of specialized knowledge, metacommunication, metacognition, and task reconceptualization (Järvelä and Salovaara, 2004). These skills are not easily taught through memorizing and fact finding using textbooks, which are the prevailing methods for learning basic skills. In fact finding, for example, the goal of the activity is most often invisible to students and the focus tends to be on tasks (Hewitt, 2001).

The shift in perspective concerning learning and cognition that CSCL provides is, in part, a result of the raised expectations in a knowledge-based society. The labor market of today demands: (1) specialized (domain-specific) skills and (2) an ability to work in teams (the capacity to integrate different types of knowledge and skills through collaboration). Specialized knowledge is important because the labor market is fragmented and interwoven in complex ways. The demands for skills in collaboration and knowledge integration (e.g., critically evaluate information resources found on the World Wide Web (WWW)) have come to the foreground over the past 10 years, making the teaching of communication, information seeking, and collaboration more important than ever.

CSCL is about teaching and learning the knowledge and skills required for participation in the knowledge-based society in concert with the basic skills they rely upon. The view we present here is consistent with those of scholars who argue that the needs for specialized knowledge and collaboration skills must be met with a comprehensive approach (Järvelä and Salovaara, 2004; de Jong, 2006; Scardamalia and Bereiter, 2006).

CSCL is also a result of the widespread use of Web-based information systems and their acceptance by a broad group of actors at all levels in the education sector and by many workplaces (e.g., learning management systems and discussion forums). Two specific directions in educational research that have taken advantage of CSCL are ICT as mediators of accumulated knowledge (Paavola and Hakkarainen, 2005) and ICT as cultural tools (Wertsch, 1991; Ludvigsen and Mørch, 2003).

This article covers the major issues, research approaches, and questions concerning CSCL. We start by providing an overview of the field, including a presentation of key events and directions. Then we provide an overview of some important results grouped into two research approaches. Next, an overview of DBR and its implications for CSCL is provided. In closing, we identify the remaining open issues and point out some directions for further research.

Background

CSCL is a new and emerging field in the educational sciences (Stahl *et al.*, 2006). The term was first publicly used at an international workshop in 1989 in Maratea, Italy. The first international conference was organized in 1995 (Koschmann, 1996), and since then a biannual series of CSCL conferences has been arranged across Europe,

North America, and Asia. In 2006, the *International Journal of Computer-Supported Collaborative Learning* (IJCSCL) brought-out its inaugural issue.

Broadly speaking, there are two main traditions within the learning sciences: cognitive psychology and the situated/sociocultural perspective. The former is based on the information-processing perspective (e.g., Anderson, 1993) and the latter on American pragmatism (e.g., Dewey, Mead, Garfinkel, and Schön,) and Soviet psychology (e.g., Vygotsky, Leontiev, Luria, and Wertsch). In CSCL studies, methods and techniques from both traditions are used and sometimes blended (e.g., interaction analysis). However, within each tradition there are unique interpretations of key concepts, methods, and empirical design.

Technical advances in computer science have contributed to CSCL in various ways. For example, researchers in computer-supported cooperative work (CSCW) have developed groupware systems that have been adopted for educational purposes (e.g., Stahl, 2006). Groupware provide shared spaces (Bannon and Bødker, 1997) on the WWW for storing and sharing information (messages, documents, pictures, and videos) and engaging the learners in social interaction (Girgensohn and Lee, 2002). When adopted in schools, they allow teachers and learners to interact online using a variety of communication and collaboration tools. Examples of shared spaces are Basic Support for Collaborative Learning (BSCL) (Stahl, 2006), Future Learning Environment (FLE) (Muukkonen *et al.*, 1999), and Knowledge Forum (Scardamalia and Bereiter, 2006).

The relationship between computer support (CS) and collaborative learning (CL) in CSCL is complex as a result of the broad scope of the research questions, the multiplicity of approaches, and the plethora of educational technologies. This complexity needs to be unraveled in order to provide a more comprehensive account of the field. Although technology has had an enormous influence on CSCL, educational technologies should not be thought of as recipes for organizing teaching and learning. Similarly, the term CL does not imply that learning in small groups is better than individual learning. They are both needed and depend on each other. Findings indicate that detailed analyses of talk are necessary to understand how collaboration is carried out (Arnseth and Ludvigsen, 2006). It is not a question of an either/or situation, but rather how to identify specific situations that require mastery of new skills and design scaffolds for those situations. The common denominator is Vygotskian epistemology, which states that social interaction precedes learning and cognition at the level of the individual. To design for this requires CSCL tools and pedagogical models that foster social interaction and ease the transition from social interaction to learning and development. In this way, CSCL both represents a subfield in educational research and broadens the scope of educational research since it interacts with computer science and information systems.

Research Approaches in CSCL

We have grouped mainstream CSCL research into systemic and dialogical approaches (Arnseth and Ludvigsen, 2006). This distinction gives us the possibility to provide a more aggregated picture of what we know about research in CSCL.

Systemic Approach

The systemic approach concerns the generation of models of how specific features of technological tools afford or constrain collaboration, reasoning, knowledge representation, and inquiry (Dillenbourg, 1999) and to what extent these features will enhance students' capacities to solve problems in different domains (Arnseth and Ludvigsen, 2006). From a systemic approach, the analytic purpose is to identify interdependencies between quantifiable variables. The unit of analysis is the individually acting and thinking agent, and the two important cognitive processes are internalization (acquiring new or improving existing knowledge) and transfer (what is learned in one situation is applied to another similar situation). Models (often computer generated) of how individuals construct, store, retrieve, and modify information serve as explanations of these phenomena (Anderson, 1993; Greeno, 2006).

Using a systemic approach in a traditional classroom setting in mathematics and reading, Lamon *et al.* (1996) demonstrated that students with CSCL tools performed better than students without such tools. The Jasper project (The Cognition and Technology Group at Vanderbilt, 1990) also reported similar results. The researchers in this large project studied the impact of educational technology on mathematics education in North America. They found that cooperative problem solving and discussion helped to engage the students in learning. In Europe, Fischer and colleagues studied how different types of scripts and tasks impact students' CL activities (Fischer and Mandl, 2005). Computational scripts were used to scaffold actions, and social scripts, such as role distribution, were used to organize turn taking. The authors found that scripts were useful for scaffolding learning and knowledge construction. However, these findings did not hold for all conditions (these conditions are further discussed in the last section of the article).

One of the most influential approaches within the systemic approach is knowledge building developed by Scardamalia and Bereiter (2006). Knowledge building is a model for distributed CL that is based on how professional scientists work to solve problems. The authors developed CSCL tools to support knowledge building (Computer-Supported Intentional Learning Environment (CSILE), Knowledge Forum). The latest version includes a Web-based shared space (WebCSILE). A further development of the Knowledge Forum is FLE (Muukkonen *et al.*, 1999).

The activities students engage in when involved in knowledge building can be formulated as a scientific-inquiry process, and many studies have been conducted using this approach (e.g., Hewitt, 2001). The phases of scientific inquiry include problem identification, proposing personal theories or hypotheses, experimentation, critical evaluation, data interpretation, scientific explanation, and summarizing. The studies in this area demonstrate that students who are engaged in knowledge building develop a deeper understanding of the domain under study. However, not all students benefit from it (Ludvigsen and Mørch, 2003). This may be related to the approach used, since a shortcoming in many of the studies is the timeframe adopted, which may range from a few hours to a few days. A consequence of this brevity is that conversational data is analyzed without taking into account the historical context of the interaction, which unfolds over time. The implication of such an approach is that the students' learning trajectories become less visible in the analysis (Crook, 1998; Rasmussen, 2005).

de Jong (2006) summarized recent research in scientific inquiry learning. He found that a number of students learn more effectively and develop deepening knowledge when supported with CSCL tools. The recommendation de Jong proposes is that it is possible to design scaffolding mechanisms into CSCL environments that enhance students' learning. On the other hand, the results also show that most students have problems using predefined structures and processes adopted from professional science. An explanation for this difficulty is that the students do not have sufficient background knowledge to grasp the significance of the scientific inquiry process, and prefer instead to use everyday interpretations of scientific phenomena. Using a professional model of science to scaffold a learning environment provides a certain kind of insight, but it also generates new problems that are not easily resolved with a systemic approach.

In summary, the systemic approach gives useful guidelines for how we can build scaffolds for cognitive processes like hypothesis generation, data interpretation, and scientific explanation. However, this model-based approach to learning and cognition needs to be supplemented by a situational approach from a social and cultural perspective to provide a full account of CSCL.

Dialogic Approach

The dialogic approach is based on the idea that learning is a socially organized activity. The unit of analysis is a group of individuals interacting to accomplish a shared goal. Key concepts are mediation, artifacts and tools, and social practice, and mediation by tools to support learning is essential. It is through talk and interaction with significant others that we can understand how participants use tools and resources in learning and cognition. Externalization is seen as the main cognitive activity. The dialogic approach is influenced by research in situated learning and sociocultural perspectives (Greeno, 2006; Vygotsky 1986; Rommetveit, 1992; Valsiner and van der Veer, 2000; Wertsch, 1991). A basic premise is that both physical and abstract tools mediate human activities, and the main abstract tool is language (Vygotsky, 1986). The use of tools for learning is not only goal driven, but can also be seen in connection with how tools connect us with the past (predecessor artifacts) and with the future (unexplored potentials). The tools span both spatial and temporal dimensions.

In a study performed by Mercer and Wegerif (1999), students were exposed to a set of ground rules for communication. These rules included the use of arguments, disputes, clarifications, and explanations. The students and teachers were trained to talk together in specific ways in order to develop shared knowledge about a specific phenomenon of interest. In a series of interventions, the ground rules became a focus of the inquiry and previously implicit structures, like norms for participation, became explicit and transparent. This increased the probability for the kind of talk Mercer and Wegerif (1999) refer to as exploratory talk. Exploratory talk is characterized by the mutual development of problems and ideas over time as a result of reflection and elaboration. They designed learning environments and new types of tasks to support these activities to promote more productive interactions in classrooms. It is further suggested that productive interaction needs to be understood not only as sequences of interaction, but as part of a broader context of institutional activities and sociocultural developments (Crook, 1998; Arnseth and Ludvigsen, 2006).

An example of a micro-study using the dialogic approach is the study of the effects of copy and paste on learning productivity. The cognitive effort involved in using copy and paste for text production and school presentations is low. As a result, many students use this technique uncritically. Some scholars have argued that it does not promote learning and should be discouraged (Hewitt, 2001; Kumpulainen and Wray, 2002). Using the dialogic approach, we can study this phenomenon in conjunction with how participants use the tools they have at their disposal to identify how the talk among the participants unfold as a result of tool mediation and emergent intermediate processes. Rasmussen (2005) found that students used copied texts as resources to deepen and broaden their understanding of the subject they studied.

Another finding concerning the use of the dialogic approach is that tasks are often open ended and cannot be taken for granted (Rasmussen, 2005). When studying how talk emerges in interaction as an analytic approach, the task needs to be constructed among the participants (Linell, 1998). The effect of this is that understanding the task becomes a learning activity in its own right, and this will stimulate the development of a higher-order skill (task conceptualization). When we assume that students working together share goals, task reconceptualization should be seen as an outcome of the activities rather than part of the premises for working together.

Suthers (2005) has identified intersubjective meaning making (Rommetveit, 1992) as one of the unique areas that CSCL is well equipped to support, and he suggests CSCL researchers undertake studies that attempt to understand how intersubjective meaning making impacts learning and how it can be mediated by technology affordances (Norman, 1999) embedded in CSCL tools. Suthers (2005) defines intersubjective meaning making as a joint composition of interpretations of a dynamically changing context. With this proposal, he provides a bold attempt to go beyond an information-sharing conception of CL. Technological affordances for exploratory learning and cooperative problem solving are proposed to support this process.

In summary, a dialogic approach to CSCL provides new analytic concepts to analyze how students and teachers interact in collaborative learning. The dialogic approach gives broader insights and explanations concerning the development of traditional skills, and pays particular attention to skills such as those for communication, coordination, information seeking, information sharing, collaboration, negotiation, critiquing, and decision making, and how to design CSCL tools to support these activities.

Design-Based Research

Pedagogical Design

DBR has influenced research methodology in CSCL. DBR provides a solution for one of the dilemmas that confront researchers in the field – on the one hand, understanding how people learn, particularly within school settings, and on the other designing ways to ensure that learning will happen in a better manner in these settings (Brown, 1992; Collins *et al.*, 2004). The development of DBR has been on theoretical and methodological levels. On the methodology level, DBR suggests partnerships among researchers and educators with the goals of conducting rigorous and reflective inquiry, testing, and refining innovative learning environments, and defining new design principles based on previous research (Sandoval and Bell, 2004). On the theoretical level, design principles are the practical application of what we know about learning. As such, DBR does not provide direction for which research approach would be appropriate. Both the systemic and the dialogic approaches could be used.

Technology Design

The link between DBR and technology design is harder to establish. This is a result of the focus on theoretical and methodological issues (not well integrated with technological issues) and the difficulty involved in creating

design principles that are practically useful for technology developers. There is an implied link between design principles and technology affordances in that the latter operationalize the former. However, this is a normative assumption upheld by some CSCL researchers, arguably strongest in the systemic tradition. Although many educational researchers agree that the basic principles of the sociocultural approach are important for the design of learning environments, the adoption of these principles have been hampered by a complex chain of elaborations before the principles can be used for developing specific tools. This is an important area for further work in CSCL (e.g., Suthers, 2005).

The basic idea of design principles in DBR is that we make use of what we know about previous research on learning when we design new learning environments. Although there is not an exact correspondence between the design principles proposed based on previous empirical studies and the design of an innovation for a new setting, the idea that the designers try to support the learning processes and anticipate its outcomes in specific directions is likely to succeed over time. For example, the principle of deep learning can be found in many CSCL environments, in various forms (e.g., Linn *et al.*, 2004, Scardamalia and Bereiter, 2006). de Jong (2006) provides a recent overview.

The operationalization of design principles into technology affordances works best for principles that lend themselves to tool support, such as scaffolding (Wood *et al.*, 1976). This principle has been successfully incorporated into many CSCL tools, often in the form of automated feedback and/or guidance. Technology scaffolds takes advantage of regularities of:

- subject domains (Fischer *et al.*, 1991);
- knowledge types and scientific inquiry (Muukkonen *et al.*, 1999; de Jong, 2006);
- presence of others, group awareness, and social networks (Kreijns and Kirschner, 2004); and
- feedback and advice for online collaboration (Soller *et al.*, 2005; Mørch *et al.*, 2005).

One debate among technology developers concerns the degree to which computerized feedback should simulate or provide higher-level representations of user-interaction data before output (feedback or guidance) is generated. Soller *et al.* (2005) suggest three levels of feedback: mirroring (awareness), metacognitive tools, and guidance. This gradually increases the system's interpretation of the user data and consequently requires the users to be equally critically aware of the feedback generated.

Another debate explores to what extent automated feedback should be proactive, reactive, or requested (Mørch *et al.*, 2005). A system that provides sentence openers and step-by-step guidance is proactive. If it allows wrong actions to be taken before it gives hints and critique, it is reactive. If the system does not take any suggestive action on its own at all, but allows the learner to request guidance upon demand, it is requested (Mørch *et al.*, 2005). All three intervention strategies are important in CSCL environments, but not at the same time. The equation for balancing the three strategies depends on the complexity of the knowledge domain to be supported (e.g., the severity of making a wrong move vs. stimulating explorative learning) and the choice of research approach (systemic vs. dialogic).

Open issues and Directions for Further Work

In the 1990s, many people discussed how technology and the Internet would revolutionize schools and educational institutions. Now, after a 10-year period, these assumptions seem rather opaque and romantic. The CSCL research has, to a large degree, provided insight concerning the condition under which we can expect students to develop deep knowledge using innovative technology support. A reasonable interpretation for the CSCL field across the different traditions we have surveyed in this article emphasizes that such capacity needs to be cultivated over a number of years, and it is dependent on the design of the learning environment, the social norms of the actors involved, and the institutional settings (Krange and Ludvigsen, 2008).

Two of the more general tendencies in complex CSCL environments are the following: first, that teachers and students need to engage deeply in specific problem-solving activities in order to learn concepts that are part of their actual knowledge development; second, that such a deep engagement often involves disagreement, identifying problems and conflicting ideas that need to be resolved (problematizing), and providing explanations, negotiations, etc. However, disagreement is not always a necessary condition. In exploratory talk, for example, reciprocal elaboration also serves as a means for engaging in deep learning. We need to conceptualize tensions, breakdowns, alignments, and elaborations as basic activities for learning to become productive for students over a long period of time.

Improving educational settings, with the scaffolding techniques for collaborative learning, is one of the aims of CSCL. This improvement includes pedagogical models and technological tools for problematizing tasks, hypothesis generation, elaboration, judgment about resources from the Internet, interpretation of data, evaluation of performance (metacognition), deliberate perspective shifts, etc. This is likely to be accomplished by scaffolding at the level of action and activities in classrooms, and supported by CSCL tools. The approaches developed by the CSCL community deal with micro-level phenomena and educational practices as seen from the teachers' and learners' points of view. In this way, CSCL has contributed to how schools can become better places for teaching and learning, and it is through the adoption and use of technology as a mediating artifact that it has achieved this status (Rasmussen, 2005; de Jong, 2006; Scardamalia and Bereiter, 2006). The historical tensions between old and new social practices create grounds for further development. It is the cognitive, social, historical, and institutional aspects, in combination, that must be taken into account for us to understand how we can improve the learning condition for students.

The systemic and the dialogical approaches to CSCL provide directions for how educational practices can and should be changed. However, an ongoing issue concerns how to constructively combine them without over simplification. Carefully designed (e.g., model-based) CSCL environments are important for improving our understanding of learning with ICT tools, but the analysis should be done from multiple perspectives, drawing on a broader set of student skills. Only by taking multiple perspectives as a starting point can we identify commonalities across approaches that enrich our understanding of social interaction and its relationship with learning and cognition, as well as how to design new learning environments that enhance both productive learning and cognitive performance.

Acknowledgments

We want to thank InterMedia, The University of Oslo, and the Competence and Media Convergence (CMC) program at the university for financing our work with this article.

See also: Classroom Discourse and Student Learning; Learning in a Sociocultural Perspective.

Bibliography

Anderson, J. R. (1993). *Rules of Mind*. Hillsdale, NJ: Erlbaum.

Andriessen, J., Baker, M., and Suthers, D. (eds.) (2003). *Arguing to Learn: Confronting Cognitions in Computer-Supported Collaborative Learning Environments*. Dordrecht: Kluwer.

Arnseth, H. C. and Ludvigsen, S. (2006). Approaching institutional contexts: Systemic versus dialogical research in CSCL. *International Journal of Computer-Supported Collaborative Learning* **1**(2), 167–185.

Bannon, L. and Bødker, S. (1997). Constructing common information spaces. *Proceedings of the European Conference on Computer Supported Cooperative Work* (ECSCW'97), pp 81–96. Dordrecht: Kluwer.

Brown, A. L. (1992). Design experiments: Theoretical and methodological challenges in creating complex interventions in classroom settings. *Journal of the Learning Sciences* **2**(2), 141–178.

Collins, A., Joseph, D., and Bielaczyc, K. (2004). Design research: Theoretical and methodological issues. *Journal of the Learning Sciences* **13**(1), 15–42.

Crook, C. (1998). Children as computer users: The case of collaborative learning. *Computers and Education* **30**(3 and 4), 237–247.

de Jong, T. (2006). Scaffolds for scientific discovery learning. In Elen, J. and Clark, D. (eds.) *Handling Complexity in Learning Environments: Research and Theory*, pp 107–128. London: Elsevier Science.

Dillenbourg, P. (ed.) (1999). *Collaborative Learning: Cognitive and Computational Approaches*. Amsterdam: Pergamon Press.

Fischer, G., Lemke, A. C., Mastaglio, T., and Morch, A. (1991). The role of critiquing in cooperative problem solving. *ACM Transactions on Information Systems* **9**(2), 123–151.

Fischer, F. and Mandl, H. (2005). Knowledge convergence in computer-supported collaborative learning: The role of external representation tools. *Journal of the Learning Sciences* **14**(3), 405–441.

Girgensohn, A. and Lee, A. (2002). Making web sites be places for social interaction. *Proceedings of the ACM 2002 Conference on Computer Supported Cooperative Work*, pp 136–145. New York: ACM Press.

Greeno, J. G. (2006). Learning in activity. In Sawyer, R. K. (ed.) *The Cambridge Handbook of The Learning Science*, pp 79–96. Cambridge: Cambridge University Press.

Hewitt, J. (2001). From focus on tasks to a focus on understanding: The cultural transformation of a Toronto classroom. In Koschmann, T., Hall, R., and Miyake, N. (eds.) *CSCL 2. Carrying Forward the Conversation*, pp 11–41. Mahwah, NJ: Erlbaum.

Järvelä, S. and Salovaara, H. (2004). The interplay of motivational goals and cognitive strategies in a new pedagogical culture. A context oriented and qualitative approach. *European Psychologist* **9**(4), 232–244.

Koschmann, T. (1996). Paradigm shifts and instructional technology: An Introduction. In Koschmann, T. (ed.) *CSCL: Theory and Practice of an Emerging Paradigm*, pp 1–23. Mahwah, NJ: Lawrence Erlbaum.

Krange, I. and Ludvigsen, S. (2008). What does it mean? Students' procedural and conceptual problem solving in CSCL environment designed within the field of science education. *International Journal of Computer supported collaborative learning* **3**, 25–51.

Kreijns, K. and Kirschner, P. A. (2004). Designing sociable CSCL environments. In Strijbos, J. W., Kirschner, P. A., and Martens, R. L. (eds.) *What We Know about CSCL: And Implementing It in Higher Education*, pp 3–31. Boston, MA: Kluwer /Springer.

Kumpulainen, K. and Wray, D. (eds.) (2002). *Classroom Interaction and Social Learning. From Theory to Practice*. London: Routledge/ Falmer.

Lamon, M., Secules, T., Petrosino, A., *et al.* (1996). Schools for thought: Overview of the project and lessons learned from one of the sites. In Schauble, L. and Glaser, R. (eds.) *Innovations in Learning: New Environments for Education*, pp 243–288. Mahwah, NJ: Erlbaum.

Linell, P. (1998). *Approaching Dialogue: Talk, Interaction and Contexts in Dialogical Perspectives*. Amsterdam: John Benjamins.

Linn, M. C., Bell, P., and Davis, E. A. (2004). Specific design principles: Elaborating the scaffolded knowledge integration framework. In Linn, M., Davis, E. A., and Bell, P. (eds.) *Internet Environments for Science Education*, pp 315–341. Mahwah, NJ: Erlbaum.

Ludvigsen, S. R. and Mørch, A. (2003). Categorisation in knowledge building: Task specific argumentation in a co-located CSCL environment. In Wasson, B., Ludvigsen, S., and Hoppe, U. (eds.) *Designing for Change in Networked Learning Environments. Proceedings of the International Conference on Computer Support for Collaborative Learning*, pp 67–76. Dordrecht: Kluwer.

Mercer, N. and Wegerif, R. (1999). Is 'exploratory talk' productive talk? In Littleton, K. and Light, P. (eds.) *Learning with Computers. Analysing Productive Interaction*, pp 79–101. London: Routledge.

Mørch, A., Jondahl, S., and Dolonen, J. (2005). Supporting conceptual awareness with pedagogical agents, information systems frontiers.

Special Issue. *Computer Supported Collaborative Learning Requiring Immersive Presence* **7**(1), 39–53.

Muukkonen, H., Hakkarainen, K., and Lakkala, M. (1999). Collaborative technology for facilitating progressive inquiry: Future learning environment tools. In Hoadley, C. and Roschelle, J. (eds.) *Proceedings for: Computer support for Collaborative Learning. Designing New Media for a New Millennium: Collaborative Technology for Learning*, pp 406–415. Stanford University, CA: Erlbaum.

Norman, D. A. (1999). Affordances, conventions and design. *Interactions* **6**(3), 38–43.

Paavola, S. and Hakkarainen, K. (2005). The knowledge creation metaphor: An emergent epistemological approach to learning. *Science and Education* **14**, 537–557.

Rasmussen, I. (2005). Project Work and ICT: A Study of Learning as Trajectories of Participation. PhD Thesis, InterMedia, University of Oslo, Norway.

Rommetveit, R. (1992). Outlines of a dialogically based social–cognitive approach to human cognition and communication. In Wold, A. H. (ed.) *The Dialogical Alternative: Towards a Theory of Language and Mind*, pp 19–44. Oslo: Scandinavian University Press.

Sandoval, W. A. and Bell, P. (2004). Design-based research methods for studying learning in context: Introduction. *Educational Psychologist* **39**(4), 199–201.

Scardamalia, M. and Bereiter, C. (2006). Knowledge building: Theory, pedagogy, and technology. In Sawyer, R. K. (ed.) *The Cambridge Handbook of The Learning Science*, pp 97–118. Cambridge: Cambridge University Press.

Soller, A., Martinez, A., Jermann, P., and Muehlenbrock, M. (2005). From mirroring to guiding: A review of state of the art technology for supporting collaborative learning. *International Journal of Artificial Intelligence in Education* **15**, 261–290.

Stahl, G. (2006). *Group Cognition: Computer Support for Building Collaborative Knowledge*. Cambridge, MA: MIT Press.

Stahl, G., Koschmann, T., and Suthers, D. (2006). Computer-supported collaborative learning. In Sawyer, R. K. (ed.) *The Cambridge Handbook of The Learning Science*, pp 409–425. Cambridge: Cambridge University Press.

Suthers, D. D. (2005). Technology affordances for intersubjective learning: A thematic agenda for CSCL. In Koschmann, T., Suthers, D., and Chan, T. W. (eds.) *Proceedings of Conference on Computer Supported Collaborative Learning 2005*, pp 662–671. Mahwah, NJ: Erlbaum.

The Cognition and Technology Group at Vanderbilt (1990). Anchored instruction and its relationship to situated cognition. *Educational Researcher* **19**(6), 2–10.

Valsiner, J. and van der Veer, R. (2000). *The Social Mind: Construction of the Idea*. Cambrigde, MA: Cambrigde University Press.

Vygotsky, L. (1986). *Thought and Language*. Cambridge, MA: MIT Press.

Wertsch, J. V. (1991). *Voices of the Mind. A Sociocultural approach to Mediated Action*. Cambridge, MA: Harvard University Press.

Wood, D., Bruner, J. S. and Ross, G. (1976). The role of tutoring in problem solving. *Journal of Child Psychology and Psychiatry* **17**, 89–100.

Further Reading

Brown, J. S. (2000). *The Social Life of Information*. Boston, MA: Harvard Business School Press.

Personal Epistemology in Education

I Bråten, University of Oslo, Oslo, Norway

What Is Personal Epistemology?

Epistemology, the study of knowledge and knowing, has absorbed philosophers from ancient times. As a branch of philosophy, epistemology concerns the nature, origins, and limitations of knowledge, as well as the justification of truth claims. Recently, educational researchers have become interested in the theories and conceptions of knowledge and knowing that students hold, with the term personal or folk epistemology used to distinguish the lay person's view about knowledge and knowing from the trained philosopher's view (Hofer and Pintrich, 2002; Kitchener, 2002). Thus, personal epistemology essentially refers to the theories or beliefs that students (and other individuals) hold about knowledge and the process of knowing (Hofer and Pintrich, 1997, 2002). Likewise, epistemic theories or beliefs refer to individuals' views about knowledge and knowing (i.e., the epistemic).

How Does Personal Epistemology Develop?

Most educational research on personal epistemology has been rooted in Perry's (1970) longitudinal interview studies at Harvard, resulting in a scheme describing the development of personal epistemology during the college years. Several researchers have continued Perry's (1970) effort to identify developmental stages or sequences in students' personal epistemology, mostly through the use of interviewing methodology (e.g., Baxter Magolda, 1992; King and Kitchener, 1994; Kuhn, 1991). This line of research has generally described a developmental trajectory beginning with a dualist view where knowledge is seen as either right or wrong and where it is possible to know what is right with certainty. This is followed by a period of multiplicity where multiple conflicting views are acknowledged and accepted as equally valid. Finally, a more evaluativistic perspective develops where individuals acknowledge that there is no absolutely certain knowledge but still believe that it is possible to evaluate competing knowledge claims and justify claims through the use of supporting evidence.

While educational researchers have been most concerned with development in personal epistemology during adolescence and early adulthood, some research has also been conducted with children. Such research has linked the development of personal epistemology to children's theory of mind and also identified a predualistic stage of egocentric subjectivism where children believe that their own perspective is the only perspective (e.g., Burr and Hofer, 2002). Moreover, research conducted at younger ages has identified progression through the developmental stages observed in college students regardless of the age of the participants. Such repetition of previously passed stages, possibly several times from childhood to adulthood, suggests that the development of personal epistemology is recursive rather than linear, with recursion possibly occurring when students enter new educational contexts (e.g., traverse from elementary to secondary and from secondary to postsecondary education) (Muis et al., 2006). However, other plausible explanations for the developmental-recursiveness puzzle also exist, for example, that development varies with the kind of facts considered (Hallett et al., 2002).

What Are the Dimensions of Personal Epistemology?

Some researchers have been less interested in the development of personal epistemology than in its dimensionality. This approach was pioneered by Schommer (1990), who described personal epistemology as a system of more or less independent beliefs about certain knowledge (ranging from the belief that knowledge is absolute and unchanging to the belief that knowledge is tentative and evolving), simple knowledge (ranging from the belief that knowledge is best characterized as isolated bits and pieces to the belief that knowledge is best characterized as highly integrated concepts), omniscient authority (ranging from the belief that knowledge is handed down by authority to the belief that knowledge is derived from reason), quick learning (ranging from the belief that learning takes place quickly or not at all to the belief that learning is gradual), and fixed ability (ranging from the belief that ability to learn is given at birth to the view that ability to learn can be increased). Using a questionnaire to examine the described system, Schommer and associates identified factors corresponding to all the proposed dimensions except omniscient authority, even though this factor structure has not been consistently replicated by other researchers (e.g., Bråten and Strømsø, 2005; Hofer, 2000; Qian and Alvermann, 1995).

Whereas the three first dimensions in Schommer's (1990) conceptualization fall under the cited definition of personal epistemology as theories or beliefs about the nature of knowledge (certain knowledge and simple knowledge) and knowing (omniscient authority), the two remaining dimensions are more controversial because they mainly concern beliefs about learning (quick learning) and intelligence (fixed ability). Hofer and Pintrich (1997) therefore placed quick learning and fixed ability outside the realm of personal epistemology and purified the construct by considering two dimensions concerning the nature of knowledge (what one believes knowledge is) and two dimensions concerning the nature or process of knowing (how one comes to know). In their conceptualization of personal epistemology, the dimensions certainty of knowledge and simplicity of knowledge, both concerning the nature of knowledge, correspond to the dimensions certain knowledge and simple knowledge as described by Schommer (1990). Within the area of nature of knowing, the dimension source of knowledge, in part paralleling omniscient authority in Schommer's belief system, ranges from the conception that knowledge originates outside the self and resides in external authority, from which it may be transmitted, to the conception that knowledge is actively constructed by the person in interaction with others. Finally, the dimension justification for knowing, also concerning the nature of knowing, refers to how individuals evaluate and justify knowledge claims. This dimension ranges from justification through observation and authority, or on the basis of what feels right, to the use of rules of inquiry and the evaluation and integration of multiple sources.

Even though the dimensionality proposed by Hofer and Pintrich (1997) is currently the most authoritative view on the dimensionality of personal epistemology, and as such widely recognized by researchers in the field, the conceptually derived dimensions have not been unequivocally empirically verified through factor analysis (Hofer, 2000). However, use of qualitative methodologies such as observations and interviews (Hofer, 2004a) or think-aloud protocols (Hofer, 2004b) indicates that all the four dimensions proposed by Hofer and Pintrich (1997) are represented in students' epistemic thinking.

Hofer and Pintrich (1997) conceptualized individuals' epistemic beliefs to be theory-like, that is, integrated and coherent rather than existing as more or less independent beliefs, as Schommer (1990) originally suggested. Regarding this issue, recent evidence suggests that the various dimensions of personal epistemology may exist and operate independently, meaning that a student may hold what could be characterized as a more sophisticated belief on one dimension (e.g., that knowledge is integrated) and, at the same time, hold what could be characterized as a more naive belief on another dimension (e.g., that knowledge is unchanging) (Buehl and Alexander, 2005).

Is Personal Epistemology Domain General, Domain Specific, or Both?

Whereas initial educational research was based on the assumption that epistemic beliefs were independent of academic domains, implying, for example, that students would hold the same beliefs about knowledge and knowing in mathematics as they would in education, some studies conducted in the 1990s started to question this assumption. Those studies could be divided into between-subjects investigations, where students majoring in different domains were compared with respect to their epistemic beliefs, and within-subjects investigations, where the same students were asked about their epistemic beliefs in different domains. Buehl and Alexander (2001) found that most existing evidence supported the view that epistemic beliefs varied as a function of academic domains and, moreover, that such variation was related to domain structuredness (e.g., between mathematics as a well-structured domain and education as an ill-structured domain). However, Buehl and Alexander (2001) also argued that students' epistemic beliefs were not solely domain specific, that is, students could simultaneously hold both domain-specific and more domain-general or overarching epistemic beliefs.

A later review by Muis *et al.* (2006) confirmed that this is not an issue of either–or. Of the 19 studies that they reviewed, eight between-subjects investigations and 11 within-subjects investigations, 17 established evidence for domain specificity on one or more of the dimensions of personal epistemology, with six of those 17 studies also indicating some degree of domain generality. The review by Muis *et al.* (2006) also confirmed that epistemic belief similarities and differences across domains were related to whether the compared domains were similar or different with respect to structuredness, as well as whether they were similar or different on the hard–soft and the pure–applied dimensions. In general, students seem to view knowledge as more certain and integrated and more readily accept experts as sources of knowledge in well-structured or hard domains such as mathematics than in ill-structured or soft domains such as education.

The conclusion that personal epistemology includes levels of both domain generality and domain specificity was further supported by Buehl and Alexander (2005), who used cluster analysis to compare the student profiles that emerged from different dimensions of personal epistemology across the domains of mathematics and history. While the distinct epistemic belief profiles that emerged differed across the two domains, there was also some consistency in students' profile membership in mathematics and history, with this finding also consistent with a dual-level conception of personal epistemology. Moreover, a useful distinction may concern domain and topic-specific epistemic beliefs. Just as domain knowledge and topic knowledge may form subcategories of formally acquired or schooled knowledge, with domain knowledge referring to the breadth of one's knowledge about a domain (e.g., psychology or history), and topic knowledge representing the depth of one's knowledge about particular contents or concepts within a domain (e.g., intelligence or World War II) (Alexander *et al.*, 1991), beliefs about knowledge and knowing in a domain may be distinguished from epistemic beliefs about topics within domains. As an example of such a topic-specific approach to personal epistemology, Trautwein and Lüdtke (2007) used questionnaire items to examine students' epistemic beliefs about specific scientific theories, for example, about biological theories concerning natural selection and extinction of the dinosaurs, respectively. It was found that epistemic beliefs differed considerably across theories. At the same time, a small but statistically significant association between topic-specific epistemic beliefs and more general epistemic beliefs about scientific knowledge was found. Likewise, Bråten (2008) described research on topic-specific epistemic beliefs concerning student views on knowledge about climate change and how one comes to know about climate.

There is a clear need to further examine how different levels of personal epistemology develop in interaction and how they operate together to promote or constrain various aspects of student motivation and learning. Possibly, personal epistemology at different levels of specificity has strongest impact on facets of academic learning at comparable levels of specificity (Schraw, 2001). Clearly, the consideration of various levels of personal epistemology also implies that measures of personal epistemology become tailored to particular levels.

The Role of Personal Epistemology in Student Motivation, Cognition, and Performance

Schommer's (1990) departure from the developmental paradigmatic approach to personal epistemology and her introduction of quantitative assessment in the form of a paper-and-pencil questionnaire initiated an important line of research on relations between personal epistemology and other academic constructs. In accordance with Schommer's (1990) initial findings, quite a few other studies have linked epistemic beliefs to students' text-based learning and comprehension (e.g., Buehl and Alexander, 2005), with this body of research generally indicating that beliefs that have traditionally been located at the naive ends of epistemic belief continuums (e.g., beliefs that knowledge is certain or simple) are related to poorer learning and comprehension. Other findings show that more naive epistemic beliefs are negatively related to argumentative reasoning (e.g., Kuhn, 1991), conceptual change learning (e.g., Qian and Alvermann, 1995), and graded academic performance (e.g., Wood and Kardash, 2002).

Such relations between epistemic beliefs and student learning, comprehension, and performance may well be mediated by the use of cognitive and metacognitive strategy use, as several researchers have documented that personal epistemology is related to students' strategic processing (for review, see Muis, 2007).

Bråten (2008) noted that research on personal epistemology and text-based learning and comprehension had almost exclusively focused on students' reading of one single text, and, moreover, that most research on personal epistemology and aspects of learning had been conducted in traditional print environments rather than in new technological environments. As personal epistemology may be particularly important when students work on complex learning tasks (Spiro *et al.*, 1996), these limitations are not trivial.

Regarding the reading of multiple texts, Rukavina and Daneman (1996) provided some early evidence that students holding more sophisticated epistemic beliefs about the complexity of knowledge were better equipped to integrate ideas across two texts presenting conflicting information on a topic. Later, Bråten and Strømsø (2006) provided new evidence that at least adult college readers are able to deal adequately with the challenge of integrating information from multiple, even conflicting, texts, provided that they hold relatively sophisticated beliefs about the nature of knowledge and knowing. Otherwise, even college readers may be better off when encountering the same content in an integrated textbook format.

Regarding the importance of personal epistemology when learning with hypermedia technology, Jacobson and Spiro (1995) provided preliminary evidence that students who believed in simple knowledge had problems handling the nonlinear and multidimensional nature of an ill-defined hypertext system. Bendixen and Hartley (2003) provided additional evidence to suggest that students' epistemic beliefs play an important role in hypermedia-learning environments. Moreover, Hofer (2004b) reported that when students thought aloud during online searching, those expressing naive epistemic beliefs were likely to pursue the searching task in a brief and perfunctory way, not seeing the need for additional sources or reflecting on the credibility and accuracy of the sources they located. Finally, Bråten and colleagues (e.g., Bråten *et al.*, 2005) found that students' epistemic beliefs predicted their Internet-based learning activities. In brief, the more naive beliefs students held about Internet-based knowledge and knowing, the more naive they seemed to be about the ease with which relevant Internet-based sources could be identified and used, also displaying an overreliance on the Internet as a communication tool and overestimating the value of virtual exchanges at the expense of real-life encounters. Given the importance of being able to construct integrated meaning from multiple textual sources in today's knowledge society, with those sources more often than not located in complex computerized information systems, further research on the role played by personal epistemology in such endeavors is greatly needed.

Thus far, fewer studies have addressed relations between personal epistemology and academic motivation than between personal epistemology and academic cognition and performance. However, Bråten and Strømsø (2004, 2005) reported that naive epistemic beliefs were negatively related to adaptive motivational beliefs such as mastery goal orientation, self-efficacy, and interest. Conversely, Buehl and Alexander (2005) identified subgroups based on epistemic belief profiles and showed that clusters characterized by more sophisticated patterns of epistemic beliefs had higher levels on both expectancy and value components of academic motivation.

Although there is a fairly solid research base for asserting the importance of personal epistemology for student motivation, cognition, and performance, the complexity of the relationships among those constructs are not very well understood. As Schraw (2001) noted, structural models that specify the direct and indirect linkages among academic constructs, including epistemic beliefs, should be generated and then tested empirically through structural equation modeling to examine such complex relationships collectively.

How Can Personal Epistemology Be Assessed?

Perry (1970) and other later researchers primarily interested in the development of personal epistemology (e.g., Baxter Magolda, 1992; King and Kitchener, 1994) mainly conducted lengthy in-depth interviews to provide thick descriptions of how individuals' beliefs about knowledge and knowing change over time. For example, King and Kitchener (1994) have conducted structured interviews about ill-structured real-life problems or dilemmas, for example, about news or food additives, asking participants about their views on such problems and how they would justify their views. The interview tool used by these researchers is called the reflective judgment interview, with research providing evidence for the validity and reliability of this tool.

However, the possibility for doing larger-scale investigations of personal epistemology greatly increased with Schommer's (1990) introduction of a questionnaire allowing for group administration and statistical analyses of student scores. Schommer's epistemological beliefs questionnaire assesses personal epistemology at a domain-general level. Modifications of the questionnaire have tried to improve its psychometric qualities. However, the dimensionality of personal epistemology has been somewhat different across the modifications, and the internal consistency reliabilities (Cronbach's Alphas) for the

dimensions measured with those instruments have sometimes been smaller than required. Still, Schommer's questionnaire has been the most widely used quantitative assessment of personal epistemology.

Research on the domain-generality versus domain-specificity issue eventually led to the construction of domain-specific personal epistemology questionnaires. First, a modified version of Schommer's domain-general questionnaire was developed where about every third item explicitly mentioned the domain (e.g., mathematics or science) that the student should keep in mind when completing the questionnaire (Schommer and Walker, 1995). However, Hofer (2000) constructed a measure more specifically devised to assess domain-specific epistemic beliefs, where each item on the questionnaire referred to a particular field or subject matter (psychology or science) as a frame of reference (e.g., in this field, knowledge is certain.). Likewise, Buehl et al. (2002) developed a self-report measure specifically devised to test for domain-specific epistemic beliefs, with the items focusing on either mathematics or history. In their more recent work, Buehl and Alexander (2005) have selected and combined items from the two above-mentioned domain-specific measures, the discipline-focused epistemological belief questionnaire (DFEBQ; Hofer, 2000) and the domain-specific beliefs questionnaire (DSBQ; Buehl et al., 2002). Buehl and Alexander (2005) reported that the resulting domain-specific questionnaire captured the dimensions of certainty, simplicity, and source of knowledge in mathematics as well as in history.

As existing measures of personal epistemology primarily focused on conventional-print environments rather than new technological environments, Bråten et al. (2005) designed the Internet-specific epistemological questionnaire (ISEQ), a questionnaire specifically assessing beliefs about Internet-based knowledge (what one believes knowledge is like on the Internet) and Internet-based knowing (how one comes to know on the Internet), with this questionnaire especially suitable for studying relations between personal epistemology and learning with hypermedia or Internet technologies. As mentioned above, some researchers have also started to construct questionnaires that assess epistemic beliefs at a topic-specific level, for example, concerning specific theories within domains (Trautwein and Lüdtke, 2007) or specific scientific topics (Bråten et al., in press; Stahl and Bromme, 2007).

Assessment of personal epistemology through survey methodology relies heavily on Likert-type rating scales where individuals express their degree of agreement with beliefs about knowledge and knowing. One issue with such scales is whether they can capture the complex and multifaceted nature of personal epistemology dimensions, particularly the source of knowledge and justification of knowing dimensions (Hofer, 2004b). Another issue is whether they are suitable for measuring all the different epistemic positions identified within the developmental approach (i.e., dualistic, multiplistic, and evaluativistic positions) (Hofer, 2004b; see also, Muis *et al.*, 2006). Given such limitations, there has been a call for more qualitative, dynamic assessments of personal epistemology. One such approach, used by Hofer (2004b), involves having students think aloud during actual learning and knowledge construction and then analyzing the think-aloud protocols for instances of epistemic thinking (see also, Mason and Boldrin, 2008). Another possibility, also used by Hofer (2004a), is to use ongoing observations of classroom discourse combined with student interviews to examine how students' personal epistemology unfolds over time in the context of subject-matter instruction.

Finally, multi-method approaches combining quantitative and qualitative data sources may be especially valuable when assessing personal epistemology (e.g., Hofer, 2006; Schraw, 2001). For example, combining the use of questionnaires with in-depth interviewing may not only lead to a refinement of existing questionnaires (Hofer, 2006), but also allow for a triangulation of data that can give both researchers and educators a more complete picture of student epistemic beliefs.

Educational Implications

Schraw (2001) noted that one educational implication that might follow from the existing research on personal epistemology is that teachers should be helped to understand and change their own epistemic beliefs. According to Schraw (2001), teachers' beliefs affect their curricular and pedagogical decisions, and such decisions may, in turn, affect student epistemic beliefs (see also, Schraw and Olafson, 2003). This was partly confirmed in a qualitative study where Hofer (2004a) combined observations and interviews in two versions of introductory-level college chemistry. Hofer (2004a) observed dramatic differences in pedagogical approaches and implicit messages about knowledge and knowing in the two courses that she studied, also showing that students' existing epistemic beliefs were influenced by the instruction they experienced. Hammer and Elby (2002) suggested that innovative pedagogical approaches where class discussion is more typical than lectures, and where students are engaged in activities of design and construction to accomplish authentic tasks, are more likely than traditional pedagogical approaches to activate sets of epistemic resources that are productive for learning.

According to Muis *et al.* (2006), however, the dominant epistemologies of educational domains (e.g., of science or history education) often seem to reinforce the beliefs that knowledge consists of right answers and unquestionable facts possessed by authorities and transmitted to students. In history, for example, students typically engage in the gathering of factual information about different topics, without much evaluation or questioning of the validity of that information. This concentration on accumulating historical facts may be reinforced by teacher beliefs in knowledge and knowing in history as the memorization and reproduction of factual information (cf., VanSledright, 2002). Instead, students need to be taught that there may be multiple opinions about historical events, with these opinions backed by varying evidence. Moreover, students need help to understand that interpretations of historical events can be justified by the amount of evidence that they account for, and that all available sources should be considered, not only a few select ones (Wolfe and Goldman, 2005).

Thus, given that teachers' epistemic beliefs in many instances seem to be less sophisticated than desirable, it is indeed an important task to try to promote belief change in teacher students as well as in more- and less-experienced teachers. Preliminary evidence suggests that this is not an impossible task. For example, Gill *et al.* (2004) showed that teachers may revise their existing epistemic beliefs through the reading of refutational text especially designed for this purpose.

Regarding the development of more sophisticated epistemic beliefs in students, Schraw (2001) suggested that schools should encourage an ongoing discussion and evaluation of such beliefs. In particular, Schraw argued that schools should try to promote critical-thinking skills and conceptual change among students, for example, by encouraging cooperative learning where students can discuss and evaluate their own epistemic beliefs. There is currently some research to underpin these suggestions, indicating that having students struggle to understand complex issues by reading texts presenting them with multiple perspectives on a topic, integrated with discussions of both text content and their current epistemic thinking, may bring about belief change. Thus, Valanides and Angeli (2005) observed that students who read a text presenting opposing views on a controversial topic and then discussed the text content, reflected on their thinking abut the issue, and evaluated their thinking in light of principles for critical thinking, developed more sophisticated epistemic beliefs after the intervention. Accordingly, Kienhues *et al.* (2008) found that students who held naive epistemic beliefs concerning the scientific topic of genetics considered knowledge about this topic to be more complex and variable after reading a text focusing on the uncertainties of genetic fingerprinting. Bråten (2008) argued that the reading of multiple texts containing contrasting perspectives on a topic would be a good starting point for reflection on both content and epistemic beliefs in relation to that content, with such reading and concomitant collective reflection presumably having the potential to foster the belief revision and conceptual change that many students seem to need.

Since personal epistemology seems to vary across domains, helping students become aware of their own epistemic beliefs, as well as develop more sophisticated beliefs, should probably take place within the frameworks of particular domains or even topics within domains. That is, an important part of instruction in a domain should concentrate on challenging students' existing beliefs about knowledge and knowing in the domain and, moreover, help them develop more sophisticated, expert-like beliefs about the nature of knowledge and the processes or methods of knowing within that domain. According to Hofer (2006), helping students develop from multiplicitism to evaluativism is a particularly difficult instructional task in postmodern educational environments.

See also: Knowledge Domains and Domain Learning; Learning as Inquiry; Learning Strategies; Metacognition; Problem Solving and Human Expertise; Self-Regulated Learning and Socio-Cognitive Theory.

Bibliography

Alexander, P. A., Schallert, D. L., and Hare, V. C. (1991). Coming to terms: How researchers in learning and literacy talk about knowledge. *Review of Educational Research* **61**, 315–343.

Baxter Magolda, M. B. (1992). *Knowing and Reasoning in College: Gender-Related Patterns in Students' Intellectual Development.* San Francisco, CA: Jossey-Bass.

Bendixen, L. D. and Hartley, K. (2003). Successful learning with hypermedia: The role of epistemological beliefs and metacognitive awareness. *Journal of Educational Computing Research* **28**, 15–30.

Bråten, I. (2008). Personal epistemology, understanding of multiple texts, and learning within internet technologies. In Khine, M. S. (ed.) *Knowing, Knowledge, and Beliefs: Epistemological Studies across Diverse Cultures*, pp 351–376. New York: Springer.

Bråten I., Gil, L., Strømsø, H. I., and Vidal-Abarca, E. (in press). Personal epistemology across cultures: Exploring Norwegian and Spanish university students' epistemic beliefs about climate change. *Social Psychology of Education.*

Bråten, I. and Strømsø, H. I. (2004). Epistemological beliefs and implicit theories of intelligence as predictors of achievement goals. *Contemporary Educational Psychology* **29**, 371–388.

Bråten, I. and Strømsø, H. I. (2005). The relationship between epistemological beliefs, implicit theories of intelligence, and self-regulated learning among Norwegian post-secondary students. *British Journal of Educational Psychology* **75**, 539–565.

Bråten, I. and Strømsø, H. I. (2006). Effects of personal epistemology on the understanding of multiple texts. *Reading Psychology* **27**, 457–484.

Bråten, I., Strømsø, H. I., and Samuelstuen, M. S. (2005). The relationship between internet-specific epistemological beliefs and learning within internet technologies. *Journal of Educational Computing Research* **33**, 141–171.

Buehl, M. M. and Alexander, P. A. (2001). Beliefs about academic knowledge. *Educational Psychology Review* **13**, 385–418.

Buehl, M. M. and Alexander, P. A. (2005). Motivation and performance differences in students' domain-specific epistemological belief profiles. *American Educational Research Journal* **42**, 697–726.

Buehl, M. M., Alexander, P. A., and Murphy, P. K. (2002). Beliefs about schooled knowledge: Domain specific or domain general? *Contemporary Educational Psychology* **27**, 415–449.

Burr, J. E. and Hofer, B. K. (2002). Personal epistemology and theory of mind: Deciphering young children's beliefs about knowledge and knowing. *New Ideas in Psychology* **20**, 199–224.

Gill, M. G., Ashton, P., and Algina, J. (2004). Authoritative schools: A test of a model to resolve the school effectiveness debate. *Contemporary Educational Psychology* **29**, 389–409.

Hallett, D., Chandler, M. J., and Krettenauer, T. (2002). Disentangling the course of epistemic development: Parsing knowledge by epistemic content. *New Ideas in Psychology* **20**, 285–307.

Hammer, D. and Elby, A. (2002). On the form of a personal epistemology. In Hofer, B. K. and Pintrich, P. R. (eds.) *Personal Epistemology: The Psychology of Beliefs about Knowledge and Knowing*, pp 169–190. Mahwah, NJ: Erlbaum.

Hofer, B. K. (2000). Dimensionality and disciplinary differences in personal epistemology. *Contemporary Educational Psychology* **25**, 378–405.

Hofer, B. K. (2004a). Exploring the dimensions of personal epistemology in differing classroom contexts: Student interpretations during the first year of college. *Contemporary Educational Psychology* **29**, 129–163.

Hofer, B. K. (2004b). Epistemological understanding as a metacognitive process: Thinking aloud during online searching. *Educational Psychologist* **39**, 43–55.

Hofer, B. K. (2006). Beliefs about knowledge and knowing: Integrating domain specificity and domain generality: A response to Muis, Bendixen, and Haerle (2006). *Educational Psychology Review* **18**, 67–76.

Hofer, B. K. and Pintrich, P. R. (1997). The development of epistemological theories: Beliefs about knowledge and knowing and their relation to learning. *Review of Educational Research* **67**, 88–140.

Hofer, B. K. and Pintrich, P. R. (eds.) (2002). *Personal Epistemology: The Psychology of Beliefs about Knowledge and Knowing.* Mahwah, NJ: Erlbaum.

Jacobson, M. J. and Spiro, R. J. (1995). Hypertext learning environments, cognitive flexibility, and the transfer of complex knowledge: An empirical investigation. *Journal of Educational Computing Research* **12**, 301–333.

Kienhues, D., Bromme, R., and Stahl, E. (2008). Changing epistemological beliefs: The unexpected impact of a short-term intervention. *British Journal of Educational Psychology* **78**, 545–565.

King, P. M. and Kitchener, K. S. (1994). *Developing Reflective Judgment: Understanding and Promoting Intellectual Growth and Critical Thinking in Adolescents and Adults.* San Francisco, CA: Jossey-Bass.

Kitchener, R. F. (2002). Folk epistemology: An introduction. *New Ideas in Psychology* **20**, 89–105.

Kuhn, D. (1991). *The Skills of Argument.* Cambridge: Cambridge University Press.

Mason, L. and Boldrin, A. (2008). Epistemic metacognition in the context of information searching on the web. In Khine, M. S. (ed.) *Knowing, Knowledge, and Beliefs: Epistemological Studies across Diverse Cultures*, pp 377–404. New York: Springer.

Muis, K. R. (2007). The role of epistemic beliefs in self-regulated learning. *Educational Psychologist* **42**, 173–190.

Muis, K. R., Bendixen, L. D., and Haerle, F. C. (2006). Domain-generality and domain-specificity in personal epistemology research: Philosophical and empirical reflections in the development of a theoretical framework. *Educational Psychology Review* **18**, 3–54.

Perry, W. G. (1970). *Forms of Intellectual and Ethical Development in the College Years: A Scheme.* New York: Holt, Rinehart, and Winston.

Qian, G. and Alvermann, D. (1995). Role of epistemological beliefs and learned helplessness in secondary school students' learning science concepts from text. *Journal of Educational Psychology* **87**, 282–292.

Rukavina, I. and Daneman, M. (1996). Integration and its effect on acquiring knowledge about competing scientific theories from text. *Journal of Educational Psychology* **88**, 272–287.

Schommer, M. (1990). Effects of beliefs about the nature of knowledge on comprehension. *Journal of Educational Psychology* **82**, 498–504.

Schommer, M. and Walker, K. (1995). Are epistemological beliefs similar across domains? *Journal of Educational Psychology* **87**, 424–432.

Schraw, G. (2001). Current themes and future directions in epistemological research: A commentary. *Educational Psychology Review* **13**, 451–464.

Schraw, G. and Olafson, L. (2003). Teachers' epistemological world views and educational practices. *Issues in Education* **8**, 99–148.

Spiro, R. J., Feltovich, P. J., and Coulson, R. L. (1996). Two epistemic world-views: Prefigurative schemas and learning in complex domains. *Applied Cognitive Psychology* **10**, S51–S61.

Stahl, E. and Bromme, R. (2007). The CAEB: An instrument for measuring connotative aspects of epistemological beliefs. *Learning and Instruction* **17**, 773–785.

Trautwein, U. and Lüdtke, O. (2007). Predicting global and topic-specific certainty beliefs: Domain-specificity and the role of the academic environment. *British Journal of Educational Psychology* **77**, 907–934.

Valanides, N. and Angeli, C. (2005). Effects of instruction on changes in epistemological beliefs. *Contemporary Educational Psychology* **30**, 314–330.

VanSledright, B. (2002). *In Search of America's Past: Learning to Read History in Elementary School*. New York: Teachers College Press.

Wolfe, M. B. W. and Goldman, S. R. (2005). Relations between adolescents' text processing and reasoning. *Cognition and Instruction* **23**, 467–502.

Wood, P. K. and Kardash, C. (2002). Critical elements in the design and analysis of studies of epistemology. In Hofer, B. K. and Pintrich, P. R. (eds.) *Personal Epistemology: The Psychology of Beliefs about Knowledge and Knowing*, pp 231–260. Mahwah, NJ: Erlbaum.

Further Reading

Khine, M. S. (ed.) (2008). *Knowing, Knowledge, and Beliefs: Epistemological Studies across Diverse Cultures*. New York: Springer.

Learning in a Sociocultural Perspective

R Säljö, Göteborg University, Göteborg, Sweden

Introduction

Issues of learning and development were at the heart of the attempts by Vygotsky (1896–1934) to take psychology out of what he described as its 'crisis.' He developed his ideas by dialoguing with the theoretical perspectives presented by many of the distinguished scholars who were active during the rich and dynamic period of psychology of the early twentieth century: Piaget, Janet, Thorndike, Pavlov, Freud, Bühler, and others who we now conceive as Grand Theorists. He was also eager to challenge the basic ideas of the influential schools of psychology of the time, such as behaviorism, pragmatism, and Gestalt psychology. Vygotsky carefully and critically scrutinized the conceptions of learning and development, underpinning these diverse traditions, and pointed to where they, in his opinion, were flawed. Some of these traditions he saw as idealistic and speculative rather than scientific; others he accused of being too reductionistic and failing to address the fundamental problems of consciousness and how the human mind develops and is transformed through social experience. (Informative accounts of the development of Vygotsky's ideas have been written by Bruner, 1985; Kozulin, 1986; and Leontiev, 1997).

One way to understand some of Vygotsky's revolutionary ideas on learning and development is to listen to his critique of the dominant tradition of his day in the Soviet Union: pavlovian reflexology. Reflexology, like behaviorism, represents a view of learning which from a philosophical perspective can be described as associationism. The core idea is that learning can be reduced to understanding the associations between stimuli and responses, the so-called S → R connection. This link between a stimulus (the presence of food) and a response (salivation by the dog in Pavlov's famous experiments) was conceived as the atom of learning. Through the principle of conditioning, which implies that a new stimulus (in Pavlov's case, a bell) is introduced to elicit a response, learning takes place. What was previously a natural response is now a conditioned, that is, learned response. In this tradition, more advanced behaviors can be understood as chains of increasingly complex connections between stimuli and responses. Vygotsky viewed this experimental approach to the study of psychological phenomena, although scientific, as insufficient for understanding how human beings learn and develop. Indeed, the adherence to this perspective on human psychological functioning was a significant part of the 'crisis.' This approach is only relevant for explaining what he referred to as the 'lower psychological functions,' that is, those elementary processes which are largely biological and given to us by nature, as it were. A genuinely psychological understanding of phenomena such as learning and development must grapple with specifically human modes of thinking and acting, where language and other cultural tools play a decisive role. These are the "higher psychological functions" (Vygotsky, 1978), which are social, historical, and cultural in their origin and nature.

The Sociocultural Approach

Vygotsky formulated his ideas during a short and hectic period of about ten years. His style of writing and the richness and originality of his ideas led the philosopher Stephen Toulmin to refer to him as the Mozart of psychology in a review of *Mind in Society* when it was published in 1978. Together with his colleagues A R Luria (1902–77) and A N Leontiev (1904–79) he formed the famous troika that was to have a profound influence on psychology and allied disciplines. The history of the sociocultural tradition is also fascinating. The research and the ideas were dormant during the dark ages of political oppression in the East and the intellectual hegemony, even monotony, of behaviorism in the West. The interest resurfaced in a major way in the 1970s and 1980s, thanks to the efforts of Luria and Leontiev and scholars in the West such as Jerome Bruner, Michael Cole, and Jim Wertsch. Today, the influence of the legacy of Vygotsky is stronger than ever and his writings form a rich and inspiring source for developing our understanding of human learning.

One important clue to understanding the pillars on which Vygotsky tried to build a new, and in his view more productive, approach to the study of learning and development can be found in the terms which have been used by his followers to characterize his approach. Some authors refer to it as a sociocultural approach, while others use the terms cultural–historical or sociohistorical. Cole (1996) uses Vygotsky's ideas as a foundation for what he refers to as cultural psychology. All these expressions communicate something significant about Vygotsky's original intellectual project: he wanted to study the relationships between the sociocultural and sociohistorical development of human activities and societies on the one hand, and, on the other, what these transformations imply for learning and development of individuals during ontogeny (i.e., their life span). In other words, he wanted to understand how a biological being becomes a sociocultural being equipped with language and a range of cultural and intellectual skills relevant for social life – skills that have no counterpart in any other species.

Mediation and Cultural Tools

One of Vygotsky's core ideas is that human beings, unlike animals, learn and develop by using cultural tools. Such tools, "language, different forms of numeration and counting, mnemotechnic techniques, algebraic symbolism, works of art, writing, schemes, diagrams, maps" (Vygotsky, 1997: 85) are the products of the development of practices in society over time. They are sociocultural also, in the sense that the nature of these tools may vary between societies. For instance, in some languages one uses some kind of phonetic alphabet for writing, others have syllabic and/or logographic writing systems. These writing systems are different cultural tools, each with their own particularities when it comes to how reading and writing are carried out. In a historical perspective most societies have not used writing at all. Growing up in the latter kind of environment implies that many human activities have to be done differently from what we are used to. For example, one cannot make notes to remember and there can be no such thing as a book of law as an element of legal practices.

Cultural tools develop through an evolutionary process, that is, they have a sociogenesis (de Graaf and Meier, 1994). This idea of the sociogenesis of tools, and of psychological processes, is central to a sociocultural perspective. Vygotsky made a distinction between intellectual/mental (although he used the term psychological) tools and technical or physical tools. Mental tools are symbolic systems used for activities such as writing, counting, measuring, and so on. Examples of physical tools, that is, artifacts, would be rulers, computers, hammers, compasses, etc. (Säljö, 1999). However, and as Cole (1996) argues very convincingly, the distinction between these two kinds of tools is difficult, maybe even pointless, to uphold; a mini-calculator or an abacus is an artifact but both these artifacts, although in different manners, incorporate intellectual tools such as number systems and rules for performing calculations. This ability of externalizing intellectual tools into physical tools is another example of a unique human talent of considerable significance for learning.

At the level of individual action, cultural tools serve as instruments of thinking and acting, to use Vygotsky's own expression. They enter into the flow of human actions and transform the manners in which we reason, communicate, and carry out all kinds of activities. From a psychological point of view, it is one thing to carry out multiplications of four-digit numbers with two decimals as mental arithmetic, another to do it with paper and pencil, and yet another to do it with a mini-calculator (Säljö *et al.*, 2006).

The manners in which we perform such operations differ radically in these situations. What is impossible to do as mental arithmetic becomes almost trivial when there is a calculator present.

In the language of sociocultural theory, cultural tools mediate the world for us in social practices. This notion of mediation is one of the most central concepts in the sociocultural approach. By learning to use cultural tools, we appropriate (Wertsch, 1998) portions of the accumulated experiences and knowing of our society. When learning how to make calculations using decimals or learning how to use a compass, we take over some of the insights and practical knowing that have emerged in our society. These tools are not the inventions of the individual; rather, we come to know and master them because they are used in the society in which we are socialized – and we use many such tools without knowing where they came from or how they emerged. Thus, all readers of this text are familiar with intellectual tools such as percent, decimals, and the = sign, but we may have no idea of their sociogenesis. We take them over as they are, and in this sense the world is pre-interpreted for us. When tools change, such as when we begin to use calculators for complex multiplications, remediation takes place.

For Vygotsky, language is the prime mechanism for mediating what happens in the world, it is "the tool of tools" as he puts it. The relationship between language and thought was one of his most prominent interests, and there are many reasons for this focus on language. One reason why language is so significant for learning and development, both at the collective and the individual level, is that it simultaneously serves as the link between people in interactive settings, and as a tool for thinking. This is how our thinking is socialized or, to put it even stronger, humanized. One of the most quoted passages from Vygotsky's work is the following, where he makes this point:

> Every function in the child's cultural development appears twice: first, on the social level, and later, on the individual level; first *between* people (*interpsychological*), and then *inside* the child (*intrapsychological*). This applies equally to voluntary attention, to logical memory, and to the formation of ideas. All the higher functions originate as actual relationships between human individuals. (Vygotsky, 1978: 57; italics in original)

This formulation indicates how Vygotsky attempted to solve the problem of creating a link between the inner world (thinking) and the outside world (interaction with others). Through language, cultural tools are appropriated (or in Vygotsky's terms: internalized) by individuals in social interaction. Thus, in a sociocultural perspective, thinking is seen as a kind of inner speech carried out by means of cultural tools that we first encountered in communicative practices (Vygotsky, 1986). To think is to engage in internal dialogs with semiotic tools.

Language is also the prime mechanism of semiotic mediation, that is, thinking by means of signs. Sign-mediated communication is another uniquely human phenomenon which, for instance, behaviorist interpretations of learning are unable to deal with. Learning as conceived in behaviorism implies that the organism (be it a human being or an animal) responds directly to stimuli in the external world, that is, in an unmediated manner. Sign-mediated communication instead implies that people think in a roundabout way (Vygotsky, 1994: 61) by means of cultural tools. We, metaphorically speaking, engage with the world via cultural tools when we communicate and perform physical activities.

In passing it should be pointed out that Vygotsky in no way denied the significance of the biological basis of human cognitive and psychological functioning. In fact, in many of his writings, he explores various features of animal cognition, in particular the thinking of primates, and he had a strong interest in such comparative research. But he was adamant in his insistence on the fact that human thinking and learning cannot be reduced to biological processes. Humans are unique in the sense that they think, communicate, and work through cultural tools, and it is at this level that we have to study learning and development if our interest is in human psychological functioning. The sociocultural development is "not a simple continuation" of the biological one. On the contrary, when people begin to appropriate cultural tools through communication with those around them, the *"nature of development itself changes,* from biological to sociohistorical" (Vygotsky, 1986: 94; italics in original). In this sense, "animals are incapable of learning in the human sense of the term," since *"human learning presupposes a specific social nature and a process by which children grow into the intellectual life of those around them"* (Vygotsky, 1978: 88; italics in original). The evolutionary psychologist Donald (2001) expresses this idea of the relationship between biology and culture even more strongly when he argues that the human brain is a biological structure which has been 'hi-jacked' by culture for cultural and interactional purposes.

Learning and Development: the Zone of Proximal Development

Another idea which is central to the sociocultural tradition, and which differs from other perspectives, is the focus on the change and dynamics of psychological processes. In fact, Vygotsky argued that when studying human beings, one always studies change. This idea he developed as a critique of the research of, among others, Piaget and his stage theory and of the representatives of traditional intelligence testing such as Binet. An assumption of such theories is that "learning trails behind development" (Vygotsky, 1978: 80). This implies that "[d]evelopment or maturation is viewed as a precondition of learning but never as a result of it" (Vygotsky, 1978). From the point of view of educating children this implies that development is seen as a more fundamental process; children can only learn it when they are at the required stage of maturation. Instruction, thus, should be adapted to the developmental level of the child.

For Vygotsky, and from a sociocultural perspective, the opposite assumption, that is, that learning is constitutive of development, is more productive. It is by appropriating cultural tools that children develop and become familiar with the accumulated knowing and skills of their community. When children begin to appropriate the basics of addition and subtraction, they become familiar with specific cultural tools and "this provides the basis for the subsequent development of a variety of highly complex internal processes in children's thinking" (Vygotsky, 1978: 90). Expressed differently, through learning the development of the child is set in motion in a specific direction. However, learning is not identical with development; rather, it is a necessary prerequisite for the child to develop "culturally organized, specifically human psychological functions" (Vygotsky, 1978).

These ideas of the dynamics of human thinking, and that learning contributes to development, are incorporated into the famous concept of the zone of proximal development (ZPD). Throughout his short life, Vygotsky had a strong interest in education and wanted to offer an alternative way of thinking about pedagogical practices to the ones offered by, for instance, stage theories and behaviorism. Instead of seeing maturation as a necessary prerequisite for learning, one should consider the manner in which children (or adults) appropriate cultural tools. This is done gradually and through the support the learner receives in social interaction by more expert partners. Thus, for the individual there is a 'zone' in which his or her familiarity with how to use a cultural tool is still at an early stage. Vygotsky (1978: 86) defined ZPD as:

> *the distance between the actual developmental level as determined by independent problem solving and the level of potential development as determined through problem solving under adult guidance or in collaboration with more capable peers.* (italics in original)

What this idea implies at a very concrete level is that when people are allowed to cooperate with more capable peers, their performance is usually much better than when they work alone. When a child is struggling with understanding the basics of addition and subtraction, support by a teacher or a parent will assist the child in understanding how to proceed when dealing with specific problems. These hints and suggestions may be indirect and subtle but when the adult and the child share a certain interpretation of the task, the child can make productive use of the skills of the more expert person. More capable partners will thus 'scaffold' (Wood *et al.*, 1976) the activities of less experienced members of an activity.

The ZPD can be conceived as a developmental path in which the child's appropriation of a cultural tool is still partial, and where external support will be necessary to accomplish a task such as tying a knot (Nilholm and Säljö, 1996) or solving a puzzle (Wertsch, 1985). But it can also be seen as the zone in which a child is particularly sensitive to instruction from a more knowledgeable partner. It is within this zone that the child is able to profit from the assistance provided by the adult in order to develop a more independent understanding of the cultural tool and how to use it in a specific setting.

The ZPD has served as an inspiration for important developmental work in education in many contexts. The attempts to develop reciprocal teaching and guided cooperative learning by the late Ann Brown and her colleagues (Brown, 1993) is one example of this. In reciprocal teaching, the role of the teacher is "to scaffold the involvement of learners in the discussion by providing the explanation, modeling, support, and feedback that will – in time – enable full participation of students" in activities such as understanding texts and other cultural tools. The idea of the ZPD has also been used as an underlying notion for the view of learning as a process of increasing participation in social practices emphasized by scholars such as Rogoff (1990). In much of this work there is also a critique of the rather one-sided view of the adult–child relationship that Vygotsky presents, where the child is always the dependent part and the adult is in control of the progress of the activity. Several of these scholars, for instance, Rogoff in her analyses of guided participation, instead emphasize the joint efforts by all parties of maintaining mutual understanding and shared perspectives on the world when engaging in conversations. This critique also draws inspiration from the more dialogical interpretations of learning and social interaction which have emerged during recent years when Vygotskian ideas have been combined with the dialogical perspective on language and interaction that is at the heart of Bahktin's approach to human communication (Wertsch, 1991).

Language, Learning, and the Formation of Mind

The most well-known publication by Vygotsky is his book *Thought and Language*. It was originally published in the final year of his life and has appeared in a number of English translations. The first English version, a highly abbreviated one, appeared in 1962 and more extended versions were published in 1986 and 1997 (the latter one with the title *Thinking and Speech*). In this volume, which undoubtedly is one of the most influential books in the fields of learning and development, Vygotsky explores fundamental problems of the relationships between thinking, communication, and the formation of mind. His ambition is to scrutinize the role that language and communication play in human ontogeny, and he touches on several significant issues that pertain to how the mind is shaped by social experience.

Vygotsky's emphasis on the role of linguistically mediated communication is rooted in his conviction of the role that semiotic mediation plays in the formation of human thinking and social interaction. It is through semiotic mediation that we develop the abilities characteristic of higher psychological functioning. We learn conceptual knowledge, how to remember, how to monitor our own activities and put them under conscious control, and a range of other sociocultural skills. Much of what we learn would in modern psychological parlance be described as meta-cognitive or meta-communicative skills; we learn to structure our own activities and the world through language (Rommetveit, 1985). The emphasis on these kinds of skills reflects Vygotsky's conviction that as human beings we not only live in the world; rather, we are also able to reflect on it and develop knowledge about what we do (cf. Cole, 1996: 120). Language is the most significant tool in such processes.

From the educational point of view, one particularly interesting analysis concerns that of the distinction between the acquisition of spontaneous concepts and scientific concepts, respectively. We appropriate spontaneous concepts (brother, sister, and family) in everyday interaction, that is, we learn them from below, metaphorically speaking. Other concepts (one example that Vygotsky uses is Archimedes' law) we have to learn through some form of explicit instruction or guidance. Somebody has to explain to us what the term and the concept mean, and appropriation then proceeds in a top-down fashion; we descend from the abstract to the concrete (cf. Kozulin, 1998: 48). Thus, understanding them implies learning to contextualize a particular class of phenomena by means of an abstract principle. Supporting this specific type of learning is the responsibility of schooling and the teacher. This is one of the reasons why schooling is so important, and why the specific learning practices of schooling are different from what we find in other settings. Thus, Vygotsky objected to Piaget's view that children, when engaged in self-directed learning and experimentation, will come to master scientific concepts. Such learning, Vygotsky argued, presupposes guidance by someone who masters the relevant discourses. A significant role for schooling is to introduce children to those parts of the accumulated knowledge of our society that is not available through everyday practices.

Vygotsky and the Development of Education

In the debates on learning and development Vygotsky's sociocultural approach has become central. The theory has become part of many introductory books in psychology and education, and has found its way into discussions about pedagogy. An interesting dimension of the legacy of Vygotsky concerns his impact on education. Already in the Soviet period there were many who attempted to develop pedagogical practices that were rooted in Vygotsky's thinking. The success of these experiments is not convincing. In fact, many of these attempts now strike us as highly problematic. The notion of a scientific approach to education often resulted in a kind of scientism with what appears to have been rather sterile, even authoritarian, teaching patterns dominated by adults. Children were, to some extent, treated as objects of teaching rather than active participants and contributors to their own learning. In recent developments in educational research, however, Vygotskian ideas have become important for approaches to teaching and learning that emphasize the situated nature of knowing and the necessity of actively engaging learners in the process of appropriating knowledge and skills in cooperation with adults and in various kinds of learning communities. The work by Brown and Rogoff and their colleagues mentioned earlier are but two examples of many contemporary attempts to take Vygotskian ideas into educational practices. This is also an important reminder of a point that John Dewey repeatedly made: theoretical principles are not enough for creating successful educational practices. This move from theoretical insights to pedagogical practices *per se* requires extensive work. But for anyone struggling with these important issues, the sociocultural approach is a rich and promising companion.

See also: Language and Literacy in Educational Settings; Vygotsky and Recent Developments.

Bibliography

Brown, A. L. (1993). First-grade dialogues for knowledge acquisition and use. In Forman, E. A., Minick, N., and Stone, C. A. (eds.) *Contexts for Learning. Sociocultural Dynamics in Children's Development*, pp 32–57. New York: Oxford University Press.

Bruner, J. S. (1985). Vygotsky: A historical and conceptual perspective. In Wertsch, J. V. (ed.) *Culture, Communication and Cognition: Vygotskian Perspectives*, pp 21–34. Cambridge, MA: Cambridge University Press.

Cole, M. (1996). *Cultural Psychology: A Once and Future Discipline*. Cambridge, MA: The Belknap Press.

de Graaf, W. and Meier, R. (eds.) (1994). *Sociogenesis Reexamined*. New York: Springer.

Donald, M. (2001). *A Mind so Rare. The Evolution of Human Consciousness*. New York: Norton.

Kozulin, A. (1986). Vygotsky in context. In Vygotsky, L. S. (ed.) *Thought and Language*, pp XI–LVI. Cambridge, MA: The MIT-Press.

Kozulin, A. (1998). *Psychological Tools. A Sociocultural Approach to Education*. Cambridge, MA: Harvard University Press.

Leontiev, A. N. (1997). On Vygotsky's creative development. In Rieber, R. and Wollock, J. (eds.) *The Collected Works of L.S. Vygotsky: Volume 3. Problems of the Theory and History of Psychology*, pp 9–32. London: Plenum Press.

Nilholm, C. and Säljö, R. (1996). Co-action and situation definitions. An empirical study of problem solving in mother–child interaction. *Learning and Instruction* **6**(4), 325–344.

Rogoff, B. (1990). *Apprenticeship in Thinking: Cognitive Development in Social Context*. New York: Oxford University Press.

Rommetveit, R. (1985). Language acquisition as increasing linguistic structuring of experience and symbolic behaviour control. In Wertsch, J. (ed.) *Culture, Communication, and Cognition: Vygotskian Perspectives*, pp 183–204. Cambridge: Cambridge University Press.

Säljö, R. (1999). Learning as the use of tools: A sociocultural perspective on the human-technology link. In Littleton, K. and Light, P. (eds.) *Learning and Computers: Analysing Productive Interactions*, pp 144–166. London: Routledge.

Säljö, R., Eklund, A -C., and Mäkitalo, Å. (2006). Reasoning with mental tools and physical artifacts in everyday problem solving. In Verschaffel, L., Dochy, F., Boekaerts, M., and Vosniadou, S. (eds.) *Instructional Psychology: Past, Present and Future Trends*, pp 73–90. Oxford: Pergamon.

Vygotsky, L. S. (1978). *Mind in Society: The Development of Higher Psychological Processes*. Cambridge, MA: Harvard University Press.

Vygotsky, L. S. (1986). *Thought and Language*. Kozulin, A. (trans.) Cambridge, MA: MIT-Press.

Vygotsky, L. S. (1994). The problem of the cultural development of the child. In van der, Veer, R. and Valsiner, J. (eds.) *The Vygotsky Reader*, pp 57–72. Oxford: Blackwell.

Vygotsky, L. S. (1997). The instrumental method in psychology. In Reiber, R. and Wollock, J. (eds.) *The Collected Works of L.S. Vygotsky. Volume 3: Problems of the Theory and History of Psychology*, pp 85–89. London: Plenum Press.

Wertsch, J. V. (1985). *Vygotsky and the Social Formation of Mind*. Cambridge, MA: Harvard University Press.

Wertsch, J. V. (1991). *Voices of the Mind: A Sociocultural Approach to Mediated Action*. Cambridge, MA: Harvard University Press.

Wertsch, J. V. (1998). *Mind as Action*. New York: Oxford University Press.

Wood, D., Bruner, J. S., and Ross, G. (1976). The role of tutoring in problem-solving. *Jounal of Child Psychology and Psychiatry* **17**, 89–100.

Further Reading

Daniels, H. (2008). *Vygotsky and Research*. New York: Routledge.

Daniels, H., Cole, M., and Wertsch, J. (eds.) (2007). *The Cambridge Companion to Vygotsky*. New York: Cambridge University Press.

Kozulin, A., Gindis, B., Ageyev, V. S., and Miller, S. M. (eds.) (2003). *Vygotsky's Educational Theory in Cultural Context*. Cambridge: Cambridge University Press.

Mercer, N. (2000). *Minds and Words: How we Use Language to Think Together*. London: Routledge.

Valsiner, J. (2000). *Culture and Human Development: An Introduction*. Thousand Oaks, CA: Sage.

Wells, G. (1999). *Dialogic Inquiry. Towards a Sociocultural Practice and Theory of Education*. Cambridge: Cambridge University Press.

Situative View of Learning

A Collins, Northwestern University, Evanston, IL, USA
J G Greeno, University of Pittsburgh, Pittsburgh, PA, USA

Glossary

Cognitive apprenticeship – A method of teaching school subjects that embodies many of the practices of apprenticeship training, such as modeling, coaching, and careful observation of the learner's practice.

Community of practice – A group of people participating together to carry out different activities, such as garage bands, ham-radio operators, recovering alcoholics, and research scientists.

Goal-based scenario – Educational settings where learners are given real-world tasks and the support they need to carry out such tasks; they can be set either in computer-based environments or naturalistic environments.

Legitimate peripheral participation – Describes the relationship of apprenticeship learners who have access to the practices that they are expected to learn and to genuine participation in the activities and concerns of the group.

Situative – A perspective on cognition, learning, and education that analyzes processes of interaction, in which individuals participate, along with other material and informational systems.

Many practices of conventional schooling consider knowledge and skill as discrete structures of cognition that can be adequately transferred from teachers to students in classrooms and studied in laboratories. Knowing and thinking, in this view, are assumed to go on in individual minds isolated from the complexity of the world outside, from which abstract knowledge can be successfully distilled. However, a growing body of research that considers cognition and learning in activities outside of specialized learning environments is undermining the plausibility of these presuppositions (e.g., Brown *et al.,* 1989; Engeström, 2001; Greeno *et al.,* 1996; Hutchins, 1995a; Lave and Wenger, 1991; Nersessian *et al.,* 2003; Rogoff, 1990; Rogoff and Lave, 1984). This research supports the view that knowing and learning by individuals are inextricably situated in the physical and social contexts of their acquisition and use. It is a mistake to think that classrooms or laboratory experiments produce knowledge or follow principles of learning that are somehow context free. Cognition and learning by individuals always occur in a context; the issue has to be what the context is, not whether there is one.

For most of the last half-century, active research programs have been studying structures and processes of social interaction, as well as cognitive processes of representing and transforming information. However, these research programs have been largely separate from each other. Situative research and theorizing attempts to unify the two perspectives of individual cognitive theory and the analysis of interactional structures and processes. The primary level of a situative analysis is an activity system, in which one or more individuals participate along with material and informational resources in the environment. Cognitive processes are understood as aspects of the practices of a community or group. Studies include analyses of perceiving (Goodwin, 1996), remembering (Hutchins, 1995b), reasoning and understanding (Greeno and van de Sande, 2007; Ochs *et al.,* 1996), and learning (Bowers *et al.,* 1999; Engeström, 2001; Engle, 2006; Stenning *et al.,* 2002). In these analyses, successful cognitive performances are considered as part of an interactive system, and analyses focus on how the multiple participants coordinate their contributions. Information structures, which the individual cognitive perspective attributes to individual minds, are attributed in the situative perspective to the interacting group as achievements of communication that enter the group's common ground (cf. Clark, 1996). Such analyses do not preclude also having analyses of the same events that focus on one or more individual participants, identifying their respective contributions to the interactions, and explaining these in terms of their individual capabilities, and with other participants and systems considered as the context (cf. Bowers *et al.,* 1999; Hatano and Inagaki, 2003).

If knowing is understood as successful situated participation, then many conventional assumptions must be questioned. In particular, a situative theory of knowing challenges the widely held belief that abstraction of knowledge from situations is the key to transferability. An examination of the role of situations in structuring knowledge suggests that abstraction and explication provide an inherently impoverished and often misleading view of knowing. Knowing by an individual is fundamentally a capability of the person to interact in the world. In this view, hypotheses or assessments of an individual's or group's knowing are about their capabilities for interacting in situations. Hypotheses that represent knowledge only as abstract propositions do not capture the densely interwoven nature of knowing.

The situative perspective views knowing as distributed among people and their environments, including the objects, artifacts, tools, books, and the communities of which they are a part. Analyses of activity focus on processes of interaction of individuals with other people and with physical and technological systems. Several research traditions have contributed to the situative perspective. The best established of these is ethnography, including the study of cultural practices and patterns of social interactions, as well as discourse analysis and conversation analysis in activity theory, sociolinguistics, anthropology, and sociology. Another research tradition is ecological psychology, which studies behavior as physical interaction in which animals, including people, participate in physical and technological systems. A third research tradition is situation theory in logic and philosophy, which analyzes meaning and action as relational systems and is developing a reformulation of logic to support these relational analyses. Knowing in this perspective is both an attribute of groups that carry out cooperative activities and an attribute of individuals who participate in the groups. Learning by a group or individual involves becoming attuned to constraints and affordances of the material and social systems with which they interact. Discussions of motivation in this perspective often emphasize engagement of individuals with the functions and goals of the community, including interpersonal commitments and ways in which individuals' identities are enhanced or diminished by their participation.

Apprenticeship and Identity

When knowing is viewed as practices of communities and of the abilities of individuals to participate in those practices, then learning is the strengthening of those practices and participatory abilities. Systems in which individuals learn to participate in social practices are very common, and include apprenticeship and other forms of being initiated into the practices of a group. Lave and Wenger (1991) reviewed several studies of learning by newcomers to communities of practice and concluded that a crucial factor in the success of such a system is that learners must be afforded legitimate peripheral participation, which involves access to the practices that they are expected to learn and genuine participation in the activities and concerns of the group. Lave and Wenger characterized learning of practices as processes of participation in which beginners are relatively peripheral in the activities of a community, and as they become more experienced and

adept, they progress toward fuller participation. A crucial issue in the nature of learning is whether, and in what ways, the peripheral participation of beginners is legitimate. They described four cases of learning by newcomers and emphasized how learners' identities derive from being part of the community as they become more fully participating members in the community. They also noted that an apprenticeship relationship can be unproductive for learning, as in a case of meat cutters they cited, where the apprentices worked in a separate room and were isolated from the working community. For an environment of apprenticeship to be a productive environment of learning, learners need to have opportunities to observe and practice activities in order to progress toward fuller participation.

The degree to which people participate fully and are respected by other members of a community determines their sense of identity (Lave and Wenger, 1991; Wenger, 1998). The fully participative roles are those that most directly contribute to the collective activities and knowledge of the community. The motivation to participate more fully in a community of practice can provide a powerful incentive for learning. Smith (1988) argued that children learn to read and write if the people they admire read and write. That is, they will want to join the literacy club and will work hard to become members. Learning to read is part of becoming the kind of person they want to become. Identity is central to deep learning.

An important aspect of learners' identities is the way in which they are positioned in the participant structures (Phillips, 1972) of learning activities. An important distinction by Pickering (1995) involves different kinds of agency, called conceptual and disciplinary. Students who are positioned with a disciplinary agency only participate as receivers and reproducers of the established meanings and procedures of the discipline, and their learning is evaluated only by whether they can perform procedures and explanations correctly. Students who are positioned with conceptual agency are expected to question and adapt concepts and methods of the discipline. For example, they might construct understandings that utilize disciplinary concepts in novel ways or consider alternatives to standard definitions of concepts. As an example, research by Boaler (2002) compared learning of mathematics in two English secondary schools and found that students who learned primarily through investigations understood mathematics as a general resource for understanding and problem solving, whereas students whose learning was primarily mastery of set procedures understood mathematics as a set of rules to be followed.

Wenger (1998) argued that people participate in a variety of communities – at home, at work, at school, and in hobbies. In his view a community of practice is a group of people participating together to carry out different activities, such as garage bands, ham-radio operators, recovering alcoholics, and research scientists.

> For individuals, it means that learning is an issue of engaging in and contributing to the practices of their communities. For communities, it means that learning is an issue of refining their practice and ensuring new generations of members. For organizations, it means that learning is an issue of sustaining the interconnected communities of practice through which an organization knows what it knows and thus becomes effective and valuable as an organization (Wenger, 1998: 7, 8).

The view that learning occurs through participation is at the root of the practices of apprenticeship, where apprentices are guided and supervised by masters. In successful apprenticeship learning, masters teach by showing apprentices how to do a task (modeling), and then helping them as they try to do it on their own (coaching and fading). Lave and Wenger (1991) emphasized how an apprentice's identity derives from becoming part of the community of practitioners. The motive for becoming a fuller participant in a community of practice can provide a powerful motivation for learning. Of course, what is learned in apprenticeship may not generalize easily to other contexts. Collins *et al.* (1989) attempted to characterize how the modeling, coaching, and fading paradigm of apprenticeship might be applied to learning the cognitive subjects of school in an approach they called cognitive apprenticeship.

Educational Applications of the Situative View

A major goal of educational reform is to have students participate more actively and legitimately in learning communities, including participation in formulating and evaluating questions and problems, and constructing and evaluating hypotheses, evidence, arguments, and conclusions (Brown and Campione, 1996). Abilities for participating in these activities have to be learned, and the research literature on that kind of learning is sparse. Several projects have been focused on creating classroom practices of discussion and inquiry, and the investigators in those projects have discussed some aspects of the process of establishing norms and expectations by the students that support productive collaborative learning (Cohen, 1986; Lampert, 1990; Slavin, 1983).

In the view of learning as coming to participate more fully in a community of practice, transfer is often thought to be a problematic issue (e.g., Anderson *et al.*, 1996). Viewed in the situative perspective, transfer can occur when learning leads to better performance or learning of new practices within a community (e.g., for school communities this might mean working on new problems or accomplishing new kinds of tasks) or outside the community (e.g., for school these might be work environments such as those studied by Beach (1995) and Saxe (1990)). Many of the resources and supports that occur within a community of practice do not carry over to a different community, and so the problem of transfer becomes one of marshalling the resources needed to be successful in a new environment. This requires sophisticated social and information-processing skills, which are the kinds of skills that businesses think they will need in the future.

In a view of transfer in the situative perspective proposed by Greeno *et al.* (1993), transfer depends on constraints and/or affordances that are invariant under the transformations that change the learning situation into the transfer situation. For transfer to occur, learners must become attuned to those invariants in their initial learning. One of the ways to be attuned is to have an abstract representation that can be applied in the new situation, but this is only one possible way for attunement to occur, and may not be the typical way to generalize many learned activities (Greeno, 1997).

Although the situative view insists that all cognition and learning are situated, learning designers who take a situative perspective generally attend to the activity settings in which learning is to occur. For example, in goal-based scenarios (Schank *et al.*, 1994, Nowakowski *et al.*, 1994) learners are given real-world tasks and the scaffolding they need to carry out such tasks. They can be set either in computer-based environments or naturalistic environments. In one computerized goal-based scenario, learners are asked to advise married couples as to whether their children are likely to have sickle-cell anemia, a genetically linked disease. In order to advise the couples, learners must use the facilities in the system to find out how different genetic combinations lead to the disease and run tests to determine the parents' genetic makeup. There are scaffolds in the system to support the learners, such as various recorded experts who offer advice. Other goal-based scenarios support learners in a wide variety of challenging tasks, such as putting together a news broadcast, solving an environmental problem, or developing a computer-reservation system. Goal-based scenarios make it possible to embed cognitive skills and knowledge in the kinds of contexts where they are to be used. Therefore, people learn not only the basic competencies they will need, but also when and how to apply these competencies.

Video and computer technology has enhanced the ability to create simulation environments where students are learning skills in context. A novel use of video technology is the Jasper series developed by the Cognition and Technology Group (1997) at Vanderbilt University to teach middle-school mathematics. In a series of 15–20-min videos, students are put into various problem-solving contexts: for example, deciding on a business plan for a school fair or a rescue plan for a wounded eagle. The problems are quite difficult to solve and reflect the complex problem solving and planning that occurs in real life. Middle-school students work in groups for several days to solve each problem. Solving the problems develops a much richer understanding of the underlying mathematical concepts than the traditional school-mathematics problems.

Another novel use of technology is the curriculum developed by the middle-school mathematics through applications project (MMAP) at the Institute for Research on Learning (Goldman and Moschkowich, 1995; Greeno *et al.*, 1999). The leading activities in the MMAP curriculum are design problems, supported by software that provide computer-aided design environments in which students design floor plans of buildings, models of population growth and decline, lexicographic codes, or geographical analyses of environmental quality. Mathematical reasoning and problem solving involving topics such as proportional reasoning, linear and exponential functions, and geometrical properties of geographical space are required for successful progress in the design activities. Printed curriculum materials are provided to support teachers in organizing activities for students to encounter, recognize, and learn important mathematical concepts and methods.

These kinds of learning tasks are different from most school tasks, because the contexts of most school tasks lack characteristics of practices that occur outside of school. Imagine learning tennis by being told the rules and practicing the forehand, backhand, and serve without ever playing or seeing a tennis match. If tennis were taught that way, it would be hard to see the point of what you were learning. But in school, students are taught algebra and Shakespeare without being given any idea of how they might be useful in their lives. That is not how a coach would teach you to play tennis. A coach might first show you how to grip and swing the racket, but very soon you would be hitting the ball and playing games. A good coach would have you go back and forth between playing games and working on particular skills – combining global learning with focused local knowledge. The essential idea in the situative view of learning is to consider learning and cognition as participation in an activity system. This view supports designers' and educators' efforts to tightly couple a focus on accomplishing authentic tasks with a focus on the underlying competencies needed to carry out the tasks.

See also: Learning in a Sociocultural Perspective.

Bibliography

Anderson, J. R., Reder, L. M., and Simon, H. A. (1996). Situated learning and education. *Educational Researcher* 25(4), 5–11.

Beach, K. (1995). Activity as a mediator of sociocultural change and individual development: The case of school-work transition in Nepal. *Mind, Culture, and Activity* 2, 285–302.

Boaler, J. (2002). *Experiencing School Mathematics: Traditional and Reform Approaches to Teaching and Their Impact on Student Learning*. (revised and expanded edition). Mahwah, NJ: Erlbaum.

Bowers, J., Cobb, P., and McClain, K. (1999). The evolution of mathematical practices: A case study. *Cognition and Instruction* 17, 25–64.

Brown, A. L. and Campione, J. (1996). Psychological theory and the design of innovative learning environments: On procedures, principles, and systems. In Schauble, L. and Glaser, R. (eds.) *Innovations in Learning: New Environments for Education*, pp 289–325. Mahwah, NJ: Erlbaum.

Brown, J. S., Collins, A., and Duguid, P. (1989). Situated cognition and the culture of learning. *Educational Researcher* 18(1), 32–42.

Clark, H. H. (1996). *Using Language*. Cambridge: Cambridge University Press.

Cognition and Technology Group (1997). *The Jasper Project: Lessons in Curriculum, Instruction, Assessment, and Professional Development*. Mahwah, NJ: Erlbaum.

Cohen, E. G. (1986). *Designing Groupwork*. New York: Teachers College Press.

Collins, A., Brown, J. S., and Newman, S. E. (1989). Cognitive apprenticeship: Teaching the crafts of reading, writing, and mathematics. In Resnick, L. B. (ed.) *Knowing, Learning, and Instruction: Essays in Honor of Robert Glaser*, pp 453–494. Hillsdale, NJ: Erlbaum.

Engeström, Y. (2001). Expansive learning at work: Toward an activity theoretical reconceptualization. *Journal of Education and Work* 14, 133–156.

Engle, R. A. (2006). Framing interactions to foster generative learning: A situative explanation of transfer in a community of learners classroom. *Journal of the Learning Sciences* 15, 451–498.

Goldman, S. and Moschkowich, J. (1995). *Environments for Collaborating Mathematically: The Middle-School Mathematics through Applications Project. CSCL '95 Proceedings*. Hillsdale, NJ: Erlbaum.

Goodwin, C. (1996). Transparent vision. In Ochs, E., Schegloff, E. A., and Thompson, S. A. (eds.) *Interaction and Grammar*, pp 370–404. Cambridge: Cambridge University Press.

Greeno, J. G. (1997). On claims that answer the wrong questions. *Educational Researcher* 26(1), 5–17.

Greeno, J. G., Collins, A., and Resnick, L. B. (1996). Cognition and learning. In Berliner, D. C. and Calfee, R. C. (eds.) *Handbook of Educational Psychology*, ch. 2, pp 15–46. New York: Macmillan.

Greeno, J. G., McDermott, R., Cole, K., *et al.* (1999). Research, reform, and aims in education: Modes of action in search of each other. In Lagemann, E. and Shulman, L. (eds.) *Issues in Education Research: Problems and Possibilities*, pp 299–335. San Francisco, CA: Jossey-Bass.

Greeno, J. G., Smith, D. R., and Moore, J. L. (1993). Transfer of situated learning. In Detterman, D. K. and Sternberg, R. J. (eds.) *Transfer on Trial: Intelligence, Cognition, and Instruction*, pp 99–167. Norwood, NJ: Ablex.

Greeno, J. G. and van de Sande, C. (2007). Perspectival understanding of conceptions and conceptual growth in interaction. *Educational Psychologist* 42, 9–23.

Hatano, G. and Inagaki, K. (2003). When is conceptual change intentional? A cognitive-sociocultural view. In Sinatra, G. M. and Pintrich, P. R. (eds.) *Intentional Conceptual Change*, pp 377–406. Mahwah, NJ: Erlbaum.

Hutchins, E. (1995a). *Cognition in the Wild*. Cambridge, MA: MIT Press.

Hutchins, E. (1995b). How a cockpit remembers its speeds. *Cognitive Science* 19, 265–288.

Lampert, M. (1990). When the problem is not the question and the solution is not the answer: Mathematical knowing and teaching. *American Educational Research Journal* 17, 29–64.

Lave, J. and Wenger, E. (1991). *Situated Learning: Legitimate Peripheral Participation*. Cambridge: Cambridge University Press.

Nersessian, N. J., Kurz-Milcke, E., Newstetter, W. C., and Davies, J. (2003). Research laboratories as evolving distributed cognitive systems. In Alterman, R. and Kirsh, D. (eds.) *Proceedings of the Twenty-Fifth Annual Conference of the Cognitive Science Society*, pp 857–862. Mahwah, NJ: Erlbaum.

Nowakowski, A., Campbell, R., Monson, D., *et al.* (1994). Goal-based scenarios: A new approach to professional education. *Educational Technology* **34**(9), 3–32.

Ochs, E., Gonzales, P., and Jacoby, S. (1996). "When I come down I'm in the domain state": Grammar and graphic representation in the interpretive activity of physicists. In Ochs, E., Schegloff, E. A., and Thompson, S. A. (eds.) *Interaction and Grammar*, pp 328–369. Cambridge: Cambridge University Press.

Phillips, S. U. (1972). Participant structures and communicative competence: Warm Springs children in community and classroom. In Cazden, C. B., John, V. P., and Hymes, D. (eds.) *Functions of Language in the Classroom*, pp 370–394. New York: Teachers College Press.

Pickering, A. (1995). *The Mangle of Practice*. Chicago, IL: University of Chicago Press.

Rogoff, B. (1990). *Apprenticeship in Thinking: Cognitive Development in Social Context*. New York: Oxford University Press.

Rogoff, B. and Lave, J. (1984). *Everyday Cognition: Its Development in Social Context*. Cambridge, MA: Harvard University Press.

Saxe, G. (1990). *Culture and Cognitive Development: Studies in Mathematical Understanding*. Hillsdale, NJ: Erlbaum.

Schank, R. C., Fano, A., Bell, B., and Jona, M. (1994). The design of goal-based scenarios. *Journal of the Learning Sciences* **3**(4), 305–346.

Slavin, R. E. (1983). *Cooperative Learning*. New York: Longman.

Smith, F. (1988). *Joining the Literacy Club*. Portsmouth, NH: Heinemann.

Stenning, K., Greeno, J. G., Hall, R., Sommerfeld, M., and Wiebe, M. (2002). Coordinating mathematical with biological multiplication: Conceptual learning as the development of heterogeneous reasoning systems. In Baker, M., Brna, P., Stenning, K., and Tiberghien, A. (eds.) *The Role of Communication in Learning to Model*, pp 3–48. Mahwah, NJ: Erlbaum.

Wenger, E. (1998). *Communities of Practice: Learning, Meaning, and Identity*. New York: Cambridge University Press.

Further Reading

McLellan, H. (1996). *Situated Learning Perspectives*. Englewood Cliffs, NJ: Educational Technology Publications.

COGNITION: RECENT TRENDS

Attention in Cognition and Early Learning

Cognition and Emotion

Memory

Intelligence

Concept Learning

Problem Solving and Human Expertise

Problem Solving and Reasoning

Knowledge Domains and Domain Learning

Metacognition

Attention in Cognition and Early Learning

M Heimann, Linköping University, Linköping, Sweden; The Swedish Institute for Disability Research, Linköping, Sweden; The Norwegian Network for Infant Mental Health, Oslo, Norway
T Tjus and K Strid, University of Gothenburg, Gothenburg, Sweden

"From a psychological view, attention includes changes from sleepiness to high alertness, from focused OR to a single object to unfocused awareness of the general scene, from responsiveness to external event to responses driven by the achievement of a particular goal."

(Posner and Rothbart, 2007a: 16)

A child's ability to direct his or her attention drives awareness; only objects and events attended to will enter the child's mind. In this sense, attention processes are essential for learning and cognitive development. Attention influences and is, in turn, influenced by various brain systems, an interaction that creates priorities affecting both perception and action. Thus, alertness and the way attention regulates, or is regulated by brain functions become highly relevant for all domains of learning. Without attention it becomes difficult, if not impossible, to take in new and important information. We, adults and children, are active in selecting what to attend to and what to ignore – a process that becomes more and more voluntary during development.

The view of an infant as passive, incapable of communicating and remembering, and unaware about self and others has changed radically during the last 50 years. Typically, developing infants have a sensory system, which makes them capable of perceiving and interacting with the environment promoting communication, emotional exchange, and signals for caretaking. In addition to this sensory system, they use their own body as a vehicle, not only for exploration of themselves, that is, building sensory motor schemas, but also for assembling information about other individuals. To learn from and understand other people and socially relate to them is crucial for a healthy development. Therefore infants' face processing is seen as an early indicator of this social attending. Newborns prefer face-like patterns suggesting an innate mechanism favored in brain processing. Furthermore, by 4 months infants look longer if there is a mutual eye gaze with the adult compared to averted eye gaze. Also, auditory perception in 6-month-old infants is linked to sensitive detection of human voices, such as discrimination of phoneme segments, both in native and foreign languages. However, at the age of 12 months this ability declines showing that early on our brain is prepared for a general language acquisition, but that exposure to one language with its specific prosodic and phonetic patterns reduces this capacity.

Attention in Infancy

All sensory systems are functional at or before birth and of these, the visual system is probably both the best-understood and least-mature system. It is actually a difficult task for the newborn infant to respond to visual stimuli. When a newborn infant acts on complex visual information, as evident when the neonate imitates facial movements, the infant responds in spite of the fact of the immaturity of the visual system: Jerky eye movements make it hard to control vision and it is difficult for the immature system to capture fast-moving objects. In short, the infant's control of fixation is mostly not under voluntary control at birth and, during the first months of life, infants cannot resist being drawn to certain patterns. Visually, the newborn infant is attracted to high spatial frequencies (e.g., checkerboard pattern and edges), to slowly moving objects (moving stimuli are more attractive than static ones), and to face-like patterns. The attraction to edges provides necessary input for the visual cortex to develop (input helps to organize cell columns in visual cortex) while the attraction to face-like patterns guides the infant toward the social world.

All nonvisual sensory systems are also functional at birth but their role in early attentional processes is less well studied, although auditory attention probably is as important as vision for early development. Hearing is essential both for language learning and for making the social world interesting. The newborn infant recognizes human voices at birth (in fact, a fetus can learn to identify the mothe's voice several weeks post-partum) and the melody of the mother tongue is identified within the first weeks. The human voice, especially the female voice, attracts the infants' attention both to the social world and to language.

Selective Attention

Selective attention develops rapidly over the first months of life. The newborn infant has less oculomotor control, less control over attentional shifts, and is attracted by salient details in perceptual displays. A neonate is not able to understand a partly occluded object as a unity and reacts only to direct visible information. It becomes a very difficult task if the neonate must identify a center-occluded object – the infant sees only the top and the bottom part of the object – in order to solve a task. This does not imply that a newborn child is not able to take in the relevant information, only that during the first months of life, perception and attention is more driven by environmental input (exogenous processes) coupled with biologically driven subcortical processes. Slowly, vision becomes more and more cortically controlled, acuity develops, the visual field increases, the eyes become better coordinated and inspection times decrease. A shift is usually seen around 2–3 months making the infant more visually competent when inspecting new objects, and, maybe most important, the child now becomes able to partake in prolonged face-to-face interactions with the caregiver.

The problem with perceptual completion, to see an object as a whole in spite of the fact that it is partly occluded, also changes during the first months of life. Some capacity is observable already at 2 months but it is not until 4–5 months that the ability to solve perceptual-completion problems can be expected to be robust. Interestingly, children at 3 months seem to be in a transition phase. A recent study (Amos and Johnson, 2006) identified two groups of children, perceivers and non-perceivers: the children who were able to perceive unity (i.e., they solved the perception-completion task) used a more efficient strategy when solving a visual search task. These differences may stem from the possibility that the two groups reflect different stages in early brain development. Selective attention makes it possible for the child to become an active participant in his/her development and early differences in this ability might have an impact on later cognitive development.

The capacity to attend selectively is also related to disengagement, an ability that develops rapidly over the first months of life. As depicted in **Figure 1**, infants younger than 2 months tend to focus on one stimulus at a time. If a second stimulus is added to the visual display while the first stimulus is still visible, the infant is more or less unable to make a gaze shift. However, by 3–4 months, this is no longer a problem.

Selective looking and habituation have dominated research on infant attention. Generally, the length of looking declines during infancy, especially from 3 to 4 months and onward. Younger infants need longer inspection time (familiarization) than older infants; studies indicate a negative correlation between visual recognition and the inspection time needed. Selective attention has also been used to study auditory attention (e.g., the ability to discriminate between specific sound signals or between mothe's voice and a stranger's voice).

Phases of Attention

Behavioral Phases

Attention in infancy is usually described as made up of three or four distinct phases representing different underlying processes (see **Figure 2**): The first phase, AR (AR), reflects the physiological readiness of the organism to react to any stimuli. Usually AR varies from deep sleep to active wakefulness through several intermediate phases. A characteristic of the young infant is that state changes occur often and rapidly, which affects the manner in which early attention is modulated. Without adequate AR, no attention can take place. During the second phase, usually called orienting (OR) or selective attention, the infant's attention is directed toward specific stimuli, that is, an interesting event is identified and the system becomes prepared for further inspection. Sustained attention (SA), phase three, reflects a phase of active information processing or encoding. SA is often described as a voluntary

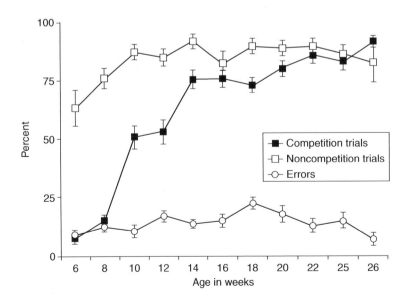

Figure 1

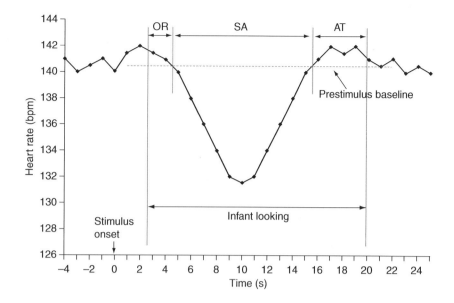

Figure 2

process and it has been linked to anterior brain systems. The final phase of attention, attention termination (AT), on the other hand, is linked to disengagement processes reflecting continuous looking after cessation of any active information processing. AT has been proposed to reflect the posterior brain system identified by Posner and colleagues and the disengagement processes have been observed to be a stronger prediction of recognition than sustained attention, at least for static stimuli.

Attention: Brain Networks

A recent attempt by Posner and Rothbart (2007b) to integrate behavioral studies of attention with current findings within cognitive neuroscience indentifies three neural networks that underlie central aspects of attention: orient, alert, and executive attention.

Alerting signifies that the child is in a state of readiness for reacting to new incoming stimuli. From a biological point of view, alerting has been linked to subcortical processes (thalamus) as well as to right parietal and right frontal areas. Norepinephrine is the main neurochemical modulator...

Orienting means that attention algins with incoming sensory signals and that some information is selected. It is activated by posterior parts of the brain, mostly the parietal lobe (e.g., the superior parietal lobe) but also some frontal (frontal eye fields) and subcortical areas (superior colliculus). The main neurochemical component is acetylcholine.

Executive attention indicates the ability to monitor responses, thoughts, and feelings, processes that not only involve mainly anterior brain areas (frontal cortex) but also some parts of the basal ganglia. It is hypothesized that

executive attention plays an important role in the ability of the developing self to regulate positive and negative affect. Dopamine is the main neurochemical modulator.

The more posterior parts of the attentional system develop relatively early. Thus, the young infant is more able to alert and orient than to show executive attention, although it takes time for these systems to become fully mature as well. The first signs of the executive system can be noted toward the end of the first year, but it will take 8–10 years for it to reach adult-like levels.

All three networks – especially the executive network – are essential for the infant to develop an ability to display effortful control, that is, to self-regulate one's own behavior.

Aspects of Attention

Novelty

Novel objects and novel locations affect attention from birth although the parallel process of familiarity also exerts a strong influence on attention during the first months of life. Behaviorally, novelty preference can be reliably observed from approximately 4–6 months of age. Identification of new information leads to faster and more reliable OR, activates the alerting system, recruits available relevant brain resources (working memory and sustained attention), and prepares the system to encode a new file (transfer information to long-term memory).

The identification of a new object is governed by two processes. The first process to emerge is the ability to identify a new location. This ability is related to the control of eye movements and is, in some form, present at birth. It is observable through inhibition of return (IOR), which means that the visual system resists going back to a previous location; new locations are more attractive. The second process, the identification of a new object, is a slower-developing visual skill. It is usually established by 4–6 months and is related to the development of object recognition. This ability is observable through visual recognition memory.

Visual Recognition Memory

From 3 to 4 months and onward, the infant's ability to process new information has proved to be robust. This can be shown in paired-comparison experiments or tests when the child's preferential looking pattern is observed. Typically, a child prefers new information (a novel stimulus) in comparison with familiar information, which makes it possible for the researcher to calculate a novelty preference score. This score provides an index of the child's visual recognition memory, because the child has to remember the familiar target in order to show a preference for the novel one. Measures of novelty preference/visual recognition memory in early infancy have been found to be a significant predictor of later intelligence quotient (IQ) as well as of nonverbal communication and language (e.g., Colombo, 1993; Bornstein and Sigman, 1986). As an example, it has been reported that visual recognition memory measured in infancy predicts receptive language at 3 years even when controlling for general IQ. These results suggest that attentional and memory capacities tapped by visual recognition memory as measured by novelty preference are important for later developing communication skills.

Visual recognition memory seems to tap into the very basic functions of our nervous system but exactly how these early attentional and memory processes affect later cognitive processes are still unexplained. One clue to an explanation has been proposed by Colombo and collaborators who found that, at 4 months, attention termination explained more of the observed variance in a novelty recognition task than sustained attention. The research group interprets their findings as supporting the "hypothesis that individual differences in the disengagement underlie the relation between look duration and cognitive performance in early to mid infancy" (Colombo *et al.*, 2001: 1605).

Face Processing

Human infants show a preference for faces right from birth, a tendency that seems to be especially strong for moving face-like stimuli (Johnson, 2005). This has been interpreted by some as indicating a pre-wired system molded by evolution. Such a system is described as being controlled by subcortical parts of the visual system functional at birth making the face a highly salient stimulus for the newborn. Thus, the child is endowed with an in-built perceptual attention grabber for faces. Although the propensity for faces among newborns is not debated, the mechanism is. In a series of studies, Simion and co-workers have provided support for an alternative view. They argue that the infant is not born with a pre-wired schematic configuration for faces but with a "domain-general bias towards configurations with more elements in the upper than lower half (i.e., top-heavy patterns)" (e.g., Cassia *et al.*, 2004: 379). The conflict between these two contrasting views is not resolved; we still do not know exactly how to describe the mechanism responsible for making newborn babies especially attracted to the human face.

Furthermore, observations also suggest that infants are better at processing female than male faces, a finding that probably stems from the fact that infants have much more experience in processing female faces. However, conclusive studies addressing this interpretation are still lacking. Finally, over the course of the first year, infants begin to process naturally looking faces in the same fashion as adults do; that is, they analyze faces in a holistic gestalt-like fashion. While 4-month-old children focus more on internal facial features, 10-month-old children use a holistic strategy. Children at 6 months seem to be in a transition phase using both strategies.

Attention and Learning

The Directed-Attention Model

Memory span of objects is around one item at 6 months and two to three items at 1 year. This means that infant learning and infants' complex social responses are carried out with a memory and attention system that is very limited compared to older children and adults. A model for how this can be achieved has been proposed by Reid and Striano (2007) who outlines a five-stage directed-attention model of infant social cognition. The model describes five perceptual stages that infants typically will master within the first year of life. The model is tentative but provides an ambitious attempt to integrate known perceptual and cognitive abilities and skills with the amazing social competence seen in the human infant. In brief, the proposed stages or phases are:

1. *Detection of socially relevant organisms.* Infants are born with a nervous system that directs them toward the social world. They are sensitive to distinctions between animate and inanimate objects, they prefer moving stimuli to static, biological motion to nonbiological motion, they are sensitive to the human voice, to rhythm, and they imitate (mimic) facial gestures.

2. *Identification of socially relevant organism.* The process to differentiate individual persons starts immediately at birth. The newborn infant rapidly learns to identify the mothe's voice, smell, and face. More complex responses, such as imitation, are also used early on (from 6 weeks) to identify persons.

3. *Assessment of the locus of attention.* Once the socially relevant organism has been detected infants start to "attend towards characteristic that index the locus of attention of the observed organism" (Reid and Striano, 2007: 105). Eye and head movements provide important information to the infant in early social interactions. The infant's predisposition to enter into the social interactions with the caregiver is probably driven by intrinsic and biologically based motives to communicate with other humans.

4. *Detection of object-oriented attention.* Already at 4 months infants can use an adult's gaze to learn about objects and, by 8–9 months, objects become parts of highly motivating joint-attention encounters. Objects or an aspect of the environment that has been highlighted through joint attention with an adult will become more salient to the infant who will direct more of his or her attention to those objects/areas. The first sign of an emerging declarative memory is observed at 6 months through the child's ability to act on a memorized representation after a delay (deferred imitation).

5. *Inference of goals and/or prepare response.* Toward the end of the first year, infants begin to respond differently to accidental and intentional action. The child now starts to understand that people have goals that motivate their actions. The capacity of working memory increases, which makes it possible for the child to hold more than one piece of information online simultaneously.

Dyadic Attention

The interaction between a parent and the infant is characterized by rhythm, intimacy, and emotional exchange, the so-called proto-conversations. This interaction is encouraged by the mother through smiles and increased gaze in such a way that the interaction is prolonged and infants are active partners in this interaction, creating turn-taking sequences. Both mother and infant are sensitive to the contingency and quality of this interaction and have already created expectancies of specific patterns of communication from each other. This is evidenced by using still-face conditions where mother is either not responding to infant's communication or by using double-video-technique showing pre-recorded interaction creating unsynchronized turn-taking from both partners. Furthermore, infants very early learn to anticipate, not only contingent communicative patterns, but also contingent behavior from

their mothers. When infants' distress is accompanied by parents soothing, the association between AR, parents' response, and subsequent relief is easily learned – soothing is anticipated by the infant already at 4 months of age.

This intrinsic communication with human beings could not be enhanced without the infant exploring the physical environment. With an increasing ability of motor control, the child will experiment with its own actions on objects such as mobiles and thereby develop an early understanding of agency according to physical cause and effect. With the growth of contingent perception, the infant is able to accompany this physical agency into detection of cause and effect/reciprocity with partners into further developed nonverbal turn-taking sequences – both vocal and with objects (like pushing a ball back and forth). This means that infants are able to coordinate their attention with another person and understand the framework in which communication takes place between two persons.

Triadic Attention/Joint Attention

Nine-month-old infants begin to understand that actors are pursuing goals and they combine the awareness of outside objects, events, and persons in order to share and coordinate their attention or perception of goal activities, the so-called joint attention. By performing joint activities such as building a tower of bricks or rolling a ball back and forth, the infants understand the concept of sharing goals. This is accompanied by attention skills such as following the other persons' eye-gaze or pointing in order to direct others' attention to objects in the surrounding, or trying to modify a persons' behavior with gestures.

Attention skills that are initiated by the child (e.g., pointing) develop slightly later than behaviors that are responses to others (e.g., gaze-following). The capacity to direct another persons' gaze to objects by the infants' own interest develops between 9 and 12 months and infants can use the pointing gesture for different purposes, for both sharing attention and requesting.

It has been argued that declarative pointing, in contrast to imperative pointing, relies on the understanding of others as mental agents and is driven by a motivation to share attention and interest with other persons; it has therefore been suggested to be especially difficult. In typically developing infants, the motivation to share attention and interest is probably strong and declarative gestures are common, in contrast to children with social impairments like autism. Experiment with 12-month-olds has revealed that the social context is crucial for the amount of points the infant makes. Only when the adult was active in sharing the infants' attention to the event the infant pointed at, the infants' pointing increased. The interpretation of this result was that the infant did not only want to direct the adult's attention, but also wanted to share this attention.

It has been shown in several studies that the capacity for joint attention is an important precursor to later-developing language and cognitive skills. Together with early memory measures (e.g., visual recognition memory and deferred imitation) joint attention probably lays the ground for later-emerging social cognition including intentional understanding.

Understanding Intentions

Humans are special in their capacity to understand others' intentions. This is obvious when children pass false-belief tasks when they are about 4 years old. It can be argued that infants, by the time they begin to follow and direct others attention, have acquired some understanding of others as intentional agents and that other people act on the basis of their own view of the world. From 6 months of age, infants follow another person's gaze to objects in the surrounding environment but they have been shown to pay more attention to where the head is turning, while older infants pay more attention to the eyes indicating understanding of the adult's intentions. When adults turn to an object with their eyes open or closed it was observed that infants by the age of 12 months looked at the target if the adult turned to it with open eyes but did not do so if the person turned to it with eyes closed.

Furthermore, studies have revealed that infants in their second year understand the intention behind an action and not only the action they actually have seen; when 18-month-old infants were observing an action that the adult failed to perform they did not imitate the failure, instead they performed the complete action. Another evidence for early intentional understanding is that 9-month-old infants show anger and distress toward an adult who is unwilling to give them a toy, but not to an adult who is unable to do it.

Compensatory Systems and Plasticity

Questions have been raised whether the sensory system can compensate for a deficit in one area, since it is striking how blind people can use auditory and tactile cues for orienting themselves and getting information. In one study, it was shown that spatial tuning of tactile attention is more accurate in early blind compared to sighted individuals when areas for Braille reading are stimulated, suggesting a compensatory scaffolding for individuals who have experienced visual deprivation from birth or early infancy. The plasticity of the brain making it possible to overcome deficits may be underlined by the fact that the sensory systems work together, especially, according to the dimensions of space, time, and intensity. This so-called redundant, amodal information is seen as a cornerstone of perceptual development, for example, when an adult takes a child's hands and uses them for clapping, auditory, visual, and tactile systems are involved, discerning both rhythm and rate to the child.

Conclusion

With increasing age, looking and attention come more and more under voluntary control. The child becomes more able to decide what to focus on; he or she will, by 4–5 years of age, be able to choose to attend to information even if it is boring. However, attention never becomes completely voluntary. Processes like novelty preference and habituation influence attention throughout life.

In the future, knowledge might be increased by detecting specific genes influencing attention, maybe even specific genes for each network or various attentional processes (see Posner *et al.*, 2007). This might help us gain a better understanding of how attention develops, how experience and biology co-act to create alertness and sustained attention, or the ability to initiate attention in another person – knowledge that will also be highly relevant for children with known disabilities such as ADHD or autism spectrum disorders.

See also: Cognition and Emotion; First Language Acquisition; Neuroscience Bases of Learning.

Bibliography

Amos, D. and Johnson, S. P. (2006). Learning by selection: Visual search and object perception in young infants. *Developmental Psychology* 42, 1236–1245.

Bornstein, M. H. and Sigman, M. D. (1986). Continuity in mental development from infancy. *Child Development* 57, 251–274.

Cassia, V. M., Turati, C., and Simion, F. (2004). Can a nonspecific bias to more top-heavy pattern explain newborn's face preference? *Psychological Science* 15, 379–383.

Colombo, J. (1993). *Infant Cognition: Predicting Later Intellectual Functioning*. Newbury Park, CA: Sage.

Colombo, J., Richman, W. A., Shaddy, J., Greenhoot, A. F., and Maikranz, J. (2001). Heart rate-defined phases of attention, look duration, and infant performance in the paired-comparison paradigm. *Child Development* 72, 1605–1616.

Johnson, M. H. (2005). *Developmental Cognitive Neuroscience*, 2nd edn. London: Blackwell.

Posner, M. I. and Rothbart, M. K. (2007a). *Educating the Human Brain*. Washington, DC: American Psychological Association.

Posner, M. I. and Rothbart, M. K. (2007b). Research on attention networks as a model for the integration of psychological science. *Annual Review of Psychology* 58, 1–23.

Posner, M. I., Rothbart, M. K., and Sheese, B. E. (2007). Attention genes. *Developmental Science* 10(1), 24–29.

Reid, V. M. and Striano, T. (2007). The directed attention model of infant social cognition. *European Journal of Developmental Psychology* 4, 100–110.

Further Reading

Bahrick, L. E., Lickliter, R., and Flom, R. (2004). Intersensory redundancy guides the development of selective attention, perception, and cognition in infancy. *Current Directions in Psychological Science* 13(3), 99–102.

Butcher, P. R., Kalverboer, A. F., and Geuze, R. H. (2000). Infants' shifts of gaze from central to peripheral stimulus: A longitudinal study of development between 6 and 26 weeks. *Infant Behavior and Development* 23, 3–21.

Colombo, J. (2002). Infant attention grows up: The emergence of a developmental cognitive neuroscience perspective. *Current Directions in Psychological Science* 11, 196–200.

Farroni, T., Csibra, G., Simion, F., and Johnson, M. H. (2002). Eye contact detection in humans from birth. *PNAS* 99, 9602–9605.

Forster, B., Eardley, A. F., and Eimer, E. (2007). Altered tactile spatial attention in the early blind. *Brain Research* 1131, 149–154.

Fridlund, A. J. (1997). The new ethology of human facial expression. In Russell, J. A. and Fernández-Dols, J. M. (eds.) *The Psychology of Facial Expression*, pp 103–127. Cambridge: Cambridge University Press.

Gomes, H., Molholm, S., Christodoulou, C., Ritter, W., and Cowan, N. (2000). The development of auditory attention in children. *Frontiers of Bioscience* 5, 108–120.

Grossman, T. and Johnson, M. H. (2007). The development of the social brain in human infancy. *European Journal of Neuroscience* 25, 909–919.

Johnson, M. J. and Morton, J. (1991). *Biology and Cognitive Development: The Case of Face Recognition*. Oxford, UK: Blackwell.

Johnson, P. J. (2004). Development of perceptual completion in infancy. *Psychological Science* 15, 769–775.

Kuhl, P. K. (2004). Early language acquisition: Cracking the speech code. *Nature Reviews Neuroscience* 5, 831–843.

Laucht, M., Becker, K., and Schmidt, M. H. (2006). Visual exploratory behaviour in infancy and novelty seeking in adolescence: Two developmentally specific phenotypes of DRD4. *Journal of Child Psychology and Psychiatry* 47, 1143–1151.

Moore, D. G., Goodwin, J. E., George, E., Axelsson, E. L., and Braddick, F. M. B. (2007). Infants perceive human point-light displays as solid forms. *Cognition* 104, 377–396.

Paterson, S. J., Heim, S., Friedman, J. T., Choudhury, N., and Benasich, A. A. (2006). Development of structure and function in the infant brain: Implications for cognition, language and social behaviour. *Neuroscience and Biobehavioral Reviews* 30, 1087–1105.

Ramsey-Rennels, J. L. and Langlois, J. H. (2006). Infant's differential processing of female and male faces. *Current Directions in Psychological Science* 15, 59–62.

Rose, S. A., Feldman, J. F., and Jankowski, J. J. (2004). Infant visual recognition memory. *Developmental Review* 24, 74–100.

Schwarzer, G., Zauner, N., and Jovanovic, B. (2007). Evidence of a shift from featural to configural face processing in infancy. *Developmental Science* 10, 452–463.

Smith, L., Fagan, J. F., and Ulvund, S. E. (2002). The relation of recognition memory in infancy and parental socioeconomic status to later intellectual competence. *Intelligence* 30, 247–259.

Striano, T., Chen, X., Cleveland, A., and Bradshaw, S. (2006). Joint attention social cues influence infant learning. *European Journal of Developmental Psychology* 3, 289–299.

Trevarthen, C. and Aitken, K. (2003). Regulation of brain development and age-related changes in infants' motives: The developmental function of regressive periods. In Heimann, M. (ed.) *Regression Periods in Human Infancy*, pp 107–184. Mahwah, NJ: Erlbaum.

Cognition and Emotion

F Pons, University of Oslo, Oslo, Norway
M de Rosnay, University of Sydney, Sydney, NSW, Australia
F Cuisinier, University of Paris Ouest, Nanterre, France

Introduction

What is the causal impact of emotion on cognition, and of cognition on emotion? Although this question is as classical as the one about, for example, the relation between nature and nurture, or consciousness and unconsciousness, it is not possible at this time to find a mapping of its possible answers within the fields of educational and psychological sciences. The investigation of the causal relation between cognition and emotion within these fields can be characterized as a disparate archipelago of research islands each somewhat isolated from the others and often covered or surrounded by an almost impenetrable fog. This article presents a representative map of this territory.

Why is it important to address the nature of the causal relation between cognition and emotion? The reasons are multiple. First, this question is interesting as a fundamental concern of human psychology that has attracted relatively little empirical attention. Of more than 200 000 psychological and educational publications (articles, book chapters, and books) including in their title the terms cognition or emotion (or equivalent terms such as intelligence, intellect, reasoning, mood, feeling, or affect), less than 4% include both terms (source PsycINFO and ERIC, May 2009). Moreover, of this 4%, almost all investigate cognition and emotion as the cause or the effect of a third phenomenon (e.g., the impact of gender on cognition and emotion or the impact of cognition and emotion on music). Few studies address the causal relation between cognition and emotion and, when they do, it is typically in one direction. Second, a better understanding of the causal relation between cognition and emotion could improve our understanding of both phenomena via the analyses of a sometimes underestimated dimension of their nature; that is, the emotional nature of cognition and the cognitive nature of emotion. Third, within pragmatic or applied contexts, such as educational settings, these two phenomena are currently assessed independently; for instance, educational attainment and behavioral/emotional problems are known to be linked but are treated as separate domains. Improved understanding of the relation between children's cognitive and emotional development should contribute to the elaboration of integrated methods for assessment and treatment or intervention; not just for atypical children, for all those within an educational setting. Last but not least, most cognition and emotion researchers and professionals within psychology and education recognize that cognition and emotion are in some sort of relation. Yet, most of the time, such individuals are quite ignorant of each other's expertise or hold false beliefs about one another even when they work in the same institution. For these four reasons, among others, the simultaneous consideration of cognition and emotion, and the nature of their relation, has much to offer.

Why does the nature of the relation between cognition and emotion still remain so open today? There are at least two reasons: the oldness of the schism between these two domains of psychological and educational enquiry, and the relative youth of affective sciences (i.e., the scientific study of emotions, moods, and feelings, and their constitutive elements). Indeed, the failure to provide integrated accounts of cognition and emotion as psychological phenomena has its roots in the history of philosophy, within which there is a classical distinction between reason and the passions, reason having been given pride of place in philosophical enquiry. Solomon explains the persistent failure to integrate these two domains as a function of the inferior role accorded to emotion, beginning with Plato, and the fact that emotion and cognition have been treated as though they are different kinds, thereby excluding the necessity of simultaneous consideration (Solomon (2000) in Lewis and Haviland-Jones (2000)). Pascal (1670/1998) eloquently captured this latter distinction when he said, "The heart has its reasons that the reason does not know."

Contemporary cognitive science continues to be dominated by a preoccupation with cognition as a cold phenomenon. Predominantly, emotion is not considered or it is viewed as a confounding variable. When emotional and cognitive phenomena are considered together, emotion is often treated as a heating process, not directly integrated with cognition but causing spikes in temperature that interfere with cognitive processes.

The cognition–emotion dualism is to a great extent perpetuated methodologically within contemporary psychological and educational sciences. Indeed, in experimental sciences, you cannot study everything at the same time; it is very difficult to be simultaneously deep and broad. The fine-grained questions of experimental sciences need focused methods and are, in many cases, deeply connected to certain procedures such as reaction time or failure–success paradigms. By contrast, the study of emotion has relied to a great extent on subjective self-report at one end of a spectrum, and expressive behaviors (e.g., facial expressions) or physiological measures (e.g., blood volume pulse) at the other end of the spectrum. Such methodological disparities are lessening as a function of the rapid growth in neuroscientific methods (e.g., functional magnetic resonance imaging (fMRI), positron emission tomography (PET), second-generation electroencephalography (EEG)) but it remains unclear when we will be able to identify and assess both cognitive and emotional functions unfolding in real time: this is a goal for the future. In the meantime, cognitive scientists and emotion researchers very often talk a different talk and walk a different walk.

As indicated earlier, the affective sciences are still relatively young. It is also notable that they have to some extent define themselves against a backdrop of cognitivism – just as the cognitive scientists once defined themselves against behaviorism. Whereas the demise of behaviorism opened the way to studying cognitive processes within the black box, the affective revolution no longer considers persons merely as cognitive processors, more or less similar to Turing machines, and has allowed scientists to ask what was happening in the heart of people: emotion has become an object of scientific enquiry to be described, explained, predicted, and even transformed. At one end of the methodological spectrum, private, conscious experiences such as feelings and moods and their self-report via introspection are again considered as legitimate scientific objects and methods. At the other end of the spectrum, neuroscientific methods raise the possibility that scientists will find some of the physical correlates of peoples' subjective experiences, thus reinforcing their status as a legitimate object of scientific enquiry. Such methods may also undermine the dominant dualistic attitude in psychological and educational sciences regarding the mind–body relationship: they open a space where the study of emotion can take place (as the missing link) between the mind and the body.

The rest of the article is divided into four sections. We start with a short discussion about the meaning of emotion and cognition. Then we discuss the straightforward conceptions of the causal relationship between cognition and emotion: cognition as a cause of emotion, and emotion as a cause of cognition. In the conclusion, we speculate about the circular causal relationship between cognition and emotion and about some promising future research and intervention programs.

The Problem of Definition

Problems surrounding the meaning of cognition and emotion are at least as old as psychological and educational sciences. The question of how to define these terms is sometimes construed as a false problem with no existence, a real problem with no solution, or a problem with as many solutions as people trying to resolve it! It is not the

function of the article to offer a definitive definition for each term but, rather, to consider how the two constructs have been related to one another. Nevertheless, it is important to set out the scope of these terms as they are used in the psychological and educational sciences. Indeed, many misunderstandings and conflicts centered on the relation between cognition and emotion are related to the absence of a common understanding of the phenomena in question and to the overgeneralization of some quite specific definitions.

Here, cognition refers to the different forms of knowledge (e.g., belief, thought, etc.) that we have and, critically, to the mental functions (e.g., systems, schemas, processes, etc.) making the acquisition, storage, retrieval, transformation, and use of this knowledge possible, for example, memory, attention, intelligence, language, mental imagery, and so on. This knowledge can be empirically or logically true or false, real or unreal, and more or less certain. It can be more or less simple or complex, sensory or symbolic, temporary or permanent, general or specific, conscious or unconscious, controllable or uncontrollable, and universal or idiosyncratic. Importantly, it is traditionally held that knowledge is (usually implicitly) rule bound or structured and that the mental functions operate in accordance with such rules; for example, knowledge of language implies some form of syntax (that is consciously inaccessible to language users without formal education). Finally, such knowledge and mental functions are considered as interrelated states and processes of the mind (e.g., subjective experience of the color red), the body (e.g., neuronal correlates associate with the perception of the color red), and the culture (e.g., words to represent the color red: red, rød, rojo, rouge, etc.).

Emotion, on the other hand, is a class of feelings directed to objects, where objects include persons, things, and situations, both real and imagined. Emotions can be pleasant or unpleasant and more or less intense or moderate, but they can be differentiated from sensations and states of bodily arousal because of their inherent aboutness (i.e., intentionality) and their close connection with actions (Kenny, 1963). Emotions can be more or less basic (e.g., happiness, anger, fear, sadness, disgust, or surprise) or complex (e.g., guilt, shame, pride, jealousy, and mixed emotions), sensory or symbolic/abstract, temporary (e.g., sadness about a specific event) or enduring (e.g., an ongoing depressive mood), conscious or unconscious, controlled or uncontrolled, general or specific, and universal (e.g., fear of death) or idiosyncratic (Spanish Duende, Portuguese Saodade, etc.). Not all these aspects of emotion are uncontested, of course, but they fall under the common sense notion of emotion and the emotional lives of persons. Emotions are generally thought to be organized in that they are discrete (particularly in childhood) and they have their own natural history: certain situations and thoughts, as well as expressions and states of the body, are universally constitutive of specific emotions presumably because of our evolutionary origins (Darwin, 1872/1899; Ekman, 1999 in Dalgleish and Power, 1999; Lazarus, 1991). Finally, emotions are interrelated states and processes of the mind (e.g., subjective experience of happiness about or of something), of the body (heart rate changes, respiration rate, muscle tension, pupil dilatation, etc.), and of the culture (e.g., the social and cultural norms related to the feeling of anger).

In the foregoing discussion, we have provided a sketch of emotion that is clearly cognitive in some sense: That is, the inherent aboutness of emotion entails that an emotion has cognitive content. For example, we are scared of the ferocious dog or happy about recent political events. The object of an emotion (e.g., the ferocious dog) and the beliefs on which an emotion is founded (e.g., that ferocious dogs may do us an injury) have a conceptual rather than a causal relation to the emotion (see Solomon, 2000 in Lewis and Haviland-Jones (2000) for a discussion). In the following sections, however, we take as a starting point the historical assumption that emotion and cognition may be treated as separable phenomena that may stand in a cause or effect relations to one another – an assumption that may ultimately unravel.

Before we embark on this discussion, however, consider some research that suggests that emotional responses can occur before there is time for any cognitive processing (even unconscious). For example, LeDoux (1996) demonstrated that some emotional answers, taking place within a few milliseconds (e.g., fear of already known stimuli) result from an immediate mid- and lower-brain (i.e., the amygdala and the thalamus) response to a stimulus and can be produced without the involvement of the cortex, where cognitive processes are assumed to take place. It should be noted, however, that LeDoux also showed that learning a new emotional reaction to a stimulus involves the (sensory) cortex and therefore, it is reasoned, some cognitive processing, until this emotional reaction is completely automatic. Interestingly, to the best of our knowledge, no experimental study has tried to demonstrate that cognitive answers can be produced without being linked to emotion (e.g., without the emotional areas of the brain being involved), though this seems entirely plausible.

Cognition as a Cause of Emotion

Until 30 years ago, explanations of emotional phenomena had been preoccupied mainly with the body. Two hypotheses were then in competition: the James-Lange and the Cannon. In a nutshell, the former postulated that emotions resulted from subjective perceptions of bodily states (e.g., we are sad because we cry) and the latter postulated almost the opposite (e.g., we cry because we are sad). The debate about the relation between the subjective experiences of emotions and their body correlates is still very much alive

(e.g., Cacioppo et al., (2000) in Lewis and Haviland-Jones, 2000; Damasio, 1994; Ekman and Rosenberg, 2005).

With the affective revolution, however, attention shifted to the role of cognition – specifically, the role of cognitive appraisal or evaluation. Schachter and Singer (1962) were among the first to give an empirical demonstration of the existence of this kind of appraisal. They injected people with adrenaline. One group was told that the injection would have an impact on their heart beat (which was true) while a second that it would have no impact (which was untrue). Although, the two groups had the same bodily experience (increase of heart beat), only the second group of people reported feeling emotions. Moreover, when the second group was exposed to a happy person, they reported happiness, and anger when exposed to an angry person (these emotions were feigned by actors present in the room with the subject).

The cognitive-appraisal hypothesis has been the object of active debate (see Lazarus, 1982, 1984 in Lazarus, 1991; Zajonc, 1980 in Zajonc, 1984) and criticism (see Reisenzein (1983) for a review): is cognition (whether conscious or not) a necessary (albeit nonsufficient) condition of emotion? Nevertheless, the basic premise that cognitive appraisal often has an influence (both as an antecedent and as a modulator) on emotional experience (whether that be the valence of the emotion experienced or the level of emotional arousal) found numerous empirical supports (e.g., Frijda, 1986; Roseman, 1984; Scherer, 1984; Smith, 1989), and underpins those cognitive-psychotherapy theories that aim to alter the cognitive-appraisal process in emotional disorders (e.g., Beck, 1976). Several dimensions of the cognitive appraisal of stimuli have been identified: novelty/familiarity, valence, goal/need significance, coping potential, and compatibility with personal and cultural norms (e.g., Kappas (2006) and Scherer et al., (2001) for reviews). For example, a stimulus that is appraised as pleasant (valence) and acceptable (according to personal and cultural norms) could result in feeling happiness.

While there are many variants of cognitive appraisal, they are unified in stressing a very tight and, in most cases, subjectively instantaneous connection between an experienced emotion and the beliefs or thoughts that accompany it. There is, however, another sense in which our emotional experience is affected by our understanding of circumstances: in addition to knowing things about the situations in which we feel emotions, we also have knowledge of emotions (of their nature, causes, consequences, and possibilities of regulation) which has a tremendous potential to impact on our emotional experience by changing the nature of the relation we have to the emotion eliciting circumstances or the emotion itself (e.g., see for reviews, de Rosnay et al., 2008; Haga et al., 2008; Harris, 2006; Pons et al., 2005). For example, between 4 and 5 years of age, children begin to understand the effect of memories on emotions. They realize that the intensity of anger decreases over time; looking at a picture of a lost loved one can reignite sadness; or thinking about a positive past event can cause joy. Development brings further emotion insights. From about 8 years of age, even sooner under certain conditions, children begin to understand how feelings can be regulated via the use of cognitive strategies such as the cognitive re-evaluation of the situation (e.g., "that's not the end of the world") and the re-orientation of attention (e.g., "let's think about something positive"); thus children demonstrate conscious knowledge of the influence of thought process (cognition) on emotions. Consider as an example the well-documented association between depression and the understanding of the strategies to regulate feelings: children and adolescents who think that the use of strategies such as rumination and passivity are better to deal with negative emotions than strategies such as reevaluation of the situation or re-focusing show more depressive symptoms.

Furthermore, there is accumulating evidence that children's knowledge about emotions has an impact on their emotional experiences and well-being in a social context. This impact has been identified in both preschool and school children (see Pons *et al.*, 2005 for a review). For example, young children who better understand situation–emotion regularities (e.g., feeling happy when receiving a gift or sad when breaking a toy) are also the most popular with their day-care friends. At 5 years of age, children who are better able to recognize basic emotions are also the most popular with their classmates 1 or 2 years later. The relationship between emotion understanding and social functioning is also seen in middle childhood: 9-year-old children (particularly girls) with a good understanding of negative emotion-regulation strategies are considered, by their classmates and teachers, to be the most socially competent.

Surprisingly, there is relatively little research on the impact of school achievement on emotion. Some studies reveal a complex pattern of relations between positive and negative emotions, and school performance and self-evaluation of academic competencies. The link seems to be stronger between emotions and self-evaluation of academic competencies than between emotions and actual school performances (Gumora and Arsenio, 2002).

Emotion as a Cause of Cognition

It is widely held, in some form or another, that our emotions put us in some kind of meaningful relation to the world: A big ferocious dog is not just a fast-moving, big-toothed, furry creature; it is something to be feared because it is a potential threat to our well-being. How, then, does this meaningful relation between the person experiencing the emotion and the world influence our cognition? The answer to this question, within psychological and educational sciences, is twofold: emotional arousal is considered to be motivational, and emotional valence is considered to be a compass that guides our cognition.

At a general level, emotional arousal has an impact on cognition because it mobilizes the mind, as well as the body and the culture, to act and react (e.g., fear prepares the mind, the body, and the culture for fight or flight). This motivational function is the only one recognized by Piaget (1954/1981). He acknowledged that the intellect needs emotional arousal, which can speed up or slow down the functioning of the intellect and therefore its development. In 1908, Yerkes and Dodson postulated that an appropriate level of emotional arousal is needed to achieve an optimal level of cognitive performance. Too much anxiety (high arousal) or not enough interest (low arousal) might have a negative impact on the cognitive functions. They also postulated a functional relation between emotional arousal and task demands: the more difficult the task, the lower the level of emotional arousal required to reach the optimum level of cognitive performance.

Emotion not only makes cognition move but also orients its movement. Emotional arousal provides energy, whereas emotional valence gives the direction for cognition to move and therefore to develop. This is well illustrated by the behaviorist research tradition. Most classical and operant conditioning would not be possible without emotional valence: Emotional reactions (more or less positive or negative) to a stimulus (more or less conditioned or unconditioned) very often determine the behavioral response to it such as the appearance, disappearance, prioritization, and transformation of the (cognitive) behavior. This compass function of emotional valence for cognition is also recognized by Freud (1905/2002). The expressed or repressed drive coming from the Id not only gives its energy to the cognitive self but also orients (e.g., activation and inhibition) its functioning and development (in collaboration with the cognitive super-ego).

Numerous experimental studies have demonstrated the impact of emotional arousal and valence on cognition (e.g., memory, attention, and creativity). For example, when shown a list of positive and negative words, most people recall more positive words. If these people are clinically depressed, however, then they will tend to recall more negative words especially when these words have a clear negative valence (death, cancer, war, etc.). In a similar vein, typical people recall more elements of a story when the emotional valence of the story matches their own current mood, especially when the story is sad and they are in a sad mood while reading the story. It should be noted that when typical people are in a neutral mood, they remember more positive than negative elements of the story (e.g., Matt *et al.* (1992) for a review). It is as if, by default, when we are feeling nothing or at least at peace, our memory has an emotionally positive orientation, which may be adaptive. Other studies have also shown that the recall of information is facilitated when the mood of the person is the same at encoding and recall, irrespective of the emotional valence of this information. This effect is stronger when the information is autobiographical. For example, the recall of a list of neutral words is facilitated if the person is in a sad mood bold when trying to learn (encoding) and to recall this list (see Eich and Forgas, (2003) for a review). Such findings may help to explain why the recall of a traumatic autobiographical event is facilitated when people are already in a negative mood – a vicious cycle recognized by many schools of psychotherapy (Beck, 1976).

Emotional arousal and valence also have a direct impact on attentional processes (Eysenck *et al.* (2007); MacLeod (2005) for reviews). People with mood disorders pay more attention to information (words, pictures, faces, etc.) with an emotional valance matching their mood. For example, depressed people have the tendency to pay more attention to their personal characteristics (internal locus of control) when explaining their failures (e.g., because who I am, what I did, or what I said) and they pay more attention to their environment (external locus of control) to explain their success (e.g., because of luck, fate, or external events). In stark contrast to typical people, those who are clinically anxious (phobia, posttraumatic stress disorder (PTSD), etc.) direct their attention more toward threatening words (cancer, evil, death, etc.) than neutral words (house, picture, chair, etc.). When confronted with homonym words (e.g., batter-pancake vs. batter-assault), non-anxious people have the tendency to activate the neutral meaning of the word, whereas anxious people have the tendency to activate the negative meaning.

A person's level of emotional arousal and the valence of their emotional experience may also play an important role when constructing new information. Projective tests such as the Thematic Apperception Test (TAT) and the Rorschach are partially built on this assumption. It is argued, for example, that people's emotions determine, via a process of projective identification, their interpretation of reality, especially when this reality is ambiguous (ambiguous inkblots could be interpreted as a loving mother, a threatening father, a lost child, an unfaithful partner, etc.). Attachment theory (Bowlby, 1969/1997) presents us with an interesting illustration of this phenomenon. It is widely held that distinctive patterns of emotion co-regulation in infancy, so-called attachment styles (i.e., secure, ambivalent, avoidant, and disorganized), continue to inform the child's understanding of relationships much later on via enduring cognitive representations of such relationships (i.e., internal working models). Thus, if presented with a quasi-ambiguous picture of a mother and father leaving a child as they go on holiday for 2 weeks, children's understanding and construal of the events depicted are to a great extent determined by their emotional attachment style in infancy.

Of course, emotions may have an impact on other aspects of memory, attention, and creativity (e.g., research on flashbulb memories and autobiographical memory) and more generally on cognition (e.g., intelligence, language, perception, and moral reasoning). It should also be noted that most studies of the impact of emotion on cognition were conducted with adults (e.g., Brennen *et al.*, 2007; Overskeid, 2000). However, findings with children seem to confirm those obtained with adults.

Indeed, a substantial number of studies have shown that emotions such as anxiety (but also joy, pride, shame, and fear) have an impact on several aspects of learning at school: achievement, motivation, interest, goals, metacognition, etc. These studies showed that this impact may differ from one academic domain to another (i.e., mother tongue, mathematics, arts, etc.) and from one pupil to another (i.e., individual differences due to gender) (see Lafortune and Pons 2005 in Pons *et al.* (2005); and Schutz and Pekrun, (2007) for reviews). For example, induced positive mood in children (e.g., a compliment about clothes) improves their performance in a block-design task, which is a classical measure of intelligence. Anxiety can prevent pupils from exercising all of their capacities and can, in some cases, prevent them from doing any mathematical reasoning altogether. Anxiety also influences the functioning of metacognition. Certain students feel that when mathematical explanations are given, a veil, even a wall, suddenly appears in front of them, stopping them from reaching the concentration level necessary for understanding what they are being shown. They are thus prevented from engaging in the metacognitive processes necessary to solve the problems. More generally, these studies showed that pupils' emotional competences (i.e., their capacity to experience, recognize, express, control the expression of, regulate the experience of, and understand emotions) have an impact on their school achievement.

Until quite recently, most of the studies on the impact of emotions at school had been almost exclusively focusing on pupils. Lately, a new line of research has emerged which suggests some interesting relations. Positive emotions experienced by teachers are related to the level of support from parents and colleagues, and to pupils' cooperative behaviors and learning achievement. Teachers' negative emotions (e.g., anger, frustration, or sadness) stem from the absence of support from colleagues and parents, and are related to pupils' disruptive behaviors. Teachers' emotions also vary according to their professional experience and the academic level of their teaching: Novice teachers report more anxiety than experienced teachers and primary school teachers report more sadness and helplessness than secondary school teachers (often related to their pupils' life difficulties). In sum, the emotional constellation of the teacher may significantly influence the educational environment of the classroom.

Conclusion

The aforementioned studies demonstrate how cognition and emotion can work together. Cognition and emotion may be thought of as two different languages, to represent and communicate about the world (ourselves, others, the physical world, etc.) that coexist within all typical individuals: Every person is emotionally and cognitively bilingual.

While illustrating impressive relations between cognition and emotion, many of the aforementioned studies actually make it difficult to know which is causally antecedent. The allocation of cause, in many cases, may depend on the moment you are taking the snapshot in the flow of the person's subjective experience (e.g., "I am anxious, which makes me focus my attention on anxious information, which in return reinforces my anxiety, which in return makes me focus on anxious information, etc.").

We may also speculate on the fact that, as a function of the situation (context, circumstances, etc.) and the individual (personality, level of development, etc.), either cognition or emotion may be dominating the individual's mental functioning and, further, that the absence of this circularity would be dysfunctional for the individual.

Until quite recently, pedagogy had focused its attention almost exclusively on the cognitive dimension of the mind, for pupils and teachers. There are at least two challenges for researchers and professionals in education and psychology. The first is the development of reliable and valid, but also realistic and interdisciplinary, methodologies to improve emotional competences within school settings. This applies to children and adolescents in relation to their school achievement, and also to teachers in relation to their teaching skills. Today, few if any of these methodologies have been properly developed, let alone evaluated for their reliability and validity. There is a need for interventions that make a discernable impact on pupils' and teachers' emotional competences and bring about stable long-term positive changes in pupils' school achievement and teachers' pedagogical competences. The second challenge is to introduce emotional competences (i.e., the abilities to experience, recognize, express, control the expression of, regulate the experience of, and understand emotions) in the standard curriculum of preschool and compulsory school, and in the training programs of the teachers. This implies strong political decision. Indeed, the introduction of emotion pedagogy at school is still often seen as irrelevant when there are no existing problems – the object and goal of the school institution being still often considered as cognitive and instructive rather than emotional and educative. This change in thinking about the importance of emotions at school also implies a reorganization of pupils' and teachers' curriculum, teachers already having much to teach and learn. Such reorganization can be quite problematic not only because it is a source of change (and that can cause some resistance) but also because it implies that some topics which are currently taught have to be reduced within the curriculum and may be even eliminated.

Summary

Three main results can be abstracted from the educational and psychological studies discussed in this article:

1. Some (old) emotional reactions can be elicited without the intervention of cognition (via a direct biological appraisal of the stimulus and without the involvement of the cortex). Surprisingly, the opposite (i.e., cognition without emotion) has not yet been so well documented; this absence perhaps being due to the fact this documentation is too trivial (or impossible). Some researchers have been tempted by an overgeneralization of these no-causal findings. However, the fact that cognition and emotion are sometimes not causing one another (or that they are not the only cause of one another) does not imply that they are never causing one another.
2. Indeed, numerous studies have demonstrated that many emotional reactions and modulations are caused by the individual's cognitive appraisal of the stimuli coming from his/her body, mind, and environment. They have also demonstrated a robust relationship between children's cognitive understanding of emotions (including the possibility to regulate emotions) and their social and emotional well-being.
3. Numerous studies have equally demonstrated that emotional arousal and/or valence have an impact on memory (encoding, storage, and retrieval of existing information), attention (activation and inhibition of existing information), and creativity (elaboration of new information). They have also shown that the impact of emotional arousal on cognition is not linear and that the impact of positive and negative emotional valences is not symmetrical. Emotional arousal has to be neither too low nor too high to have an optimum impact on cognition (i.e., not an additional burden for cognitive executive functions) and the impact of negative emotions on cognition seems clearer than the impact of positive emotions.

While illustrating impressive relations between cognition and emotion, many of the studies discussed in this article actually make it difficult to know which is causally antecedent. The allocation of cause, in many cases, may depend on the moment you are taking the snapshot in the flow of the person's subjective experience (e.g., "I am depressed, which makes me focus my attention on depressive information, which in return reinforces my depression, which in return makes me focus on depression information"). We may also speculate on the fact that, as a function of the situation (context, circumstances, etc.) and the individual (personality, level of development, etc.), either cognition or emotion may be dominating the individual's mental functioning and, further, that the absence of this circularity would be dysfunctional for the individual.

Finally, although most of the studies reported here have been conducted in laboratories, an increasing number of studies seems to confirm, with some nuances, the mutual impact of cognition and emotion on pupils and teachers. In the future, it would be interesting to further investigate this mutual impact of cognition and emotion at school. Such investigations could have a positive influence on pupils' school achievement and on the quality of teachers' teaching. It would also test the validity of our understanding of the relation between cognition and emotion. Indeed, one thing is to demonstrate the logical coherence and the empirical correspondence of our understanding; another is to demonstrate that our understanding can change pragmatically the world of practice for the best.

See also: Cognition: Overview and Recent Trends.

Bibliography

Beck, A. (1976). *Cognitive Therapy and the Emotional Disorders*. New York: Meridian.
Bowlby, J. (1969/1997). *Attachment and Loss. Volume 1: Attachment*, 2nd edn. Sydney: Random House.
Brennen, T., Dybdahl, R., and Kapidzic, A. (2007). Trauma-related and neutral false memories in war-induced posttraumatic stress disorder. *Consciousness and Cognition* **16**, 877–885.
Dalgleish, T. and Power, M. (eds.) (1999). *Handbook of Cognition and Emotion*. Chichester: Wiley.
Damasio, A. (1994). *Descartes' Error: Emotion, Reason and the Human Brain*. New York: Putnam.
Darwin, C. (1872/1899). *The Expression of the Emotions in Man and Animals*. New York: D Appleton (Plain Label Books).
de Rosnay, M., Harris, P., and Pons, F. (2008). Emotion understanding and developmental psychopathology in young children. In Sharp, C., Fonagy, P., and Goodyer, I. (eds.) *Social Cognition and Developmental Psychopathology*, pp 343–385. Oxford: Oxford University Press.
Eich, E. and Forgas, J. (2003). Mood, cognition, and memory. In Healy, A. and Proctor, R. (eds.) *Handbook of Psychology: Experimental Psychology*, vol. 4, pp 61–83. Hoboken, NJ: Wiley.
Ekman, P. and Rosenberg, E. (eds.) (2005). *What the Face Reveals? Basic and Applied Studies of Spontaneous Expression Using the Facial Action Coding System (FACS)*. Oxford: Oxford University Press.
Eysenck, M., Derakshan, N., Santos, R., and Calvo, M. (2007). Anxiety and cognitive performance: Attentional control theory. *Emotion* **7**(2), 336–353.
Freud, S. (1905/2002). *The Joke and Its Relation to the Unconscious*. London: Penguin Books.
Frijda, N. (1986). *The Emotions*. Cambridge: Cambridge University Press.
Gumora, G. and Arsenio, W. (2002). Emotionality, emotion regulation and school performance in middle school children. *Journal of School Psychology* **40**, 395–413.

Harris, P. (2006). Social cognition. In Kuhn, D., Siegler, R., Damon, W., and Lerner, R. (eds.) *Handbook of Child Psychology: Vol 2. Cognition, Perception, and Language*, 6th edn., pp 811–858. Hoboken, NJ: Wiley.
Haga, S., Kraft, P., and Corby, E. (2008). Coming to terms with emotion regulation: A cross-cultural exploration of antecedents and well-being outcomes. *Journal of Happiness Studies*.
Kappas, A. (2006). Appraisal are direct, immediate, intuitive, and unwitting... and some are reflective.... *Cognition and Emotion* **20**(7), 952–975.
Kenny, A. (1963). *Action, Emotion and Will*. Thetford: Lowe and Brydone.
Lazarus, R. S. (1991). *Emotion and Adaptation*. Oxford: Oxford University Press.
LeDoux, J. (1996). *The Emotional Brain: The Mysterious Underpinnings of Emotional Life*. New York: Simon and Schuster.
Lewis, M. and Haviland-Jones, J. (eds.) (2000). *Handbook of Emotions*. New York: Guilford Press.
MacLeod, C. (2005). The Stroop Task in clinical research. In Wenzel, A. and Rubin, D. (eds.) *Cognitive Methods and Their Application to Clinical Research*, pp 41–62. Washington, DC: American Psychological Association.
Matt, G., Vasquez, C., and Campbell, W. (1992). Mood-congruent recall of affectively toned stimuli: A meta-analytic review. *Clinical Psychological Review* **12**, 227–255.
Overskeid, G. (2000). The slave of the passions: Experiencing problems and selecting solutions. *Review of General Psychology* **4**, 284–309.
Pascal, B. (1670/1998). *Œuvres Complètes*. Paris: Gallimard.
Piaget, J. (1954/1981). *Intelligence and Affectivity. Their Relationship during Child Development*. Palo Alto, CA: Annual reviews.
Pons, F., Hancock, D., Lafortune, L., and Doudin, P. -A. (eds.) (2005). *Emotions in Learning*. Aalborg: Aalborg University Press.
Reisenzein, R. (1983). The Schachter theory of emotion: Two decades later. *Psychological Bulletin* **94**(2), 239–264.
Roseman, I. (1984). Cognitive determinants of emotions: A structural theory. In Shaver, P. (ed.) *Review of Personality and Social Psychology*, vol. 5, pp 11–36. Beverly Hills, CA: Sage.
Schachter, S. and Singer, J. (1962). Cognitive, social and physiological determinants of emotional state. *Psychological Review* **69**, 379–399.
Scherer, K. (1984). On the nature and function of emotion: A component process approach. In Scherer, K. and Ekman, P. (eds.) *Approaches to Emotion*, pp 293–318. Erlbaum: Hillsdale.
Scherer, K., Schoor, A., and Johnstone, T. (eds.) (2001). *Appraisal Processes in Emotion: Theory, Methods, Research*. Oxford: Oxford University Press.
Schutz, P. A. and Pekrun, R. (eds.) (2007). *Emotion in Education*. Burlington: Elsevier.
Smith, C. (1989). Dimensions of appraisal and physiological response in emotion. *Journal of Personality and Social Psychology* **56**, 339–353.
Zajonc, R. (1984). On the primacy of affect. *American Psychologist* **39**, 117–123.

Further Reading

Braisby, N. and Gellatly, A. (eds.) (2005). *Cognitive Psychology*. Oxford: Oxford University Press.
Davidson, R., Scherer, K., and Goldsmith, H. (eds.) (2003). *Handbook of Affective Sciences*. Oxford: Oxford University Press.
Manstead, N., Frijda, N., and Fischer, A. (eds.) (2004). *Feelings and Emotions: The Amsterdam Symposium*. Cambridge: Cambridge University Press.
Saarni, C. (1999). *The Development of Emotional Competence*. New York: Guilford Press.

Memory

S Magnussen and T Brennen, University of Oslo, Oslo, Norway

Glossary

Declarative memory – An essential property of declarative memory is that one is conscious of what one is remembering. Such memories are, by their very nature, verbal. For example, one can talk about one's experiences, and about new words that one has learned.

Episodic memory – Personal experiences and events are stored in episodic memory (see declarative memory).

False memory – A memory that appears real to the rememberer, but is not based on veridical experience is referred to as a false memory. They can be induced in the laboratory, but they are also prevalent in everyday situations, sometimes with drastic legal and interpersonal consequences.

Forgetting – It is the inability to recall an episode or a skill that was previously learned. In forgetting of declarative memory (*quod vide*), it is suspected that many failures to recall are in fact due to a failure to access a still-existent memory trace.

Memory systems – In contrast to previous schools of thought in psychology, where memory was considered to be unitary, in cognitive psychology one considers memory to be a multifaceted set of modules. There is a host of evidence to suggest that we possess many different types of memory.

Nondeclarative memory – We are not aware of everything that affects our behavior. These nonconscious effects of previous experience are evidence of nondeclarative memory. Also, our memory for motor skills, such as walking, typing, and skiing, is nondeclarative because motor skills are essentially nonverbal.

Perceptual representation system – Conceived of as the interface between perception and memory, it is a basic memory system storing perceptual information that enables us to perceive the world as meaningful.

Priming – Things that you have just seen, heard or thought about will facilitate thoughts about related concepts. This expression of memory is referred to as priming.

Semantic memory – Believed to be stored separately from personal experiences or episodes, semantic memory refers to a person's general knowledge of the world (see episodic memory).

Working memory – A coordinated set of short-term memory mechanisms that allow us to consciously manipulate what we are thinking about at any given moment.

Memory is a central part of the brain's attempt to make sense of experience, and to tell coherent stories about it. These tales are all we have of our past, so they are potent determinants of how we view ourselves and what we do. Yet our stories are built from many ingredients. Snippets of what actually happened, thoughts about what might have happened, and beliefs that guide us as we attempt to remember. Our memories are the powerful but fragile products of what we recall from the past, believe about the present, and imagine about the future   (Schacter, 1996: 308).

A few years ago, a Norwegian newspaper (*Dagbladet, Magasinet*, 27 March, 2004) reported the story of Dodo, a young man of Asian origin who, in January 2003, woke up on the freezing ground in a small village in Switzerland with his well-equipped rucksack nearby, stuffed with expensive clothes and a money belt containing US$5000, but no identity papers or tickets and with absolutely no personal memory. Dodo wandered around in Europe for some weeks, and, for reasons he could not explain, somehow managed to travel to Oslo, Norway. His memory loss of the time before he woke up in Switzerland is massive, he has no idea who he is, and he did not recognize his own face in the mirror. He had even lost his native language – he spoke heavily accented English but not any Asian language; the only thing he knew about himself was that he smoked Camel and liked pop music.

Dodo suffers from the condition of retrograde amnesia. That is, he has lost his memory in the sense people usually use the term memory, the recollection of private experiences and facts we have learned about the world. But Dodo remembered many things, he remembered what cigarettes were for, the workings of photographic equipment, he understood the value of money, was able to buy food, and mastered the skill of traveling by public transport. So he could make use many of the things he had learned. This type of selective memory impairment is a main argument cited by memory researchers in support of the idea that memory rather than being a single cognitive process or system, is a collective term for a family of neurocognitive systems that store information in different formats (Schacter *et al.*, 2000; Tulving, 2002).

Varieties of Human Memory

Modern taxonomies distinguish between several forms of memory, or memory systems. An important distinction is drawn between declarative memory, which refers to the conscious recollection of facts and personal experiences, and nondeclarative memory, which refers to behavior changes resulting from previous experiences that may or may not be accompanied by conscious recollection (see **Figure 1**).

The story of Dodo illustrates well the central role of declarative memory in human life. This young man had lost not only his personal past – his autobiographical memories – but also large parts of his general knowledge of the world and even his ability to speak his native language. Thus, the systems or forms of memory that we term episodic and semantic memory are heavily affected. Episodic memory is assigned a special role in human life: it is unique in the sense that memories are associated with a place and a time, and is, according to Tulving (2002), the only known example of a process where the arrow of time is turned back and the past can be re-experienced, a feat probably unique to humans. Without episodic memory, the mental representation that psychologists call the self – the organization of personal memories in a historical context – is lost. Obviously, this is what had happened to Dodo; however, his nondeclarative memory seemed largely intact.

In nondeclarative memory, the effects of previous experiences and exercises manifest themselves directly in behavior; the individual learning sessions may be vaguely remembered or be completely inaccessible to conscious recollection. Procedural memory is responsible for the maintenance of the cognitive and motor skills that we have acquired throughout life, from knowing how to eat with a knife and fork to the mastery of swimming, cycling, or driving a car, as well as the advanced skills of playing billiards or playing a saxophone. Conditioning is a basic memory system that in humans is particularly important in tying emotional reactions to external stimuli or situations. For example, in phobic reactions, anxiety is triggered by the phobic stimuli but the person is typically not aware of the learning episodes in which the connection between the emotion and stimulus was established. Similarly, a piece of music, or a specific odor may evoke romantic feelings without an accompanying experienced-memory episode. Perceptual learning, or the perceptual representation system (PRS), enables us to perceive the world consisting of meaningful entities, because in order to produce a perceptual experience, online sensory signals must join stored representations, and this linking is part of the perceptual process itself. To see is to recognize, or to realize that you do not recognize. Tulving and Schacter (1990) also identified priming as an expression of non-declarative memory, coupled to the PRS. In priming, the person's performance on a specific task is facilitated (or inhibited) by the previous presentation of related information. For example, perceptual identification of a portrait as representing Hillary Clinton is speeded by the prior presentation of a picture of Bill Clinton, compared to the prior presentation of a picture of, say, the Pope.

An important feature of the memory systems concept is the idea that the various systems store information in different formats, and the information stored in one format is not directly translatable into other formats. This implies that the information stored in one system is not immediately accessible to other systems. However, assuming that the memory systems operate independently and in parallel, most experiences would be recorded and stored in parallel in different formats, and the memory performance assisted by several memory systems working in concert (Tulving, 2002).

Another basic distinction in memory theory is the division between a short-term memory mechanism that is the seat of consciousness and active processing, and is able to store limited quantities of information for a limited period of time, and a long-term memory mechanism that stores unlimited amounts of information for unlimited periods of time (Atkinson and Shiffrin, 1968). The short-term memory mechanism is currently associated with

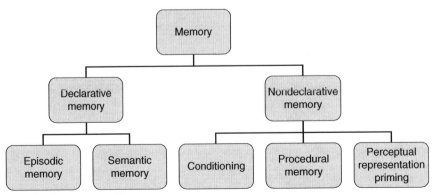

Figure 1 A common textbook taxonomy of human memory.

Baddeley's (1986, 2003) concept of working memory, a coordinated set of mechanisms that combine incoming nformation with information retrieved from long-term memory with the assistance of three support systems that actively manipulate verbal, visuo-spatial, and episodic information. The concept of working memory is closely associated with the concept of attention; only those pieces of information that are actively attended to, enter memory. Since the capacity of attention and working memory is limited, it follows that only part of the potentially available information confronting us at any time is registered, and much of the information that is registered is immediately forgotten. In a sense, most of the things we believe we have forgotten, never really entered a durable memory system.

In the context of education and everyday life, it is long-term memory that is the important aspect of memory.

Metaphors and Models of Memory – Strategies of Research

In the attempt to understand memory, scientists as well as laymen are forced to try to describe something that is not directly observable. We may be aware of some of the processes that take place during learning, and similarly of the processes that take place when we attempt to search for a piece of information in memory, but we have little access to the processes that mediate between encoding and retrieval. In order to make sense of the phenomena to which we have little access, both laymen and researchers tend to use metaphors and analogies, many of which are borrowed from the physical world (Magnussen et al., 2007).

Koriat et al. (2000) pointed out that the study of memory following Ebbinghaus (1885) has been dominated by a storehouse metaphor, in which discrete items of information are stored and later retrieved, and which tends to evaluate memory in terms of the number of items that are retained (or lost). The storehouse metaphor invites an interest in the number of stored items. An effective store is one that contains many items, retains these items for long periods of time, and allows easy access to them. Memory then is evaluated in terms of its quantity – how much is retained, how much is lost.

Quantitative aspects of memory are frequently of great interest in everyday life, and research relevant to the classroom and academic achievement typically follows this strategy. However, an alternative approach to the study of memory, derived from the correspondence metaphor and that can be traced to the work of Bartlett (1932), evaluates memory performance in terms of the correspondence between the original event and the memory of it; the accuracy of the memory report. A high-quality memory is more faithful to the remembered event than an inferior memory, and contains fewer distortions and errors. Sometimes people remember events that

never happened. The assessment of memory correspondence should therefore start with the output – what the person reports – rather than with the input – what actually happened. An output-bound assessment reflects the accuracy of what is remembered – how much of what the person reports did in fact occur (Koriat et al., 2000). In many real-life situations, such as in court, there is greater concern with the accuracy of the report than with the amount of information reported.

The Seven Sins of Memory

The modern study of the accuracy of episodic memory has convincingly disproved another popular metaphor, the idea of memory as a video recorder taping and replaying the original events. Episodic memory does not reproduce, it constructs, and the reconstruction of previous episodes is based on information from many sources with the assistance of many neural systems (Rubin, 2006). As some of the sources of information used in the construction of episodic memories are external to the original event, memory accuracy suffers. In a widely read book, Schacter (2001) identifies seven factors that he terms the "seven sins of memory," which are at the origin of the tricks that episodic memory plays on us. The sins are: absent-mindedness; to be encoded into episodic memory, a piece of information or an event that must be attended to. When focal attention is diverted or attention is switched to auto-pilot, information may be missed, and the event is not properly remembered because the information was never registered in the first place. Transience refers to fact that memories fade. Some memories fade rapidly, others fade more slowly, depending on a number of factors, but no memory gets better over time. The general course of memory decay, first described by Ebbinghaus (1885), is the negatively accelerated function shown in **Figure 2(a)**, which represents the long-term forgetting of ordinary life events. However, as illustrated by **Figure 2(b)**, frequently studied or over-learned material shows very little decay, and some extraordinary life events, in particular dramatic and traumatic experiences, appear to be very resistant to fading and rather obey the sin of persistence. In fact, some memories we would like to forget, haunt us for the rest of our lives. And sometimes information that we know that is not forgotten – it is on the tip of the tongue – is unavailable to memory because of a failure of retrieval; this is the sin of blocking. Memories not only fade, they are subject to influences from several sources. The human mind is suggestible, our memories of events and facts are influenced by information from external sources, from what we read, and from what other people tell us. Memories may be biased in various ways. For example, our memories of the past depend on or are colored by the present, or as Schacter (2001) puts it, "the way we were depends upon the way we are." The sin of misattribution refers to the confusions and

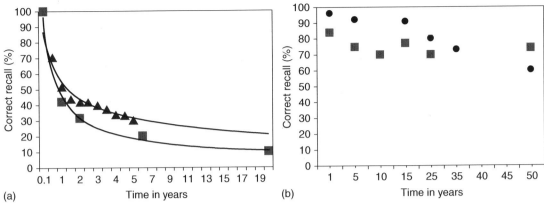

Figure 2 (a) Memory for personally experienced everyday events, (▲) and (■). (b) Very long-term memory for over-learned material, obtained by asking participants to match pictures of high-school classmates' faces to their names, (●), and testing participants' ability to translate unused Spanish vocabulary learned in school to English, (■). Despite the fact that we treasure our autobiographical memories and they play an integral role in our personal identity, we become incapable of bringing to mind the specifics of most of what we experience within a year or so of it happening. By contrast, multiple repeated exposures to something that is quite unimportant for one in later life and never practiced or recalled can allow access to memories decades later. This may be seen as paradoxical until one realizes that motivation to remember is not always as important as the amount of practice one has put in to learning something. (a) Adapted from Wagenaar, W. (1986). My memory: A study of autobiographical memory over six years. *Cognitive Psychology* **18**, 225–252 and White, R. (2002). Memory for events after twenty years. *Applied Cognitive Psychology* **16**, 603–612. (b) Adapted from Bahrick, H. P., Bahrick, P. O., and Wittlinger, R. P. (1975). Fifty years of memories for names and faces: A cross-sectional approach. *Journal of Experimental Psychology: General* **104**, 54–75 and Bahrick, H. P. (1984). Semantic memory content in permastore: Fifty years of memory for Spanish learned in school. *Journal of Experimental Psychology: General* **113**, 1–29.

mistakes we often make concerning the source of a particular piece of information, confusions of times, people, and places, and in the extreme case, the confusion of genuine memory and fantasy that gives rise to false memories.

Memory in Everyday Contexts

Ebbinghaus' (1885) pioneering studies investigated his own memory for nonsense syllables, and a century later, as cognitive psychology became the dominant school in psychology in the 1970s, the typical experiment on memory still clearly bore Ebbinghaus' imprint: university undergraduates sat in a darkened lab and learned long lists of words. A degree of discomfort with the potential lack of relevance of these experiments for understanding life outside the lab, led to a push for memory research to be more ecologically valid, and the study of applied memory has since grown into a very active research field. Drawing on the correspondence metaphor of memory, a key underlying question in this field has been, on how accurate is our memory, as it is used in everyday life. Another change has been in the types of material used. breaking out of the verbal learning tradition (learning lists of words), a concerted research effort over the past 20 years has, for instance, tried to shed light on our ability to remember more real-life stimuli, like people, and events we have experienced in our lives, a skill that Dodo apparently no longer possesses.

How do we remember people? A person represents an extremely complex and multifaceted biological stimulus:

while we most often recognize a person from their face, we can also judge who a person is from their name, their voice, their gait, besides many other potential routes. It turns out that the complexity of the stimulus is reflected in the diversity of memory representations we have for people. Not all types of person information are equally memorable either. In particular people's names pose a problem when it comes to recall. All readers will have experienced the tip-of-the-tongue phenomenon for a name, when one is unable to recall a name but feels that one might recall it at any time, and may be able to give partial information about the missing word. This phenomenon occurs particularly for people's names, and its frequency increases with age (Schwartz, 2002; Valentine *et al.*, 1996). On the other hand, our ability to distinguish between faces and to recognize that the one you are looking at now is one you have seen before is prodigious. This is perhaps not surprising from an evolutionary point of view: humans are social animals and there is a strong need to distinguish between family, friends, and enemies. On the other hand, more recent research in the applied memory tradition has cast doubt on our face-recognition skills in some practical situations. For instance, the use of credit cards with a picture of the holder's face is now widespread, but Kemp *et al.* (1997) have shown that, in fact, shop assistants are terrible at detecting that the face on the card does not match the person holding the card.

How much of our lives do we remember? Cognitive psychologists would agree with the sentiments of the novelist Milan Kundera who pointed out that in fact we are only able to recall a vanishingly small proportion of the events in our lives. While we do of course remember many individual events from our lives, much of our memory appears to be based on generalized averages of similar events, so that while you may only be able to specifically recall a few of the times you have been to the Odeon cinema, you may know very well where you usually park, what sort of films you see, who you go with, and what snacks you buy. A systematic approach to answering the question was taken by Wagenaar (1986) who wrote down one incident from his life each day over a period of 4 years. When subsequently tested, he found that being cued by the who, what, or where of an event was more powerful a cue than when, and that single piece of information (who, what, or where) triggered recall of the incident only on about 50% of occasions for the first year and declined to 20% after 4 years. Multiple cues triggered over 60% of memories, even after 4 years, and even cases where he had apparently forgotten the incident completely could be recalled in cases when another person was central in the incident and could be asked to provide more cues. Thus, it is a case of the glass being half-full or half-empty: even events which were thought to be completely forgotten turned out to be retrievable, but on the other hand, normal cues failed to trigger a majority of memories. Results from Wagenaar's (1986) together with results from a similar study carried out across a 20-year interval by White (2002) are shown in **Figure 2(a)** and illustrate the dramatic decline of ordinary everyday memories. White (2002) tested his memory by having an assistant read event descriptions picked randomly, and he decided if he remembered the event vividly, vaguely, or not at all. At all testing times, most of the remembered events were vaguely remembered, and he encountered not a single case where an event forgotten at one time was remembered at a later time. Assuming the conditions of retrieval are the same at different testing points, memory does not improve over time.

False Autobiographical Memories

In the 1990s, the science of memory was the subject of a fierce debate in scientific journals, newspapers, and courts of law. A phenomenon that was first observed in the United States but that has since spread to other countries is that cases of alleged child-abuse were being brought to court by the victims, years and even decades later, because the victims had previously been unable to retrieve the memories. This was a powerful and deeply shocking claim that split psychology into those who thought of these memories as recovered, and those who thought of them as false, the so-called memory wars.

Since Bartlett's seminal research on how our memory for narrative introduces errors that fit in with the rest of our knowledge, memory research has known about the malleability of our memories for events. Due to the memory wars, such memory illusions have been much studied over the past decade, showing that under certain circumstances, we can become convinced that, several years previously, one had been up in a hot air balloon, or had knocked over a punch bowl at a wedding when these events simply had not happened (Loftus, 2003). The key ingredients appear to be that one believes the authority telling one the information, and that one is given time to try to retrieve the information: over time, the false memories come to feel real to the rememberer. When it turns out that in many documented cases of recovered memories of child–abuse, the victim had been in therapy with a clinician who believed that symptoms of depression and anxiety in fact are the manifestation of early child-abuse, there is the very real possibility that the often grotesque and implausible accounts were genuinely believed by the rememberer but nonetheless entirely false, produced by the combination of an authority figure, the therapist, and several practice sessions in which to recover the memories. A number of documented cases show that false memories may be quite dramatic, as for example, remembering being witness to a murder that never happened (Goodman et al., 2007). Modern research also fails to support the idea that early traumatic childhood experiences can be stored in a detailed fashion but repressed or blocked from consciousness, only later to be exhumed by therapeutic exercises. Rather, well-controlled studies show that such memories obey the sin of persistence (Goodman et al., 2003).

Knowledge of the constructive nature of autobiographical memory is important for many professions, especially those dealing with psychiatric patients, children, and other groups with little power. The vulnerability of autobiographical or episodic memory is also the focus of another important area of applied memory research, the study of factors affecting the reliability of eyewitness testimony (Loftus, 2003; Wells et al., 2006). In the interrogation room and in court, failures to remember are less damaging to the judicial process than are memory errors; absence of memory points nowhere, memory errors may point in the wrong direction.

Memory in the Classroom

One of the secrets to creating robust long-term memories, already shown by Ebbinghaus' experiments and known to centuries of teachers, is repetition or over-learning. Schoolchildren spend a lot of time in classrooms learning from teachers and books. The vast majority of children in the West spend upward of a decade of their lives in such a system. It is generally agreed that education is a good thing, but the exams that are used to test that the requisite knowledge has been acquired often take place within a few months of the teaching, which begs the question of the fate of this knowledge in the long term. How much of the Spanish vocabulary that you learned in high school can you still recall? What about the fate of your university degree that you haven't used since your graduation exams? Seminal research by Harry Bahrick has shown that we are able to recall surprising amounts of knowledge even several decades after learning (see for example, Bahrick, 1984). Lots of material seems to become unavailable within the first year of learning. About 2 years after studying a topic, people are able to perform at around 50% of the level they were at when they stopped studying, but the surprising finding is that up to 50 years later, one performs at about the same level as one did 2 years after: very little forgetting appears to occur after an initial period. Similar results have been reported for mathematics, Spanish, and for cognitive psychology, so that this function appears to reflect general properties of the long-term semantic memory system, or permastore as Bahrick termed it (**Figure 2(b)**).

Another question is that of how best to study to ensure long-term learning. In the light of the prevailing orthodoxy in education, it might be surprising to some that a body of evidence has built up recently to suggest that the best way to study for a test is to test oneself. For instance, Roediger and Karpicke (2006) asked participants to read and learn a short essay. After all participants had read the passage through, one group was then given a test on what they had remembered, whereas the other group reread the passage. There was then a final memory test given, either 5 min, 2 days, or a week subsequent to the reading. After 5 min, those participants who had reread the passage performed better than the other group. However those tested after 2 days and those tested after a week had the opposite pattern: an extra opportunity to study the material led to worse memory compared to those who were tested also in the first phase (see **Figure 3**). The message from this study and many replications is clear: the very act of testing improves performance. It is to be hoped that educational systems will confront the challenge to incorporate the consequences of this finding into their classrooms: testing is not only a way of assessing students' performance, it also a way of facilitating their learning.

The Future for Memory Research

Memory research finds itself at the touching point between basic and applied research. On the one hand, it is becoming more integrated into neuroscience, with studies using cognitive tasks in conjunction with brain imaging methods, for instance. On the other hand, the emphasis on an understanding of memory in everyday contexts is strengthening. Up to now, the findings of memory research have been relatively slow to get out to practical situations. This is unfortunate because the focus

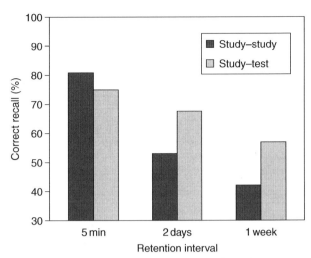

Figure 3 Having heard a story they were trying to learn, some participants were immediately tested on what they could recall, while others had a second chance to learn the story. Five minutes later, the second-chance group (the dark column) had better recall, but of potential importance to educationalists, the immediate-test group (the light column) did better on tests 2 and 7 days later. Adapted from Roediger, H. L. and Karpicke, J. D. (2006). Test-enhanced learning – taking memory tests improves long-term retention. *Psychological Science* **17**, 249–255.

in recent decades on more applied sides of memory – how it is actually used in daily settings – has produced important results, which, at the risk of hyperbole, would appear important to be more widely known about. For all in the legal system, from the police to jury members, the studies showing that people can be induced to create false memories in themselves, should be required reading. Similarly, for the educational system, the generalized, positive gains obtained by the very act of testing someone's knowledge should become more widely known, and integrated into teaching systems.

See also: Cognition and Emotion; Cognition: Overview and Recent Trends; Problem Solving and Human Expertise.

Bibliography

Atkinson, R. C. and Shiffrin, R. M. (1968). Human memory: A proposed system and its control processes. In Spence, K. W. and Spence, J. T. (eds.) *The Psychology of Learning and Motivation,* vol. 1, pp 89–195. New York: Academic Press.

Baddeley, A. D. (1986). *Working Memory.* Oxford: Oxford University Press.

Baddeley, A. D. (2003). Working memory. Looking back and looking forward. *Nature Neuroscience Reviews* **4**, 829–839.

Bahrick, H. P. (1984). Semantic memory content in permastore: Fifty years of memory for Spanish learned in school. *Journal of Experimental Psychology:General* **113**, 1–29.

Bartlett, F. (1932). *Remembering.* Cambridge: Cambridge University Press.

Ebbinghaus, H. (1885). *Über das Gedächtnis*. Leipzig: Dunker.

Goodman, G. S., Ghetti, S., Quas, J. A., *et al*. (2003). A prospective study of memory for child sexual abuse: New findings relevant to the repressed memory controversy. *Psychological Science* **14**, 113–118.

Goodman, G. S., Magnussen, S., Andersson, J., *et al*. (2007). Memory illusions and false memories in real life. In Magnussen, S. and Helstrup, T. (eds.) *Everyday Memory*, pp 157–182. Hove: Psychology Press.

Kemp, R., Towell, N., and Pike, G. (1997). When seeing should not be believing: Photographs, credit cards and fraud. *Applied Cognitive Psychology* **11**, 211–222.

Koriat, A., Goldsmith, M., and Pansky, A. (2000). Toward a psychology of memory accuracy. *Annual Review of Psychology* **51**, 481–537.

Loftus, E. (2003). Our changeable memories: Legal and practical implications. *Nature Neuroscience Reviews* **4**, 231–234.

Magnussen, S., Endestad, T., Koriat, A., and Helstrup, P. (2007). What do people believe about memory, and how do they talk about memory? In Magnussen, S. and Helstrup, T. (eds.) *Everyday Memory*, pp 5–25. Hove: Psychology Press.

Roediger, H. L. and Karpicke, J. D. (2006). Test-enhanced learning – taking memory tests improves long-term retention. *Psychological Science* **17**, 249–255.

Rubin, D. C. (2006). The basic-systems model of episodic memory. *Perspectives on Psychological Science* **1**, 277–311.

Schacter, D. L. (1996). *Searching for Memory: The Brain, the Mind, and the Past*. New York: Basic Books.

Schacter, D. L. (2001). *The Seven Sins of Memory: How the Mind Forgets and Remembers*. Boston, MA: Houghton Mifflin.

Schacter, D. L., Wagner, A. D., and Buckner, R. L. (2000). Memory systems of 1999. In Tulving, E. and Craik, F. I. M. (eds.) *The Oxford Handbook of Memory*, pp 627–643. Oxford: Oxford University Press.

Schwartz, B. L. (2002). *Tip-of-the-Tongue States: Phenomenology, Mechanism and Lexical Retrieval*. London: Erlbaum.

Tulving, E. (2002). Episodic memory: From mind to brain. *Annual Review of Psychology* **53**, 1–25.

Tulving, E. and Schacter, D. L. (1990). Priming and human memory systems. *Science* **247**, 301–306.

Valentine, T., Brennen, T., and Brédart, S. (1996). *The Cognitive Psychology of Proper Names: The Importance of Being Ernest*. London: Routledge.

Wagenaar, W. (1986). My memory: A study of autobiographical memory over six years. *Cognitive Psychology* **18**, 225–252.

Wells, G. L., Memon, A., and Penrod, S. D. (2006). Eyewitness evidence: Improving its probative value. *Psychological Science in the Public Interest* **7**, 43–75.

White, R. (2002). Memory for events after twenty years. *Applied Cognitive Psychology* **16**, 603–612.

Further Reading

Bahrick, H. P., Bahrick, P. O., and Wittlinger, R. P. (1975). Fifty years of memories for names and faces: A cross-sectional approach. *Journal of Experimental Psychology: General* **104**, 54–75.

Cohen, G. (2004). *Memory in the Real World*, 2nd edn. Hove: Psychology Press.

Kundera, M. (2002). *Ignorance*. New York: Harper Collins.

Magnussen, S. and Helstrup, T. (eds.) (2007). *Everyday Memory*. Hove: Psychology Press.

McNally, R. J. (2003). *Remembering Trauma*. Cambridge, MA: Harvard University Press.

Toglia, M. P., Read, J. D., Ross, D. F., and Lindsay, R. C. L. (eds.) (2007). *The Handbook of Eyewitness Psychology. Vol. I, Memory for Events*. London: Erlbaum.

Tulving, E. and Craik, F. I. M. (eds.) (2000). *The Oxford Handbook of Memory*. Oxford: Oxford University Press.

Squire, L. and Kandel, E. R. (1999). *Memory. From Mind to Molecules*. New York: Freeman.

Intelligence

R J Sternberg, Tufts University, Boston, MA, USA

Glossary

Crystallized intelligence – One of two major subfactors of general intelligence, it represents the accumulation of knowledge over the life span of the individual and may be measured by tests in areas such as vocabulary, general information, and achievement (cf. fluid intelligence).

Deviation intelligence quotients (IQs) – A means of determining intelligence test scores, based on deviations from an average score, calculated such that the normative equivalent for the median score is 100, about 68% of the scores are computed to fall between 85 and 115, and about 95% of the scores fall between 70 and 130; strictly speaking, they are not IQs because no quotient is involved (cf. mental age and ratio IQ).

Emotional intelligence – The ability to perceive and express emotion, assimilate emotion in thought, understand and reason with emotion, and regulate emotion in the self and others.

Fluid intelligence – One of two major subfactors of general intelligence, it represents the acquisition of new information or the grasping of new relationships and abstractions about known information (may be measured, e.g., by timed tests involving analogies, series completions, or inductive reasoning; cf. crystallized intelligence).

Heritability coefficient – The degree to which heredity contributes to individual differences in intelligence, expressed in terms of a number on a scale from 0 to 1, such that a coefficient of 0 means that heredity has no influence on variation among people, whereas a coefficient of 1 means that heredity is the only influence on such variation.

Intelligence – The ability to implement goal-directed adaptive behavior.

Mental age – A means of indicating a person's level of intelligence (generally in reference to a child), based on the individual's performance on tests of intelligence, by indicating the chronological age of persons who typically perform at the same level of intelligence as the test-taker (used less frequently today than in the past; cf. deviation IQs, intelligence, and ratio IQ).

Mental retardation – Low level of intelligence, usually reflected by both poor performance on tests of intelligence and poor adaptive competence (the degree to which a person functions effectively within a normal situational context).

Ratio IQ – A means of indicating performance on intelligence tests, based on a quotient of mental age divided by chronological age, times 100 (cf. deviation IQs).

Reaction range – The broad limits within which a particular attribute (e.g., intelligence) may be expressed in various possible ways, given the inherited potential for its expression in the particular individual.

Theory of multiple intelligences – A theory suggesting that intelligence comprises eight distinct constructs – bodily–kinesthetic intelligence, interpersonal intelligence, intrapersonal intelligence, linguistic intelligence, mathematical–logical intelligence, musical intelligence, naturalist intelligence, and spatial intelligence – that function somewhat independently, but may interact to produce intelligent behavior.

Triarchic theory of successful intelligence – A theory of intelligence that asserts that intelligence comprises three aspects, which deal with the relationship of intelligence to the internal world, to experience, and to the external world.

Theories of Intelligence

Implicit Theories

How do psychologists or educators know about what intelligence is? One way they find out is by asking people. For example, they might ask experts. What do experts say?

In a 1921 symposium on the definition of intelligence, an American psychologist, Lewis M. Terman, emphasized the ability to think abstractly. Another American psychologist, Edward L. Thorndike, emphasized learning and the ability to give good responses to questions. In a similar 1986 symposium, however, psychologists generally agreed on the importance of adaptation to the environment as the key to understanding both what intelligence is and what it does. They also emphasized learning skills and understanding one's own cognitive processes. Therefore, adaptation, learning, and metacognition (i.e., understanding oneself) won the day.

In a set of studies published in 1981, Robert J. Sternberg and his colleagues asked laypeople in the United States what they thought intelligence was. Three factors emerged from their responses: practical problem solving, verbal ability, and social competence. The conceptions that arise depend, however, on who is asked.

Robert J. Sternberg and his colleagues have studied implicit theories in various cultures. In comparable studies done in Taiwan, four factors prevailed: cognitive skills, getting along with other people, understanding oneself, and knowing when to and when not to show that one is smart. In other studies conducted in Kenya, cognitive skills also were emphasized less than in the West. In contrast, obedience, respect, and understanding people were emphasized more.

Most theories of intelligence are explicit rather than implicit. They are elicited not by asking people what they mean by intelligence, but rather, by having people perform tasks believed to require intelligence. There are several different kinds of explicit theories.

Psychometric Theories

Psychometric theories have generally sought to understand the structure of intelligence: What form does it take, and what are its parts, if any? Such theories have generally been based on and tested by the use of data obtained from tests of mental abilities. These tests include assessments of vocabulary, numerical reasoning, analogical reasoning, and visualization of what forms would look like if they were rotated in space.

The first major psychometric theories were proposed by the British psychologist Charles E. Spearman. In a 1904 article, Spearman argued that just two kinds of factors underlie virtually all individual differences in test scores. Spearman called the first and more important kind of factor the general factor or g. It was said to pervade performance on all tasks requiring intelligence. The second kind of factor, according to Spearman, was specific to each test. However, what exactly is g? In 1927, Spearman proposed it might be something he labeled mental energy.

An American psychologist, L. L. Thurstone, instead suggested that seven factors, or primary mental abilities, underlie individual differences in mental test performance: verbal comprehension (knowledge of vocabulary and in reading); verbal fluency (writing and producing words in response to a prompt, such as words beginning with the letter d); number (solving simple arithmetical computation and reasoning problems); spatial visualization (mentally visualizing and manipulating objects); inductive reasoning (completing a number or letter series); memory (remembering people's names or faces); and perceptual speed (rapidly proofreading to discover typographical errors in a typed text).

Raymond B. Cattell and John B. Carroll, among others, suggested that abilities are hierarchical. At the top of the hierarchy is g, or general ability. Below g in the hierarchy are successive levels of gradually narrowing abilities, ending with Spearman's specific abilities.

Cattell suggested that general ability can be divided into two basic abilities, fluid and crystallized. Fluid abilities are the reasoning and problem-solving skills measured by tests such as the analogies, classifications, and series completions. Crystallized abilities derive from fluid abilities and are viewed as their products, which include vocabulary, general information, and knowledge about specific fields. John L. Horn suggested that crystallized ability more or less increases over the life span, whereas fluid ability increases in the earlier years and decreases in the later ones.

John B. Carroll proposed a three-stratum model of intelligence. It is considered by some to be the most definitive psychometric model of intelligence because it is based upon reanalyses of hundreds of data sets. According to this model, general ability is at the top of a hierarchy of abilities. At the next lower stratum are various broad abilities (including learning and memory processes and the effortless production of many ideas). At the bottom of the hierarchy are many narrow, specific abilities, such as spelling ability and reasoning speed.

J. P. Guilford, an American psychologist, proposed a structure-of-intellect theory, which, in its earlier versions, postulated 120 abilities. For example, in an influential 1967 work, Guilford argued that abilities can be divided into five kinds of operations, four kinds of contents, and six kinds of products. These various facets of intelligence combine multiplicatively for a total of $5 \times 4 \times 6$, or 120 separate abilities. An example of such an ability would be cognition (operation) of semantic (content) relations (product), which would be involved in recognizing the relation between lawyer and client in the analogy problem, lawyer:client::doctor:? In 1984, Guilford increased the number of abilities proposed by his theory, raising the total to 150.

In an address to the American Psychological Association in 1957, Lee J. Cronbach proposed that psychologists unite the two disciplines of scientific psychology – experimental and differential (the study of individual differences). His proposal led to cognitive theories of intelligence, which are derived and tested by experimental means.

Underlying most cognitive approaches to intelligence is the assumption that intelligence comprises a set of mental representations (e.g., propositions and images) of information and a set of mental processes that can operate on the representations. A more intelligent person is assumed to mentally represent information better and also to operate more quickly on these representations than a less intelligent person does.

In 1975, Earl B. Hunt, Clifford E. Lunneborg, and J. Lewis showed that a critical ability underlying verbal intelligence is that of rapidly retrieving lexical information, such as letter names, from memory. A few years later, Robert J. Sternberg identified key mental processes alleged to underlie many cognitive tasks, especially ones involving inductive reasoning. The processes included, among others, encoding stimuli, inferring relations between stimuli, and applying what one has learned.

Ian Deary and his colleagues have sought to understand intelligence through the study of inspection time. They have found that more intelligent individuals can discriminate the lengths of the lines with lesser stimulus duration (inspection) times than less intelligent individuals can.

Two leaders in the field of cognitive psychology, Allen Newell and Herbert A. Simon, used computers to model intelligence. The underlying idea is that computers can, in some sense, show a kind of intelligence similar to that shown by humans. In 1972, Newell and Simon proposed a general theory of problem solving, much of which was implemented on the computer. It involves heuristics such as means–ends analysis, whereby one seeks, at each step of problem solving, to reduce as much as possible the distance between the solution and where one is in the problem.

Marcel Just and Patricia Carpenter showed that complex intelligence test items, such as figural matrix problems involving reasoning with geometric shapes, could be solved by a computer program at a level of accuracy comparable to that of human test-takers.

The models described above are serial-processing models, whereby the computer takes steps in sequence. David E. Rumelhart and Jay L. McClelland, proposed what they call parallel distributed processing models of the mind. These models postulate that many types of information processing occur at once, rather than just one at a time.

Perhaps the dominant cognitive approach today is one that stresses the role of working memory in intelligence. Patrick Kyllonen, Randall Engle, and others have suggested that the main source of differences in performance on intellectual tasks is in people's differential working-memory capacities, that is, their ability to remember and manipulate recently presented information in their minds.

Cognitive-Contextual Theories

Cognitive-contextual theories deal with the way cognitive processes operate in various environmental contexts. Two of the major theories of this type have been proposed by Howard Gardner and Robert Sternberg.

In 1983, Gardner proposed a theory of what he called multiple intelligences. In the 1999 version of the theory, the multiple intelligences include, at minimum, linguistic, logical–mathematical, spatial, musical, bodily–kinesthetic, naturalist, interpersonal, and intrapersonal intelligences. Gardner has also speculated about the existence of an existential intelligence.

An alternative theory, also taking into account both cognition and context, is Sternberg's triarchic theory of successful intelligence. According to Sternberg, intelligence has three aspects. These aspects relate intelligence to what goes on internally within a person, what goes on in the external world, and to experience, which mediates between the internal and external worlds.

The first aspect is the set of cognitive processes and representations that form the core of all thought. Sternberg has distinguished three kinds of processes: those involved in deciding what to do and, later, in deciding how well it was done; those involved in doing what one has decided to do; and those involved in learning how to do it in the first place. The second aspect is the application of these processes to the external world. According to Sternberg, mental processes serve three functions in the everyday world: adaptation to existing environments, the shaping of existing environments into new ones, and the selection of new environments when old ones prove unsatisfactory. According to the theory, more successful intelligent persons are not just those who can execute many cognitive processes quickly or well. Greater intelligence is additionally reflected in knowing what one's strengths and weaknesses are and capitalizing upon strengths while remedying or compensating for weaknesses. Successfully intelligent persons, then, find a niche in which they can operate effectively.

The third aspect of Sternberg's triarchic theory is the integration of the internal and external worlds through experience. One measure of intelligence is the ability to cope with relatively novel situations. The abilities to cope with relative novelty and to automatize cognitive processing are seen as interrelated: The more a person is able to automatize the tasks of daily life, the more mental resources there are left to cope with novelty.

Peter Salovey and John Mayer proposed the construct of emotional intelligence. It was popularized by Daniel Goleman in a 1995 book. It is the ability to perceive accurately, appraise, and express emotion; the ability to access and/or generate feelings when they facilitate thought; the ability to understand emotion and emotional knowledge; and the ability to regulate emotions to promote emotional and intellectual growth. Several tests are now available to measure emotional intelligence. They generally show modest to moderate correlations with conventional tests of intelligence. They also predict various forms of real-world behavior.

Biological Theories

Biological theories are based in the neuropsychological functioning that produces, or at least is correlated with, intelligent behavior. Several biological approaches have been proposed.

One approach has been the investigation of the types of intellectual performance as related to the regions of the brain from which they originate. An American researcher in this area, Jerre Levy, found that the left hemisphere is superior in analytical functioning, of which a prime example is the use of language. The right hemisphere is superior in many forms of visual and spatial performance and tends to be more synthetic and holistic in its functioning than the left.

A second approach to research has involved the use of brain-wave recordings to study the relation between these waves and either performance on ability tests or in various kinds of cognitive tasks. Researchers, such as British researcher P. G. Caryl, have found a relationship between certain aspects of electroencephalogram (EEG) and event-related potential (ERP) waves and scores on standard psychometric tests of intelligence.

A third and approach involves the measurement of blood flow in the brain, which is a fairly direct indicator of functional activity in brain tissue. In such studies, the amount and location of blood flow in the brain is monitored while subjects perform cognitive tasks. Using positron emission tomography (PET), Richard Haier discovered that people who perform better on conventional tests of intelligence often show less activation in relevant portions of the brain than those who do not perform as well. This pattern of results suggests that the better performers find the tasks easier and thus invoke less effort than the poorer performers do.

Development of Intelligence

There have been diverse approaches to studying the development of intelligence. Psychometric theorists, for instance, have sought to understand how intelligence develops in terms of changes in the factors of intelligence over time and changes in the amounts of the various abilities that children have. For example, the concept of mental age was popular during the first half of the twentieth century. A given mental age was believed to represent an average child's level of mental functioning for a given chronological age. Thus, an average 10-year-old would have a mental age of 10, but an above-average 8-year-old or a below-average 12-year-old might also have a mental age of 10 years. The concept of mental age has fallen into disfavor, however, and is used only rarely now. The concept does not work well over a chronological age of roughly 16. Moreover, its assumption of perfectly smooth continuous mental development is questionable.

The Theory of Jean Piaget

Jean Piaget, a Swiss psychologist, suggested that the child explores the world, observes regularities, and makes generalizations, much as a scientist does. Two fundamental cognitive processes are alleged to work in a somewhat reciprocal fashion. Assimilation involves incorporating new information into an already existing cognitive structure. Accommodation involves forming a new cognitive structure to incorporate new information. Cognitive development, according to Piaget, represents a dynamic equilibrium between these two processes of assimilation and accommodation.

Piaget also postulated that there are four major periods in intellectual development. The first, the sensorimotor period, extends from birth until roughly 2 years of age. During this period, a child learns how to modify reflexes to make them more adaptive, coordinate actions, retrieve hidden objects, and, eventually, to begin representing information mentally. During the second, preoperational period, from about 2 to 7 years of age, a child experiences the growth of language and mental imagery. He or she also learns to focus on single perceptual dimensions, such as color and shape. The third, concrete-operational period, is from about 7 to 12 years of age. It is the period during which a child develops an important set of skills that are referred to as conservation skills. The child will recognize that substances stay the same in amount, regardless of their form. Finally, children emerge into the fourth, formal-operational period, which begins at about age 12 and continues throughout life. The formal-operational child develops thinking skills in all logical combinations and learns to think with abstract concepts.

The Theory of Lev Vygotsky

Lev S. Vygotsky, a Soviet psychologist, suggested that intellectual development may be largely influenced by a child's interactions with others: a child sees others thinking and acting in certain ways and then internalizes and models what is seen. Vygotsky also proposed the notion of a zone of proximal development (ZPD), which is the range of ability between a person's observable level of ability and the person's latent capacity. This latent capacity is not directly observable, but may be detected by providing a context in which the latent capacity may be revealed and expressed. The ZPD is sometimes termed the zone of potential development.

Measuring Intelligence

Early Historical Background

The publication of Charles Darwin's *The Origin of Species* in 1859 had a profound effect on many lines of scientific work. Darwin suggested that the capabilities of humans are, in some sense, continuous with those of lower animals. Hence, they can be understood through scientific investigation. One person who was strongly influenced by Darwin's thinking was his cousin, Sir Francis Galton. For 7 years – between 1884 and 1890 – Galton maintained a laboratory at the South Kensington Museum in London. For a small fee, visitors could have themselves measured on a variety of psychophysical tasks. These tasks included weight discrimination and sensitivity to musical pitch. Galton believed that these tests measured more than just psychophysical abilities. He believed that psychophysical abilities are the basis of intelligence and, hence, that his tasks were measures of intelligence. Galton's intelligence test, therefore, required a person to perform simple tasks, such as deciding which of two weights was heavier or showing how forcefully he could squeeze his hand. The Galtonian tradition was taken to the United States by the psychologist James McKeen Cattell.

The Intelligence Quotient Test

A more influential tradition of mental testing was developed in France by Alfred Binet and his collaborator, Theodore Simon. In 1904, the minister of public instruction in Paris named a commission to study or create tests that would insure that mentally retarded children received an adequate education. The minister was also concerned that certain children were being placed in classes for the retarded not because they were retarded, but because they had behavior problems, and teachers did not want them in their classrooms. Binet and Simon proposed that tests of intelligence should measure skills such as judgment, comprehension, and reasoning – the same kinds of skills measured on most intelligence tests today. Binet's early test was taken to the United States by a Stanford University psychologist, Lewis Terman, whose version came to be called the Stanford-Binet test. This test has been revised frequently and continues to be in use.

The Stanford-Binet test and others similar to it have traditionally yielded, at the very least, an overall score referred to as an intelligence quotient (IQ). In its most recent form, this test as well as the Wechsler Adult Intelligence Scale and the Wechsler Intelligence Scale for Children yield an overall IQ and other scores as well.

More recent tests of intelligence have expanded the range of abilities tested. For example, in 1997, J. P. Das and Jack Naglieri produced a test, the Cognitive Assessment System, based on a theory of intelligence first proposed by a Russian psychologist, Alexander Luria. The test measures planning abilities, attentional abilities, and simultaneous and successive processing abilities.

IQ was originally computed as the ratio of mental age to chronological (physical) age, multiplied by 100. It is thus sometimes referred to as a ratio IQ. For example, if a child of age 8 had a mental age of 10 (i.e., performed on the test at the level of an average 10-year-old), the child was assigned an IQ of $(10/8) \times 100$, or 125. If the 8-year-old had a mental age of 6, the child's IQ would be $(6/8) \times 100$, or 75. A score of 100, whereby the mental age equals the chronological age, is average.

As discussed above, the concept of mental age has fallen into disrepute, and few tests continue to involve the computation of mental ages. Many tests still yield an IQ, but it is most often computed on the basis of statistical distributions. The scores are assigned on the basis of what percentage of people of a given group would be expected to have a certain IQ. Scores computed in this way are called deviation IQs.

The Distribution of IQ Scores

Intelligence test scores follow an approximately normal distribution, meaning that most people score near the middle of the distribution of scores. Scores drop off fairly rapidly in frequency in either direction from the center of the distribution. For example, on the IQ scale, about two-thirds of all scores fall between IQs of 85 and 115, and about 95% of scores fall between 70 and 130. Put another way, only one out of 20 scores differs from the average IQ (100) by more than 30 points.

It has been common to associate certain levels of IQ with labels. For example, at the upper end, the label gifted is sometimes assigned to people with IQs over a certain point, such as 130. In addition, at the lower end, mental retardation has been classified into different degrees depending upon IQ; therefore, for example, IQs of 70–84 have been classified as borderline retarded, 55–69 as mildly retarded, 40–54 as moderately retarded, 25–39 as severely retarded, and IQs below 25 as profoundly retarded.

Many psychologists now believe that IQ represents only a part of intelligence, and intelligence is only one factor in both mental retardation and giftedness. Most current definitions of mental retardation stress adaptive skills as well as IQ and also emphasize attributes such as creativity, motivation, and achievement in conceptions of giftedness.

The Heritability and Malleability of Intelligence

Historically, intelligence has been viewed as a more or less fixed trait. This view conceives intelligence as something people are born with. The function of development is thus to allow this genetic endowment to express itself. A number of investigators have suggested that intelligence is highly heritable, and that it is transmitted through the genes. Heritability is here defined as the proportion of individual-differences variance that is genetically transmitted. Other investigators believe that intelligence is minimally heritable, if at all. Most authorities take an intermediate position. However, all agree that heritability operates within a reaction range, meaning that a given genotype for intelligence can result in a wide range of phenotypes, depending on how environmental factors interact with genetic ones.

Several methods are used to assess the heritability of intelligence. The most well known is perhaps the study of identical twins reared apart. For a variety of reasons, identical twins are occasionally separated at or near birth. If the twins are raised apart, and if it is assumed that when twins are separated, they are randomly distributed across environments (often a dubious assumption), then the twins would heritably have in common all of their genes, but none of their environment, except for chance environmental overlap. As a result, the correlation between their performances on tests of intelligence can provide an estimate of the proportion of variation in test scores due to heredity. Another method of computing the hereditary effect on intelligence involves comparing the relationship between intelligence test scores of identical twins and those of fraternal twins.

It appears that roughly half the variation in intelligence test scores is caused by hereditary influences. However, Robert Plomin and others have shown that the heritability of intelligence increases with age, suggesting that genetic factors become more important and environmental factors less important to individual differences in intelligence with increasing age. In adulthood, heritability may reach as high as 70% or more. The estimates are computed, for the most part, on the basis of intelligence test scores, so that the estimates are only for that part of intelligence measured by the tests. An interesting recent finding by Eric Turkheimer and his colleagues is that heritability appears to be substantially higher in higher social classes than in lower social classes.

Whatever the heritability factor of IQ, an entirely separate issue is whether intelligence can be increased. The work by a New Zealand researcher, James Flynn, has shown that, in the middle and later twentieth century, scores on intelligence tests rose rather steadily throughout the world. The precise reason for the increase is unknown, although speculations include better education, better nutrition, and advances in technology.

Despite the general increase in scores, average IQs continue to vary across both countries and different socioeconomic groups. For example, many researchers have found a positive correlation between socioeconomic status and IQ, although they disagree over the reason for the relationship. Most psychologists agree that differences in educational opportunities play an important role, and some investigators believe that there is a hereditary basis for the difference as well. However, there is simply no broad consensus on the issue of why the differences exist.

Again, the differences are based on IQ, not broadly defined intelligence.

No matter how heritable intelligence is, some aspects of it are still malleable. Heritability of a trait is a separate issue from its malleability. For example, height is not only highly heritable, but also highly modifiable by nutrition and other environmental factors. Thus, with intervention, even a highly heritable trait can be modified. There is a growing body of evidence suggesting that aspects of intelligence also can be modified. Intelligence, in the view of many psychologists, is not merely a fixed trait. A program of training in intellectual skills can increase some aspects of a person's level of intelligence. No training program – no environmental condition of any sort – is likely to make a genius of someone with low measured intelligence. However, some gains are possible, and a number of programs have been developed for increasing intellectual skills. A main trend for psychologists working in the intelligence field has been to combine testing and training functions in order to enable people to optimize their intelligence. Such work needs to take into account technological advances because the very existence of technology changes the nature of intelligence. Today, skills in computer literacy and database management, which were needed only rarely 50 years ago, have become important. Therefore, the nature of intelligence is, to some extent, a moving target, one that researchers in the field must constantly track.

See also: Cognition: Overview and Recent Trends; Vygotsky and Recent Developments.

Further Reading

Binet, A. and Simon, T. (1916). *The Development of Intelligence in Children*. Baltimore, MD: Williams and Wilkins.

Carroll, J. B. (1993). *Human Cognitive Abilities: A Survey of Factor-Analytic Studies*. New York: Cambridge University Press.

Cattell, R. B. (1971). *Abilities: Their Structure, Growth, and Action*. Boston, MA: Houghton Mifflin.

Ceci, S. J. (1996). *On Intelligence*. Cambridge, MA: Harvard University Press.

Cronbach, L. J. (1957). The two disciplines of scientific psychology. *American Psychologist* **12**, 671–684.

Deary, I. J. (1999). Intelligence and visual and auditory information processing. In Ackerman, P. L., Kyllonen, P. C., and Roberts, R. D. (eds.) *Learning and Individual Differences: Process, Trait, and Content Determinants*, pp 111–130. Mahwah, NJ: Erlbaum.

Deary, I. J. and Caryl, P. G. (1997). Neuroscience and human intelligence differences. *Trends in Neurosciences* **20**, 365–371.

Engle, R. W., Kane, M. J., and Tuholski, S. W. (1999). Individual differences in working memory capacity and what they tell us about controlled attention, general fluid intelligence, and functions of the prefrontal cortex. In Miyake, A. and Shah, P. (eds.) *Models of Working Memory: Mechanisms of Active Maintenance and Executive Control*, pp 102–134. Cambridge: Cambridge University Press.

Gardner, H. (1983). *Frames of Mind: The Theory of Multiple Intelligences*. New York: Basic Books.

Gardner (1999). *Intelligence Reframed: Multiple Intelligences for the 21st Century*. New York: Basic books.

Guilford, J. P. (1950). Creativity. *American Psychologist* **5**(9), 444–454.

Haier, R. J., Siegel, B., Tang, C., Abel, L., and Buchsbaum, M. S. (1992). Intelligence and changes in regional cerebral glucose metabolic rate following learning. *Intelligence* **16**(3–4), 415–426.

Horn, J. L. (1994). Theory of fluid and crystallized intelligence. In Sternberg, R. J. (ed.) *The Encyclopedia of Human Intelligence,* vol. 1, pp 443–451. New York: Macmillan.

Hunt, E. B., Lunneberg, C., and Lewis, J. (1975). What does it mean to be high verbal? *Cognitive Psychology* **7**, 194–227.

Jensen, A. R. (1998). *The g Factor: The Science of Mental Ability*. Westport, CT: Praeger/Greenwood.

Just, M. A. and Carpenter, P. A. (1992). A capacity theory of comprehension: Individual differences in working memory. *Psychological Review* **99**, 122–149.

Kyllonen, P. C. (1996). Is working memory capacity Spearman's g? In Dennis, I. and Tapsfield, P. (eds.) *Human Abilities: Their Nature and Measurement*, pp 49–75. Mahwah, NJ: Erlbaum.

Mayer, J. D. and Salovey, P. (1993). The intelligence of emotional intelligence. *Intelligence* **197**, 433–442.

Neisser, U. (ed.) (1998). *The Rising Curve*. Washington, DC: American Psychological Association.

Newell, A. and Simon, H. A. (1972). *Human Problem Solving*. Englewood Cliffs, NJ: Prentice-Hall.

Piaget, J. (1972). *The Psychology of Intelligence*. Totowa, NJ: Littlefield-Adams.

Plomin, R. (1997). Identifying genes for cognitive abilities and disabilities. In Sternberg, R. J. and Grigorenko, E. L. (eds.) *Intelligence, Heredity, and Environment*, pp 89–104. New York: Cambridge University Press.

Preiss, D. D. and Sternberg, R. J. (2006). In everyday life, tool-free abilities do not exist. *Educational Technology* **46**(2), 43–47.

Spearman, C. (1904). 'General intelligence,' objectively determined and measured. *American Journal of Psychology* **15**(2), 201–293.

Spearman, C. (1927). *The Abilities of Man*. New York: Macmillan.

Sternberg, R. J. (1990). *Metaphors of Mind: Conceptions of the Nature of Intelligence*. New York: Cambridge University Press.

Sternberg, R. J. (1997). *Successful Intelligence*. New York: Plume.

Sternberg, R. J. (ed.) (2000). *Handbook of Intelligence*. New York: Cambridge University Press.

Sternberg, R. J. (2003). *Wisdom, Intelligence, and Creativity Synthesized*. New York: Cambridge University Press.

Sternberg, R. J. (2004). Culture and intelligence. *American Psychologist* **59**(5), 325–338.

Sternberg, R. J., Conway, B. E., Ketron, J. L., and Bernstein, M. (1981). People's conceptions of intelligence. *Journal of Personality and Social Psychology* **41**, 37–55.

Sternberg, R. J., Grigorenko, E. L., and Kidd, K. K. (2005). Intelligence, race, and genetics. *American Psychologist* **60**(1), 46–59.

Terman, L. M. and Merrill, M. A. (1937). *Measuring Intelligence*. Boston, MA: Houghton Mifflin.

Thurstone, L. L. (1938). *Primary Mental Abilities*. Chicago, IL: University of Chicago Press.

Turkheimer, E., Haley, A., Waldron, M., D'Onofrio, B., and Gottesman, I. I. (2003). Socioeconomic status modifies heritability of IQ in young children. *Psychological Science* **14**, 623–628.

Vygotsky, L. S. (1978). *Mind in Society: The Development of Higher Psychological Processes*. Cambridge, MA: Harvard University Press.

Concept Learning

S J Unsworth, San Diego State University, San Diego, CA, USA
D L Medin, Northwestern University, Evanston, IL, USA

In what follows, we use concept to refer to a mental representation and category to refer to the set of entities or examples picked out by the concept. It is generally accepted that instances of a concept are organized into categories. Almost all theories about the structure of categories assume that, roughly speaking, similar things tend to belong to the same category and dissimilar things tend to be in different categories. For example, robins and sparrows both belong to the category bird and are more similar to each other than they are to squirrels or pumpkins. Similarity is a pretty vague term, but most commonly it is defined in terms of shared properties or attributes. Although alternative theories assume concepts are structured in terms of shared properties, theories differ greatly in their organizational principles.

Theories of Concept Representation and Learning

The Classical View

The classical view assumes that concepts have defining features that act like criteria or rules for determining category membership. For example, a triangle is a closed geometric form of three sides with the sum of the interior angles equaling 180°. Each of these properties is necessary for an entity to be a triangle, and together these properties are sufficient to define triangle.

A fair amount of research has examined people's knowledge about object categories such as bird, chair, and furniture and this evidence goes against the classical view. Not only do people fail to come up with defining features, but also they do not necessarily agree with each other (or even with themselves when asked at different times) on whether something is an example of a category. Philosophers and scientists also have worried about whether naturally occurring things such as plants and animals (so-called natural kinds) have defining features. The current consensus is that most natural concepts do not fit the classical view.

The Probabilistic View

The major alternative to the classical view is the probabilistic view which argues that concepts are organized around properties that are characteristic or typical of category members but crucially, they need not be true of all members. That is, the features are only probable. For example, most people's concept of bird may include the properties of building nests, flying, and having hollow bones, even though not all birds have these properties (e.g., ostriches and penguins). The probabilistic view has major implications for how we think about categories. First, if categories are organized around characteristic properties, some members may have more of these properties than other members. In this sense, some members may be better examples or more typical of a concept than others. For example, it has been found that the more frequently a category member's properties appeared within a category, the higher was its rated typicality for that category. Robins were rated to be very typical birds and penguins rated as very atypical birds. A second implication is that category boundaries may be fuzzy. Nonmembers of a category may have almost as many characteristic properties of a category as do certain members. For example, whales have a lot of the characteristic properties of fish, and yet they are mammals. Third, learning about a category cannot be equated with determining what the defining features are because there may not be any.

Typicality: Central tendency versus ideality

Is typicality only based on central tendency? Although typicality effects are robust (and problematic for the classical view), other research shows that the underlying basis for typicality effects may vary with both the kind of category being studied and with the population being studied. While the internal structure of taxonomic categories is based primarily on the central tendency (or the average member) of a category, the internal structure of goal-derived categories, such as things to wear in the snow, is determined by some ideal (or the best possible member) associated with the category. The best example of snow clothing, a down jacket, was not the example that was most like other category members; instead, it was the example with the maximum value of the goal-related dimension of providing warmth.

One might think that ideals will only come into play when the category of interest lacks the natural similarity structure that characterizes common taxonomic categories, such as bird, fish, and tree. However, for tree experts (people who know a lot about trees, such as landscapers, parks workers, and taxonomists), the internal structure of the category tree is organized around the positive ideal of height and the negative ideal of weediness. The best examples of tree are not trees of average height but trees of extraordinary height (and free of weedy characteristics like having weak limbs, growing where they are not wanted, and being susceptible to disease).

Indeed, research does suggest that people who have considerable knowledge in a domain tend to base typicality judgments on ideals and not on the number of typical features. For example, for Itzá Maya adults living in the rainforests of Guatemala, the best example of bird is the wild turkey which is culturally significant, prized for its meat, and strikingly beautiful. The fact that US tree experts based typicality on ideals suggests that it is not just that the Itzá have a different notion of what typicality means. It has also been found that Native American and European American fishermen's typicality judgments were based on ideals, although those ideals differed somewhat across groups.

Prototype versus exemplar theories

If categories are not represented in terms of definitions, what form do our mental representations take? One suggestion about how concepts are represented is known as the family resemblance principle. The general idea is that category members resemble each other in the way that family members do. A simple summary representation for such a family resemblance structure would be an example that possessed all the characteristic features of a category. The best example is referred to as the prototype.

In a prototype model of categorization, classifying a new example is done by comparing the new item to the prototype. If the candidate example is similar enough to the prototype for a category, it is classified as a member of that category. More detailed analyses, however, show problems with prototypes as mental representations. Prototype theory implies that the only information abstracted from categories is the central tendency. A prototype representation discards information concerning category size, the variability of the examples, and correlations among attributes, and people can use all three of these types of information.

An alternative approach, which is also consistent with the probabilistic view, assumes that much more information about specific examples is preserved. This approach appropriately falls under the general heading of exemplar theories. Exemplar models assume that people initially learn some examples of different concepts and then classify a new instance on the basis of how similar it is to the previously learned examples. The idea is that a new example reminds the person of similar old examples and that people assume that similar items will belong to the same category. For example, suppose someone is asked whether large birds are more or less likely to fly than small birds. He/she will probably answer "less likely," based on retrieving examples from memory and noting that the only nonflying birds one can think of are large (e.g., penguin and ostrich).

Quite a few experiments have contrasted the predictions of exemplar and prototype models. In head-to-head competition, exemplar models have been considerably more successful than prototype models. Why should exemplar models fare better than prototype models? One of the main functions of classification is to allow one to make inferences and predictions on the basis of partial information. Relative to prototype models, exemplar models tend to be conservative about discarding information that facilitates predictions. For instance, sensitivity to correlations of properties within a category enables finer predictions: from noting that a bird is large, one can predict that it cannot sing. In short, exemplar models support predictions and inferences better than do prototype models.

More recent research has pointed to three major limitations of these simple forms of prototype and exemplar models:

1. they have narrowly focused on categorization and have paid little attention to how other conceptual functions, such as communication and inference, may affect concept representation and learning;
2. they view learning as a passive accumulation of statistical information rather than an active learning that may reflect particular learner goals; and
3. they pay little attention to how theoretical notions and causal reasoning organize learning.

With respect to the second point, we have just reviewed evidence from a number of populations, indicating that typicality is driven by ideals and that later learning builds on earlier learning. If category ideals tend to be learned first then they will have an important role in the development of categories, and modelers are beginning to shift to this more active view of learning. With respect to the role of theories, there is evidence that using (abstract) similarity relations may be likely to be a strategy of last resort, used only when more relevant information is unavailable. Let us examine the theory view in a bit more detail.

The Theory View

A number of researchers have argued that the organization of concepts is knowledge based (rather than similarity based) and driven by intuitive theories about the world. The idea that concepts might be knowledge based rather than similarity based suggests a natural way in which concepts may change – namely, through the addition of new knowledge and theoretical principles. There is also good evidence that these theories help determine which abstract and observable features learners pay attention to. We have a different set of categories for mental disorders now than we had 100 years ago, in part because our knowledge base has become more refined. Often knowledge of diseases develops from information about patterns of symptoms to a specification of underlying causes. For example, the advanced stages of syphilis were treated as a mental disorder until the causes and consequences of this venereal disease were better understood. Recently, it has been shown that clinical psychologists organize their knowledge of mental disorders in terms of rich causal theories and that these theories (and not the atheoretical diagnostic manual they are supposed to use) guide their diagnostic classification and reasoning.

Domain Specificity

Several constraints have been hypothesized to mold concept formation in different domains, including the domains of biology, psychology, mathematics, and physics. The current consensus is that the potential for variation in conceptual knowledge across cultural communities is mediated by universal constraints on learning and the ways in which they interact with culture-specific experiences. Concepts are the building blocks of thought and one way to understand the flexibility of concept learning is to consider whether people in different cultures think differently. Usually, this question is tied up with the question of whether and how language influences thought and we will not give a separate treatment of this issue. Of course, if thought processes of two cultural groups were radically incommensurable, one would quickly realize that there were dramatic differences but feel at something of a loss to explain them. The fact that one part of learning a foreign language involves finding out what term or word is used in that language to refer to bird, or fish, or chair, or Tuesday, or mother suggests that comparable concepts and categories are in play. Nevertheless, culture affects learning and knowledge construction. Rather than provide a comprehensive catalog of the various principles constraining knowledge construction in each domain, we present a few detailed accounts of cultural research on concept formation, using for illustration cross-cultural conceptions of plants and animals (the domain of folk biology) and counting and calculation (the domain of folk mathematics).

Concept Learning in the Domain of Biology

The field of folk biology is blessed with many intriguing and important issues that lend themselves to an analysis in terms of culture and cognition. Biological concepts are believed to be processed and organized according to evolved cognitive structures that are functionally autonomous with respect to biological information, and for this reason are thought of as belonging to a separate domain of cognitive processing. Building on decades of work in ethnobiology, research has shown that a few key principles guide the recognition and organization of biological information in similar ways across cultures, although important variation is produced by differences in expertise and other cultural factors.

First, there is marked cross-cultural agreement on the hierarchical classification of living things, such that plants and animals are grouped according to a ranked taxonomy with mutually exclusive groupings of entities at each level. For instance, across cultural groups, the highest level of taxonomic organization includes the most general categories, such as the folk kingdom rank (which includes groupings, such as plants and animals), and lower levels distinguish between increasingly greater degrees of specificity (e.g., life forms, such as tree or bird; generic species level, such as oak or blue jay). Furthermore, the generic species (in local settings the vast majority of genera are represented by a single species, so we use this term) level appears to be consistently privileged for inductive inference when generalizing properties across plants and animals (it is the most abstract level for which inductive confidence is strong and only minimal inductive advantage is gained at more subordinate levels). There is also cross-cultural agreement in the assumption that the appearance and behavior of every generic species is caused by an internal biological (and usually unspecified) essence that is inherited from the birth parents and is responsible for kindhood persistence in the face of physical and developmental transformation.

However, there is also considerable variability within these universal constraints in concept formation as a function of both experience with the natural world and cultural salience (two highly related factors). For instance, the basic level (the level at which they possess the greatest knowledge) for urban undergraduates is the life form (e.g., bird, fish, and tree), but for groups that have more direct experience with the natural environment and greater expertise, the basic level corresponds to the generic species level.

The remarkable cross-cultural agreement in the structure of folk biological organization is, at the same time, culturally variable. Correlations across groups of 0.70 appear quite strong but explain less than half the variance. Although some of these differences might be attributed to experience, other findings implicate cultural differences. For instance, when asked to sort biological kinds into categories, individuals from different communities vary not only in their taxonomic sorting but also in the degree to which they spontaneously sort along ecological dimensions. This difference is not as predictable on the basis of expertise alone. For example, Menominee Native American fisherman and European American fishermen, who both live in rural Wisconsin and have equivalent expertise about fish and fish habitats, differ in that Menominee fishermen are significantly more likely to sort in terms of ecological relationships.

Similar differences in ecological orientation have been found for children from these communities, such that Menominee children were more likely to reason about shared properties between living things using ecological relations, relative to rural European American children. In turn, rural European American children were more likely to employ ecological-based reasoning for shared properties than were urban children. In short, differences in ecological orientation reflect a confluence of experience-based and culturally based factors in folk biological thought.

Cultural differences in cognitive processing, concept representation, and behavior can be thought of as reflecting routines of practices or habits of the mind. Cultural groups establish practices over time, and the history of these practices may lead to regularities in the ways groups participate in the everyday activities within their communities. These practices may be associated, implicitly or explicitly, with different epistemologies that determine what sorts of things are presupposed, go without saying, and seem natural. For example, European Americans tend to conceive of nature as something external, to be cared for, and respected; in contrast, Native Americans are more likely to see themselves as part of nature. These sorts of presuppositions are likely to be embedded in curricula and school practices and represent a challenge to students from cultures and communities that do not share them.

Cultural practices are not immutable, static traits that are attached to participants (a view which can lead to overly deterministic views of cognition), but exist in tension with emergent goals, practices, and situationally specific affordances. Thus, one might design a biology curriculum for Native American students emphasizing ecological relationships, but then build on this base to suggest the value of other forms of organization (e.g., taxonomic). There is increasing evidence that taking advantage of the cultural practices that children bring to the classroom leads to better motivation, identification with learning, and academic performance.

Concept Learning in the Domain of Mathematics

Folk biological research has tended to compare different cultural groups and to identify robust similarities (and differences) in reasoning and representation. Studies of mathematical concepts have expanded on this strategy by using developmental comparisons and analyzing similarities between human and nonhuman species to identify universal or core principles. The domain of mathematics spans a wide variety of concepts, including numerosity, geometry, trigonometry, and so on.

We will limit our review to numerosity, counting, and calculation. A great deal of evidence suggests that for humans and other species there are evolved principles that assist in the representation of numerosity, and

that different principles can constrain representations in particular ways, depending on the set size of elements. Importantly, however, it has been proposed that the systems for large and small numerosity can interact for humans in ways not possible for nonhuman species. Number words and verbal counting may link together systems for small and large numerosities so that, through counting, distinctions can be made between large numerosities that differ in as little as one element.

The flexibility in concepts of numerosity afforded by natural language leads to questions about variability in representations of numerosity and counting as a function of language and other cultural inputs. Some innovative research has examined the different counting systems that have emerged in different cultural communities throughout the world. For instance, before contact with Western culture in 1940, the Oksapmin people in the West Sepik province of Papua New Guinea used a 27-body-part count system, beginning with the thumb on one hand and enumerating discrete points along the upper half of the body (including head and shoulders) and ending on the little finger on the other hand. Counting past 27 involves moving back along the same 27 points until the desired numerosity is reached. In addition, as individuals become more involved in the cash economy, this counting system becomes coopted for arithmetic calculations in addition to or in the place of enumeration and, in some cases, is even transformed to a base-10 system. Although cultural differences in counting systems are well established, not much work has examined the impact of these systems on the representation of numerosity.

Other research has examined the ways in which mathematical concepts, such as calculation processes and representations, are shaped by context-specific goals and culture-specific practices. For instance, grocery shoppers engage in mathematical calculations in response to specific shopping-related goals, and these calculations depend on the resources and environmental tools available to the shopper in the grocery store. Examples have been reported in which a shopper who, upon suspecting a price error for a block of cheese, sorted through a bin of cheese to find a block of similar weight and noted the difference in price that confirmed his suspicions. Had the bin of cheese not been available, the shopper would have had to mentally calculate the correct price based on listed-price-per-weight information.

An important issue is the relation between these sorts of out-of-school goal related strategies and in-school mathematics learning. Community-specific goals can lead to a greater frequency and, therefore, greater proficiency for some calculations over others. For example, research has shown that 10–12-year-old children in Brazil with little or no education, who sold candy in urban streets, were highly likely to use ratio calculations during vending activities and were better at ratio comparisons than same-aged children with formal education experience. Other work has revealed that African American middle school and high-school students vary in the extent to which they engage in mathematical calculations to evaluate basketball performance because of differences in the structure of the practice of basketball and level of commitment to basketball. High-school students were more likely to calculate formal statistics (such as average and percent) of their own and others' basketball performance, and these calculations were higher when ways of keeping and reporting basketball statistics were increasingly available to students. This work points out that the players' use and approach to mathematics during their everyday cultural practice may differ dramatically from the approach taken to school mathematics – the use of mathematics in a student's own cultural context is often more engaging. Related work with the children of sugarcane farmers found complementary tendencies to approach mathematical problem solving in different ways depending upon the value ascribed to the context or practice in play.

Conclusions

Concept learning is one of the most exciting and fundamental research areas within cognitive science because it concerns the very building blocks of thought. Early models which assumed that category learning consists of the accumulation of information about entities in the world have been superseded by approaches which stress that learning is in the service of goals, that it is guided by evolved, domain-specific constraints, and molded by cultural practices.

See also: Knowledge Domains and Domain Learning; The Adult Development of Cognition and Learning.

Further Reading

Anderson, J. R. (1990). *The Adaptive Character of Thought.* Hillsdale, NJ: Erlbaum.
Atran, S., Medin, D., and Ross, N. (2005). The cultural mind: Environmental decision making and cultural modeling within and across populations. *Psychological Review* **112**, 744–776.
Barsalou, L. W. (1985). Ideals, central tendency, and frequency of instantiation as determinants of graded structure in categories. *Journal of Experimental Psychology: Learning, Memory, and Cognition* **11**, 629–654.
Berlin, B. (1992). *Ethnobiological classification.* Princeton, NJ: Princeton University.
Carey, S. (1985). *Conceptual Change in Childhood.* Cambridge, MA: Bradford Books.
Gutierrez, K. D. and Rogoff, B. (2003). Cultural ways of learning: Individual traits or repertoires of practice. *Educational Researcher* **32**, 19–25.
Hauser, M. D. and Spelke, E. (2004). Evolutionary and developmental foundations of human knowledge. In Gazzaniga, M. (ed.) *The Cognitive Neurosciences, III,* pp 853–864. Cambridge: MIT Press.
Keil, F. (1989). *Concepts, Kinds, and Cognitive Development.* Cambridge, MA: MIT Press.
Lave, J. (1988). *Cognition in Practice.* New York: Cambridge University Press.
Medin, D. and Atran, S. (2004). The native mind: Biological categorization and reasoning in development and across cultures. *Psychological Review* **111**, 960–983.
Murphy, G. L. (2002). *The Big Book of Concepts.* Cambridge, MA: MIT Press.
Nasir, N. (2000). ''Points ain't everything'': Emergent goals and average and percent understandings in the play of basketball among African-American students. *Anthropology and Education Quarterly* **31**, 283–305.
NRC/National Research Council (2000). *How People Learn: Brain, Mind, Experience, and School: Expanded Edition.* Washington, DC: National Academies Press.
NRC/National Research Council (2005). *How Students Learn: History, Math, and Science in the Classroom.* Washington, DC: National Academies Press.
Rosch, E. and Mervis, C. B. (1975). Family resemblance: Studies in the internal structure of categories. *Cognitive Psychology* **7**, 573–605.
Saxe, G. B. (1999). Cognition, development, and cultural practices. *New Directions for Child and Adolescent Development* **83**, 19–35.
Saxe, G. (2006). The mathematics of child street vendors. *Child Development* **59**, 1415–1425.
Smith, E. and Medin, D. (1981). *Categories and Concepts.* Cambridge, MA: Harvard University Press.

Problem Solving and Human Expertise

T J Nokes and C D Schunn, University of Pittsburgh, Pittsburgh, PA, USA
M T H Chi, Arizona State University, Tempe, AZ, USA

Glossary

Absolute methods – A research methodology that consists of an in-depth examination of high-level experts, usually in a task specific to their domain of expertise (e.g., playing a game of chess for chess experts).

Chunk – A unit of knowledge that is composed of several smaller units of information.

Declarative knowledge – This consists of descriptions about the world including facts, strategies, and principles, and is commonly referred to as knowing that.

Knowledge compilation – A cognitive mechanism hypothesized to interpret declarative knowledge into a set of specific procedural rules given a particular goal.

Procedural knowledge – This consists of information for how to perform particular actions to accomplish task goals, and is commonly referred to as knowing how.

Relative methods – A research methodology that consists of comparing more- to less-experienced participants, often in a neutral task not typically practiced in their domain of expertise (e.g., recalling chess positions for chess experts).

Schema – A hierarchical knowledge structure that includes prototypical information about the type of problem, including declarative knowledge of objects, facts, strategies, and constraints and may also include procedural operators for solving the problem.

Problem solving is a critical cognitive activity that permeates many aspects of our day-to-day lives. We solve problems at home, school, and work ranging from the simple – such as figuring out the tip on a bill – to the complex – such as planning the logistics of a family trip. Problems sometimes have clear goals and steps you can take (as in algebra problems), but sometimes have vague goals or ambiguity about what solution methods are possible. The latter are called ill-structured problems and are considered much more difficult than well-structured problems. Developing expertise in problem solving is critical to the success of a wide range of human activities, including pursuits in science, art, business, and politics. As our society becomes ever-more technologically diverse and

sophisticated, experts are sought in more and more specialized fields. Having a scientific explanation of expert performance is needed to understand its development and to facilitate its acquisition. Knowing what to teach influences the methods of teaching. Expertise research is an area that provides a basis for determining what needs to be taught. Our purpose in writing this article is to provide an integrative review of the psychological research on expert problem solving by taking a close look at what it is, how it is acquired, and the implications for education and instruction.

We structure the article around two interrelated themes. First, that expertise can be understood from an information-processing perspective by focusing on the role of knowledge, its content, and the cognitive processes that bring that knowledge to bear during problem solving. Second, that expert performance is acquired through deliberate practice (Ericsson *et al.*, 1993). This view that expertise can be decomposed into a set of knowledge structures that are learned has implications for how to structure learning environments in order to facilitate its acquisition. In the rest of this article, we explore these themes beginning with a brief review of the methods used to examine expertise, followed by a detailed analysis of how expertise impacts each stage of problem solving. We then review the research on its acquisition with a focus on the underlying cognitive processes. In the final section, we discuss current directions and implications for instruction.

Methods

Researchers have typically used one of two approaches to study expertise, what Chi (2006) has called absolute and relative methods. Absolute methods consist of an in-depth examination of high-level experts, usually in a task specific to their domain of expertise, such as playing a game of chess for chess experts. Defining the level of expertise occurs through established criteria for a particular domain. For some domains, there are written criteria (a rating or scoring system) to determine rank, such as in chess. In other domains, expertise is determined by a certain level of professional achievement, such as becoming a professional ballet dancer, physicist, or a commercial airline pilot. The absolute approach is aimed at providing an in-depth description of the knowledge and cognitive processes underlying expert performance. This approach includes both observational studies as well as historical analyses of famous cases (e.g., James Clerk Maxwell; Nersessian, 1992). Relative methods involve comparing more- to less-experienced participants, often in a neutral task outside of their domain expertise, such as recalling chess positions for chess experts. The advantage of this approach is that it can uncover the structures and processes of performing the task, and not merely the ways that experts can excel. Both approaches have made extensive use of verbal protocols to obtain detailed data as to the thinking processes that accompany expert (and novice) performance (Ericsson, 2006).

These approaches have produced a wealth of findings on the nature of expertise (for general reviews see the section titled 'Further reading'). In the next section, we draw upon this literature to examine the impact of expertise on problem solving. We begin by describing a general theory of problem solving and then at each stage of the process describe the differences between expert versus novice performance and the explanations to account for those differences.

Expert Problem Solving: Major Findings

Most theories of human problem solving consist of some formulation of the following seven stages:

1. problem categorization,
2. construction of a mental representation of the problem,
3. search for the appropriate problem-solving operators (e.g., strategies or procedures),
4. retrieval and application of those operators to the problem,
5. evaluation of problem-solving progress and solution,
6. iterating stages 1–4 if not satisfied with progress/solution, and finally
7. storage of the solution (e.g., Newell and Simon, 1972).

These stages may not be strictly sequential, but may be iterative. In the following subsections, we describe the expertise findings relevant to each stage and discuss the theories proposed to account for them (see **Figure 1** for an illustration of the problem-solving stages and the impact of expertise on each one).

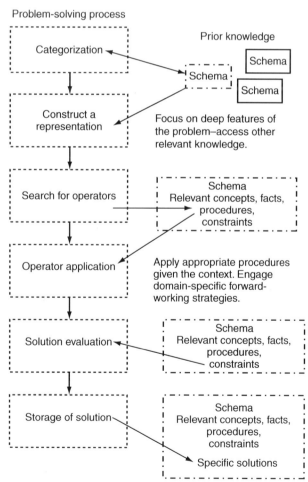

Figure 1   The impact of expertise on each stage of the problem-solving process.

Problem Categorization

The first stage involves the categorization of the problem. This stage is critical as it impacts all subsequent problem-solving processes, such as determining what knowledge to use and what strategies are relevant. For example, after a statistician categorizes a statistics problem as a permutations problem, she or he can proceed by retrieving and applying the appropriate formula to solve it. Much research has shown that experts' domain knowledge actually influences problem perception. When experts are presented a problem or task relevant to their domain of expertise, they see the problem in terms of prior meaningful patterns of information. For example, Chase and Simon (1973a, 1973b) found that expert chess players recalled more than novices on a memory task in which they were briefly presented a game scenario that they had to reconstruct. The experts recalled approximately four times as many pieces as the novices but only for scenarios that were from real games; when the scenario consisted of randomly placed pieces, experts performed at the same level as the novices. It was hypothesized that the experts' prior knowledge facilitated the recognition and recall of domain-relevant patterns, or chunks, of information from the scenarios (see **Figure 2** for an example of chunks in chess). These chunks provide experts useful ways to perceive and reason about large amounts of domain-relevant information.

Similar effects have been shown in research on medical expertise. For example, Lesgold *et al.* (1988) compared expert to novice physicians as they diagnosed X-ray films of the lungs. The physicians were asked to draw on the X-rays to identify the important features of their diagnosis. Both groups noticed abnormalities associated with a collapsed lung. However, experts were much more likely to identify the correct shape and size of the abnormality, whereas novices identified abnormalities that were approximately half the size of those identified by the experts. This work shows that experts and novices can perceive a problem very differently even when looking at the exact same stimulus. This finding that expert knowledge impacts problem perception has been found in a variety of tasks and domains including: architecture (Akin, 1980), mathematics (Silver, 1979), and naturalistic decision-making (NDM) tasks such as a fireman determining the safety of a room in a burning building (Klein, 1998).

A related effect is the finding that experts are more likely than novices to categorize problems at a deep level of abstraction (or function), whereas novices are more likely to categorize problems based on the surface features. For example, in the seminal work by Chi *et al.* (1981) experts and novices were asked to sort physics word problems based on their similarity. Experts sorted them according to their underlying physics principles, such as Newton's second

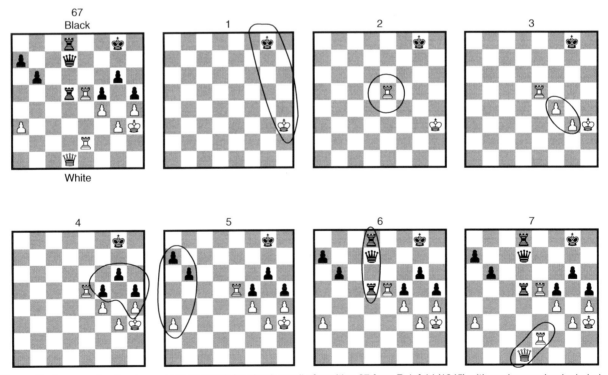

Figure 2 An example of a chess master's chunk-by-chunk recall of position 67 from Reinfeld (1945) with each new chunk circled. From Chase, W. G. and Simon, H. A. (1973). The minds eye in chess. In Chass, W. G. (ed.) *Visual Information Processing*, pp 215–281. New York: Academic Press. With permission from Elsevier.

law, whereas novices sorted them based on their surface features such as inclined planes or pulleys. Similar results have been shown in mathematics, where novices categorized algebra problems on the basis of the problem content (e.g., river problems), whereas more experienced students categorized them based on the underlying equation or principle (Silver, 1979). This effect has been found in a number of domains, including computer programming (Adelson, 1981), medicine (Groen and Patel, 1988), and engineering design (Moss, *et al.*, 2006) among others.

These results have typically been explained by the hypothesis that experts' problem schemas are organized differently than novices. Schemas are hierarchical knowledge structures that include prototypical information about the type of problem, including declarative knowledge of objects, facts, strategies, and constraints, and may also include the procedural operators for solving the problem (Marshall, 1995). Expert schemas are hypothesized to include many principle or structural features of the problem type, whereas novice schemas include few structural features and shallower, surface features. Schemas play a critical role in categorizing a problem. See **Figure 1** for the interactive role schemas play in both problem perception and construction of the problem representation. Next, we discuss how experts and novices construct a mental representation of the whole problem.

Construction of a Representation

After a problem has been categorized, the problem solver can begin to elaborate their mental representation that goes beyond the given information of the task environment. For some simple or well-practiced tasks (e.g., puzzle-type tasks, NDM tasks, and procedural skills), this step happens as rapidly as categorization but for other complex, multistep problems, such as those in physics or ill-structured tasks such as design tasks, constructing a mental representation is an iterative process that takes time to develop. Constructing a representation involves specifying the important features of the task such as the relevant objects, operators, and constraints. When experts are solving complex or ill-structured problems, they approach them qualitatively, first examining and elaborating the givens of the problem and then refining that representation. For example, Voss and Post (1988) examined how experts and novices in political science solved an open-ended problem on how to increase crop productivity in the Soviet Union. They showed that experts spent more time than novices in developing their representation of the problem by elaborating the history and causal factors underlying the problem.

These results are consistent with the schema account of expertise in which experts' schematic knowledge provides access to additional knowledge and strategies to help elaborate and develop the initial problem representation. This process has been hypothesized to be highly interactive (Chi *et al.*, 1981). Based on the initial categorization, the activated schema can provide additional information, strategies, constraints, and expectations to further characterize and elaborate the problem representation that may in turn activate other relevant schemas. For very complex problems, this process may take several iterations. Consistent with the categorization results described earlier, McDermott and Larkin (1978) (see also Reimann and Chi, 1989) have proposed that physicists construct problem representations at different levels of abstraction including: literal, naive, scientific (qualitative), and algebraic (see **Table 1** for a description of each level). Differences in levels of representation have also been shown in medicine where experts represent text descriptions of patient cases with an abstract situation model, whereas novices represent them more at the text-based (or surface) level (Groen and Patel, 1988).

Not only does expert knowledge facilitate the development and elaboration of the problem representation, but research also shows these representations are very durable. Experts have been shown to quickly encode problems and are able to easily access that representation even after disruption, whereas novices often take much longer to encode and re-represent a problem (Ericsson and Kintsch, 1995). The durability of expert memory and encoding has been shown in a variety of domains, including bridge (Charness, 1979), medicine (Norman *et al.*, 1989), and computer programming (McKeithen *et al.*, 1981). To account for these findings, Ericsson and Kintsch postulate that experts have developed effective long-term working memories that use very specific cues in the task environment to reliably retrieve prior knowledge structures (chunks and schemas).

Table 1   Four different levels of abstraction in representing physics problems

Representation level	Description
Literal	Representations containing keywords from the text.
Naive	Representations containing literal objects and their spatial relationships, often accompanied by a sketch of the situation.
Scientific	Representations containing idealized objects (points, bodies) and physical concepts (forces, momenta).
Algebraic	Equations containing physical concepts and their relationships.

From Reimann, P. and Chi, M. T. H. (1989). Human expertise. In Gilhooly, K. J. (ed.) *Human and Machine Problem Solving*, pp 161–191. New York: Plenum, with permission from Springer.

Application of Problem-Solving Procedures

After a problem representation has been constructed, the problem solver can then access and apply the appropriate problem-solving strategies and procedures to solve it. Experts have been shown to have more reliable access than novices to domain-specific solution procedures for well-practiced problem types. For simple problems, they make decisions faster and more accurately than novices. Research has also shown that experts and novices use different types of strategies when solving simple problems. Experts are more likely to use forward-working strategies for well-practiced problems, whereas novices use backward-working strategies. Forward-working strategies consist of working toward the solution from the domain principles. For example, physics experts first identify the principles for the task and then apply the domain-specific strategies and procedures, working step-by-step toward the solution (Simon and Simon, 1978). In contrast, novices have been shown to use general problem-solving heuristics, such as means–ends analysis to work backward from the problem goal (e.g., a sought value in physics or math). However, strategy use for both experts and novices critically depends on the relationship between prior knowledge and the task. Experts may also use general problem-solving methods and backward-working strategies when solving very novel tasks in the domain (e.g., physicists in their own research).

Solution Evaluation and Storage

Solution evaluation is the process of assessing a problem solution. Research has shown that experts spend more time than novices evaluating their solutions to make sure they satisfy task constraints (Groen and Patel, 1988; Voss and Post, 1988). Experts are also more likely than novices to identify and correct errors. For example, historians given a problem outside their subdomain are more likely than novices to seek additional resources and information to revise their initial framing of the problem, whereas novices are more likely to proceed with their initial incorrect assumptions (Wineburg, 1998). This research suggests that experts have developed better meta-cognitive skills (i.e., reflective monitoring) than novices for domain-relevant tasks. These skills may be particularly useful when adapting their knowledge to novel tasks in the domain.

After a solution has been generated it can be stored for later use. Much research shows that prior knowledge has a large impact on what is learned. For example, it is easier for experts to acquire new knowledge in the domain than for novices. Baseball experts have better recall than novices after listening to the broadcast of a novel baseball game (Spilich et al., 1979) and expert pilots recall more than novices after listening to new air traffic control messages (Morrow et al., 2001). Experts' rich, well-organized knowledge structures enable them to easily incorporate (assimilate) new information into their prior knowledge.

Summary

Theoretical accounts of expert–novice differences are primarily articulated in the representation and organization of expert knowledge. Not only do experts have more conceptual and procedural knowledge than novices, but their knowledge is also organized in ways that facilitate effective problem solving. They are able to quickly recognize large chunks of domain-relevant information, see the deep features of the problem, and effectively elaborate their initial problem representations. They can apply domain-specific strategies, efficiently monitor their problem-solving progress by refining and correcting solutions, and can learn new domain-relevant information easier than novices. In the next section, we briefly review the theoretical accounts of how this knowledge is acquired.

Acquisition of Expertise

Much research shows that a minimum of 10 years of daily deliberate practice is necessary to develop expertise in most domains (Ericsson et al., 1993). Ericsson and colleagues refer to deliberate practice as

> repeated experience in which the individual can attend to the critical aspects of the situation and incrementally improve her or his performance in response to knowledge of results, feedback, or both from a teacher (Ericsson et al., 1993: 368).

This perspective emphasizes how the type and structure of practice is critical to the acquisition of expert performance. In contrast to this perspective is the view that expertise is due to some talent or innate ability. The talent perspective, originally proposed by Galton (1869), is the notion that psychological traits, like physical traits, are inherited and family lineage (i.e., genes) strongly influences the person who achieves expert performance. Most modern formulations of this perspective hypothesize that expertise is the result of a complex interaction between genetic dispositions and experience (e.g., Simonton, 1999). Given that the talent perspective has received limited empirical support (see Howe et al., 1998 for a discussion and commentary) and much research shows that expert advantages are due to their domain knowledge (and not general reasoning or memory abilities), we focus on the cognitive learning processes that give rise to this knowledge.

Expert knowledge is composed of both declarative and procedural components. Declarative knowledge consists of descriptions about the world, including facts, strategies, and principles, and is commonly referred to as knowing that. Procedural knowledge consists of information for how to perform particular actions to accomplish task goals, and is commonly referred to as knowing how. Different learning processes have been hypothesized to account for the acquisition of these two types of knowledge. Learning declarative knowledge has been hypothesized to occur through observation, comprehension processes for oral and written discourse, induction, analogy, inference, and self-explanation (see Chi and Ohlsson, 2005 for a recent review of the learning mechanisms that lead to the acquisition of complex declarative knowledge). The key point is that declarative knowledge can be acquired through a number of reflective cognitive processes. Learning environments (e.g., classroom instruction) can be structured to facilitate its acquisition by including and improving these processes.

The acquisition of procedural knowledge or skill is hypothesized to occur through the repeated practice of a particular task or problem (Anderson, 1982, 1987). Fitts (1964) has characterized skill acquisition into three stages of performance, including the cognitive, associative, and automatic stages. During the cognitive stage, a person applies declarative knowledge to solve a problem and performance is characterized as being slow, effortful, and error prone. In domains such as mathematics and physics, novices rely heavily on declarative knowledge from prior examples to solve new problems (e.g., VanLehn, 1998). Students often apply this knowledge by making an analogy between the current problem they are solving and a previous problem that was solved similarly or had similar content. In the associative stage, the skill is practiced and performance becomes faster, more accurate, and less susceptible to interference. In this stage, students rely less on examples and more on applying learned rules to solve the problem. In the automatic stage, the skill has become proceduralized and is characterized by the fast application of the knowledge (or rules) with little or no errors and requires minimal cognitive resources.

Research on skill acquisition has revealed a power-law relationship between the amount of practice and performance. Generally, it shows that performance improves most when first learning a task, followed by decreasing learning gains as practice continues until performance asymptotes. However, the pattern of learning is more specific than the fast-then-slow pattern: when plotted on a logarithmic scale, the power-law relationship is revealed as an exact straight line. This exact relationship has been shown to be a very general phenomenon and has been observed in a variety of activities from learning to roll cigars to learning to solve math problems (see Proctor and Dutta, 1995 for a review). See **Figure 3** for a real-world example of the power-law relationship.

One mechanism hypothesized to account for procedural learning is knowledge compilation (Anderson, 1987). Knowledge compilation acts as a translation device that interprets, or compiles, declarative knowledge into a set of specific procedural rules given a particular goal. As those

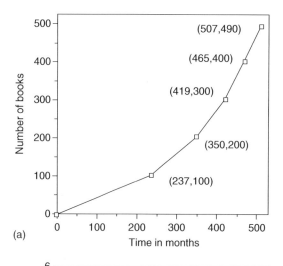

(a)

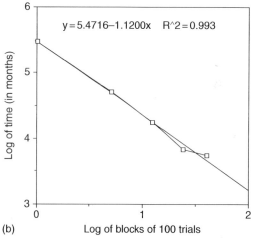

(b)

Figure 3 An illustration of the power-law relationship for the development of Professor Asimov's professional writing skills. (a) The number of books Professor Isaac Asimov wrote as a function of time in months. (b) The time to complete 100 books as a function of practice, plotted with logarithmic coordinates on both axes. From Ohlsson, S. (1992). The learning curve for writing books: Evidence of Professor Asimov. *Psychological Science* **3**, 380–382. With permission from Wiley-Blackwell.

procedures (rules) get repeatedly applied they become concatenated or chunked together into more compact rules. This mechanism shows how cognitive processing changes from relying on the interpretation and retrieval of declarative knowledge to embedding that knowledge into a set of procedural rules that become more compact with use. The result is a context-specific representation of the skill that can be quickly and efficiently executed.

In sum, research has shown that the acquisition of expert performance requires extended deliberate practice in the domain. Expert knowledge is composed of both declarative and procedural knowledge and research on learning has shown that declarative knowledge can be acquired through multiple cognitive pathways, whereas procedural knowledge comes from the repeated practice of a task. This view suggests that the type and structure of the learning environment are critical to the acquisition of expert performance. In the final section, we discuss two extensions to the traditional paradigm for research on expertise.

Current Directions

Current research extends the traditional paradigm in a number of ways. In this section, we focus on two: collaborative expertise and using expert–novice differences to determine targets of learning. In recent work, Schunn and colleagues (Tollinger *et al.*, 2006) had the unique opportunity to examine how over 50 NASA scientists worked together to plan the day-to-day operations of the two Mars rovers (Mars Explorer Rover Mission). The scientists' daily task was to analyze the data from the previous day and then come up with a plan for what experiments the rovers would conduct on the next day. They found that the amount of planning decreased across days and followed a learning curve similar to those typically observed for the acquisition of individual expertise, suggesting that expertise can also be acquired at the group level. Initial analyses suggest that the speedup in planning was due to both cognitive factors, such as individual knowledge chunking, plan reuse, and reducing task uncertainty, as well as social factors, such as coordinating information with others and the effect of leadership on the group.

In other recent work, Nokes *et al.* (2006) conducted a laboratory experiment on the effect of expertise on collaborative problem solving. They examined both expert and novice pilots' problem-solving performance when either working alone or with another participant of the same level of expertise. They found that experts working in pairs showed much larger collaborative benefits than novices working together, particularly for complex problem-solving tasks. Analysis of verbal protocols revealed that expert collaborative performance was supported by both domain knowledge (e.g., elaborating each other's contributions) and collaborative skill (e.g., acknowledging and restating the partner's contributions). The pilot and NASA scientist work extends the traditional paradigm and asks how expertise impacts cognitive and social processes at both the individual and the group level.

A second direction focuses on using expertise research to help identify targets of learning for novices. For example, Mestre and colleagues have used some of the classic findings in physics expertise (e.g., Chi *et al.*, 1981) to develop an instructional intervention to help students adopt similar strategies to that of the experts (Dufresne *et al.*, 1992; Mestre *et al.*, 1993). In one study, students were instructed to perform conceptual analyses vis-à-vis a computer interface that was based on the way experts strategize and solve problems, by first identifying the appropriate principles, justifying the use of those principles, and then articulating the solution procedures. They found that this type of strategizing improved student's conceptual understanding and subsequent problem solving compared to control conditions where students used more traditional approaches to solve problems (e.g., textbook instruction). This research provides one example for how findings from the expertise literature can be used to help improve instructional techniques.

Conclusions

In this article, we reviewed the psychological research on expertise in human problem solving. We saw that expert knowledge impacts each stage of the problem-solving process from problem perception to solution storage. Expert knowledge is composed of both declarative and procedural knowledge and is organized into knowledge structures (e.g., chunks and schemas) that facilitate the categorization and construction of a mental representation of the problem, support the selection of appropriate strategies and procedures, provide constraints to evaluate problem-solving progress, and provide a framework to effectively store new information about the domain. These knowledge structures are acquired through deliberate practice, and learning environments can be designed to facilitate their acquisition. Future work should build upon this rich knowledge base to further advance theories of learning and instruction.

Acknowledgments

Preparation of this paper was supported by Grant SBE0354420 from the Pittsburgh Science of Learning Center and Grant R305B070085 from the Institute of Education Sciences.

See also: Concept Learning; Memory; Metacognition.

Bibliography

Adelson, B. (1981). Problem solving and the development of abstract categories in programming languages. *Memory and Cognition* **9**, 422–433.

Akin, O. (1980). *Models of Architectural Knowledge*. London: Pion.

Anderson, J. R. (1982). Acquisition of cognitive skill. *Psychological Review* **89**, 369–403.

Anderson, J. R. (1987). Skill acquisition: Compilation of weak-method problem solutions. *Psychological Review* **94**, 192–210.

Charness, N. (1979). Components of skill in bridge. *Canadian Journal of Psychology* **33**, 1–50.

Chase, W. G. and Simon, H. A. (1973a). The minds eye in chess. In Chass, W. G. (ed.) *Visual Information Processing*, pp 215–281. New York: Academic Press.

Chase, W. G. and Simon, H. A. (1973b). Perception in chess. *Cognitive Psychology* **4**, 55–81.

Chi, M. T. H. (2006). Two approaches to the study of experts' characteristics. In Ericsson, K. A., Charness, N., Feltovich, P. J., and Hoffman, R. R. (eds.) *The Cambridge Handbook of Expertise and Expert Performance*, pp 21–30. Cambridge, UK: Cambridge University Press.

Chi, M. T. H., Feltovich, P. J., and Glaser, R. (1981). Categorization and representation of physics problems by experts and novices. *Cognitive Science* **5**, 121–152.

Chi, M. T. H. and Ohlsson, S. (2005). Complex declarative learning. In Holyoak, K. J. and Morrison, R. G. (eds.) *The Cambridge Handbook of Thinking and Reasoning*, pp 371–399. Cambridge: Cambridge University Press.

Dufresne, R. J., Gerace, W. J., Hardiman, P. T., and Mestre, J. P. (1992). Constraining novices to perform expertlike analyses: Effects on schema acquisition. *Journal of the Learning Sciences* **2**, 307–331.

Ericsson, K. A. (2006). Protocol analysis and expert thought: Concurrent verbalizations of thinking during experts' performance on representative tasks. In Ericsson, K. A., Charness, N., Feltovich, P. J., and Hoffman, R. R. (eds.) *The Cambridge Handbook of Expertise and Expert Performance*, pp 223–241. Cambridge, UK: Cambridge University Press.

Ericsson, K. A. and Kintsch, W. (1995). Long term working memory. *Psychological Review* **102**, 211–245.

Ericsson, K. A., Krampe, R. T., and Tesch-Romer, C. (1993). The role of deliberate practice in the acquisition of expert performance. *Psychological Review* **100**, 363–406.

Fitts, P. M. (1964). Perceptual-motor skill learning. In Melton, A. W. (ed.) *Categories of Human Learning*, pp 243–285. New York: Academic Press.

Galton, F. (1869). *Hereditary Genius: An Inquiry into Its Laws and Consequences*. London: Julian Friedman Publishers.

Groen, G. J. and Patel, V. L. (1988). The relationship between comprehension and reasoning in medical expertise. In Chi, M. T. H., Glaser, R., and Farr, M. J. (eds.) *The Nature of Expertise*, pp 287–310. Hillsdale, NJ: Erlbaum.

Howe, M. J. A., Davidson, J. W., and Sloboda, J. A. (1998). Innate talents: Reality or myth? *Behavioral and Brian Sciences* **21**, 399–442.

Klein, G. (1998). *Sources of Power: How People Make Decisions*. Cambridge, MA: MIT Press.

Lesgold, A., Rubinson, J., Feltovich, P., *et al.* (1988). Expertise in a complex skill: Diagnosing X-ray pictures. In Chi, M. T. H., Glaser, R., and Farr, M. J. (eds.) *The Nature of Expertise*, pp 311–342. Hillsdale, NJ: Erlbaum.

Marshall, S. (1995). *Schemas in Problem Solving*. New York: Cambridge University Press.

McDermott, J. and Larkin, J. H. (1978). Re-representing textbook physics problems. In *Proceedings of the 2nd National Conference of the Canadian Society for Computational Studies of Intelligence*. Toronto: University of Toronto Press.

McKeithen, K. B., Reitman, J. S., Reuter, H. H., and Hirtle, S. C. (1981). Knowledge organization and skill differences in computer programmers. *Cognitive Psychology* **13**, 307–325.

Mestre, J. P., Dufresne, R., Gerace, W. J., Hardiman, P. T., and Touger, J. S. (1993). Promoting skilled problem solving behavior among beginning physics students. *Journal of Research in Science Teaching* **30**, 303–317.

Morrow, D. G., Menard, W. E., Stine-Morrow, E. A. L., Teller, T., and Bryant, D. (2001). The influence of expertise and task factors on age differences in pilot communication. *Psychology and Aging* **16**, 31–46.

Moss, J., Kotovsky, K., and Cagan, J. (2006). The role of functionality in the mental representations of engineering students: Some differences in the early stages of expertise. *Cognitive Science* **30**, 65–93.

Nersessian, N. J. (1992). How do scientists think? Capturing the dynamics of conceptual change in science. In Giere, R. N. (ed.) *Cognitive Models of Science: Minnesota Studies in the Philosophy of Science,* vol. XV, pp 3–44. Minneapolis, MN: University of Minnesota Press.

Newell, A. and Simon, H. A. (1972). *Human Problem Solving*. Englewood Cliffs, NJ: Prentice-Hall.

Nokes, T. J., Meade, M. L., Morrow, D. G., and Stine-Morrow, E. A. L. (2006). Investigating the effect of domain knowledge on collaborative problem solving. In Sun, R. and Miyake, N. (eds.) *Proceedings of the 28th Annual Cognitive Science Society*, pp 2572. Vancouver, CA: Cognitive Science Society.

Norman, G. R., Brooks, L. R., and Allen, S. W. (1989). Recall by expert medical practitioners and novices as a record of processing attention. *Journal of Experimental Psychology: Learning, Memory, and Cognition* **15**, 1166–1174.

Proctor, R. W. and Dutta, A. (1995). *Skill Acquisition and Human Performance*. Thousand Oaks, CA: Sage.

Reimann, P. and Chi, M. T. H. (1989). Human expertise. In Gilhooly, K. J. (ed.) *Human and Machine Problem Solving*, pp 161–191. New York: Plenum.

Silver, E. A. (1979). Student perceptions of relatedness among verbal problems. *Journal of Research in Mathematics Education* **10**, 195–210.

Simon, D. P. and Simon, H. A. (1978). Individual differences in solving physics problems. In Siegler, R. (ed.) *Thinking: What Develops?* Hillsdale, NJ: Erlbaum.

Simonton, D. K. (1999). Talent and its development: An emergenic and epigenetic model. *Psychological Review* **106**, 435–457.

Spilich, G. J., Vesonder, G. T., Chiesi, H. L., and Voss, J. F. (1979). Text processing of domain-related information for individuals with high and low domain knowledge. *Journal of Verbal Learning and Verbal Behavior* **14**, 506–522.

Tollinger, I., Schunn, C. D., and Vera, A. H. (2006). What changes when a large team becomes more expert? Analyses of speedup in the Mars exploration rovers science planning process. *Paper Presented at the Human Computer Interaction Consortium.* Frasier, CO.

VanLehn, K. (1998). Analogy events: How examples are used during problem solving. *Cognitive Science* **22**, 347–388.

Voss, J. F. and Post, T. A. (1988). On the solving of ill-structured problems. In Chi, M. T. H., Glaser, R., and Farr, M. J. (eds.) *The Nature of Expertise*, pp 261–285. Hillsdale, NJ: Erlbaum.

Wineburg, S. (1998). Reading Abraham Lincoln: An expert/expert study in the interpretation of historical texts. *Cognitive Science* **22**, 319–346.

Further Reading

Chi, M. T. H., Glaser, R., and Farr, M. J. (eds.) (1988). *The Nature of Expertise.* Hillsdale, NJ: Erlbaum.

Ericsson, K. A. (ed.) (1996). *The Road to Excellence: The Acquisition of Expert Performance in the Arts and Sciences, Sports, and Games.* Mahwah, NJ: Erlbaum.

Ericsson, K. A., Charness, N., Feltovich, P. J., and Hoffman, R. R. (eds.) (2006). *The Cambridge Handbook of Expertise and Expert Performance.* Cambridge, UK: Cambridge University Press.

Ericsson, K. A. and Smith, J. (1991). Prospects and limits of the empirical study of expertise: An introduction. In Ericsson, K. A. (ed.) *Toward a General Theory of Expertise*, pp 1–38. Cambridge, UK: Cambridge University Press.

Problem Solving and Reasoning

R E Mayer, University of California, Santa Barbara, CA, USA

Problem solving and reasoning are frequently in the spotlight of educational reform. In addition to remembering information, students must be able to use what they have learned to solve new problems. A major goal of education is to help students become effective problem solvers, that is, people who can generate useful and original solutions when they are confronted with problems they have never seen before.

Definitions

A problem consists of a given state (i.e., a description of the current situation), a goal state (i.e., a description of the desired situation), and a set of operators (i.e., rules for moving from one state to another). A problem occurs when a situation is in one state, the problem solver wants it to be in another state, and there are obstacles preventing a smooth transition from one state to another. Duncker (1945: 1) defined a problem in the following way: "A problem arises when a living creature has a goal but does not know how this goal is to be reached." Although Duncker's definition is still valid, it must be updated to include the possibility of problem solving by machines, and so the term problem solver can refer to both living creatures and machines.

Problem solving occurs when a problem solver engages in cognitive activity aimed at overcoming a problem. Duncker (1945: 1) noted that "when one cannot go from the given situation to the desired situation simply by action, then there has to recourse to thinking" and "such thinking has the task of devising some action which may mediate between the existing and desired situations." Similarly, Polya (1981: ix) defined problem solving as "finding a way out of a difficulty, a way around an obstacle." In developing computer simulations of problem solving, Newell and Simon (1972) defined problem solving as a search for a path between the given and goal states of a problem. Mayer (1992) summarized three major elements in a definition of problem solving: (1) problem solving is cognitive because it occurs internally within the problem solver's cognitive system, (2) problem solving is a process, because it involves manipulating or performing operations on the problem solver's cognitive representations, and (3) problem solving is directed, because the problem solver is attempting to achieve some goal. In short, problem solving is directed, cognitive processing aimed at finding a way to achieve a goal.

What is the relation between problem solving and other high-level cognitive processes such as thinking and reasoning? Thinking can be broken down into two types – directed and nondirected thinking. Problem solving is a common and pervasive type of thinking, namely, directed thinking in which the thinker engages in cognitive processing aimed at achieving some goal. On the contrary, in nondirected thinking, the thinker engages in cognitive processing that is not aimed at achieving some goal, such as daydreaming or the abnormal thinking of autistic or schizophrenic people. In general, the terms problem solving and thinking can be used interchangeably, with the recognition that nondirected thinking is excluded.

Reasoning can be viewed as a type of problem solving, and is required in deductive reasoning tasks and inductive reasoning tasks. In deductive reasoning, the problem solver is given premises and must apply the rules of logic to derive a conclusion. For example, if you know all four-sided polygons are quadrilaterals and all squares are four-sided polygons, you may logically conclude, all squares are quadrilaterals. In inductive reasoning, the problem solver is given a series of instances or events or examples and must infer a rule. For example, after learning the Spanish words *la casa, el libro, la escuela, el perro, la muchacha,* and *el muchacho,* you may conclude that the article la goes with words ending in a and the el goes with words ending in o, a grammatical rule that is not without exceptions in Spanish.

Finally, creative thinking occurs when a problem solver generates ideas and critical thinking occurs when a problem solver evaluates them. Two important criteria in creative and critical thinking are that the ideas must be original and useful.

Types of Problems

An important distinction – based on the clarity of the problem statement – can be made between well-defined problems and ill-defined problems. A well-defined problem has a clear given state, a clear goal state, and a clear set of allowable operators. For example, finding the value of x in an algebraic equation such as $2x + 5 = 8$ is a well-defined problem because the given state is the equation, the goal state is a value for $x = $ ___, and the operators are defined by the rules of algebra and arithmetic. In contrast, an ill-defined problem has a poorly specified given state, goal state, and/or operators. For example, choosing an appropriate education for a career path is an ill-defined problem because the goal and allowable operators are not clearly specified. Most problems encountered in school are well-defined problems, whereas most crucial problems in everyday life are ill-defined.

Another important distinction – based on the knowledge of the problem solver – can be made between routine and nonroutine problems. Routine problems are identical or very similar to problems that the problem solver already knows how to solve, and therefore require what Wertheimer (1959) called reproductive thinking – reproducing responses that have been produced previously. For example, a routine problem for most high school students is "5 + 5 = ___" or "The headquarters of the United Nations is located in the city of _____." In the strictest sense, routine problems do not conform to the definition of problem, since they do not include an obstacle between the given and goal states. In contrast, nonroutine problems are different from any problems that the problem solver already knows how to solve and therefore require what Wertheimer (1959) called productive thinking – creating a novel solution. Examples for most high school students include writing a computer program to compute the mean and standard deviation of a sample, or working out why Spanish explorers waited several centuries before colonizing California. In school, students often work on routine problems called exercises; however, most important problems in everyday life are nonroutine.

A third distinction can be made between problems requiring convergent and divergent thinking. Convergent thinking problems have a single correct answer that can be determined by applying a procedure or retrieving a fact from memory. Examples include arithmetic computation problems and answering factual questions. Divergent thinking problems have many possible answers, and so the problem solver's job is to create as many solutions as possible (Guilford, 1967). Classic examples include uses problems, such as "List all the possible uses of a brick," and consequences problems, such as "List all the consequences of humans having six rather than five fingers." Creativity can be measured in terms of the originality and usefulness of the answers, and divergent thinking skills, which underlie creativity, are taught in courses on creative thinking (Sternberg, 1999). Although divergent thinking is the hallmark of creativity, most school-based problems require convergent thinking.

Cognitive Processes and Types of Knowledge in Problem Solving

Problem solving can be divided into two major phases: problem representation and problem solution. Problem representation involves building a mental representation of the problem, and includes the cognitive process of representing (i.e., building a situation model, that is, a mental representation of the situation described in the problem). Problem solution involves devising and carrying out a plan for solving the problem, and includes the cognitive processes of planning (i.e., devising a plan), executing (i.e., carrying out the plan), and monitoring (i.e., tracking the effectiveness of the plan).

The cognitive processes involved in problem representation and problem solution may interact, rather than occur in linear order. For example, a student may be given the following word problem: "Sarah has three marbles. David has two more marbles than Sarah. How many marbles does David have?" In representing the problem, the student must translate each sentence into an internal mental representation, such as "Sarah's marbles = 3" and "David's marbles = Sarah's marbles + 2," and mentally integrate them into a situation model, such as a spatial representation consisting of a bar for Sarah's marbles (3 units high), a bar on top of it for the difference between Sarah's and David's marbles (2 units high), and a bar next these for David's marbles (indicating that Sarah's marbles and the difference set of marbles are subsets of David's marbles). Planning involves determining the operations to be performed, such as determining that 3 and 2 must be added together. Executing involves carrying out the operation(s), such as computing that 5 is the sum of 3 and 2. Monitoring involves detecting when a plan is not working, a step was not executed correctly, or an answer is questionable. Although school instruction tends to emphasize execution of basic skills, students' major difficulties are in learning how to represent problems, devise plans, and monitor problem-solving processes.

Several types of knowledge are required for successful problem solving: facts, concepts, procedures, strategies, and beliefs (Anderson *et al.*, 2001; Mayer, 2008). Facts are elements of a factual knowledge about the world, such as, "There are 1000 milliliters in a liter." Concepts are principles or models (which are elements of conceptual knowledge) such as, "In the number 567, 6 refers to the number of tens," or categories or schemas (which are elements of schematic knowledge), such as knowing that "What is probability of flipping a fair coin three times and getting heads all three times?" is a joint probability problem. Procedures are step-by-step processes, such as knowledge of the procedure for long division used for 252 divided by 12. Strategies are general methods for problem solving, such as knowing how to break a problem into smaller parts. Beliefs are thoughts about one's cognitive processing, such as believing, "I am good at solving statistics problems." Facts and concepts are useful in the process of representing; procedures are useful for the process of executing; and strategies and beliefs are useful for planning and monitoring. Although instruction may tend to emphasize facts and procedures, all five kinds of knowledge are needed to support problem solving.

Rigidity in Thinking

A major obstacle to effective problem solving is rigidity in thinking. For example, in some problem-solving situations, the problem solver must use an object in a new way, such as using a brick as a doorstop or using a pencil as a bookmark. When a problem solver can only conceive of using an object in its most common function, then the problem cannot be solved. Duncker (1945) used the term functional fixedness to refer to a situation in which a problem solver cannot think of a using an object in a new function that is required to solve the problem. Another example of rigidity occurs when a problem solver uses a well-learned procedure on a problem for which the procedure is inappropriate. For example, if a student solved a long series of arithmetic story problems that all contain the word 'more' and require adding the numbers together, the student may incorrectly carry out this same addition procedure for a new problem that actually requires subtracting the numbers from one another. Luchins (1942) used the term *einstellung* (or problem-solving set) to refer to this phenomenon. A goal of instruction in problem solving is to help students avoid rigid thinking.

Problem-Solving Transfer

Transfer is the effect of prior learning on new learning. When the new learning task is a problem to solve, we can use the term problem-solving transfer to refer to the effect of prior learning on solving a new problem (Mayer and Wittrock, 2006). Positive transfer occurs when previous learning helps you on a new task, whereas negative transfer occurs when previous learning hurts you on a new task. For example, if you have learned arithmetic, it should be easier for you to solve an arithmetic word problem – which would indicate positive transfer. If you learned to drive on the right side of the road in the United States, you may experience negative transfer in trying to learn to drive on the left side of the road in Australia. How does transfer work? This has been a central research question in psychology and education since Thorndike's (1931) (Thorndike and Woodworth, 1901) pioneering work in the early 1900s, and has generated three alternative explanations: general transfer, specific transfer, and mixed transfer. General transfer is the idea that learning task *A* can help you on task *B*, even if *A* and *B* have nothing specifically in common. For example, the doctrine of formal discipline (which is a classic theory of general transfer) posited that learning certain school subjects, such as Latin and geometry, would improve students' minds in general and thereby help them on unrelated tasks in the future. The doctrine of formal discipline was used to justify the establishment of Latin schools, in which the curriculum consisted of learning Latin, Greek,

geometry, and similar subjects. In one of the first experiments in the field of educational psychology, Thorndike (1931) (Thorndike and Woodworth, 1901) was able to show that students who learned Latin did not perform any better in learning bookkeeping than did students who had not learned Latin. Subsequent research (Singley and Anderson, 1989) also found little support for the idea of general transfer. In contrast, specific transfer is the idea that learning task *A* will help you in task *B* only to the degree that *A* and *B* have identical elements in common. Thus, learning Latin may help you learn Spanish because some of the verb conjugations are similar and many of the words are similar. The theory of specific transfer is problematic for educators because it suggests that students need to learn every specific piece of knowledge they will ever need.

Mixed transfer is a compromise between general and specific transfer that involves specific transfer of a general principle, that is, mixed transfer occurs when a learner abstracts a general principle from learning *A* and is able to apply it to solving a new problem *B*. The transfer is specific because both *A* and *B* can be solved by the same general principle but what is being transferred is a general principle rather than specific behaviors. For example, if students learn to make sense out text passages by producing summaries, this general method can be transferred to the task of making sense out of a new text passage. Research on teaching of cognitive strategies shows that students can benefit from learning general strategies such as summarizing in reading comprehension (Pressley and Woloshyn, 1995).

Promoting positive transfer is a fundamental goal of education, that is, educators seek to help students learn in ways so that they will be able to use what they have learned to solve new problems. Mayer and Wittrock (2006) have described seven ways to promote problem-solving transfer: load-reducing methods, such as helping students build automaticity in basic skills; structure-based methods, such as using concrete models; schema-based methods, such as using advance organizers or pretraining; generative methods, such as encouraging learners to engage in elaboration or self-explanation; guided discovery methods, such as providing hints as someone solves a problems; modeling methods, such as providing worked examples; and teaching thinking skills, such as training people to use effective methods and strategies.

The Distinction between Productive and Reproductive Thinking

Why is it that some people invent clever solutions when confronted with a problem, whereas others do not? The Gestalt psychologist, Wertheimer (1959) attempted to answer this question by distinguishing between two kinds of thinking mentioned above, namely productive thinking and reproductive thinking. Productive thinking involves producing a novel solution when confronted with a problem, whereas reproductive thinking occurs when problem solvers use solution procedures that they already know as a result of solving previous problems.

For example, Wertheimer (1959) described two ways of learning how to find the area of a parallelogram – learning by rote and learning by understanding. In learning by rote (or rote learning), the student is taught to measure the height, measure the base, and then multiply height times base. According to Wertheimer, students who learn by rote perform well on retention tests, such as finding the area of similar parallelograms, and poorly on transfer problems, such as finding the area of an unusually shaped parallelogram. In contrast, students who learn by understanding (or by meaningful learning) are encouraged to discover that the parallelogram can be converted into a rectangle by cutting the triangle off one end and moving it to the other end. Students who learn by understanding are expected to perform well on both retention and transfer tests. Thus, rote learning leads to reproductive thinking (as measured by retention tests) whereas meaningful learning leads to productive thinking (as measured by transfer tests).

The Nature of Insight

Insight is the cognitive process by which a problem solver suddenly moves from a state of not knowing how to solve a problem to a state of knowing how to solve a problem (Mayer, 1995). Insight plays a crucial role in creative thinking (Sternberg, 1999), in which a problem solver invents novel solutions to a problem. How does insight work? Gestalt psychologists and others have offered five somewhat interrelated explanations (Mayer, 1995): insight as completing a schema, insight as sudden visual reorganization, insight as reformulation of a problem, insight as removing mental blocks, and insight as finding a problem analog. Selz, working in the early 1900s in the Netherlands, produced psychology's first explanation of insight as completing a schema (Frijda and De Groot, 1982). For example, when given a problem such as "What is a coordinate of baseball?" a problem solver may say, "Let's see. Baseball is a sport. Another sport is football, so football is the answer." In this case, the problem solver is not following a chain of associations, but rather is trying to build a cognitive structure that has a superset (sport) linked to two subsets that are co-ordinates (baseball and one more), so coming up with an answer amounts to completing a schema. The idea that meaningful learning requires active construction by the learner is the fundamental theme of many current theories of learning (Bransford *et al.*, 1999).

Kohler, also working in the early 1900s, provided evidence that insight is a process of sudden visual reorganization in which the problem solver literally sees how all the parts of the problem fit together (Kohler, 1925).

For example, when an ape was put in an area that had stackable crates on the floor and bananas hanging overhead out of reach, the ape looked around and then in an apparent flash of insight, suddenly stacked the crates to form a sort of ladder leading to the bananas. This approach is consistent with current interest in using computer-assisted visualizations and concrete representations to help people understand how various systems work.

Duncker (1945) described insight as a reformulation of the problem, particularly a restatement of the givens or the goal in a new way. For example, in the tumor problem, you are asked to free a person of an inoperable stomach tumor by using "rays which destroy organic tissue at sufficient intensity" (p. 1). In order to solve the problem, the problem solver must restate the goal as, "lower the intensity of the rays as they pass through the healthy tissue," which leads to the solution of having many weak rays all converge on the tumor. This approach is consistent with the current idea that the most difficult aspect of problem solving is mentally representing the problem in a productive way.

Duncker (1945) also described insight as a process of removing mental blocks, that is, of being able to use an object in way that is different from its conventional use. For example, in the candle problem, the problem solver is given a box containing candles, a box containing tacks, and a box containing matches, and is asked to mount a lighted candle on a wall. The solution – involving using a box as the base, which is tacked into the wall – is much more difficult if the objects are in the boxes rather than next to them. According to Duncker, presenting the objects in the boxes creates functional fixedness – the tendency to be able to conceive of only one use of an object even though a problem solution requires using an object in a new way. Removing mental blocks is a key focus of current programs aimed at teaching thinking skills.

Finally, Wertheimer (1959) offered a fifth explanation of insight – finding a problem analog – in which the problem solver abstracts a general principle from one problem and applies it to a new one. Thinking by analogy is still an important theme in cognitive science, and is the basis for more current views of problem-solving transfer (Holyoak, 2005).

A sixth explanation – insight as nothing new – holds that solving insight problems is no different from solving other problems (Weisberg and Suls, 1973), although Metcalfe and Wiebe (1987) have shown that problem solvers use qualitatively different thinking processes for insight problems and routine problems.

Problem Space and Search Processes

Information-processing theories of problem solving focus on constructing a problem space and finding a path through the problem space (Newell and Simon, 1972;

Novick and Bassok, 2005). A problem space consists of a representation of the initial state, goal state, and all intervening states. For example, the problem space for solving the equation, $2X - 5 = X$, has this equation as the initial state, and $X = \_\_\_$ as the goal state. Two of the intervening states, directly after the initial state are $2X = X + 5$ and $2X - X - 5 = 0$, which were created by applying legal operators such as add 5 to both sides or subtract X from both sides. Similarly, other states are created by applying operators to these states, and so on.

Once a problem is represented as a problem space, the problem solver's task is to search for a path from the initial state to the goal state. Means-ends analysis is a search strategy in which the problem solver works on one goal at a time; if that goal cannot be achieved directly, the problem solver sets a new goal of removing barriers, and so on. This search strategy is commonly used in computer simulations of problem solving and is consistent with the way that beginners solve problems.

Problem Solving in Realistic Situations

Although classic research focused mainly on solving artificial puzzles or formal syllogisms, cognitive science research on problem solving and reasoning has been shifting toward realistic situations including everyday problem solving, expert problem solving, and problem solving in subject areas (Ericsson *et al.*, 2006; Holyoak and Morrison, 2005).

Research on everyday thinking shows that people rarely use school-taught methods to solve problems encountered outside of school (Lave, 1988; Nunes *et al.*, 1993). For example, to determine the best buy in a supermarket – such as 90 cents for a 10-ounce can of peanuts or 45 cents for a 4-ounce can – the school-taught procedure is compute the unit cost of each item (i.e., 9 cents vs. 11.25 cents, respectively). However, Lave (1988) found that people almost never used the school-taught procedure; instead, they invented arithmetic procedures suited to the situation, such as the ratio strategy in which the problem solver notes that the larger one is a better buy because it costs twice as much and gives you more than twice as many ounces.

Research on expert problem solving compares differences in how novices and experts solve problems in domains such as physics, medical diagnosis, computer programming, and the game of chess. For example, when Larkin (1983) asked experts and novices to think aloud as they solved physics problems, she found that experts were more likely to focus on underlying physics concepts (such as forces and weights) whereas novices focused on surface characteristics (such as pulleys and ropes). Similarly, when Chi *et al.* (1981) asked experts and novices to sort physics problems into groups, experts sorted problems based on their underlying physics principle (such as conservation of energy), whereas novices sorted the problems based on

their surface characteristics (such as inclined planes and springs). Results of expert–novice studies suggest that experts represent and solve problems differently from novices, and so instruction can focus on helping novices think more like experts.

Another example of problem solving in realistic situations involves psychologies of subject matter, that is, research on problem solving in subject areas, such as reading, writing, mathematics, science, and history (Mayer, 2008). Instead of asking, how do people think in general, researchers ask, how do people think about testing a scientific theory, solving a mathematics word problem, or explaining why a historical event happened, or how do people think as they create an essay or make sense out of a printed passage. This approach suggests that instruction in subject matter areas should focus on helping students learn the cognitive processes and strategies required for successful problem solving.

See also: Cognition: Overview and Recent Trends; Knowledge Domains and Domain Learning.

Bibliography

Anderson, L. W., Krathwohl, D. R., Airasian, P. W., *et al.* (2001). *A Taxonomy for Learning, Teaching, and Assessing: A Revision of Bloom's Taxonomy of Educational Objectives*. New York: Longman.

Bransford, J. D., Brown, A. L., and Cocking, R. R. (1999). *How People Learn*. Washington, DC: National Academy Press.

Chi, M. T. H., Feltovich, P. J., and Glaser, R. (1981). Categorization and representation of physics problems by experts and novices. *Cognitive Science* **5**, 121–152.

Duncker, K. (1945). On problem solving. *Psychological Monographs* **58**(270), 3.

Ericsson, K. A., Feltovich, P. J., and Hoffman, R. R. (eds.) (2006). *The Cambridge Handbook of Expertise and Expert Performance*. New York: Cambridge University Press.

Frijda, N. H. and de Groot, A. D. (1982). *Otto Selz: His Contribution to Psychology*. Hague: Mouton.

Guilford, J. P. (1967). *The Nature of Human Intelligence*. New York: McGraw-Hill.

Holyoak, K. J. (2005). Analogy. In Holyoak, K. J. and Morrison, R. G. (eds.) *The Cambridge Handbook of Thinking and Reasoning*, pp 117–142. New York: Cambridge University Press.

Holyoak, K. J. and Morrison, R. G. (eds.) (2005). *The Cambridge Handbook of Thinking and Reasoning*. New York: Cambridge University Press.

Kohler, W. (1925). *The Mentality of Apes*. New York: Liveright.

Larkin, J. H. (1983). The Role of Problem Representation in Physics. In Gentner, D. and Stevens, A. L. (eds.) *Mental Models*, pp 75–98. Mahwah, NJ: Erlbaum.

Lave, J. (1988). *Cognition in Practice*. Cambridge, UK: Cambridge University Press.

Luchins, A. (1942). Mechanization in problem solving. *Psychological Monographs* **54**(248), 6.

Mayer, R. E. (1992). *Thinking, Problem Solving, Cognition*, 2nd edn. New York: Freeman.

Mayer, R. E. (1995). The search for insight: Grappling with Gestalt psychology's unanswered questions. In Sternberg, R. J. and Davidson, J. E. (eds.) *The Nature of Insight*, pp 3–32. Cambridge, MA: MIT Press.

Mayer, R. E. (2008). *Learning and Instruction*. Upper Saddle River, NJ: Merrill Prentice Hall.

Mayer, R. E. and Wittrock, M. C. (2006). Problem solving. In Alexander, P. A. and Winne, P. H. (eds.) *Handbook of Educational Psychology,* 2nd edn, pp 287–304. Mahwah, NJ: Erlbaum.

Metcalfe, J. and Wiebe, D. (1987). Intuition in insight and non-insight problem solving. *Memory and Cognition* **15**, 238–246.

Newell, A. and Simon, H. A. (1972). *Human Problem Solving.* Englewood Cliffs, NJ: Prentice-Hall.

Novick, L. R. and Bassok, M. (2005). Problem solving. In Holyoak, K. J. and Morrison, R. G. (eds.) *The Cambridge Handbook of Thinking and Reasoning*, pp 321–350. New York: Cambridge University Press.

Nunes, T., Schliemann, A. D., and Carraher, D. W. (1993). *Street Mathematics and School Mathematics*. Cambridge, UK: Cambridge University Press.

Polya, G. (1981). *Mathematical Discovery*. New York: Wiley.

Pressley, M. and Woloshyn, V. (1995). *Cognitive Process Instruction*, 2nd edn. Cambridge, MA: Brookline Books.

Singley, M. K. and Anderson, J. R. (1989). *The Transfer of Cognitive Skill*. Cambridge, MA: Harvard University Press.

Sternberg, R. J. (1999). *Handbook of Creativity*. New York: Cambridge University Press.

Thorndike, E. L. (1931). *Human Learning*. New York: Century.

Thorndike, E. L. and Woodworth, R. S. (1901). The influence of improvement in one mental function upon the efficiency of other functions. *Psychological Review* **8**, 247–261.

Weisberg, R. W. and Suls, J. (1973). An information processing model of Duncker's candle problem. *Cognitive Psychology* **4**, 255–276.

Wertheimer, M. (1959). *Productive Thinking*. New York: Harper and Collins.

Knowledge Domains and Domain Learning

L Maggioni and P A Alexander, University of Maryland, College Park, MD, USA

Glossary

Conditional knowledge – A state of knowledge that pertains to when and where knowledge (declarative or procedural) could or should be applied. For this reason, it has been described as "knowing when and where".

Declarative knowledge – Involves factual information and is the state of knowledge referred to as "knowing what".

Disciplinary knowledge – Represents the specialized knowledge associated with a foundational discipline (e.g., history or mathematics) and includes a specific taxonomy, vocabulary, concepts, theories, research methods, and standards of justification aligned with that discipline. It is knowledge of an academic discipline that is taught; a specialized field, or study, or particular branch of learning.

Discourse knowledge – A type of conceptual knowledge that is more particularly about language and its use.

Heuristics – Refer to general guidelines and practices that facilitate a systematic approach to a task and thus favor arriving at a solution (e.g., identifying the data of a problem, looking for related problems, and checking the results).

Knowledge domain – Refers to the part of the world investigated by a specific discipline. Such knowledge is characterized as the object (e.g., plants, numbers, or the past) of a specific body of knowledge (e.g., botany, mathematics, or history).

Metacognition – Typically defined as knowledge of knowledge; knowledge about one's cognition and the regulation of that cognition.

Misconception – An erroneous, sometimes naïve, idea or theory that can seriously hinder understanding.

Procedural knowledge – Described as "knowing how." Procedural knowledge is, in effect, that state of knowledge encompassing certain processes, strategies, or routines.

Schemata – (pl. of schema) Knowledge structures that are interconnected with and embedded in, one another. The term schemata has been associated with the organization of conceptual knowledge or used to represent all one knows about the physical, social, or mental world.

Second-order knowledge – Refers to concepts regarding how historical knowledge is generated (i.e., the doing of history), such as evidence, accounts, change, and cause.

Skill – A procedure that has been routinized or habitualized, a mental habit that prompts specific actions in front of simple and highly familiar situation, usually operating at an unconscious level.

Strategy – A mental operation or technique, employed to solve problems or to enhance performance. Some strategies are called general, because they can be successfully applied across various domains, while others are called specific, because they target a specific domain or task within a domain.

Substantive knowledge or first-order knowledge – Refers to concepts that identify clusters of kinds of things in the world and, as such, they refer to what a discipline is about (e.g., market, migration, revolution). Such knowledge implies understanding of the rule that guides the formation of those clusters and being able to identify instances of that rule across time and space.

Although educational psychologists' interest in how knowledge develops within specific domains has fluctuated across time, formal education throughout the world is organized around particular fields of studies, and students soon come to characterize their experience of school in terms of subject matters. Thus, in education, domains seem to make a difference. The term knowledge domain refers to the part of the world investigated by a specific discipline. In other words, the domain can be characterized as the object (e.g., plants, numbers, or the past) of a specific body of knowledge (e.g., botany, mathematics, or history).

Herein, we offer a survey of the development of increasingly specialized disciplines and of the corresponding identification of ever-narrower knowledge domains. In particular, we consider the cultural trends that accompanied these changes and the major influences on the structure of formal education. Subsequently, we turn to consider the characteristics of learning and generating knowledge within specific domains. Specifically, we consider the findings of educational research in understanding the processes of learning and teaching in history, mathematics, and science. We also include contributions regarding the processes of reading and writing, given their relevance in the school curriculum and the tendency in educational research to conceptualize these activities as domains of learning in their own right.

The Development of Disciplines

Besides being characterized by its systematic knowledge of a particular domain, each discipline is also distinguished by a specific way of thinking about associated phenomena. Thus, disciplinary knowledge includes a specific taxonomy, vocabulary, concepts, theories, research methods, and standards of justification. Histories of science, such as those offered by Fehl (1966), Hall and Hall (1988), and Libby (1917) illustrate that disciplines developed over the centuries as privileged pathways toward an understanding of almost any topic. The reciprocal influences between the prevalent cultural climate, disciplinary developments, and formal education are well exemplified by cultural histories of Western education, such as the one composed by Butts (1955).

These studies concur in affirming that organized bodies of knowledge arose in conjunction with the human needs of gaining understanding of the world, establishing some control on the physical environment, and organizing social life. In ancient Egypt, for example, efforts toward controlling and predicting the floods of the Nile fostered remarkable advances in geometry and astronomy. However, it was in the Greek cities of Asia Minor and, later, Athens that the investigation of philosophers into the nature and origin of the universe introduced the method of rational inquiry that so deeply influenced the development of knowledge in Western civilization.

In fact, Western thought owes much of its systematization of knowledge to the Greeks and to their reliance on critical reason in speculating about the origin and nature of the universe. The Greeks came to regard rationality as the human faculty allowing the acquisition of knowledge and truth; hence, the intellectual formation afforded by mathematics and philosophy was considered a privileged road to knowledge and learning and acquired centrality in education.

Over time, increased complexity in the knowledge and skills characterizing competence in specific areas fostered the development of formal instruction and the establishment of schools as separate institutions. The process of organization of knowledge was greatly favored by reliance on the written form, a practice adopted relatively soon by the liberal arts, but not by the practical arts. In the practical arts, informal apprenticeship remained the prevalent way of passing technical skills from one generation to the next. On the other hand, formal education tended to focus on those bodies of knowledge that were systematically organized in written form.

The importance of accurate definitions in furthering thoughts and the power accorded in Athenian life to those who could speak effectively prompted the development of grammar and rhetoric. The need to think clearly encouraged the development of logic or dialectics. In addition, Greek philosophy began to organize into bodies of knowledge studies regarding the ultimate reality of things (metaphysics), the theory of knowledge (epistemology), human nature and human conduct (ethics, political science, economics, sociology, and psychology), the physical world (astronomy, geography, physics, mechanics, hydraulics, mineralogy, and botany), and the living world (zoology, physiology, and anatomy). The search for intellectual discipline and the problems investigated by the developing sciences favored the progress in the field of mathematics and the refinement and systematization of theories and concepts in arithmetic, geometry, and trigonometry. In addition, Greek inquiry extended to the human past, investigating the causes of historical events and thus laying the foundation of history. Finally, although the fine arts were not organized into systematic bodies of knowledge, the Greeks cultivated several forms of literary criticism, thus giving systematic organization to the theory of art and esthetics.

Roman culture widely drew from Greek thought, furthering the systematization of knowledge and its organization in forms suitable for teaching. By the end of the fourth century, the liberal arts had been circumscribed to the study of compendia (written in Latin) of those Greek works deemed suitable to the spiritual and intellectual development of the pupils. Specifically, the trivium, that is, the elementary liberal art curriculum, included grammar, rhetoric, and logic. The higher liberal arts, or quadrivium, mainly incorporated mathematical studies and comprehended arithmetic, geometry, astronomy, and music. The boundaries of these disciplines did not necessarily include the same content that they comprise in modern times. For example, grammar also involved the study of poetry and literature. In addition, the content reflected changes in the Roman intellectual climate. For instance, the purpose of rhetoric changed from preparation to active participation in the debates over public policies to the study of elegant language to be employed in public celebrations. At the same time, the Romans did not tend to value the sciences for their own sake, but applied the theoretical knowledge gained from the Greeks in geometry, astronomy, and natural philosophy to the solution of practical problems.

The disciplines included in the trivium and the quadrivium continued to constitute the backbone of knowledge during the Middle Ages. However, many changes were made in each of the seven disciplines in response to the varying needs and interests of the time. Latin increasingly became the language of educated people; hence, grammar gained preponderance among the elementary liberal arts during the Early Middle Ages when the non-Latin people began to take part in the intellectual life of Europe. Nonetheless, Medieval Latin became increasingly different from classical Latin, reflecting the influence of the various languages spoken by the European peoples. Rhetoric lost most of its celebratory purpose and focused on the use of the written language for drawing up legal and feudal documents. Logic was increasingly identified with the rules of deductive thinking and, essentially, became distinguished from philosophy.

Arithmetic, geometry, and astronomy saw important developments during the Middle Ages. The cultural exchanges with the Arab world and the translation of the most important Greek, Arab, and Hindu works into Latin laid the foundations for the scientific and mathematical investigations of later centuries. Within the quadrivium, music retained its theoretical nature, even if its performance gained importance in medieval life. Although knowledge of the Greek tradition was praised by Christian philosophers for the contribution it gave to truth, and thus as an aid to the understanding of God and the soul, the intellectualism of pursuing knowledge for knowledge's sake was rejected. In the Benedictine tradition, where the monastery became the home of practical agriculturalists, as well as of religious, artists, and scholars, the alliance between learning and concrete reality foreshadowed the importance of factual knowledge and the relation between science and technology that came to characterize modern science.

Beginning in the twelfth century, teachers and students began to organize themselves into guilds for protections against the king, the bishop, or anyone else who tried to control them. Over time, the term *universitas* began to refer specifically to guilds of teachers (faculties) and students. Reflecting the articulation of knowledge of the time, the typical guilds of teachers were the faculties of liberal arts, law, medicine, and theology. Specific universities became famous for one specific faculty, thus deeply influencing the development of a particular discipline. In addition, the university system fostered an expansion of the liberal arts curriculum, adding the works of Aristotle on the physical sciences, ethics, politics, and metaphysics. The system also promoted the institutionalization of the educational curriculum (with its degrees, licenses to teach, exams, and titles) and, thus, the grouping of studies into separate faculties.

The Renaissance celebrated the return to the classics (Latin, Greeks, and Hebrew) and highly regarded rhetoric as a way to cultivate polite letters and expression. Logic fell in disrepute due to the humanist opposition to scholasticism. However, these changes had a deeper effect on the content of the trivium and quadrivium than on the disciplines taught in the universities, where medieval philosophy conserved its predominance. In the sciences, humanists turned away from the deductive methods of argumentation and advocated the use of the inductive method (observations of facts and generalization).

The belief that the method of induction is the proper method to gain scientific knowledge is at the root of the classification of human knowledge provided by Francis Bacon in the seventeenth century. Here, the disciplines came to be mainly characterized as histories of nature, collections of descriptions regarding a vast array of natural phenomena. At the same time, a method common to all sciences began to take shape. The scientist should observe nature, collect facts, identify their common qualities, and express these similarities in general formulas. Empiricism highlighted the patient work of scientists in acquiring facts. However, it dismissed the guiding role of theory in deciding observations and experiments. Although the almost exclusive reliance on induction disappeared in later work on method by Descartes, the uniqueness of the scientific method to gain knowledge was not challenged. In fact, the certitude granted by mathematics was upheld as the goal of scientific knowledge, and the scientific method was considered applicable and appropriate to all fields of human thought.

Whereas in the physical sciences this new method of gaining knowledge proved compatible with the emergence of a unitary principle of explanation, that is, the mechanism, a close relation between abstract thought and scientific investigation failed to surface in the biological sciences. The complexities involved in studying living things and the philosophical impossibility of reconciling the existence of human soul with a completely mechanistic physiology supported the specificity of different bodies of knowledge.

The search for natural laws was extended to the study of society and political economy during the era of Enlightenment. The rules for scientific data gathering also began to be applied in the field of the social sciences, and historians began to identify progress as the fundamental law of history. This process was furthered by the role played by Darwinism in the biological science, where the process of change assumed a central explanatory role. From biology, the idea that change is an inherent part of natural and human development influenced the social sciences and their methodological approach, which increasingly tried to emulate the scientific approach of the natural sciences. In the nineteenth century, the rise of positivism in philosophy further promoted the assumption that reality obeys general and universal laws. The purpose of the disciplines became to discover by observation and experimentation relationships able to explain nature, the universe, human nature, and social institutions. Psychology, anthropology, and scientific medicine were all deeply influenced by this way of thinking.

In the nineteenth century, the effect on education of the increasingly important role attributed to the sciences in the overall knowledge landscape was delayed by the lingering humanist belief that a truly liberal education has to be strongly based on a deep acquaintance with the classics. Secondary instruction was particularly successful in protecting this view; in contrast, in the universities, and especially in Germany, where professors and students were recognized for their remarkable degree of independence and freedom, mathematics and science became the dominant studies during the second half of the nineteenth century.

In the American colleges and universities, the attempt to extend to all fields of knowledge the application of the scientific method and the rise of professional organizations of scholars and specialists in various fields encouraged the subdivision of traditional bodies of knowledge into specialized subjects. What, at the beginning of the century, was studied under the label of natural history was, by the end of the century, subdivided into the various biological and natural sciences, thus including botany, zoology, physiology, psychology, paleontology, ornithology, entomology, and anthropology. Natural philosophy was articulated into specialized physical sciences (astronomy, physics, chemistry, mineralogy, geology, meteorology, and physical geography); similarly, history, economics, political sciences, sociology, and anthropology acquired their own specificity within the field of moral philosophy.

The scientific discoveries of the twentieth century in astronomy and physics challenged the positivistic assumptions of a rigid and indestructible matter, obedient to rigid laws. More generally, these new insights questioned the close correspondence between what the universe is really like and the picture rendered by science at a certain point in time, and brought the debate about the epistemic status of scientific knowledge to the forefront. At the same time, and almost paradoxically, the process of disciplinary subdivision went even further as scholars tended to specialize in ever-narrower aspects of one discipline. However, as noted by Easton and Schelling (1991), real-world problems are rarely confined to a specific knowledge domain and the parceled understandings afforded by the increasing specialization do not easily reassemble into a unitary view of the issue at hand. Proposed solutions include interdisciplinary training and teamwork within specific research topics, although the point of departure for these attempts at integration tends to remain the specialized knowledge granted by the various disciplines.

On one hand, the overview of the development of disciplinary knowledge showed that a certain partition of the world in different domains reflects broad cultural and institutional trends. On the other hand, the nature of the object investigated makes specific methodological choices more effective and fruitful than others, thus characterizing each discipline as a specific way of knowing. In the next section, we turn to consider the influence that these differences in thinking have on learning and teaching.

Domain Learning

Do teaching and learning differ across domains? As documented by Shulman and Quinlan (1996), educational psychologists' answer to this question has changed considerably across time. During the first two decades of the twentieth century, the answer has been mainly in the affirmative. In particular, Dewey (1902/1916) advocated the need to psychologize the subject matter of the studies by making explicit the research work that generated knowledge in a specific domain and by referring it to the present experience of the child. His experimental research was thus located within the naturalistic setting of the laboratory school.

In the next decades, following the lead of researchers such as Thorndike, educational psychologists' interest shifted toward the search for general theories of learning. Even when their research was nested within a particular subject matter, the general theoretical framework constrained the analysis of the disciplinary tasks. In addition, the controlled experiment in laboratory setting became the preferred methodological approach, further detaching psychological research from the educational setting.

Beginning in the 1980s, subject matters regained centrality. For instance, studies on classroom teaching increased understanding of the importance of pedagogical content knowledge. Further, comparisons between novices and experts uncovered the role played by heuristics typical of a certain discipline in the performance on domain-specific tasks. Moreover, the classroom, with its complexities, came to be considered a viable and preferred setting for studying these issues. Overall, researchers found that performance of domain-specific tasks calls for particular psychological processes. These findings spurred investigations of what pedagogical practices can best favor the development of these processes and thus improve students' learning.

In the ensuing sections, we consider some of the outcome of this research for the domains of reading, writing, history, mathematics, and science. Traditionally, these domains occupy a large portion of the educational curriculum, especially in the early years. Thus, it is not by chance that a large body of research about domain learning focused on these areas. We also mention a few controversial issues regarding the translation of research results into pedagogical practice. A general review of the work of educational psychologists in regard to learning within these specific domains may be found in the relevant chapters of the first and second editions of the *Handbook of Educational Psychology* (Alexander and Winne, 2006; Berliner and Calfee, 1996). Alexander (2006) offers an introductory overview of these topics.

Reading

Theories of learning have played a critical role in identifying what is meant by reading and writing, and, more generally, by literacy. Thus, definitions of reading span from the ability to decode (i.e., breaking the linguistic code) and encode (i.e., convert written signs fluently into meaning) to being well learned in a variety of topics as well as in a set of cultural practices (with more or less emphasis on the power structure engrained in them). The method chosen to study the process of reading and writing contributed to influence the definition of literacy also. For example, the exclusive focus on observable behavior characterizing research in the behaviorist tradition precluded the possibility to study understanding. Thus, these researchers mainly focused on handwriting, grammar, word recognition, and perception of print. Further, assuming that meaning is inherent in the text and the individual's role consists in uncovering it, understanding was mainly studied by observing vocabulary and recall. The pedagogical implications of this approach, still present in current curricula, include the suggestion to break the reading process into steps and to teach reading as a series of skills and subskills.

As well exemplified by Bruner (1990), the cognitive revolution focused on explaining mental processes; thus, understanding how meaning was generated became crucial. However, within the cognitive tradition, researchers conceived meaning in different terms. Specifically, the researchers working within the framework of information-processing theory assumed that meaning is transported from the author to the readers, while constructivists posited that meaning is constructed by the readers on the basis of information provided by the author.

This difference notwithstanding, cognitive psychologists fostered understanding of how individuals make sense of information conveyed by texts. By investigating the nature of readers' schemata and how information was organized in memory, researchers studied the role of background knowledge (Anderson and Pearson, 1984). Other studies focused on how different texts work, paying attention to their various structures (e.g., narrative or expository; Alexander and Kulikowich, 1994). Finally, research on the control that individuals maintain during meaning making has explored individuals' knowledge of their own cognitive processes (i.e., metacognition). In particular, researchers investigated individuals' knowledge of the tasks and goals required by reading or writing (i.e., declarative knowledge), of the strategies that allow one to pursue these goals (i.e., procedural knowledge), and individuals' awareness of how, when, and where to use a specific strategy (i.e., conditional knowledge; Garner, 1987). This work provided the background for research in strategy instruction and, limits notwithstanding, shifted the attention of educational psychologists from product to process.

Finally, cognitive psychologists fostered understanding of two basic processes of reading: phonemic awareness and automaticity. Phonemic awareness is the ability to think and manipulate sounds and plays a central role in the study of reading development. Automaticity regards the ability to process perceptual information necessary to the decoding of print with a minimum cognitive load, thus freeing attention for meaning-making purposes; within this process, accuracy and speed emerged as good predictors of comprehension (Stanovich, 1990). These findings suggest the soundness of a balanced reading program, in which mastering basic processes and meaningful engagement with text reinforce each other.

The social constructivist perspective highlighted the social dimension of learning. Thus, the definition of text was extended beyond the printed words to include conversation, media, and, more generally, social discourse. This perspective also implied a crucial epistemological shift since it defined knowledge as the consensus reached by the community of knowledgeable peers for the time being. Thus, according to this view, the external world may exist, but knowledge is not defined by a correspondence to it anymore (Bruffee, 1986). Such a view also suggested that thinking is an internalized version of conversation; thus, learning happens first on the social plane and, subsequently, is internalized by the individual (Vygotsky, 1934/1986). Pedagogically, this perspective advocated practices such as reciprocal teaching and whole language approach. This framework also drew attention on the influence of the context on the meaning-making process.

Writing

The importance of writing for communication, learning, and knowledge transmission can hardly be overstated. However, the scientific study of the process of writing is relatively recent (Graham, 2006). In the previous section, we considered the influence of different theoretical approaches on the study of literacy in general and described their pedagogical suggestions in terms of reading. In this section, we focus on the body of research that specifically addressed the writing process and on its pedagogical implications.

Mainly relying on analyses of think-aloud protocols collected from individuals of different ages and levels of expertise while composing texts, researchers in this domain emphasized that writing is a self-directed process. Often proceeding in a nonlinear fashion, this process requires individuals to simultaneously attend to several cognitive demands and, thus, entails a high level of effort. Although most of the research focused on cognitive processes, motivational and contextual factors were also found to influence writing (e.g., competence beliefs and environmental support).

Most theorists view writing as the interplay of three main components (Hayes and Flower, 1980). The first comprises factors external to the writer, such as topic, audience, and text produced so far. The second component regards the cognitive processes involved in writing and includes planning (e.g., setting goals, generating ideas, and organizing ideas into a plan), text production (e.g., translating plans into a written text), and reviewing (critically reading the text, determining how to address emerged problems, and editing). The final component is the writer's long-term memory, which includes knowledge of the topic, of the intended audience, and of rhetorical devices, as well as general plans to perform the writing task.

This body of research suggests that teaching writing should address all its components (Hillocks, 1986). In particular, direct teaching of strategies for planning and revising has proven particularly effective (Graham, 2005). At the same time, mastering of basic skills such as handwriting and spelling is also crucial to allow individuals to attend to the multiplicity of writing demands.

The learning environment can sustain students' development of writing strategies by offering appropriate scaffolding and peer interactions. Finally, increased awareness of the processes of reading and writing, of their differences as well as of their similarities, can foster the development of programs that facilitate development in both domains (Shanahan, 2005).

History

Although there is general agreement in identifying the domain of history with the past, psychological research has associated strikingly different processes to learning in history. In the first decades of the twentieth century, for example, learning history was viewed as the acquisition of temporal perspective and moral ideals (Hall, 1911), the maturation of chronological and causal thinking (Judd, 1915), and the development of historic sense (Bell, 1917).

Educational researchers, overall, agreed that learning history could not be reduced to answering factual questions; however, they also realized that this component of learning was the easiest to test. Behaviorism further restricted the study of domain-specific topics; in the case of history, research was limited to study how to apportion facts in order to facilitate memorization. It was only with the cognitive revolution that the attention of researchers focused on the psychological processes involved in learning history (Wineburg, 1996).

Aided by the use of qualitative methodologies, educational psychologists explored learners' background knowledge in an attempt to uncover beliefs and conceptions that may have fostered or hindered thinking in history (e.g., ideas about time and chronology, sparse information about historical people and events, and beliefs about the nature of history). They also studied how historians and novices generated historical understanding while reading primary and secondary sources about specific events (Wineburg, 2001).

This body of research suggested that learning history entails developing familiarity with concepts and ideas that allow a description of the past (i.e., substantive knowledge) and also becoming acquainted with the strategies employed by historical inquirers to research and interpret the past (i.e., procedural knowledge). In particular, the development of historical knowledge includes not only being able to answer who, what, when, where, and how questions about the past (i.e., first-order knowledge), but also developing an understanding of concepts such as causation, change, historical significance, empathy, evidence, and account that allow historical investigators to interpret the past (i.e., second-order knowledge; Lee, 2005).

By comparison, procedural knowledge regards being able to use strategies such as assessing the status of sources, corroborating sources, contextualizing events, constructing evidence-based arguments, and writing accounts (VanSledright and Limón, 2006). The difference of these processes with the experience of memorization of information commonly associated to learning history is striking.

Although research in the past 20 years has increased understanding of the process of learning history and highlighted its specificity, the intense debate about the role of history in the school curriculum makes it difficult to translate these findings into pedagogical practice. In schools, the goal of developing historical thinking is often countered by the will to use history to build a collective, national identity. While the first purpose is well served by pedagogical approaches that foster a view of history as a critical inquiry into the past, the second is better pursued by the transmission of a specific narrative viewed as coinciding with the past. In addition, more research is needed to understand how to prepare teachers to be able to foster historical thinking in their students.

Mathematics

Historically, the characterization of mathematics evolved from a science of numbers and space to a science of patterns. More recently, the view of mathematics as a human activity defined within historical, cultural, and social contexts also emerged. In psychological research, specific aspects of mathematics learning were often used for studying general theories and pedagogical approaches. However, the specificity of thinking within this domain was usually ignored (De Corte et al., 1996).

As surfaced in other domains considered herein, different psychological theories of cognitive development espoused distinctive views of mathematics, used a various array of research methodologies, focused on particular aspects of mathematics learning, and thus reached different pedagogical conclusions. Behaviorism and connectionism, for example, favored drill and practice of well-defined information, skills, and associations.

The view of mathematics learning changed remarkably with the cognitive revolution, shifting the focus on the processes involved in thinking mathematically. In characterizing the domain, researchers highlighted the dual nature of mathematics. Rooted in the perception and description of the order of objects and events, once mathematics succeeds in modeling these structures through a process of symbolical representation, these representations become amenable to study in an abstract fashion, independent from their real-world roots. The pedagogical consequence of acknowledging this feature of the domain is a shift of focus from computation to modeling (i.e., the thinking of the mathematician; Davis, 1992).

A second characteristic of the domain regards the fact that, historically, mathematical concepts evolved hierarchically through a series of restructuring of previously developed concepts, definitions, and functions. The parallel with the Piagetian characterization of cognitive growth through a series of restructuring engendered by a situation of disequilibrium perhaps explains why mathematics was so often used by cognitive psychologists to study general cognitive development. Pedagogically, this feature of the domain supports practices that help the child relive the developmental process of the discipline (Freudenthal, 1991). This indication does not suggest that children need to reinvent the product of this development (e.g., the definition of rational numbers), rather that they have to trod the same cognitive path of people facing mathematical problems (e.g., abstracting and formalizing).

Finally, development in mathematics requires that individuals are comfortable with multiple modes of representation (e.g., verbal/syntactic, visual/spatial, and formal/symbolic) and fluent in translating from one system to the other. In particular, researchers theorized that mathematical thinking implies the interplay of external representations (e.g., language, symbols on a page, and objects), and internal mental processes, which include internal representations, affective processes, and executive functions (e.g., planning, and monitoring; Goldin, 1992). Pedagogically, this theory suggests that learning mathematics means fostering the development of internal representations well connected and consistent with conventional external representations; fluid movement across different systems of representation also needs to be promoted.

In schools, mathematics is often associated to doing mathematics rather than thinking mathematically. Thus, problem solving takes a central place in the curriculum and a large body of research in mathematics focused on investigating this process. From these studies, it emerged that problem solving involves the interplay of four factors: domain-specific knowledge, heuristic methods, metacognitive knowledge, and affection (beliefs and emotion).

Domain-specific knowledge refers to definitions, formulas, symbols, algorithms, and concepts typical of the domain. Although this knowledge in experts is well organized and thus flexibly accessible, misconceptions and defective skills often hinder problem solving in novices. In addition, experts tend to categorize problems according to their mathematical structure, whereas novices focus on problem surface characteristics (Chi *et al.*, 1988; Confrey, 1990).

Heuristics are general guidelines that facilitate a systematic approach to the task and thus favor arriving at a solution (e.g., identifying the data of the problem, looking for related problems, and checking the results). However, knowledge of isolated heuristics is usually not very helpful. Research suggests that a more successful approach requires teaching heuristics concurrently with metacognitive skills and while exposing students to a variety of situations, so that learners may understand when and how to use a certain heuristic (Schoenfeld, 1992).

Metacognitive knowledge regards knowledge of one's own cognitive functioning and self-monitoring of these cognitive activities. Skilled problem solvers demonstrate high control of their actions, including planning and monitoring, and, if necessary, make the required corrections to a previously implemented strategy. Finally, affective components of problem solving include beliefs about the self and about mathematics, and emotions such as interest in the task (McLeod, 1990). Research on problem solving has shown that it is possible to teach students to plan and monitor more effectively (Schoenfeld, 1985). In addition, when the learning environment is structured in such a way as to favor reflective practice and talk among students about their thinking, mathematical learning is usually improved (Lampert, 1990).

Science

Reflecting a trend evidenced in other domains, the definition of what it means to learn science and of what psychological processes are central to its development has been influenced by theories of cognitive development. The meaning of learning science has increasingly broadened to include an understanding of substantive concepts and of the nature of science, logical reasoning, procedures used to develop scientific explanations, and metacognitive awareness (Linn *et al.*, 1996).

Comparisons between expert and novice thinking demonstrated that novices' knowledge is organized around concrete factors (e.g., formulas), while experts' knowledge tends to be hierarchically organized around abstract elements (Chi *et al.*, 1981). Beginning in the late 1970s, researchers increasingly distinguished between the development of logical skills and that of scientific concepts (Pfundt and Duit, 1991). In addition, research extended beyond the acquisition of science information to investigate learners' ideas about the nature of science (Hestenes, 1992). The acknowledgment of the role of metacognition in learning paralleled this shift in focus, suggesting that monitoring one's own cognition is an important component in learning science, once one abandons the idea that science consists of universal truth contained in textbooks (White, 1988).

The interpretation of students' misconceptions also changed; previously conceptualized as instances signaling faulty reasoning on the students' part, these ideas began to be interpreted as alternative intuitions or framework to model the world. Researchers noted that students' misconceptions may originate from inaccurate implications drawn from accurate observations, with a focus on inessential characteristics of phenomena, or on the adoption of standards of evidence and views of science markedly different from those espoused by the scientific community (Kuhn *et al.*, 1988).

From these insights, two lines of research developed; the first focused on conceptual change and the second, on the restructuring of knowledge. Consistent to the Piagetian theory, conceptual change tended to be promoted by using cognitive conflict as a mechanism to foster scientific understanding. More recently, researchers studied what can motivate students to change their current understandings and found that, in addition to facing disconcerting evidence about their current concepts, students also need to confront clear alternatives (Strike and Posner, 1985). This new approach prompted teachers to focus on fostering and guiding the reasoning process of students while they investigate phenomena, rather then contradicting the conclusions they reach.

The investigation of experts' organization of scientific knowledge showed that scientists often use qualitative models (e.g., free-body diagrams) as an aid in problem solving. They also tend to chunk knowledge in patterns that can be used in a variety of situations, developing production rules that link a condition (e.g., the object in contact has different temperature) to a consequent action (e.g., the objects will tend toward equilibrium). In addition, experts tend to entertain several models of scientific phenomena and to choose which one to rely on according to the specific problem they face (Reif and Larkin, 1991).

Studies of novices found that students often entertain conflicting interpretations of scientific phenomena. Some researchers hypothesized that students' scientific knowledge tends to be fragile and fragmented (diSessa, 2002); other studies showed that students tend to contextualize their views, applying one set of ideas to interpret phenomena within the classroom context and another set to deal with the same instance out of class (Gilbert and Boulter, 2000). In addition, novices' ability to generalize a model across a range of experiences is usually limited.

These findings supported a change in the goals set for science education, with the focus shifting from acquiring science information and concepts to developing the ability to scientifically reason about phenomena (Linn and Eylon, 2006). Pedagogically, this view suggests that students are exposed to a variety of explanatory models and provided with criteria for selecting among them according to the problem considered. Far from engaging students in inquiry or discovery activities for their own sake, this approach highlights the development of background knowledge, modeling and discussion of key processes and strategies, instructional guidance, feedback, use of evidence to test one's own ideas, and monitoring of one's progress (Alexander, 2006).

Concluding Thoughts

The roots of current disciplines and domains of study reach well back in history. These areas of knowledge and practice have not only reflected societies and cultures of their time, but have also influenced them, especially through formal educational systems. The differences in domains continue to shape the landscape of academic practice due to their inherent and socially constructed nature. Here, we have explored several of those features that define contemporary domains and their instantiation in educational practice.

See also: Concept Learning; Learning to Read; Reading Comprehension: Reading for Learning; Writing, Advanced; Writing, Early.

Bibliography

Alexander, P. A. (2006). *Psychology in Learning and Instruction*. Upper Saddle River, NJ: Pearson/Merrill Prentice Hall.

Alexander, P. A. and Kulikowich, J. M. (1994). Learning from physics text: A synthesis of recent research. *Special Issue: Print-Based Language Arts and Science Learning. Journal of Research in Science Teaching* **31**, 895–911.

Alexander, P. A. and Winne, P. H. (eds.) (2006). *Handbook of Educational Psychology*, 2nd edn. Mahwah, NJ: Erlbaum.

Anderson, R. C. and Pearson, P. D. (1984). A schema-theoretic view of basic processes in reading comprehension. In Pearson, P. D., Barr, R., Kamil, M., and Mosenthal, P. (eds.) *Handbook of Reading Research*, vol. 1, pp 255–293. New York: Longman.

Bell, J. C. (1917). The historic sense. *Journal of Educational Psychology* **8**, 317–318.

Berliner, D. C. and Calfee, R. C. (eds.) (1996). *Handbook of Educational Psychology*. New York: Simon and Schuster/Macmillan.

Bruffee, K. A. (1986). Social construction, language, and the authority of knowledge: A bibliographic essay. *College English* **48**, 773–790.

Bruner, J. (1990). *Acts of Meaning*. Cambridge, MA: Harvard University Press.

Butts, F. R. (1955). *A Cultural History of Western Education: Its Social and Intellectual Foundations*, 2nd edn. New York: McGraw-Hill.

Chi, M. T., Feltovich, P., and Smith, E. L. (1981). Categorization and representation of physics problems by experts and novices. *Cognitive Science* **5**(2), 121–152.

Chi, M. T., Glaser, R., and Farr, M. J. (eds.) (1988). *The Nature of Expertise*. Hilldale, NJ: Erlbaum.

Confrey, J. (1990). A review of the research on student conceptions in mathematics, science, and programming. In Cazden, C. B. (ed.) *Review of Research in Education,* vol. 16, pp 3–55. Washington, DC: American Educational Research Association.

Davis, R. B. (1992). Reflections on where mathematics education now stands and on where it may be going. In Grouws, D. A. (ed.) *Handbook of Research on Mathematics Teaching and Learning*, pp 724–734. New York: Macmillan.

De Corte, E., Greer, B., and Verschaffel, L. (1996). Mathematics teaching and learning. In Berliner, D. C. and Calfee, R. C. (eds.) *Handbook of Educational Psychology*, pp 491–549. New York: Simon and Schuster/Macmillan.

Dewey, J. (1902/1916). *The Child and the Curriculum*. Chicago, IL: University of Chicago Press.

diSessa, A. A. (2002). Why ''conceptual ecology'' is a good idea. In Limón, M. and Mason, L. (eds.) *Reconsidering Conceptual Change: Issues in Theory and Practice*, pp 29–60. Dordrecht: Kluwer.

Easton, D. and Schelling, C. S. (eds.) (1991). *Divided Knowledge:Across Disciplines, across Cultures*. Newbury Park, CA: Sage.

Fehl, N. E. (1966). *Science and Culture*. Hong Kong: Chung Chi Publications.

Freudenthal, H. (1991). *Revisiting Mathematics Education*. Dordrecht: Kluwer.

Garner, R. (1987). *Metacognition and Reading Comprehension*. Norwood, NJ: Ablex.

Gilbert, J. K. and Boulter, C. J. (2000). *Developing Models in Science Education*. Dordrecht: Kluwer.

Goldin, G. A. (1992). On developing a unified model for the psychology of mathematical learning and problem solving. In Geeslin, W. and Graham, K. (eds.) *Proceedings of the Sixteenth Annual Meeting of the International Group for the Psychology of Mathematics Education*, vol. 3, pp 235–261. Durham, NC: University of New Hampshire Press.

Graham, S. (2005). Strategy instruction and the teaching of writing: A meta-analysis. In MacArthur, C., Graham, S., and Fitzgerald, F. (eds.) *Handbook of Writing Research*, pp 187–207. New York: Guilford.

Graham, S. (2006). Writing. In Alexander, P. A. and Winne, P. H. (eds.) *Handbook of Educational Psychology*, pp 457–478. Mahwah, NJ: Erlbaum.

Hall, A. R. and Hall, B. M. (1988). *A Brief History of Science*. Ames, IA: Iowa State University Press.

Hall, G. S. (1911). *Educational Problems*, vol. II. New York: Appleton.

Hayes, J. and Flower, L. (1980). Identifying the organization of writing processes. In Gregg, L. and Steinberg, E. (eds.) *Cognitive Processes in Writing*, pp 3–30. Hillsdale, NJ: Erlbaum.

Hestenes, D. (1992). Modeling games in the Newtonian world. *American Journal of Physics* **60**(8), 732–748.

Hillocks, G. (1986). *Research on Written Composition: New Directions for Teaching*. Urbana, IL: National Council of Teachers of English.

Judd, C. H. (1915). *Psychology of High-School Subjects*. Boston, MA: Ginn.

Kuhn, D., Amsel, E., O'Loughlin, M., and Schauble, L. (1988). *The Development of Scientific Thinking Skills, Developmental Psychology Series*. Orlando, FL: Academic Press.

Lampert, M. (1990). When the problem is not the question and the solution is not the answer: Mathematical knowing and teaching. *American Educational Research Journal* **27**, 29–63.

Lee, J. P. (2005). Putting principles into practice: Understanding history. In Donovan, M. S. and Bransford, J. D. (eds.) *How Students Learn: History in the Classroom*. Washington, DC: The National Academies Press.

Libby, W. (1917). *An Introduction to the History of Science*. Boston, MA: Houghton Mifflin.

Linn, M. C. and Eylon, B. (2006). Science education: Integrating views of learning and instruction. In Alexander, P. A. and Winne, P. H. (eds.) *Handbook of Educational Psychology*, pp 511–544. Mahwah, NJ: Erlbaum.

Linn, M. C., Songer, N. B., and Eylon, B. (1996). Shifts and convergences in science learning and instruction. In Berliner, D. C.

and Calfee, R. C. (eds.) *Handbook of Educational Psychology*, pp 438–490. New York: Simon and Schuster/Macmillan.

McLeod, D. B. (1990). Information-processing theories and mathematics learning: The role of affect. *International Journal of Educational Research* **14**, 13–29.

Pfundt, H. and Duit, R. (1991). *Students' Alternative Frameworks,* 3rd edn. Kiel: Institut für die Pädagogik der Naturwissenschaften (Institute for Science Education at the University of Kiel).

Reif, F. and Larkin, J. H. (1991). Cognition in scientific and everyday domains: Comparison and learning implications. *Journal of Research in Science Teaching* **28**(9), 733–760.

Schoenfeld, A. H. (1985). *Mathematical Problem Solving*. New York: Academic Press.

Schoenfeld, A. H. (1992). Learning to think mathematically: Problem solving, metacognition, and sense-making in mathematics. In Grouws, D. A. (ed.) *Handbook of Research on Mathematics Teaching and Learning*, pp 334–370. New York: Macmillan.

Shanahan, T. (2005). Relations among oral language, reading, and writing development. In MacArthur, C., Graham, S., and Fitzgerald, J. (eds.) *Handbook of Writing Research*, pp 171–185. New York: Guilford.

Shulman, L. S. and Quinlan, K. M. (1996). The comparative psychology of school subjects. In Berliner, D. C. and Calfee, R. C. (eds.) *Handbook of Educational Psychology*, pp 399–422. New York: Simon and Schuster/Macmillan.

Stanovich, K. E. (1990). A call for an end to the paradigm wars in reading research. *Journal for Reading Behavior* **22**, 221–232.

Strike, K. A. and Posner, G. J. (1985). A conceptual change view of learning and understanding. In West, L. H. and Pines, A. L. (eds.) *Cognitive Structure and Conceptual Change*, pp 211–231. Orlando, FL: Academic Press.

VanSledright, B. and Limón, M. (2006). Learning and teaching social studies: A review of cognitive research in history and geography. In Alexander, P. A. and Winne, P. H. (eds.) *Handbook of Educational Psychology*, pp 545–570. Mahwah, NJ: Erlbaum.

Vygotsky, L. S. (1934/1986). *Thought and Language*. Kozulin, A. (trans.) Cambridge, MA: MIT Press.

White, R. T. (1988). Metacognition. In Keeves, J. P. (ed.) *Educational Research,Methodology and Measurement:An International Handbook*, pp 70–75. Oxford: Pergamon.

Wineburg, S. (1996). The psychology of learning and teaching history. In Berliner, D. C. and Calfee, R. C. (eds.) *Handbook of Educational Psychology*, pp 423–437. New York: Simon and Schuster/Macmillan.

Wineburg, S. (2001). *Historical Thinking and other Unnatural Acts: Charting the Future of Teaching the Past*. Philadelphia, PA: Temple University Press.

Further Reading

Donald, J. (2002). *Learning to Think: Disciplinary Perspectives*. San Francisco, CA: Jossey-Bass.

Elby, A. (2001). Helping physics students learn how to learn. *Physical Education Research: American Journal of Physiology Supplement* **69**(7), 54–64.

Gardner, H. (1999). *The Disciplined Mind: What All Students Should Understand*. New York: Simon and Schuster.

Harris, R. W. (1960). *Science, Mind, and Method*. Oxford: Basil Blackwell.

Hashweh, M. (1996). Effects of science teachers' epistemological beliefs in teaching. *Journal of Research in Science Teaching* **33**(1), 47–63.

Hirst, R. H. (1973). Liberal education and the nature of knowledge. In Peters, R. S. (ed.) *Philosophy of Education*, pp 87–101. Oxford: Oxford University Press.

Larkin, J., McDermott, J., Simon, D. P., and Simon, H. A. (1980). Expert and novice performance in solving physics problems. *Science* **208**(20), 1335–1342.

Messer-Davidow, E., Shumway, D. R., and Sylvan, D. J. (eds.) (1993). *Knowledges:Historical and Critical Studies in Disciplinarity.* Charlottesville, VA: University Press of Virginia.

Moll, L., Amanti, C., Neff, D., and Gonzales, N. (1992). Funds of knowledge for teaching: Using a qualitative approach to connect homes and classrooms. *Theory into Practice* **31**, 132–141.

Seixas, P. (2000). Schweigen! die Kinder! Or, does postmodern history have a place in the schools? In Stearns, P. N., Seixas, P., and Wineburg, S. (eds.) *Knowing, Teaching, and Learning History,* pp 19–37. New York: New York University Press.

VanSledright, B. (2002). *In Search of America's Past: Learning to Read History in Elementary School*. New York: Teachers College Press.

Venezky, R. L. (1984). The history of reading research. In Pearson, P. D., Barr, R., Kamil, M., and Mosenthal, P. (eds.) *Handbook of Reading Research,* vol. 1, pp 3–39. New York: Longman.

Wilson, S. M. (1990). Mastodons, maps, and Michigan: Exploring uncharted territory while teaching elementary school social studies. *Report No. 24*. Elementary Subjects Center Series, Michigan State University.

Wineburg, S. and Wilson, S. (2001). Wrinkles in time and place: Using performance assessment to understand the knowledge of history teachers. In Wineburg, S. (ed.) *Historical Thinking and other Unnatural Acts:Charting the Future of Teaching the Past*, pp 173–214. Philadelphia, PA: Temple University Press.

Metacognition

L Baker, University of Maryland, Baltimore County, Baltimore, MD, USA

Glossary

Cognitive monitoring – It refers to any activity aimed at evaluating or regulating one's own cognitions, including planning, checking, self-testing, assessing one's progress, and correcting one's errors.

Comprehension monitoring – It refers to metacognitive control in reading or listening, which involves deciding whether or not one understands (evaluation) and taking appropriate steps to correct comprehension problems that are detected (regulation).

Executive function – It is the cognitive system that controls and manages other cognitive processes, is associated with frontal lobe functioning, and includes processes typically regarded as metacognitive in nature, such as planning, monitoring, and error correction and detection.

Metacognition – It refers to thinking about thinking; knowledge about cognition and regulation of cognition; knowledge about person, task, and strategy variables that affect performance in a given domain; and cognitive monitoring and control.

Metacomprehension – It refers to understanding one's understanding, that is, realizing that one has understood.

Metamemory – It is knowledge about memory and control of memory, that is, appraisal of one's memory on a given task.

Other-regulation – It refers to regulation of the behaviors and cognitive activities of one individual by another, usually more knowledgeable; it involves Vygotsky's proposed sequence of other-regulation to self-regulation.

Reciprocal teaching – It is an approach to foster cognitive and metacognitive strategies in reading that involves peer collaboration; students are taught to use strategies of predicting, clarifying, summarizing, and questioning.

Self-regulation – It is the ability to control one's own behavior and cognitive activities; self-regulated learning is self-directed, intrinsically motivated, and under the deliberate, strategic control of the learner; it involves effective use of processes included within the regulatory component of metacognition, such as planning, monitoring, and evaluating.

Self-system – It is the cluster of motivational and affective processes that influence why we do what we do; it includes self-perceptions, attributions for performance outcomes, goals for engaging in an activity, and achievement motivation.

Definitional Issues

A question of ongoing interest and importance is how and when students develop knowledge and control of their cognitive processes. This higher-level cognition was given the label metacognition by the American developmental psychologist John Flavell in the mid-1970s. Metacognition is concerned with our ability to reflect on our own thinking, and in an academic context it includes knowledge about ourselves as learners, about aspects of the task, and about strategy use. Metacognition also involves self-regulation of our own cognitive efforts, including planning our actions, checking the outcomes of our efforts, evaluating our progress, remediating difficulties that arise, and testing and revising our strategies for learning.

The construct of metacognition has had wide appeal and wide applicability, stimulating a great deal of research across a broad spectrum of disciplines. Research today spans the subdisciplines of educational, developmental, cognitive, clinical, social, comparative, and cognitive psychology, as well as related fields such as neuroscience, linguistics, and second language learning, special education, and speech and communication disorders. Once developmental psychologists began to study metacognition in the 1970s, the construct quickly attracted the attention of educational researchers seeking an explanation for why some students fared better in school than others. The consistent finding for more than 30 years has been that students who are more successful in a domain exhibit higher levels of metacognitive knowledge about the domain and are more skilled at regulating their cognitive processes. Instructional interventions to promote metacognition quickly became popular and remain so today. The focus in this article is on metacognition in educational contexts.

Metacognition has been defined in different ways, and that of course affects how it has been studied. The term literally means thinking about thinking. John Flavell and Ann Brown initially defined metacognition as knowledge about cognition and regulation of cognition.

This two-component conceptualization of metacognition has been widely but not exclusively used since then by educational researchers. Some have restricted the term to the knowledge component, whereas others have restricted it to the control component. For example, researchers within the cognitive–experimental tradition use a definition proposed by Thomas Nelson that includes two components, monitoring and control. Two closely related constructs are associated with the control aspect of metacognition: self-regulation and executive functioning. The term self-regulation is often used by educational psychologists to refer to the use of skills included within the regulatory component of metacognition, such as planning, monitoring, and evaluating. (Developmental psychologists have a broader definition of self-regulation that encompasses impulse control.) Executive function is a term with origins in cognitive psychology and neuroscience. It includes processes typically regarded as metacognitive in nature, such as planning, monitoring, and correcting and detecting errors, and it is typically linked to frontal lobe functioning in the brain.

Whereas metacognition once was studied solely in terms of how it is related to cognition, it is now recognized that one cannot understand how and why people perform as they do on cognitive tasks without an examination of motivational and affective as well as metacognitive factors. Accordingly, many contemporary researchers examine the role of the self-system, which includes motivation, perceived competence, and attributional beliefs, in conjunction with metacognition and cognition.

Origins of Metacognition

Much of the research on metacognition in educational contexts is descriptive in nature, documenting developmental and individual differences in knowledge and control. Less often do researchers address basic questions about the mechanisms of metacognitive growth. Nevertheless, it is now widely agreed that the origins of metacognition lie at least in part in social interactions. Russian psychologist Lev Vygotsky proposed that children first learn how to engage in cognitive tasks through social interaction with more knowledgeable others, usually parents or teachers. The expert initially takes the responsibility of regulating the novice's activity by setting goals, planning, evaluating, and focusing attention on what is relevant. Gradually, the expert gives over more and more responsibility to the novice as the novice becomes capable of assuming it, until finally the novice internalizes the regulatory mechanisms and can perform without expert assistance. Many successful interventions aimed at fostering metacognition draw on Vygotsky's proposed sequence from other-regulation to self-regulation.

Whereas Vygotsky emphasized expert–novice interactions, another influential social perspective is that of Swiss psychologist Jean Piaget, who emphasized the importance of peer interactions. Piaget argued that peers challenge one another's thoughts and thus advance cognitive development. Discussion and collaboration help students to monitor their own understanding and build new strategic capabilities. Instructional interventions often supplement an emphasis on individual cognition with an emphasis on peer support for monitoring, reflection, and revision. These interventions, too, have met with success, providing validation for the perspective that metacognition has its origins in social interaction.

It is important not to overlook maturation as a further contributor to metacognitive growth. Adolescence is a period of major development in the prefrontal cortex, the portion of the brain involved in executive function. As noted previously, executive function includes metacognitive processes such as planning and monitoring. The prefrontal lobes are the last portions of the brain to develop, with maturation not complete until late adolescence or early adulthood. This late maturation helps explain why limitations in metacognitive control are still apparent in high school and college students.

Methods for Assessing Metacognition

Considerable controversy exists as to the best ways to measure metacognition. Methods vary in part depending on the theoretical orientation of the researcher. Methods also must be selected with developmental considerations in mind. Therefore, a variety of approaches have been used to study metacogniiton. Each approach has limitations, so it is advisable to use multiple measures that converge on the construct.

Verbal Reports

The most frequently used approach to assess both metacognitive knowledge and metacognitive control is to ask students directly about what they know or what they do while engaging in cognitive activities. Such self-reports have been collected in a variety of ways. For assessing metacognitive control, participants may be asked to think aloud about what they are doing and thinking as they solve a problem or read a text or they may be asked to provide written comments periodically throughout the session. Participants may alternatively be asked to complete checklists of strategies they used in a given task after its completion, or they may complete questionnaires or study-strategy inventories.

Whereas verbal reports are but one way for assessing metacognitive control, they are the primary basis for collecting information about metacognitive knowledge, either through interviews or questionnaires. John Flavell's early study of metamemory that fueled the interest in metacognition used a structured interview format. Questionnaires were subsequently developed, often based on interview findings or think-aloud protocols. The major limitation of such approaches is that there is not necessarily a correspondence between what people say they do and what they actually do. Comparisons of general questionnaire responses with performance measures on a given task often yield rather low correlations. In addition, students, particularly children, often respond according to what they think they should say, rather than what they actually believe or do. Nevertheless, despite their limitations, there is a general consensus that verbal reports can be valid and reliable sources of information about cognitive processes when elicited and interpreted according to established guidelines.

Most questionnaires designed to assess metacognition are domain specific (e.g., reading or mathematics), but a few are intended to be more domain general. A domain-specific inventory might tap a student's understanding of variables that affect reading outcomes and of strategies that are effective for comprehending text. A domain-general inventory might assess an individual's knowledge about cognition (including declarative, procedural, and conditional knowledge) and regulation of cognition (including planning, monitoring, debugging, and evaluating learning). Relatively few well-validated and reliable instruments are available for research or practical use.

Online Processing Measures

Metacognitive control is frequently studied by asking students to engage in a task and collecting process measures as the task is being completed. For example, to assess metacognitive control during reading, a passage may be presented to the reader on a computer screen. Patterns of movement through the text are collected automatically, revealing whether the reader paused at a particular point, whether he or she looked back at previous text, whether he or she jumped ahead. These measures are often supplemented by asking readers to reflect on what they were thinking, or by giving them comprehension questions and then relating outcomes to the processing measures. Computer technology has similarly been used to capture processing during writing tasks and during mathematical problem solving. An advantage of these approaches is that they reveal what students do instead of what they say they do. However, the naturalness of the cognitive task is often disrupted by the specialized technology demands.

Judgments of Learning and Predictions of Performance

In judgments of learning (JOL) tasks, students are presented with to-be-learned material, such as a list of words or a passage, and then they are given a test over the material. They are then asked to judge how well they learned the material or how well they answered the comprehension questions (often referred to as an index of metacomprehension). Judgments of learning are then examined in relation to actual performance.

A related approach, often referred to as knowledge monitoring, involves presenting students with material and asking them how well they think they would perform on a test. For example, they might be presented with a list of vocabulary words and be asked how many they would be able to define, or a set of math problems and asked how many they can solve. They are then asked to complete the task, and their performance is compared to their predictions.

These types of tasks are more likely to be used in research conducted by cognitive psychologists interested in basic processes than by educational researchers concerned with more applied issues. Nevertheless, the approach has its origins in seminal research on memory monitoring, and research on studying (applied memory) often includes assessments of test readiness.

Metacognition in Specific Academic Domains

Most of the research on metacognition is focused on a particular academic domain, in recognition that metacognition is largely domain specific. In other words, a student may have a great deal of metacognitive knowledge about reading, but that knowledge does not necessarily generalize to mathematics. This section addresses research findings on metacognition as it has been studied in reading, writing, mathematics, and science.

Metacognition in Reading

Research on metacognition in reading began in the 1970s, shortly after the publication of Flavell's seminal studies on metamemory. Pioneers in this area of research were Ann Brown and Scott Paris. Reading is the academic domain most frequently studied, and so it is given more attention in this article than the other content areas.

Studies of metacognitive knowledge

Much of the research on metacognitive knowledge about reading uses structured interview procedures adapted from Flavell's metamemory work. In a typical study, children are interviewed about their knowledge of person, task, and strategy variables involved in reading. The pattern that has been found consistently is that younger readers have little awareness that they must attempt to make sense of text. They focus on reading as a decoding process, rather than as a meaning-getting process. Ability-related differences in knowledge about reading, like developmental differences, have been documented in countless studies, across age groups ranging from early childhood through later adulthood. Students' metacognitive knowledge about reading, whether assessed through interviews, questionnaires, or verbal reports, remains an active and important area of inquiry.

Studies of comprehension monitoring

Effective text comprehension requires an important metacognitive control component known as comprehension monitoring. Comprehension monitoring involves deciding whether or not we understand (evaluation) and taking appropriate steps to correct whatever comprehension problems we detect (regulation). Research has shown that students of all ages often are ineffective at monitoring their understanding of text. These difficulties are perhaps most apparent when students are asked to read information text, such as science and history textbooks. Failures to evaluate and regulate understanding reduce the likelihood of meaningful learning.

The majority of studies of comprehension monitoring over the years have used the error-detection paradigm. In this approach, errors or problems are deliberately introduced into texts, and various indices are used to determine whether readers notice the problems and attempt to resolve them. For example, readers may be asked to underline or report detected errors, or online processing measures may reveal longer pauses when readers encounter problematic text. Caution is needed in interpreting these studies because of students' propensity to believe texts are true and well structured and because of their reluctance to acknowledge comprehension difficulties. Moreover, some types of errors are more likely to be reported than others; for example, younger and less-skilled readers are more likely to evaluate their understanding using a word-level criterion than an internal-consistency criterion.

Studies aimed at fostering metacognitive skills

Intervention studies began to be implemented in the 1980s, providing solid evidence that metacognitive knowledge and control could be enhanced through direct instruction. Comprehensive classroom reading interventions incorporated metacognitively oriented instruction, with the goal not of enhancing metacognition *per se*, but rather of promoting students' reading comprehension by increasing their metacognition. Interventions that use some variant of reciprocal teaching, in which peers collaborate to learn and apply strategies of predicting, clarifying, summarizing, and questioning, have yielded substantial effects on reading comprehension. The research

base for the effectiveness of metacognitive intervention is now so strong that professional organizations and national panels recommend that metacognition be included in reading comprehension curricula.

Metacognition in Writing

Metacognition plays a role in the production of text as well as in the comprehension of text. Research on metacognition in writing has followed a similar course to that on reading. In the 1980s, researchers began to compare the metacognitive knowledge and control of more-skilled and less-skilled writers. Across all age groups, clear differences are apparent in students' conceptions of writing, their knowledge of the writing process, and their abilities to implement effective control strategies. For example, better writers focus more on the function of writing, whereas poorer writers focus more on form. When asked about their conceptions of writing, better writers discuss the qualities of good writing, such as having a clear beginning, middle, and end, whereas poorer writers discuss spelling all of the words correctly. Skilled writers have higher-order awareness of the writing process, such as awareness of the need for clarity, organization, and audience sensitivity, whereas less-skilled writers tend to focus on lower-order processes dealing with spelling, grammar, and punctuation.

Interest in metacognitive control of writing coincided with the publication of a cognitive process model of writing by Linda Flower and John Hayes in the early 1980s. The model includes three recursive processes: planning, translating (sentence generation), and revising, all of which are controlled by a monitor or executive component. Research has demonstrated consistent differences in how expert and novice writers handle the planning and revision processes. For example, experts are more likely to have global goals for their writing that take into account the communicative purpose of the task, and they revise at a global level. In contrast, novices seldom have overall plans for their writing and their revisions are typically made at a sentence-by-sentence level.

Also, as with reading, classroom interventions have been devised and implemented to increase students' metacognitive awareness and control of writing processes. Many of these interventions aim to reduce the cognitive processing demands on less-skilled writers by providing prompts, cues, and scaffolds. Marlene Scardamalia and Carl Bereiter developed an approach known as procedural facilitation that has proven effective with elementary school students and has been adapted up through the college level. Prompts are provided to remind students of the steps in the planning process, for example, or things that need to be taken into account when revising a paper. Often the translation demands are reduced so that students who are overly focused on spelling, punctuation, and handwriting do not get bogged down with the lower-level components (e.g., a word processing system is used).

Metacognition in Mathematics

Research on metacognition in mathematics also began to appear in the 1980s. As with reading and writing, attention focused on both knowledge and control and on students of all ages. A paper by Alan Schoenfeld in 1987 was particularly influential in bringing metacognition to the attention of mathematics educators (What's all the fuss about metacognition?). Schoenfeld presented evidence from the college-level math course he taught that showed that many students did not reflect on the problem-solving strategies they used and that they frequently failed to connect the solutions they obtained with the real world.

Mathematical strategy knowledge includes basic knowledge of algorithms and heuristics, as well as metacognitive awareness of strategies to help in comprehending problem statements, organizing information or data, planning solution attempts, executing plans, and checking results. Even first-grade children have some specific strategy knowledge about math, but students seldom monitor their approaches to problem solving until much later. At first, problem solving is often taken one step at a time, and students show little understanding of the general principles of the problems. This is similar to the sentence-level focus of young writers who approach the task without an overall plan.

Just as students must monitor their comprehension of what they read, so too must they monitor their cognitive processes while doing math. Consider the different levels at which one may monitor the adequacy of a solution to a word problem. One may evaluate the results of arithmetic procedures carried out to obtain an answer; such monitoring could occur simply by checking the arithmetic involved (e.g., subtracting an addition result). One may evaluate whether the procedure one has chosen is correct. This requires some semantic analysis of the text, whether rereading the entire text or simply finding a key word. One may also evaluate the sensibleness of the problem itself. This involves looking at the relations expressed in the text and making a decision about whether those relations make sense. Research has shown difficulties in monitoring at all three levels, with younger and poorer math students more likely to focus on the low-level calculation standard of evaluation. These results are comparable to the reading and writing research, which shows novices more likely to evaluate low-level aspects of the task (e.g., decoding or spelling).

Metacognitive research in mathematics also includes a line of work focused on students' judgments of whether they will be able to solve problems correctly and judgments of which problems they succeeded in answering correctly. When judgments or predictions are compared with actual performance, the general pattern of results is that younger and less skilled students are less accurate in monitoring their abilities than their older and higher-achieving peers.

As with literacy, professional organizations now advocate that reflection and metacognition be central components of mathematics teaching. Classroom interventions have been devised and successfully implemented to help students plan, monitor, and evaluate their own thinking during mathematical problem solving. The National Council of Teachers of Mathematics in the United States emphasized the importance of writing as a way of helping students reflect: "writing in mathematics can also help students consolidate their thinking because it requires them to reflect on their work and clarify their thoughts about the ideas" (NCTM, 2000: 61). Research has shown the value of peer collaboration and discussion in enhancing mathematics performance, as students make their cognitive processes, assumptions, and strategies explicit. Consistent with a Piagetian constructivist perspective, the cognitive conflicts that may arise as students justify their approaches are effective in stimulating cognitive and metacognitive growth.

Metacognition in Science

The body of research on metacognition in science focuses primarily on the reading of scientific texts; the research results are comparable to those already discussed in the domain of reading. Scientific problem solving is clearly another academic endeavor where metacognitive knowledge and control are critical, but it is much less researched. The term metacognition may be absent from the following statement in the National Science Education Standards (NSES) in the United States, but there can be no doubt as to the central concern: "Engaging students in inquiry helps students develop an appreciation of 'how we know' what we know in science" (p. xx). The standards call for teachers to guide students to understand the purposes for their own learning and to develop their abilities to assess and reflect on their own scientific accomplishments. They also call for providing students with opportunities to apply standards of scientific practice to their own and others' scientific efforts.

Summary and Conclusions

It might be tempting to conclude from this brief review of metacognition within specific academic domains that metacognition is domain general. This conclusion may be drawn because the developmental and individual differences that have been revealed across domains are conceptually similar. Nevertheless, correlations in performance across domains are often rather low. It is therefore important not to assume that metacognitive skills can and should be fostered in settings devoid of academic content.

It also might be tempting to conclude that the relation between metacognition and cognition is uni-directional, given the evidence that metacognitive training can promote greater achievement in a given domain. However, reciprocal causation is most likely; that is, improvements in metacognition contribute to improvements in cognition (reading, writing, problem solving, etc.), which in turn contribute to further improvements in metacognition.

One of the reasons why young students exhibit limited metacognitive awareness and control is because the basic processes needed to carry out the activity are not yet routinized or fluent. For example, beginning readers who must allocate all of their processing capacity to decoding have little cognitive capacity left to devote to meaning construction, let alone evaluate the adequacy of the meaning that was constructed. With repeated experience, readers learn to decode and to monitor their comprehension sufficiently well that they do not have to allocate attention to the processes; it is only when an obstacle is noted that attention is directed to the problem area. Automaticity is also critical to mathematical performance – students need to be sufficiently fluent with basic number facts so that simple addition and subtraction do not take up the cognitive resources needed for higher-level conceptual processes. Similarly, monitoring and evaluation of ongoing processes need to become automatic, so that they can proceed without deliberate attention. The same logic follows for writing. In other words, students should be able to proceed with a cognitive activity fluently and automatically, with metacognitive control processes reaching conscious awareness only at times when they must be deployed.

When students have knowledge and control of their own cognitive processes, learning is enhanced. This holds regardless of the domain of learning, whether reading, writing, science, or any other activity that involves thinking. Educators across disciplines now have the common goal of fostering metacognitively sophisticated learners, and the means to accomplish this goal appear to be similar: (1) Scaffolded instruction should take place embedded within a meaningful context. (2) Metacognition should not be promoted as an end in itself but rather as a means of promoting learning and achievement. (3) Students should be taught to apply a critical stance toward the information they encounter, overcoming the common tendency to accept at face value the accuracy and plausibility of information conveyed to them by perceived authorities. (4) Students should be given opportunities to work collaboratively with their peers on common problems and tasks and to articulate their cognitive and metacognitive processes.

Although the construct of metacognition is now widely known in the educational research community, empirical findings still look a great deal like they did when metacognition first became an area of inquiry. For example, studies conducted in the current decade reveal that 8–10-year-olds rely almost exclusively on word-level criteria for evaluating their understanding, replicating the findings of more than 20 years earlier. Similarly, young students' conception of a good reader as one who reads quickly without making any mistakes is the same as that identified almost 30 years earlier. These patterns are troubling because they illustrate how slowly advances in research knowledge are translated into changes in classroom practice that in turn bring about changes in student outcomes.

See also: Knowledge Domains and Domain Learning; Personal Epistemology in Education; Problem Solving and Human Expertise; Self-Regulated Learning and Socio-Cognitive Theory; Vygotsky and Recent Developments.

Further Reading

Baker, L. (2004). Reading comprehension and science inquiry: Metacognitive connections. In Saul, W. (ed.) *Crossing Borders in Literacy and Science Instruction: Perspectives on Theory and Practice*, pp 239–257. Newark, DE: International Reading Association.

Baker, L. (2005). Developmental differences in metacognition: Implications for metacognitively-oriented reading instruction. In Israel, S. E., Block, C. C., Bauserman, K. L., and Kinnucan-Welsch, K. (eds.) *Metacognition in Literacy Learning: Theory, Assessment, Instruction, and Professional Development*, pp 61–79. Mahwah, NJ: Erlbaum.

Baker, L. (2008). Metacognitive development in reading: Contributors and consequences. In Mokhtari, K. and Sheorey, R. (eds.) *Reading Strategies of First- and Second-Language Learners: See How They Read*, pp 25–42. Norwood, MA: Christopher Gordon.

Baker, L. and Brown, A. L. (1984). Metacognitive skills and reading. In Pearson, P. D., Kamil, M., Barr, R., and Mosenthal, P. (eds.) *Handbook of Research in Reading*, vol. 1, pp 353–395. New York: Longman.

Baker, L. and Cerro, L. (2000). Assessing metacognition in children and adults. In Schraw, G. and Impara, J. (eds.) *Issues in the Measurement of Metacognition*, pp 99–145. Lincoln, NE: Buros Institute of Mental Measurements, University of Nebraska.

Carr, M. and Biddlecomb, B. (1998). Metacognition in mathematics from a constructivist perspective. In Hacker, D. J., Dunlosky, J., and Graesser, A. C. (eds.) *Metacognition in Educational Theory and Practice*, pp 69–91. Mahwah, NJ: Erlbaum.

Chambres, P., Izaute, M., and Marescaux, P.-J. (eds.) (2002). *Metacognition: Process, Function and Use*. Boston, MA: Kluwer.

Desoete, A. and Veenman, M. (eds.) (2006). *Metacognition in Mathematics Education*. Hauppauge, NY: Nova Science.

Hacker, D. J., Dunlosky, J., and Graesser, A. C. (eds.) (1998). *Metacognition in Educational Theory and Practice*. Mahwah, NJ: Erlbaum.

Hartman, H. J. (ed.) (2001). *Metacognition in Learning and Instruction: Theory, Research and Practice*. New York: Springer.

Israel, S. E., Block, C. C., Bauserman, K. L., and Kinnucan-Welsch, K. (eds.) (2005). *Metacognition in Literacy Learning: Theory, Assessment, Instruction, and Professional Development*. New York: Erlbaum.

McCormick, C. (2003). Metacognition and learning. In Reynolds, W. M., Miller, G. J., and Weiner, I. B. (eds.) *Handbook of Psychology: Volume 7, Educational Psychology*, pp 79–102. New York: Wiley.

NCTM (2000). *Principles and Standards for School Mathematics*. Reston, VA: National Council of Teachers of Mathematics.

Schraw, G. and Impara, J. (eds.) (2000). *Issues in the Measurement of Metacognition*. Lincoln, NE: Buros Institute of Mental Measurements.

Sitko, B. M. (1998). Knowing how to write: Metacognition and writing instruction. In Hacker, D. J., Dunlosky, J., and Graesser, A. C. (eds.) *Metacognition in Educational Theory and Practice*, pp 93–115. Mahwah, NJ: Erlbaum.

Van Haneghan, J. P. and Baker, L. (1989). Cognitive monitoring in mathematics. In McCormick, C. B., Miller, G., and Pressley, M. (eds.) *Cognitive Strategy Research: From Basic Research to Educational Applications*, pp 215–238. New York: Springer.

Wong, B. Y. L. (1999). Metacognition in writing. In Gallimore, R., Bernheimer, L. P., MacMillan, D. L., Speece, D. L., and Vaughn, S. (eds.) *Developmental Perspectives on Children with High Incidence Disabilities*, pp 183–198. Mahwah, NJ: Erlbaum.

LEARNING: RECENT TRENDS

Learning Strategies

Technology and Learning

Learning as Inquiry

Cooperative Learning

Learning Strategies

C E Weinstein and J Jung, The University of Texas at Austin, Austin, TX, USA
T W Acee, Texas State University – San Marcos, San Marcos, TX, USA

Glossary

Comprehension monitoring – This occurs when learners check their understanding of something they are trying to learn using some form of self-assessment.

Domain-dependent learning strategies – The learning strategies that are specific to a particular content area or type of academic task.

Domain-independent learning strategies – The learning strategies that are widely applicable across content areas and academic tasks.

Elaboration strategies – The deep-level strategies used to build bridges or meaningful connections between what the learner is trying to learn and their prior knowledge, experience, attitudes, and/or beliefs.

Learning strategies – Any behavioral, cognitive, metacognitive, motivational, or affective process or action that facilitates understanding, learning, and meaningful encoding into memory.

Organization strategies – The deep-level strategies used to meaningfully translate or transform information into a configuration or form that creates some sort of coherent scheme that makes the information more understandable and easier to encode and remember.

Rehearsal strategies – The surface-level repetition strategies used to memorize discrete information or hold information in working memory so that it can be processed further.

Self-regulation learning strategies – The strategies used by learners to control, manage, and oversee cognitive, motivational, emotional, and environmental factors that influence learning.

Our desire to understand our world and learn what we need to know and do to survive and thrive has existed since the origin of mankind on the earth. However, it is only since the 1970s that the psychological study of the strategies we use to learn about our world began in earnest. In the broadest sense, a learning strategy is any behavioral, cognitive, metacognitive, motivational, or affective process or action that facilitates understanding, learning, and meaningful encoding into memory. The problem with such a broad definition is that it includes almost any psychological variable. Everything affects learning to at least some extent. For this reason, educational psychologists study variables that have been found to have the greatest direct or indirect impact on learning and encoding into memory, and that can be modified by some type of training or educational intervention. This second criterion excludes some variables such as personality traits because, although they may affect learning, they are not amenable to change by an educational intervention (however, we can teach students learning strategies that reduce the negative impact of some individual variables such as impulsivity or attention deficit disorders).

The major categories of learning strategies include: cognitive information acquisition and processing strategies, motivational strategies, self-regulation and monitoring strategies, affect regulation strategies, and behavioral strategies. Several of these strategies are discussed further after the presentation of a brief historical overview of this area. This is followed by a discussion of the ways in which models of strategic and self-regulated learning incorporate learning strategies, how learning strategies are assessed, and types of instruction used to teach learning strategies.

Historical Overview

From the time humans first appeared on the earth, they were concerned about learning and memory. Some anthropologists have hypothesized that cave drawings were at least in part an attempt to learn and remember animal migrations and the seasons for different foods. They may also have been a way to help the young learn the knowledge, culture, and norms of life as it then existed. The Greeks are famous for the development of mnemonic devices, or mental memory aids, some of which are still used today (e.g., using the ABC song in the United States to learn the alphabet, associating a new item we are trying to remember with an existing image, or the first letter mnemonic HOMES (Huron, Ontario, Michigan, Erie, and Superior) to remember the five Great Lakes in America). In the 1800s and early 1900s many parlor entertainers at parties or gatherings would use mnemonics to perform prodigious feats of learning and memory. Today, advertising experts use mnemonic tunes and phrases to help people remember to buy their brand when they see it in a store.

For the first half of the twentieth century the study of mnemonics or any other cognitive learning strategy lay dormant as the overwhelming charge of behaviorism swept through psychology. Behaviorists, in their attempt to make psychology a science, rejected not only philosophical or introspective methods of research but also any theoretical or empirical work involving mental processing. The world of environmental manipulations, reinforcement, and extinction had little interest in the black box (mind).

It was not until the late 1960s and 1970s that the study of mental processes made its way back into psychological theories and research. Once again, mnemonics played a key role. Some of the earliest studies during this period focused on mnemonics but this time, once it was established that they were not just parlor tricks, the focus shifted to why and how mnemonics worked and what we could learn about human information processing from them. What cognitive processes were involved in the creation and use of mnemonics? What fundamental information did this give us about human information processing? In the 1970s, this work was greatly enriched by other early researchers in the area of what we now call cognitive educational psychology. For example, a major influence was the work of John Flavell and his colleagues who developed the concept of metacognition, or thinking about our thinking. Basically, metacognition is thinking that focuses on knowledge, self-reflection, and analyses of how we think and learn. As a direct result of this early work examining cognition, variables that might influence cognition and the degree to which cognition might or might not be influenced through some form of educational intervention, the area of learning strategies developed as a field of study.

Types of Learning Strategies

There is general agreement about the basic types of learning strategies as originally codified by Weinstein and Mayer (1986) and expanded upon by continuing theoretical and research work in this area. The development of interactive models of strategic and self-regulated learning at all educational levels has, however, changed the ways we explore, study and teach students how to use learning strategies. This is discussed further later in this article.

Rehearsal Strategies

These are the most basic of all learning strategies and can be used most effectively in the first stages of building a knowledge base in a content domain. Rehearsal strategies are most useful for basic memorization, processing new information at a surface level, but are not generally useful for creating a deep and sophisticated understanding of the material. Researchers differentiate between passive

rehearsal, which is not very effective for most learning tasks, and active rehearsal, which can be more beneficial. Passive rehearsal is based on early mental muscle models of learning which assumed that the mind is like a muscle – the more you practice, the more you will build up the strength of your memory. It involves learners repeating something over and over until they remember it (similar to the use of flash cards) or using other memory aids, such as mnemonics. While these methods may be useful for learning discrete bits of information (e.g., isolated facts and lists of information), they are not very effective as learning strategies for more complex content or learning tasks involving reasoning. In addition, these methods do not contribute efficiently to the integration of new information one is trying to learn with existing knowledge and expertise, a major goal for many learning tasks.

Active rehearsal, while using some of the same methods as passive rehearsal, differs in terms of the goals for using this strategy. In passive rehearsal, repetition is the end point of the process, while in active rehearsal, repetition is used as an enabling tool to hold onto information so that it can be further processed and encoded into more stable areas of memory. Highlighting important information in class notes or a textbook and then reviewing the highlighted material at a future time would be examples of using repetition to help learn the content by creating additional opportunities to further process it. Even something like flash cards could be used for active repetition, if the goal was to continue thinking about and encoding the information on the cards.

Elaboration Strategies

Elaboration strategies are the largest and most diverse category of learning strategies. Fundamentally, elaboration involves building bridges or connections between what the learner is trying to learn and their prior knowledge, experience, attitudes, and beliefs. Building these bridges forces the learner to actively process the new information and it is this engagement that is believed to be the core cognitive mechanism involved in reaching learning goals. It is not just the elaborations that result from using these strategies but the process of creating those elaborations that facilitates meaningful encoding into memory. In addition, elaboration has been found to increase related variables such as task focus and concentration, task interest and enjoyment, motivation, and positive attitudes and emotions toward the learning content and task itself.

Elaboration learning strategies take many forms depending on the nature of the content, the learning task, and the learner's individual differences and learning goals. The most basic forms of elaboration involve paraphrasing and summarizing. Even though these are fundamentally a form of repetition, unlike rehearsal strategies, they are not simple verbatim recall which does not involve higher-level cognitive processes. To paraphrase or summarize what a student is trying to learn requires some degree of encoding and transformation of the targeted information so active cognitive engagement is required. More advanced and complex forms of elaboration include: using everyday experience to try to understand a new concept, applying what the student is learning to new and diverse tasks, trying to teach the material to someone else, perspective taking, visualization, using a problem-solving strategy in a new context, creating analogies, using compare-and-contrast methods to highlight the differences and similarities between two related concepts, and creating and responding to questions about the material being studied.

Research has shown that the active processing involved in using elaboration strategies is what is key to learning and that the specific elaboration strategy used for a learning task is not as important. However, it has been shown that it is important for students to learn a repertoire of diverse strategies so that they can both develop their preferences and have alternative strategies to fall back on if their preferences do not work for a particular learning task. This issue also relates to what strategies students should learn and in what context they should learn them. The instructional issues this raises are discussed further in later sections.

Organization Strategies

Organization strategies involve translating or transforming information into another configuration and creating some sort of scheme to provide structure to this new way of characterizing or representing the information. These strategies are used to organize information into meaningful categories, hierarchies, and sequential structures so that it can be visualized, analyzed, understood, and encoded meaningfully into memory. Similar to elaboration strategies, organization strategies facilitate deep processing of the information and meaningful encoding into memory. By organizing the new information the learner is actively engaged with the material and it is believed that this active engagement underlies much of the benefit of using organization strategies. In addition, the product that results can be used in the future to review and deepen understanding. Moreover, similar to elaboration, organization strategies have been found to increase related variables such as task focus and concentration, task interest and enjoyment, motivation, and positive attitudes and emotions toward the learning content and task itself.

Creating outlines, concept maps, and concept matrices are types of organizational strategies. Creating an outline involves organizing material into a hierarchical structure with a logical flow using an outline format (e.g., I. Thesis statement; A. Major point; 1. Supporting detail). Creating concept maps is another organizational strategy that is

used to graphically represent relationships among and between concepts. For example, connecting concepts with arrowed lines and identifying those relationships with phrases such as: results in, contributes to, decreases, is a defining attribute of, or is a subcategory of is a common type of organization strategy. Creating concept matrices refers to graphically organizing information about related concepts into a matrix of rows and columns in order to learn and analyze those concepts (e.g., organizing the names of concepts in the first column, concept definitions in the second column, and examples of the concepts in the third column). Organizational strategies have been found to help students analyze, learn, and remember their course material at a deep level. Research suggests that the effectiveness of organization strategies derives not only from the active processing that is required to create the organizational structure but also from the product itself since it can be later used for review, as a study aid, or incorporated into a larger and more encompassing scheme in that knowledge domain.

Self-Regulation Learning Strategies

Self-regulation learning strategies are used by students to control, manage, and oversee cognitive, motivational, emotional, and environmental factors that influence learning (both positively and negatively). Goal-setting/planning, implementing/monitoring, and evaluating both process and outcomes are types of self-regulation strategies. Goal-setting/planning refers to setting learning goals and planning for how one will reach those goals (e.g., choosing one rehearsal strategy, two elaboration strategies, and one organizational strategy that will be used to reach the learning objectives for an upcoming exam). Implementing/monitoring involves implementing these learning plans and monitoring the pursuit of the learning goals (e.g., implementing and monitoring a plan to summarize each section of a textbook). Evaluating the success of one's strategic approaches to achieve a learning goal is another type of self-regulation strategy (e.g., evaluating whether or not the cost in time of creating a concept map was worth the payoff in learning). Self-regulation learning strategies can help students fine-tune their strategic approaches to reaching their learning goals and develop more effective and efficient study routines. These strategies can also be used to oversee and manage the regulation of motivational, emotional, and environmental variables that influence learning.

Metacognitive Strategies – Comprehension Monitoring

An important component of self-regulation involves using metacognitive strategies for learning. Within this broad area, the most relevant type of metacognitive strategy for the purposes of this article is comprehension-monitoring strategies. Basically, comprehension monitoring involves checking our understanding of something we are trying to learn using some form of reviewing or self-testing. Comprehension strategies both support and contribute to meaningful learning. Without them, learning could be incomplete or errors might persist undetected. Reviewing and self-testing also contribute to knowledge consolidation and integration across topics. Using mental reviews, going over notes and course materials, thinking of potential questions to guide reading or help prepare for an exam, trying to use new information in novel ways, and trying to apply a principle or method are all important methods for checking understanding, consolidating new knowledge, and integrating related information (both from what is being learned and from what is already known). Although comprehension-monitoring strategies include many of the strategies discussed under elaboration, the purpose is different. When learning new content material, using a strategy like applying a principle is designed to enhance understanding and encoding into memory. When applying a principle such as a comprehension-monitoring strategy, the goal is to see if that understanding and accessible memory encoding has been established.

Need for a Learning Strategies Repertoire

Rehearsal, elaboration, and organization strategies can be used to help students actively process and learn new information. However, students differ over which learning strategies work best for them both within and across different types of learning tasks and contexts. For this reason, it is important that students learn and develop a repertoire of learning strategies both within and across all three of these categories so that they can mindfully develop their preferences and have a range of strategies to fall back on if their preferences do not work.

Domain-Independent Strategies Versus Domain-Dependent Strategies

In current theory, research, and practice, the applicability, or generalizability, of particular learning strategies to different learning content areas or tasks is still being debated. The general issue is whether it is best for students to learn domain (content or task)-specific strategies (e.g., strategies for solving a particular type of physics problem or learning a new vocabulary term in a foreign language) or more generalizable, or domain (content or task)-independent strategies that can be applied to many content areas (e.g., how to approach an

unfamiliar textbook or using self-testing to check your understanding of what you are learning). In fact, if you think about it in terms of a generalization gradient, they are really just different points on the line. If the strategy has a narrower domain of applicability (i.e., it can only be used for a relatively small number of learning or performance activities), then it is domain dependent. If, on the other hand, it can be used in a wide variety of situations or content areas, then it has a wide domain of applicability and is domain independent. Like many controversies, it appears that it takes a bit of both to help students become self-regulating, strategic learners. Some strategies may be more effective and efficient for the content and tasks in one particular academic area, while others may be helpful for a wider variety of academic areas and tasks.

Learning Strategies in Models of Strategic and Self-Regulated Learning and College Readiness

The study of learning strategies has evolved from an isolated area of study into a critical component of most models of strategic and self-regulated learning. This integration of learning strategies into more complex and interactive models of academic learning is exemplified by the work of Pintrich (2004), Weinstein *et al.* (2004), and Zimmerman and Schunk (2001). As an example of these theoretical models that guide much of the current research and instructional development designed to help students become more strategic and self-regulated learners, the most recent version of the Model of Strategic Learning (MSL) developed by Weinstein *et al.* (2006) is briefly discussed (see **Figure 1**).

Model of Strategic Learning

Similar to other recent models, the MSL is a multidimensional, interactive model where the focus is on the interactions among the components rather than the simple effects of one or two elements. Even many of the recent advances in statistical analyses are based on the need for analyzing interactive models. The core of the model (within the triangle) is the learner and all of the individual differences, self-system variables, and long-term goals learners bring to any learning event. In addition, most meaningful learning is goal-driven and the model will be used in different ways by students with different learning tasks and goals.

The variables outside the rectangle (e.g., requirements of the task and instructor expectations) are important variables for completing a learning activity but they are not usually under the student's direct control. The three

The Model of Strategic Learning

Requirements of the current learning activity, assignment, or test

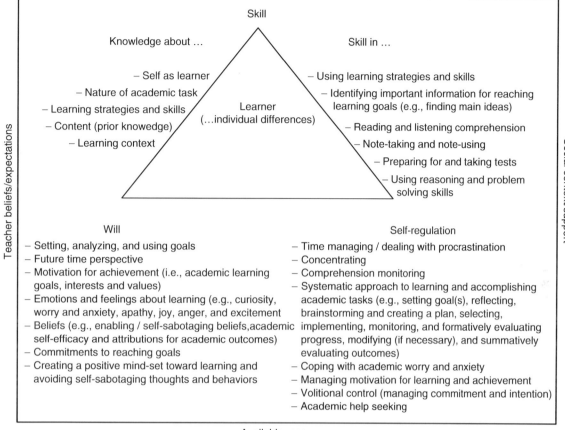

Figure 1 The Model of Strategic Learning.

main components of the model are listed at the three points of the triangle: skill, will, and self-regulation. Skill focuses on declarative (knowing what to do), procedural (knowing how to do it), and conditional (knowing when to use the strategies) knowledge that students need to develop in order to become more strategic learners (e.g., not only knowing about different learning strategies but also knowing how to use them effectively and when it is most appropriate to use a particular strategy). Will focuses on attitudes, beliefs, and goals that help students thrive and persist when faced with roadblocks to learning (e.g., setting specific and challenging, yet realistic, learning goals and avoiding or coping with self-sabotaging beliefs and attitudes). The self-regulation component focuses on managing the learning process and one's own cognition, motivation, and emotion related to the task (e.g., time management, comprehension monitoring, and coping with anxiety). For any given learning task, the student must take into account variables from each of the three components. Like the systems of the body, variables related to skill, will, and self-regulation need to function

together in order to facilitate strategic learning. Which elements of each component will be most important to think about or use for completing a task will be largely determined by the learner's goals, prior knowledge, past experiences, and the nature of the task.

Assessment of Student Learning Strategies

Purposes for Assessment

The primary purpose of most learning strategy instruments is to identify students' knowledge and use of learning strategies in order to:

1. investigate correlational and causative relations with other variables, such as motivational goal types, class participation, or academic performance;
2. identify students' strengths and weaknesses in different areas of learning strategies to identify students who might need additional instruction in the areas where they scored low;

3. use as a pre–post and/or delayed outcome measure for interventions designed to teach learning strategies;
4. provide information to educators about individual needs of their students so they can target part of their instruction to helping their students learn or enhance their use of learning strategies; and
5. help developmental educators, student affairs counselors, and advisors who work with at-risk students to identify students who may be at risk of failure or dropping out from higher education settings because of their lack of knowledge and use of learning strategies so that they can be placed in learning strategies courses or other types of interventions.

Approaches and Instruments Used to Assess Students' Learning Strategies Knowledge and Use

There are a number of experimental and published instruments that assess students' knowledge and use of learning strategies. These instruments use some type of self-report method, usually involving some type of instrument or questionnaire. Some studies do have students describe or explain their strategies as they are using them, or just after completing a learning task, but these assessment methods still rely on self-report. While the limitations of self-report methods have been repeatedly documented, it remains the best method for providing a window on the mind.

Some of the more commonly used measures include: The Learning and Study Strategies Inventory (2nd edition) by Weinstein *et al.* (2002), the Learning and Study Strategies Inventory – High School Version (2nd edition) by Weinstein and Palmer (1990), the Motivated Strategies for Learning Questionnaire by Pintrich *et al.* (1991), the Approaches and Study Skills Inventory for Students by Entwistle (1997), the Learning Process Questionnaire by Biggs (1987), the Survey of Study Habits and Attitudes, Form C by Brown and Holtzman (1984), and the Study Behavior Inventory by Bliss *et al.* (2000).

Teaching of Learning Strategies

Another controversy in the current literature focuses on the best way to teach students about learning strategies and how to use various learning strategies. This controversy also relates to the debate over the domain of applicability issue and whether we should teach content-dependent or content-independent strategies. Proponents on one side of the controversy believe that learning strategies should be taught in content courses, such as math, history, or biology, and not as a separate course. Proponents on the other side of the controversy believe that learning strategies should be taught as part of a course or

training program in strategic or self-regulated learning. Recent research literature indicates that both groups are right – for students who are highly deficient in their knowledge and use of learning strategies, an adjunct course is best. For students who already have some level of skill, refining their knowledge and skills in content-dependent settings appears to be more helpful.

However, the most powerful instructional model appears to be a combination of the two. Using an adjunct course to help teach students general knowledge and skills in using strategies with a broad domain of applicability combined with what Weinstein has called the metacurriculum in content courses. Basically, a metacurriculum involves purposefully teaching learning strategies while also teaching course content. It can be as simple as paraphrasing a lesson and then teaching the class to do the same thing on their own to check their understanding, or as complex as teaching students how to develop, implement, monitor, and modify a test-preparation plan for an upcoming exam. For example, implementing a metacurriculum would involve not only teaching students what to learn in a history course but also how to learn and think like an historian.

Concluding Statement

It has often been said that the present belongs to those who have learned but the future belongs to those who are learning. Increasing longevity and our increasingly complex and technologically sophisticated world requires that students be prepared to be lifelong learners throughout the different stages of their life span. Having an extensive repertoire of learning strategies is one step toward helping individuals become more effective and efficient learners.

See also: Knowledge Domains and Domain Learning; Metacognition; Personal Epistemology in Education; Self-Regulated Learning and Socio-Cognitive Theory.

Bibliography

Biggs, J. B. (1987). *The Learning Process Questionnaire (LPQ): Manual.* Hawthorn: Australian Council for Educational Research.
Bliss, L. B., Kerstiens, G., and Marvin, R. (2000). *The Study Behavior Inventory (Version 2.0).* Torrance, CA: Androgogy Associates.
Brown, W. F. and Holtzman, W. H. (1984). *Survey of Study Habits and Attitudes, Form C.* New York: Psychological Corporation.
Entwistle, N. J. (1997). *The Approaches and Study Skills Inventory for Students (ASSIST).* Edinburgh: University of Edinburgh Centre for Research on Learning and Instruction.
Pintrich, P. R. (2004). A conceptual framework for assessing motivation and self-regulated learning in college students. *Educational Psychology Review* **16**(4), 385–407.
Pintrich, P., Smith, D., Garcia, T., and McKeachie, W. (1991). *Motivated Strategies for Learning Questionnaire.* The University of Michigan: National Center for Research to Improve Postsecondary Teaching and Learning.

Weinstein, C. E. and Mayer, R. E. (1986). The teaching of learning strategies. In Wittrock, M. C. (ed.) *Handbook of Research on Teaching*, 3rd edn., pp 315–327. New York: Macmillan.

Weinstein, C. E. and Palmer, D. R. (1990). *Learning and Study Strategies Inventory-High School Version*. Clearwater, FL: H & H Publishing.

Weinstein, C. E., Schulte, A., and Palmer, D. R. (2002). *The Learning and Study Strategies Inventory*, 2nd edn. Clearwater, FL: H & H Publishing.

Weinstein, C. E., Tomberlin, T. L., Julie, A. L., and Kim, J. (2004). Helping students to become strategic learners: The roles of assessment, teachers, instruction, and students. In Ee, J., Chang, A., and Tan, O. (eds.) *Thinking about Thinking: What Educators Need to Know*, pp 282–310. Singapore: McGraw-Hill.

Zimmerman, B. J. and Schunk, D. H. (eds.) (2001). *Self-Regulated Learning and Academic Achievement: Theoretical Perspectives*, 2nd edn. Mahwah, NJ: Erlbaum.

Further Reading

Biggs, J. and Tang, C. (2007). *Teaching for Quality Learning at University*, 3rd edn. Berkshire: Open University Press/McGraw-Hill.

Boekaerts, M., Pintrich, P. R., and Zeidner, M. (eds.) (2000). *Handbook of Self-Regulation.* San Diego, CA: Academic Press.

Boekaerts, M., Renninger, K. A., Sigel, I. E., Damon, W., and Lerner, R. M. (2006). Self-Regulation and Effort Investment. Wiley: Hoboken, NJ.

Dembo, M. H. and Sell, H. (2007). *Motivation and Learning Strategies for College Success: A Self-Management Approach*, 2nd edn. Erlbaum: Mahwah, NJ.

Flavell, J. H. (1979). Metacognition and cognitive monitoring: A new area of cognitive-developmental inquiry. *American Psychologist* **34**(10), 906–911.

Janac, K., Kipperman, D., and Linder, D. (1997). *Learning Strategies Matrix.* http://edweb.sdsu.edu/courses/ET650_online/MAPPS/Strats.html (accessed August 2009).

Jones, B. F. and Idol, L. (1990). *Dimensions of Thinking and Cognitive Instruction*. Hillsdale, NJ: Erlbaum.

McNamara, D. S. (2007). *Reading Comprehension Strategies: Theories, Interventions, and Technologies*. Mahwah, NJ: Erlbaum.

New Horizons for Learning (2002). *Teaching and Learning Strategies*. http://www.newhorizons.org/strategies/front_strategies.html (accessed August 2009).

Paris, S. G. and Paris, A. H. (2001). Classroom applications of research on self-regulated learning. *Educational Psychologist* **36**(2), 89–101.

Schunk, D. H. and Zimmerman, B. J. (eds.) (2007). *Motivation and Self-Regulated Learning: Theory, Research and Application*. Mahwah, NJ: Erlbaum.

Weinstein, C. E. and Hume, L. M. (1998). *Study Strategies for Lifelong Learning*. Washington, DC: American Psychological Association.

Weinstein, C. E., Meyer, D. K., Van Mater Stone, G., and McKeachie, W. J. (2006). Teaching students how to learn. In McKeachie, W. J. and Svinicki, M. (eds.) *Teaching Tips: Strategies, Research, and Theory for College and University Teachers*, 12th edn, pp. 300–317. Lexington, MA: Houghton Mifflin.

Wolters, C. A. (2003). Regulation of motivation: Evaluating an underemphasized aspect of self-regulated learning. *Educational Psychologist* **38**(4), 189–205.

Relevant Websites

http://www.howtostudy.org – How to Study.

http://www.muskingum.edu – Muskingum, CAL Learning Strategies Database.

http://www.studygs.net/index.htm – Studies Guides and Strategies.

Technology and Learning

B Means and J Roschelle, SRI International, Menlo Park, CA, USA

Glossary

Agent – A software program that assists the user in performing some task, taking into account the nature of the user and the situation.

Asynchronous communication technology – Any technology designed to support an exchange of messages with posting and reading occurring at different times; examples include email and blogs.

Avatar – A graphic representation of oneself that a user either creates or chooses to represent his/her identity online; for example in a chat room or multiplayer game.

Clickers – Devices use to register a response as part of a classroom response system.

Immersive environment – A computer-created scene or world that gives the user the sensation of being within the scene rather than being outside of it.

Information and communication technology – A general term encompassing computer hardware and software as well as their application.

Instructional management software – System that manages the gathering, processing, and display of student data from computer-based instruction.

Online learning – Learning that occurs over the Internet.

Open source – A computer program for which the source code is made available for free use and modification by others.

Podcast – Digital media file (either audio or video) distributed over the Internet for download and playback on a mobile device or personal computer.

Recommendation system – Software that uses information about a user, in conjunction with data on the opinions and choices of all users of the system, to identify and present items or products that are likely to interest the user.

Response system – Hardware and software that enable members of a class or audience to respond simultaneously to a question from an instructor or presenter, who receives a tabulation or other representation of the aggregated responses.

Social networking site – A Web site that supports building online communities by having users post a public or semi-public representation of themselves and indicate other users with whom they wish to share information; examples include Facebook, Twitter and MySpace.

Synchronous communication system – Systems in which all users are logged on at the same time; examples include videoconferencing, Internet telephony and instant messaging.

Virtual manipulative – A software representation of a thing or system that the user can interact with.

Advances in information and communication technology (ICT) have enabled its use to support teaching, learning, and assessment both within and outside of schools. The current state of access to ICT within schools and ways in which ICT is used are described below. At the same time, it is noted that the increased use of ICT in schools has not produced the dramatic changes in pedagogy and learning content that some technology proponents had predicted. Formal educational systems impose curriculum standards, high-stakes tests, and criteria for promotion or selection into educational programs at higher grade levels that reinforce continuity in educational approaches. Research on the implementation of ICT in schools and classrooms has found that elements outside the technology – including principal support, teacher training, the design of the learning activity in which ICT is used, and assessment practices – influence the extent to which ICT is used and its effectiveness as a tool for learning. Thus, those who would like to see ICT transform the nature of education are still waiting for the long-promised radical shift. Reformers can point to current technology trends as potential sources of major change, however. These technology trends include the increasing availability of open-source course content on the Internet; the dramatic rise of collaborative, user-generated content (termed Web 2.0); and the high level of engagement triggered by immersive, multi-user games with complex structures and highly realistic, dynamic graphics.

Spread of Technology Within Schools

Few areas of education have experienced as much change over the last 15 years as the use of ICT to support learning. In 1994, when the prior edition of this encyclopedia was published, the World Wide Web was in its infancy. At that time, only 35% of public schools in the United States had Internet access anywhere in the building and just 3% of instructional classrooms had a computer connected to the Internet. By 2005, in contrast, 94%

of instructional rooms had computers with Internet access (Wells and Lewis, 2006). The United States was not alone in making a major investment in technology in schools during this time frame. By 2006, schools in the 22 countries participating in the SITES 2006 international survey had, on average, one computer with Internet access for every seven students (Law *et al.*, 2008).

During the same time period, the cost of computing power dropped dramatically, and smaller, lighter computing devices became available in the form of personal digital assistants, MP3 players, mobile phones, and tablet PCs. Today's iPhone is vastly more powerful than a top-of-the-line 1994 desktop computer.

Further, advances in projection technology have made it feasible to provide bright, lightweight projectors to every classroom. Indeed, many classrooms go beyond projectors to provide an electronic whiteboard on which the teacher can write or draw, interact with computer applications, and access resources on the Internet.

The declining cost of computers and the increase in digital resources for learning have led a number of schools, districts, and countries to launch one-to-one computing initiatives to provide every student with a computer. For example, in 2005 Australia launched a AU$1.2-billion plan to provide every secondary student in years 9–12 with a computer. At the same time, it must be acknowledged that the playing field with respect to access to ICT that can support learning is still not level. A survey of principals in 56 countries participating in the 2006 PISA assessment of 15-year-olds, for example, found that schools in the 14 countries with the strongest technology infrastructures had an Internet computer for roughly every three or four students, while the 14 countries with the least technology had an Internet computer for every 25 or more students, and three countries reported no instructional computers with Internet access in their schools.

There is no doubt that technology will continue to become more available to teachers and students. The more difficult challenge has proven to be the design, development, and dissemination of educationally meaningful learning activities supported by technology.

School Uses of Technology for Learning

Technology use within schools has been promoted since the mid-1980s. Early predictions of how personal computers and learning software would transform education, however, have given way to an appreciation of the complexity of technology integration and of educational change. Some critics have argued variously that ICT has had no significant impact on schools (Cuban *et al.*, 2001) or that it has had negative impacts (Healey, 1999). Even so, technology continues to be a part of school instruction, albeit a less common instructional practice

than more traditional pedagogies such as teacher lecture or question-and-response cycles.

In a 2005 survey of US teachers, 45% reported requiring their students to use technology once a week or more (Bakia *et al.*, 2008). The most often teacher-reported weekly uses of technology were to practice or review mathematics or reading topics, enrichment activities in mathematics and reading, and taking tests or quizzes online. Student use of technology for their school work does not necessarily occur within school, however. Across the 40 countries with students' participating in the PISA 2006 survey, only 9% of 15-year-olds reported using a computer at school almost every day. Even among countries with the largest number of Internet computers in classrooms, none had as many as a third of its students reporting use of a computer at school on a daily basis. In contrast, 75% or more of students in more than a third of the participating countries reported home use of computers on a daily basis.

Typical Uses

Observers of ICT in schools often contrast uses that seek to make the current system more efficient (e.g., by providing for more practice or feedback in the same amount of time) with those that seek to fundamentally change or transform the nature of teaching and learning (Means *et al.*, 2004). Among the types of applications that most educators would consider enhancements of efficiency are uses of new technologies for transmitting information (such as lectures offered online); skills practice software for reading, mathematics, and second language learning; and instructional management systems that keep track of the mastery status of every student on a set of skills or content standards. These technology uses can be incorporated into classrooms as they are currently constituted without fundamentally changing the nature of what is taught or interactions between students and teachers. Likewise, many large-scale installations of electronic whiteboards have succeeded only in reproducing existing teaching practice using a new medium. In contrast, technologies that structure and scaffold independent inquiry and design activities on the part of individual students or groups of students and those that are designed to support collaborative knowledge-building activities require changes in the content of learning and in the roles of teachers and students.

While case study research tends to highlight more innovative, transformative uses of technology (some of which will be described below), large-scale surveys provide a more representative picture of what teachers are asking students to do with ICT. In teacher surveys conducted during the first wave of microcomputer use in schools in the mid-1980s, the most commonly reported student uses of technology were as part of computer literacy and programming classes and for drill-and-practice in basic skills (Becker, 1985). Twenty years later, a 2005 national teacher survey in the United States (Bakia *et al.*, 2008) found that teaching technology as a subject was no longer a major emphasis: rather the dominant pattern of school technology use was a combination of general productivity software and continued use for basic skills development. The most frequent uses of technology across grade levels were word processing, Internet research, and reading or mathematics skills practice, with each of these practices occurring once or more a week in the classes of about a third of all teachers. The fourth most common practice – use of software to teach content in a subject other than mathematics or reading – was reported as a weekly occurrence in just 16% of classrooms.

Potential uses of technology within classrooms extend far beyond the typical uses described above. Across a wide range of subject areas, technology has been used to organize and individualize student instruction, provide a motivating, realistic context for learning, give students access to a broad range of resources, and structure learning tasks in ways that reduce the load on memory and stimulate use of analytic strategies and reflection. Some of these uses are described in more detail below.

Subject-Specific Uses of ICT

Reading

Software has been developed to foster emergent literacy in preschool children through word and alphabet games. More broadly, ICT can support creation of an environment that supports young children's literacy skills through the creation of literacy props such as signs, tickets, and cards that can be used in play-like activities involving literacy skills. In addition, commercial software products aimed at developing phonemic awareness and phonics skills are broadly available. Research on the effectiveness of such products has produced mixed results and suggests that the child's entering skill level, the nature of the non-ICT-based instruction offered, and the phonetic regularity of the child's language may be factors in explaining why some studies find an advantage of software use while others do not.

There is a greater body of supportive research for the use of technology to support struggling readers with the development of greater reading fluency and comprehension. Software can present students with a text to read and provide a digitized spoken presentation of the text synchronized with the child's utterances. When the child has difficulty with a word, these systems typically have mechanisms for helping to analyze the word or presenting it orally so that the child can continue reading. Speech recognition systems are now capable of processing a young reader's spoken word and determining whether or not corrective feedback is in order. Such reading support systems help students acquire needed reading practice, and many students appreciate the patience and privacy of a computer-based system.

Software systems can also support students' vocabulary learning and comprehension through hyperlinks to definitions or illustrations of unfamiliar words or concepts. Some systems provide summaries of main ideas or periodic comprehension checks to help students monitor their level of understanding. Interactive Strategy Training for Active Reading and Thinking (iSTART), for example, is a web-based program that uses animated agents to teach comprehension strategies such as paraphrasing, predicting, and elaboration. Universal Design for Learning (UDL) is an approach in which instructional materials are designed with optional supports so that they can be used effectively by the broadest possible spectrum of learners (Rose and Meyer, 2002), including those with disabilities. These supports include many of the kinds of mechanisms discussed above (text to speech translation, glossaries, prompts for strategic reading strategies) plus an electronic log of the student's work. Research on the application of UDL to learning from science texts has found that having students manipulate electronically presented diagrams of key concepts or having the support of computer agents enhances students' concept learning (Dalton and Strangman, 2006).

Writing

As noted above, the most pervasive use of technology within schools is as a productivity tool, making word processing software the leading educational application. Numerous studies have compared the composition and editing skills of students with and without access to technology. A 1993 meta-analysis of the early word processing studies (Bangert-Drowns, 1993) found a modest but significant positive effect of word processing on overall writing quality. More recent studies of the effects of giving students a personal laptop have found a positive effect on student writing skills (Kulik, 2003; Penuel, 2006).

Mathematics

Graphing calculators have been the leading technology in mathematics classrooms; most secondary students in the United States and several other countries have access to a graphing calculator. While some critics have warned that the introduction of calculators into mathematics instruction will lead to an inappropriate de-emphasis on calculation skills, mathematics educators recommend that the calculators be used not as a substitute for skill learning but to support students when they are engaged in learning mathematical concepts. Calculators can handle calculations and graph construction, freeing students' cognitive resources to concentrate on solution strategies and understanding concepts. Other software tools supporting students' mathematics problem solving include the Geometer's Sketchpad and Cabri Géomètre, which can be used to support students' exploration and development of geometry proofs, and Tinkerplots and Fathom, which provide tools for organizing, analyzing, and representing data in ways that support understanding of statistics. SimCalc MathWorlds, a research-based tool, similarly provides representations that support students' learning of concepts in Algebra and the transition to Calculus. Advanced calculators incorporate Computer Algebra Systems, which can support students in reasoning about algebra strategically, while allowing the calculator to handle tedious rewriting of symbols. Libraries of virtual manipulatives provide similar capabilities to explore mathematical situations and concepts, but within a narrower focus. Overall, these tools provide support for both calculation and representation of mathematical concepts.

Cognitive tutors represent another advance in the use of ICT in mathematics learning. A cognitive tutor observes the step-by-step process of a students' problem solving and intervenes when the student deviates from an expert solution process. Carnegie Tutors are available for pre-algebra, algebra I and II, geometry, and integrated mathematics. Half a million students in roughly 2600 US schools have used one or more of these tutors.

The commercial market also contains many examples that reflect earlier computer-assisted instruction approaches. These approaches typically present students with tutorials and then offer feedback and hints as students solve problems.

Recent advances in classroom networking are leading to mathematical tools that allow groups of students to participate in constructing mathematical objects. For example, the commercial TI-Navigator system allows students to simultaneously submit graphs or equations to the teacher and offers the teacher controls to compare and contrast students' work. Research projects have been exploring the potential of collaboration with such specifically mathematical tools.

Second language learning

Technology has played a significant role in many language classrooms since the language labs of the 1960s. While software designed to teach a language and provide practice opportunities remains available and popular in CD-ROM form, the rise of Internet usage within schools has ushered in a new era with a wider range of learning activities in support of second-language learning. In addition to the option of formal language instruction, students can practice and enhance their second language skills by working with original materials such as newspaper articles, blogs, and speeches, developed for the purpose of communication rather than language teaching, available on the Internet in the language they are learning. Opportunities for language classes to interact online with native speakers of the language they are studying have become commonplace. Hybrid language classes, which combine elements of face-to-face instruction and online learning, have become increasingly popular.

Science

Technology tools have become essential to the practice of science, and this change in the nature of the profession has influenced science instruction. Probes and sensors connected to computers, online databases, computer simulations, and models are central to the practice of scientific fields such as physics, biochemistry, and environmental science. Versions with appropriate interfaces and simplifications for education purposes have been developed for many of these, while in other cases students use the same tools as science professionals. In addition to supporting measurement and data storage and analysis, these technology-based tools provide access to phenomena that occur at a size or timescale that would be difficult or impossible for the unaided human to apprehend and, in some cases, involve dangers that make them inappropriate for classroom use. Students can interact with computer-based simulations of viral epidemics, for example, providing a context demonstrating the real-world relevance of science concepts while protecting students from the real world's hazards.

A number of ICT-supported science education programs involve having students interact with scientists working in the field that students are studying. Features such as email, electronic chat, webcasts, and bulletin boards have been used to support student–scientist interactions in programs, including Kids as Global Scientists, GLOBE, BioKids, Project FeederWatch, and Hands-on Universe. In these programs, students are expected to collect scientific data using scientist-developed protocols and to contribute their findings to a shared database on the World Wide Web. In BioKids, for example, students use personal digital assistants (PDAs) with special software to record the animal life within a study site near their school (Songer, 1996). Because the data are entered into a database shared with other schools, data can be aggregated across schools within the same city, or at a state or regional level. Students can then use BioKids data to address questions about changes in biodiversity over time or in different areas of their state.

Another set of technology-supported tools specific to science learning are systems that build in supports for science inquiry skills. The Knowledge Integration Environment (KIE) and Web-based Inquiry Science Environment (WISE), both developed at the University of California, Berkeley, present students with prompts, reminders, and organizational devices that they use as they explore scientific issues and controversies (Linn, 2006).

Rapidly Growing Uses

Open-source online resources and curriculum materials

One of the biggest transformations wrought by the World Wide Web is the increased availability of the world's cultural, historical, and information resources.

The treasures of major museums such as the Louvre and the British Museum are available to anyone with an Internet connection. History students can inspect original documents such as manifests of ships engaging in the slave trade or Leonardo de Vinci's notebooks.

Beyond access to information and artifacts, the Web also offers educational resources organized into units or learning activities and increasingly, entire courses that a school or individual may choose to use. Many educational jurisdictions have organized collections of instructional resources and learning activities keyed to their content standards. The governments of Australia and New Zealand, for example, have collaborated in supporting The Learning Federation, which develops educational content tied to those countries' curricula, and makes it available online to schools at no cost. Curriki is a community web site where educators can post K-12 open-source lesson plans and curriculum materials for review, modification, and use by other teachers. Intended as a global resource, the Curriki site comes in Spanish, French, Hindi, and Bahasa (the native language of Indonesia) as well as English versions. At the tertiary level, the Open Courseware Consortium (OCW) organized by the Massachusetts Institute of Technology (MIT) has made materials from 1800 courses from major universities available online at no cost. While online collections offer teachers access to impressive resources, teachers often have too little time to search for appropriate resources and too little expertise to assemble a coherent plan of instruction from a library of fragmentary resources.

Online learning and virtual schools

Web-based online learning has been well-established in tertiary education and corporate training since the 1990s. More recently, this use of technology has become a significant part of K-12 education as well. A survey of US school districts commissioned by the Sloan Consortium (Picciano and Seaman, 2007) estimated that 700 000 US public school students were taking online courses in school year 2005–06 – a tripling of K-12 online learners in the 3 years following a National Center for Educational Statistics survey of districts concerning their online course offerings in 2002–03 (Setzer and Louis, 2005). Most of the online courses taken by K-12 public school students at the time of the survey were at the high school level, but the practice now is spreading to lower grades.

In addition to online course offerings through conventional schools, there are also increasing numbers of K-12 school programs that are entirely online. By fall 2007, 28 of the 50 US states had online virtual high school programs (Tucker, 2007). The Florida Virtual School, the first statewide public virtual school in the United States, had 64 000 secondary and middle school students enrolled in online classes in 2008–09.

Online learning has become popular because of its potential for providing more flexible access to content and instruction at any time, from any place. Online learning is often selected with goals such as (1) increasing the availability of learning experiences for learners who cannot or choose not to attend traditional face-to-face offerings, (2) assembling and disseminating instructional content more cost-efficiently, or (3) enabling instructors to handle more students, while maintaining learning outcome quality that is equivalent to that of comparable face-to-face instruction.

Different technology applications are used to support different models of online learning. One class of online learning models uses asynchronous communication tools (e.g., e-mail, threaded discussion boards, and newsgroups) to allow users to contribute at their convenience. Synchronous technologies (e.g., webcasting, chat rooms, and desktop audio/video technology) are used to approximate such face-to-face teaching strategies such as delivering lectures and holding meetings with groups of students. Early online learning applications tended to implement one model or the other, but current online learning applications tend to combine multiple forms of synchronous and asynchronous online, as well as occasional face-to-face, interactions.

Frequent assessment and individualization of learning

Some of the earliest learning software, developed in the 1960s by Patrick Suppes at Stanford University, incorporated the principle of individualizing the material presented to a learner based on that particular learner's state of knowledge. Proponents of mastery learning (an instructional approach organized around specific learning objectives with learning time allowed to vary so that each student works on an objective until he or she has mastered it) quickly appreciated the value of ICT for supporting their instructional approach. While current generations of instructional software are built in new programming languages and have more sophisticated interfaces, much of the mathematics and reading software for elementary and secondary students is a revision of early computer-assisted instruction (CAI) content developed with a mastery learning design. Common software features include reports for teachers showing each student's performance and a summary of the performance of the whole class, organized by curriculum standard or instructional objective.

The increased accountability pressures around mathematics and reading achievement ushered in by the No Child Left Behind Act of 2001 in the United States and similar legislation in other countries has sparked more widespread interest in frequent assessment of students on the content and skill objectives that are part of the accountability system. Even for schools where none of the instruction in reading and mathematics takes place on computer, it has become common for students to take frequent interim or benchmark tests to see where the student is with respect to accountability standards at a point where there is still time to provide extra services or focused instruction on areas of weakness. In many cases, these assessments are provided on computer and scored almost instantaneously. Instructional management software helps teachers and school leaders maintain records and generate reports of interim assessment data. Mislevy and colleagues describe technology's role in supporting the systematic design of assessments and assessment delivery.

Technology is also enabling the development and use of formative assessments. Formative assessments are those that provide feedback to the learner and the instructor that is used to advance learning. Such assessments are most effective when conducted in close proximity to the relevant learning experience and when they have been designed based on research on how people learn the content being assessed. Such assessments reveal both what a student does not understand and why it is not understood. The advantage of technology is in extending the range of situations or tasks that can be presented to the student so that more complex skills and the students' ability to integrate multiple concepts and skills can be assessed. Complex, multi-step problems, data sets, simulations, and models can be incorporated into technology-based assessments, and not just the student's final answer to the problem but each step taken in addressing the problem can be recorded automatically. Pellegrino describes examples of research-based formative assessments in reading, science, and mathematics. Bennett describes how these same technology capabilities are starting to extend the range of skills addressed by assessments designed for large-scale administration, such as the Keystage 3 ICT Assessment Tasks developed by England's National Assessment Agency and new science assessments being studied for potential incorporation into the National Assessment of Educational Progress (NAEP) in the United States.

Emerging Uses

Technology changes at a much more rapid pace than education, and whenever a new technology emerges, there are those who want to see it applied in schools. Experimentation with mobile phones, podcasts, and social networking sites as educational tools are ongoing. Three major themes in emerging research and development on educational technology are collaborative knowledge building through Web 2.0 applications, immersive environments and games for learning, and interactive classroom communication systems. A common thread among these three themes is increased opportunities for contribution and participation.

Web 2.0

Although without a precise definition, the term Web 2.0 was coined to cover what are considered second-generation

Internet sites, distinguished by their dynamic content shaped by multiple users. It includes social networking sites such as MySpace, recommendation systems such as that used by Amazon.com, and community-developed resources such as Wikipedia. Within an education context, Web 2.0 applications engage students in working with others (other students, instructors, or content experts) to explore and build knowledge around concepts or phenomena. The WISE science learning environment described above is an example of a Web 2.0 educational application as is the Knowledge Forum, developed at the Ontario Institute for Studies in Education (Scardamalia and Bereiter, 2006).

The Knowledge Forum software environment is a multimedia database that allows students, teachers, and external mentors to post notes containing information, questions, or interpretations. It was designed to promote knowledge-building discourse – the kind of exchange of information, conjectures, questions, and interpretations one would expect to see in a research laboratory (Scardamalia and Bereiter, 2006). The software provides a set of labels including 'my theory,' 'new information,' 'this theory explains,' and 'this theory does not explain' to scaffold students' efforts to make sense of and build theories about the content of their shared database. The software also provides 'views,' which are alternative organizations of the database contents – for example, categorization of cases on the basis of different features or on the basis of chronology or consistency/inconsistency with a certain theory or school of thought. Knowledge Forum has been used with groups ranging from kindergartners to graduate students and professionals (Scardamalia and Bereiter, 2006) and in a range of countries, including Canada, the United States, Finland, and Hong Kong.

Immersive environments and games

A second technology trend with potential to influence education is the increasing realism and interactivity offered by multi-user virtual environments. While some critics decry the amount of time that young people spend on multi-player online games such as World of Warcraft, others argue that the level of engagement engendered by such games can and should be harnessed for educational purposes (Federation of American Scientists, 2006). A number of so-called serious games have been developed to demonstrate the educational potential of this approach (Barab *et al.*, 2004; Steinkuehler, 2006). River City, for example, is an environment in which students learn middle school science concepts by acting as a character (an avatar) in a simulated eighteenth-century city where the citizens are falling ill at an alarming rate. Students use their knowledge of biology along with the results of tests conducted online with equipment such as virtual microscopes to investigate the mechanisms through which the disease is spreading (air, water, or insects). Students collaborate to write up their research findings as a report to River City's mayor. River City's developers believe that the power of such virtual environments lies in their ability to situate student learning in an authentic context while providing scaffolding through system prompts and input from experts that is gradually faded as students acquire stronger inquiry skills.

Interactive classroom communication systems

Another long-standing trend in classroom technology has been increased use of student response systems or clickers. In their simplest form, these devices allow students to simultaneously vote on a multiple-choice question posed by the teacher. The votes can be anonymously collected and displayed as a histogram, indicating the proportion of students that selected each answer. This facility, on its own, has little impact on learning. However, it can support new pedagogical strategies, such as Peer Instruction (Crouch and Mazur, 2001), that increase learning. In Peer Instruction, for example, the instructor uses the feedback to focus student attention on the cognitive contrast between the two most frequent answers to the question. The students are asked to work in pairs to convince each other of the correct answer. This process of argumentation often results in students' convergence toward the correct response. In addition, response systems provide feedback to the teacher, who can use this feedback to adjust instruction.

Classroom communications systems now go considerably beyond simple multiple-choice responses. For example, researchers have developed participatory simulations in which all students take the role of an agent in a simulation. Further, using a networked classroom communication system such as the TI-Navigator, students can contribute mathematical expressions, graphs, data sets, and other mathematical objects to a common shared display. In another research prototype, GroupScribbles, students can contribute handwritten notes (like familiar office sticky notes) to a shared group display, enabling many forms of collaborative brainstorming and critique.

Evidence of the Effects of ICT on Teaching and Learning

Parents and teachers report that students' motivation for learning increases with the use of ICT, and most believe that ICT enhances students' learning. Rigorous evidence regarding the effects of ICT on objectively measured learning outcomes is harder to come by, however.

Evaluating the effectiveness of technology is complex because there are so many different technologies and even more ways in which technologies can be used. Some have argued for trying to isolate the effects of technology *per se*

by providing exactly the same pedagogy and content with and without technology in an experimental design (Clark, 1983). ICT proponents argue that this is a self-defeating strategy, however, because the most important reason to use ICT in instruction is to support kinds of learning that cannot be accomplished without it (making an all-other-things-equal control condition logically impossible).

A recent meta-analysis of controlled studies comparing learning outcomes for online and face-to-face classes, found that students learned more in classes that included online learning activities (Means *et al.*, 2009). The researchers noted, however, that the classes that combined online and face-to-face elements differed from the conventional face-to-face classes not just in terms of the additional instructional medium but also in terms of differing content, instructional strategies, and learning time.

Increasingly, researchers see technology as infrastructural and not itself as an intervention. New computing power, networking, and displays provide the capability to create new instructional activities, but without those new activities, the infrastructure *per se* adds little to teaching and learning. Further, new technology-enabled instructional activities often require additional teacher professional development and new forms of assessment. Hence, a modern perspective emphasizes systems of instruction which build upon the new infrastructural possibilities offered by ICT.

Systems of instruction include both ICT components and curriculum, teacher training, and other supports. The strongest and best-designed studies have examined such technology-supported systems of instruction in large numbers of classrooms with random assignment of teachers or classes to experimental and control conditions. The effectiveness of the SimCalc MathWorlds software and associated instructional activities and teacher development was evaluated in a randomized controlled trial involving 95 middle school mathematics teachers. Students who used SimCalc attained a better understanding of rate and proportionality than did similar students in control classes.

In contrast, a randomized control trial conducted by the US Department of Education involving 16 different commercial mathematics and reading software applications found no effect of software use on either reading or mathematics learning (Dynarski *et al.*, 2007). A potentially critical feature of the US Department of Education study is that schools and teachers were left to their own devices to determine how they would implement the commercial software; there was no R&D organization helping teachers develop an instructional system to integrate the software with the rest of their instructional program. Moreover, because every school had teachers in both the experimental and the control conditions, a schoolwide program of support for software implementation was not possible.

Effective Implementation of Technology-Supported Learning

A number of large-scale teacher surveys have provided insights into the characteristics of teachers and school environments associated with teacher integration of ICT into instruction. Survey data suggest that teachers who themselves have stronger ICT skills are more likely to have students engage in ICT-supported activities for their classes. The extent to which teachers have their students use ICT is larger also for teachers who have participated in professional development around technology integration and for those whose school leaders promote the use of technology (Zhao *et al.*, 2002). There are also teacher characteristics with no obvious connection to technology use that nevertheless predict the extent of technology integration in a teacher's classroom. Teachers with constructivist or student-centered teaching philosophies have their students use technology more often than do other teachers (O'Dwyer *et al.*, 2005). Teachers who engage in a broader range of professional activities (collaborating with colleagues around instructional issues in their school, participating in professional activities outside the school, and acting as leaders in professional activities) are significantly more likely than other teachers to have their students use technology weekly or more often (Becker and Riel, 2000). Teacher leaders are particularly likely to have their students use ICT in more sophisticated ways involving knowledge building, problem solving, and collaboration (Riel and Becker, 2008).

Beyond the question of the extent to which ICT is being used in schools and classrooms, there is the broader system-level question of the educational goals its use is addressing. UNESCO (2008) has provided a framework describing different strategies for using ICT to support education reform. The technology literacy strategy aims to harness technology to increase the basic skills of the populace and also to increase students' skill in using ICT, often through taking a specific course taught by a specialized technology teacher. The knowledge deepening strategy seeks to prepare students to use ICT to address complex high-priority problems in the real world, and implementations of this strategy include student use of digital resources and technology tools to address complex problems in a content area (e.g., by exploring a simulation of a watershed in science class). Finally, the knowledge creation strategy involves teaching and using technology in ways that prepare students to become innovators through developing the problem solving, communication, collaboration, and critical thinking skills that are often called twenty-first-century skills.

Law , elsewhere in this encyclopedia, suggests that the skills that teachers need with respect to ICT vary for these different strategies. The technology literacy strategy requires only a few teachers with strong ICT skills to help students acquire technology fluency. The knowledge deepening approach, in contrast, requires all teachers to have not just basic technology competency but also a knowledge of available technology resources in their subject area and an understanding of how these resources can be used to enhance learning in this domain. The knowledge creation strategy requires teachers to be able to move beyond teaching the content conventionally covered in their subject area to develop learning activities that provide the opportunity to learn and refine twenty-first-century skills. Law suggests that execution of this strategy requires a school's staff to be able to use technology to support their communication and collaboration with each other and to manage and analyze student assessment data. Hinostroza, Labbe, and Lopez describe how ICT can be used to support the learning that teachers must do to support such educational reform strategies.

Some researchers have reasoned that acquisition of twenty-first-century skills and the likelihood that these skills will be applied outside of school can be increased through learning experiences that place students in an active role within a collaborative group working with a realistic or situated problem context. By making the context of learning similar to the contexts within which students will apply their learning (i.e., complex problems that transcend disciplinary boundaries, problem-solving teams with differentiated roles, ICT supports for information finding, reasoning, and communication), educators expect to promote inquiry skills while also making learning activities more motivating and increasing the likelihood that acquired skills and dispositions will transfer to real-world situations.

Use of Technology for Learning Outside of School

As noted above, ICT is becoming increasingly ubiquitous in young peoples' lives and is in fact more common outside of school than inside. Some observers have expressed strong concern about potentially harmful social and physical side effects of excessive technology use, but available empirical research suggests a more balanced view, with some areas of risk and general benefits.

Collins and Halverson suggest that people have many experiences involving searching for and synthesizing information from disparate sources, and using ICT to expand one's cognitive capacity outside of school. Through the Internet, young people engage in communities of individuals with like interests, engage in sophisticated gaming, and acquire new knowledge and skills when they need them (see also Jenkins *et al.*, 2006). Collins and Halverson see the world moving toward a culture of lifelong learning with ICT playing a pivotal role in supporting learning activities, a majority of which will occur outside of brick-and-mortar schools.

It is also possible that in-school and out-of-school learning activities will develop new lines of convergence supported by technology. Signs of this are apparent in the growth in online learning connected to educational institutions. Several universities offering their courses online have reported that the largest single group of online learners consists of regular residential students who prefer the anywhere/anytime quality of the online course to sitting in a lecture hall. In K-12 education, some school districts are offering both classroom-based and online versions of key secondary school courses. In addition to those students opting for the online version from the beginning, there are students taking the classroom-based course who avail themselves of the online learning option for part of the course after becoming ill or needing to travel. Increasingly, students as well as adult learners will expect to be able to access tailored learning resources when and where they want them.

Conclusion

ICT has become increasingly prominent in schools, and many classrooms now have processing power, networking apabilities, and projected displays that were barely imaginably two decades ago. However, technology is infrastructural and by itself has produced few changes in teaching and learning. Effective use of this new infrastructure depends on systems of instruction that include cognitive tools, pedagogical activities, teacher professional development, and appropriate forms of assessment. Many systems of instruction incorporate the capability of technology to provide increased interactivity and feedback. Further, the most successful systems of instruction have been subject-matter-specific. Reading, mathematics, and science each require specific kinds of software and approaches. The Internet is also making it possible to provide original source content, for example, from museums, directly to the classroom. Emerging approaches to ICT include immersive games, collaborative Web 2.0 applications, and classroom communication systems – all means to increase student participation and collaboration in learning. Still, the evidence that technology improves learning is rather thin. Additional research is needed that tests technology in the context of full instructional systems with adequate implementation support.

Bibliography

Bakia, M., Yang, E., and Mitchell, K. (2008). *National Educational Technology Trends Study: Local-Level Data Summary*. Washington, DC: US Department of Education.

Barab, S., Thomas, M., Dodge, T., Carteaux, R., and Tuzun, H. (2004). Making learning fun: Quest Atlantis, a game without guns. *Educational Technology Research and Development* **53**(1), 86–108.

Bangert-Drowns, R. L. (1993). The word processor as an instructional tool: A meta-analysis of word processing in writing instruction. *Review of Educational Research* **63**, 69–93.

Becker, H. J. (1985). How schools use microcomputers: Results from a national survey. In Chen, M. and Paisley, W. (eds.) *Children and Microcomputers: Research on the Newest Medium*, pp 87–107. Beverly Hills, CA: Sage.

Becker, H. and Riel, M. (2000). *Teacher Professional Engagement and Constructivist-Compatible Computer Use*. Report #7 Teaching, Learning and Computing: 1998: National Survey. Available online at the Center for Research on Information Technology and Organizations, University of California, Irvine.

Clark, R. E. (1983). Reconsidering research on learning from media. *Review of Educational Research* **53**(4), 445–449.

Crouch, C. H. and Mazur, E. (2001). Peer instruction: Ten years of experience and results. *Physics Teacher* **69**, 970–977.

Cuban, L., Kirkpatrick, H., and Peck, C. (2001). High access and low use of technologies in high school classrooms: Explaining an apparent paradox. *American Educational Research Journal* **38**(4), 813–834.

Dalton, B. and Strangman, N. (2006). Improving struggling readers' comprehension through scaffolded hypertexts and other computer-based literacy programs. In McKenna, M. C., Labbo, L. D., Kieffer, R. D., and Reinking, D. (eds.) *International Handbook of Literacy and Technology*, vol II, pp 75–92. Mahwah, NJ: Erlbaum.

Dynarski, M., Agodini, R., Heaviside, S., *et al.* (2007). Effectiveness of reading and mathematics software products: Findings from the first student cohort. *Report to Congress. NCEE 2007-4006*. Washington, DC: US Department of Education.

Federation of American Scientists (2006). *Harnessing the Power of Video Games for Learning*. Washington, DC: Federation of American Scientists.

Healey, J. M. (1999). *Failure to Connect: How Computers Affect Our Children's Minds – and What We Can Do About It*. New York: Simon and Schuster.

Jenkins, H., Clinton, K., Purushotma, R., Robinson, A. J., and Weigel, M. (2006). *Confronting the Challenges of Participatory Culture: Media Education for the 21st Century*. Chicago, IL: The MacArthur Foundation.

Kulik, J. A. (2003). *Effects of Using Instructional Technology in Elementary and Secondary Schools: What Controlled Evaluation Studies Say*. Arlington, VA: SRI International.

Law, N., Pelgrum, W. J., and Plomp, T. (2008). *Pedagogy and ICT Use in Schools around the World: Findings from the IEA SITES 2006 Study*. Hong Kong: University of Hong Kong, Comparative Education Research Centre.

Linn, M. (2006). The knowledge integration perspective on learning and instruction. In Sawyer, R. K. (ed.) *Cambridge Handbook of the Learning Sciences*, pp 243–264. Cambridge: Cambridge University Press.

Means, B., Roschelle, R., Penuel, W., Sabelli, N., and Haertel, G. (2004). Technology's contribution to teaching and policy: Efficiency, standardization, or transformation? In Floden, R. E. (ed.) *Review of Research in Education*, vol. 27, pp 3–56. Washington, DC: American Educational Research Association.

Means, B., Toyama, Y., Murphy, R., Bakia, M., and Jones, K. (2009). *Evaluation of Evidence-Based Practices in Online Learning: A Meta-Analysis and Review of Online-Learning Studies*. Washington, DC: US Department of Education.

O'Dwyer, L. M., Russell, M., and Bebell, D. (2005). Identifying teacher, school, and district characteristics associated with middle and high school teachers' use of technology. A multilevel perspective. *Journal of Educational Computing Research* **33**(4), 369–393.

Penuel, W. R. (2006). Implementation and effects of 1:1 computing initiatives: A research synthesis. *Journal of Research on Technology in Education* **38**(3), 329–348.

Picciano, A. G. and Seaman, J. (2007). *K-12 Online Learning: A Survey of U.S. School District Administrators*. Boston, MA: Sloan Consortium.

Riel, M. and Becker, H. (2008). Characteristics of teacher leaders for information and communication technology. In Voogt, J. and

Knezek, G. (eds.) *International Handbook of Information Technology in Primary and Secondary Education*, pp 397– 417. New York: Springer.

Rose, D. and Meyer, A. (2002). *Teaching Every Student in the Digital Age: Universal Design for Learning*. Alexandria, VA: ASCD.

Scardamalia, M. and Bereiter, C. (2006). Knowledge building: Theory, pedagogy, and technology. In Sawyer, R. K. (ed.) *Cambridge Handbook of the Learning Sciences*, pp 97–115. Cambridge: Cambridge University Press.

Setzer, J. C. and Louis, L. (2005). *Distance Education Courses for Public Elementary and secondary School Students: 2002-03 (NCES 2005-010)*. Washington, DC: National Center for Education Statistics.

Songer, N. B. (1996). Exploring learning opportunities and coordinated network enhanced classrooms: A case of kids as global scientists. *Journal of the Learning Sciences* **5**(4), 297–327.

Steinkuehler, C. A. (2006). Massively multiplayer online video gaming as participation in a discourse. *Mind, Culture, and Activity* **13**(1), 38–52.

Tucker, B. (2007). *Laboratories of Reform: Virtual High Schools and Innovation in Public Education*. Washington, DC: Education Sector Reports.

UNESCO (2008). ICT competency standards for teachers: Policy framework. CI02007/WS/21. http://portal.unesco.org (accessed August 2009).

Wells, J. and Lewis, L. (2006). *Internet Access in U.S. Public Schools and Classrooms: 1994–2005 (NCES 2007-020)*. Washington, DC: National Center for Education Statistics, US Department of Education.

Zhao, Y., Pugh, K., Sheldon, S., and Byers, J. (2002). Conditions for classroom technology innovations. *Teachers College Record* **104**(3), 482–515.

Further Reading

Becker, H. J., Ravitz, J., and Wong, Y. (1999). Teacher and teacher-directed student use of computers and software. *Technical Report #3: Teaching, Learning, and Computation, 1998 National Survey*. Irvine, CA: University of California at Irvine.

Condi, R. and Munro, B. (2007). *The Impact of ICT in Schools – A Landscape Review*. Coventry: Becta Research.

Means, B. (2008). Technology's role in curriculum. In Connelly, F. M., He, M. F., and Phillion, J. (eds.) *Sage Handbook of Curriculum and Instruction*, pp 123–144. Thousand Oaks, CA: Sage.

Nunnery, J. A., Ross, S. M., and McDonald, A. (2006). A randomized experimental evaluation of the impact of Accelerated Reader/Reading Renaissance implementation on reading achievement in grades 3 to 6. *Journal of Education for Students Placed at Risk* **11**(1), 1–18.

Roschelle, J. M., Pea, R. D., Hoadley, C. M., Gordin, D. N., and Means, B. M. (2000). Changing how and what children learn in school with computer-based technology. *Children and Computer Technology* **10**(2), 76–101.

Smith, M. S. (2009). Opening education. *Science* **323**, 89–93.

Learning as Inquiry

S R Goldman, J Radinsky, S Tozer and D Wink, University of Illinois, Chicago, IL, USA

Learning as Inquiry

Inquiry as a purposeful approach to teaching and learning – sometimes called inquiry-based learning, or discovery learning, or inquiry-based teaching – is at least as old as Socrates. In the *Republic*, Socrates uses questioning techniques to prove to his students that anything worthy of the name knowledge had to be constructed by the learner through processes of questioning and answering. Teaching-as-telling could produce imitation, but not real knowledge. Even in arithmetic, he says, "No one uses it rightly; no one treats it as something that can truly lead to [knowledge of] reality." (Plato in *Sterling and Scott*, 1985: 216, 523-a).

What is now called Socratic method was, in Plato's telling, actually various approaches to using inquiry to help students learn. Chief among these were guided inquiry, in which the teacher already knew the answer but was posing questions so that the student might discover, construct, or even recover knowledge (as in the *Meno*), and shared inquiry, in which the teacher knew what questions to pose but was joining students in pursuit of an answer that even the teacher did not yet know. In either case, the teacher's expertise lay in the method of finding answers, and his role was to help students learn that method, as well as the answers to which that inquiry method might lead. As Socrates said of the act of teaching, "[S]ome things are likely to provoke thought and some not" (*Republic*, 218, 524-d).

In short, inquiry learning foregrounds the question rather than the answer and places the locus of learning in the learner, not in the material that can be transmitted by the teacher. Although there are many approaches to inquiry learning, addressing all the core subjects taught in schools, these approaches share a defining feature: the learner's engagement with the processes of answering one or more questions. The learner, the teacher, or the learning material can frame the question and the answer is developed from that point. This is a common design feature of inquiry-based curriculum materials for pre-K-12 schools. Ultimately, answers to questions do matter. However, in inquiry learning, the processes of inquiry are valued for their particular impact on the learner's knowledge, skills, and dispositions toward learning itself. Educators and researchers find that these learning outcomes differ from those that arise when the learner focuses primarily on an answer to be memorized, a skill to be used algorithmically, or something otherwise learned apart from the process of arriving at that answer for him or herself.

The early history of public schools in the United States included little use of inquiry methods, Socratic or otherwise. Rather, rote memorization, recitation, and repetition were the primary approaches to teaching in rural and urban schools. In the twentieth century, progressive educators such as John Dewey began to explore how forms of inquiry learning could be implemented in public and private schools. "The rise of what is called new education and progressive schools," Dewey wrote in *Experience and Education* "is of itself a product of discontent with traditional education. In effect it is a criticism of the latter" (Dewey, 1959: 4). In books such as *How We Think* (first published in 1910); *Democracy and Education* (first published in 1916); *Logic: The Theory of Inquiry* (first in 1938); and *Experience and Education* (also in 1938), Dewey so shaped contemporary thinking about the role of inquiry in teaching and learning that in 1992 Donald Schön titled an analysis of Dewey's influence 'The theory of inquiry: Dewey's legacy to education'.

Like Plato, Dewey began with a notion of what it means to know something, rather than what it means to teach it or learn it. In contrast to Plato, for whom wisdom and virtue were the highest forms of knowing, Dewey focused on scientific knowing as the model for knowledge. For Dewey, science was an instructive model because it produced consensus about scientific answers only through shared agreement about the methods of inquiry needed to reach those answers. Dewey saw that the methods of science were essential for arriving at warranted knowledge, just as Plato saw that the methods of philosophical inquiry were indispensable for arriving at truth. In this way, Dewey wrote in *Experience and Education* of "scientific method as the pattern and ideal of intelligent exploration and exploitation of the potentialities inherent in experience" (1959: 108).

Dewey therefore saw the domain of science as particularly useful in thinking about teaching and learning in schools. To teach science as static subject matter, as opposed to teaching it through processes of inquiry, was not to teach science at all. To teach science meant that students needed to engage in the methods of inquiry essential to science, at whatever level their development would permit. Without using the term inquiry learning, in *Experience and Education*, Dewey described some of its particulars and challenges.

Adaptation of the method to individuals of various degrees of maturity is a problem for the educator, and the constant factors in the problem are the formation of ideas, acting upon ideas, observation of the conditions which result, and organization of facts and ideas for future use. The ideas, the activities, the observations, or the organization are not the same for a 6-year-old person as they are for a 12- or 18-year-old, to say nothing of the adult scientist (Dewey, 1959: 112).

Dewey claimed that the experience of such learning differed markedly from the experience of more traditional learning approaches, and that the nature and quality of experience influenced the nature and quality of learning. Traditional learning approaches fostered rote learning and recitation of information as evidence of learning. Such shallow understanding would be less likely with inquiry-learning approaches. Students would not simply learn new subject-matter knowledge; they would also learn habits of mind – the disposition to form and pursue questions, the tendency to think critically and analytically, a reflective stance toward experience, and an interest in learning itself. Most importantly, he argued, these habits of mind are critical to future learning.

Collateral learning in the way of formation of enduring attitudes, of likes and dislikes, may be and often is more important than the spelling lesson or lesson in geography or history that is learned. These attitudes are fundamentally what count in the future. The most important attitude that can be formed is that of the desire to go on learning. (Dewey, 1959: 49)

Dewey and other progressive educators believed that such habits of mind were important to adult participation in a democratic society, which places a premium on individual as well as collective problem solving and decision making. In *Democracy and Education*, Dewey popularized the notion of the classroom as a community and as a laboratory for democracy, where groups of students could engage in shared problem solving and making decisions together under a teacher's guidance. *Democracy and Education* applied this thinking explicitly to a range of school subjects beyond science, demonstrating that different domains of knowledge afford different opportunities for students to engage in different kinds of learning – and that inquiry could be motivated and guided by student interests based on the prior experiences they brought to the classroom.

Despite the inquiry-learning influence of progressive-era educators, at no time in the twentieth century could it be said that inquiry teaching and learning were dominant in American public schools. Throughout the late twentieth century, studies of American classrooms typically documented modes of instruction that centered on teacher dissemination of information through presentation and books, rather than on students' engagement in inquiry methods, either guided or shared. However, research on learning over the past 40 years generated a renewed interest in inquiry learning in that it demonstrates that the learner is an active participant in the learning process. The active view of the learner contrasts with the behaviorist tradition and its view of the learner as a passive recipient of knowledge, the view that pervades traditional classroom instruction.

Contemporary Classrooms and Inquiry Learning

Inquiry-focused education was simply not compatible with behaviorist traditions and instructional approaches based on the passive learner. Transmission from the teacher to the student was the dominant instructional philosophy, with metaphors of students as sponges or empty containers dominating education. However, findings from cognitive and social research conducted over the past 40 years painted a different picture of the learner and the role of disciplinary communities of practice. This research showed that learners were active participants in the acquisition and construction of knowledge and that learning was a social, interpersonal activity, not just an individual act. These characteristics were manifest in the functioning of communities of practice in the discipline. Furthermore, twenty-first-century society is a knowledge society with an increasing basis in technology. In a knowledge society, inquiry learning is an essential skill for successful and productive functioning. People need to be able to formulate appropriate questions and seek out their answers. Therefore, at the beginning of the twenty-first century, inquiry-based learning is increasingly evident in classroom instructional programs, albeit in many diverse forms.

Examples abound of both guided inquiry and shared inquiry, from unique teacher-invented learning exercises to commercial, mass-produced curricula that support teachers' use of inquiry learning in many different subject areas. The diversity of these reflect different strategies to include purposeful questioning by learners about a system, whether it is for learning about a discipline or learning to use knowledge obtained from a discipline. In addition, classrooms vary in the nature of the teachers, the students, the resources available, and the degree to which the school environment supports the independence that teachers need for inquiry teaching. This means that particular inquiry curricula are implemented in different ways in different classrooms and different student outcomes result. Implementation that is not completely faithful does not necessarily compromise the benefits of inquiry, although that is often the case.

Relationships between Professional Inquiry and Inquiry Learning in Schools

Many educators and scholars, usually following or responding to Dewey, have examined the nature of the relationship between professional communities of inquiry and their K-12 classroom counterparts. There are clearly essential differences between these two communities: professional inquiry is conducted by an exclusionary community of people who have undergone extensive training and apprenticeship, while classroom communities are by definition inclusive, lacking in specialized training, and unfamiliar with many aspects of the domain. Professional inquiry involves well-established procedures for vetting claims, such as peer review, while classroom inquiry results in fragmentary claims that may lack complete information and lead to unwarranted arguments.

Beyond these differences in the participants and their backgrounds, disciplinary and classroom practices also differ in their epistemological assumptions. Scientists, historians, and other researchers investigate questions with the goal of creating new knowledge, challenging or clarifying existing assumptions. This contrasts sharply with the most common classroom goal of inquiry, that is, to help students acquire knowledge that is assumed to be already well established among more knowledgeable others outside the classroom community of inquirers. In this sense, the products of professional inquiry – understandings that are seen as tentative and subject to challenge within professional inquiry communities – are treated as something quite different by classroom communities, namely as established and unimpeachable facts.

Another difference lies in the source of authority in each community. Of necessity, a single authority (the teacher) exists in classrooms to serve as arbiter and facilitator of all inquiry activity. In contrast, complex hierarchies of authority exist within professional communities, with any member of the community vested with the authority to challenge any proposition made by any other. In this sense, classroom communities of inquiry may be seen as both more egalitarian, in that all students have nominally equal status, yet also more authoritarian, in that the teacher holds a position of ultimate authority which can only be challenged with his or her own consent.

In light of these differences, the appropriate relationship of inquiry activity in the classroom to professional inquiry is not self-evident. Some educators seek ways to simulate aspects of professional inquiry practices in classrooms and scaffold the knowledge and skills required to engage in them. Others attempt to simplify overly complex aspects of investigations, an effort that can have the unfortunate consequence of changing which cognitive processes are engaged by the inquiry process, sometimes turning inquiry into rote procedural execution. Still others seek to create ways for students to engage as peripheral participants in the actual work of scientific communities. In contrast, other approaches focus on the act of problematizing the conceptual content of the domain itself, rather than in the trappings of real-world investigations, seeing this activity as the most important relationship between professional communities of inquiry and the work done by students in classrooms. Finally,

there are those that question the relevance of the professional practices of scientists for the design of science instruction, instead focusing on the nature of inquiry as a knowledge-building practice that can be enacted in classrooms based on the experiences, lives, and cultures of the members of the classroom community itself.

Implementing Inquiry in Classrooms

The range of conceptions of inquiry that exist mean that, unsurprisingly, inquiry-based instruction takes on many forms in classrooms. It varies from single-classroom innovations designed by the teacher to large-scale curricula distributed by publishing houses or educational research-and-development institutions. Many of the established inquiry curricula share certain characteristic approaches to designing materials and learning experiences to scaffold classroom inquiry. At the same time, the particular characteristics of inquiry vary depending on the domain and, sometimes, the subdomains of inquiry (e.g., science, history, mathematics; biology, ecology, and physics) to reflect the epistemological orientation of the content area.

Inquiry Cycles

Notable among characteristic approaches to inquiry is the use of inquiry cycles that emphasize (to different degrees) the iterative relationship among research questions, investigation procedures, findings, and new or modified research questions. Such inquiry cycles typically move through a problematizing phase (engagement, posing of the challenging task), an investigation phase (e.g., guided inquiry within small groups), a feedback phase (e.g., analysis and reflection), and a revision phase based on the feedback. For example, the Inquiry Island curriculum and instructional approach includes six elements: 'question, hypothesize, investigate, analyze, model, evaluate', and returning to question. A similar circular model underlies the design of the inquiry-support software Symphony. It represents an investigation process as being constituted of five steps: develop problem, collect data, visualize data, model data, and review progress. A similar five-phase cycle for younger children consists of engage, prepare to investigate, investigate, prepare to report, and report. Important to the inquiry cycle is a driving question to necessitate collaborative investigation, communication of findings, and generation of work products that learners can talk about and use as a basis for feedback and revision.

Participation in these types of inquiry cycles in science supports students' long-term engagement with their own learning. Each phase presents "different learning opportunities and teaching challenges" . . . and "different types of thinking and activity on the part of the students and the teacher; hence, each phase has a unique role to play in supporting the development of scientific knowledge and ways of knowing" (Magnusson and Palincsar, 2005: 428). Within each phase, instruction emphasizes the metacognitive knowledge relevant to the work students will be doing, including the what, when, and why (i.e., the procedural and conditional knowledge) necessary for students' developing expertise and ownership of strategies and concepts taught and applied appropriately to the content learning. Instruction itself takes the form of a gradual release of responsibility, in which teachers and students are co-participants in the learning process. As students gain more knowledge and control over strategies taught, they assume greater responsibility for the full learning cycle. The development of the metacognitive or reflective skills and habits needed to manage the complexity of these inquiry projects is often an explicit instructional goal.

Many inquiry-oriented interventions include the use of software or other highly structured materials to constrain and enable particular kinds of thinking and activity. This is in part because inquiry teaching often involves long-term projects with multiple phases and types of activity, requiring students to reason across many experiences to make sense of their investigation.

Some educators emphasize the value of more open-ended or student-driven inquiry processes as an alternative to sequential or otherwise highly structured investigations. In the domain of mathematics, applications of concepts to the real world are not the only way for students to engage in inquiry. Instead, students can engage in constructing solutions to problems about the conceptual issues of mathematics themselves and discover new relationships in mathematics. Given the opportunity to engage with such problems when learning mathematics, children's inquiry replicates elements of argumentation and reasoning used by mathematicians, suggesting modes in which inquiry learning aligns to inquiry in a field. Conversely, it may be most important that students engage in discourse that draws out the unseen knowledge, assumptions, and experiences they bring into the classroom from their home cultures and lives into the classroom. The investigation of any science phenomenon through science talk that both values students' understandings and challenges them to establish evidence for claims has the potential to become a focus of authentic scientific inquiry.

Although science and mathematics instruction are the most common home of inquiry curricula, other subject areas are increasingly providing examples of inquiry. For example, inquiry projects in history engage middle-school students in generating explanations for historical events, using historical documents to gather evidence to support or refute particular explanations, and critiquing one another's interpretations. In one such investigation, students tried to establish the precise seat which Rosa Parks refused to surrender on a Montgomery bus, the incident that triggered the anti-segregation bus boycott of 1955.

Design projects in the domain of engineering emphasize inquiry and prioritize the work of creating an actual designed artifact as a key component of the inquiry process. These inquiry projects include not only design and artifact production but also phases of experimentation, testing, communication of results, and communal negotiation of the nature of the problem being addressed and the relative qualities of competing designs. This form of inquiry emphasizes knowledge as a building tool and brings out the usefulness of knowledge to solve problems.

Inquiry learning also can be found in the study of literature. Cultural modeling scaffolds high school students' investigations of great American novels. This approach helps students develop inferences about layered meanings in the novel, supporting them with evidence drawn from the text. Knowledge building is an approach that provides computer tools for developing inferences about texts, giving and receiving feedback, and building connected knowledge across a community of inquirers. Finally, collaborative reasoning and book clubs engage youngsters of elementary school age in conducting inquiries into moral and social dilemmas often faced by the characters in literary works written for the young reader.

Challenges for Inquiry Learning in Classrooms

Research and development efforts over the past 15 years have brought to light several challenges that arise in conducting inquiry learning in the classroom, as well as approaches to dealing with the challenges. The four challenges discussed below echo the issue Dewey raised regarding the adaptation of the inquiry method so that it is implemented in classrooms in developmentally appropriate ways.

1. Providing sets of resources that enable students to understand the problem, including sources that provide information essential to solving the problem. Many informational text sources are too complex from a conceptual, vocabulary, and often grammatical perspective for students to be able to use them successfully. Some approaches provide students with strategies designed to assist them in understanding the key concepts and relations among the concepts. Examples of these are 'Questioning the Author, Leslie's Notebook', text annotation, and concept webs or mapping. Other approaches find or adapt more complex sources so that the concepts are accessible to the target student group. Still others move away from traditional written texts as sources of information and use alternative media, such as video and dialog, to present the information. Embedded data and embedded teaching are examples. The issue of accessibility of text resources may be more problematic in some

disciplines than in others due to the importance placed on working with primary source documents.

2. Ensuring accessibility of the processes of thinking about the information and using it to address the problem to be solved. Students need to develop both the language for structuring acceptable arguments in a discipline and the processes for generating the content from sources. A number of scaffolding tools assist students in this. Some help students organize, sort, and categorize information, while others prompt for explanation, thinking, and reflection and some enable both.

3. Understanding and being able to use a discipline's representational formalisms. These include maps, various forms of data arrays (e.g., graphs and tables), equations and formulas, and dynamic and static physical models, for example, of chemical elements and their behavior. Efforts to introduce these formalisms to students include various technology-based modeling environments of dynamic graphs and chemistry phenomena. In addition, several groups of researchers make the issue of data representation a major focus of their work with school-age children.

4. Creating or providing relevant and meaningful problems that students care about. Such problems increase the likelihood that students will engage in intentional, conscious processes of learning complex ideas. A number of major development projects have produced inquiry materials rooted in significant societal, local, or personal needs and research indicates that these are engaging to students.

There are three challenges that relate to the classroom instructional context and the importance of the teacher in providing guidance to the inquiry process.

1. Teachers preparedness to guide inquiry-learning projects. Effective guidance of inquiry-learning activities requires that teachers understand the process and content of the inquiry. They must also understand how students are likely to engage with the inquiry and the problems and strategies that arise in moving students' thinking forward. Accordingly, many inquiry development projects include both development of curricula for students and teacher professional development. Some development efforts involve teachers as collaborators and, in so doing, create both professional development opportunities and curriculum materials.

2. Changing the norms of classroom discourse from the traditional pattern of teacher initiation, student response, and teacher evaluation (called I-R-E) to those of reasoned arguments in which claims are made and supported with evidence in ways appropriate to the discipline. A related change in classroom discourse patterns concerns the kinds of questions that teachers ask. Known-answer questions predominate in traditional classrooms: Teachers ask questions that they already know the answers to and students know that the teacher knows the answer. When teachers ask questions to which there are not known answers, students have something genuine to contribute to the classroom discourse and become more engaged and energized. Such questions engage students in inquiry rather than test their knowledge. Making these changes in the patterns of classroom discourse is often challenging for teachers who typically have had little opportunity to experience this form of interaction themselves. Professional development institutes often model and provide opportunities for teachers to engage in more inquiry-oriented discourse.

3. Related to changing instructional interactions is the challenge of moving from the informal language of everyday life to more precise technical language of the discipline. As students engage in inquiry processes, their descriptive language needs to move toward the language used in the disciplines. For example, words such as conjecture, hypothesis, evidence, data, and conclusion take on specific meanings in the context of discipline-based inquiry. Yet, many of these words have less formalized meanings in the everyday world. Developing inquiry learning involves acquiring a good command of the ways in which members of the disciplinary community use these terms and expressions. Guiding the inquiry-learning process involves introducing and modeling the use of the language as much as the understanding of the content.

Although the challenges of doing inquiry in classrooms are substantial, there is an increasing body of evidence that instruction and materials can be designed to engage students with inquiry-learning problems over extended periods of time. This engagement produces evidence of student learning on assessments closely aligned with the inquiry-learning situations as well as on more generic achievement tests.

See also: Classroom Discourse and Student Learning; Cognition: Overview and Recent Trends; Knowledge Domains and Domain Learning; Problem Solving and Human Expertise; Problem Solving and Reasoning; Situative View of Learning.

Bibliography

Dewey, J. (1959). *Experience and Education*. New York: MacMillan.
Magnusson, S. J. and Palincsar, A. S. (2005). Teaching to promote the development of scientific knowledge and reasoning about light at the elementary school level. In Bransford, J. D. and Donovan, S. (eds.) *How Students Learn*, pp 421–474. Washington, DC: National Academy of Sciences.
Plato (1985). *The Republic*, Sterling, R. W. and Scott, W. C. (trans). New York: W.W. Norton.

Further Reading

Barab, S., Zuiker, S., Warren, S., *et al.* (2007). Situationally embodied curriculum: Relating formalisms and contexts. *Science Education* 1–33. http://www.interscience.wiley.com (accessed June 2009).

Cognition and Technology Group at Vanderbilt (1997). *The Jasper Project: Lessons in Curriculum, Instruction, Assessment, and Professional Development*. Mahwah, NJ: Erlbaum.

Dewey, J. (1966). *Democracy and Education*. New York: Free Press.

Goldman, S. R. (2005). Designing for scalable educational improvement. In Dede, C., Honan, J. P., and Peters, L. C. (eds.) *Scaling up Success: Lessons Learned from Technology-Based Educational Improvement*, pp 67–96. San Francisco, CA: Jossey-Bass.

Kolodner, J., Camp, P. J., Crismond, D., *et al.* (2003). Problem-based learning meets case-based reasoning in the middle-school science classroom: Putting learning by design into practice. *Journal of the Learning Sciences* **12**, 495–547.

Lee, C. D. (2001). Is October Brown Chinese? A cultural modeling activity system for underachieving students. *American Educational Research Journal* **38**(1), 97–141.

Linn, M. C., Davis, E. A., and Bell, P. (eds.) (2004). *Internet Environments for Science Education*. Mahwah, NJ: Erlbaum.

Marx, R. W., Blumenfeld, P. C., Krajcik, J. S., *et al.* (2004). Inquiry-based science in the middle grades: Assessment of learning in urban systemic reform. *Journal of Research in Science Teaching* **41**, 1063–1080.

Nemirovsky, R., Rosebery, A., Solomon, J., and Warren, B. (2004). *Everyday Matters in Science and Mathematics: Studies of Complex Classroom Events*. Mahwah, NJ: Erlbaum.

Reiser, B. J., Tabak, I., Sandoval, W. A., *et al.* (2001). BGuILE: Strategic and conceptual scaffolds for scientific inquiry in biology classrooms. In Carver, S. M. and Klahr, D. (eds.) *Cognition and Instruction: Twenty-Five Years of Progress*, pp 263–305. Mahwah, NJ: Erlbaum.

Scardamalia, M., Bereiter, C., and Lamon, M. (1994). The CSILE Project: Trying to bring the classroom into World 3. In McGilly, K. (ed.) *Classroom Lessons: Integrating Cognitive Theory and Classroom Practice*, pp 201–228. Cambridge, MA: MIT Press.

Songer, N. B., Lee, N., and McDonald, S. (2003). Research towards an expanded understanding of inquiry science beyond one idealized standard. *Science Education* **87**, 490–516.

Stevens, R., Herrenkohl, L. R., Bell, P., and Wineburg, S. (2005). The comparative understanding of school subjects: Past, present, and future research agenda. *Review of Educational Research* **75**, 125–157.

White, B. Y. and Fredericksen, J. R. (2005). A theoretical framework and approach for fostering metacognitive development. *Educational Psychologist* **4**, 211–223.

Relevant Website

http://www.thinklinklearning.com – Adventures of Jasper Woodbury.

http://www.biokids.umich.edu – BioKids.

http://www.ciera.org – Book Club Plus.

http://csr.ed.uiuc.edu – Collaborative Reasoning.

http://www.k12science.org – Down the Drain.

http://www.worldwatcher.northwestern.edu – GEODE (Geographic Data in Education).

http://www.hi-ce.org – Investigating and Questioning Our World.

http://www.knowledgeforum.com – Knowledge Forum.

http://www.perseus.tufts.edu – Perseus Project.

http://www.literacymatters.org – Questioning.

http://www.simcalc.umassd.edu – SimCalc.

http://www.globe.gov – The Globe Program (Global Learning and Observations to Benefit the Environment).

http://www.jasonproject.org – The Jason Project.

http://wwwthinkertools.org – Thinkertools.

http://www.wise.berkeley.edu – Web-based Inquiry Science Environment (WISE).

Cooperative Learning*

R E Slavin, Johns Hopkins University, Baltimore, MD, USA

Cooperative learning refers to a set of instructional strategies in which students work together in small groups to help each other learn academic content. Cooperative learning methods vary widely in their details: group sizes may be from two to several; group members may have individual roles or tasks, or they may all have the same task; and groups may be evaluated or rewarded based on group performance or the average of individual performances, or they may simply be asked to work together.

In one form or another, cooperative learning has been used and studied in every major subject, with students from preschool to college, and in all types of schools. It is used at some level by hundreds of thousands of teachers. One national survey in the 1990s found that 79% of elementary teachers and 62% of middle school teachers reported regular use of cooperative learning (Puma *et al.*, 1993). Antil *et al.* (1998) found that 93% of a sample of teachers reported using cooperative learning, with 81% reporting daily use.

There have been hundreds of studies of cooperative learning focusing on a wide variety of outcomes, including academic achievement in many subjects, second-language learning, attendance, behavior, intergroup relations, social cohesion, acceptance of classmates with handicaps, attitudes toward subjects, and more (see Slavin, 1995; Johnson and Johnson, 1998; Rohrbeck *et al.*, 2003).

This article focuses on research on achievement outcomes of cooperative learning in elementary and secondary schools, and on the evidence supporting various theories to account for effects of cooperative learning on achievement.

Theoretical Perspectives on Cooperative Learning

While there is a fair consensus among researchers about the positive effects of cooperative learning on student achievement, there remains a controversy about why and how cooperative learning methods affect achievement, and, most importantly, under what conditions cooperative learning has these effects. Different groups of researchers investigating cooperative learning effects on achievement begin with different assumptions and conclude by explaining the achievement effects of cooperative learning in terms that are substantially unrelated or contradictory.

In earlier work, Slavin (1995) identified motivationalist, social cohesion, cognitive developmental, and cognitive elaboration as the four major theoretical perspectives on the achievement effects of cooperative learning.

The motivationalist perspective presumes that task motivation is the single most impactful part of the learning process, asserting that the other processes, such as planning and helping, are driven by individuals' motivated self interest. Motivationalist-oriented scholars focus more on the reward or goal structure under which students operate, even going so far as to suggest that under some circumstances, interaction may not be necessary for the benefits of cooperative goal structures to manifest (Slavin, 1995). By contrast, the social cohesion perspective (also called social interdependence theory) suggests that the effects of cooperative learning are largely dependent on the cohesiveness of the group. This perspective holds that students help each other learn because they care about the group and its members and come to derive self-identity benefits from group membership (Johnson and Johnson, 1998). The two cognitive perspectives focus on the interactions among groups of students, holding that in themselves, these interactions lead to better learning and thus better achievement. Within the general cognitive heading, developmentalists attribute these effects to processes outlined by scholars such as Piaget and Vygotsky. Work from the cognitive elaboration perspective asserts that learners must engage in some manner of cognitive restructuring (elaboration) of new materials in order to learn them. Cooperative learning is said to facilitate that process. One reason for the continued lack of consensus among cooperative learning scholars is that each perspective tends to approach the topic without reference to the body of similar work from other perspectives and without attending to the larger picture.

This article offers a theoretical model of cooperative learning processes which intends to acknowledge the contributions of work from each of the major theoretical perspectives. It places them in a model that depicts the likely role each plays in cooperative learning. This work further explores conditions under which each may operate, and suggests research and development needed to advance cooperative learning scholarship so that educational practice may truly benefit from the lessons of 30 years of research.

The alternative perspectives on cooperative learning may be seen as complementary, not contradictory. For example, motivational theorists would not argue that the cognitive theories are unnecessary; instead, they would

---

* Portions of this paper are adapted from Slavin, 1995.

assert that motivation drives cognitive process, which in turn produces learning. They would argue that it is unlikely that over the long haul, students would engage in the type of elaborated explanations found by Webb (2008) to be essential to profit from cooperative activity, without a goal structure designed to enhance motivation. Similarly, social cohesion theorists might hold that the utility of extrinsic incentives must lie in their contribution to group cohesiveness, caring, and pro-social norms among group members, which could in turn affect cognitive processes.

A simple path model of cooperative learning processes, adapted from Slavin (1995), is diagrammed in **Figure 1**, below. It depicts the main components of a group learning interaction, and represents the functional relationships among the major theoretical approaches to cooperative learning.

This diagram of the interdependent relationships among each of the components begins with a focus on group goals or incentives based on the individual learning of all group members. That is, the model assumes that the motivation to learn and to encourage and help others to learn activates cooperative behaviors that will result in learning. This would include both task motivation and motivation to interact in the group. In this model, motivation to succeed leads to learning directly, and also drives the behaviors and attitudes that lead to group cohesion, which in turn facilitates the types of group interactions – peer modeling, equilibration, and cognitive elaboration, which yield enhanced learning and academic achievement. The relationships are conceived to be reciprocal, such that as task motivation leads to the development of group cohesion, that development may reinforce and enhance task motivation. By the same token, the cognitive processes may become intrinsically rewarding and lead to increased task motivation and group cohesion.

Each aspect of the diagramed model is well represented in the theoretical and empirical cooperative learning literature. All have well-established rationales and some supporting evidence. What follows is a review of the basic theoretical orientation of each perspective, a description of the cooperative learning mode each prescribes, and a discussion of the empirical evidence supporting each.

Four Major Theoretical Perspectives on Cooperative Learning and Achievement

Motivational Perspectives

Motivational perspectives on cooperative learning presume that task motivation is the most important part of the process, believing that the other processes are driven by motivation. Therefore, these scholars primarily focus on the reward or goal structures under which students operate (see Slavin, 1995). From a motivationalist perspective (e.g., Johnson and Johnson, 1998; Slavin, 1983, 1995), cooperative incentive structures create a situation in which the only way group members can attain their own personal goals is if the group is successful. Therefore, to meet their personal goals, group members must both help their groupmates to do whatever enables the group to succeed, and, perhaps even more importantly, to encourage their groupmates to exert maximum efforts. In other words, rewarding groups based on group performance (or the sum of individual performances) creates an interpersonal reward structure in which group members will give or withhold social reinforcers (e.g., praise and encouragement) in response to groupmates' task-related efforts (see Slavin, 1983).

The motivationalist critique of traditional classroom organization holds that the competitive grading and informal reward system of the classroom creates peer norms opposing academic efforts (see Coleman, 1961). Since one student's success decreases the chances that others will succeed, students are likely to express norms that high achievement is for nerds or teachers' pets. However, by having students work together toward a common goal, they may be motivated to express norms favoring academic achievement, to reinforce one another for academic efforts.

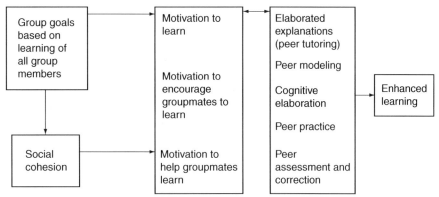

Figure 1 A model of achievement effects of cooperative learning. Adapted from Slavin, R. E. (1995). *Cooperative Learning: Theory, Research, and Practice*, 2nd edn. Boston, MA: Allyn and Bacon.

Not surprisingly, motivational theorists build group rewards into their cooperative learning methods. In methods developed at Johns Hopkins University (Slavin, 1994, 1995), students can earn certificates or other recognition if their average team scores on quizzes or other individual assignments exceed a preestablished criterion. Methods developed by Johnson *et al.* (1998) and his colleagues at the University of Minnesota often give students grades based on group performance, which is defined in several different ways. The theoretical rationale for these group rewards is that if students value the success of the group, they will encourage and help one another to achieve.

Empirical support for the motivational perspective

Considerable evidence from practical applications of cooperative learning in elementary and secondary schools supports the motivationalist position that group rewards are essential to the effectiveness of cooperative learning, with one critical qualification. Use of group goals or group rewards enhances the achievement outcomes of cooperative learning if and only if the group rewards are based on the individual learning of all group members (Slavin, 1995). Most often, this means that team scores are computed based on average scores on quizzes which all teammates take individually, without teammate help. For example, in Student Teams-Achievement Divisions, or STADs (Slavin, 1994), students work in mixed-ability teams to master material initially presented by the teacher. Following this, students take individual quizzes on the material, and the teams may earn certificates based on the degree to which team members have improved over their own past records. The only way the team can succeed is to ensure that all team members have learned, so the team members' activities focus on explaining concepts to one another, helping one another practice, and encouraging one another to achieve. In contrast, if group rewards are given based on a single group product (e.g., the team completes one worksheet or solves one problem), there is little incentive for group members to explain concepts to one another, and one or two group members may do all the work (see Slavin, 1995).

In assessing the empirical evidence supporting cooperative learning strategies, the greatest weight must be given to studies of longer duration. If well executed, these are bound to be more realistically generalizable to the day-to-day functioning of classroom practices. A review of 99 studies of cooperative learning in elementary and secondary schools that involved durations of at least 4 weeks compared achievement gains in cooperative learning and control groups. Of 64 studies of cooperative learning methods that provided group rewards based on the sum of group members' individual learning, 50 (78%) found significantly positive effects on

achievement, and none found negative effects (Slavin, 1995). The median effect size for the studies from which effect sizes could be computed was +0.32 (32% of a standard deviation separated cooperative learning and control treatments). In contrast, studies of methods that used group goals based on a single group product or provided no group rewards found few positive effects, with a median effect size of only +0.07. Comparisons of alternative treatments within the same studies found similar patterns; group goals based on the sum of individual learning performances were necessary to the instructional effectiveness of the cooperative learning models (e.g., Fantuzzo *et al.*, 1989, 1990).

Social Cohesion Perspective

A theoretical perspective somewhat related to the motivational viewpoint holds that the effects of cooperative learning on achievement are strongly mediated by the cohesiveness of the group. The quality of the group's interactions is thought to be largely determined by group cohesion. In essence, students will engage in the task and help one another learn because they identify with the group and want one another to succeed. This perspective is similar to the motivational perspective in that it emphasizes primarily motivational rather than cognitive explanations for the instructional effectiveness of cooperative learning. However, motivational theorists hold that students help their groupmates learn primarily because it is in their own interests to do so. Social cohesion theorists, in contrast, emphasize the idea that students help their groupmates learn because they care about the group. A hallmark of the social cohesion perspective is an emphasis on teambuilding activities in preparation for cooperative learning, and processing or group self-evaluation during and after group activities. Social cohesion theorists have historically tended to downplay or reject the group incentives and individual accountability held by motivationalist researchers to be essential. They emphasize, instead, that the effects of cooperative learning on students and student achievement depend substantially on the quality of the group's interaction (Battisch *et al.*, 1993). For example, Cohen (1994: 69, 70) stated "if the task is challenging and interesting, and if students are sufficiently prepared for skills in group process, students will experience the process of groupwork itself as highly rewarding . . . never grade or evaluate students on their individual contributions to the group product." Cohen's (1994) work, as well as that of Sharan and Sharan (1992) and Elliot Aronson (Aronson *et al.*, 1978) and his colleagues, may be described as social cohesiveness theories. Cohen, Aronson, and the Sharans all use forms of cooperative learning in which students take on individual roles within the group, which Slavin (1983) calls "task specialization" methods. In Aronson's Jigsaw method, students study material on one of four or five topics distributed among the group members. They meet in expert groups to share information on their topics with members of other teams who had the same topic, and then take turns presenting their topics to the team. In the Sharans' Group Investigation method, groups take on topics within a unit studied by the class as a whole, and then further subdivide the topic into tasks within the group. The students investigate the topic together and ultimately present their findings to the class as a whole. Cohen's Finding Out/ Descubrimiento program has students play different roles in discovery-oriented science activities.

One main purpose of the task specialization used in Jigsaw, Group Investigation, and Finding Out/Descubrimiento is to create interdependence among group members. In the Johnsons' methods, a somewhat similar form of interdependence is created by having students take on roles as checker, recorder, observer, and so on. The idea is that if students value their groupmates (as a result of teambuilding and other cohesiveness-building activities) and are dependent on one another, they are likely to encourage and help one another to succeed.

Empirical support for the social cohesion perspective

There is some evidence that the achievement effects of cooperative learning depend on social cohesion and the quality of group interactions (Battisch *et al.*, 1993). The achievement outcomes of cooperative learning methods that emphasize task specialization are less clear. Research on the original form of Jigsaw has not generally found positive effects of this method on student achievement (Slavin, 1995). One problem with this method is that students have limited exposure to material other than that which they studied themselves, so learning gains on their own topics may be offset by losses on their groupmates' topics. In contrast, there is evidence that when it is well implemented, Group Investigation can significantly increase student achievement (Sharan and Shachar, 1988). In studies of at least 4 weeks' duration, the Johnson *et al.* (1998) methods have not been found to increase achievement more than individualistic methods unless they incorporate group rewards (in this case, group grades) based on the average of group members' individual quiz scores (see Slavin, 1995). Studies of forms of Jigsaw that have added group rewards to the original model have found positive achievement outcomes (Mattingly and Van Sickle, 1991).

Research on practical classroom applications of methods based on social cohesion theories provides inconsistent support for the proposition that building cohesiveness among students through teambuilding alone (i.e., without group incentives) will enhance student achievement. In general, methods which emphasize teambuilding and group process, but do not provide specific group rewards based on the learning of all group members, are no more effective than traditional instruction in increasing achievement (Slavin, 1995), although there is evidence that these methods can be effective if group rewards are added to them.

Cognitive Perspectives

The major alternative to the motivationalist and social cohesiveness perspectives on cooperative learning, both of which primarily focus on group norms and interpersonal influence, is the cognitive perspective. The cognitive perspective holds that interactions among students will in themselves increase student achievement for reasons which have to do with mental processing of information rather than with motivations. Cooperative methods developed by cognitive theorists involve neither the group goals that are the cornerstone of the motivationalist methods nor the emphasis on building group cohesiveness characteristic of the social cohesion methods. However, there are several quite different cognitive perspectives, as well as some which are similar in theoretical perspective, but have developed on largely parallel tracks. The two most notable of these are described in the following sections.

Developmental perspectives

One widely researched set of cognitive theories is the developmental perspective (e.g., Damon, 1984). The fundamental assumption of the developmental perspective on cooperative learning is that interaction among children around appropriate tasks increases their mastery of critical concepts. Vygotsky (1978: 86) defines the zone of proximal development as "... the distance between the actual developmental level as determined by independent problem solving and the level of potential development as determined through problem solving under adult guidance or in *collaboration with more capable peers*" (emphasis added). In his view, collaborative activity among children promotes growth because children of similar ages are likely to be operating within one another's proximal zones of development, modeling in the collaborative group behaviors more advanced than those they could perform as individuals.

Similarly, Piaget (1926) held that social-arbitrary knowledge – language, values, rules, morality, and symbol systems – can only be learned in interactions with others. Peer interaction is also important in logical–mathematical thought in disequilibrating the child's egocentric conceptualizations and in providing feedback to the child about the validity of logical constructions.

There is a great deal of empirical support for the idea that peer interaction can help nonconservers become conservers. Many studies have shown that when conservers and nonconservers of about the same age work collaboratively on tasks requiring conservation, the nonconservers generally develop and maintain conservation concepts (see Bell *et al.*, 1985). From the developmental perspective, the effects of cooperative learning on student achievement would be largely or entirely due to the use of cooperative tasks. In this view, opportunities for students to discuss, argue, and to present and hear one another's viewpoints constitute the critical elements of cooperative learning with respect to student achievement.

Empirical evidence for the developmental perspective

Despite considerable support from theoretical and laboratory research, there is little evidence, from classroom experiments conducted over meaningful time periods, that pure cooperative methods, which depend solely on interaction, do produce higher achievement. However, it is likely that the cognitive processes described by developmental theorists are important mediating variables, which can help explain the positive outcomes of effective cooperative learning methods (Slavin, 1995).

Cognitive elaboration perspectives

A cognitive perspective on cooperative learning quite different from the developmental viewpoint is one which might be called the cognitive elaboration perspective. Research in cognitive psychology has long held that if information is to be retained in memory and related to information already in memory, the learner must engage in some sort of cognitive restructuring, or elaboration of the material (Wittrock, 1986). One of the most effective means of elaboration is explaining the material to someone else. Research on peer tutoring has long found achievement benefits for the tutor as well as the tutee (Devin-Sheehan et al., 1976). In this method, students take roles as recaller and listener. They read a section of text, and then the recaller summarizes the information while the listener corrects any errors, fills in any omitted material, and helps think of ways by which both students can remember the main ideas. The students switch roles on the next section.

Empirical evidence for the cognitive elaboration perspective

Donald Dansereau and his colleagues at Texas Christian University have found in a series of brief studies that college students working on structured cooperative scripts can learn technical material or procedures far better than can students working alone (O'Donnell, 1996). Dansereau and his colleagues found in a series of studies that while both the recaller and the listener learned more than did students working alone, the recaller learned more (O'Donnell and Dansereau, 1992). This mirrors both the peer-tutoring findings as well as those of Noreen Webb (2008), who discovered that the students who gained the most from cooperative activities were those who provided elaborated explanations to others. In this research as well as in Dansereau's, students who received elaborated explanations learned more than those who worked alone, but not as much as those who served as explainers. Studies

of reciprocal teaching, in which students learn to formulate questions for each other, have generally supported its positive effects on student achievement (Palincsar et al., 1987; Rosenshine and Meister, 1994; O'Donnell, 2000).

Structuring Group Interactions

There is some evidence that carefully structuring the interactions among students in cooperative groups can be effective, even in the absence of group rewards. For example, Meloth and Deering (1992) compared students working in two cooperative conditions. In one group, students were taught specific reading comprehension strategies and given think sheets to remind them to use these strategies (e.g., prediction, summarization, and character mapping). In the other group, students earned team scores if their members improved each week on quizzes. A comparison of the two groups on a reading comprehension test found greater gains for the strategy group.

However, there is also evidence to suggest that a combination of group rewards and strategy training produces much better outcomes than either alone. Fantuzzo et al. (1992) directly made a comparison between rewards alone, strategy alone, and a combination, and found the combination to be by far the most effective. Further, the outcomes of dyadic learning methods, which use group rewards as well as strategy instruction, produced some of the largest positive effects of any cooperative methods, much larger than those found in studies that provided groups with structure but not rewards. As noted earlier, studies of scripted dyads also find that adding incentives adds to the effects of these strategies (O'Donnell, 1996). The consistent positive findings for Cooperative Integrated Reading and Composition (CIRC) (Stevens et al., 1987), which uses both group rewards and strategy instruction, also argue for this combination.

Reconciling the Four Perspectives

The model shown above in **Figure 1** illustrates how group goals might operate in enhancing the learning outcomes of cooperative learning. Provision of group goals based on the individual learning of all group members might affect cognitive processes directly, by motivating students to engage in peer modeling, cognitive elaboration, and/or practice with one another. Group goals may also lead to group cohesiveness, increasing caring and concern among group members and making them feel responsible for one another's achievement, thereby motivating students to engage in cognitive processes which enhance learning. Finally, group goals may motivate students to take responsibility for one another independently of the teacher, thereby solving important classroom organization problems and providing increased opportunities for cognitively appropriate learning activities. Scholars whose theoretical orientations deemphasize the utility of extrinsic rewards attempt to intervene directly on mechanisms identified as mediating variables in the model described earlier. For example, social cohesion theorists intervene directly on group cohesiveness by engaging in elaborate teambuilding and group processing training. Cognitive theorists would hold that the cognitive processes that are essential to any theory relating cooperative learning to achievement can be created directly, without the motivational or affective changes discussed by the motivationalist and social cohesion theorists.

From the perspective of the model diagrammed in **Figure 1**, starting with group goals and individual accountability permit students in cooperative learning groups to benefit from the full range of factors that are known to affect cooperative learning outcomes. While group goals and individual accountability may not always be absolutely necessary, to ignore them would be to ignore the tool with the most consistent evidence of positive effects on student achievement.

In summary, although cooperative learning has been studied in an extraordinary number of field experiments of high methodological quality, there is still much more to be done. Cooperative learning has the potential to become a primary format used by teachers to achieve both traditional and innovative goals. Research must continue to provide the practical, theoretical, and intellectual underpinnings to enable educators to achieve this potential. This article has advanced a cohesive model of the relationships among the important variables involved in the functioning of cooperative learning. It offers a framework for discussion and continued debate while calling for a move away from competitive attempts to explain this complex phenomenon toward a unified theoretical model which can guide future research efforts and inform education practice.

Acknowledgment

This work was supported by funding from the Institute of Education Sciences, US Department of Education (Grant No. R305A040082).

See also: Vygotsky and Recent Developments.

Bibliography

Antil, L. R., Jenkins, J. R., Wayne, S., and Vadasy, P. F. (1998). Cooperative learning: Prevalence, conceptualizations, and the relation between research and practice. *American Educational Research Journal* **35**(3), 419–454.

Aronson, E., Blaney, N., Stephan, C., Sikes, J., and Snapp, M. (1978). *The Jigsaw Classroom*. Beverly Hills, CA: Sage.

Battisch, V., Solomon, D., and Delucci, K. (1993). Interaction process and student outcomes in cooperative learning groups. *Elementary School Journal* **94**(1), 19–32.

Bell, N., Grossen, M., and Perret-Clermont, A.-N. (1985). Socio-cognitive conflict and intellectual growth. In Berkowitz, M. (ed.) *Peer Conflict and Psychological Growth*, pp 88–112. San Francisco, CA: Jossey-Bass.

Cohen, E. G. (1994). *Designing Groupwork: Strategies for the Heterogeneous Classroom*, 2nd edn, pp 69–70. New York: Teachers College Press.

Coleman, J. (1961). *The Adolescent Society*. New York: Free Press.

Damon, W. (1984). Peer education: The untapped potential. *Journal of Applied Developmental Psychology* **5**, 331–343.

Devin-Sheehan, L., Feldman, R., and Allen, V. (1976). Research on children tutoring children: A critical review. *Review of Educational Research* **46**(3), 355–385.

Fantuzzo, J., King, J., and Heller, L. (1992). Effects of reciprocal peer tutoring on mathematics and school adjustment: A component analysis. *Journal of Educational Psychology* **84**(3), 331–339.

Fantuzzo, J. W., Polite, K., and Grayson, N. (1990). An evaluation of reciprocal peer tutoring across elementary school settings. *Journal of School Psychology* **28**, 309–323.

Fantuzzo, J. W., Riggio, R. E., Connelly, S., and Dimeff, L. A. (1989). Effects of reciprocal peer tutoring on academic achievement and psychological adjustment: A component analysis. *Journal of Educational Psychology* **81**, 173–177.

Johnson, D., Johnson, R., and Holubec, E. (1998). *Cooperation in the Classroom*. Boston: Allyn & Bacon.

Johnson, D. W. and Johnson, R. T. (1998). *Learning Together and Alone: Cooperative, Competitive, and Individualistic Learning*, 5th edn. Boston, MA: Allyn and Bacon.

Mattingly, R. M. and Van Sickle, R. L. (1991). Cooperative learning and achievement in social studies: Jigsaw II. *Social Education* **55**(6), 392–395.

Meloth, M. S. and Deering, P. D. (1992). The effects of two cooperative conditions on peer group discussions, reading comprehension, and metacognition. *Contemporary Educational Psychology* **17**, 175–193.

O'Donnell, A. M. (1996). The effects of explicit incentives on scripted and unscripted cooperation. *Journal of Educational Psychology* **88**, 74–86.

O'Donnell, A. M. (2000). Interactive effects of prior knowledge and material format on cooperative teaching. *Journal of Experimental Education* **68**(2), 101–108.

O'Donnell, A. M. and Dansereau, D. F. (1992). Scripted cooperation in student dyads: A method for analyzing and enhancing academic learning and performance. In Hertz-Lazarowitz, R. and Miller, N. (eds.) *Interaction in Cooperative Groups: The Theoretical Anatomy of Group Learning*, pp 120–144. New York: Cambridge University Press.

Palincsar, A. S., Brown, A. L., and Martin, S. M. (1987). Peer interaction in reading comprehension instruction. *Educational Psychologist* **22**, 231–253.

Piaget, J. (1926). *The Language and Thought of the Child*. New York: Harcourt Brace.

Puma, M. J., Jones, C. C., Rock, D., and Fernandez, R. (1993). Prospects: The congressionally mandated study of educational growth and opportunity. *Interim Report*. Bethesda, MD: Abt Associates.

Rohrbeck, C. A., Ginsburg-Block, M. D., Fantuzzo, J. W., and Miller, T. R. (2003). Peer-assisted learning interventions with elementary school students: A meta-analytic review. *Journal of Educational Psychology* **94**(20), 240–257.

Rosenshine, B. and Meister, C. (1994). Reciprocal teaching: A review of research. *Review of Educational Research* **64**, 490–530.

Sharan, S. and Shachar, C. (1988). *Language and Learning in the Cooperative Classroom*. New York: Springer.

Sharan, Y. and Sharan, S. (1992). *Expanding Cooperative Learning through Group Investigation*. New York: Teachers College Press.

Slavin, R. E. (1983). When does cooperative learning increase student achievement? *Psychological Bulletin* **94**, 429–445.

Slavin, R. E. (1994). *Using Student Team Learning*, 2nd edn. Baltimore, MD: Johns Hopkins University, Center for Social Organization of Schools.

Slavin, R. E. (1995). *Cooperative Learning: Theory, Research, and Practice*, 2nd edn. Boston, MA: Allyn and Bacon.

Stevens, R. J., Madden, N. A., Slavin, R. E., and Farnish, A. M. (1987). Cooperative integrated reading and composition: Two field experiments. *Reading Research Quarterly* **22**, 433–454.

Vygotsky, L. S. (1978). *Mind in Society*, Cole, M., John-Steiner, V., Scribner, S., and Souberman, E. (eds.). Cambridge, MA: Harvard University Press.

Webb, N. M. (2008). Learning in small groups. In Good, T. L. (ed.) *21st Century Education: A Reference Handbook*, pp 203–211. Los Angeles, CA: Sage.

Wittrock, M. C. (1986). Students' thought processes. In Wittrock, M. C. (ed.) *Handbook of Research on Teaching*, 3rd edn, pp 297–314. New York: Macmillan.

LEARNING – LANGUAGE, READING, AND WRITING

Language and Literacy in Educational Settings

Neuroscience of Reading

Learning to Read

Reading Comprehension: Reading for Learning

First Language Acquisition

Second Language Learning

Writing, Early

Writing, Advanced

Language and Literacy in Educational Settings

V G Aukrust, University of Oslo, Oslo, Norway

Glossary

Genre or register – It refers to the constellation of lexical and grammatical features that characterize particular uses of language.

Lexicon or vocabulary – It is the body of words used in a particular language or in a particular sphere of activity.

Morphology – It is the way in which words are formed and related to each other. Morphology is therefore the subsystem of the smallest units of meaning in a language – words and parts of words.

Narrative – It is a sequence of language or words that describe a sequence of events.

Phonology – It refers to the sound system of a language which involves the rules for combining sounds.

Pragmatics – It refers to the rules of language use, and the way members of a community use language to accomplish their intentions and achieve their goals. It includes systems of commonly held conventions and constraints in interpersonal and institutional relations and purposes (e.g., indirect forms of expression in which the meaning is inferred rather than stated explicitly in polite conversation).

Semantics – It refers to the the ways in which language conveys meaning.

Syntax – It is the system of phrases and clauses that are used to create sentences.

Word recognition – It refers to how phonological and visual–orthographic information is combined for the identification of individual words in a text.

Language plays an essential part in education. It is a prerequisite for most of the learning that takes place in schools. Language is also a set of complex cognitive and linguistic skills that schools foster. The role of language in learning has attracted educational researchers from various disciplines, such as linguistics, psychology, sociology, and anthropology. Moreover, across the disciplines, perspectives on the role of language in learning have been underpinned by a number of different theoretical contributions. In examining the role of language in education, this article asks the following questions:

1. How is language learned? In responding to this question, emphasis is placed on two major perspectives on language learning: the cognitive and the sociocultural perspectives.
2. What is the role of language in literacy acquisition? Most researchers agree that language and literacy are integrated systems, and that language is the primary system. But, more precisely, how does research based on the cognitive and the sociocultural perspectives relate language to literacy?
3. What is the role of language in subject-matter learning? Although most researchers agree on the importance of language for literacy learning, the role of language in subject-matter learning that is not reading is less obvious and much less examined. This article examines the impact of academic language on subject-matter learning.

Most children around the world learn more than one language. Several languages may be spoken at home and the child will learn to use them and switch between them, or the child will learn to use one language at home and perhaps another language (the majority language) in the community and school. Many children will also learn one or several foreign languages in school. The multilingual learning situation of most children is not addressed here. A large body of research has addressed the early phases of language learning, emphasizing continuities and discontinuities in the transition from being a child communicating through natural (rather than conventional) vocalizations that are interpreted by the child's caretakers, to the child that acquires and uses conventional vocabulary and syntactical structures, and follows pragmatic rules. This article addresses first-language learning from an age when language has been acquired in at least a rudimentary form.

How Is Language Learned?

Approaches to the study of language rest within a broader set of approaches related to human learning. Recent reviews of learning theories often distinguish between three broad views on learning: the behaviorist/empiricist view, the cognitive/rationalist view, and the situative/pragmatist–sociohistoric view (Greeno *et al.*, 1996). These are distinct traditions in educational theories and practices and are presented here as behavioral, cognitive, and sociocultural perspectives. The behaviorist perspective has played an important role in language research in the past; the cognitive and sociocultural perspectives are contemporary comprehensive accounts of language learning and they will be the focus of this article.

There are significant variations within each of these last two broad perspectives in terms of their theoretical positions and the questions they have asked, as well as points of contact and overlapping issues between them.

Language learning theories vary and can be distinguished in the following ways:

1. Theories that concentrate on how the task of language learning is conceptualized, and by how they define what it means to know a language. Does it primarily have to do with developing the conceptual basis for language use, or being able to participate fluently in everyday linguistic practices?

2. Theories that relate to the nature/nurture dimension. How children acquire language has long been contended: on one side, Chomskian linguistic generative structuralists articulate a nativist position in which basic presuppositions are claims about the poverty of the stimulus. This means that however rich the input is, children can never extract the underlying structural rules of grammar from it. On the other side are psychologists who have a functional approach focused on social inputs and child strategies. Most theories of language development acknowledge both an inborn and a learning component, but differ in the emphasis they give to these elements.

3. Theories that pay attention to the individual versus the community or culture in which the child grows up.

4. Theories that look at different aspects of language. Language is a complex system with subsystems such as phonology, morphology, semantics, lexicons, and pragmatics. Are phonological skills that support children's word processing basic in language learning, or should the language researcher turn to how children learn to express their intentions in language, acquire meaning, and learn the pragmatics of language use in their speech communities?

5. Theories that examine how the relationship between language and literacy is conceptualized.

The Behaviorist Perspective on Language Learning

There are many different hypotheses concerning language acquisition that fall under the general heading of behaviorism. All these approaches share a common focus on the observable aspects of language behavior. Learning is seen as the formation, strengthening, and adjustment of associations between stimuli and responses. Behaviorist perspectives on language learning following from Skinner explain language through two major types of conditioning – classical and operant – and through imitation and shaping (Bohannon and Warren-Leubecker, 2001). Language learning takes place when stimuli in the environment become associated with internal responses, which then become associated with overt behavior through the

application of classical and operant conditioning, imitation, and shaping. Operant conditioning is the learning principle that explains productive speech. Simply put, behavior that is rewarded tends to be repeated by the learner. Behaviorists assume that caregivers reward children when their speech, or parts of it, most closely approximate adult speech. Children's word combinations are assumed to be acquired in much the same way as single words, through shaping, imitation training, and rewards. The hypothesis is that smaller units must be mastered as a prerequisite for more complex units. Therefore analysis of complex tasks into learning hierarchies has been used in designing instruction sequences.

The behaviorist perspective is on the very end of the nature/nurture continuum, emphasizing the role of experience in language learning. Behaviorists focus on how the small units of language are acquired, and how more complex learning outcomes build on these. The behaviorists' view has been criticized for relying too much on simple principles to explain language development. The idea that smaller behavioral units must be mastered as a prerequisite for more complex units has also been questioned. Moreover, caretakers have not been found to consistently provide rewards for grammatically correct utterances or punishment for incorrect ones. Rather, they respond to the content of the utterance. In spite of its significance in the history of language-learning research, behavioral views play a minor role in contemporary educational research, compared to cognitive and sociocultural perspectives which we now turn to.

The Cognitive Perspective on Language Learning

The process of language acquisition by children remains one of the critical issues for contemporary cognitive theory. Within the cognitive perspective, learning is considered as change in conceptual and cognitive structures. Various theoretical contributions – connectionism, constructivism, and the sociocognitive approach – have contributed to the cognitive perspective on language. In this article, the sociocognitive contribution is included in the group of cognitive studies because of its commitment to study individuals, even though sociocognitive research has incorporated sociocultural ideas of the mediated mind, and its conceptual contributions such as intention reading, perspective taking, and communicative collaboration have impacted sociocultural views on language learning. The three theoretical examples of the cognitive perspective in this article share assumptions regarding the importance of the individual as the processor of input from the environment. They differ in their views on the relative role of innate conditions versus environmental input in language learning, and in the relative emphasis on individual versus social and cultural dimensions in explaining learning.

Connectionism

Connectionism emphasizes constraints on the processing of information and the experience-driven reorganization of lower-level behavior into more complex patterns. Connectionists argue against the need to postulate abstract rule systems to explain emerging regularities in language use (cf. Chomsky and the generative structuralists) and emphasize the role of experience or input. The question is how a system like the brain, given streams of input from the structured world, comes to discover that structure. For example, when children start to produce the past tense of verbs they initially get them correct (e.g., she went), and then they begin to make errors (e.g., she goed). This has been cited as evidence for the theory that linguistic development proceeds in stages that reflect the children's acquisition of rules (first learn the word, e.g., went, then acquire the rule about the past tense, and finally discover that rules have exceptions – the two-route way to verb learning). A connectionist simulation of children acquiring knowledge of the use of the past tense showed that they used a mixture of correct and erroneous past tenses in a way that was not stage-like (the one-route way to verb learning).

Constructivist approaches

The constructivist model emphasizes the child's ability to actively organize and construct knowledge. Piaget's influence on conceptual learning as the basis for language learning has been considerable. Piaget focused on the conceptual structures that children develop and which their language presupposes and builds on. Generally, the constructivist approach following from Piaget stresses that language is only one of many complex cognitive skills that children acquire.

Sociocognitive approaches

Although the cognitive perspective on learning has traditionally focused its attention on the individual's learning processes, such as the development of cognitive structures, and has regarded social interaction as only one factor influencing learning, more attention has been paid recently to the social context in which learning occurs. Tomasello (1999) and Nelson (1996) have contributed to these recent developments within the cognitive perspective.

Tomasello emphasizes on children's sociocognitive skills that enable them to participate with others in joint attention, and learn from others, to understand the communicative intentions of others, to take the perspective of others in interpreting and using language, and to collaborate communicatively. Children apply sociocognitive skills to acquire and use language – skills of joint attention, intention reading, perspective taking, and communicative collaboration. Tomasello presents a two-way relationship between children's social cognition and their language. Their

sociocognitive skills support their language acquisition, but engaging in linguistic communication leads them to create new sociocognitive skills such as taking the perspective of the other. Cultures shape the development of children, especially through the intentional instruction of others. According to Tomasello, grammar, regardless of its language, is a perspective-taking device, learned in part by the human capacity to see experience from someone else's perspective.

Similarly, Nelson's sociocognitive theory emphasizes the relationships between cognitive development and language. Language is not separable from cognitive development, and cognitive development cannot be detached from language. Nelson takes as a starting point that the primary cognitive task of the child is to make sense of his or her situated place in the world in order to participate in its activities. She argues that, for the child, knowledge of the object world is embedded within knowledge of the sociocultural world, with the basic task for the child being to predict activities. She introduced the idea of participatory interactions, referring to children taking part in activities without fully understanding them. Through participation they learn their parts and acquire knowledge about them. The meaning of words and language forms such as narrative is acquired through participation in social discourse and it requires extensive practice. When internal language representations come into play, thinking in language emerges.

The Sociocultural Perspective on Language Learning

Sociocultural views of language learning emphasize the social nature of learning (also known as situative, pragmatist, sociolinguistic views, and as social constructivism and cultural psychology). This article foregrounds three contributions that are related: the Vygotskian tradition, sociolinguistic research with an emphasis on language socialization, and ethnographic studies of discursive practices in homes and schools. These three sociocultural branches represent a family of related frameworks. They share the approach that the unit for studying language is the socially situated individual. In this group of approaches, language learning is based on children's repeated participation in everyday activities with other more-competent participants. Through extended engagement in activities with others who are more knowledgeable or expert, children transform the specific means for realizing these activities into individual skills.

The Vygotskian tradition

According to Wertsch (1985), there are three major lines of thought in Vygotskian sociocultural theory. First, to understand a psychological phenomenon, such as language or literacy learning, it is necessary to understand the origin of the phenomenon and the processes by which it is acquired. Vygotsky referred to it as genetic or developmental analysis. Central to this analysis is the conception that any competence appears on the scene twice, first as an intermental capacity between the language-learning child and more competent others, and subsequently through a process of internalization as an intramental capacity in the child. Second, for Vygotsky, mind is social in nature and constituted through language-based social interactions with others. Third, human action is mediated by signs and tools – primarily psychological tools such as language. Researchers working with the Vygostkian idea of internalization have recently included the Bakhtinian notion of appropriation to emphasize the active making-of-one's own that is part of the process of learning language (Aukrust, 2001).

The child's developing capacities are seen as internalization or appropriation of the society's practices via the support of adults or more knowledgeable peers. Through guided participation, children appropriate cultural tools such as language, literacy practices, and social rituals. Children's participation and subsequent development are mediated by the symbolic tools and resources that constitute their learning environments. The metaphorical term scaffolding has become common for this guided assistance that supports the child's growing linguistic participation in everyday routines and formats. Scaffolded assistance in the zone of proximal development supports children's development into the practices deemed important in their culture. Studies of play (Bruner, 1983) and book reading (Snow and Goldfield, 1983) have shown that children's early language acquisition takes place within structured and repeated scaffolded interactions in familiar routines.

Sociolinguistic approaches emphasizing language socialization

Language socialization studies emphasize the complex social norms that govern the use of specific language constructions. These studies clearly define the implicit and explicit socialization practices involved in the child's developing language.

The term language socialization refers to the interactional processes through which a child develops the competence required for participation in the social life of a particular community, including routine cultural practices, such as language and literacy activities. Language socialization research builds on the view that acquiring a language is part of a much larger process of becoming a member of society. The language socialization paradigm is concerned with two phenomena: how children are socialized to use language, and how they are socialized through the use of language.

Ochs and Schieffelin (1995) argue that language socialization accounts for children's grammatical development in terms of the indexical meanings of grammatical forms. Children are viewed as tuned into certain lexical meanings of grammatical forms, which link those forms to, for example, the social identities of interlocutors. They may use a form they do not hear often because it is indexically appropriate to use it. A language socialization approach relates children's use and understanding of linguistic forms to how information is linguistically presented within and across socially recognized situations.

Ethnographic studies

Ethnographic studies emphasize that language always takes place in a specific social and cultural setting. Acquisition of language and literacy is conceptualized as a gradual process of adopting local cultural practices. This group of studies, closely related to the language socialization approach, was developed originally as part of linguistic anthropology. This research demonstrated the cultural specificity of language and literacy socialization practices and their developmental consequences in the transition from home-based to school-based activities (cf. Heath's study below).

During the last two decades, ethnographic studies have examined the characteristics of language learning in the multiparty interaction of classrooms (for review, see Cazden, 2001; Wolf et al., 2006). Many classroom activities are created through classroom discourse, and therefore its role is important in the creation of learning environments and thus of individual learning. This group of studies has been concerned with children's pragmatic learning – their learning of discourse participation. The most common participant structure in classrooms is described as initiative–response–feedback (IRF), initiative–response–evaluation (IRE), triadic dialog, and recitative conversation. In its characteristic form, this participant structure comprises three moves: initiative (I), usually in the form of a teacher's question which often relates to known information; response (R) where the student answers the question; and feedback (F) or evaluation (E), where the teacher follows up or comments on the student's response. A number of international studies have documented that classroom conversations displaying the IRF structure serve to control the students and make them passive within an asymmetrical balance of power: it is the teacher who controls the theme, gives the questions to the students, and the opportunities for them to answer, and it is the teacher who evaluates the answers. However, several recent studies have also emphasized the learning potential in the IRF sequence and have concluded that the relationship between the students' responses and the teachers' feedback is a decisive factor in establishing shared background knowledge. Educators have also explored more complex classroom discourse under terms such as reciprocal teaching (Brown et al., 1996) and dialogic enquiry (Wells, 1999), which refer to discursive activity in classrooms that permits the co-construction of meaning between teachers and students.

Comparing the Cognitive and Sociocultural Perspectives

Cognitive and sociocultural perspectives differ in the ways they conceptualize language learning, in their relative emphasis on innate versus learned aspects of language learning, in the role of the individual versus the collective in language learning, and in which aspects of language they are focused.

How is the task of language learning conceptualized?

In the cognitive perspective, language is a system that must be acquired in terms of a processing system. For the majority of theorists working within the cognitive perspective, learning is a process of acquiring new representations that gradually take on a more decontextualized quality. This is the task the individual child faces when acquiring language, but there is considerable variation among researchers working within the cognitive perspective when it comes to how this task is conceptualized – from the constructivist tradition following Piaget, who addresses individual construction, to the culturally embedded approaches of Tomasello and Nelson.

For the sociocultural researcher, language is a system of cultural practices into which the child is gradually socialized. Language learning is not so much a process of incorporating information or individual construction, but a process of socialization in which the novice gradually participates more and engages in cultural practices. These two main perspectives therefore differ in their view of what it is to know a language (concepts, schemas, networks, versus participation in social activity). The sociocultural perspective tends to disregard acquisition of decontextualized knowledge and emphasizes increasingly competent and fluent participation in cultural routines.

What is the relative emphasis of innate versus acquired aspects of language learning?

Although the innate versus acquired dimension of language development has historically received much attention in language development research, neither the cognitive nor the sociocultural perspectives have a one-sided stance in this question. In the extent to which these issues are discussed in the cognitive and sociocultural research literature, the argument seems to be that young children are biologically predisposed to interact with their environments, but that the effects of language input, and the language structure and culture on children's developing language systems, suggest an enormous susceptibility on the part of the language learners to the effects of input.

Studies applying a cognitive perspective tend to expect that relatively little higher-level knowledge is innate. They tend to emphasize how lower-level learning mechanisms lead to higher-level concepts and rule-governed behavior.

The connectionists propose a combined nativist and input-sensitive language-learning system; similarly, the sociocognitivists emphasize that children are biologically prepared for culture (Tomasello), but that their participation in culture supports acquisition of new cognitive and linguistic skills. They start with the premise that language serves cognitive and social functions of human life, and claim that the structures of language emerge from its functions. Generally, socioculturalists do not speak about input as such, but focus on the culturally or institutionally embedded interactions in which children participate. The analytic focus is not on the child receiving input to process, but on ways of participating fluently and competently in significant cultural routines surrounding the child.

What is the role of the individual versus the social or collective in language learning?

The primary analytic level of the cognitive perspective is the individual processing information. The sociocultural perspective often distinguishes between three analytic levels: individual development, social interaction, and the cultural activities in which both take place. Sociocultural studies commonly view individual development as changed ways of participation in social interaction embedded in cultural activities. The individual level is therefore not the primary focus when socioculturalists explain individual change or learning. Although the sociocognitive approach is concerned with how culture enters the young mind and with how thinking becomes culturally mediated when it emerges in language, its focus is on the child constructing this knowledge.

As there is variation along the individual–collective continuum between the cognitive and the sociocultural perspectives, there is also variation within each of these perspectives regarding the conceptualization of the individual as active versus fairly passive and about the focus of the social interaction.

The cognitive perspective on learning language consists of a number of approaches that differ in the importance they attribute to the individual versus the social context. At one end of the continuum is Piagetian constructivism, which emphasizes the individual's mental processes in the construction of meaning. At the other end of the continuum is the sociocognitive approach, which pays more attention to the social context in which the individual is constructing knowledge. Piaget highlighted the child as an active constructor of knowledge and conceptual structures, whereas connectionism tends to view the child as a receiver of information. Also the sociocognitive approach emphasizes the actively constructing child, but unlike the Piagetian tradition, the research focus is on the child making use of culturally embedded meanings.

While the cognitive perspective pays attention to the individual and distinguishes between individual children and the cultures into which they are born, the sociocultural perspective turns primary attention to social/institutional/cultural opportunities and constraints for learning, and emphasizes the role of social experience and cultural tools in a child's developing language skills. Learning is a matter of how people transform through participation in the activities of their communities. Within the sociocultural perspective, studies differ when it comes to their specific focus on social/cultural analysis, whether transformed participation is studied within dyadic interaction (often characteristic of many Vygotskian-based language learning studies), within cultural activities (Heath, 1983; Ochs and Schieffelin, 1995), or power relationships (many ethnographic studies of classroom interaction).

Which aspects of language learning are focused on most?

The cognitive and sociocultural perspectives differ in their orientation to the aspects of language that are studied. The former perspective has a long tradition of interest in grammar, whereas the latter has primarily addressed social meanings, genres, and the mediating role of language. For example, cognitive research on word learning tends to focus on the number of semantic features the child knows, whereas socioculturalists emphasize the child's usage of a word across various contexts and performance rather than generalized knowledge. It is worth noting that sociocognitive theory has offered significant work on language-mediated narrative thinking and on children's acquisition of socially and culturally embedded word meanings, while research within the sociocultural perspective has examined children's functional learning of grammar, from the starting point that grammatical forms are linked to social meaning and social identities.

What is the Role of Language in Literacy Acquisition?

Literacy is not acquired in the same way as language and needs to be taught. There is consensus in the field of literacy research that language plays a major role in reading and writing, and that these activities are fundamentally linguistic activities. But what is the role of language in literacy? We now turn to how this relationship is conceptualized within the cognitive and sociocultural perspective. Various bidirectional relationships exist between oral language and literacy, but the impact of reading on language is not addressed here.

Language in Literacy: The Cognitive Perspective

Researchers who study literacy from cognitive and psycholinguistic orientations generally agree that literacy draws upon multiple interrelated skills, including oral language, phonological awareness, knowledge of the graphic features of print, and an understanding of how sounds map into print. Cognitive research, particularly within psycholinguistics, has identified components of skills that need to be mastered in order to become a qualified reader. Within the cognitive perspective, literacy has been analyzed as a combination of skills to encode information from text into mental representations of letters and words, to recognize the words and activate representations of their meanings, to combine representations of words into phrases and sentences, and to form representations of the propositions they cover.

Early predictors of reading comprehension are word recognition and oral language skills. Two processes are involved in word recognition: a visual process and a phonological decoding process, which concerns the correspondences between printed letters and the sounds of the language, especially phonemes (the small sound units within spoken words). Research in alphabetic reading has developed the consensus that phonological decoding is a routine part of skilled word recognition. How the phonological and visual–orthographic information combines for the identification of individual words has been the focus of much research within the cognitive tradition, reflecting theoretical debates about how to conceptualize the cognitive mechanisms of word recognition. In addition to supporting word recognition, phonological processing supports cognitive processes such as comprehension and memory of the text. It is well documented that word recognition is an important source of individual variation in reading. In word recognition, accuracy and fluency are crucial for processing meaning. Fluency enables readers to access and apply relevant higher thinking skills for comprehension.

Moreover, reading comprehension is predicted by oral language which again is comprised of multiple skills. As noted, phonological skills are precursors to literacy. The importance of phonological awareness (the ability to reflect upon and manipulate the sound structure of spoken language) is well documented. Moreover, vocabulary has long been known to be predictive of later-reading comprehension. One of the most robust findings in the field of literacy research is actually the high correlation between vocabulary and reading comprehension. Also, variability in syntax skills has been found to be related to reading. Finally, knowledge of discourse types (expository text, narrative) predicts comprehension. Good comprehenders tend to have a more advanced understanding of various discourse types, which helps them interact with texts strategically and construct meaning successfully. Two types of extended discourse – explanations and narratives – have received much attention in literacy research, and children's exposure to such discourse has been linked to literacy-related outcomes. Over all and in sum, it is widely agreed that specific and multiple oral-language skills prepare children for comprehension.

Phonological processing and oral-language skills influence different aspects of reading acquisition at different times. The association between oral language – particularly vocabulary – and reading has been found to be greater for the later years, from fourth grade on. This does not mean that oral-language skills have no importance for early reading. Oral-language skills seem to have an indirect relationship with phonological processing as early as kindergarten and across the early years of schooling.

Language in Literacy: The Sociocultural Perspective

Within the sociocultural perspective, literacy practices are considered part of social practices, the most fundamental unit of analysis of human action within the field. Sociocultural researchers often adopt a broad view of literacy and have also proposed multiple literacies, such as digital literacy and science literacy.

Language is considered the most significant resource for creating and reproducing meaning and is an essential feature of social practices. Human knowledge is stored in discourse, systematically organized systems of language in which meaning is produced according to certain semiotic principles. Socioculturalists' emphasis on language and literacy recognizes the role of mediational means in understanding human collective and individual action.

Two important contributions to the role of language in literacy within the sociocultural perspective are considered: Heath's anthropological study of continuities and discontinuities in ways with words in home and school, and the new literacy studies (Gee, 1996).

Heath (1983) described how children in different communities in the USA learned their community's way of using language in everyday social practices. She suggested that each community had specific ways of socializing members. For example, Heath found that children from Trackton, a mostly African-American community, and Roadville, a mostly white community, exhibited very different story-telling behaviors. Heath documented how children learned to use language and how their use of language established their identity, roles, and relationships among family and friends. Following these children into their schools, she documented how their distinct ways of learning language affected their integration into academic life. Most critical to academic success were certain ritualized uses of language, such as the assignment of labels to objects and responses to questions about events already known to the questioner. She also described how children from some communities were encouraged to look at letters and books at home. The children developed a familiarity with texts that supported their learning in school. The study reports on continuities and discontinuities in literary practices at home and school, and underlines the many relationships between language, literacy, and academic learning, beneficial for children who experienced continuity in ways with words between home and school and detrimental for those who did not. The study finds support in more recent ethnographic studies, which have concluded that the failure of many children from low-income homes in reading results from a mismatch between home and community patterns of language and literacy use, and the uses of language and literacy typically expected in schools.

The new literacy studies took as a starting point that reading and writing only makes sense when studied in the context of social and cultural practices. This group of studies is closely related to work on situated cognition that has argued that knowledge does not reside solely in individuals' heads, but rather is distributed across the social practices (including language practices) and the various tools, technologies, and semiotic systems that a given community of practice uses in order to carry out its activities. Learning to read and write is to become a participant in literate social practices, and further learning is a matter of changing patterns of participation in literacy practices. The new literacy studies pays attention to different styles of oral language use and the various types of literacy that are tied to specific domains, such as science in classrooms, or to specific sociocultural groups. Cognition is studied in terms of how thinking is mediated by the physical and social environment, various semiotic systems, and different sorts of tools.

The Role of Language in Literacy – The Two Perspectives Compared

In the cognitive perspective, language plays an important role in reading comprehension. Various oral skills have been examined, and many of them, such as vocabulary, phonological processing, syntactic skills, and discourse knowledge, showed a relationship to reading outcomes. Though there is much developmental continuity between language and literacy, and though language is a strong predictor of later literacy, there are also discontinuities and differences, the most important being that literacy needs to be taught to be acquired.

Research based on the sociocultural perspective does not apply a skills approach to literacy. Literacy is not considered an individual accomplishment, but a social practice to which communities and schools socialize children. Texts and other cultural tools mediate the ways people communicate and think in a culture. The formation of literate identities and the acquisition of academic social languages are important achievements in literacy education. Moreover, the sociocultural perspective does not differentiate sharply between language, artifacts such as the alphabetic system and texts, and social practices. Artifacts are conceived as forms of human knowledge and as mediating resources that structure social practices as well as human thinking.

This article has culled out some differences in how researchers within the cognitive and sociocultural fields respond to questions of the role of language in literacy. When it comes to reading programs, there are many examples of researchers who draw from both the individual skills and the social practices perspective. An example is reciprocal teaching which is partly Piaget based and partly Vygotsky based, and is a cognitive apprenticeship model for teaching reading comprehension within communities of learners (Brown *et al.*, 1996). Teachers and students take turns leading a discussion that includes four types of strategic activities: predicting, questioning (making up a question on the main idea in the text), summarizing, and clarifying.

The Role of Language in Learning Subject Matter: Academic Language

While much research has examined relationships between language and literacy, less is known about the impact of language on learning subject matter in general, outside the mediating role of reading for learning. This final section turns to the role of academic language in children's discipline learning. Both the cognitive and the sociocultural perspectives have paid attention to academic language, the former with a focus on the particular language skills required to cope with textbooks and classroom discourse, the latter related to genres or registers as mediating tools for learning. While the term academic language represents a fairly recent attempt at identifying those qualities of language that support acquisition of content-area knowledge, a variety of terms have been used to capture the same language qualities, and these are reviewed briefly first:

1. *Decontextualized language.* Decontextualized language is talk that goes beyond the here and now, and relies on language to convey information about other times and places. The term was frequently used in child language research from a cognitive and psycholinguistic perspective in the 1980s and 1990s. Offering oral definitions is, for example, a discourse task in which children need to rely on their decontextualized language skills. The term has also been used to point out similarities in spoken and written language. Oral stories, in which the speaker does not presuppose shared knowledge with the interlocutors, take on some of the characteristics of written language: they have a relatively complete message, adequate explicit references, and an assumed audience that does not share much background information with the writer. These characteristics are all examples of decontextualized language skills. Advocates of the sociocultural perspective have argued that all language use is contextualized in social practices. They have also suggested

applying the term recontextualized to messages that do not presuppose shared background knowledge.

2. *Extended discourse.* Extended discourse is the term suggested in child language research to cover much of the same meaning as decontextualized language. The term extended has two meanings. First, it emphasizes sustained use of language, such as in conversations, as opposed to simple directives – that is, talk that extends over several utterances or turns. Second, it refers to talk that extends the here and now. Narratives and explanations are examples of extended discourse that children participate in and that have been found to support their development of oral language and reading. Making convincing arguments and providing formal definitions are also examples of extended discourse.

3. *Cognitive Academic Language Proficiency* (CALP). The distinction between cognitive academic language proficiency (CALP) and basic interpersonal communicative skills (BICS) was proposed by Cummins (1979) to draw attention to the time required by immigrant children to acquire second-language conversational fluency (BICS) compared with grade-appropriate academic proficiency which was needed for school learning. Conversational fluency was often acquired within about 2 years of exposure to the second language, whereas academic aspects of the second language required a much lengthier process to be learned.

4. *Accountability talk.* The term accountability talk is used to point out various features of types of talk that support reading comprehension. These three features are:

   - *Accountability to accurate knowledge.* Participants make use of specific and accurate knowledge, recognize the kind of knowledge required to address a topic and appropriate evidence for claims and arguments, and show commitment to getting it right.
   - *Accountability to rigorous thinking.* Participants use strategies to present arguments and to challenge each other's reasoning, synthesize several sources of information, construct explanations, formulate hypotheses, and apply generally accepted standards of reasoning.
   - *Accountability to the learning community.* Participants make efforts to ensure that all participants understand the ideas and positions shared, elaborate and build on each other's ideas and work to clarify or expand propositions, and ask each other questions aimed at clarifying propositions (Cazden, 2001; Wolf *et al.*, 2006).

Academic Language in Cognitive versus Sociocultural Perspectives

Academic language in the cognitive/psycholinguistic perspective

Academic language has various typical features: the interpersonal stance is detached or authoritative, the information load is dense, the organization of information involves explicit marking of text structures (metadiscourse), and at the lexical level academic language is diverse and precise, including terms that are discipline-specific as well as terms used academically across disciplines. Moreover, these linguistic features must be combined with additional cognitive achievements: genre mastery, mastery of argumentative strategies, and content-area knowledge (Snow and Uccelli, 2009). Academic language, like all linguistic communication, involves challenges at the level of self-representation, of representing a message, and of constructing discourse.

Academic language in the sociocultural perspective

Within this perspective, academic language is integrated with social identities and social practices and is at the core of school-based literacy (Gee, 2004). Academic language is part of social languages which again are defined as ways of using language so as to enact a particular socially situated identity and carry out a particular socially situated activity. School success is based on the ability to cope with academic language, which is different from everyday language in face-to-face conversation. Science has, for example, been conceptualized as a special-purpose language. To acquire an academic social language, students must be willing to see the acquisition of the academic social language as a gain (gaining traits, categorizations, etc.) and also accept certain losses (attitudes, interests, values left out by the speaker/writer).

What is academic language: Summary

Even in the early grades, children are expected to learn new information from content-area texts, so failure to understand the academic language of those texts can hinder their access to new information. Academic language is often defined as the language used in textbooks and in schools, that is, academic language is defined by the context in which it appears. In addition, academic language has special linguistic features, puts specific demands on self-representation (the cognitive/psycholinguistic perspective), and is integrated with the enactment of social identities (the sociocultural perspective).

Concluding Comments

The behaviorist perspective was historically a main line of development in the psychology of learning and played a significant role in the study of language learning in the 1950s and 1960s. The cognitive perspective became influential in research on learning and cognition in the 1970s, while recent developments like connectionism and socio-cognitive research continue to vitalize the study of language learning. The sociocultural perspective is the youngest of the three, but defines an area of educational research with

vital activity during the last decades. In their broad review of the field of learning and cognition, Greeno et al. (1996) discuss potential future developments and relationships between these theoretical perspectives. One possibility is that the different views will live side by side, complementing each other and analyzing processes of learning at different levels of aggregation. Another possibility is a somewhat more competitive relation among the perspectives, in which one perspective can provide a kind of synthesis of the others. One salient theoretical question for the study of how language is learned and how it impacts literacy and academic school learning will be the continuing clarification of relations among research perspectives.

See also: Attention in Cognition and Early Learning; First Language Acquisition; Learning in a Sociocultural Perspective; Learning to Read; Reading Comprehension: Reading for Learning; Second Language Learning; Vygotsky and Recent Developments.

Bibliography

Aukrust, V. G. (2001). Agency and appropriation of voice: Cultural differences in parental ideas about young children's talk. *Human Development* **44**, 235–249.

Bohannon, J. N. and Warren-Leubecker, A. (2001). Theoretical approaches to language acquisition. In Gleason, J. B. (ed.) *The Development of Language*, pp 254–314. Columbus, OH: Merrill.

Brown, A., Metz, K., and Campione, J. (1996). Social interaction and individual understanding in a community of learners: The influence of Piaget and Vygotsky. In Tryphon, A. and Vonèche, J. (eds.) *Piaget–Vygotsky: The Social Genesis of Thought*, pp 145–171. Hove: Psychology Press.

Bruner, J. S. (1983). *Child's Talk: Learning to Use Language*. New York: W. W. Norton.

Cazden, C. (2001). *Classroom Discourse: The Language of Teaching and Learning*. Portsmouth: Heinemann.

Cummins, J. (1979). Cognitive/academic language proficiency, linguistic interdependence, the optimum age question and some other matters. *Working Papers on Bilingualism* **19**, 121–129.

Gee, J. P. (1996). *Social Linguistics and Literacies: Ideology in Discourses*. London: Taylor and Francis.

Gee, J. P. (2004). Language in the science classroom: Academic social languages as the heart of school-based literacy. In Yerrick, R. (ed.) *Establishing Scientific Classroom Discourse Communities: Multiple Voices of Teaching and Learning Research*, pp 19–38. Mahwah, NJ: Erlbaum.

Greeno, J. G., Collins, A., and Resnick, L. (1996). Cognition and learning. In Berliner, D. C. and Calfee, R. C. (eds.) *Handbook of Educational Psychology*, pp 15–46. New York: Macmillan Library Reference USA.

Heath, S. B. (1983). *Ways with Words: Language, Life, and Work in Communities and Classrooms*. Cambridge: Cambridge University Press.

Nelson, K. (1996). *Language in Cognitive Development: Emergence of the Mediated Mind*. Cambridge: Cambridge University Press.

Ochs, E. and Schieffelin, B. (1995). The impact of language socialization on grammatical development. In Fletcher, P. and MacWhinney, B. (eds.) *The Handbook of Child Language*, pp 73–94. Oxford: Blackwell.

Snow, C. E. and Goldfield, B. A. (1983). Turn the page please: Situation-specific language acquisition. *Journal of Child Language* **10**, 551–569.

Snow, C. E. and Uccelli, P. (2009). The challenge of academic language. In Olson, D. and Torrance, N. (eds.) *The Cambridge Handbook of Literacy*, pp 112–113. Cambridge: Cambridge University Press.

Tomasello, M. (1999). *The Cultural Origins of Human Cognition*. Cambridge, MA: Harvard University Press.

Wells, G. (1999). *Dialogic Inquiry. Towards a Sociocultural Practice and Theory of Education*. Cambridge: Cambridge University Press.

Wertsch, J. (1985). *Vygotsky and the Social Formation of Mind*. Cambridge, MA: Harvard University Press.

Wolf, M., Crosson, A. C., and Resnick, L. (2006). *Accountable Talk in Reading Comprehension Instruction*. Los Angeles, CA: Center for the Study of Evaluation, University of California.

Further Reading

Bakhtin, M. (1986). *Speech Genres and other Late Essays*. Austin, TX: University of Texas Press.

Chomsky, N. (1957). *Syntactic Structures*. Hague: Mouton.

Dickinson, D. and MaCabe, A. (2001). Bringing it all together: The multiple origins, skills, and environmental supports of early literacy. *Learning Disabilities Research and Practice* **16**, 186–202.

Griffin, T., Hemphill, L., Camp, L., and Palmer, D. (2004). Oral discourse in the preschool years and later literacy skills. *First Language* **24**, 123–147.

Piaget, J. (1959). *The Language and Thought of the Child*. London: Routledge/Kegan Paul.

Skinner, B. F. (1957). *Verbal Behaviour*. Englewood Cliffs, NJ: Prentice-Hall.

Snow, C. E., Burns, M. S., and Griffin, P. (1998). *Preventing Reading Difficulties in Young Children*. Washington, DC: National Academy Press.

Stone, C. A. (2004). Contemporary approaches to the study of language and literacy development. In Stone, C. A., Silliman, E. R., Ehren, B. J., and Apel, K. (eds.) *Handbook of Language and Literacy. Development and Disorders*, pp 3–24. New York: Guilford Press.

Street, B. (ed.) (2001). *Literacy and Development: Ethnographic Perspectives*. London: Routledge.

Vygotsky, L. (1986). *Thought and Language*. Cambridge, MA: MIT Press.

Wertsch, J. (1998). *Mind as Action*. New York: Oxford University Press.

Neuroscience of Reading

U Goswami, University of Cambridge, Cambridge, UK

Glossary

EEG – Electroencephalography, a time sensitive imaging method based on direct measurement of electrical brain activity.
fMRI – Functional magnetic resonance imaging, a spatial imaging method based on blood flow.
MEG – Magnetoencephalography, a time sensitive imaging method based on the magnetic fields generated by electrical brain activity.

Introduction

The neural demands made by learning to read appear to be very similar in different languages. Current neuroimaging research suggests that the core neural systems involved are the same across languages, and that the atypical neural processing characteristic of children with developmental dyslexia is also highly similar across languages. Current neuroimaging technologies are able to provide information about the time processes in reading (electroencephalography (EEG) technology), information about the parts of the brain that are involved in reading (functional magnetic resonance imaging (fMRI) technology), and information about the temporal sequential activation of different neural regions (magnetic source imaging (MSI)). Connectivity analyses also provide important information on the white matter tracts (information highways in the brain) that develop to support successful word recognition.

The most prevalent neuroimaging technologies used with children work in different ways and provide different kinds of information. In EEG, sensitive electrodes are placed on the child's scalp and brain electrical activation is recorded directly. The sensitive electrodes can measure the low-voltage changes in networks of neurons caused by cells communicating with each other (an electrochemical process). EEG is very time sensitive, and is able to record changes in brain activity at the millisecond level. For example, EEG can pinpoint the exact time at which a child recognizes a word. However, EEG signals are difficult to localize, hence the neural regions responsible for word recognition are not revealed by this technique. A second prevalent measure – currently the most dominant measure in use with children – is fMRI. fMRI measures changes in blood flow in the brain, through detecting the magnetic resonance signal generated by the protons of water molecules in neural cells. This generates a blood oxygenation level-dependent (BOLD) response. The BOLD response peaks over time, and relative activation in different neural regions will be recorded. Images are typically acquired over 0.5–several seconds, and so fMRI lacks the millisecond temporal resolution of EEG. However, fMRI offers very good spatial resolution, indicating where exactly in the brain reading-related neural activity takes place. Finally, MSI depends on a combination of magnetoencephalography (MEG) and MRI. MEG measures the magnetic fields generated by the electrical activity in the brain rather than the electrical activity itself (the latter is measured by EEG). These magnetic fields are tiny; they are 1 billion times smaller than the magnetic field generated by the electricity in a light bulb. By combining this information with MRI scans – which detect changes in blood flow – both the time course and the spatial localization of brain activity is possible. There are currently very few MSI studies of children's reading.

The Development of Reading

The history of behavioral research on reading acquisition in English reveals considerable debate about the extent to which visual processes versus phonological processes are critical for learning to read. For example, in the 1970s there was debate concerning the relative contribution of Phonecian (code-breaking) versus Chinese (visual memorization) reading-acquisition strategies. Developmental dyslexia was assumed to be a primarily visual disorder, conceptualized as a congenital word blindness. More recently, behavioral researchers have proposed stage or phase models of reading acquisition in English, in which early logographic or visual memorization strategies are replaced by code-breaking or phonological recoding strategies, with a final phase of automatic orthographic word recognition. Dual-route models of reading acquisition were also popular. These models assumed that, developmentally, children could choose to learn to read by either whole-word-based strategies (a visual or direct route to meaning) or by using grapheme–phoneme assembly (a phonological or indirect route to meaning). It was also assumed that developmental dyslexia could either reflect visual-orthographic difficulties in developing a sight vocabulary (surface developmental dyslexia), or difficulties in learning to recode words using letter-sound rules (phonological surface dyslexia). Most of these ideas are looking increasingly dated with the advent of brain imaging.

Brain imaging studies available at the time of writing suggest that reading begins primarily as a phonological process. In the earliest phases of reading acquisition, it is the neural structures for spoken language that are particularly active. As reading expertise develops, an area in the visual cortex originally named the visual word-form area (VWFA) becomes increasingly active (Cohen and Dehaene, 2004). Although described as processing visual forms, this area is not a logographic system that accesses meaning directly from a holistic pattern. Although close to the visual areas that are active during picture naming, the VWFA is also active during nonsense word reading (reading aloud nonlexical forms, such as tegwump). Nonsense words do not have visual word forms in the mental lexicon, hence the VWFA is thought to store orthography–phonology connections at different grain sizes. Orthographic sequences and their connections to sound appear to be stored at both the whole-word and sub-word level.

Many behavioral studies in developmental psychology have demonstrated the critical role of phonological awareness in learning to read (see Ziegler and Goswami, 2005, for a recent review). Phonological awareness is thought to develop from natural language-acquisition processes. Word learning is exponential between the ages of 1 and 6 years, and in order for the brain to represent each learned word as a distinct and unique sequence of sounds, the mental lexicon must incorporate knowledge of the sound elements that comprise a particular word, and the order in which these elements occur. Behavioral studies across languages have shown that a child's awareness of these sound elements at different linguistic levels (syllable, onset–rime, and phoneme) predicts the acquisition of reading (see Ziegler and Goswami, 2005, for a review). Further, training phonological awareness has positive effects on reading acquisition across languages, particularly when it is combined with training about how letters or letter sequences correspond to sounds in that language (e.g., Schneider *et al.*, 2000). Children with developmental dyslexia across languages appear to have specific problems in detecting and manipulating component sounds in words, called a phonological deficit (e.g., Snowling, 2000).

Neuroimaging Studies of Learning to Read

There are still relatively few neuroscience studies of children who are learning to read. Most neuroimaging studies of reading have been carried out with adults (see Price and McCrory, 2005, for a recent synthesis). Adult fMRI studies show a very consistent picture concerning the neural networks that underpin skilled reading. Skilled word recognition appears to depend on a left-lateralized network of frontal, temporoparietal, and occipitotemporal regions – whatever language is being read. However, there is some additional recruitment of visuospatial areas for languages with nonalphabetic orthographies (e.g., left middle frontal gyrus for Chinese, see meta-analysis by Tan *et al.* (2005)). The frontal, temporoparietal, and occipitotemporal regions essentially comprise the language, cross-modal, and visual areas of the brain. At a very simple level, semantic and memory processing is thought to occur in temporal and frontal areas, auditory processing in temporal areas, visual processing in occipital areas, and cross-modal processing in parietal areas. Data on neural timing from EEG studies suggest that the brain has decided whether it is reading a real word or a nonsense word within 160–180 ms of presentation. This has been demonstrated both for children and adults across languages (e.g., Csepe and Szucs, 2003; Suaseng *et al.* 2004).

Studies of children using fMRI have tended to use a restricted range of tasks. These include asking participants to read single words and then comparing brain activation to a resting condition with the eyes closed; asking participants to pick out target visual features while reading print or false font (false font is made up of meaningless symbols matched to letters for visual features like the ascenders in the letters b, d, and k); making phonological judgments while reading words or nonsense words (e.g., "do these items rhyme?": leat and jete), and making lexical decisions (e.g., pressing a button when a word is presented, and a different button when a nonsense word is presented). Nevertheless, the developmental studies that have been completed demonstrate a high degree of consistency between the neural networks recruited by novice and expert readers. For example, work by Turkeltaub and colleagues used fMRI and the false-font task to compare neural activation in English-speaking children and college students aged from 7 to 22 years (Turkeltaub *et al.*, 2003). This task was selected because 7-year-olds can perform it as well as adults, meaning that changes in reading-related neural activity are likely to reflect developmental differences rather than differences in task expertise. Turkeltaub and colleagues reported that adults activated the usual left hemisphere sites, including left posterior temporal and left inferior frontal cortex. They then restricted the analyses to children younger than 9 years of age. In this instance, the main area engaged was the left posterior superior temporal cortex. This region is traditionally considered the focus of phonological activity, and is thus thought to be active during grapheme phoneme translation. As reading developed, activity in left temporal and frontal areas increased, while activity previously observed in right posterior areas declined. This pattern was interpreted as showing that reading-related activity in the brain becomes more left-lateralized with development.

In further analyses focusing only on the younger children, the researchers investigated the relationships between three core phonological skills and word processing. The three core phonological skills are usually taken to be phonological awareness, phonological memory, and rapid automatized naming (RAN). Turkeltaub and colleagues calculated partial correlations between activated brain regions and each of these three measures while controlling for the effects of the other two measures. They reported that the three different measures correlated with three distinct patterns of brain activity. Brain activity during phonological awareness tasks appeared to depend on a network of areas in the left posterior superior temporal cortex and the inferior frontal gyrus. The level of the children's phonological skills modulated the amount of activity in this network. Activity in the inferior frontal gyrus increased with reading ability. This area is also a key phonological area (Broca's area) – important for the motor production of speech. Phonological short-term memory (digit span) appeared to depend on a different neural network, including left intraparietal sulcus – the dominant site of working memory in adults – the middle frontal gyri (bilaterally), and right superior temporal sulcus. RAN appeared to depend on a different, bilateral network including right posterior superior temporal, right middle temporal, and left ventral inferior frontal gyri. Other studies report increasing engagement of the VWFA as reading ability increases. This suggests that the VWFA is a kind of skill zone – with greater activation reflecting increasing expertise with orthography–phonology connections (see Pugh, 2006, for an overview).

A similar developmental picture emerges from an fMRI study of 119 typically developing readers in the age range 7–17 years by Shaywitz and colleagues (Shaywitz et al., 2007). This study used a rhyme-decision task (e.g., "do these items rhyme?": leat and kete), and a visual line orientation task (e.g., "Do [\\V] and [\\V] match?"). Shaywitz and his colleagues reported that networks in both left and right superior and middle frontal regions were more active in younger readers. Activity in these networks declined as reading developed. In contrast, activity in the left anterior lateral occipitotemporal region increased as reading developed. This region includes the putative VWFA. Hence both Turkeltaub et al. (2003) and Shaywitz et al. (2007) report decreased right hemisphere involvement as reading develops. The difference in the behavioral tasks used (e.g., false font vs. rhyme judgment) may explain why somewhat different neural networks became less active.

Overall, therefore, current neuroimaging data appear to support a single route model of reading development. Neuroimaging data suggest that phonological recoding to sound rather than logographic recognition is the key early reading strategy, accompanied by an incremental process of developing orthographic–phonological connections at different grain sizes in the VWFA. This reflects the development of an orthographic lexicon containing both whole words and fragments of familiar words

such as orthographic rimes (Pugh, 2006). The VWFA is not a logographic or visual lexicon, able to support Chinese processing or a direct route from printed word to meaning postulated by dual-route theory.

Neuroimaging Studies of Developmental Dyslexia

The Networks Recruited for Reading

Neuroimaging studies of adult readers with developmental dyslexia suggest biological unity with regard to the affected neural networks. These studies report atypical activation in the three important neural sites for reading – namely, the left posterior temporal regions, the left inferior frontal regions, and the left occipitotemporal regions (such as the VWFA) (e.g., Paulesu et al. (2001), for a comparison of Italian, French, and English-speaking adult dyslexics). Further, neuroimaging studies carried out with children with developmental dyslexia report a similar pattern to adult studies (e.g., Shaywitz et al., 2002, 2007; Simos et al., 2000). However, when interpreting neural differences in developmental studies, it is important to ensure that behavioral performance in the tasks being used is equivalent. If children with dyslexia are worse in such tasks than control children, then any differences in neural activity could reflect differing levels of expertise rather than the neural differences that are core to being dyslexic.

In one of the first developmental studies, Shaywitz et al. (2002) studied 70 children with dyslexia, mean age of 13 years, and compared them to 74 11-year-old typically developing controls (although the controls were not matched for reading level). The children lay in the fMRI scanner while performing a variety of reading-related tasks – namely, letter identification (e.g., Are t and V the same letter?), single-letter rhyme (e.g., Do V and C rhyme?), nonword rhyming (e.g., Do 'leat' and 'jete' rhyme?), and reading for meaning (e.g., Are 'corn' and 'rice' in the same semantic category?). Brain activity in each condition was contrasted with activity in a baseline condition; the line-orientation task (e.g., do [\\V] and [\\V] match?). Shaywitz et al. (2002) reported that the children with developmental dyslexia showed underactivation in the core left temporoparietal networks, with older dyslexics showing overactivation in right inferior frontal gyrus. The children with developmental dyslexia also showed increased activation in right temporoparietal networks. However, some of the differences found in brain activation could have reflected differing levels of expertise with the tasks. For example, for the nonword-rhyming measure, the controls (79% correct) were significantly better at the task than the children with dyslexia (59% correct). In a subsequent study of an expanded sample, Shaywitz et al. (2007) used in-magnet nonword-reading ability as a covariate to control for this problem. Shaywitz and colleagues compared 113 dyslexic children in the age range of 7–18 years to the 119 typically developing readers discussed above in the nonword rhyme and visual line-orientation tasks. Compared to the typically developing children, the dyslexic children showed no age-related increase in the activity of the VWFA. Instead, activity both in the left inferior frontal gyrus (speech articulation) and the left posterior medial occipitotemporal system increased, and reading did not become left-lateralized, with continued right hemisphere involvement.

Developmental Differences in the Time Course of Neural Activation

If basic word-recognition processes are delayed in developmental dyslexia, this will delay access to semantics and, therefore, affect reading comprehension. Similarly, cognitive processes such as grapheme–phoneme conversion might take longer in developmental dyslexia. EEG and MSI technologies can help us to study these questions.

One of very few longitudinal neuroimaging studies of children learning to read used MSI to gain information about developmental differences in the time course of neural activation. Simos and his colleagues studied 33 English-speaking children – 16 of whom were thought to be at high risk of developing dyslexia. The researchers compared brain activation in a letter-sound task (the child saw a letter and had to provide its sound) and a simple nonword-reading task (recoding nonwords like 'lan' to sound). Both tasks were administered at the end of kindergarten and again at the end of the first grade (see Simos et al., 2005). In kindergarten, the high-risk group were significantly slower to show neural activity in response to both letters and nonwords in the occipitotemporal region (requiring, on average, 320 ms compared to 210 ms for those not at risk). The high-risk group also showed atypical activation in the left inferior frontal gyrus when performing the letter-sound task. For this task, the onset of activity actually increased developmentally – from 603 ms in kindergarten to 786 ms in the first grade. The typically developing readers did not show a processing-time increase.

When Simos and his colleagues compared the onset of activity of the three core neural networks for reading, they found that low-risk children showed early activity in the left occipitotemporal regions. This was followed by activity in the temporoparietal regions, predominantly in the left hemisphere, and then by bilateral activity in the inferior frontal regions. In contrast, high-risk children showed little differentiation in terms of the time course of activation between the occipitotemporal and temporoparietal regions. High-risk children who were also nonresponsive to a phonological remediation package being administered during the study ($N = 3$) were distinct in showing earlier onset of

activity in the inferior frontal gyrus compared to the temporoparietal regions. Simos and colleagues commented that the increased inferior frontal activation probably reflected the role of compensatory articulatory processes. This may indicate that children with phonological difficulties rely more heavily on networks for articulation when phonological processing is required.

The Neural Effects of Remediation

Neuroimaging studies of different types of remediation for reading difficulties are consistent in showing that when targeted phonology-based interventions are used with affected children, neural activity is normalized. This indicates that levels of activation in the left-lateralized network of reading areas typically improve following such interventions (e.g., Shaywitz and Shaywitz, 2005; Simos et al., 2002; Temple et al., 2003). Most such studies rely on fMRI, and hence it is difficult to be sure how extensive such normalization really is, given that the BOLD signal reaches a peak over several seconds. Simos and his research group, therefore, used MSI to explore neural activation in eight children with developmental dyslexia who had received 80 h of intensive training with a phonological remediation package (Simos et al., 2002). MSI scans were taken during a nonword rhyme-matching task (e.g., 'yoat' 'wote'), both before the intervention and following remediation. Prior to the intervention, the dyslexic children showed the usual hypoactivation of left temporoparietal regions. Following the intervention, all eight children showed a dramatic increase in the activation of left temporoparietal regions, predominantly in the left posterior superior temporal gyrus. As will be recalled, these networks support grapheme–phoneme recoding in typically developing readers (see Turkeltaub et al., 2003). However, Simos and colleagues found that neural activity was delayed in the children with dyslexia relative to the controls even after this remediation. For example, the peak in left superior temporal gyrus activity occurred at 837 ms, on average, for the dyslexic children, and at 600 ms for the controls. Therefore, even with intensive remediation, children with dyslexia are slow to achieve the reading fluency shown by nondyslexic children.

Shaywitz and Shaywitz (2005) used retrospective examination of the large sample of children with developmental dyslexia reported in Shaywitz et al. (2002) to compare whether children at risk for reading difficulties showed different neurodevelopmental trajectories. They distinguished three groups within the sample – a group of persistently poor readers (PPR), who had met criteria for poor reading both in the second/third and in the ninth/tenth grades; a group of accuracy-improved poor readers (AIR), who had met criteria for poor reading in the second/third grades but who did not meet criteria in the ninth/tenth grades; and a control group of nonimpaired readers (C), who had never met criteria for poor reading (the participants had been studied since age 5). Shaywitz and Shaywitz reported that both the PPR and the AIR groups showed hypoactivation in neural networks in left superior temporal and occipitotemporal regions. However, the groups were distinguished by their neural activity when reading real words. The AIR group still demonstrated underactivation in the usual left posterior areas for real-word reading, whereas the PPR group activated the left posterior regions to the same extent as controls.

Shaywitz and Shaywitz then carried out further analyses based on connectivity. Connectivity analyses examine the neural areas that are functionally connected to each other during reading. The connectivity analyses suggested that reading achievement depended on memory for the PPR group, and not on the normalized functioning of the left posterior regions. The unimpaired controls demonstrated functional connectivity between left hemisphere posterior and anterior reading systems, but the PPR group demonstrated functional connectivity between left hemisphere posterior regions and right prefrontal areas associated with working memory and memory retrieval. Prospective longitudinal studies comparing patterns of neural activation and connectivity in dyslexic children as high-frequency words become over-learned would clearly be very valuable.

Conclusions

Neuroscience studies using fMRI have provided a clear picture of the neural networks that underpin reading both in typically developing and dyslexic readers. It has been shown that the functional organization of the networks for reading is similar in typical development and in dyslexia. Rather than relying on different neural networks, dyslexics show hypoactivation of crucial parts of the network of areas involved in word recognition, and an atypical pattern of continuing right hemisphere involvement. These fMRI studies are essentially correlational studies. They do not answer research questions about what goes wrong in the dyslexic brain. Neuroimaging methods that provide data on the time course of neural processing, such as MEG (MSI) and EEG, are beginning to answer such causal questions. For example, studies using MSI demonstrated that neural activation is delayed in core components of the left-lateralized reading network, and suggested that core components of the reading network may be activated in a different order in developmental dyslexia. We need more longitudinal studies to find out whether there are different neurodevelopmental routes to word recognition for dyslexic children compared to typically developing children. Only longitudinal studies can illustrate the response of a dyslexic brain to being trained to learn to read.

It is believed that the most informative studies with respect to causation in reading will be longitudinal prospective studies that use neuroscience techniques to study basic sensory processing in at-risk children. Such studies may give insight into the causes of the phonological deficit. In this regard, the most promising studies to date are those investigating basic auditory processing, using EEG and MEG methodologies. For example, a large-scale Finnish study (the Jyväskylä Longitudinal Study of Dyslexia or JLD; see Lyytinen *et al.*, 2004) has followed babies at familial risk for dyslexia since birth. EEG measures of auditory sensory processing (evoked-response potentials to speech and nonspeech cues) have been found to distinguish the at-risk babies from controls even during infancy. Hence EEG technologies may soon be able to offer robust neural markers of risk for reading difficulties, enabling much earlier intervention.

See also: Learning to Read; Neuroscience Bases of Learning; Reading Comprehension: Reading for Learning.

Bibliography

Cohen, L. and Dehaene, S. (2004). Specialization within the ventral stream: The case for the visual word form area. *NeuroImage* **22**, 466–476.

Csepe, V. and Szucs, D. (2003). Number word reading as a challenging task in dyslexia? An ERP study. *International Journal of Psychophysiology* **51**, 69–83.

Lyytinen, H., Ahonen, T., Guttorm, T., *et al.* (2004). Early development of children at familial risk for dyslexia: Follow-up from birth to school age. *Dyslexia* **10**, 146–178.

Paulesu, E., Démonet, J. F., Fazio, F., *et al.* (2001). Dyslexia: Cultural diversity and biological unity. *Science* **291**(5511), 2165–2167.

Price, C. J. and McCrory, E. (2005). Functional brain imaging studies of skilled reading and developmental dyslexia. In Snowling, M. J. and Hulme, C. (eds.) *The Science of Reading: A Handbook*, pp 473–496. Oxford: Blackwell Publishing.

Pugh, K. (2006). A neurocognitive overview of reading acquisition and dyslexia across languages. *Developmental Science* **9**, 448–450.

Sauseng, P., Bergmann, J., and Wimmer, H. (2004). When does the brain register deviances from standard word spellings? An ERP study. *Cognitive Brain Research* **20**, 529–532.

Schneider, W., Roth, E., and Ennemoser, M. (2000). Training phonological skills and letter knowledge in children at-risk for dyslexia: A comparison of three kindergarten intervention programs. *Journal of Educational Psychology* **92**, 284–295.

Shaywitz, S. E. and Shaywitz, B. A. (2005). Dyslexia (specific reading disability). *Biological Psychiatry* **57**, 1301–1309.

Shaywitz, B. A., Shaywitz, S. E., Pugh, K. R., *et al.* (2002). Disruption of posterior brain systems for reading in children with developmental dyslexia. *Biological Psychiatry* **52**(2), 101–110.

Shaywitz, B. A., Skudlarski, P., Holahan, J. M., *et al.* (2007). Age-related changes in reading systems of dyslexic children. *Annals of Neurology* **61**, 363–370.

Simos, P. G., Breier, J. I., Fletcher, J. M., Bergman, E., and Papanicolaou, A. C. (2000). Cerebral mechanisms involved in word reading in dyslexic children: A magnetic source imaging approach. *Cerebral Cortex* **10**, 809–816.

Simos, P. G., Fletcher, J. M., Bergman, E., *et al.* (2002). Dyslexia-specific brain activation profile becomes normal following successful remedial training. *Neurology* **58**, 1203–1213.

Simos, P. G., Fletcher, J. M., Sarkari, S., *et al.* (2005). Early development of neurophysiological processes involved in normal reading and reading disability: A magnetic source imaging study. *Neuropsychology* **19**(6), 787–798.

Snowling, M. J. (2000). *Dyslexia*. Oxford: Blackwell.

Tan, L. H., Laird, A. R., Li, K., and Fox, P. T. (2005). Neuroanatomical correlates of phonological processing of Chinese characters and alphabetic words: A meta-analysis. *Human Brain Mapping* **25**(1), 83–91.

Temple, E., Deutsch, G. K., Poldrack, R. A., *et al.* (2003). Neural deficits in children with dyslexia ameliorated by behavioral remediation: Evidence from functional MRI. *Proceedings of the National Academy of Sciences* **100**, 2860–2865.

Turkeltaub, P. E., Gareau, L., Flowers, D. L., Zeffiro, T. A., and Eden, G. F. (2003). Development of neural mechanisms for reading. *Nature Neuroscience* **6**(6), 767–773.

Ziegler, J. C. and Goswami, U. (2005). Reading acquisition, developmental dyslexia, and skilled reading across languages: A psycholinguistic grain size theory. *Psychological Bulletin* **131**(1), 3–29.

Learning to Read

M S Burns and J K Kidd, George Mason University, Fairfax, VA, USA

Essential Underpinnings of Reading

All beginning readers depend on language underpinnings that begin developing in the preschool years. During formal reading instruction, children continue to develop oral-language capabilities needed to approach and understand written language. As preschool children's oral language develops, their expressive oral language increases and their listening comprehension becomes more sophisticated. As this occurs, their ability to remember and use information increases and they learn how to listen differently when hearing expository text, storybooks, poems, and nonsense rhymes. They become aware of the sounds of the language and the phonemes and morphemes that comprise words. They learn the purpose of written language and the forms it takes. At a basic level, they learn how print works (concepts of print). A final but major part of an early literacy foundation is children's developing motivation to read. These essential skills and knowledge continue to develop during instruction in learning to read and as students continue to build reading competence (see **Figure 1**). Below, we elaborate on these underlying skills and knowledge.

Language and Listening Comprehension

Oral language begins in infancy and continues throughout life. It is the largest developmental domain relevant to reading. Oral-language skills form the foundation for the transition from understandings of spoken language to written language. During the preschool years, children develop their receptive language, which enables them to understand, remember, and use what they hear, as well as their expressive language, which gives them the ability to communicate their own needs and thoughts.

At the word level, young children develop speech discrimination in the languages they hear on a consistent basis. They hear words and also the separation between words, developing a sense of what a word is. They compare and contrast words, understanding that some begin with the same sounds and some end with the same sounds, developing phonological awareness. Through manipulation of this word–sound system, they begin to understand that words (speech) are made up of a sequence of sounds (phonemes) and are combined in different ways for different words. Given this opportunity and familiarity with many words, children eventually develop a mental model that enables them to break the code (i.e., understand sound–letter correspondences). Children's model for learning and understanding new words is also rooted in morphological development. During the preschool years, children learn many aspects of morphology, for example, how to form past tense and possessives. A morpheme is the smallest unit of language that carries meaning, for example, the word play has one morpheme, that is, play, and the past tense of play, played, has two morphemes play and ed. Children develop phonological awareness and later morphological awareness, metalinguistic understandings. Words are connected and syntax developed.

Central to language development is semantic development and vocabulary. Young children learn sentential semantics, how phrases and sentences are ordered to obtain meaning. Lexical semantics and vocabulary flourish around 2–3 years of age when children acquire the naming insight, realizing that words are names for things. Developing vocabulary includes not only learning new words but the interrelationships between words. Young children play with word meaning as exemplified in the childhood joke, "Why did the girl throw the butter out the window? To see a butterfly." As children build upon these skills and gain experience with storytelling, they develop a sense of narrative and hone their listening-comprehensions skills.

Forms and Uses of Written Language

During the preschool period, children begin to learn that written language comes in different forms and is used for different purposes. They learn that words are arranged on paper in different ways (e.g., the food words on a menu vs. those on a grocery list vs. those in a cookbook). They simultaneously learn that the food words in these three different forms have different functions. They learn that a storybook (i.e., fiction) is different from a book in which they are learning new information (i.e., expository text). They learn the features of a narrative, how in a narrative a sequence of events relates to the central theme of a story. They learn that a written story has specific features such as quotes in parentheses along with an indication of who is saying the information in quotes (e.g., "Let's take the bicycles," said Mary).

Knowledge of the Written Symbol System and of Print Concepts

Before they can read, children as young as 3 years know we can read certain letter strings, like BOOK,

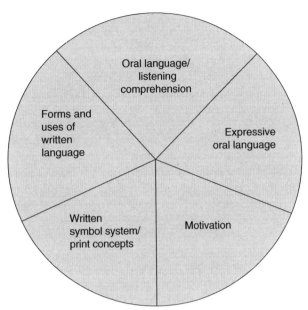

Figure 1 Essential underpinnings of reading.

but not TTTT. Young children also reliably classify BOOK as a word and 8965 as a number. They learn that it is the print in books that is read, and that it works in a certain way (e.g., in English it goes from top to bottom, left to right on the page). They learn knowledge of punctuation and letter knowledge. They develop the understanding that print can have meaning independent of immediate context.

Motivation: Becoming Enthusiastic About Reading and Writing

Literacy as a source of enjoyment takes place in the preschool years as children are read to in interactions that are positive and warm. These experiences are enhanced when the interactions address children's interests, take into account their prior knowledge, honor cultural continuity, and provide multilingual support.

Instruction That Develops Essential Underpinnings of Reading

Oral language, forms and uses of written language, knowledge of the written symbol system, concepts of print, and becoming enthusiastic about reading and writing are acquired before formal instruction in learning to read. These essential skills and knowledge continue to develop during instruction in learning to read and as students continue to build reading competence.

How do children learn the knowledge and skills during the preschool period? The social context is particularly important as young children communicate and participate in social and cultural activities, including experiences such

as storytelling, singing, and reading story books. Young children explore both the reading and writing systems when they, for example, pretend to read and write or act out stories that have been read to them. Peer play is essential. Sociodramatic play is especially important for supporting children's language. It is a time in which children use symbols for objects and participate in shared schemes with other children as they develop their play narratives. Adults enter interactions with children and teach and nudge by sharing their language, knowledge, and skills. The variety and richness of adult words (including rare words) used in those conversations influences children's use of vocabulary. Positive, warm exchanges have the most positive outcomes on children's language and literacy. Children develop their knowledge of the world and urge adults to provide new learning. These shared interactions between adults and children are sustained over time, developing depth of understanding of language and literacy.

Beginning of Formal Reading Instruction

Formal reading instruction builds upon these understandings of language and literacy that emerge as children interact with others and encounter language and literacy models in their world. When learning to read, children build upon what they know about language and text to simultaneously identify printed words and construct meaning. They draw upon their prior experiences, cultural knowledge, and developing vocabularies to make sense of the text. As they develop their abilities to decode and comprehend text, they become fluent readers who read with accuracy, prosody, and speed.

Identifying Printed Words

Identifying printed words requires knowledge of the relationship between letters and sounds and a developing repertoire of words that are recognized at sight. The development of letter–sound correspondences builds upon children's phonological sensitivity and their increasing awareness of phonemes. According to Ehri, children progress through five phases of alphabetic development. In the prealphabetic phase, children have no awareness that there is a relationship between letters and sounds. As children move to the partial-alphabetic phase, they gain an awareness of the relationship between letters and sounds, but focus their attention on the most prominent parts of words (e.g., initial letters). In the fully alphabetic phase, children know the sounds associated with the letters and blend the sounds together to pronounce the word. By the consolidated alphabetic phase, children recognize the whole word instantly and may use multiletter chunks to arrive at the word. When reaching the automatic alphabetic phase, children recognize most words by sight and are able to apply a variety of strategies to decode unfamiliar words.

Movement through these phases requires increasing knowledge about letters and their associated sounds. Children gain this knowledge in a variety of ways. A focus on phonemic awareness combined with the development of letter–sound correspondences has been found to be beneficial in initial instruction. In this approach, children are taught to segment, blend, delete, and substitute phonemes as well as match and isolate sounds and match words. As phonemic awareness is developed, the sounds associated with particular letters are introduced, reinforced, and applied. Application of children's knowledge of letter–sound correspondences can be seen in their written as well as oral representations of letter sounds. As children write to communicate their stories and ideas, writing the letters of the sounds heard reinforces the relationship between sounds and letters and provides insight into the development of letter–sound correspondences.

As children develop an awareness of letter–sound correspondences, a synthetic phonics approach that systematically teaches letters and their corresponding sounds can be helpful for some. This approach focuses on teaching the sounds associated with letters and then teaching children how to blend the sounds together to decode the word. However, many children use sequential decoding rather than synthetic phonics as they figure out unfamiliar words. Sequential decoding involves looking at all letters in an unknown word and then decoding the word by associating sounds with some but not all of the letters of the word. Children who decode in this way use what they know about letters and sounds as well as picture and context cues to predict the word. For example, children reading the sentence, "Stan pet the dog," might use their knowledge of the sounds associated with the consonants in pet and dog along with the picture of a boy petting a dog and the context of the story to help decode both unfamiliar words. Caution has to be taken to ensure that students do not develop an overreliance on pictures for decoding as the overriding goal in decoding instruction is learning the letter–sound correspondences.

For many children who have some understanding of letter–sound correspondences, an analogy approach to learning to decode words is effective. This method of instruction focuses children's attention on using patterns children know to decode unfamiliar words. This approach requires that children delete the initial consonants of a syllable, the onset, to segment the rime, the vowel and consonants that follow the vowel. For example in 'dog,' the 'd' is the onset and 'og' is the rime, and in 'Stan,' 'St' is the onset and 'an' is the rime. Once children recognize a familiar rime, they can decode unfamiliar words by substituting the onset in the known word with the onset in the familiar word. Therefore, children who can read dog, can use the familiar pattern 'og' to read an unknown word fog by substituting the 'd' for an 'f.' This use of analogy is often more efficient and effective than sounding out each letter in a word and blending them together because the vowel sounds in these patterns are fairly constant. For example, the 'a' in 'an' remains stable whether used in Stan, can, or answer. Whereas, learning sounds for 'a' is variable depending on the letters that follow it (e.g., cat, cay, car, and care).

The reliance on patterns to decode words continues as children encounter multisyllabic words. However, the use of onset and rime is not nearly as prevalent as the use of morphemes in decoding longer words. Recognizing morphemes helps children decode words using familiar patterns, such as 'jump' and 'ing' to arrive at 'jumping.' As morphemes are the smallest unit of meaning, the use of morphemic patterns is important because they not only help children decode unknown words, but these patterns also help them construct meaning. For example, children who can decode bed, know what a bed is, and understand that adding an 's' to form beds makes the word plural recognize that two or more beds are being referenced. Likewise, children who are familiar with bed and room comprehend what a bedroom is through their ability to decode and understand both morphemes.

As children's decoding skills develop, so does their ability to recognize words automatically. Developing a sight-word vocabulary involves recognizing familiar words by linking printed words with words stored in memory to remember their meanings and how to pronounce them. As children are exposed to words, connections are made between the graphemes in the spelling of the words and their associated phonemes. The word spellings are a visual representation of the words stored in memory and serve to activate the pronunciation and meaning of these words as children encounter them in print. By developing a repertoire of sight words, children are able to expend less energy on the decoding of text and can focus on constructing meaning as they read.

The goal of decoding instruction is to foster automatic word recognition and enhance reading comprehension to produce fluent readers. Effective instruction builds upon the essential underpinnings developed before formal reading instruction, recognizes the influence of motivation on children's willingness to interact with printed text, and develops decoding and comprehension skills and strategies simultaneously (see **Figure 2**). Children's knowledge of the written symbol system and print concepts supports their ability to navigate the text (e.g., directionality; meaning of punctuation; knowledge of letters, words, and sentences) and helps them understand that identifying printed words is a process of not only being able to pronounce the written word, but also of being able to associate meaning. This requires children to use what they know about oral language, including their knowledge of phonemes,

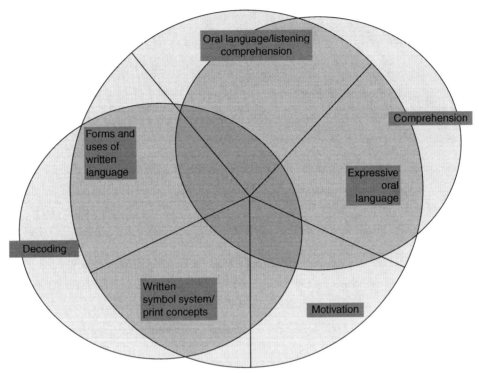

Figure 2 Formal reading instruction.

morphemes, syntax, and semantics, to read the word. For example, when encountering 'read' in print, children use sound–symbol correspondence, grammar, and the context to know how to pronounce and interpret the word. 'Read' used, pronounced, and understood in the past tense (e.g., she read the book yesterday) differs from 'read' used, pronounced, and understood in the future tense (e.g., she will read the book tomorrow). In essence, children use their knowledge of oral and written language to identify printed words to comprehend text while at the same time they rely on their comprehension of text to assist in their identification of the printed words.

Reading Comprehension

Reading comprehension occurs when readers construct meaning as they interact with the written word in an exchange of ideas between themselves and the message in the text. To comprehend text, readers rely upon their ability to decode text fluently, draw upon their extensive vocabularies, and employ comprehension skills and strategies to assist their understanding of the printed materials. This requires them to draw upon their prior knowledge and experiences to make connections between their existing knowledge and the information presented in the text. This interactive process between readers and text enables readers to understand, remember, and use information read and

is influenced by readers' purpose for reading, motivation, and social context.

When learning to read, developing fluent word recognition is important for enhancing comprehension of text. Both decoding and comprehension demand memory which has a limited capacity. Effort devoted to decoding words detracts from the ability to expend resources on understanding text. Therefore, developing automatized decoding is vital to increasing comprehension. However, a focus on word recognition should not be at the expense of an emphasis on developing vocabulary and comprehension skills and strategies. All areas need to be developed simultaneously as children learn to read.

Vocabulary and concept development is also essential to developing comprehension in children learning to read. Knowledge of words and their meanings contributes to clearer understandings of the text. When vocabulary is unknown, children rely on clues from the text, which may result in an incorrect understanding of what was read. To build a rich vocabulary that enhances comprehension, children learning to read need to be immersed in language-rich experiences, both in natural as well as instructional contexts. Exposure to a wide range of vocabulary is needed, including contextualized oral language and the decontextualized language in oral storytelling and written text. These encounters with vocabulary that begin before formal instruction (see **Figure 2**) and continue over time enable children to develop deeper understandings of words and the meanings they convey.

The ability to identify printed words and attach meaning to the words enables children to construct literal interpretations of the text. To comprehend at a deeper level, children learn to activate their prior knowledge or schema to make inferences about what they read. Children reading about a trip to the park will use information based on their own experiences to help them understand. They will rely on what they know about parks to infer information that is not explicitly stated. When the connections they make are relevant and accurate, comprehension is fostered. However, if the connections they make are not relevant or are inaccurate or past experiences with and prior knowledge about the topic are minimal or nonexistent, drawing upon existing schema can limit comprehension. Therefore, children also learn to rely on the connections they make within the text to make inferences. This is especially helpful when they have limited knowledge about or experience with the topic. For example, children reading about an activity that is not familiar might infer that the activity is fun if the text refers to the characters' laughter as they engage in the activity.

As children learn to read, they develop a repertoire of strategies that promote active engagement before, during, and after reading. Prior to reading a text, children learn to establish a goal for reading and activate their prior knowledge. Children use their prior knowledge and the existing text to make predictions as they read. Active reading involves making predictions, confirming or modifying the predictions, and making new predictions. As children make predictions and confirm or modify those predictions, they are engaged in constructing meaning. However, when children hold on to incorrect predictions, comprehension is hindered. For example, children reading a book about the South Pole might originally make the prediction that the South Pole has a warm climate because they associate south with warm. As they read about the ice and the cold temperature, children who have learned to use the information from the text to modify their predictions will realize that the South Pole is cold and will use this information while continuing to read. Whereas, children who maintain their original prediction will not understand information that is reliant on knowing that the South Pole has a cold climate.

While reading, children also learn to monitor their reading. They become aware of the text structure, the relevance of what they are reading, and their own understanding or lack of understanding of the text. They learn to moderate their pace, reread when necessary, and use different reading strategies to enhance their comprehension. Their increasing repertoire of strategies may include generating questions, visualizing the text, and paraphrasing what they read. They learn to identify important information and organize details around the main ideas. The development of their metacognitive awareness enables children to regulate their reading and become more effective readers.

Reading Fluency

As with the previous processes addressed in this piece on learning to read, fluency is dependent upon and coordinated with all the previous mentioned aspects of reading as well as decoding and comprehension (see **Figure 3**) and is emphasized in instruction at all reading levels using various levels of text difficulty. Prosody, using emphasis and variations in intonation, pausing, etc., is a feature of reading that is observed in fluent readers. To achieve prosody, readers employ their knowledge of syntactic information and processing as they use meaningful phrasing and punctuation in the text being read. As mentioned in the section on identifying printed words, morphology and phonology play important roles in achieving decoding automaticity. Prior knowledge, vocabulary, and strategic processing are central in comprehension, as depicted in **Figure 2**. These processes overlap with each other and with the essential underpinnings of language and literacy. Listening comprehension and motivation explain variance in fluency.

Specific instruction to achieve fluency includes a number of forms of repeated reading, both assisted by teachers and peers as well as technology, to be effective. Silent reading with no accounting for comprehension is an additional practice that has been used to increase the amount of absolute reading but results are mixed for use of this method. It seems that the bottom line for fluency is that absolute amount of reading is the most important factor. Caution must be taken though to make sure that absolute amount of reading is defined as reading to get meaning from the text. Word calling without understanding, even if done with accuracy and expression, does not count. Fluency instruction focusing on decoding speech and accuracy and prosody can have such an impact, that is, word calling. The reader might not be reading accurately and comprehending during this time.

Levels of Reading

When children are learning to read, the children's levels of reading and the difficulty of the text must be taken into account. Children's decoding and comprehension of text and their ability to read fluently are affected not only by their reading development, but also by the text they are reading. The difficulty or ease in reading a text is influenced by textual features, such as the size and placement of the text; the presence or lack of pictures; difficulty of the words; the complexity of the sentence structure; and the children's familiarity with the content of the text. Recognizing that texts will pose different levels of challenge for children as they learn to read, it is important to match texts with children in ways that foster reading development. To facilitate this process, texts are

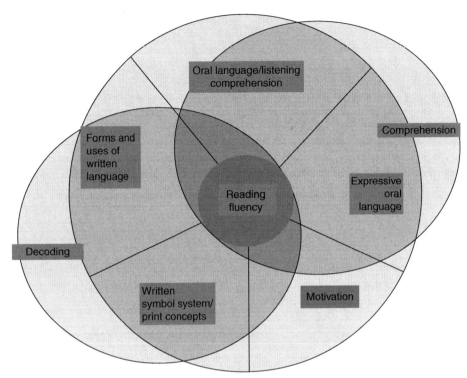

Figure 3 The fluent reader.

generally classified as being at children's independent, instructional, borderline instructional, or frustration level (see **Table 1**).

Texts at children's independent level are ones children can read fluently without assistance. Reading texts on their independent level provides children with an opportunity to practice and apply the reading strategies and skills they already possess and improves their decoding, comprehension, and fluency. Children's reading of instructional-level texts promotes reading development when support or scaffolding is provided by a more adept reader. The use of instructional-level texts during reading instruction enables teachers to instruct within the children's zone of proximal development and optimizes the potential effects of the instruction provided. This is also true when reading materials at the borderline instructional level are read during instruction. However, texts at this level require a high level of teacher support. This is often the level used when children are working with a reading specialist or tutor who can provide more intensive instruction and scaffolding. Texts at children's frustration level require such a high level of support that children typically do not benefit from instruction. With these levels in mind, teachers can enhance reading development by providing children with opportunities to read a variety of texts on their independent and instructional levels with appropriate levels of support and scaffolding.

Table 1   Children's levels of reading in relationship to text difficulty

Level	Word recognition	Comprehension
Independent	99–100%	90–100%
Instructional	95–98%	75–89%
Borderline instructional	90–94%	50–74%
Frustration	Below 90%	Below 50%

Summary

To learn to read, learners need opportunities to learn and integrate numerous underpinnings of reading, identify printed words, develop comprehension, and increase reading fluency. Underpinnings include oral expressive language, listening comprehension, forms and uses of written language, knowledge of the written symbol system, concepts of print, and becoming enthusiastic about reading and writing, motivation. These essential skills and knowledge continue to develop during formal instruction in learning to read and as students continue to build reading competence. To identify printed words, children continue to develop their understanding of the alphabetic system and apply a variety of strategies to decode unfamiliar words. To comprehend, children construct meaning as they interact with the text and draw upon their prior knowledge and experiences. Reading fluency occurs when children's decoding and comprehension enables them to read with speed, accuracy, and prosody. A focus on any one aspect of learning to read should not be at the expense of an emphasis other aspects. To the extent possible, different aspects should be integrated into instruction and the relationship among the processes should be the focus of instruction.

See also: Language and Literacy in Educational Settings; Reading Comprehension: Reading for Learning.

Further Reading

Cunningham, P. M. and Cunningham, J. W. (2002). What we know about how teach phonics. In Farstrup, A. E. and Samuels, S. J. (eds.) *What Research Has to Say about Reading Instruction*, pp 87–109.

Ehri, L. C. and McCormick, S. (1998). Phases of word learning: Implications for instruction with delayed and disabled readers. *Reading and Writing Quarterly: Overcoming Learning Difficulties* **14**(2), 135–163.

Juel, C. and Minden-Cupp, C. (2000). Learning to read words: Linguistic units and instructional strategies. *Reading Research Quarterly* **35**, 458–492.

Nagy, W. E. and Scott, J. A. (2000). Vocabulary processes. In Kamil, M. L., Mosenthal, P. B., Pearson, P. D., and Barr, R. (eds.) *Handbook of Reading Research: Vol. III*, pp 269–284. Mahwah, NJ: Erlbaum.

Pressley, M. (2000). What should comprehension instruction be the instruction of? In Kamil, M. L., Mosenthal, P. B., Pearson, P. D., and Barr, R. (eds.) *Handbook of Reading Research: Vol. III*, pp 545–561. Mahwah, NJ: Erlbaum.

Snow, C. E., Burns, M. S., and Griffin, P. (1998). *Preventing Reading Difficulties in Young Children*. Washington, DC: National Academy Press.

Snow, C. E., Griffin, P., and Burns, M. S. (eds.) (2005). *Knowledge to Support the Teaching of Reading: Preparing Teachers for a Changing World*. Indianapolis, IN: Jossey-Bass.

Snow, C. E. and Páez, M. (2004). The head start classroom as an oral language environment: What should the performance standards be? In Zigler, E. and Styfco, S. (eds.) *The Head Start Debates (Friendly and Otherwise)*, pp 215–244. Baltimore, MD: Brookes Publishing.

Tolchinsky, L. (2003). *The Cradle of Culture and What Children Know about Writing and Numbers Before Being Taught*. Mahwah, NJ: Erlbaum.

Reading Comprehension: Reading for Learning

C E Snow, Harvard Graduate School of Education, Cambridge, MA, USA

Defining Reading Comprehension

The challenge of understanding reading comprehension derives, in part, from the difficulty of defining its borders. Comprehension was defined by the Research and Development (RAND) Reading Study Group (RRSG, 2002) as "the process of simultaneously constructing and extracting meaning through interaction and engagement with print." This definition was intended to signal the importance of a number of key features of comprehension: the accurate decoding of print, a process of meaning construction through which inferences and information not available from the print are incorporated into the meaning representation, and active, motivated engagement from the reader. This definition works well for prototypical cases: the 10-year-old laughing while reading a joke book, the 15-year-old engrossed in a science fiction novel, and the 25-year-old being guided by a manual to install and run a new piece of software. The processes that occur during these prototypical comprehension events have been the subject of considerable research (see RRSG, 2002 for more detailed information about those processes), which has made clear that the success of any reading comprehension event is determined by variation on three dimensions: the text, the reader, and the task, all defined within a sociocultural context. The RRSG characterized successful comprehension as what occurs when the demands of the text, the challenges of the task, and the skills and proclivities of the reader are all well aligned, as exemplified by the prototypical cases listed above. Any pair of these dimensions can be the site of a mismatch that causes comprehension to fail and, as is described below, each introduces some ambiguity about where real reading comprehension begins and ends.

Texts

Consider a candidate text that might be found in a first grade reader:

Alex and Ali ran to the swings and jumped on.

What constitutes comprehension for this text? At a minimum, a mental representation of two individuals moving quickly toward and using some playground equipment should be conjured up, but is the inference that Alex and Ali are probably children part of the comprehension process or does that go beyond basic comprehension? Is it required that the comprehender assign genders to Alex and Ali, or that gender assignment be postponed, recognizing that Alex could be short for either Alexandra or Alexander, that Ali could be a boy's name or a nickname for Alison? If Ali is provisionally classified as a boy, is it part of comprehension processing to infer that he comes from a Muslim family, or is that an inference that goes well beyond basic comprehension? If the reader has, for example, just arrived from China and has never encountered these first names before, has that reader fulfilled expectations with the inference that these are animate creatures – perhaps as likely to be cats as children? Must the reader infer that Alex and Ali actually started swinging, or does that go beyond comprehension into the realm of prediction? Does an inference that Alex and Ali were enjoying themselves belong to the realm of comprehending this sentence or comprehending the world? In other words, what is a sufficiently elaborated representation of this simple sentence to qualify as comprehension?

The dilemmas posed by considering different levels of processing of this brief text are, of course, greatly expanded if we consider the comprehension of longer and more complex texts, from paragraphs to newspaper reports or scientific articles to entire novels, let alone trying to establish what constitutes comprehension when reading an array of texts – reports of a political speech in right-wing versus left-wing newspapers, or scientific articles reporting conflicting results, or the entire oeuvre of a novelist – in conjunction with one another. At some point between the simple sentence above and the several volumes of *Remembrance of Things Past*, the definition of comprehension shape-shifts from a simple representation of an event to deep understanding of a worldview, but fixing the boundary between those activities is not easy.

Readers

Considering students at different points in development also dictates emphasis on different aspects and levels of comprehension, whether one is motivated to design instruction, select assessments, or investigate the underlying comprehension processes. For example, researchers and practitioners focused on reading to learn for students in secondary grades must take into account the overwhelmingly important contribution to successful comprehension of students' access to relevant background knowledge. Thus, in science, social studies, and math classes, there is often considerable emphasis on ensuring that students know something about a topic (using lectures, videos, diagrams, hands-on demonstrations, or other nonliterate means) prior and as a support to their reading a text about that topic. On the other hand, researchers and practitioners more interested in early reading instruction and/or in remediation for struggling readers tend to emphasize issues related to reading and understanding the words in the text because that is where beginning readers encounter comprehension challenges, and it is often (though not always) the reason struggling readers do not comprehend well. In between these extremes of teaching beginning and struggling readers and teaching reading for learning, there is instructional emphasis on what might be thought of as simple comprehension – comprehension by students who have mastered word reading, reading texts which only make limited demands on background knowledge, but which do require (1) building and continually revising/expanding a text representation while reading, (2) making some inferences about connections among sentences and about connections to real world situations, and (3) perhaps some comprehension monitoring and comprehension repair mechanisms.

These differences related to developmental stage are also reflected in comprehension assessments, which for younger readers typically include items testing literal comprehension or basic inferencing, while items for older readers may require inferences that go farther beyond the text or draw more deeply on background knowledge (Snow, 2003). In other words, the definition of successful comprehension must be made conditional on at least the age and stage of development of the reader as well as the level and complexity of the text being read.

Task

A further complicating factor in defining successful reading comprehension has to do with the task being undertaken. There are important cultural, educational, and individual differences in the conceptualization of comprehension. In some literary and religious traditions, for example, literal memory for text is valued above interpretation of the text, whereas in others, attention to the actual words of the original text is much less important than coming to a justifiable interpretation of it, making connections to it, and even perhaps critiquing it.

Stark differences in task can be observed within cultures across disciplinary boundaries as well. For example, a science textbook is meant to be read for information, and comprehension can be said to occur when the reader expands and/or revises his/her understanding of some phenomenon by reading the information in the book; all too often, of course, the science textbook reader simply remembers the new information long enough to pass a test on it, without actually revising his/her enduring understanding. Therefore, the question that then arises is

whether this is a failure of comprehension or a failure of science learning.

In contrast, though successful comprehension of a novel read in a language arts or literature class does require learning the basics of characters, setting, and plot, just acquiring that information is not considered successful learning unless some appreciation is also engendered of the mood, the characters' and author's perspectives, the theme, the author's goal in writing the book, and other such ineffable features. One might well, in the course of reading some literary works, incidentally pick up information about scientific or historical or interpersonal topics treated in the book, and that would signal comprehension in one sense, but a literary reading would demand much more from the reader. Therefore, in literature classes, the question arises whether the dutiful student who can write an accurate plot summary of a novel, but fails to recognize, for example, that the narrator has taken an ironic stance or that the plot is a modern reenactment of the Odyssey, has failed at reading comprehension or at literary analysis.

Integrating Information about Reader, Text, and Task

Predicting comprehension success requires calculating information about the reader's stage of development, the complexity of the text being read, and the task being engaged in (see RRSG (2002) for further elaboration of each of these three aspects of any comprehension experience; **Figure 1**, reproduced from the RAND report, is a visual representation of this model). Successful comprehension occurs when these three dimensions are well

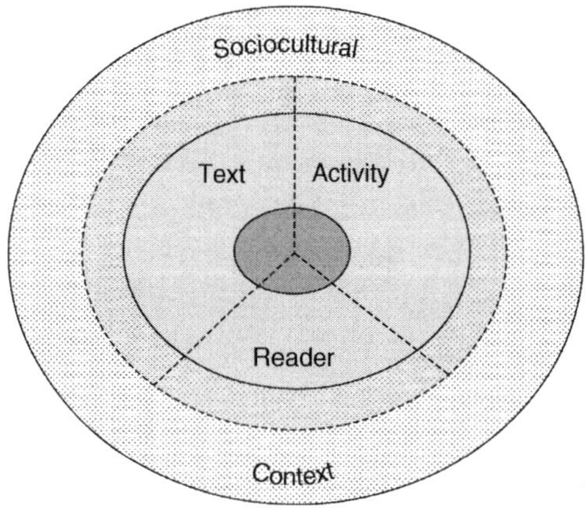

Figure 1 A heuristic for thinking about reading comprehensions devised by the Research and Development (RAND) Reading Study Group (2002) to depict the interaction of text, reader, and activity (or task) on reading comprehension.

aligned. For each of these dimensions of comprehension, though, there are simple cases and more marginal, gray areas where comprehension shades into learning or interpreting or functioning disciplinarily. The vast differences in what we would call successful comprehension across different levels of reader skill, text challenge, and task definition pose a challenge in summarizing what we know about reading comprehension, and in integrating or even providing a road map to the extensive research literature on comprehension development, assessment, instruction, and intervention.

A Taxonomy for Comprehension

For the purposes of this overview, we argue that identifying exactly where the boundary between reading comprehension and some other activity occurs is, to some extent, the individual's prerogative; even experts in the field achieve better agreement on identifying prototypical comprehension events than on placement of the boundaries. Furthermore, while the difficulty of deciding when a reading activity incorporates too many additional demands to be considered real comprehension may be obvious, there are also difficulties in deciding where comprehension begins at the bottom end, considering young readers and simple texts. What about the Jewish American or Muslim Turkish child who learns to read a sacred text, following the print faithfully while accurately pronouncing words that neither understands? It may seem obvious that this does not count as comprehension; however, what if that child has been told what the text is about, or has even been given a careful and complete translation of it? If the child is thinking of the translation while reading, is that comprehension? What if the child can understand a few of the words in the text, but has no understanding of the grammar of the written language? What if the child understands that verse, but none of the others in the book? When does reciting stop and real reading comprehension begin?

Reading comprehension might be thought of, then, as located on the radius of a set of concentric circles (see **Figure 2**). In the center circle are the basic reading processes that must be in place in order to access the text and form a mental representation of it: accurate word recognition, fluent access to word meaning, recognition of syntactic cues to sentence meaning, and short-term phonological memory. Variations of skill on these dimensions are clearly related to reading comprehension success – the reader who misidentifies words, who does not know the meaning of words in the text, who cannot parse the syntax of utterances, and who forgets the first sentence in a paragraph while reading the second will have difficulty comprehending (RRSG, 2002; Vellutino, 2003).

The second circle can be thought of as core comprehension processes – the ability to construct a mental representation of the ideas presented textually (Kintsch, 1998; Kintsch and Kintsch, 2005). Core comprehension requires text memory, making text-based inferences (e.g., tracing anaphors back to referents, keeping track of the order of events, and understanding implicit causal links), and making text-world links (e.g., bringing information about real dogs to bear in understanding what is strange and funny about a talking dog). Much early comprehension instruction focuses on helping learners activate relevant background knowledge before confronting text, on the theory that even children who have the required knowledge may not automatically access it while reading or integrate it with new information in the text. Another aspect of comprehension instruction for younger readers is a focus on self-monitoring, to ensure that the process of reading remains focused on building mental representations, and not just on reading the words.

The third circle comprises more elaborated comprehension processes, the processes involved in going beyond creating an unadorned text representation to a deeper understanding of the text. Many of the comprehension strategies that are recommended as part of comprehension instruction, for example, visualization, noting questions that arise while reading, and making text-to-text connections, are focused on these somewhat more elaborated comprehension processes. These processes also shade into ones that might be identified and taught as part of inquiry learning, such as figuring out how claims in one text relate to claims in another text, identifying the point of view a text presents, critiquing the argument in a text, and so on. In other words, rather than inquiry being a process applied to real-world phenomena, it is taken as a process to be applied to text itself. This is the theory underlying approaches to comprehension instruction such approaches to comprehension instruction as reciprocal teaching (Palincsar, 2003), questioning the author (Beck and McKeown, 2002), and reading apprenticeship (Shoenbach et al., 1999).

An outer circle comprises highly elaborated comprehension processes that overlap with disciplinary studies or deep learning from text. Whereas ordinary readers might be expected to engage in moderately elaborated comprehension for purposes of understanding murder mysteries, psychological novels, columnists' political opinion pieces, or popular science articles, highly elaborated comprehension processes can only be expected of readers operating within domains where they have developed deep background knowledge and have had disciplinary training in how to read. These would encompass the processes involved, for example, in reading for purposes of literary criticism, historiography, constructing an intellectual history, or producing a parody.

The representation of these four kinds of reading in **Figure 2** as concentric circles with clear boundaries

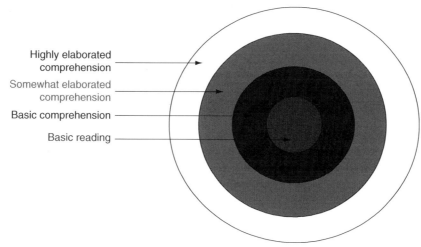

Highly elaborated
comprehension

Somewhat elaborated
comprehension

Basic comprehension

Basic reading

Figure 2 Basic reading processes, basic comprehension processes, and elaborated and highly elaborated comprehension processes represented as concentric circles, with reading comprehension located somewhere on a radius depending on the reader, text, and task.

between them should be viewed cautiously. First, there is no strong basis for placing a particular reading comprehension event on either side of the boundaries between central, elaborated, and highly elaborated comprehension processes. Second, this depiction is not meant to license an approach to reading instruction that starts in the middle and moves slowly outward; meaning construction, new learning, and interpretation should be part of the earliest literacy instruction, though these activities may be engaged in while reading texts aloud to children who are still mastering the code. Furthermore, the degree to which more sophisticated and elaborated comprehension might be expected of a lay literate versus a disciplinary literate depends, to a large extent, on the decisions a society makes about educational goals. Nonetheless, it may be useful in categorizing research, analyzing comprehension assessments, and understanding the challenges facing teachers of reading and of content areas to at least stipulate that reading comprehension is quite different when it occurs during code-focused reading as compared to reading for new learning and intellectual development.

Theories of Reading Comprehension

A few theories of reading comprehension have been particularly useful in guiding research and informing instruction. The simple view of reading (Gough and Tunmer, 1986) conceptualizes comprehension as the product of two capacities: the capacity to decode and the capacity to understand spoken language. The simple view claims, then, that comprehension is limited not only by speed and accuracy of word reading, but also by oral comprehension ability, and that if either of these abilities

is zero, then comprehension does not occur. Children following a normal developmental trajectory are subject to comprehension limitations stemming from constraints on word reading during the early years of schooling, and stemming from the limits on oral language skills thereafter. Under this view, it is clear that building oral language skills (vocabulary, comprehension of complex syntax, and comprehension of extended discourse forms) constitutes a key contribution to reading comprehension.

The simple view underemphasizes, though, the role of background knowledge and of motivation. The theory formulated by Kintsch introduces background knowledge by articulating how the textbase (the product of core comprehension processes) interacts with the mental model (the meaning representation constructed from the textbase and world knowledge; Kintsch, 1998; Kintsch and Kintsch, 2005). Kintsch (1998) also notes the importance of attending to the genre and the rules of reader–writer communication within the genre. Key in understanding the textbase and its links to the mental model, the genre, and the larger communicative act are various signals at the sentence level (e.g., after, same, and but) and the larger discourse level (e.g., headers and lists) of how the bits of information in the text are meant to be related to and integrated with one another (see also Graesser et al., 2003; RRSG, 2002).

The role of motivation is emphasized in the work of Guthrie (2003), who points out that background knowledge is likely to be richer in areas of personal interest, and that readers are more likely to persist in wrestling with text if (1) they are interested in the topic and (2) they experience self-efficacy as readers. Reader self-efficacy grows with comprehension skill, which in turn supports reading engagement, which in turn further builds comprehension skills and background knowledge.

Instruction in Reading Comprehension

Instruction in reading comprehension is much less emphasized than instruction in basic reading skills or instruction focused on content areas without attention to the challenges of reading in these areas. Given the importance of background knowledge and vocabulary to successful comprehension, young children should have access to oral language-focused instruction, in which comprehension is modeled and vocabulary and background knowledge are taught by reading aloud from both fiction and nonfiction books.

The most frequent form of comprehension-focused instruction involves teaching comprehension strategies (National Reading Panel, 2000). While strategies such as monitoring one's own comprehension, stopping to note questions that one has, and visualizing can be supportive, it is important that instruction in these strategies focus on when to use them and why they can be helpful in creating meaning representations. A focus on content teaching creates a context for introducing comprehension strategies as targeted learning tools, as happens in Guthrie's program called Concept-oriented Reading Instruction (2002) and in Reading Apprenticeship (Shoenbach *et al.*, 1999), rather than teaching them as all-purpose comprehension aides.

Intervention with Struggling Comprehenders

Providing intervention to help struggling comprehenders before they fall far behind is a key responsibility in light of the overwhelming evidence that poor comprehension is associated with reduced opportunities to learn vocabulary and general knowledge (Stanovich, 1986), difficulties in learning across academic areas (RRSG, 2002), and ultimately, frustration with schooling and a higher likelihood of failure to graduate from high school or to achieve access to higher education. A challenge in providing comprehension intervention is that poor comprehension can be a product of a breakdown in any of a wide variety of reader skills (word reading accuracy, fluency, vocabulary, background knowledge, text memory, deployment of appropriate strategies, and engagement in reading), and effective intervention requires identifying the challenge and responding to it. For adolescent learners struggling with comprehension because of difficulties with word reading or fluency, it is often difficult to access instructional materials that offer minimal textual challenge, but are engaging and of appropriate cognitive level.

Deshler *et al.* (2007) provide an extensive review of interventions for struggling comprehenders, indexed by target of the intervention as well as developmental level

and type of learner (e.g., vocabulary focus for intermediate second-language learners). Unfortunately, very few of the programs they review, many of which have solid theoretical foundations, have been extensively evaluated or analyzed to determine under which circumstances and for which subgroups of learners they are most useful.

Summary

Reading comprehension is a complex topic. Predicting success in comprehension requires knowing about the reader, about the text being read, about the task being undertaken, and about the sociocultural context in which the reading is occurring. Since reading comprehension shades into learning, constructing a worldview, and discipline-specific literacy practices, it is difficult to establish firm boundaries around comprehension; nonetheless, it is clear that more attention to comprehension is needed across the grades. In preschool and primary grades, opportunities for building vocabulary and background knowledge and practicing oral comprehension should be provided while children are learning to decode. In later grades, students need explicit instruction in how texts are constructed and how language cues signal meaning at sentential and discourse levels, as well as practice and support in wrestling with content-rich texts for well-defined and engaging purposes.

See also: First Language Acquisition; Language and Literacy in Educational Settings; Learning as Inquiry; Learning to Read.

Bibliography

Beck, I. L. and McKeown, M. G. (2002). Questioning the author: Making sense of social studies. *Educational Leadership* **60**(3), 44–47.

Deshler, D. D., Palincsar, A. S., Biancarosa, G., and Nair, M. (2007). *Informed Choices for Struggling Adolescent Readers: A Research-Based Guide to Instructional Programs and Practice*. New York: International Reading Association.

Gough, P. B. and Tunmer, W. E. (1986). Decoding, reading, and reading disability. *Remedial and Special Education* **7**, 6–10.

Graesser, A. C., McNamara, D. S., and Louwerse, M. M. (2002). What do readers need to learn in order to process coherence relations in narrative and expository text? In Sweet, A. P. and Snow, C. E. (eds.) *Rethinking Reading Comprehension*, pp 82–98. New York: Guilford.

Guthrie, J. (2003). Concept-oriented reading instruction: Practices of teaching reading for understanding. In Sweet, A. P. and Snow, C. E. (eds.) *Rethinking Reading Comprehension*, pp 115–140. New York: Guilford.

Kintsch, W. (1998). *Comprehension: A Paradigm for Cognition*. New York: Cambridge University Press.

Kintsch, W. and Kintsch, E. (2005). Comprehension. In Paris, S. G. and Stahl, S. A. (eds.) *Children's Reading Comprehension and Assessment*, pp 71–92. Mahwah, NJ: Erlbaum.

National Reading Panel (2000). *Teaching Children to Read: An Evidence-Based Assessment of the Scientific Research Literature on Reading and its Implications for Reading Instruction. Reports of the*

Subgroups, NIH Publication No. 00-4754, Washington, DC: National Institute of Child Health and Human Development.

Palincsar, A. M. (2003). Collaborative approaches to comprehension instruction. In Sweet, A. P. and Snow, C. E. (eds.) *Rethinking Reading Comprehension*, pp 99–114. New York: Guilford.

RAND Reading Study Group (RRSG) (2002). Toward an R&D program in reading comprehension. Santa Monica, CA: RAND. http://www.rand.org/pubs/monograph_reports/2005/MR1465.pdf (accessed May 2009).

Schoenbach, R., Greenleaf, C., Cziko, C., and Hurwitz, L. (1999). *Reading for Understanding: A Guide to Improving Reading in Middle and High School.* San Francisco, CA: Jossey-Bass.

Snow, C. E. (2003). Assessment of reading comprehension: Researchers and practitioners helping themselves and each other. In Sweet, A. P. and Snow, C. (eds.) *Rethinking Reading Comprehension*, pp 192–206. New York: Guilford.

Stanovich, K. E. (1986). Matthew effects in reading: Some consequences of individual differences in the acquisition of literacy. *Reading Research Quarterly* **21**(4), 360–406.

Vellutino, F. R. (2003). Individual differences as sources of variability in reading comprehension. In Sweet, A. P. and Snow, C. E. (eds.) *Rethinking Reading Comprehension*, pp 51–81. New York: Guilford.

Carnegie Corporation of New York, Washington, DC: Alliance for Excellent Education.

Brown, A. L., Armbruster, B. B., and Baker, L. (1986). The role of metacognition in reading and studying. In Orasanu, J. (ed.) *Reading Comprehension: From Research to Practice*, pp 49–76. Hillsdale, NJ: Erlbaum.

Clark, A. M., Anderson, R. C., Archodidou, A., *et al.* (2003). Collaborative reasoning: Expanding ways for children to talk and think in the classroom. *Educational Psychology Review* **15**, 181–198.

Fry, E. (2002). Readability versus leveling. *Reading Teacher* **56**(3), 286–291.

Moje, E. B., Dillon, D. R., and O'Brien, D. (2000). Reexamining roles of learner, text and context in secondary literacy. *Journal of Educational Research* **93**(3), 165–180.

Perfetti, C. A., Landi, N., and Oakhill, J. (2005). The acquisition of reading comprehension skills. In Snowling, M. J. and Hulme, C. (eds.) *The Science of Reading: A Handbook*, pp 227–247. Malden, MA: Blackwell.

Rasinski, T. V., Padak, M. D., McKeon, C. A., *et al.* (2005). Is reading fluency a key for successful high school reading? *Journal of Adolescent and Adult literacy* **49**(1), 22–27.

Sweet, A. P. and Snow, C. E. (eds.) (2003). *Rethinking Reading Comprehension.* New York: Guilford.

Further Reading

Alexander, P. A. and Jetton, T. L. (2000). Learning from text: A multidimensional and developmental perspective. In Barr, R., Kamil, M., Mosenthal, P., and Pearson, P. D. (eds.) *Handbook of Reading Research,* vol. 3, pp 285–310. New York: Longman.

Bailey, A. (ed.) (2007). *The Language Demands of School: Putting Academic Language to the Test.* New Haven, CT: Yale University Press.

Beck, I. L. and McKeown, M. G. (2001). Text talk: Capturing the benefits of read aloud experiences for young children. *Reading Teacher* **55**(1), 10–20.

Biancarosa, G. and Snow, C. (2004). Reading next: A vision for action and research in middle and high school literacy. *Report to the*

Relevant Websites

http://www.all4ed.org – Alliance for Excellent Education.
http://www.carnegie.org – Carnegie Corporation of New York.
http://www.ciera.org – Center for Intervention in Early Reading Achievement.
http://www.excelgov.org – Coalition for Evidence-Based Policy.
http://www.w-w-c.org – Department of Education, What Works?
http://www.reading.org – International Reading Association.
http://www.rand.org – RAND Reports.
http://www.sedl.org – Southwest Educational Development Laboratory (SEDL).

First Language Acquisition

N B Ratner, University of Maryland, College Park, MD, USA

Glossary

Affix – It is an element appended to a root word form, which may convey grammatical information (e.g., plural, past tense) or lexical information (e.g., un-, re-).

Dative sentence – It is a sentence form in which the normal sequence of direct object and indirect object has been inverted (e.g., I gave the present to the girl → I gave the girl the present).

Figurative language – It refers to the nonliteral use of language (e.g., a cold woman).

Finiteness – It is an attribute of verb forms that convey person, tense, number, and mood (e.g., he runs).

Formants – They are concentrations of acoustic energy caused by the resonant properties of the vocal tract that are particularly critical for distinguishing among vowels in a language.

Indirect language – They are linguistic forms that do not directly convey intended meaning, such as use of "it's hot in here" to request that someone open a window.

Inflection – It refers to a grammatical affix.

Metalinguistic ability – It is the ability to use language to talk about the characteristics and use of language.

Morpheme/morphology – A morpheme is the smallest meaningful unit in a language, for example, words and affixes; morphology is the study of word structure.

Over-extension – It is the use of a word to refer to a larger category of referents than is appropriate, for example, calling all four-legged creatures doggie.

Passive sentence – It is a sentence form in which the order of subject and object are inverted, as in John(s) loves Mary(o) → Mary is loved by John.

Phonemic awareness – It refers to the ability to appreciate the fact that spoken words are composed of individual sounds (phonemes).

Phoneme/Phonology – A phoneme is a minimally contrastive sound in a language; phonology is the study of the sound system of a language.

Phonotactics – It refers to the permissible ordering of phonemes within a language.

Pragmatics – It is the study of language use in socially appropriate ways, which may vary with context, addressee, and other factors.

Pronominal reference – It refers to the use of pronouns to refer back to previously mentioned nouns or concepts (also called anaphora or anaphoric reference).

Segmental/supra-segmental – It is the distinction between information conveyed by sounds and words (segments) and prosodic characteristics such as intonation, volume, and stress that may extend over more than one segment.

Semantics – It is the study of meaning.

Specific language impairment – It is a developmental disorder in which comprehension and use of language is below age-expectations, in the absence of observable deficits in intellectual, hearing, or motor function.

Syntax – It is the study of sentence structure and grammatical morphology.

Vocabulary burst – It refers to a stage early in children's vocabulary development during which words are learned at a very rapid pace.

The Nature of Human Language

Human languages are distinct from animal communication systems in a wide variety of ways. Among them are infinite creativity (the ability for speakers and hearers to produce and understand an infinite variety of utterances), their symbolic nature (the arbitrary relationships among words, utterances, and the concepts to which they refer), and hierarchical organization, which allows a number of levels of rules governing appropriate structure and use (see Fromkin *et al.*, 2007).

Within any language, there is a set of rules that governs appropriate use of sounds, words, grammar, and meaning. Moreover, competent language users must also master socially appropriate means of conveying and interpreting linguistic messages. Briefly, these subsystems of language knowledge consist of phonology, morphology, syntax, semantics, and pragmatics.

Phonological features of any given language specify its sound inventory (phonemes) as well as ways in which sounds may be legally combined to create well-formed words (phonotactics). The smallest units of language that convey meaning or grammatical distinctions are morphemes; for example, in English, a word such as *cats* consists of one lexical morpheme, *cat*, which can stand alone, and one grammatical morpheme to signal the plural. Languages have large numbers of lexical (or open class) morphemes, and a much smaller and delimited number of grammatical morphemes (closed class), which may stand alone (such as *the* or *can*), or must be attached to lexical morphemes (such as the plural, past tense, possessive, etc.)

Mastery of syntax requires appropriate use of morphology as well as any rules governing the ordering of elements in sentences and their smaller constituents, such as noun and verb phrases. Some languages, such as Finnish, permit fairly free word order, while others are highly constrained. In addition, languages may differ in basic word order; for example, English tends to employ subject–verb–object as its canonical ordering, while the Philippine language Tagalog is primarily verb–subject–object.

Meaning in language can be conveyed by the meanings of individual words (as in knowing what the word *chair* refers to), as well as the order in which words are combined to reflect themes such as subject and object (most readers will readily appreciate that "John loves Mary" does not necessarily mean that "Mary loves John"). Finally, the meanings of sentences often go beyond the strict interpretation of their words and syntax. Pragmatic intent is obtained by evaluation of the sentence within a context to ascertain its function within conversation – whether one's objective is to inform, warn, request action, etc., as might variously be the case in hearing someone say, "It's late." All of these rule systems must be adequately mastered in order for the child to function as a capable speaker–hearer of a language.

Techniques in Understanding Language Development

Facts about the typical milestones in language acquisition are obtained from a variety of sources. Historically, diary data and small, longitudinal studies offered the first insights into stages and strategies in child language development. This tradition has been continued with the broad use of open access data archives such as the Child Language Data Exchange System (CHILDES, http://childes.psy.cmu.edu) by developmental psycholinguists to investigate new questions about children's behaviors using existing data from a broad variety of languages and populations.

Observational data are augmented by experimental or quasi-experimental studies in which production or comprehension of various language targets is elicited. More recently, the use of electrophysiological measures, such as event-related potentials (ERPs), eye tracking, and functional magnetic resonance imaging (fMRI), have

enabled researchers to explore the underlying substrates of infant and child linguistic performance (Karmiloff and Karmiloff-Smith, 2001).

Milestones in Speech and Language Development

Despite some degree of individual variation in timing and sequencing of the development of specific linguistic abilities, there is considerable uniformity in children's language development. This predictability in sequencing permits educators and other professionals working with infants and children to apply developmental expectations to assessment and, if necessary, intervene with children not meeting typical pacing or sequencing of skill development (Oller *et al.*, 2006). Knowledge of typical developmental milestones also permits educators to construct appropriate curricular goals and strategies for all activities involving language and reading which build upon earlier linguistic skill development.

Pre-Linguistic Achievements

Language learning begins right from the womb. There is evidence that a fetus can be conditioned to recognize the rhythm and cadence of stories repeatedly read aloud in the last trimester of pregnancy; shortly after birth, use of non-nutritive sucking paradigms show that babies demonstrate a marked preference for the voices of their own mothers, and samples of conversational speech in their own language, rather than a foreign language or dialect.

In early infancy, babies show a capacity to distinguish linguistic contrasts used by all the world's languages, rather than merely their own. For example, they can distinguish contrasts in voicing, place, and manner of consonants, as well as between vowels very similar in formant characteristics. However, by approximately 10 months of age, such discrimination ability wanes, as the infant begins to narrow contrasts to those used by his or her native language. Concurrently, their expressive babble begins to reflect segmental (sound) and suprasegmental (prosodic) characteristics of the ambient language or languages to which they are exposed.

Use of a number of laboratory paradigms has shown that the very young infant is able to begin to discriminate individual words within the conversational speech stream, as well as features within utterances that signal possible word boundaries, an important skill that will enable the child to begin to map early vocabulary and grammar. This ability to segment the speech signal is critical because even infant-directed speech typically takes the form of multiword sentences, with few words produced in isolation. Some milestones in segmentation skills occur relatively early. For example, typically developing infants usually can discriminate their own names from similar-sounding foils, even in noise, by 4 months of age, while children later diagnosed with developmental language disorders may not show such ability. By 7–8 months of age, if an infant is familiarized with a novel word in isolation, she will listen longer to short spoken passages containing that word, and the inverse is also true. This discrimination is quite precise, and infants will not falsely respond to words that are similar, but differ by only one speech sound. Segmentation is not an all-or-none skill, and appears to rely on development of sensitivity to certain language-specific cues, such as the typical stress patterns within words and among words in sentences, as well as more general statistical regularities (such as co-occurrences of sounds or syllables). Word discovery progressively enables further and finer segmentation of elements in input, creating a circular relationship between segmentation and lexical development, with segmentation skill leading to enhanced word-learning, which in turn improves segmentation skill and future word learning.

Speech segmentation abilities may be quite delayed in children with identifiable syndromes known to be accompanied by significant cognitive and linguistic deficits, supporting the idea that segmentation may be a necessary precursor to normal language development. Infants who appear to be developing normally but fail to show typical segmentation abilities have significantly poorer language outcomes than infants who succeed in these tasks.

Production and Understanding Prior to First Words

Infant babble and conversational turn taking during vocal interactions with caretakers increasingly reflect the typically developing child's knowledge of both the shape of the ambient language as well as pragmatically appropriate eye gaze and gestures; these patterns appear to be mutually reinforcing, with more vocal children typically receiving a greater degree of conversational input from their caretakers. Failure for infants to develop appropriate eye-contact, reciprocal vocalization patterns, and gesture may be an early indicator of developmental delay, particularly autism spectrum disorder.

Typical early babble uses prosodic features of the language to convey pragmatic intent, such as requesting, notice, or displeasure, well before actual identifiable words are used for such functions; this pattern of vocalization is sometimes called jargon. By about 10 months of age, many infants will have developed proto-words, phonetically consistent forms that are regularly used to convey a particular message.

At about this same age, an important change occurs in infants' social cognition. They begin to intuit other people's thoughts, desires, and goals (sometimes called a theory of mind). They follow the direction of a point (unlike animals, who will simply fixate on the hand doing the pointing), and will begin to follow others' gaze to an object or action of interest. Both behaviors signal the infant's ability to engage in joint attention. The pattern of responsiveness by both infants and adults is important to the rate of language development; inability of the infant to engage in joint attention is a marker of developmental delay, while the adult's ability to discern the infant's interest in objects or activities and comment on them contingently and responsively has been linked to more rapid achievement of early linguistic milestones.

The Nature of Early Word Production and Comprehension

Well before the production of first recognizable words of the language, usually at 12–15 months of age, infants use their segmentation skills to construct a fairly broad receptive vocabulary that can be assessed using parental report inventories. First words are usually not pronounced in an adult-like fashion, but are used consistently to convey intent. Across most languages that have been observed, first words are highly likely to be names of objects or people (a preference for nouns) that they actively interact with (rather than being merely the most frequently used word in a language), but individual children may show a preference for more conversational vocalizations, such as greetings, or terms used in play with adults. Semantic representation of first words is likely to be under-specified, leading to over-extension, in which words are applied to an overly broad category of referents (e.g., *doggie* for many additional types of four-legged, furry animals). However, word learning is governed by a number of principles that seem quite uniquely human, such as a tendency to associate labels with the entirety of a reference, rather than one of its component features, and the presumption that new words refer to novel, rather than known, referents.

Infants and toddlers comprehend more words than they tend to produce, and show good evidence of understanding general rules of syntax (such as preferred word order of the language, signaling the difference between "Big Bird pushes Ernie" and "Ernie pushes Big Bird") in laboratory tasks well before they produce multi-word utterances themselves. By 2 years of age, the typically developing child will have achieved at least a 50-word expressive vocabulary (the average is approximately 200) and begin to combine words into two-word utterances. Children who have failed to reach this stage by 24 months are significantly at risk for a variety of communicative disorders, although a substantial proportion of late talkers do appear to recover and later function within the normal range.

Early two- and three-word utterances are likely to lack appropriate grammatical affixes in a language such as

English, in which they are relatively sparse. Acquisition of the relatively closed set of grammatical morphemes in English has been tracked extensively, beginning with Roger Brown and his colleagues at Harvard in the early 1960s, and it follows a relatively consistent order and trajectory (see **Table 1**).

Classic studies, such as that conducted by Jean Berko in the late 1950s demonstrate that the learning of these morphemes represents abstraction and generalization of rules which can be extended to novel exemplars (see **Figure 1**) and even mis-applied to exceptional forms

Table 1 Typical order of acquisition for 14 common English morphemes

Morpheme	Example
Present progressive	Baby crying
Prepositions in/on	Cookie on table; Mommy in car
Regular plural	Cats, dogs, dishes
Past irregular (learned as lexical items)	Early examples: came, fell, broke, sat, went
Possessive	Daddy's car
Uncontractible copula	Eve is girl
Articles (a, the)	See the kitty, Give a cookie
Past regular	Hugged, kissed, patted, cried
Third person regular	Boy runs, doggie barks
Third person irregular	He does/has it
Uncontractible auxiliary	I am going.
Contractible copula	What's that
Contractible auxiliary	Puppy's eating

Mastery may span from 1 year and 6 months to 4 years in typically developing children.
Adapted from Brown (1973).

The wug test

This is a wug

Now there is another one.
There are two of them.
There are two—.

Figure 1 The Wug test.

(e.g., when a child says *foots* or *wented*), rather than rote memorization of items the child has overheard. Among the most difficult morphemes are those conveying tense and finiteness, and these continue to be problematic for children later diagnosed with specific language impairment. Children learning highly inflected languages will show earlier productive use of grammatical elements, even during the single-word stage.

While it may take many months for the child to compile the initial 50-word vocabulary, this achievement is usually followed by what some have termed a vocabulary burst, in which hundreds of words are acquired within a very short space of time. Most children entering kindergarten have vocabularies upward of 14 000 words, which may represent both unique roots as well as morphologically complex forms such as un+comfort-abl+y.

Combining Words into Utterances

In English, mastery of basic sentence forms tends to proceed from those types of utterances requiring few verbal auxiliaries, such as the imperative, to those that require manipulation of, or changes and additions to the typical components in declarative sentences, as in negative utterances (*He is/isn't going, I like/don't like spinach*), and finally, those that additionally require re-ordering or permutation of elements, as in questions (*Is he going?, Doesn't he like ice cream?*) Mastery of wh-questions (e.g., *Where is he going?*) requires additional skills, including further understanding of the specific meanings conveyed by question terms such as *what, when, where,* and *why,* with the latter requiring perhaps the greatest level of sophistication.

Progressively longer and more complex utterances are formed by conjoining, using conjunctions, and embedding. Conjoining is typically first observed in object clauses, then subject clauses ("He likes cookies and milk vs. Daddy and Mommy are coming home"). The conceptually simpler conjunctions such as *and* are mastered before those requiring higher levels of understanding of causality (*because*), time (*before/after*), or conditionality (*if*). Prior to full understanding of such terms, the child is likely to respond to clauses linked using later-learned conjunctions using an order-of-mention strategy, in which the first clause is presumed to occur before the second.

In a language such as English, which shows a strong preference for subject–verb–object ordering, sentences deviating from this order are likely to lead to misinterpretation, or reliance on conceptual plausibility. Thus, inaccurate comprehension of the subjects of verbs in passives ("Big Bird (object) is pushed by Ernie (subject)"), direct objects (DO) and indirect objects (IO) in datives ("Mary showed the baby (IO) the kitty (DO)" vs. the more canonically ordered "Mary showed the kitty (DO) to the baby (IO)"), center-embedded relative clauses ("The man who lives next to my sister is a doctor"), and other exceptional constructions (e.g., "The boy is easy to see"), is quite likely, at ages up to 8 years or so, depending upon situational context and other cues provided by the specific words in the sentence.

Later Acquisitions

As the child nears kindergarten entry and progresses through the early school years, refinements occur in phonological, lexical, and grammatical skills. Residual problems in adult-like pronunciation of late-acquired sounds (in English, e.g., sounds such as /r/ and /l/, consonant clusters containing these sounds, and /s/) subside before age 8 years. In lexical development, the ability to comprehend relative terms (those with no fixed meaning, that require perspective, such as *big* or *daughter*), and those which convey abstract concepts (such as *honest*) emerges, as does the awareness that words may be ambiguous (having more than one meaning). This last skill enables elementary school-aged children's growing appreciation of jokes and riddles. The ability to decompose and assemble multi-morphemic forms (e.g., *anti+dis+establish+ment+arianism* or *mono+the+ism*) will continue across the school years and is critical to continued development of linguistic skills required of skilled readers. Skilled readers will also need to expand vocabulary mappings to include figurative and metaphorical uses of language common to advanced literary forms.

Other skills required in the academic setting include the ability to make sound–symbol associations (phonemic awareness) in the child's language and orthography necessary for the decoding of the written word. Fluency in word decoding will need to be achieved in order for the child to retrieve the meanings of utterances before information fades from the short-term memory store.

Written language skills will require mastery of more complex language forms than those typically used in conversation, and the student's writing will increasingly demonstrate frequent use of compound and complex sentences. In addition, success in writing for academic purposes will depend upon the child's ability to comprehend complex text, including passages with long-distance pronominal references (also known as anaphoric reference, as in "The European colonization of the Americas in the fifteenth and sixteenth centuries resulted in progressive decimation of native populations, as it introduced diseases to which they had no natural resistance..."). Students are also expected to demonstrate metalinguistic knowledge of terminology for the forms they already understand and produce (e.g., notions such as subject–verb agreement). Finally, both oral and written assignments will require them to demonstrate facility with different genres of language use, such as narratives and formal expository text. Most classroom writing assignments will also require the child to comprehend text more linguistically sophisticated

than that he or she conventionally produces, and to then paraphrase that information into a unique, but accurate recast of the original wording found in source materials.

While even the youngest child has control over a variety of pragmatic functions, including the ability to request, argue, explain, engage in appropriate turn taking, etc., socially appropriate use of language continues to develop over the school years. Acceptable ways to convey politeness or deference will grow from relatively simple strategies (such as the use of *please*) to the use and comprehension of indirect forms (as in knowing that the phrase, "Yum, that looks good" is an appropriate way to convey a desire to receive a bite of the coveted food item).

Cross-Linguistic Variation in Profiles of First-Language Acquisition

It is both theoretically and practically relevant to understand that patterns of acquisition in one language do not necessary map directly to others. The order in which aspects of grammar, in particular, are learned in a specific language may be impacted by a number of factors. These may include the pervasiveness of a linguistic concept (e.g., whether or not verbs are invariably marked for person and number as in Spanish, contrasted with relatively sparse marking in English). Other considerations may include conceptual simplicity of a grammatical form (whether a language distinguishes between singular and plural only, or requires some marking of physical number), and whether or not a grammatical rule is relatively uniform or is characterized by numerous exceptions. The study of different trajectories seen in languages which differ typologically can do much to identify which aspects of acquisition appear dependent upon language-specific features, generalized cognitive development and ability, or input characteristics, and which appear relatively uniform regardless of the language being learned. When relatively invariant patterns or strategies emerge across language differing widely in their rule systems, they provide evidence of innate predispositions that govern the process of language acquisition (see section titled 'Theories of language acquisition').

Practically speaking, knowledge of the specific stages and strategies in acquisition of individual languages enables the important process of assessing the adequacy of children's progress in language learning, and the identification and remediation of delayed or disordered language development. It is already abundantly clear that even within a single language, dialectal variation may compromise the sensitivity or appropriateness of language-assessment instruments. Additionally, because concepts and rules are acquired at different points and in differing orders across languages, a simple translation of a test written in English, for example, regardless of its solid psychometric properties when used with English-speaking children, will be inappropriate in assessing the development of a child learning Spanish or Urdu.

Individual Variation

While the many generalizable patterns of language learning within a specific language community enable us to have appropriate expectations of children of a given age, individual variation does exist in how children approach the task of language acquisition. Some children appear to be more attracted to learning the names of things early in lexical development, while some appear more attuned to the social and conversational uses of language. Some children appear to map the prosodic characteristics of adult language when producing early utterances, while others appear to pay more attention to the segmental properties of target words. Some children appear to make relatively rapid progress in acquiring an initial vocabulary, while some appear to accumulate first words more slowly. However, precocious language learners do not appear to keep their verbal advantage over the life span. In contrast, a significant number of slower language learners do continue to experience long-term delay (see section titled 'Developmental language disorders').

Theories of Language Acquisition

Given the rapidity with which a child learns his or her first language, it is not surprising that multiple theories of language acquisition have been advanced and debated. The traditional contrast has been between those researchers and theorists who attribute the major impetus in language development to innate or nativist predispositions and those who reserve a relatively larger role for social-interactionist factors, such as the nature, quality, and quantity of verbal interaction the child receives. The first approach is most classically associated with Noam Chomsky and Steven Pinker, while the second is often attributed to Jerome Bruner and Catherine Snow. In most respects, the contrast between the positions is artificial. There clearly appear to be features of language learning, particularly in the domains of syntax and the course of phonological development, that are constrained by innate strategies and are not very easily accounted for by aspects of the nature of input addressed to the child, nor generalized cognitive strategies. In contrast, aspects of a language such as its vocabulary and pragmatic conventions can only be learned through exposure, although some aspects of lexical learning appear constrained by apparently innate strategies.

Additional theories of language learning often appeal to more generalized cognitive strategies for the discovery and abstraction of linguistic rules and regularities. Among them are connectionist models of language acquisition, which liken the process to that seen in learning by computing networks. Researchers most highly identified with what might be termed an information-processing approach include Brian MacWhinney and the late Elizabeth Bates.

Developmental Language Disorders

Estimates vary, but between 6% and 10% of preschool and school-aged children demonstrate problems in language acquisition. Some delayed or deviant skills may be attributable to primary problems in intellectual development, hearing impairment, or autism spectrum disorder, but others appear relatively unique to language, thus leading to a diagnosis of specific language impairment (SLI). SLI has significant ramifications for later educational achievement, as it shows high co-morbidity with dyslexia, but also impacts later-reading/writing skills development and use that are reliant upon linguistic knowledge. Chief among these are the abilities to make phoneme–grapheme correspondences, decode complex multi-morphemic words, as well as to comprehend and use complex syntax. Weaknesses in decoding ambiguity, following pronominal reference and resolving metaphorical and figurative usages of language are common.

Early identification of language-learning disorders and appropriate intervention are crucial during the preschool and early elementary school years because of impacts on later school achievement. SLI is highly heritable and children at familial risk should be carefully monitored.

See also: Attention in Cognition and Early Learning; Classroom Discourse and Student Learning; Language and Literacy in Educational Settings; Learning to Read; Writing, Early.

Bibliography

Brown, R. (1973). *A First Language*. Cambridge, MA: Harvard University Press.

Fromkin, V., Rodman, R., and Hyams, N. (2007). *An Introduction to Language*, 8th edn. Boston, MA: Thomson Wadsworth.

Karmiloff, K. and Karmiloff-Smith, A. (2001). *Pathways to Language*. Cambridge, MA: Harvard University Press.

Oller, J. W., Oller, S., and Badon, L. (2006). *Milestones: Normal Speech and Language Development across the Lifespan*. San Diego, CA: Plural.

Further Reading

Berko, J. (1958). The child's learning of English morphology. *Word* **14**, 150–177.

Gleason, J. B. and Ratner, N. B. (2008). *Language Development*, 7th edn. Boston, MA: Allyn and Bacon.

Golinkoff, R. and Hirsh-Pasek, K. (1999). *How Babies Talk: The Magic and Mystery of Language Acquisition*. New York: Dutton/Penguin.

Hoff, E. (2005). *Language Development*, 4th edn. Boston, MA: Thomson Wadsworth.

Hulit, L. and Howard, M. (2006). *Born to Talk: An Introduction to Speech and Language Development*, 4th edn. Boston, MA: Allyn and Bacon.

Jusczyk, P. (1997). *The Discovery of Spoken Language*. Cambridge, MA: MIT Press.

Nippold, M. (1998). *Later Language Development: The School-Age and Adolescent Years*, 2nd edn. Austin, TX: Pro-Ed.

Paul, R. (2006). *Child Language Disorders: From Infancy through Adolescence*, 3rd edn. St. Louis, MO: Mosby/Elsevier.

Traxler, M. and Gernsbacher, M. (2006). *Handbook of Psycholinguistics*. Amsterdam: Academic.

Relevant Website

http://www.childes.psy.cmu.edu – The CHILDES (child language data exchange) Project.

Second Language Learning

J S Arnfast and J N Jørgensen, University of Copenhagen, Copenhagen S, Denmark
A Holmen, Aarhus University, Copenhagen NV, Denmark

Theories of Second Language Acquisition

Contrastive Linguistics

The first major paradigm of language-acquisition theory was the behaviorist–structuralist school which was informed by the contrastive hypothesis. This was built on the observation that learners with common mother tongues developed similar difficulties with specific foreign languages. The general principle of the hypothesis was that difficulties in second- or foreign-language learning were caused by structural differences between the mother tongue of the learner and the language to be acquired. The hypothesis had two degrees (Wardhaugh, 1970). The strong version claimed to be able to predict the difficulties of learners on the basis of a contrastive analysis, that is, a systematic comparison of the structures of the two languages involved. The original contrastive hypothesis was closely related to structuralist linguistics and its emphasis on *langue* (Lado, 1957). The view on learning was that of behaviorist psychology. Language was considered a set of habits, and second-language learning was a task which primarily involved a change of habits. The mother tongue of the learner would, in its capacity as a set of habits, interfere with the learner's new language (Weinreich, 1953). Contrastive analysis of entire languages were planned and carried out. Depending on the structural salience of the features involved, contrastivists also found that they were able to determine different degrees of difficulty. James (1980) suggests that contrastive analysis can be used by curriculum planners and teachers in their preparation, but not necessarily as a wholesale explanation of difficulties. Based on studies of learners' actual difficulties, however, a criticism of the contrastive hypothesis developed. It was found that difficulties predicted by contrastive analysis sometimes never appeared, and in other cases, difficulties arose which contrastive analysis did not explain. Furthermore, so-called errors came to be seen as necessary steps in the acquisition of a language (Corder, 1967). Many error analyses were carried out in order to shed light on real-life difficulties of learners. In some cases, the characteristics of the target language (L2) appeared to be more important than the mother tongue (Hyltenstam, 1978). The focus soon shifted to the study of the L2 performance of the learner as a language in its own right, a so-called interlanguage (*interlingua* or approximative system, Richards, 1974). An interlanguage has a grammar which follows universal principles just like any other grammar; it is just more variable.

This understanding of language differed from traditional structuralist linguistics. Interlanguage studies further led to theorizing over the patterns of acquisition of second-language learners. This theorizing was likewise far removed from the behaviorist view of learning, it concentrated on cognitive aspects of language acquisition.

A Cognitive Approach to Second Language Acquisition

The cognitive approach to language acquisition has its starting point in the human brain's capacity for processing and organizing information. The central notion that (second) language learning is skill learning opens the field to psychological accounts of the processes leading to language acquisition. The first major contributions (e.g., McLaughlin, 1987) to the upcoming field were to a certain extent based on the L1 (first language)-acquisition studies of Slobin (1985). Slobin argued that the mind is programmed to process information which is perceptually salient, and to organize this information according to specific operating principles eventually leading to language learning. This explains cross-linguistic similarities in first-language acquisition. In later studies Slobin (1996) points to a close connection between language typology and language processing. A process similar to Slobin's earlier studies was believed to work for second-language learning (Andersen, 1990), and different models were proposed to account for the information processing necessary for the automatization of second-language learners' linguistic knowledge and fluent speech. Both McLaughlin's (1987) information-processing model and Anderson's (1985) adaptive control of thought are related to this line of research. Like L1-acquisition, second-language acquisition (SLA) is considered to follow a concise developmental order by which certain parts or features of the language are acquired before others (e.g., Givón, 1985). These thoughts are further elaborated in Pienemann's (1998) processability theory, which claims that language acquisition follows similar patterns even across language families. In cognitively oriented language-acquisition studies, the role of memory is taken into consideration in more detail. Such studies also drew on cognitive psychology in order to investigate the limits of perception, that is, how many different items the brain is capable of processing. Short-term memory is able to process only a limited amount of new information at a time, and by ways we can still only hypothesize about, information is stored in the long-term memory after being processed repeatedly and thereby automatized. However, when information is stored in long-term memory, it is considered difficult to retrieve it for further processing, for instance, if the structure of the linguistic information is incomplete (i.e., incomplete morphology, syntax, or pronunciation). Krashen (1985) attempted to formulate a comprehensive theory for SLA, consisting of five major hypotheses. His comprehensive theory has been criticized for being difficult to test empirically. Nevertheless, the discussions it has raised have been fruitful for the further development of the field. One of the outcomes of Krashen's comprehensive theory was the extension of the input hypothesis proposed by Long (1985), in the field generally known as the interaction hypothesis. Through studies from the 1980s onward, Long pointed to the interesting differences in conversations carried out among native speakers compared to conversations involving both a native speaker and a learner. Conversations and communicative difficulties and how they were managed were studied through conversation analysis. They showed a significant use of conversational strategies (e.g., repetitions, repairs, requests for clarification, and comprehension checks) by both parties to ensure that the meaning and content of the conversation were not lost due to misunderstandings. During language acquisition, through negotiation of meaning, the learner focuses on content as well as form (Long and Robinson, 1998). The idea that language is learned through interaction, and thus tied to a social practice, is part of a wider pedagogical movement which shifts the focus from teaching to learning. The learner is considered an active part of a learning process. Schmidt and Frota (1986) point to the importance of consciousness and noticing as central phenomena in the language-acquisition process. Noticing specific aspects of language is closely linked to cognitive development as well. Through the 1980s, this interactionist approach was further developed. The notion of communicative strategies which accounted for the psycholinguistic aspects of interaction from comprehension to production was widely discussed, e.g., Kellerman and Bialystok (1997).

Motivation

Two major paradigms dominated the studies of motivation in language learning from the beginning of the 1970s. One was the view on motivation considered in terms of instrumentality and integrativeness (Gardner and Lambert, 1972). According to this view the motivational drive to learn a second language is the prospect of achieving specific goals (e.g., job or education) by learning the language (instrumental motivation), or the drive stems from a desire to adapt the culture and habits associated with the language (integrative motivation). The other paradigm distinguished between intrinsic versus extrinsic motivation (Deci and Ryan, 1985). This approach is more sociopsychological. Motivation is considered the outcome of individual regulation of behavior. Extrinsic motivation is connected with the demands and expectations formulated by persons (e.g., parents or teachers) in the individual's surroundings under the promise of reward or the threat of punishment. As the individual becomes more and more socialized into a certain behavior, the motivation to fulfill specific expectations would come from within (intrinsic motivation). In both paradigms, the relation between the motivation types is complex, as one type may be dominant in some situations, but not in others.

Dörnyei and Ottó (1998) express the idea that motivation could be subject to change during the learning process. They introduce time as a factor in their model. The learner regularly adjusts her or his goals and strategies according to an ongoing evaluation. Noels et al. (2000) point to a strong correlation between instrumental motivation and external regulation (parallel to the extrinsic–intrinsic motivation paradigm). Travels, friendship, and knowledge are all involved, and important. Norton (2000) points to the complex relationship between identity, language learning, and setting, including socioeducational and socioeconomic factors as relevant to the development of the individual's motivation to learn a new language. Norton's introduction of the concept of social investment reflects the complex conditions that govern motivation.

Social Theory in SLA

With the sociolinguistic turn in SLA research, focus shifted from seeing language learning as the gradual development of a language system in individuals to a perspective on language learners as language users in real-life environments. Dominant cognitive theories were replaced by or supplemented with sociocultural theories focusing on actual language use. One characteristic aspect of learners' second-language use is the high level of variability in their interlanguage at any given time, that is, their use of different versions of the same language construction (e.g., marker of past tense in verbs). In the 1980s and early 1990s, results from a number of descriptive case studies on variability were analyzed in the SLA literature to discuss the theoretical concept of acquisition. Among others, Tarone (1988) and Ellis (1994) discussed how accurate the use of a linguistic form must be in order to say that the learner has acquired the basic rule. Another consequence of the rise of sociocultural theories in SLA research was a focus on the model of communication evoked in different approaches. Whereas the majority of cognitive studies as well as early sociolinguistic studies were based on a transmission model of communication, sociocultural studies assumed an interactionist perspective. Firth and Wagner (1997) argue that a dialogic view on language is a fundamental concept in modern SLA research, thus criticizing the traditional view on language as monologic in nature. A third and partly related aspect of sociocultural theories is the focus on the social environment of language learning and on the interplay between language learners and their community. Based on Hymes (1972), an ethnographic approach to language learning implies seeing learning as socially and collaboratively constructed in interaction in different contexts or speech events. Different speech events provide learners with different opportunities for interaction, affordances (van Lier, 2000), as they draw on different communicative patterns and are governed by social hierarchies and power relations. In instructed second-language learning, there is typically an orientation toward target norms in the social context and in the dialog between student and teacher. However, recent studies show that other less-institutionalized kinds of interaction also develop as participants negotiate their social identity through individual style or group patterns (e.g., through new rituals, Rampton, 1999).

This has brought about discussions of the role of normativity in second-language learning, similar to the debate on socialization in child-language studies (e.g., Ochs, 1996). Insofar as language learning consists of picking up conversational routines or adjusting to specific norms of language use, both learner and child may be seen as apprentices moving from the periphery toward the center of a community through interaction with experts (Lave and Wenger, 1991). Although normativity is an important characteristic of instructed second-language learning, views on language learning as a uniform process of approaching predefined target norms have come under attack from poststructuralists who see learning as "a nonlinear and relational human activity, co-constructed between humans and their environment, contingent upon their position in space and history, and a site of struggle for the control of social power and cultural memory" (Kramsch, 2002: 5). According to this sociocultural or ecological position, the sociolinguistics of second-language learning is not restricted to background variables which explain the speed and rate of success in the process of language learning. It is placed at the core of theories on the dynamics of language learning. Language is seen as part of the complex and dynamic processes of social membership, culture, and identity. Language learning is not only a matter of individual capability, but also of opportunities for interaction at the microsocial level and of power relations and linguistic norms at the macrosocial level. The role of social interaction is to provide supporting structures or scaffolding for individual competencies and thus to mediate language learning through communicative patterns and other semiotic tools (van Lier, 2000; Lantolff, 2000). At the macrosocial level, language proficiency is developed in social settings shaped by social structures and orders of discourse. Language development interacts with identity issues, such as the manifestation of agency in a negotiation of competing

subject positions in conflicting discourse communities (Canagarajah, 2004). Due to the increasing complexity of modern multilingual and multicultural societies, both learners and native speakers belong to several speech communities with a range of membership roles. Consequently, the idea of the native speaker is criticized for being a political rather than a theoretical concept. Kramsch (1998) replaces it with the concept of intercultural speaker and Dabelsteen and Jørgensen (2004) with the concept of the languager.

Interlanguage

Selinker (1972) introduced the term interlanguage to refer to the language produced by a learner, seen as a unique linguistic system different from the learner's L1 and from the target language, but using elements from both. The term describes learner language as systematic, and yet as dynamic and transitional. The gradually growing complexity of learner language is seen as a continuum of interlocking systems.

Since the 1980s, the term interlanguage has come to be used with different meanings: On the one hand, it refers to the mental grammar which the learner constructs while developing a second or foreign language. The learner's competence at any given time is hypothesized to be the guiding principle behind instances of language use. On the other hand, the term refers to the learner's actual language use in a social situation. The understanding is that learner language is a systematic variety of language (Færch et al., 1984). According to both uses, deviations in learner language use are not seen as imperfect learning, but rather as signs of learning through hypothesis testing or as linguistic expressions of social identity.

Acquisition and Variation

SLA leads to variation in the L2 production of learners. Interlanguage is a highly variable phenomenon which changes with a range of factors, including oscillating precision, in reaching the target-language norms. In addition to this, SLA leads to variation which is sociolinguistically related in the way L1 variation is. Around 2000 minority groups of young second-language speakers of majority languages in the European cities developed styles which were marked as minority-related, but nevertheless also used by young majority members (Kotsinas, 2000). It remains to be seen whether these phenomena develop into ethnolects of the majority languages, or perhaps socially stigmatized urban varieties.

Variation in the production of learners may also involve loans and code switching. Contrary to conventional wisdom in traditional textbooks on language learning and language teaching, switching may be productive for the understanding between learners, or between learners and native speakers (Arnfast and Jørgensen, 2003). The learner may achieve on several levels by code switching away from the L2 in an otherwise L2 conversation. Switching can be a strategy to maintain fluency, and therefore obtain at the level of social relations. It may also represent a learning strategy to expand the learner's knowledge of L2 – or the culture in which the L2 is being learned. In learner groups, perhaps, particularly school classes, the L2 may come to represent specific values (or stereotypes) which can be exploited in the everyday interaction among the learners (Rampton, 1999) in code switches into the L2 during otherwise L1 interaction. An intricate and complex pattern of code choice by young Londoners is described by Rampton (1995) as crossing which involves both English, Punjabi, Creole English, and other varieties. Crossing is characterized by the fact that the speakers do not necessarily know very much of the languages from which they borrow in their interactions. Similarly, Turkish-Danish students switch between a range of different languages, several of which have been taught to them, in what has been termed languaging (Dabelsteen and Jørgensen, 2004). Languaging is the use of linguistic items and features – regardless of where they belong – by human beings in order to achieve communicative goals.

Code switching and crossing are (as yet) controversial phenomena which are often discouraged by language instructors. There could be a future development in language-acquisition research which attempts to demonstrate to what extent learners can achieve by employing all the linguistic skills they have.

Age and SLA

The relationship between child SLA and adult SLA is a crucial problem in acquisition theory and empirical studies. Behaviorism formulated the critical-age hypothesis which states that language learning changes profoundly with the lateralization of the brain in adolescence, and the individual's ability to acquire new language deteriorates, and the acquisition of the mother tongue must be well under way before the age of 13, or the acquisition will never be complete (Lenneberg, 1967). This has also been applied to acquisition of a second language. The theory has been criticized, for one, because experiments have shown that adults acquire some aspects of language faster than children. On the other hand, the end result apparently is more native-like, the earlier a continuous acquisition has begun. A crucial review article is by Long (1990). Long concludes that the concept of a critical period is not irrelevant. However, it is not one specific period, but a continuum of maturation which affect different aspects of language at different times. He relates the maturational constraints to a physiological process, myelination, an ongoing process which renders the nervous system less

flexible, and which runs parallel with the automatization of linguistic features. The effect of age on language learning is a richly discussed issue (e.g., Singleton and Lengyel, 1995). Evidence for the critical-age hypothesis is found in studies which conclude that adults fail to acquire second-language features which are different from their L1 (e.g., Schachter, 1996). Evidence against the hypothesis is presented and reviewed by Bialystok (1997). Abrahamsson and Hyltenstam (2004) find evidence that neither young learners nor adult learners achieve complete native-like command of a second language, and like Long, they cite physiological reasons. Burgo (2006) reaches a similar conclusion. A different perspective of age-related differences has its focus on the identity work performed by learners when investing personal resources in acquiring a second language. The reactions of particularly adult learners range from rejection of, and isolation from, the second language and the cultures associated with it to completely embracing the language and cultures (Norton, 2000). Identities ascribed to learners, especially minority learners, by society at large may also affect the outcome of the learning process (McKay and Wong, 1996). Expectations as well as identities affect young learners and adult learners differently, and may affect motivations differently.

Second-Language Learning and Foreign-Language Learning

The distinction between foreign- and second-language learning is traditionally considered to be a matter of learning environment and the possibility to encounter, outside a formal learning setting, the language being learnt. The distinction between the two becomes clearer, when the who, how, what, and why are compared.

Foreign-language learning is generally directed to students, usually children or adolescents in primary and secondary school, who are taught the primary *lingua franca* of their country as a part of their general education. At a later stage within the educational system, foreign-language learning is either a goal in itself (e.g., Scandinavian philology in Asia) or a means to qualify other educational goals (e.g., studying German in order to read philosophers in the original language or to specialize in business school). In most countries, the number and selection of foreign languages offered in the educational system is determined by historical, political, cultural, and sociolinguistic factors. Outside the educational system, foreign-language learning is most often associated with adult education on a leisure-time basis, and rarely with special instruction for instrumental reasons. The second-language learner, on the other hand, is typically considered to be an immigrant (or in some cases the children of immigrants), learning the language that plays an institutional and social role in the community

(Ellis, 1994). Learning a second language may take place in formal settings (e.g., language courses) in the target country, or in the informal settings of the workplace, contact with authorities or social institutions, or other specific communities of practice. In this way, second-language learning takes place in a much more complex setting and under much more complex conditions than foreign-language learning. Since the 1990s, the distinction between formal and informal second-language learning tends to be regarded as a question of sociolinguistic setting. In this view, it is important to consider the interaction between the two settings, with an overlap between the two.

With the ongoing globalization of communication, it is no longer possible to regard foreign-language learning as an activity isolated from the community where the language in question is spoken as the primary means of communication. School classes communicate with other classes in twin towns, students seek out communities of interest on the Internet, and possibilities of traveling are expanding, just to mention a few. This promotes intrinsic motivation to improve specific linguistic and communicative skills in order to participate in social activity – real or virtual.

Second-Language Learning for School

In schools, language is not only taught, but also used in specific ways to transmit and reproduce relevant knowledge in relevant ways. This develops the specialized academic registers of school. At the same time, language is used to socialize children into (what counts as) competent citizens. Thus, language is both a means and an end to school activities. Language is also an instrument which links children's everyday experiences and cultural and family background with relevant school categories and learning practices, through recontextualization of their knowledge (Bernstein, 1990). Schools make use of a communicative code which draws on the social and thematic priorities that are given in the local context, and which overlaps only little with the functions of everyday language. For younger children, schools tend to link their language use with bodily activities, visual and sensory support, etc. to provide a physical basis for new concepts. For older children, the development of new conceptual categories is predominantly based on linguistic cues and explanations. Other kinds of problem solving, for example, math activities, also become gradually more dependent on the child's mastery of the relevant semiotic systems. The role of language is crucial in understanding why schooling in general is intellectually and socially difficult for children who do not master the communicative code of the school, and why the so-called fourth-year slump (e.g., Thomas and Collier, 2001) marks the onset of a growing gap between high- and low-performing students. As a consequence, language plays an important role in counteracting children's problems with school.

For minority students, who attend school in their second language, the situation is often particularly difficult. It takes several years to achieve high proficiency in a new language across several domains (Cummins, 2001), and especially to develop the academic language suited for educational purposes. The learning situation of the minority children is often hampered by lack of response to their special linguistic needs. Many school systems are misled by a monolingual, common-sense view on language learning, which claims that it is a limited process shared by all learners regardless of their age, social, or linguistic background. According to this view, learning will eventually lead to the same outcome, whether it takes place before or after school starts. As a consequence, there is a political pressure toward preschool language learning in several industrialized countries. The logic behind this is the idea that an earlier introduction of the majority language leads to better results. This idea has been termed the fallacy of early start by Skutnabb-Kangas (2000). The idea draws on a simplistic, quantitative view on language learning. It is in line with another common fallacy – that so-called natural acquisition of language automatically develops into school language. According to this, children pick up everyday language through interaction in the playground and gradually transform this into the academic language of schools. Crawford (2000) among others has cautioned against the so-called sink-or-swim-method in which minority children are left to cope on their own with the intellectually and linguistically demanding learning of curriculum without instructional support. In this situation, efficient language learning may be hampered by gate keeping and silencing (Santa Ana, 2004). This may lead to social marginalization and – at a very practical level – to reduced opportunity of using the target language in situations that could have promoted learning.

The quantitative perspective is challenged by a view on language proficiency as a complex and dynamic combination of skills, knowledge, and reflexivity, relevant for both majority and minority children. In order to change the situation of educational underachievement in general, the role and norms of language must be made explicit in the classroom. Discourses must be established which may form the bridge between students' everyday language and prior knowledge on the one hand and their development of the academic school registers on the other (Gibbons, 2006). For minority children, this must include strategies to incorporate the actual multilingualism of the students' environment as part of their learning potential (Thomas and Collier, 2001).

See also: First Language Acquisition; Language and Literacy in Educational Settings.

Bibliography

Abrahamsson, N. and Hyltenstam, K. (2004). Mognadsbegränsningar och den kritiska perioden för andraspråksinlärning. In Hyltenstam, K. and Lindberg, I. (eds.) *Svenska som andraspråk*, pp 221–258. Lund: Studentlitteratur.

Andersen, R. (1990). Models, processes, principles and strategies: Second language acquisition inside and outside the classroom. In Van Patten, B. and Lee, J. (eds.) *Second Language Acquisition – Foreign Language Learning*, pp 45–68. Clevedon, UK: Multilingual Matters.

Anderson, J. (1985). *Cognitive Psychology and its Implications*, 2nd edn. New York: Freeman.

Arnfast, J. S. and Jørgensen, J. N. (2003). Code-switching as a communication, learning, and social negotiation strategy in first-year learners of Danish. *International Journal of Applied Linguistics* **13**(1), 23–53.

Bernstein, B. (1990). *The Structuring of Pedagogic Discourse*. London: Routledge.

Bialystok, E. (1997). The structure of age: In search of barriers to second language acquisition. *Second Language Research* **13**, 116–137.

Burgo, C. (2006). Maturational constraints in SLA. LL Journal **1**(1), 12–25, http://ojs.gc.cuny.edu/index.php/lljournal/article/viewFile/burgo/64 (accessed August 2009).

Canagarajah, S. (2004). Multilingual writers and the struggle for voice in academic discourse. In Pavlenko, A. and Blackledge, A. (eds.) *Negotiation of Identities in Multilingual Contexts*, pp 266–289. Clevedon, UK: Multilingual Matters.

Corder, S. P. (1967). The significance of learners' errors. *International Review of Applied Linguistics* **4**, 161–170.

Crawford, J. (2000). *At War with Diversity. US Language Policy in an Age of Anxiety*. Clevedon, Avon: Multilingual Matters.

Cummins, J. (2001). *Language, Power and Pedagogy. Bilingual Children in the Crossfire*. Clevedon, UK: Multilingual Matters.

Dabelsteen, C. and Jørgensen, J. N. (eds.) (2004). *Languaging and Language Practices. Copenhagen Studies in Bilingualism 36*. Copenhagen: University of Copenhagen.

Deci, E. and Ryan, R. M. (1985). *Intrinsic Motivation and Self-Determination in Human Behavior*. New York: Plenum Press.

Dörnyei, Z. and Ottó, I. (1998). Motivation in action: A process model of L2 motivation. *Working Papers in Applied Linguistics* (Thames Valley University) **4**, 43–69.

Ellis, R. (1994). *The Study of Second Language Acquisition*. Oxford: Oxford University Press.

Firth, A. and Wagner, J. (1997). On discourse, communication and (some) fundamental concepts in SLA research. *Modern Language Journal* **81**(3), 286–300.

Færch, C., Haastrup, K., and Phillipson, R. (1984). *Learner Language and Language Learning*. Copenhagen: Gyldendal.

Gardner, R. and Lambert, W. (1972). *Attitudes and Motivation in Second Language Learning*. Rowley, MA: Newbury House.

Gibbons, P. (2006). *Bridging Discourses in the ESL Classroom. Students, Teachers and Researchers*. London: Continuum.

Givón, T. (1985). Function, structure and language acquisition. In Slobin, D. (ed.) *The Crosslinguistic Study of Language Acquisition*, 2, pp 1005–1027. New York: Erlbaum.

Hyltenstam, K. (1978). *Progress in Immigrant Swedish Syntax. A Variability Analysis*. Lund: University of Lund.

Hymes, D. (1972). Models of the interaction of language and social life. In Gumperz, J. and Hymes, D. (eds.) *Directions in Sociolinguistics*, pp 35–71. New York: Holt, Rinehart and Winston.

James, C. (1980). *Contrastive Analysis*. London: Longman.

Kellerman, E. and Bialystok, E. (1997). On psychological plausibility in the study of communication strategies. In Kasper, G. and Kellerman, E. (eds.) *Communication Strategies: Psycholinguistic and Sociolinguistic Perspectives*, pp 31–48. London: Longman.

Kotsinas, U.-B. (2000). *Kontakt, variation och förändring – studier i Stockholmsspråk*. Stockholm: Almqvist and Wiksell.

Kramsch, C. (1998). The privilege of the intercultural speaker. In Byram, M. and Fleming (eds.) *Language Learning in Intercultural Perspective: Approaches through Drama and Ethnography*, pp 16–33. Cambridge: Cambridge University Press.

Kramsch, C. (ed.) (2002). How can we tell the dancer from the dance? In *Language Acquisition and Language Socialization*, pp 1–30. London: Continuum.

Krashen, S. (1985). *The Input Hypothesis: Issues and Implications*. Harlow: Longman.

Lado, R. (1957). *Linguistics across Cultures*. Ann Arbor, MI: University of Michigan Press.

Lantolf, J. P. (ed.) (2000). *Sociocultural Theory and Second Language Learning*. Oxford: Oxford University Press.

Lave, J. and Wenger, E. (1991). *Situated Learning. Legitimate Peripheral Participation*. Cambridge: Cambridge University Press.

Lenneberg, E. H. (1967). *Biological Foundations of Language*. New York: Wiley.

Long, M. H. (1985). Input and second language acquisition theory. In Gass, S. and Madden, C. (eds.) *Input and Second Language Acquisition*, pp 377–393. Rowley, MA: Newbury House.

Long, M. (1990). Maturational constraints on language development. *Studies in Second Language Acquisition* **12**(3), 251–285.

Long, M. H. and Robinson, P. (1998). Focus on form: Theory, research and practice. In Doughty, C. J. and Williams, J. (eds.) *Focus on form in Second Language Acquisition*, pp 15–41. Cambridge: Cambridge University Press.

McKay, S. L. and Wong, S.-L. C. (1996). Multiple discourses, multiple identities: Investment and agency in second-language learning among Chinese adolescent immigrant students. *Harvard Educational Review* **66**(3), 577–608.

McLaughlin, B. (1987). *Theories of Second Language Learning*. London: Edward Arnold.

Noels, K. A., Pelletier, L. G., Clément, R., and Vallerand, R. J. (2000). Why are you learning a second language? Motivational orientations and self-determination theory. *Language Learning* **50**, 199–218.

Norton, B. (2000). *Identity and Language Learning. Gender, Ethnicity and Educational Change*. London: Longman.

Ochs, E. (1996). Linguistic resources for socializing humanity. In Gumperz, J. and Levinson, S. C. (eds.) *Rethinking Linguistic Relativity*, pp 407–437. Cambridge: Cambridge University Press.

Pienemann, M. (1998). *Language Processing and Second Language Development: Processability Theory*. Amsterdam: John Benjamins.

Rampton, B. (1995). *Crossing. Language and Ethnicity among Adolescents*. London: Longman.

Rampton, B. (1999). Deutsch in inner London and the animation of an instructed foreign language. *Journal of Sociolinguistics* **3**(4), 480–504.

Richards, J. C. (ed.) (1974). *Error Analysis. Perspectives on Second Language Acquisition*. London: Longman.

Santa Ana, O. (ed.) (2004). *Tongue-Tied. The Lives of Multilingual Children in Public Education*. Lanham: Rowman and Littlefeld.

Schachter, J. (1996). Maturation and the issue of universal grammar in second language acquisition. In Ritchie, W. and Bhatia, T. (eds.) *Handbook of Second Language Acquisition*, pp 159–193. San Diego, CA: Academic Press.

Schmidt, R. and Frota, S. (1986). Developing basic conversational ability in a second language: A case-study of an adult learner. In Day, R. (ed.) *Talking to Learn: Conversation in Second Language Acquisition*, pp 237–326. Rowley, MA: Newbury House.

Selinker, L. (1972). Interlanguage. *International Review of Applied Linguistics* **10**, 209–231.

Singleton, D. and Lengyel, Z. (eds.) (1995). *The Age Factor in Secondg Language Acquisition*. Clevedon, Avon: Multilingual Matters.

Skutnabb-Kangas, T. (2000). *Linguistic Genocide in Education – or Worldwide Diversity and Human Rights*. Mahwah, NJ: Erlbaum.

Slobin, D. (ed.) (1985). *The Crosslinguistic Study of Language Acquisition*, vol. 1–2. Hillsdale, NJ: Erlbaum.

Slobin, D. I. (1996). From 'thought and language' to 'thinking for speaking'. In Gumperz, J. and Levinson, S. C. (eds.) *Rethinking Linguistic Relativity*, pp 70–96. Cambridge: Cambridge University Press.

Tarone, E. (1988). *Variation in Interlanguage*. London: Edward Arnold.

Thomas, W. and Collier, V. (2001). National study of school effectiveness for language minority students long-term academic achievement. http://www.crede.org/research/llaa/1.1_final.html (accessed August 2009).

Van Lier, L. (2000). From input to affordance: Social-interactive learning from an ecological perspective. In Lantolf, J. (ed.) *Socio-Cultural*

Theory and Second Language Learning, pp 245–259. Oxford: Oxford University Press.

Vygotsky, L. (1978). *Mind in Society. The Development of Higher Psychological Processes*. Cambridge, MA: Harvard University Press.

Wardhaugh, R. (1970). The contrastive analysis hypothesis. *TESOL Quarterly* 4(2), 123–130.

Weinreich, U. (1953). *Languages in Contact. Findings and Problems*. The Hague: Mouton.

Further Reading

Byram, M. (1997). *Teaching and Assessing Intercultural Communicative Competence*. Clevedon, UK: Multilingual Matters.

Dörnyei, Z., Csizér, K., and Németh, N. (2006). *Motivation, Language Attitudes, and Globalisation: A Hungarian Perspective*. Clevedon, UK: Multilingual Matters.

Writing, Early

B E Hagtvet, University of Oslo, Oslo, Norway

Writing as a Multimodal Phenomenon

An increasing awareness, during the 1970s, with regard
to preschool children's literacy learning led to a growing
body of research on early writing during the last part of
the twentieth century. These studies complemented the
work of pioneers Montessori (1971), Luria (1978), and
Vygotsky (1978). They also marked a new era in literacy
research – by highlighting how literacy emerges during
preschool and early schooling, and by emphasizing children's early writing as an interdisciplinary field with great
educational implications.

Writing is a social practice – an act of communication that
uses script to compose messages. Similar to reading, writing
basically consists of two skills: the ability to use a notational
system (i.e., the alphabetic code) and the ability to handle
word messages. Over the past decades, research on early
writing has been prolific – covering the development of
graphic script as well as the skills needed to write down
verbal messages. There has also been a focus on linguistic
and cognitive knowledge in the interface between oral and
written modalities. For example, studies of the emerging
notational system, of how early scribbling is transformed
into letters via drawings and various graphic symbols, have
shed light on the development of children's understanding
of language as a system, and on the relationships between
phonemes and graphemes. The research has also examined
differences between drawing and writing and between signs
and letters, as well as how older preschoolers and young
school children tackle orthographic spelling and spelling
rules. Furthermore, researchers have focused on the process
of constructing verbal messages, on how children act, speak,
and interact while transforming speech into written script.
There have been studies of how children make use of pencils,
computers, and toys in writing, and of how written language
learning is culturally embedded with the script mediated by
significant adults and peers in the child's environment.

Research on early writing has drawn attention to not
only the understanding of emerging literacy, but also to
the importance of the preschool years in literacy learning.
In defining early literacy, there is no need to make a strong
distinction about the point in time that children start
formal writing instruction at school. Children – around
the world – start school at different ages, and different
school systems emphasize formal introduction to literacy
differently. Thus, the term early writing is defined here
more pragmatically as the period prior to a child mastering
the conventional writing system with a certain consistency.

Disciplinary and Theoretical Roots

Prior to the 1970s, the idea of early writing was mainly
associated with writing as a motor activity or with early
spelling using alphabetic script. In some cases, it was also
associated with the skills of young fluent readers, that is,
children who taught themselves to read and write prior
to formal schooling (Clark, 1976). Only in rare cases was
early writing seen as an integral part of developmental
theory – first and foremost by Luria and Vygotsky. The
research was typically anecdotal and conducted in natural
settings at home and in school.

In the 1970s, there was a major shift toward a broader
concept of writing. The concept of emergent literacy was
coined – reflecting an interest in the study of how literacy
emerges during the preschool years. Writing was now
more often studied ethnographically by focusing writing
practices in different contexts: in nursery school, in collaborative play, or in informal situations in children's
homes (Clay, 1975; Teale and Sulzby, 1986). In addition,
children's creative spellings, that is, how children come
to terms with the alphabetic and orthographic rules of
the notational system by child-driven explorations, was
focused upon (Read, 1986; Treiman, 1993).

Generally, the development of writing skills has been
studied from four main perspectives (Tolchinsky, 2004):

1. The sociocultural approach originated in the early
   work of Vygotsky (1978) and Luria (1978). Focusing
   on written language as tools of linguistic and cognitive
   change in the development of the individual, their
   work contributed to moving the study of early writing
   to the scientific arena of higher-order psychological
   functions. In a literate society, a child is surrounded
   by print that is brought to the child by adults and more
   competent peers mediating the written language. These
   ideas of Vygotsky's about mediated learning have inspired
   much modern pedagogy, for example, that writing skills
   are learned while children collaborate and interact verbally
   with adults or more competent peers, and that tools
   (artifacts) such as words, pencils, lap tops, and symbolic
   toys are crucial mediating elements. Moreover, they
   have vitalized research on how children construct ideas
   about written language via writing practices, through
   collaborative writing, children's think alouds, and verbal
   dialogs during writing.

2. The psychogenetic approach dates back to the theoretical
   and methodological work of J. Piaget and was recreated in
   the field of early writing by the groundbreaking work of

E. Ferreiro and her collaborators (e.g., Ferreiro and Teberosky, 1983). With a constructivist point of departure, this strand of research focuses on how children achieve mastery of the script by exploring and experimenting with the script as an object. Children reconstruct the conventions of written language through processes of assimilation and accommodation (see this). They build hypotheses about connections between oral and written language that are not idiosyncratic but developmentally ordered. By making use of controlled tasks in combination with clinical interviews, researchers within this line of research have shed light on how children's growing knowledge of literacy may be described in terms of developmental stages and how each stage reflects a dominant or favored strategy of writing.

3. The emergent literacy approach typically involves ethnographic researchers studying how literacy emerges during the writing process in classrooms and families in various cultures and social contexts. A primary concern is how children's emergent graphic signs are influenced by their interaction with parents or peers, or by their talking to themselves during the writing process, and how drawing, talking, and writing interact during the writing process (e.g., Bissex, 1980; Clay, 1975; Dyson, 1989; Teale and Sulzby, 1986). Often influenced by sociocultural theory of learning, researchers within this line of research have highlighted phenomena such as children's self-regulatory speech during writing, scaffolding interactions, writing conferences, etc. (e.g., Graves, 1983). However, ethnographic researchers have expanded this paradigm by focusing more broadly on literacy events, that is, on learning to write as an event with specific purposes that are culturally defined by certain ways of relating to other participants and by expected text topics and structures, such as how children (and adults) collaborate in composing a letter or a story (Heath, 1983). Shedding light on cultural variations and on the importance to literacy of both family literacy and classroom practices, this strand of research has had great implications for educational practice, for example, in the ramifications of terminology such as classroom events.

4. Approaches focusing on invented spelling typically concentrate on the product and process of writing in a more restrictive sense than the above-mentioned approaches. Spelling is seen as one component of writing (Treiman and Cassar, 1996) and concerns the ability to write words in accordance with orthographic rules. In line with this narrow definition, the term invented spelling regards child-driven activities, referring to the children's own experimentation with meaning-form links and with connections between spoken and written language (Read, 1986). Many will side with Richgels' (1995: 99) definition of invented spelling as children's ability to "sound units in words and associate letters with those units in a systematic though

non-conventional way before being taught to spell or read." However, the term is also used with broader meanings (Saada-Robert, 2004), blurring its distinction from terms such as invented or emergent writing. Invented spelling typically regards a later developmental period, when the child experiments with the conventional notational system, that is, the alphabetic system, while invented writing typically refers to a larger developmental period including also pre-alphabetic periods. Important issues relating to research on invented spelling in the last 20–30 years include: the role of phonology and morphology in early spelling, the development of spelling, including the roles of logos, children's names, and letter naming in children's creative attempts to break the alphabetic code. More recently, there have been comparative studies of how orthographic systems influence early spellings (Nunes and Hatamo, 2004).

Within each of these approaches, there are large variations, and the distinguishing criteria are more pragmatic than logical. The four approaches have inspired researchers theoretically and methodologically. In practice, research projects transcend theories and methodologies. For example, while the process of writing within a sociocultural paradigm is commonly studied by ethnographic methodology (observation, interviews, etc.), semi-structured, test-oriented methods associated with the microgenetic approach of the Piagetian constructivist paradigm are also used. While invented spelling is quite often studied by test-oriented procedures, for example, dictation of single words over time, it may also be studied ethnographically via spontaneous writing of informal notes.

Stages of Early-Writing Development

Despite differences associated with specific characteristics of scripts and languages across orthographies and cultures, certain universal periods or stages of writing skills may be revealed, for example, in Hebrew (Levin and Landsmann, 1987), Italian (Pontecorvo and Zuccermaglio, 1989), Spanish (Ferreiro and Teberosky, 1983), English (Clay, 1975), German (Brügelmann, 1999; Valtin, 1997), French (Jaffré and David,1998), Norwegian (Elsness, 2001; Hagtvet, 2003), and Swedish (Liberg, 1993). These developmental periods share similarities with Piagetian stages to the effect that the strategies used by children at each stage determine the characteristics of that particular stage. However, this does not imply that the individual child makes consistent use of one strategy at the time. Rather, a child typically makes use of multiple strategies cutting across different stages, so the borders between stages are variable. Nevertheless, at a specific point in time, there appears to be a domination in a child's preference for one specific strategy, even though it may be used inconsistently.

So, a developmental stage is a period when there is a domination of a specific strategy.

Stages of early writing have been described using various terminologies depending on the focus of study and classification criteria for a stage. The basis for the developmental description below is a combined set of criteria reflecting qualities associated with the process and the product of writing (Hagtvet, 1989, 2003).

Prephonetic writing

In prephonetic writing, the graphic signs do not refer to phonetic entities in the child's speech. They reflect a weak awareness about the linguistic segments that constitute sentences (words, syllables, and phonemes). Serving a multitude of functions, prephonetic writing has been operationalized differently, depending on the perspective taken by the researcher and on the focus of study, for example, pretend writing, preliterate spelling (Henderson and Templeton, 1986), visual writing (Valtin, 1997), and precommunicative writing (Ellis, 1997). It is often produced as an imitation of adult writing or in symbolic play (pretend writing). Written from memory, the graphic signs are visual renderings of reality (visual writing) – often with an unfocused intention of communicating (precommunicative). However, even young children typically intend to communicate when writing. Therefore, the term precommunicative does not necessarily capture the essence of this early stage.

Children's early drawings and scripts symbolize referents, and drawing is seen as a precursor of scripts. According to Vygotsky: " . . . A child's memory does not yield a simple depiction of representational images at this age. . . . A major feature of this mode is a certain degree of abstraction, which any verbal representation necessarily entails. . . . drawing is graphic speech that arises on the basis of verbal speech. This gives us reasons for regarding children's drawing as a preliminary stage in the development of written language" (Vygotsky, 1978: 112–113). A big leap in development takes place when children come to understand that graphic signs can represent objects or events, for example, big circles, much text, or large letters refer to big, many, or long objects (Ferreiro and Teberosky, 1983).

Three different types of scripts are typically seen during this prephonetic stage reflecting different substages or subperiods:

Scribbling and symbols with no similarity with letters

This form has also been labeled figurative writing (Valtin, 1997) alluding to the symbolic and imaginative nature of early script. Its relation to the referent is initially imprecise reflecting a weak understanding of the relationships between segments of speech and graphic scripts. At an early age (typically before age 3), scribbling is not differentiated from drawing. It is performed

rather arbitrarily – similar to an imitation of the writing movement observed in adults and for a purpose that appears to be an accompaniment to speech. Somewhat later, the scribbling becomes loaded with meaning – as observed when children follow their text with eyes and fingertips while reading their newly written text (Sulzby, 1986). Slowly, the graphic signs take on a more advanced, symbolic content – representing a more conscious and verbalized interpretation of things and events in the real world (around age 4). This is illustrated in **Figure 1** Leonard, age 3.4, has been asked to draw a picture, to write what he has drawn, and to write his name. Leonard's reading of his texts indicates that he differentiates between his drawing ("many big snakes"), his writing of the word snake, and his name (Leo). Four months previously, he did not know the difference between drawing and writing, and when asked to write his name, he said he did not know how to.

Letters in rows that represent words

When letters are written more or less randomly on the page, children typically remember and experiment with the form of the letters, but without phonetic awareness.

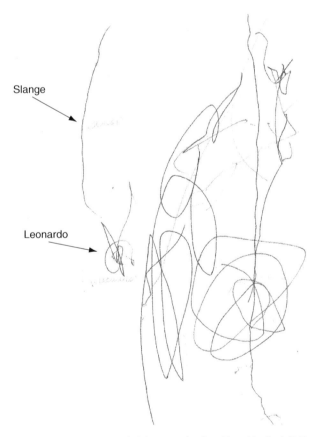

Slange

Leonardo

Figure 1 Leonard, age 3.4 draws and writes. From Hagtvet, B. E. (2003). *Språkstimulering. Tale og skrift i førskolealderen.* (Language stimulation. Speech and literacy before school age.) Oslo: Cappelen Akademisk.

Copying letters as pictures (sometimes from memory), this strategy has also been termed visual or logographic. **Figure 2** illustrates how letters may be used as pictures in a row when writing a Christmas card.

Global writing

When words are written as word pictures, the graphic scripts may be labeled global writing. Based on visual memory, this form of writing is still logographic. Own names and names of friends and family members are common among early words written by young children, but logos read on signs and posters (e.g., MILK, SHELL, and COKE) are also typical. This early writing of names commonly sets the stage for alphabetic exploration. Because these early names and word pictures are familiar and well-known in content – and, in most cases, emotionally important – they commonly act as catalysts for active and self-driven identification of phonemes in words. Slowly, children who regularly explore letter-sound relations in word pictures discover the alphabetic principle while writing.

Semiphonemic writing

Semiphonemic writing makes use of a phonetic strategy, but in a phonemically imprecise way: the child signals an awareness of the relationship between the phonological system and the script by means of graphic signs, pretend letters, or letters. An early phase of this developmental pattern is illustrated in **Figure 3** where Helene has written the sentence, *Helene liker is* (Helene likes ice cream). When reading the sentence, she underlines the syllabic pattern and rhythm of the sentence by means of voice punctuations and by tapping her finger tip on the relevant parts of the text revealing an awareness of the correspondence between word length and length of text: "*He-le-ne li-ker is*".

The discovery that different marks or signs in the text represent different aspects of speech (usually around

ages 3–4) is seen by Vygotsky as a shift in the development of written language from drawing things to drawing speech. From then on, spoken language disappears as the intermediate link between the world and the text, and written language slowly becomes as directly perceived as spoken language.

When letters are used in the semiphonemic stage, they are not copies of letters as pictures like they are in the prephonetic stage. Letters now represent sound patterns (sentences, words, onset, rhymes, and syllables) or language sounds (phonemes), and they now have a functional meaning to the child: they are used as building blocks in making word messages.

The writing of language sounds (phonemes) is a late phase in the semiphonemic stage. From then on, the writing becomes more and more phonemically oriented. First, the most prominent phoneme in the word is written down; each phoneme typically representing a larger unit of phonemes, for example, HS for house. The omission of vowels is a typical characteristic, as is the incorrect sequencing of phonemes or mirror imaging of words, for example SKRM for Markus.

Many children depend on letter naming during this early phonemic writing, for example, MSE (mess) or HLP (help) (Treiman and Cassar, 1997). However, this strategy may also be a barrier to proper phonemic writing by making the vowels less visible, which may explain why vowels are commonly omitted during this stage, for example, KM (come).

Phonemic writing

During the phonemic stage, children can identify phonemes in words, combine them with relevant graphemes, and write the graphemes in correct sequence. In early phonemic writing, children typically write as they say, tending to use this strategy systematically without

Figure 2 Experimenting with letters when writing a Christmas card, Christoffer, age 5.8. From Hagtvet, B. E. (2003). *Språkstimulering. Tale og skrift i førskolealderen.* (Language stimulation. Speech and literacy before school age.) Oslo: Cappelen Akademisk.

Figure 3 Syllabic writing, Helene, age 4.0.

orthographic information or spelling rules. This can yield charming examples such as RUDF? (Are you deaf?) (Bissex, 1980). They understand the alphabetic principle, but apply it orthodoxically phonemically . . .

Analyses of how early phonemic writing deviates from the adult norm have revealed that children's errors are quite logical. Children appear to actively construct a system of spelling patterns in accordance with the logic provided by their current level of skills. For this reason, it has been argued that spelling errors are windows into the child's written-language awareness, that is, to the systemic understanding of how the phonological structure of language matches the graphic structure of the script (Read, 1986).

Writing with conventional orthography

Increased experience with phonemic writing typically triggers children's interest in text and an acceleration of reading activities. This, in turn, generates an increased familiarity and awareness of the orthographic system and facilitates the inclusion of orthographic patterns in their writing (Treiman, 1994). The phonemic writing is then transformed into an orthographically driven process where orthographic representations are coordinated with phonological strategy. Jaffré and David (1998) see this developmental span from phonemic to orthographic spelling as two sub-phases, the first being a second logographic phase (in contrast to the logographic or visual phase described above). This is a phase where phonographic and morphological knowledge becomes integrated. Morphological knowledge is inherent in the orthographic system; it is based on rules and semantic insights. The second phase is the final orthographic phase.

The increasing awareness that the same sound can be spelled in one way when it represents one morpheme or has one grammatical meaning and in another way when it represents other ones, is demonstrated by children's unconventional or invented spellings (Read, 1986; Treiman, 1993). Children's spellings of regular past tense in English are good illustrations of this: the morphological rule being that past verbs end in-ed. In a longitudinal study of English children (Nunes et al., 1997), children around age 6 ignored this ending and wrote past tense phonetically, for example, KIST for kissed. This was followed by an intermediate period when the children tended to avoid the ed-ending. Then, they used it too often, including non-verbs and irregular past verbs – in addition to some, but far from all, regular verbs. This phase is illustrated by the spellings of a boy aged 7.5 years: DRESD (dressed), FILLD (filled), SLEPED (sleeped), SOLED (sold), NECSED (next), and SOFED (soft). Following this period of overgeneralization, the children used the past tense with past verbs only, finally restricting its use to regular past tense verbs (Bryant and Nunes, 2004).

Individual Variations

Universality of stages

The extent to which these stages (prephonetic, semiphonemic, phonemic, and orthographic) are universal is debatable. Differences in language, culture, and school systems, no doubt, affect development. Literacy varies in importance and emphasis in different cultures (Heath, 1983). However, evidence suggests that despite cultural diversity, children in literate societies go through the same stages, but at a different pace (see above). Generally, there appear to be surprisingly many commonalities across cultures, languages, and orthographies.

In addition, there are similarities in the onset of literacy development. It has been observed that the integration of scripts in children's drawings is suggestive of an increased interest in the written language on the part of the child. The universality of this observation, at least within the Western hemisphere, is illustrated in **Figure 4** where drawings by two girls age 5.4 are presented. Nicola grew up in New Zealand in the early 1970s while Benedicte grew up in Norway in the early part of this millennium. Nicola started school at age 5, while Benedicte started at age 7. Despite these differences of time and culture, their approach to early writing is surprisingly similar – in particular, in the style of their drawings and in their writing as an integral part of their drawing.

Variations within cultures

Despite general similarities, there are also noticeable differences – such as in the differences between boys and girls. Boys are often reported by their nursery school teachers to be less interested in paper-and-pencil activities than girls are. However, this may be an effect of the task more than biological differences. When encouraged to write on topics that appeal to them and allowed to make use of their own script, boys quite often produce more imaginative and detailed writing and drawings than girls do (Hagtvet, 2003). This is illustrated in **Figure 5** where Carl, age 5.3 has drawn a picture of the lives of sea animals and made up an explanatory text.

Girls appear generally less oriented toward details and events in the real world in their early writing. They are more inclined to tell stories about people, often inspired by fairy tales, such as tales about the prince and the princess, or a girl below a blue sky with a yellow sun as in **Figure 6**.

Carl and Melanie (Clare) approach the writing task differently, yet it is hard to rate one above the other. There are intragender differences as well. However, the gender differences in early writing are so striking that they invite more research attention – in particular, because boys tend to fall increasingly behind girls in literacy skills, according to recent international comparative studies (Programme for International Student Assessment (PISA)). Careful studies

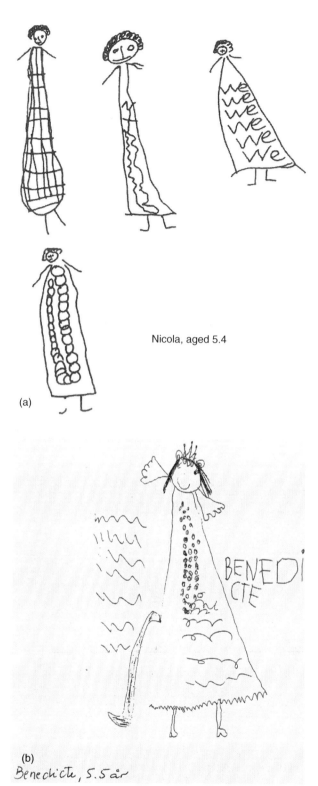

Nicola, aged 5.4

(a)

(b)

Benedicte, 5.5 år

Figure 4 Integrating scripts in drawings, Nicola, age 5.4 (New Zealand) and Benedicte (Norway), age 5.5. (a) Adapted from Clay, M. M. (1975). What Did I Write? Beginning writing behaviour. Heinemann: Auckland. (b) Adapted from Hagtvet, B. E. (2003). *Språkstimulering. Tale og skrift i førskolealderen*. (Language stimulation. Speech and literacy before school age.) Oslo: Cappelen Akademisk.

(a)

(b)

Carl, 5.3år leser:
Der står haiene og der delfinene
og der står de derre bena
og så de derre bollene
også de der reunde ballene
også den gule ballen
også de små lekene
og regn og stener og pinner
og en til
kongler og pinner

Carl, 5.3 years reads while pointing:

It says the sharks and it says the dolphins

and it says those odd feets

and then those balls

and the yellow ball

and the small toys

and rain and stones and sticks

and one more

cones and pins

(c)

Figure 5 Carl, age 5.3: A boy's drawing and text. Text showing the child's reading of written text. From Hagtvet, B. E. (2003). *Språkstimulering. Tale og skrift i førskolealderen*. (Language stimulation. Speech and literacy before school age.) Oslo: Cappelen Akademisk.

Figure 6   Melanie, age 5.0: A girl's drawing and text. Text showing the child's reading of written text: "She was about to marry. She went out to pick flowers." From Hagtvet, B. E. (2003). *Språkstimulering. Tale og skrift i førskolealderen*. (Language stimulation. Speech and literacy before school age.) Oslo: Cappelen Akademisk.

of the importance of early writing for continued motivation for reading and writing appears to be a promising line of research.

Variations across languages

During the last 10 years, studies of literacy across languages have been a major focus of research (e.g., Joshi and Aaron, 2006; Perfetti *et al.*, 1997). In learning to spell orthographically, children are challenged differently by different orthographies. The closer the orthographic system depicts the pattern of pronunciation, the smoother is the road to mastery of conventional orthographic spelling (Wimmer and Landerl, 1997). For example, children learning to spell in languages with many written markers that have no corresponding pronunciation tend to be slow in conquering these silent orthographic patterns. This was demonstrated in French speaking children who typically learn to spell the silent endings in nouns, verbs, and adjectives rather slowly (Fayol *et al.*, 1999). On the other hand, even dyslexic Norwegian-speaking children making

use of a semi-structured orthography achieved mastery of regularly spelt words quite easily while irregularly spelled words were more difficult (Hagtvet and Lyster, 2003).

Summary

In conclusion, the pace and ways at which children come to terms with alphabetic and later orthographic writing reflects biological maturation as well as differences in languages, culture, and educational practice. When encouraged to write, children typically start writing once they know how to hold a pencil or use a computer, and literacy development is further supported by interventional means. Recent studies have shown that the quality of maternal mediation of children's writing in kindergarten affects children's literacy scores 2 years later (Aram and Levin, 2004). In addition, teaching of morphological rules to deaf children with spatially based sign language as mother tongue improved their orthographical spelling of

English (Burman and Pretzlik, 2004). These are examples underscoring the importance of active mediation to early writing. Mastery of orthographic spelling and skills in constructing word messages in different genres is typically achieved following several years of schooling, but for some children – for example, for dyslexic or deaf children – this is a continuous struggle.

Bibliography

Aram, D. and Levin, I. (2004). The role of maternal mediation of writing to kindergartners in promoting literacy in school: A longitudinal perspective. *Reading and Writing: An Interdisciplinary Journal* **17**, 387–409.

Bissex, G. I. (1980). *Gnys at Wrk*. Cambridge, MA: Harvard University Press.

Brügelmann, H. (1999). From invention to convention: Children's different routes to literacy. In Nunes, T. (ed.) *Learning to Read: An Integrated View from Research to Practice*, pp 315–341. London: Kluwer Academic Press.

Bryant, P. and Nunes, T. (2004). Morphology and spelling. In Nunes, T. and Bryant, B. (eds.) *Handbook of Children's Literacy*, pp 91–118. London: Kluwer Academic Publishers.

Burman, D. and Pretzlik, U. (2004). Paths to literacy for deaf British Sign Language (BSL) users. In Nunes, T. and Bryant, B. (eds.) *Handbook of Children's Literacy*, pp 741–766. London: Kluwer Academic Publishers.

Clark, M. M. (1976). *Young Fluent Readers*. London: Heinemann.

Clay, M. M. (1975). *What Did I Write? Beginning Writing Behaviour*. Heinemann: Auckland.

Dyson, A. H. (1989). *Multiple Worlds of Child Writers*. New York: Teachers' College Press.

Ellis, N. (1997). Interactions in the development of reading and spelling; stages, strategies, and exchange of knowledge. In Perfetti, C. A., Rieben, L., and Fayol, M. (eds.) *Learning to Spell*, pp 271–294. Mahvali, NJ: Erlbaum.

Elsness, T. F. (2001). *Stavestrategier hos barn i alderen 7–8 år*. (Spelling strategies in children aged 7–8 years.) Doctoral dissertation. Department of Educational Research: University of Oslo.

Fayol, M., Thenevin, M.-G., Jarousse, J.-P., and Totereau, C. (1999). From learning to teaching to learning French written morphology. In Nunes, T. (ed.) *Learning to Read: An Integrated View from Research and Practice*, pp 43–63. London: Kluwer Academic Publishers.

Frith, U. (1985). Beneath the surface of developmental dyslexia. In Patterson, K. E., Marshall, J. C., and Coltheart, M. (eds.) *Surface Dyslexia*, pp 301–330. London: Routledge and Kegan Paul.

Graves, D. H. (1983). *Writing: Teachers & Children at Work*. London: Heinemann.

Hagtvet, B. E. (1989). Emergent literacy in Norwegian six-year-olds. From pretend writing to phonemic awareness and invented writing. In Biglmaier, F. (ed.) *Reading at the Cross-Roads. Conference Proceedings, The 6th European Conference on Reading*, 31 July to 3 August, 1989, Berlin.

Hagtvet, B. E. (2003). *Språkstimulering. Tale og skrift i førskolealderen*. Language stimulation. (Speech and literacy before school age.) Oslo: Cappelen Akademisk.

Hagtvet, B. E. and Lyster, S. A. H. (2003). The spelling errors of Norwegian good and poor decoders: A developmental cross-linguistic perspective. In Goulandris, N. (ed.) *Dyslexia in Different Languages. Cross-Linguisitic Comparisons*, pp 181–207. London: Whurr Publishers.

Heath, S. B. (1983). *Ways with Words*. Cambridge: Cambridge University Press.

Henderson, E. H. and Templeton, S. (1986). A developmental perspective of formal spelling instruction through alphabet, pattern and meaning. *Elementary School Journal* **86**(3), 305–316.

Jaffré, J.-P. and David, J. (1998). Premières experiences en littératie. (First experiences in literacy). *Psychologie et Education* **33**, 47–61.

Joshi, R. M. and Aaron, P. G. (2006). *Handbook of Orthography and Literacy*. Mahwah, NJ: Erlbaum.

Levin, I. and Landsmann, L. T. (1987). Becoming literate: Referential and phonetic strategies in early reading and writing. *European Journal of Behavioural Development* **12**, 369–384.

Liberg, C. (1993). *Hur barn lär sig läsa och skriva*. Lund: Liber Läromedel.

Luria, A. R. (1978). The development of writing in the child. In Cole, M. (ed.) *The Selected Writings of A.R. Luria*, pp 145–194. White Plains, NY: M.E. Sharpe.

Montessori, M. (1971). *The Montessori Elementary Material*. Cambridge, MA: Robert Bentley.

Nunes, T., Bryant, P., and Bindman, M. (1997). Spelling and grammar – the necsed move. In Perfetti, C. A., Rieben, L., and Fayol, M. (eds.) *Learning to Spell*, pp 151–170. Mahvali, NJ: Erlbaum.

Nunes, T. and Hatamo, G. (2004). *Morphology, Reading and Spelling: Looking across Languages*. In Nunes, T. and Bryant, B. (eds.) *Handbook of Children's Literacy*, pp 651–672. London: Kluwer Academic Publishers.

Perfetti, C. A., Rieben, L., and Fayol, M. (1997). *Learning to Spell*. Mahvali, NJ: Erlbaum.

Pontecorvo, C. and Zucc: hermaglio, C. (1989). From oral to written text: How to analyze children dictating stories. *Journal of Reading Behavior* **2**, 109–125.

Read, C. (1986). *Children's Creative Spellings*. London: Routledge and Kegan Paul.

Richgels, D. J. (1995). Invented spelling ability and printed word learning in kindergarten. *Reading Research Quarterly* **30**, 96–109.

Saada-Robert, M. (2004). Early emergent literacy. In Nunes, T. and Bryant, B. (eds.) *Handbook of Children's Literacy*, pp 575–598. London: Kluwer Academic Publishers.

Sulzby, E. (1986). Writing and reading: Signs of oral and written language organization in the young child. In Teale, W. H. and Sulzby, E. (eds.) *Emergent Literacy: Writing and Reading*, pp 50–89. Norwood, NJ: Ablex Publishing.

Teale, W. H. and Sulzby, E. (1986). Introduction: Emergent literacy as a perspective for examining how young children become writers and readers. In Teale, W. H. and Sulzby, E. (eds.) *Emergent Literacy: Writing and Reading*, pp vii–xxv. Norwood, NJ: Ablex Publishing.

Tolchinsky, L. (2004). Childhood conceptions of literacy. In Nunes, T. and Bryant, B. (eds.) *Handbook of Children's Literacy*, pp 11–29. London: Kluwer Academic Publishers.

Treiman, R. (1993). *Beginning to Spell: A Study of First Grade Children*. New York: Oxford University Press.

Treiman, R. (1994). Use of consonant letter names in beginning spelling. *Developmental Psychology* **30**, 567–580.

Treiman, R. and Cassar, M. (1996). Effects of morphology on children's spelling of final consonant cluster. *Journal of Experimental Child Psychology* **63**, 141–170.

Valtin, R. (1997). Strategies of spelling and reading of young children learning German orthography. In Leong, C. K. and Joshi, R. M. (eds.) *Cross-Language Studies of Learning to Read and Spell*, pp 175–193. London: Kluwer Academic Publishers.

Vygotsky, L. S. (1978). The prehistory of written language. In Cole, M., John-Steiner, V., Scribner, S., and Souberman, E. (eds.) *Mind in Society*, pp 105–119. Cambridge, MA: Harvard University Press.

Wimmer, H. and Landerl, K. (1997). How learning to spell German differs from learning to spell English. In Perfetti, C. A., Rieben, L., and Fayol, M. (eds.) *Learning to Spell*, pp 81–96. Mahvali, NJ: Erlbaum.

Further Reading

Farr, M. (1985). *Advances in Writing Research, Volume One: Children's Early Writing Development*. Norwood, NJ: Ablex Publishing.

Ferreiro, E. and Teberosky, A. (1983). *Literacy before Schooling*. London: Heinemann Educational Books.

Writing, Advanced

R Andrews, University of London, London, UK

Introduction

The history of teaching-of-writing approaches at advanced levels over the last 50 years or so can be characterized into two broad phases: the pre-computer phase, and the phase informed by reciprocal co-evolution with information and communication technologies.

The 1950s and 1960s saw an approach to writing which set high store by literary quality within a limited range of genres derived from nineteenth-century rhetorical categories. There was little emphasis on the processes of writing; more on the finished product and on a distanced, academic command of language types. Exercises deriving from the Renaissance and Elizabethan grammar school practice of *progymnasmata* (rhetorical models and imitation) were designed to build up competence. This period marked the high point in the teaching of formal grammar in the hope of improving writing quality and accuracy. It is against this background that much of the development in approaches to the teaching of writing at advanced levels can be gauged.

This article divides the main phases in the teaching and learning of writing at advanced levels into the decades from the 1960s to the 1980s; and from the 1980s to the present. Between these two phases, it looks at a number of different transitions that are critical to writing pedagogy.

1960s to 1980s

From the 1960s to the early 1980s there was more emphasis on expressiveness and the emergence of a personal voice in writing than in the previous decades. The foregrounding of the imaginative and creative (in a literary sense) continued, with a move away from tried and tested school genres toward experimentation. There was a celebration of self within societal contexts, best characterized by *Growth through English* (Dixon, 1967), the book emerging from the Dartmouth seminar of the International Federation for the Teaching of English in 1966. Two other key works in the late 1960s were Moffett's (1968/1987) *Teaching the Universe of Discourse*, and *Language, the Learner and the School* by Barnes *et al.* (1969/1989). The former charted the range of discourses that a student could expect to cover in formal education, with a clear indication that narrative modes and genres must come first, followed by expositional and argumentative types of writing. This work,

therefore, sat very much in the rhetorical tradition, but marked a step forward from the conventional theorizing and practice of the 1950s, where theory was ignored to taken for granted and practice fell into well-trodden ways. As Moffett states (1987, vii), in reflecting on the first edition of his book "I wanted to recast into the psychological terms of human growth those familiar but opaque academic elements such as rhetoric, logic, grammar, and literary technique…" Perhaps the most salient aspects of Moffett's hypothesis is that language development takes a course from drama through narrative and exposition to argumentation. Although such a series – with the famous sentence that "whereas adults differentiate their thought into specialized kinds of discourse such as narrative, generalization and theory, children must for a long time make narrative do for all" (my italics) (1987: 49) – seems to suggest a Piagetian fixed sequence, Moffett suggests that the strands of discourse run through young people's development concurrently. The basis in dialog and drama still feels contemporary in the light of Vygotsky's theory of cognitive development and, for example, Alexander's (2006) notions of dialogic teaching.

Language, the Learner and the School was more seminal than Moffett's work, in that it took a fresh empirical look at practice in classrooms and found it wanting in a number of respects. First, speech in the classroom was seen to be teacher dominated, with little space for pupils or students to try out ideas or expound at length. Second, although there was a higher proportion of open questions in English as a secondary school subject than in other subjects, there were fewer questions that required reasoning than in mathematics or science lessons. Third, questions asked by teachers tended to seek factual rather than reasoned answers, thus downplaying the dialogic, negotiated potential of the curriculum for learning and knowledge building. The investigations recorded in the book suggest that a closer relationship between active pupils' talk and their writing would enhance performance in both modes of communication; nevertheless, there was not only a gap between teacher and pupil discourses, but also one between pupil talk and pupil writing. However, Barnes (1989: 72) notes that "though this paper focuses on spoken language, much of what I have said applies equally to written language." In many ways, the connection between talk and writing was made, bringing an expressive, thinking-through-writing, dialogic (and potentially dialectical) character to learning to write at advanced level. Such a connection is also made in Britton (1967) and in the work of Dixon (op. cit.). The complex interdependency of speech and writing is also reflected, for example, in the work on Ong (1982/1988).

The period also marked the rise of narrative as a primary act of mind (Hardy, 1977) or even human paradigm (Fisher, 1989). Rosen (1985) continued his interest in narrative speech and writing with publications in the 1980s celebrating the power and ubiquity of narrative, not just for expressive writing in autobiography and storytelling, but also in transactional, nonfictional kinds of writing. The interest in the oddly negative nonfiction category was captured in Pavel's (1986) *Fictional Worlds*, which brilliantly charted the position of fiction in relation to other forms of writing, reading, and cultural engagement. In many ways, this period marked the beginning of the breakaway from the personal growth model of English which emphasized creative and imaginative fictional and poetic expression to a broader conception of the subject which celebrated a wider range of genres and text types, not without their own kinds of creativity, expression, and imagination (as had already been presaged by Moffett, 1968/1987).

An interest in genres and their place in the teaching of advanced writing increased in the second half of the 1980s, following the publication of Miller's (1984) article, 'Genre as social action'. The notion of genres and their importance to writing curricula and pedagogies derived from film studies and from sociological theory. Essentially, Miller's conception of genre was influential because it saw genres as constituted in social action rather than in text types. The spectrum of possibilities between the social, contextual view of genre and its more narrow textual (formal properties of texts) version has defined the debate and practices in the field, not least because it is at advanced stages in learning to write that the social and textual differentiation between kinds of writing manifests itself. One the one hand, the social, contextual view is represented in writing by Kress (1982/1994), Freedman and Medway (1994); the more linguistically focused view finds expression in the Sydney School of Australian Halliday-derived genre theory and practice, as evidenced in the work of Martin (1991), Christie (1987) and others. Excellent surveys of the field and of the contribution of genre theory to the development of writing abilities are found in Reid (1987) and Cope and Kalantzis (1993). The influence of such theory on curriculum design is felt in many countries.

A greater understanding of writing processes in expert writers that can be modeled in novice writers emerged in the 1980s to early 2000s, deriving from the work of psycholinguistic and discourse modeling by Graves (1983) and Scardamalia and Bereiter (1987). The understanding and mapping of process was reified into a formal system for teaching writing (Calkins, 1986), and creating an abreaction

(e.g. Harwayne, 2001) among those who believed it to be fossilized. The emphasis of this movement to celebrate and teach process was on drafting, editing, and peer conferencing (aided by use of word processing), aiming all the time to capture the voice in writing. Sometimes this movement was linked to or ran alongside a widening of the range of written (and spoken) forms – a development that in itself was reacting against the preponderance of a single, unified narrative/expressive mode and by taking such a wider perspective was aiming to prepare young writers for the world. Such widening of the range of discourse manifested itself in the later versions of the National Curriculum (UK) and in the Australian (specifically, the Sydney School, e.g., Christie, 2002) celebration (and calibration) of a range of genres in writing.

Transitions

There are at least three types of transition in writing at advanced levels that need to be mentioned:

1. one is concerned with the transition from literary or inward-looking textual composition to real-world discourses;
2. another is between imaginative, informational, and an often-neglected argumentative mode of writing; and
3. a third concerns the transition from primary/elementary schooling to secondary/high school, and again from school to college.

The first transition that gets too little attention is that between the classroom and the real world. Although Britton *et al.* (1975) made the distinction between poetic and transactional writing – the latter doing the work of the world and thus giving status to it – much of the writing that was practiced under that heading was informational and/or factual rather than making a difference in the world. In other words, it was inert rather than transactional. Indeed, writing curricula is often divided into creative and imaginative types of writing on the one hand, and informational and instructional writing on the other, suggesting not only that these are the two main types of writing, but also that they are somehow opposed. There are two exceptions to such reductive categorization: writing that made a difference in the world, and argumentative writing; both of which, from time to time, are temporarily given higher profile in writing curricula.

Writing that makes a difference in the world was the subject of an under-published report by Brown *et al.* (1990) which looked to develop English for the UK's Technical and Vocational Education Initiative (TVEI). The key change made to writing practices in this project was that the contexts and audiences for the writing reached beyond the classroom. For example, in one subproject, pupils were commissioned by the school librarian to survey and make recommendations to her on the journals and magazines to which the library subscribed. A 65-page report, compiled and written over 6 weeks by a group of pupils, was delivered and made a significant difference not only to the library subscriptions, but also to the number of pupils reading in the library. The composition of the report was complex and highly motivating; the accuracy was enhanced by the need for public presentation.

Work on the place of argumentative writing in the curriculum was undertaken by Andrews (1995) and Mitchell (2000), suggesting that at secondary school and at further and higher education levels, the emphasis on the formal essay was not only in need of better teaching, but could be reinvigorated and diversified by exploration of the dialogic and dialectic nature of argumentation as well. To see the basis of learning to write at advanced levels as being in dialog suggests also the close and complex connection between writing and speech. Ong's exploration of orality and of oral cultures on the one hand, and Bakhtin's notion of a dialogic imagination (Bakhtin, 1982) on the other (composed in the 1930s, but published in the West in the 1970s and early 1980s) bring a new dynamic to the learning of and teaching of writing at advanced levels. Essentially, Ong's study of the shift from oral to chirographic (writing) cultures is both historical and synchronic. He sees writing cultures returning to a second orality in which dialogic forms are preferred, and short interchanges in writing (akin to speech) become prevalent. Bakhtin's notion that all writing is created in response to some existing discourse is helpful in that it makes writing appear to be more of a cultural exchange, and more like speaking, than is usually assumed.

The transitions from primary/elementary schooling to secondary/high schools, and/or through the middle school phase constitute a particular concern for the learning and teaching of writing.

Tabor (2004) sets out the particular problems in the teaching of writing in the transition from age 11 to 12 in the English system. In a doctoral study based on the progression of four pupils, he suggests that despite efforts made to ease transition by schools and by curriculum design and implementation (e.g., the National Literacy Strategy in England, followed by the Primary and Secondary National Strategies – with their particular focus on literacy development for 11–14-year-olds), there remains a dip in performance in writing at the start of secondary schooling. Such a dip would not be of concern if the progress of pupils was recovered, but some students do not make a recovery. The problem is part of a larger issue of progression in writing at advanced levels. Tabor (2004: 18–21) provides a very useful table on conceptualizing progression in writing, drawing on many of the key works mentioned in the present account and adding others. What is particularly interesting is that few, if any, of the theories or models of writing account for progression.

1990s to the Present

The period from the mid-1990s to the present has seen a tension between the functions of writing in wider society and those in schooling and assessment. The place of writing within multimodal communication, and especially recognition of its relation with the visual (still and moving images) in popular and indeed all culture(s) has begun to be explored, inspired by writers such as Lanham (1993) or Mitchell (1986). Lanham suggested that the "turn to the visual" in the 1990s, supposedly inspired by the visual/verbal interface of computer screens, was not new but was a phenomenon that had been a preoccupation for cultural analysts since at least the medieval period (through illuminated manuscripts and textual commentaries on iconic images). Mitchell took the idea further, exploring the spectrum of means of representation from image through icon to (written) text, linking the range of media to narrative. Although both writers operate at a high level of theory, their work has been instrumental in helping us to understand the relationship between word and image, and thus the particular characteristic and functions of writing, in late twentieth-/early twenty-first-century practice both within and without the classroom.

Writing processes moved from an understanding and practice of drafting and editing to design issues (Kress, 1995). A move away from the notion of a single personal voice to a multiplicity of voices was registered; and, indeed, through the improved quality of sound on computers (not quite up to general speech recognition and instant translation-into-writing quality). The advent of the mobile learner (see Sharples et al., 2007), accessing written, visual, and audio material anytime, at anyplace, brought about an extension of academic and social space, especially for 11–16-year-olds. Writing began to be conceived as text-box filling, but not always briefly; there was much scope for extended writing, both of an in-depth and functional nature. The need for keyboarding skills became apparent as writing increasingly took place through word processing. One of the key papers of this period was by the New London Group (1996/2000): 'A pedagogy of multiliteracies: Designing social futures'. This paper put the teaching and learning of writing within a multimodal conception of literacy; and furthermore, within changing social and economic patterns in personal, working lives and with regard to citizenship. It thus would see writing as embedded within school cultures (what Sheeran and Barnes (1991) call school writing), but as critically needing to reflect wider social practices and patterns or representation in order to stay relevant and engaging for advanced writers. The pedagogic problem of engineering such a productive relationship is seen to be a question of design: designs of meaning and the available designs of the grammars of various semiotic systems, providing the basis for the act of designing and redesigning. In school practice, learning to write is often a matter of taking material from one genre (used in the social process sense) and redesigning it for another. The pedagogy of multiliteracies approach extends this conception in two ways: into the visual and other semiotic codes in hybrid combinations with the verbal spoken and written codes (often foregrounded or highlighted by information and communication technologies); and by looking for more interaction between the practices of school life and social/political practices beyond the classroom.

The major challenge posed by the place of writing in a universe of discourse, and the pedagogies associated with it, is shaping a writing curriculum for 11–19-year-olds that would:

1. Recognize the place of writing within multimodality.
2. Reengage and motivate disaffected or unengaged young people by:
   a. bringing the genres of schooling closer to the genres of the wider social world, and
   b. giving writing a range of real purposes.
3. At the same time, use the power of writing to explore depth in thought, reflection, and feeling.
4. Recognize the place of creativity and imagination in nonliterary forms of writing, as well as in literary forms;
5. Recognize and exploit the fact that writing and reading are reciprocal – investigate the similarities and differences, strengths and weaknesses of speaking and writing in different contexts and for different functions – and thus reestablish the link between speaking and writing.

The last point needs further exploration. Speaking and writing are primarily skills of language production, whereas listening and reading are primarily skills of reception.

Speaking and writing can be demanding in that they require expression, articulation, framing, and shaping. To explicate these terms briefly: expression requires motivation to speak or write and the intellectual and motor facility to do so; articulation requires clarity of intention and thought, or at least a move toward such clarity; framing requires selections from the repertoire of socially embedded and generated speech genres and text types (sometimes these genres are hybrid or newly created); and shaping requires the manipulation of language within the those frames of reference, often at the point of utterance. Expression and articulation are part and parcel of the current curriculum but both need to be reemphasized; framing derives from sociological and discourse theory (see, e.g., Tannen, 1993) as a way of making sense of the demands of meaning-making at text level; shaping derives from Britton's notion of shaping at the point of utterance (Britton, 1980), that is, giving credit to the fact that much oral and written communication is not preplanned, but is shaped at it happens.

Expression is important because it engages the self or personae and releases what may be felt and/or thought. It affords channels of communication and creates contact with others.

Articulation aims to make such communication clear. In speech terms, articulation is associated perhaps most readily with surface features such as clear enunciation of utterances; more importantly, the notion of articulation (joining) is about logical or a-logical connections between ideas, thoughts, feelings, and language, in speech and/or writing. Andrews *et al.* (2006b), in a systematic review of research on the teaching of argumentative writing at KS2 and 3, draw attention to the need for cognitive as well as linguistic work in improving writing in this mode. The findings of this report are mirrored in a recent report by the US-based Alliance for Excellent Education – see Graham and Perin (2006) – which, based on a meta-analysis of research studies, concludes there are 11 strategies for improving writing in middle and high schools, including writing strategies, summarizing, collaborative writing, specific product goals (audiences), word processing, sentence combining (cf. grammar review by Andrews *et al.*, 2006a), prewriting (planning), inquiry activities (research), and a process writing approach.

With framing and shaping, the emphasis needs to move from a focus on the end products – the frames (pedagogic scaffolds, genres, text types, and forms) and shapes that language uses and that need to be learned – to the act of framing and shaping that is at the heart of composition (literally, putting things together). Such a move will entail thinking more deeply about the early stages of composition: how ideas are formed; how they are framed; how inspirational ideas are supported by a climate for learning and development; how choices are made, early on, about the medium or media in which it is best to convey the message; how drafting and editing can be improved by critical dialog and reflection at the deeper levels of composition (structure, voice, position, and tone); how momentum and interest can be sustained; how speaking, reading, and listening can contribute to the composing process in writing; how issues of design, balance, and elegance (when is a piece finished?) can be taught and learned; and how a community of learners (speakers/writers/makers) can support such committed and high-quality composing.

One possible reason for the fact that writing performance lags behind reading for the most part is that when listening or reading, the material is given. The intellectual load on the audience or reader might be said to be lighter than when composing in speech or writing, although that load will vary with content and substance in each case. It is generally accepted that writing is the most difficult, if not the most complex, of the four language skills, requiring solitary, creative, thoughtful, accurate, and focused compositional energy; as well as a higher degree of reflective thinking and (usually) personal engagement.

Much has been done, for example, to introduce pupils to nonfiction text types, and to improve their control of stylistic features associated with them. Where practice is weaker is in generating the motivation and purpose to write; without such direction, pupils know how to write but not why they write, how to start or how to engage an audience, and how to generate and marshal ideas. Producing writing of such quality, along with other text types, is one of the keys to overall improvement in English.

It worth reciting how speaking and writing can support each other at advanced levels. First, speaking can be an important rehearsal for writing. Ideas can be discussed in pairs, small groups, in whole-class discussion, and in larger forums, then distilled, translated, and developed in writing. Such writing can be dialogic as well as monologic. Dialogic writing includes planning for Socratic dialog (question-and-answer format), colloquia, play scripts, and other dual- and multi-voiced text types. Monologic writing includes the more conventional forms such as essay, story, letter, and report, where translation from the multiple voices of speech to the single authorial voice of the writer can be more difficult.

Second, writing can be a rehearsal for speech. Individual and/or joint composition in writing can prefigure delivery in speech, as in the making of a speech, the production of an oral narrative, the composition of a persuasive case, or the scripting of a (radio) play or advertisement. Speech as a product in these cases is more than mere performance: it is part of a dialog that invites response in spoken, written, and other formats. It is in such transformation between different means of communication and different genres within those means that the day-to-day practice of English in classrooms takes place.

The problem of insufficient space for sustained speaking and writing in school curricula is compounded by assessment practices.

What is clear is that speaking and writing are central to learning in formal education because they afford the learner the ability to reflect, think, compose, and rearrange as well as respond spontaneously (particularly in the case of speech). Furthermore, as Meek (1983) proves, such emphasis on the productive language skills can be the key to improvements and even breakthroughs for weaker learners not only in speaking and writing themselves, but also in reading and listening as a result of increased motivation, commitment, and investment in making meaning in language; and increased awareness and exploitation of the reciprocity between writing/ reading, and speaking/listening.

A further phase of development in writing practices, yet to arrive, will probably see advances in speech-recognition technology that might or might not obviate the need for keyboards or writing implements. The emphasis on composing written text (expression, articulation, framing, and shaping) will shift toward oral composition, while not abandoning writing. There will be a renewed dynamic relationship between speaking and writing, with each finding their roles in a new economy of communication.

Conclusion

Writing pedagogy is in need of reform to keep up with developments in the digital age and with multimodal perspectives. In particular, there has been little research on writing development at advanced levels. There is no doubt that writing will continue to be an important mode and medium of communication in the twenty-first century. What is a matter of concern is that teachers of writing are not necessarily equipped themselves as writers at advanced levels in a wide range of genres; they thus find the teaching of writing more difficult than that of reading. This article has indicated the range of skills and capabilities required to be a competent and inspiring teacher of writing.

See also: Writing, Early.

Bibliography

Alexander, R. (2006). *Towards Dialogic Teaching*, 3rd edn. Thirsk: Dialogos.

Andrews, R. (1995). *Teaching and Learning Argument*. London: Cassell.

Andrews, R., Torgerson, C., Beverton, S., *et al.* (2006a). The effect of grammar teaching on writing development. *British Educational Research Journal* 32(1), 39–55.

Andrews, R., Torgerson, C., Low, G., McGuinn, N., and Robinson, A. (2006b). Teaching argumentative non-fiction writing to 7–14 year olds: A systematic review of the evidence of successful practice. Report. In *Research Evidence in Education Library*. London: EPPI-Centre, Social Science Research Unit, Institute of Education, University of London. http://eppi.ioe.ac.uk/reel (accessed August 2009).

Bakhtin, M. M., Holquist, M., and Liapunov, V. (1982). *The Dialogic Imagination: Four Essays*. Austin, TX: University of Texas Press.

Barnes, D., Britton, J., and Rosen, H. (1969/1989). *Language, the Learner and the School*. Harmondsworth/Portsmouth, NH: Heinemann-Boynton/Cook/Pelican.

Britton, J. (1967). *Talking & Writing: A Handbook for Teachers*. London: Methuen.

Britton, J. (1980). Shaping at the point of utterance. In Freedman, A. and Pringle, I. (eds.) *Reinventing the Rhetorical Tradition*, pp 61–66. Las Vegas: Long and Silverman.

Britton, J., Burgess, T., Martin, N., McLeod, A., and Rosen, H. (1975). *The Development of Writing Abilities (11–16)*. London: Macmillan.

Brown, J., Clarke, S., Medway, P., Stibbs, A., and Andrews, R. (1990). *Developing English for TVEI*. Leeds: University of Leeds, School of Education.

Calkins, L. M. (1986). *The Art of Teaching Writing*. Portsmouth, NH: Heinemann.

Christie, F. (1987). Young children's writing: From spoken to written genre. *Language in Education* **1**.1, 3–13.

Christie, F. (2002). *Classroom Discourse Analysis: A Functional Perspective*. London: Continuum.

Cope, B. and Kalantzis, M. (1993). *The Powers of Literacy: A Genre Approach to Teaching Writing*. London: Falmer.

Dixon, J. (1967). *Growth through English*. Oxford: Oxford University Press for the National Association for the Teaching of English.

Fisher, W. (1989). *Human Communication as Narration*. Columbia, SC: University of South Carolina Press.

Freedman, A. and Medway, P. (eds.) (1994). *Learning and Teaching Genre*. Portsmouth, NH: Heinemann.

Graham, S. and Perin, D. (2006). *Writing Next: Effective Strategies to Improve Writing of Adolescents in Middle and High Schools*. Washington, DC: Alliance for Excellent Education.

Graves, D. (1983). *Writing: Children and Teachers at Work*. Portsmouth, NH: Heinemann.

Hardy, B. (1977). *The Cool Web: The Pattern of Children's Reading*. London: The Bodley Head.

Harwayne, S. (2001). *Writing through Childhood: Rethinking Process and Product*. Portsmouth, NH: Heinemann.

Kress, G. (1982/1994). *Learning to Write*. London: Routledge.

Kress, G. (1995). *Writing the Future: English and the Making of a Culture of Innovation*. Sheffield: National Association for the Teaching of English.

Lanham, R. (1993). *The Electronic Word: Democracy, Technology and the Arts*. Chicago, IL: University of Chicago Press.

Martin, J. R. (1991). *English Text: System and Structure*. Amsterdam: John Benjamins.

Meek, M. (1983). *Achieving Literacy: Longitudinal Studies of Adolescents Learning to Read*. London: Routledge.

Miller, C. (1984). Genre as social action. *Quarterly Journal of Speech* **70**, 151–167.

Mitchell, S. and Andrews, R. (eds.) (2000). *Learning to Argue in Higher Education*. Portsmouth, NH: Boynton/Cook.

Mitchell, W. J. T. (1986). *Iconology: Image, Text, Ideology*. Chicago, IL: University of Chicago Press.

Moffett, J. (1968/1987). *Teaching the Universe of Discourse*. Portsmouth, NH: Heinemann-Boynton/Cook.

New London Group (1996/2000). A pedagogy of multiliteracies: Designing social futures. *Harvard Educational Review* **66**, 60–92. (Revised in Cope, B. and Kalantzis, M. (2000), pp 9–37.)

Ong, W. J. (1982/1988). *Orality and Literacy: The Technologizing of the Word. New Accents*, Hawkes, T. (ed.). New York: Methuen.

Pavel, T. G. (1986). *Fictional Worlds*. Cambridge, MA: Harvard University Press.

Reid, I. (ed.) (1987). *The Place of Genre in Learning: Current Debates*. Geelong: Deakin University Press, Centre for Studies in Literary Education.

Rosen, H. (1985). *Stories and Meaning*. Sheffield: National Association for the Teaching of English.

Scardamalia, M. and Bereiter, C. (1987). *The Psychology of Written Composition*. Hillsdale, NJ: Erlbaum.

Sharples, M., Taylor, J., and Vavoula, G. (2007). A theory of learning for the mobile age. In Andrews, R. and Haythornthwaite, C. (eds.) *The Sage Handbook of E-Learning Research*, pp 221–247. London: Sage.

Sheeran, Y. and Barnes, D. (1991). *School Writing: Discovering the Ground Rules*. Milton Keynes: Open University Press.

Tabor, D. (2004). *Young Writers at Transition*. London: RoutledgeFalmer.

Tannen, D. (ed.) (1993). *Framing in Discourse*. New York: Oxford University Press.

Further Reading

Andrews, R. (ed.) (2004). *The Impact of ICT on Literacy Education*. London: RoutledgeFalmer.

Beaufort, A. (1999). *Writing in the Real World: Making the Transition from School to Work*. New York: Teachers College Press.

Cope, B. and Kalantzis, M. (2000). *Multiliteracies: Literacy Learning and the Design of Social Futures*. London: Routledge.

Hillocks, G. (1995). *Teaching Writing as Reflective Practice*. New York: Teachers College Press.

Jones, R. and Wyse, D. (2000). *Teaching English, Language and Literacy*. London: Routledge.

Massey, A. J., Elliott, G. L., and Johnson, N. K. (2005). *Variations in Aspects of Writing in 16+ English Examinations between 1980 and 2004: Vocabulary, Spelling, Punctuation, Sentence Structure, Non-Standard English*. Cambridge: Assessment Directorate, Cambridge Local Examinations Syndicate.

Medway, P. (1980). *Finding a Language: Autonomy and Learning in School*. London: Chameleon.

Myhill, D. and Fisher, R. (2005). *Informing Practice in English: A Review of Recent Research in Literacy and the Teaching of English*. London: Office for Standards in Education (Ofsted).

Russell, D. R. (2002). *Writing in the Academic Disciplines*. Carbondale, IL: Southern Illinois University Press.

Sharples, M. (1999). *How We Write – Writing as Creative Design*. London: Routledge.

Vygotsky, L. (1986). *Thought and Language*. Cambridge, MA: MIT Press.

Wilkinson, A. (1986). *The Quality of Writing*. Milton Keynes: Open University Press.

Relevant Websites

http://www.caribou.bc.ca/disciplines

http://www.ifte.net – International Federation for the Teaching of English.

http://www.jslw.org – Journal of Second Language Writing.

http://www.nate.org.uk – National Association for the Teaching of English.

http://www.literacytrust.org.uk – National Literacy trust.

http://www.writingproject.org – National Writing Project.

http://www.ncte.org/prog/writing

http://www.thinkingwriting.qmul.ac.uk – Thinking Writing.

LEARNING IN CONTEXTS AND THROUGHOUT THE AGES

Gender and Schooling

Organizational Learning

The Adult Development of Cognition and Learning

Lifelong Learning

Classroom Discourse and Student Learning

Learning Outside of School

Gender and Schooling

L Yates and J McLeod, The University of Melbourne, Melbourne, VIC, Australia

Glossary

Hidden curriculum – The knowledge and understandings that students learn in school that are not part of the official syllabus curriculum, and not intentional. For example, if textbooks consistently show men in positions of authority and women in subordinate roles (or if principals are always men and infant teachers always women) this is seen as shaping girls' and boys' expectations of their pathways in and beyond school.

Social construction/social constructionist – A description of how identities are shaped and formed by social factors, such as language, roles, traditions, expectations, and the like. It is contrasted with views that see identity as solely the result of fixed biological or natural impulses and orientations.

Voice, women's voice – In educational research, voice refers to the expression of someone's identity, as communicated in many ways, not only in speech. Women's voice conveys a sense of women's distinct qualities, orientations, and differences, such as preferring humanistic rather than abstract orientations to problems.

One of the most prominent developments in educational thinking in the last three to four decades has been the rise of gender as a central issue for learning and curriculum, and for education more broadly. This reflects a world where equality between women and men is a formal expectation for education systems and where there is a good deal of monitoring and research on patterns of educational participation and achievement by gender. The attention to gender in research and policy on learning also reflects some significant changes that began in the second-half of the twentieth century, with researchers moving away from simply accepting sex differences as an explanation for different patterns to focusing in much more detail on the ways teaching practices and school arrangements interact with the characteristics and experiences girls and boys bring to learning. In this work, learning (and teaching) is understood as shaping gender as well as the converse.

A large array of different kinds of research and policy-making has been carried out on gender and learning. It can now be found in most disciplines (or foundations) that study education, in many areas of school curriculum subject-specific study, and in many different kinds of research: longitudinal, qualitative, quasi-experimental, and action-research projects as well as in large-scale data monitoring. Research on gender and school learning also encompasses a broad range of topics, including attitudes to subject areas and subject choice; the effect of the portrayal of males and females in text books; the influence of teacher and classroom language; effects of male and female teachers and role models and of different teaching methods and class arrangements; the impact of peer culture; cognitive style; assessment methods and their effects; and patterns of achievement in cohort or end-of-school examinations as well as in curriculum areas. The last four decades have seen some significant shifts of interest across the field of gender and learning: moving from debunking deficit assumptions of sex differences in the 1970s, through a broad concern with girl-friendly and inclusive approaches in the 1980s, to a new kind of concern with boys' learning in the 1990s.

The article begins with a snapshot of shifts in thinking about gender and learning and a brief comment on terms and concepts. This provides background to a mapping of key themes and dilemmas addressed in research on gender and learning, particularly following the influence of feminist and equal-opportunity reforms in many education systems from the 1970s onward.

Gender Compared to Sex Differences

The term gender itself is used in a variety of ways, and has been the subject of much debate. In general, the term gender signals an attention to the socially formed nature of male and female identities, relationships, and orientations rather than seeing these as simply inherent or biological differences. This contrasts with earlier uses of the term sex to denote differences between males and females, which often assumed such differences to be a fixed, empirical, and innate phenomenon. From the late 1970s, gender began to replace sex as the preferred descriptor of male/female identity differences, and this is seen in a shift from a focus on sex differences in learning to a focus on gender and learning.

In the sex-differences mode, researchers tended to assume that the category of sex was stable, and research was concerned to investigate its effects. In the gender-research approach, research was looking to investigate how patterns of differentiation were produced, and, in the case of learning, how practices could be changed to produce more equal outcomes. With this latter approach, learning is viewed as an outcome of the social experiences in and out of schools to which young people are exposed. Gender was differentiated from biological sex, and was used to describe differences in what students liked and did not like, what skills and knowledge they found easy and what they found difficult. If girls did not progress as well in science, for example, the explanation might be found in their preschool play with dolls rather than mechanical objects; similarly, boys' weaker literacy skills were attributed to less-early-years involvement in group and language-based play. Or it might be the result of in-school social influences, such as particular types of teaching and assessment practices that are discussed below.

Initially, in many public and policy contexts, gender was regarded as a term denoting a rather radical perspective, a code for feminist approach. Sex remained the preferred, more familiar term. However, this view of the terms has shifted markedly in the last three decades in the English-speaking world. Many official sources now label their formal policy and data categories as gender rather than sex. Simultaneously, as research on gender has continued to develop, much of it no longer takes such a strong social-constructionist position about the desires and orientations girls and boys develop in the preschool years and beyond. A range of different research traditions, from brain researchers to cultural studies practitioners, now understand human differences and developments as arising out of interactions between biological and social. On the one hand, biology and drives are seen as producing some predispositions in individuals and, on the other, social, educational, and familial environments are seen as driving how and whether these dispositions are developed (including biologically) or turned into behaviors, preferences, and outcomes. Individuals are not seen as a *tabula rasa* upon which social messages are neatly inscribed. Nevertheless, the social environment is seen as a key formative shaper of individual identities and learning outcomes because of the way it interacts with and develops inherent biological characteristics. The implication for school learning remains one that emphasizes social arrangements, in and out of school. To see gender as an important element in how learning takes place and in what learning occurs, requires attention to experiences and values developed and conveyed in families and the broader society, as well as attention to what is said and conveyed in a classroom.

In summary, since the late 1970s, there has been an explosion of research on the social construction of gender and an accompanying recognition of the importance of gender in relation to learning. This, in turn, has contributed to changes in conceptions of learning that have expanded beyond models or measures of individual cognition to include a strong focus on the sociocultural processes and contexts shaping learning. This research on learning also shows the influence of ideas coming from the new sociology of education, particularly notions such as the hidden curriculum, which drew attention to the powerful knowledge and know-how that was not part of the official syllabus and classroom program but which was a vital part of students' overall learning.

An additional point to emphasize here is that research on gender and learning is not only concerned with how gender influences learning, but also with how school learning influences gender. This is both in terms of individuals' developing sense of who they are, and what potential they have (or lack), and in terms of broader patterns of outcomes for men and women in the world. A further point is that although the definition of terms offered here explains some broad differences in how sex-differences research and gender-and-learning research have been oriented, the use of these terms is not invariable or mutually exclusive. A lot of sex-differences research still continues, and large-scale national and international testing, such as the Organization for Economic Cooperation and Development (OECD)'s Programme of International Student Assessment (PISA), continues to routinely monitor differences by sex or gender, as well as by the intersection of such differences with other social variables, such as level of parental education, country of birth, and numerous proxies for socioeconomic status.

Shifts in Focus of Work on Gender and Learning

Gender and learning became an issue for education as much because of social developments and new expectations regarding the roles of women and girls outside education research fields, as from developments within these fields. For example, the tendency for girls not to continue with mathematics and science and to do less well in some subjects had been known for some time, but to some extent was taken simply as natural. It was when different expectations about women's social outcomes were raised from the 1970s onward that researchers began to give serious attention to whether such outcomes were, in part at least, the result of how schools and teaching were organized, and that these arrangements and practices could be changed.

Initially, in its translation into school policies and practices, gender was predominantly addressed as an issue that affected girls (Yates, 1998), and in reality much discussion and policy was directed to girls rather than to gender or gender relations. The new problem was understood to be why are girls not doing as well as boys? The challenge was to expose and critique what had been taken for granted as the normal state of affairs, and to show that differences in learning expectations, opportunities, and outcomes that systematically disadvantaged one gender group were unacceptable.

Research on gender and learning initially took two main forms: exposing flaws in previous research that had seemed to prove the innate inferiority of girls compared with boys, and identifying practices in schools where girls might be given different opportunities and messages than boys (AAUW, 1992). Before the 1970s, for example, it was common for the higher achievement and retention of boys in mathematics compared with girls to be attributed to innate differences, in particular to differences in spatial cognition, with boys on average judged to be naturally more adept at this than girls. A wave of influential feminist-based research in the following decade systematically reexamined this earlier work, exposing flaws in its design and arguments and encouraging greater participation of girls in traditionally male learning domains (e.g., Kelly, 1981; Fennema and Leder, 1990; Friedman, 1995). Research on the different ways schools conveyed implicitly different messages to girls about their potential included work on language and images in textbooks and work on teachers' different kinds of interactions with male and female students, as well as peer interactions.

One example of such research investigated how children responded to teacher feedback and found this shaped the learning and sense of competence of both girls and boys. Wood (1998) reported that while boys often received negative feedback from mathematics teachers, this was usually directed at their lack of attentiveness rather than their mathematical ability. When boys received positive feedback, it was likely to be in terms of their intellectual competence. In contrast, while girls tended not to receive a lot of negative feedback, any such responses were likely to be directed to their lack of ability. Thus "for boys criticism is common ... and it does not reflect upon their competence.... Because negative feedback is rare for girls, when a girl does receive it, it forms a notable event and is likely to convey the idea, to herself and her peers, that she is not very good at the subject" (Wood, 1998: 287).

Another influential body of work examined the hidden or implicit but powerful expectations teachers held about what kind of students were the right kind of learners. Valerie Walkerdine's studies of early childhood and primary-school classrooms showed some of the complex and subtle ways in which teachers' beliefs about what good learning looked like were gendered, with boys typically regarded as potentially more disruptive in the classroom but also more risk taking and independent as learners, and girls as more cooperative and diligent but less likely to be exceptional or brilliant students (Walkerdine, 1989). Walkerdine argued that conceptions of learning and cognitive development were themselves deeply gendered and that the ideal rational learner was implicitly masculine.

In other work, a wave of interest in women's ways of knowing or women's voice sought to identify specific qualities in women and girls' learning and to devise pedagogies and forms of curriculum that would promote the realization of these qualities. The work of Carol Gilligan was particularly influential. Gilligan's (1982) revisionist account of Kohlberg's framework of moral reasoning argued that hierarchies of intellectual development had been founded on male styles of reasoning, particularly valuing abstraction and judgment. She laid out ways in which connectedness, or reasoning that included attention to human effects, can be seen not simply as a lower stage of the first hierarchy, but as a different hierarchy altogether with similar stages of complexity. The well-known American study, *Women's Ways of Knowing* (Belenky et al., 1986), influenced by Gilligan's work, argued that women had been silenced by traditional educational processes and that they were more likely to find their own voice and develop as learners when the learning is connected. This occurs when learning is connected to first-hand experience, values question posing, learning in context, and relative, context-specific truth. Such an orientation is contrasted to traditional masculine ways of learning that value objectivity, abstraction, and general principles. Considerable debate and further research followed from these attempts to identify female and male learning style, particularly in terms of whether these paid sufficient attention to differences within the category of girls, especially in relation to race and social-class differences.

By the mid-1990s, a new focus of gender research and policymaking began to emerge – the issue of boys and their learning preferences and needs (Weaver-Hightower, 2003). In part, this was motivated by concern about boys who were dropping out of school, and in part by a perception that there had been a lot of reform attention given to girls but little to boys. Some of this work took a similar form to the earlier gender-based research on girls, focusing on the disadvantaging effects of teaching methods. In the case of boys, targets included the growing need for higher levels of language skills in all subjects, and assessment practices – essay-based compared with short-answer testing – and how these interacted with patterns of achievement for boys (Epstein et al., 1998). Other research tended more toward a sex-differences approach, in emphasizing the strength of different innate drives, and questioning how well schools dealt with these. Within the boy turn in research on gender, there are some sharp disagreements about directions for boys and recommended school practices. But all the research broadly falls within a focus on gender as defined earlier in this article, because it all pays some attention to the interaction between social arrangements inside and outside schools, and the ways these produce orientations and outcomes in relation to schooling for a particular group.

The research on boys and learning is often crudely divided into pro- and anti-feminist work. Pro-feminist work rejects the idea that boys rather than girls are disadvantaged by school practices, and sees the need for attention to both. It sees its approach as building on the earlier work on girls and gender, and often focuses on the way gender (learned ways of being masculine) disadvantages boys' learning and needs to be changed. Anti-feminist approaches tend to argue that boys have replaced girls as the new disadvantaged group, and to see boys' gendered preferences as a given with which schools should work, rather than as socially constructed or sometimes detrimental. Weaver-Hightower (2003) provides a good overview of the different lines of work in this area.

Gender-Equity Reforms and Reviews

During the 1990s, after about two decades of deliberate gender-equity reform, many national governments and international agencies commissioned major studies of gender and school participation and performance (e.g., Arnot *et al.*, 1999). While there were national differences, one overwhelming finding from much of this overview research was that girls' participation and retention had increased, and that in many subject areas the average girl was performing at a higher level than the average boy. At the same time, this research drew attention to the question of who actually was the average girl or boy, and what factors other than gender were influencing school learning and educational outcomes. For example, although there were some average differences in outcomes between girls as a group and boys as a group, these were usually smaller differences than differences within the category of girls or within the category of boys, particularly in relation to socioeconomic status or social class. As noted above, the OECD's PISA continues to produce its own comparative data on these issues, showing some of the relative effects of different variables on school achievement.

The various national reviews of the effects of large-scale policy attention to gender in schooling have shown that changes in school teaching and assessment practices do produce different patterns of outcomes in relation to gender. That is, they have confirmed the understanding that changes in education practices – school teaching, learning, and assessment – are able to influence patterns of outcomes by gender. This, in turn, raises some questions that are at issue in contemporary debates about boys. Should the mandate of schooling be to produce identical patterns of outcomes for girls and boys (e.g., regardless of how hard they work)? Should teachers and teaching approaches proceed on the assumption of gender-based differences in learning preferences and styles? Should there be common or differentiated expectations of learning? How far should forms of assessment be modified to produce gender-neutral outcomes?

For example, it is generally agreed that on average boys and girls develop at different rates in the early and primary years (for discussion of this issue see MacNaughton, 2003), but the degree to which school-starting age and national age-based or year-based testing should take

account of that continues to be in some dispute in different policy settings. Similarly, a range of studies have found that boys are overrepresented in both remedial and gifted streams, where these exist, and in named learning difficulties categories, such as attention-deficit disorder, but there is debate on the extent to which social practices and assumptions in relation to gender produce such results and need to be changed.

Single Sex and Coeducation and Learning

The heightened interest in learning and achievement patterns by gender, and the recognition that school and classroom arrangements are important, has produced a continuing interest in the impact of single sex compared with coeducational arrangements. A very large number of studies have been conducted on this topic and it continues to prompt considerable scholarly, policy, and community attention (Salomone, 2003). The topic itself is an interesting case of the multifaceted way in which gender and learning come together, since whether or not a school or a classroom is girls-only or boys-only is only one of a number of important elements of the gender and learning environment, which includes the school culture overall, curriculum choices and supports, the expectations of teachers, and the expectations of students themselves and their parents. It is not surprising, then, that empirical data comparing the results of single sex and coeducation have often not been consistent between different studies or over time. However, they do show small overall indications that, controlling for other aspects of school-intake difference, single-sex groupings may have a slightly beneficial effect on girls' achievement and self-esteem and on their likelihood of choosing masculine subjects; and, further, that coeducational groupings may have a slightly positive effect on boys' achievement.

However, overall patterns here are of less significance than how particular arrangements may affect specific groups of girls or boys, or particular purposes. Some single-sex arrangements have been put in place almost as a form of action research. These include a range of experimentation with single-sex classes to encourage greater participation in certain subject areas, such as single-sex classes for girls in for mathematics in the middle years; as well as attempts to establish small alternative single-sex schools for students who are at risk, especially boys.

Gender in Interaction with Other Factors

Much research has taken place on gendered preferences and achievement in different school subjects. Such research often attends to the ways in which particular subjects themselves have gendered identities (e.g., mathematics as male, English as female) that produce different patterns of take-up and achievement. But gender is not a single or simple phenomenon, and patterns of takeup are strongly influenced by socioeconomic and ethnic backgrounds of students as well as by expectations and practices of different kinds of schools. How gender intersects with social-class background leads to well-documented differences in patterns of achievement. Based on achievement data, it would appear that the higher their socioeconomic status, the fewer disadvantages girls experience in mathematics and science and the fewer disadvantages boys experience in English. Gender relativities in learning outcomes are thus weakest – but not absent – among those with the greatest material and cultural advantages (Teese and Polesel, 2003).

Current and Emerging Issues

The kinds of monitoring and comparisons involving gender are now well established in most national systems (at least those covered by the OECD) and are likely to continue. If obvious disparities are evident, these generate a new wave of research attention to that subject area, or to parts of the education system. In recent years, for example, new technologies and particularly the more widespread use of computers have been a significant issue for learning in schools and for work opportunities beyond schools. This has produced a strong focus on gendered take-up and preferences within this work, often mirroring the kinds of work that took place earlier in relation to mathematics and science, including attention to role models, the way the subject is portrayed culturally, and in schools, peer attitudes, and assessment practices.

Within broader policy directions, the increasing emphasis on international benchmarking, school effectiveness, and more intense testing commonly includes gender as a basic category for comparison, yet often works to downplay the range of the social and identity factors that students bring into classrooms. Its emphasis tends to be on effective techniques for teaching or managing school systems, rather than social interactions within schooling and the classroom.

In terms of a global perspective, a lot of work on gender has focused on issues of access to schooling or to levels and programs within schooling systems. This research has received new impetus with the UN Millennium Development Goals, which included a target of eliminating gender disparity in primary and secondary education, preferably by 2005, and to all levels of education no later than 2015. The goals and targets here give continued attention to the ongoing strong interaction between schooling and social expectations and practices around gender. Two areas that are subject to renewed attention as part of this work are also areas of heightened concern in developed countries: bullying and sexual harassment as a hidden component of school learning; and the legitimacy or illegitimacy of promoting gender-differentiated expectations via the curriculum, including religious framing of education.

A focus on gender and learning has produced some ongoing attention to differences in what students bring to schooling as part of the learning environment, and some changing expectations of the responsibilities of schooling to acknowledge, support, or attempt to modify these. It has also produced a continuing attention to patterns of subject choice, retention, and success and failure in schooling as something that are not simply a given or produced by what students bring to the task, but in part at least an effect of what schools and teachers do, an effect of how learning environments operate for different kinds of students. The framing of research on gender and learning also reflects political differences in the questions and assumptions researchers bring to education and its relation to broader social forms, as well as changing social expectations about standards and outcomes for education for both women and men in the twenty-first century.

Bibliography

AAUW (American Association of University Women) (1992). *How Schools Short Change Girls.* New York: Marlowe.

Arnot, M., David, M., and Weiner, G. (1999). *Closing the Gender Gap: Postwar Education and Social Change.* Cambridge: Polity Press.

Belenky, M. F., Clinchy, B. M., Goldberger, N. R., and Tarule, J. M. (1986). *Women's Ways of Knowing: The Development of Self, Voice and Mind.* New York: Basic Books.

Epstein, D., Elwood, J., Hey, V., and Maw, J. (eds.) (1998). *Failing Boys? Issues in Gender and Achievement.* Buckingham, PA: Open University Press.

Fennema, E. and Leder, G. (eds.) (1990). *Mathematics and Gender.* New York: Teachers College Press.

Friedman, L. (1995). The space factor in mathematics: Gender differences. *Review of Education Research* **65**(1), 22–50.

Gilligan, C. (1982). *In a Different Voice: Psychological Theory and Women's Development.* Cambridge: Harvard University Press.

Kelly, A. (ed.) (1981). *The Missing Half: Girls and Science Education.* Manchester: Manchester University Press.

MacNaughton, G. (2003). *Shaping Early Childhood: Learners, Curriculum and Contexts.* Maidenhead: Open University Press.

Salomone, R. (2003). *Same, Different, Equal: Rethinking Single-Sex Schooling.* New Haven, CT: Yale University Press.

Teese, R. and Polesel, J. (2003). *Undemocratic Schooling: Equity and Quality in Mass Secondary Education in Australia.* Melbourne: Melbourne University Press.

Walkerdine, V. and Girls and Mathematics Unit Institute of Education (1989). *Counting Girls Out.* London: Virago.

Weaver-Hightower, M. (2003). The "boy turn" in research on gender and education. *Review of Education Research* **73**(4), 471–498.

Wood, D. (1998). *How Children Think and Learn,* 2nd edn. Oxford: Blackwell.

Yates, L. (1998). Constructing and deconstructing 'girls' as a category of concern. In MacKinnon, A., Elgvist-Saltzman, A., and Prentice, A. (eds.) *Education into the 21st Century: Dangerous Terrain for Women,* pp 155–167. London: Falmer.

Further Reading

Aikman, S. and Unterhalter, E. (eds.) (2005). *Beyond Access: Transforming Policy and Practice for Gender Equality in Education.* Oxford: Oxfam Publishers.

Berge, B-M. and Ve, H. (2000). *Action Research for Gender Equity.* Maidenhead: Open University Press.

Connell, R. W. (2002). *Gender.* Cambridge: Polity Press.

Erskine, S. W. (ed.) (1999). *Gender Issues in International Educations: Beyond Policy and Practice.* New York: Falmer.

Gilligan, C. (1982). *In a Different Voice: Psychological Theory and Women's Development.* Cambridge: Harvard University Press.

Mael, F. A. (1998). Single-sex and coeducational schooling: Relationships to socioemotional and academic development. *Review of Educational Research* **68**(2), 101–129.

OECD (Organisation for Economic Co-Operation and Development) (2008). *PISA Database 2006.* http://pisa2006.acer.edu.au/interactive.php (accessed August 2009).

United Nations (2000). *Millennium Goals: Goal 3, Promote Gender Equality and Empower Women.* http://www.un.org/millenniumgoals/gender.shtml (accessed August 2009).

Walkerdine, V. (1988). *The Mastery of Reason: Cognitive Development and the Production of Rationality.* London: Routledge.

Organizational Learning

P-E Ellström, Linköping University, Linköping, Sweden

Although organizational learning has been a subject of research within management and organizational studies at least since the early 1960s, interest in this concept has grown considerably since the late 1980s. Important driving forces for this development have been the globalization and growing corporate competition, and thereby, an increasing interest in finding alternatives to established forms of organization. This development was mirrored not least in the movement to abandon traditional Tayloristic and bureaucratic models of work organization in favor of allegedly more flexible and integrated work systems, that is, what has been characterized as high-commitment work systems. The performance of these types of new work systems is assumed to critically depend on their capacity to create favorable conditions for organizational learning.

Today the concept of organizational learning has become established not only within economic and management disciplines, but also within behavioral and social science disciplines such as psychology, education, and sociology. Considering empirical research on organizational learning, it is clear that there is and has been a predominance of studies within private companies. This is the case in spite of the fact that many of the early studies by researchers such as Argyris, Cyert, and March were also carried out in governmental agencies and educational institutions. However, over the last decade there has been an increase in the number of studies of organizational learning in, for example, schools, military organizations, public administration, political organizations, and unions. Considering education specifically, the interest in organizational learning is presently clearly visible in at least three areas of educational research: school development and innovative schools, human resource development (HRD), and workplace learning.

The Field of Organizational Learning

The field of organizational learning is characterized by an increasing diversity and specialization. In order to map key topics within the field of organizational learning, Easterby-Smith and Lyles (2003) distinguish between four subfields within the general field of organizational learning: organizational learning, the learning organization, organizational knowledge, and knowledge management. The first of these four subfields, organizational learning, refers to descriptive and explanatory studies of learning processes of and within organizations. That is, studies of organizational learning largely from an academic knowledge interest, aiming at an understanding and critique of what is.

In contrast to this, the learning organization subfield is characterized by more practical and normative knowledge interests. A learning organization is viewed as an ideal type of organization (or a vision of an organization), which has the capacity not only to facilitate the learning of its members, but also to transform this learning into continuous organizational renewal. The literature within this subfield focuses on how to create and improve the learning capacity of an organization through different types of intervention. One of the most well-known contributions to this subfield is the book on learning organizations by Peter Senge in 1990.

Turning to the remaining two subfields, the subfield called organizational knowledge refers to attempts to understand the nature of knowledge and processes of knowledge production within and between organizations. Within this subfield, there are studies of not only what has become known as knowledge work, but also studies of knowledge creation and the sharing and integration of organizational knowledge and competence. A key contribution to this subfield is the book by Nonaka and Takeuchi (1995) on knowledge creation through transformations of tacit and explicit knowledge. The subfield of knowledge management has a focus on issues related to the use of information and communication technology (ICT) to facilitate and support the acquisition, storage, sharing, retrieval, and utilization of knowledge in order to improve organizational performance.

As underlined by Easterby-Smith and Lyles (2003), it is not possible to make clearcut distinctions between these four subfields of organizational learning. For example, a critical study of processes of organizational learning within an alleged learning organization would belong to the subfield of organizational learning. Furthermore, studies of organizational learning interventions could belong both to the subfield of organizational learning and that of the learning organization depending on which knowledge interest predominates. As will be clear in the next section, it is also difficult to make clear-cut distinctions between the two subfields of organizational learning and organizational knowledge. In fact, in recent years, these two subfields have tended to merge.

Dimensions of Organizational Learning

In spite of the large number of studies on organizational learning that have been published during recent years, there is little consensus on how to define the concept of organizational learning. It is also, to say the least, a very difficult task to try to formulate a definition that could adequately cover the many meanings of organizational learning that can be found in the literature. On a general level, however, it is possible to distinguish a number of dimensions along which many definitions vary. In the text below, three such dimensions are dealt with.

Levels of Analysis

A first dimension is what is considered as the proper level of analysis, and thus, as the locus of learning. Many definitions and studies of organizational learning focus on an individual level of analysis, that is, on the learning by individuals in an organizational context (Huber, 1991; Simon, 1991). A main argument behind this approach is that basic concepts in the literature on organizational learning, for example, the concept of memory, only apply to individual subjects. In line with this, it is assumed that organizational learning is mediated through individual learning, conceived as an interplay between processes of cognition and action. Furthermore, organizational learning is assumed to imply individual learning, but not vice versa. Thus, individual learning is viewed as a necessary, but not sufficient condition for organizational learning. In relation to this view, questions arise concerning what it means when an organization learns, and how to understand the links between individual and organizational learning.

Other definitions of organizational learning focus on a collective subject, that is, on the group (the team) or the organization as the locus of learning. The basic assumption is that the group or the organization is more than a collection of individuals, and thus, that learning at a collective level is different from and not only the sum of each individual's learning. For example, Senge (1990), in his book on the learning organization, argues that the team is the fundamental level of learning in an organization. It is typically argued that the learning process of a group closely parallels that of an individual and that it can be described as cycles of cognition, action, feedback, and reflection (Edmondson, 2002).

When it comes to studies that focus on the organization as the proper level of learning, the notion of learning is typically used in a more metaphorical sense. That is, groups or organizations are assumed to learn in a way analogous to individual learning, and concepts found in theories of individual learning are extended to the group or organizational level (Hedberg, 1981). This approach has raised criticism of anthropomorphism. However, some would argue that this criticism is irrelevant, and that the notion of learning should be understood as something qualitatively different when applied to a collective entity like an organization compared to individuals. More specifically, it has been argued that organizational

learning should be interpreted from a cultural rather than from a cognitive perspective, and that the notion of organizational culture would be useful for conceptualizing the collective aspects of organizational learning, and thereby, for understanding learning at an organizational level (Cook and Yanow, 1993). Accordingly, learning is assumed to be embedded in collective assumptions and interpretative systems, routines, technologies, and cultural practices. This view comes close to what below is called a sociocultural approach to organizational learning.

A fourth level of analysis is the level of inter-organizational learning. Much research on organizational learning has concerned learning within or of organizations, where the organization has often been treated as a self-contained system with fixed boundaries that operates to a large extent independently of other organizations in the environment. Today, there is a growing interest in new forms of organization at an inter-organizational level. Networks, clusters, innovation systems, and partnerships are a few such examples. Other examples include multinational corporations and joint ventures. A number of new issues of organizational learning are raised at this level of analysis, for example, issues concerning learning and innovation, or learning under conditions of competition and cooperation. At the same time, many of the issues dealt with above are also highly relevant to this level of analysis. Presently, there are few systematic studies of learning processes and outcomes at an inter-organizational level of learning.

Although there are a lot of studies that treat organizational learning as a process that should be analyzed and studied on one or the other of the four different system levels distinguished above, there are also studies that emphasize organizational learning as an interplay between different system levels or as a multilevel process. The latter position is taken, for example, by Crossan *et al.* (1999) in an article that emphasizes that a theory of organizational learning needs to consider the individual, group, and organizational levels. The latter authors also develop a framework including four subprocesses of organizational learning that link the individual, group, and organizational levels.

Organizational Learning as Change and/or Stability

According to many definitions, organizational learning is defined as an experienced-based process of change. It is sometimes also stated or implied that organizational learning means improvements of the actions or the performance of the learning subject, whether this is an individual, a group, or an organization. However, this kind of definition raises a number of issues that need to be addressed. First, observations of changes and adaptations to environmental events do not automatically mean that these changes are the result of a learning process. On the contrary, changes in actions and improved performance may occur for a number of reasons that have little or nothing to do with learning, for example, situational factors that trigger certain changes in behavior. Second, learning processes are not always, for a number of reasons, mirrored in observable behavior. There may, for example, be situational factors such as a lack of sufficient resources or adequate tools that constrain behavior. In line with this, some scholars have defined organizational learning in terms of changes in potential behaviors rather than actual behaviors (Huber, 1991).

Third, observed changes in action may not be positively related to the performance of the individual, the group, or the organization. On the contrary, we may, in some instances, talk about negative learning in the sense that the learning outcomes may for some reason be undesirable, or in fact, negatively related to performance. That might happen if, for example, the members of a team acquire a form of learned helplessness and an accompanying lack of self-confidence. Thus, the learning process may under some conditions unintentionally result in a deterioration of individual or organizational performance. Furthermore, learning processes, whether they result in positive or negative outcomes from a performance perspective, are in many cases neither conscious nor intentional. Thus, processes of learning, change, and improvement in performance may be totally different processes that need to be clearly distinguished both conceptually and empirically.

While recognizing that learning and change may be two different processes, many researchers have defined levels of learning in terms of the character of the individual and/or organizational changes that are implied by the concept of learning. For this purpose, distinctions have been made between: (a) changes that occur within a given framework, for example, within a given set of beliefs or values or within a given organizational structure or situation, and (b) changes that represent a break with and something that goes beyond the given (Ellström, 2001). Perhaps the most well-known version of this distinction is the one made by Argyris and Schön (1978) between single-loop and double-loop learning. More recently, related and in some respects parallel distinctions have been proposed between first- and second-order learning; adaptive (reproductive) and developmental (innovative) learning; incremental and radical learning. While the former type of learning in each pair has a focus on improving or refining existing procedures or capabilities, the latter type of learning has a focus on the more radical change of institutionalized practices and the development of new capabilities.

Learning as refinement of existing structures and processes may be viewed as a way of reproducing or stabilizing an organization or a social system over time. In a sense, then, reproduction and change (transformation) of a social system may be viewed as two sides of the same coin. In line with this, arguments have been raised to the effect that it is important to find a balance between radical and incremental change or between the exploration of new alternatives and the exploitation of existing knowledge and technologies, and that the returns to fast learning and change are not all positive (March, 1991). Others would take a further step, and argue – from a cultural perspective – that organizational learning is not just about change, but also about organizational stability and the maintenance and preservation of an organization's activities and cultural practices (Cook and Yanow, 1993). Thus, organizational learning could be seen as a means for cultural reproduction as well as a means for transformation.

Content and Processes of Organizational Learning

The third dimension distinguished here concerns the content and processes of organizational learning. While content refers to what is learned (e.g., knowledge), the process of learning refers to how learning takes place. For present purposes, the following three main approaches may be distinguished with respect to the content (outcomes) and processes of organizational learning: the cognitive-behavioral approach, the sociocultural approach, and the knowledge-creating approach (cf. Paavola et al., 2004).

The cognitive–behavioral approach – an approach strongly anchored in the work of James March and his associates (e.g., March, 1991; March and Olsen, 1976) – has had a strong influence on theory and research on organizational learning for several decades. A basic assumption underlying this approach is that organizational learning is about the development and change of routines through the accumulation of experience. The key term routine includes rules, norms, procedures, strategies, and technologies that are assumed to guide actual behavior in and of organizations and their subunits. In some studies, the notion of routine is treated as explicitly formulated prescriptions. Other studies apply a broader definition and view routines as distributed procedural knowledge (knowing-how), skills, or habits. Still others broaden the view of the products of organizational learning to also include declarative knowledge (knowing-that) and mental models at the individual level, and at the organizational level interpretative systems or shared mental models and frameworks (Kim, 1993; Hedberg, 1981). Organizational learning is conceived of as a process where routines, beliefs, and actions adapt incrementally to past experience through feedback from organizational actions and their outcomes in relation to targets. Specifically, March and Olsen (1976) depict organizational learning as a cycle comprising four stages, including individual beliefs, individual action, organizational action, and environmental outcomes (responses).

The sociocultural (or situated) approach to organizational learning focuses on culture as a core concept. Rather than conceiving learning as a process of knowledge acquisition through experienced-based changes in cognition or action, there is a focus on learning as participation in work practices and activities. Furthermore, what is learned is assumed to be in a fundamental sense connected to the conditions under which it is learned, that is, it is in this sense situated. In line with this, a main tenet is that learning cannot be separated from working and other social practices where it is assumed to take place or be used (Brown and Duguid, 1991). On the contrary, learning is defined as a matter of participation in practices, and indeed, as an aspect of "legitimate peripheral participation" in "communities of practice" (Lave and Wenger, 1991). In line with this focus on participation, learning about practice is less central than learning to become a practitioner. Thus, processes of identity formation are viewed as important aspects of learning. Furthermore, learning and processes or activities (knowing) rather than content or products (knowledge) are emphasized. The sociocultural approach has received considerable attention in recent years as an alternative to the cognitive–behavioral approach, which has been criticized for a decontextualized view of knowledge, and for separating individual and organizational learning. However, critics of the sociocultural approach have, to some extent, reversed these arguments. Thus, it has been criticized for a tendency to reduce learning to an aspect of participation, thereby making it impossible to analytically separate learning and other organizational processes.

The knowledge-creating approach is based on the view that the production, transformation, and utilization of knowledge are fundamental for understanding organizational learning (Paavola et al., 2004). Learning is viewed as an interplay between intra- and inter-individual (social) processes of knowledge creation. The content of learning is knowledge or competence and mechanisms (processes) of learning are typically conceptualized as cyclical processes of problem-solving and knowledge transformation. Perhaps the most well-known framework within this approach is the model proposed by Nonaka and Takeuchi (1995). This model assumes that knowledge creation could be understood as a cyclical process of knowledge conversion based on the interaction between tacit and explicit knowledge. Four modes of knowledge conversion are distinguished: socialization, externalization, combination, and internalization. Another example of a model within this approach is the model of expansive (innovative) learning proposed by Engeström (1999). This model, based on activity theory, views learning as a cycle of epistemic or learning actions starting with the questioning of prevailing practices in an organization. The learning cycle proceeds through an analysis of the existing situation and the creation, testing, and implementation of a conceptual model of a new idea that is assumed to explain and provide a solution to the problematic situation that initiated the learning process. This model has also been used as an intervention method for facilitating innovative learning in organizations. A third example is the knowledge evolution cycle proposed by Zollo and Winter (2002) based on the evolutionary process of variation, selection, replication, and retention. Underlying this model is a distinction between three learning mechanisms called experience accumulation, knowledge articulation, and knowledge codification.

Conditions and Practices of Organizational Learning

Although organizational learning is sometimes viewed as a natural, continuous process of adaptation in response to internal or external events – processes that may not be conscious or intentional – there is much evidence that indicates that processes of learning are easily interrupted by different kinds of barriers or constraining factors. A conclusion drawn from such observations is that organizational learning needs to be consciously facilitated and supported by consciously planned interventions. Thus, it is assumed that organizations need to learn to learn. This could mean to learn to carry out processes of deliberative inquiry and reflection, and thereby, develop new routines, new knowledge, or new ways of handling a certain organizational problem or task. In accordance with such an interventionist view of organizational learning, a wide range of organizational learning interventions have been developed based on different conceptions of learning. Examples of organizational learning interventions include: project-based learning and action learning interventions based on notions of reflective practice; process consultation; dialogue meetings; open space technology; and different types of learning laboratories (Dierks et al., 2001; Easterby-Smith and Lyles, 2003).

Most organizational learning interventions are, implicitly or explicitly, based on assumptions concerning factors that are likely to constrain or facilitate organizational learning. The purpose of the intervention is of course to attempt to create favorable conditions for learning. What then, does available research tell us about conditions for organizational learning? What factors are assumed to constrain or facilitate learning? One answer to this question is the influential theoretical model proposed by March and Olsen (1976). These authors distinguish between different types of interruptions or blockages that result in restricted or incomplete learning cycles. Others distinguish between conditions related to structural factors, subjective and cultural factors, and factors related to leadership. Among structural factors, many writers underline the importance of the characteristics of the tasks that the organization is attempting to handle (e.g., task complexity and frequency). Other studies emphasize that centralized and hierarchical structures, as well as too high a degree of formalization and standardization of work processes, are likely to impede learning; in particular, when such structural conditions are combined with limited opportunities for organizational members to participate in organizational decision making. However, there are radically different views concerning the meaning and consequences of these factors for organizational learning.

Although many organizations are structured by gender, there are a few studies of gender aspects in relation to organizational learning. Rather, organizational learning has been studied as a gender-neutral process. This is the case in spite of the significance of gender in relation to other organizational processes. Considering this research, it is quite likely that organizational demographics with respect to gender – as well as in other respects – would be significant for processes of organizational learning. For example, organizations dominated by men could be expected to provide different conditions for learning compared to organizations dominated by women (Berthoin Antal *et al.*, 2001).

It is also possible to identify a number of factors with respect to subjective and cultural issues. In the analyses proposed by Argyris and Schön (1978), and in later studies, so-called defensive routines developed by individuals for protection from threatening situations are viewed as major obstacles to learning. Many writers also focus on anxiety and fear as barriers to organizational learning, and emphasize the need to create psychological safety and trust in order to counterbalance the feelings of threat and anxiety that may be provoked by organizational learning interventions. A factor that many assume is likely to facilitate learning is the extent to which the organizational culture encourages questioning and critical reflection on what is taking place in the organization. Other characteristics of an organizational culture that are considered by many as supportive of learning would include issue orientation, openness, trust, and norms that emphasize initiative and risk-taking, tolerance toward disparate views, and tolerance for admitting errors. Although conflict is assumed by some to be an obstacle to learning, many researchers would agree on the importance of conflicts as driving forces for organizational learning. An equally important factor is how conflicts are handled and resolved as part of an organizational learning process.

A recurrent issue in the literature on organizational learning is the importance of leadership as a condition for organizational learning and, conversely, the lack of adequate leadership support as an obstacle to organizational learning. Leadership support for organizational learning includes the design of an enabling learning environment in the organization, that is, an environment which has many of the structural and cultural features mentioned above. Other important leadership tasks would include the provision of organizational resources (e.g., time) for learning and the facilitation of learning on the part of organizational members both individually and collectively, for example, by asking challenging questions, stimulating intellectual curiosity, and acting as a coach or mentor (Sadler, 2001).

Power and Politics

As observed by many writers on organizational learning, issues of power and politics in relation to organizational learning have, to a large extent, been neglected in the past. This is somewhat astonishing considering that power and politics for quite a long time have been recognized as important areas within the more general field of organizational studies. The relative neglect of these issues within the field of organizational learning is also astonishing, given that many writers in this field emphasize the importance of conflicts and contradictions as essential for learning in organizations.

However, the lack of emphasis on power and politics is not uniform across the field of organizational learning. In particular, many writers, from what was previously described as a sociocultural approach and a knowledge-creating approach to organizational learning, emphasize the importance of power relations for understanding organizational learning. In line with the practice orientation of these approaches, and the view of learning as integral to everyday work practices in organizations, it is emphasized that learning practices are embedded in and are enabled or constrained within relations of power (Contu and Willmott, 2003). Consistent with this position, it has also been argued that access (or lack of access) to specific learning practices, as well as the division of labor, and thereby, available opportunities for learning, is shaped by prevailing relations of power in the organization and in society at large. The issue, then, becomes one about who participates and who is not allowed to participate in specific learning practices. Another important issue from a political perspective concerns what is valued as knowledge, and whose knowledge and ideas are recognized in an organization. Power differences between different groups in an organization, for example, between different departments or between groups with different status may be assumed to influence whose learning is recognized and acted upon.

Other important issues that have been raised and debated from a political perspective on organizational learning relate to control and ideology in organizations. According to one position, organizational learning represents the ideology of particular power groups (e.g., the management of an organization, but also different groups of experts) and it is used to mask and legitimize the interests of these groups. In addition, organizational learning is seen as a mechanism and a methodology of control that aims to discipline members of an organization (Gherardi and Nicolini, 2001). Thus, according to this view, organizational learning is a practice for the management of meaning, and a soft means for the subjugation of employees. More specifically, the latter could mean increasing the legitimacy of the organization in the eyes of the employees as regards its goals, fundamental ideology, and power structure, and thereby, contributing to increased employee loyalty with and support for the goals and values of the business. Although there are a number of articles and books that deal with these and related issues, there is a notable lack of empirically substantiated knowledge concerning these matters.

Bibliography

Argyris, C. and Schön, D. A. (1978). *Organizational Learning: A Theory of Action Perspective*. Reading, MA: Addison-Wesley.

Berthoin Antal, A., Dierkes, M., Child, J., and Nonaka, I. (2001). Organizational learning and knowledge: Reflections on the dynamics of the field and challenges for the future. In Dierkes, M., Berthoin Antal, A., Child, J., and Nonaka, I. (eds.) *Handbook of Organizational Learning and Knowledge*, pp 921–939. Oxford: Oxford University Press.

Brown, J. S. and Duguid, P. (1991). Organizational learning and communities-of-practice: Toward a unified view of working, learning, and innovation. *Organization Science* **2**, 40–57.

Contu, A. and Willmott, H. (2003). Re-embedding situatedness: The importance of power relations in learning theory. *Organization Science* **14**, 283–296.

Cook, S. D. N. and Yanow, D. (1993). Culture and organizational learning. *Journal of Management Inquiry* **2**, 373–390.

Crossan, M., Lane, H., and White, R. (1999). An organizational learning framework: From intuition to institution. *Academy of Management Review* **24**, 522–537.

Dierks, M., Berthoin Antal, A., Child, J., and Nonaka, I. (eds.) (2001). *Handbook of Organizational Learning and Knowledge*. Oxford: Oxford University Press.

Easterby-Smith, M. and Lyles, M. A. (eds.) (2003). Introduction: Watersheds of organizational learning and knowledge management. In *The Blackwell Handbook of Organizational Learning and Knowledge Management*, pp 1–15. Malden, MA: Blackwell.

Easterby-Smith, M. and Lyles, M. A. (eds.) (2003). *The Blackwell Handbook of Organizational Learning and Knowledge Management*. Malden, MA: Blackwell.

Edmondson, A. C. (2002). The local and variegated nature of learning in organizations: A group-level perspective. *Organization Science* **2**, 128–146.

Ellström, P. E. (2001). Integrating learning and work: Problems and prospects. *Human Resource Development Quarterly*, **12**, 421–435.

Engeström, Y. (1999). Innovative learning in work teams: Analyzing cycles of knowledge creation in practice. In Engeström, Y.,

Miettinen, R., and Punamäki, R. L. (eds.) *Perspectives on Activity Theory*, pp 19–38. New York: Cambridge University Press.

Gherardi, S. and Nicolini, D. (2001). The sociological foundations of organizational learning. In Dierks, M., Berthoin Antal, A., Child, J., and Nonaka, I. (eds.) *Handbook of Organizational Learning and Knowledge*, pp 35–60. Oxford: Oxford University Press.

Hedberg, B. L. T. (1981). How organizations learn and unlearn. In Nystrom, P. C. and Starbuck, W. H. (eds.) *Handbook of Organizational Design. Vol 1. Adapting Organizations to Their Environments*, pp 3–27. Oxford: Oxford University Press.

Huber, G. P. (1991). Organizational learning: The contributing processes and the literatures. *Organization Science* **2**, 88–115.

Kim, D. H. (1993). The link between individual and organizational learning. *Sloan Management Review* **35**, 37–50.

Lave, J. and Wenger, E. (1991). *Situated Learning: Legitimate Peripheral Participation*. Cambridge: Cambridge University Press.

March, J. G. (1991). Exploration and exploitation in organizational learning. *Organization Science* **2**, 71–87.

March, J. G. and Olsen, J. P. (1976). Organizational learning and the ambiguity of the past. In March, J. G. and Olsen, J. P. (eds.) *Ambiguity and Choice in Organizations*, pp 54–68. Oslo: Universitetsforlaget.

Nonaka, I. and Takeuchi, H. (1995). *The Knowledge-Creating Company: How Japanese Companies Create the Dynamics of Innovation*. Oxford: Oxford University Press.

Paavola, S., Lipponen, L., and Hakkarinen, K. (2004). Models of innovative knowledge communities and three metaphors of learning. *Review of Educational Research* **74**, 557–576.

Sadler, P. (2001). Leadership and organizational learning. In Dierks, M., Berthoin Antal, A., Child, J., and Nonaka, I. (eds.) *Handbook of Organizational Learning and Knowledge*, pp 415–427. Oxford: Oxford University Press.

Senge, P. M. (1990). *The Fifth Discipline: The Art and Practice of the Learning Organization*. New York: Doubleday.

Simon, H. A. (1991). Bounded rationality and organizational learning. *Organization Science* **2**, 125–134.

Zollo, M. and Winter, S. G. (2002). Deliberate learning and the evolution of dynamic capabilities. *Organization Science* **13**, 339–351.

Further Reading

Antonacopoulou, E., Jarvis, P., Andersen, V., Elkjaer, B., and Hoyrup, S. (eds.) (2006). *Learning, Working, Living. Mapping the Terrain of Working Life Learning*. New York: Palgrave Macmillan.

Cohen, M. D. and Sproull, L. S. (1996). *Organizational Learning*. Thousand Oaks, CA: Sage.

Easterby-Smith, M., Araujo, L., and Burgoyne, J. (1999). *Organizational Learning and the Learning Organization. Developments in Theory and Practice*. Thousand Oaks, CA: Sage.

Leithwood, K. and Seashore, K. L. (eds.) (1999). *Organizational Learning in Schools*. Lisse, PA: Taylor and Francis.

March, J. G. (1999). *The Pursuit of Organizational Intelligence*. Malden, MA: Blackwell.

Marsick, V. J. and Watkins, K. E. (1999). *Facilitating Learning Organizations*. Aldershot: Gower.

Moingeon, B. and Edmondson, A. C. (eds.) (1996). *Organizational Learning and Competitive Advantage*. London: Sage.

The Adult Development of Cognition and Learning

E A L Stine-Morrow and J M Parisi, University of Illinois at Urbana–Champaign, Champaign, IL, USA

Introduction

Cognition in adult development arises out of the dynamic interplay of (1) gains in knowledge-based systems, expertise, and skill and (2) losses in speed of processing, working memory (WM) capacity, and inhibitory control processes. These changes have important effects on the nature of learning and entail that strategies in instruction be developmentally sensitive throughout the life span. At the same time, education early in the life span shapes these lifelong trajectories, while education and engagement in work and leisure through adulthood play an important role in engendering and maintaining competencies. Our goal in this article is to examine this interaction between the adult development of cognition and education. In the following sections, we examine the nature of cognition through adulthood and consider implications for learning. We also discuss recent research suggesting lifelong plasticity in neural networks, so that education is intimately tied with successful aging.

Theories of Life-Span Development

We review learning and cognition in adulthood and aging against the backdrop of a long history in psychology and education in which adulthood has been viewed merely as the culmination of what was achieved in childhood followed by a biologically driven decline. To the contrary, contemporary theories and empirical findings suggest that there are dynamic changes in cognition, motivation, and regulatory heuristics throughout the life span.

Multidirectionality in Cognition and Intellectual Function

While there are a number of competing theories for mechanisms that underlie age-related changes in cognition, there is broad agreement that age effects on cognition can be characterized at a coarse level as the result of two competing forces. On the one hand, the senescence process drives a decline in mental mechanics, the capacity to control attention and perform basic mental computations with accuracy and speed. On the other hand, there is accumulating evidence that the brain has immense potential for plasticity into late life; therefore, experience-based articulation of knowledge systems, skill, and expertise offers potential for growth. These divergent trajectories have also been characterized in terms of fluid versus crystallized abilities, derived from the factor structure of typical tests of intellectual ability. Fluid ability is manifested in tasks that require the encoding and transformation of information and detecting underlying relationships (e.g., block design, digit symbol, inductive reasoning, and spatial orientation). Crystallized ability, or pragmatics, depends on the acquisition of culture (e.g., vocabulary, semantic memory, and world knowledge).

Beyond that first cut, there are various theories characterizing the specific nature of declines in mechanics with age. The slowing hypothesis suggests that aging brings a systematic decrease in the speed with which mental operations can be performed. The WM hypothesis posits that aging is associated with a decline in the capacity to perform basic processing operations and store their products (as might be required, e.g., as one listens to a lecture and tries to construct an understanding of what is currently being discussed and integrate it with what has come before). According to the inhibition deficit hypothesis, aging brings a decreased effectiveness in suppressing irrelevant or no-longer-relevant information, thus reducing the functional capacity of WM. Another recent variant on the WM hypothesis is the effortfulness hypothesis, which identifies sensory loss as a critical contributor to age-related deficits in mental mechanics, not simply because they diminish the quality of information coming into the cognitive system, but also because central resources are strained by effort allocated to interpret the muddy input.

At the same time, aging may bring growth in a variety of capacities. Unlike declines, which come for free as a consequence of the senescence process, growth appears to arise out of dedicated engagement with particular types of experience. Initial conceptualizations of life-span growth focused on the normative development of capacities that could be scaled within a cultural context, for example, vocabulary and areas of common knowledge (e.g., why does bread rise? Who wrote Huckleberry Finn?), termed crystallized ability. In fact, vocabulary and some aspects of verbal ability are often found to increase or show stability through adulthood, with some evidence suggesting that such growth depends on habitual engagement with literacy-based activities. More recent conceptualizations acknowledge that normative growth of knowledge within certain cultural contexts early in the life span arises out of age-graded curricula in which there can be considerable commonality in the types of experiences to which children are exposed. However, relative to childhood, experiences in adulthood are more diverse and, rather than arising out of common school curricula, are tied to occupational and leisure activities. The particularized knowledge and skill systems that develop during adulthood are key achievements during this period and are intimately tied to selective allocation of resources to particular activities. Skill systems can be maintained well into late life, with recent evidence highlighting an important role for deliberate practice.

These two dimensions of intellectual function interact in interesting ways. First, because knowledge growth and skill development require attentional control, expansion of crystallized ability, particularized knowledge, and expertise ultimately depend on fluid abilities to some extent. Consequently, early in the life span, fluid and crystallized abilities grow apace with each other. In midlife to early old age, however, these trajectories diverge; knowledge and skill can continue their upward trajectories, but at a shallower slope as it takes a greater investment in attention to achieve the same gains, relative to earlier in the life span. On the other hand, to the extent that an individual has already invested in creating knowledge structures and skill systems (regardless of age), subsequent growth in those areas can be accomplished more easily. In part, this is because of a greater efficiency in processing information when existing knowledge can support learning. Another factor that contributes to knowledge-driven learning is that knowledge can support attentional control (i.e., effective allocation of effort).

Selectivity

A hallmark of adult development is increased selectivity, the focus of effort on a subset of available options. While the earlier part of the life span is a period in which effort is allocated to hone a diverse repertoire of skills and to expand social networks, movement through adulthood brings a motivational shift toward selectivity. There are two developmental forces that drive this.

First, the decline in mental mechanics limits the resources available to promote growth; therefore, selective focus of effort will increase the likelihood that selected domains will thrive. This strategy of selective optimization is distinctively an adult skill, with evidence suggesting that well-being in later life is enhanced by mindful selection of domains to which effort will be allocated toward growth, with the acknowledgment that this will entail loss in unselected domains. Expertise and knowledge systems may enhance selectivity by enabling more efficient focus on the most relevant features of a situation.

Selectivity is also thought to be driven by a changing perspective on the temporal horizon across the life span. Time is perceived to be open ended in youth, with unlimited – and unknowable – possibilities for experience. This expansive temporal horizon engenders concerns with information acquisition, skill development, and enrichment of social networks as a strategy for preparing for an uncertain future. With movement through the life span, the temporal horizon comes into view. Time is not limitless and choices have consequences that may squander that limited resource. This salience of the temporal horizon may increase attention to emotional concerns and decrease motivation toward purely cognitive goals. This theory has been used to explain, for example, why social networks typically decrease in size but become more emotionally satisfying. One implication of this socioemotional selectivity theory for learning is that cognition itself may be used most reliably in service of emotional goals; therefore, learning is expected to be relatively enhanced in later life if it is well integrated with the socioemotional system.

Self-Regulation

Another theme that emerges in adult developmental theory is the extent to which aging brings a change in the ability to engage processing resources for learning. While adult education textbooks often proclaim that adult learning is self-directed, the ability to self-initiate and self-direct learning may well depend on the level of existing knowledge and skill in the domain. In fact, one theory of cognitive aging holds that it becomes more difficult to self-initiate processing and that age-related difficulties in learning can be ameliorated to a large extent by the availability of environmental supports to guide processing.

Beliefs about one's capacity to accomplish cognitive and intellectual tasks appear to play a critical role in learning throughout the life span, but these may be particularly important in later adulthood and old age. Two related constructs that have received a lot of attention in the literature are self-efficacy and perceived control, each of which appears to be domain specific (e.g., one can conceive of being able to master health-related behaviors, but be undone by a cognitive task like filing a tax form). Self-efficacy is the confidence that one can execute the behavior or process necessary to achieve the desired outcome; perceived control is a multidimensional construct defining beliefs about the locus of control for achieving desired outcomes, with internal control reflecting beliefs of personal efficacy in achieving outcomes, and external control (chance or power others) reflecting beliefs that control of achievement rests with other sources. Relative to younger adults, older adults are sometimes found to have reduced levels of self-efficacy and may be more likely to believe that there are other people who will be able to control cognitive outcomes. To some extent, certain effects of aging are beyond our control; therefore, such beliefs may arise, in part, from an overgeneralization of a veridical perception. Another factor that may contribute to these beliefs is negative aging stereotypes, which can be internalized, and thus reduce effort to cognitive performance. In any case, such beliefs can become self-fulfilling prophecies. In fact, individual differences in self-efficacy and control beliefs can often account, in part, for age differences in cognitive performance, effects that are themselves sometimes mediated by strategy utilization.

Learning through Adulthood

Memory and Aging

Memory is among the first cognitive domains to be studied through adulthood and it remains a complex and vibrant literature. Memory is often conceptualized as involving three stages: encoding of information into a relatively durable trace, retention, and retrieval of the information into consciousness. Memory failure is among the most prevalent of aging stereotypes, and with aging, many adults complain about a difficulty with memory. In fact, age differences in memory performance can depend, to a large degree, on the task conditions, the materials, and the educational levels of the samples compared. Semantic memory (e.g., the meanings of words) and retrieval of well-learned information can show great resilience throughout the life span. By contrast, episodic memory, the ability to associate information with a particular learning context, may show pronounced age differences under some circumstances.

Deficits have been attributed, in part, to the demands that effective encoding places on mental mechanics and attentional control. Normatively, in an episodic memory task, older adults may be less likely to encode information in a way that is organized, elaborate, and distinctive. Critically, older learners have a more difficult time forming new arbitrary associations. Fairly modest interventions (e.g., instruction in organizational strategies) can improve memory performance. Interestingly, even though memory training can improve performance into very late life, training gains are typically greater among the young, suggesting that it is ultimately age-graded declines in mental mechanics that limit how well these strategies can be implemented.

Age changes in the effectiveness of episodic memory can also be attributed to retrieval. For example, age deficits in memory performance are often exaggerated in free recall relative to recognition or cued recall, a difference that presumably resides in the reduced demands to generate the information. In recognition, older adults are more likely to rely on familiarity rather than direct recollection.

Difficulty with name retrieval is one of the more common memory complaints. Aging does bring more tip-of-the-tongue experiences, in which an individual knows the word he/she wants to say but is unable to retrieve any of the phonological information. This is most likely to happen for relatively rare words or for infrequently encountered names. Happily, these are most typically resolved, even among older adults.

Learning from Text

Learning from text is often conceptualized as involving distinct processing systems that operate in concert to construct different facets of the language representation. At the surface level, individual lexical items (words) are encoded from the orthographic or acoustic signal and their meanings are activated. The semantic representation can be described in terms of integrated ideas (or propositions) that establish relationships among concepts described by the text, a representation called the textbase. Knowledge plays a role in facilitating integration, enabling elaborative inference, and evoking a simulation of the situation suggested by the text. Consistent with the divergent age trajectories of mechanics and knowledge-based processes, age deficits are more likely for the resource-consuming aspects of language processing.

Understanding words

Vocabulary often shows an increase with age, particularly among those who are regularly exposed to text; therefore, word recognition and word-level comprehension appear to be highly resilient in reading. Visual-processing declines can impact reading rate, especially if the font is small or hard to decode. In speech processing, declines in auditory processing can make spoken word recognition more demanding; therefore, more acoustic information is needed to understand individual words. Such effects may not merely disrupt encoding of the surface form, but also tax WM resources that would otherwise be used to construct a representation of the text's meaning. For example, elders with normal and impaired hearing listening to a word list interrupted periodically to report the last word presented may show negligible differences; however, if asked to report the last three words, the hearing-impaired elders will show deficits. The explanation for such a provocative finding is that the hearing-impaired elders overcome a sensory loss at some attentional cost so as to exert a toll on semantic and elaborative processes that enhance memory. Presumably, the same mechanisms operate in ordinary language processing. At the same time, there is evidence that older adults can take differential advantage of context in the recognition of both spoken and written words, especially in noisy environments. One area of difficulty that older adults may have in word processing is in deriving the meaning of novel words from context, with research showing that older adults are likely to infer more generalized and imprecise meanings relative to the young, a difference that can be largely accounted for in terms of declines in mental mechanics.

Textbase processing

Older adults typically show poorer memory for the content expressed directly by the text. Processes used to construct the textbase (e.g., to instantiate and integrate concepts in the text, essentially an associative memory task) are among the most resource-consuming of those required in learning from text and are, hence, the most vulnerable to aging. When reading is self-paced, older adults require more time for effective propositional encoding (e.g., as indexed by effective reading time, the time allocated per idea unit recalled). In listening, when the pace is controlled by the speaker, older adults may have particular difficulty in understanding and retaining the information, especially as informational density is increased or in noisy environments. Older adults appear to have no difficulty drawing anaphoric inference (i.e., correctly identifying the referent when the pronoun is used to refer to a noun that was introduced earlier) over short distances, but may find it difficult when the pronoun and referent are separated by intervening text. Thus, the general impression from this literature is that the semantic (textbase) representation is more fragmented and less distinctive as a function of aging.

There is an important exception to age declines in text memory that appears to derive from socioemotional selectivity. That is, memory for text may be very good if it is consonant with emotional goals or if the task is embedded in a social context. For example, it has been reported that emotional content in narratives (e.g., characters' emotional reactions) is well retained among older readers relative to emotion-neutral information. It has also been reported that age differences in narrative memory may be minimized if there is a social goal (e.g., tell a story to a child) as opposed to an information-acquisition goal (e.g., recall the text to an experimenter).

Situation model

Aside from deriving ideas directly from the text, learning from the text also involves elaboration on these ideas based on existing knowledge. Some theories focus on the perceptual quality of this level of representation, which gives rise to a perceptual simulation of the events described by the text. Therefore, for example, in narrative understanding, readers track goals and emotional reactions of characters as well as their movement through space and time. Behavioral methods to study this level of representation include probe recognition for objects in the narrative, as well as reading time, both of which show subtle effects of situation model processing. Readers are slower to verify the existence (in the narrative world) of objects that are spatially distant from the protagonist relative to those that are nearby. Readers also slow down when new characters are introduced, or when there is a spatial discontinuity (e.g., the locus of narrative events shifts from the village to the castle) or a temporal discontinuity (e.g., The next day...). When the text describes a goal to be achieved (e.g., Susan intends to buy her mother a purse for her birthday), the goal is activated in memory until it is achieved; therefore, concepts related to the goal are more quickly verified as long as the goal is open (e.g., purse will be more quickly verified if Susan can find the purse when she goes to the store relative to a condition in which she could not find one). To the extent that these paradigms have been used to explore adult age differences in situation model processing, there has been very little evidence of developmental differences in situation construction and updating; if anything, attentional allocation to situation construction may increase with aging. This is important because it suggests that the experiential aspects of reading and language understanding

(i.e., the phenomenal experience of entering the world described by the discourse) are resilient or even enhanced through adulthood. In addition, to the extent that perceptual simulation is required to understand expository or procedural text (e.g., how the heart works or how to put together a grill), the preservation of situation model processing may enable authentic learning from text – even if measures of explicit recall might suggest otherwise.

Older adults may particularly rely on the situation model to support textbase processing. For example, in ambiguous text (e.g., "The strength and flexibility of this equipment is remarkable. Not everyone is capable of using it even though most try at one point or another..."), older readers take differential advantage of titles (e.g., driving a car) that disambiguate the meaning to facilitate processing. Since the title renders the situation instantly transparent, both younger and older adults are more efficient in reading when it is available; however, older adults show this effect to a larger degree.

To the extent that the hallmark of situation model processing is an integration of textbase content with knowledge, one might expect that older adults would be particularly adept at inferential processing; however, this is not always the case. While older adults are more likely to draw elaborative inferences (e.g., in recall, to annotate their recollections with personal experiences or related information learned in another context), if inference is constrained so that it requires retrieval of textbase content, age deficits are the norm.

Discourse structures and context

Beyond sentence processing, different genres of text have characteristic forms. For example, narratives typically begin by introducing a setting and characters and proceed to describe a series of episodes in which goals or problems are introduced to be resolved, and so on. Expository texts have certain characteristic forms of argumentation (e.g., problem–solution and thesis–evidence). Older readers generally appear to track these larger discourse structures in the same way as the young. Adult readers have also been shown to benefit from explicit instruction in discourse forms to enhance memory and understanding.

Cognitive Reserve: Lifelong Effects of Education

Differential Developmental Trajectories as a Function of Education

A growing body of evidence suggests that there is a relationship between early educational experiences and cognitive development in adulthood. Numerous studies linking education and cognition have found that greater educational attainment is associated with higher levels of cognitive performance and lower risk for the development of Alzheimer's disease. Although the mechanisms for education–cognition relationships remain unclear, four plausible explanations have been suggested, which may be operative individually or interactively. First, educational level may be a marker for innate levels of vitality or for capacities that are developed very early in the life span, such that those who are initially more able are also more likely to succeed in the educational system. Second, educational experiences early in the life span may expand neural networks, so as to create a lifelong cognitive reserve that enables relatively high levels of cognitive functioning even as the senescence process winnows neural connections later in life. Third, early educational experiences may be related to cognition through their association with socioeconomic status; therefore, it is socioeconomic advantage that enables lifelong conditions (e.g., nutrition, leisure that affords regular exercise, and medical care) that promote health and, thereby, successful cognitive aging. Finally, educational attainment may afford self-regulatory skill that promotes lifelong mental stimulation. Since educational experiences often lead to occupational, professional, and leisure experiences that provide intellectual challenge in domains in which one is invested, it may be that lifelong patterns of mental stimulation promote neural health, thereby engendering cognitive vitality. It is this latter possibility that is particularly exciting, and an important thrust of recent research in psychology, cognitive neuroscience, and education.

Cognitive and Neural Plasticity

In fact, there is growing evidence from animal models and human research that exposure to stimulating environments promotes neural growth and cognitive vitality. Studies that have administered cognitive training or practice sessions have revealed that the cognitive abilities of older adults show considerable plasticity. For example, the Advanced Cognitive Training for Independent and Vital Elderly (ACTIVE) trial is a randomized clinical trial to examine the effectiveness and durability of cognitive interventions on basic cognitive processes (memory, reasoning, and speed of processing). Results to date indicate that, in spite of the fact that each intervention has targeted a domain tapping into mental mechanics, training effects are ability specific (e.g., increased speed of processing does not transfer to better reasoning or memory). Interestingly, these effects have been shown to be durable up to 5 years. Such data not only provide evidence for the modifiability of cognitive abilities into late life, but also demonstrate that training effects may be highly selective.

On the other hand, certain conditions appear to enhance executive control (e.g., the ability to switch between two tasks) that may ultimately have the potential to affect a relatively wide array of activities. For example, aerobic exercise can increase executive function throughout adulthood. Recent evidence suggests that language processing may impact this control function as well, with several recent demonstrations of enhanced executive function among fluent bilinguals who habitually manage two language systems.

There may be limits to plasticity very late in the life span, with some training studies showing reduced effects with increasing age. Such findings highlight the dynamic nature of change during adulthood, and also imply that cognitive vitality past the age of 85 or 90 years may depend on the cognitive reserve established up to that point.

Neuroimaging studies offer further insight into how the brain is shaped by learning and experience, in particular, showing effects that are specific to experience. For example, adults with long-term experience in navigation show enhanced neural development in brain regions thought to be responsible for spatial processing (posterior hippocampus). Experimental studies in which individuals are randomly assigned to receive training in a particular skill (e.g., juggling and videogames) show distinctive patterns of change in neural structure and function (e.g., among jugglers, bilateral expansion of mediotemporal and left posterior parietal areas, thought to be responsible for visual storage and processing).

At the same time, older adults may show compensatory patterns of resource allocation and neural recruitment. In a number of different task domains, neuroimaging data have provided evidence that older adults show reduced hemispheric asymmetry in activation patterns, demonstrating expanded recruitment of brain regions from both hemispheres. Older adults, especially those with relatively better performance, are likely to show greater activation of the prefrontal cortex, suggesting that successful cognitive performance may increasingly require executive attentional control with age. Interestingly, recent research also suggests that increased frontal recruitment with aging may be exaggerated among those with relatively high levels of education, providing some support for the self-regulatory account of education–cognition relationships.

Conclusion

This article has discussed the dynamic interplay between cognitive development and educational experiences throughout the life span, so that trajectories of adult cognitive development must shape educational practices and educational practices can promote cognitive vitality. Within this framework, education throughout the life span becomes a public health issue.

Sociologists have distinguished between age-segregated and age-integrated social structures. In age-segregated structures, permissible social roles are tightly tied to chronological age (e.g., education during youth and work during midlife). Within developed countries, advances in medicine and health practices have stimulated a worldwide shift in demographics toward older populations, such that age segregation is no longer a tenable model. Life is simply too long now: effective work cannot rest on temporally removed education, and intellectual engagement is critical to vitality at every stage of the life span.

See also: Cognition and Emotion; Cognition: Overview and Recent Trends; Memory; Problem Solving and Human Expertise; Problem Solving and Reasoning.

Further Reading

Baltes, P. B. (1997). On the incomplete architecture of human ontogeny: Selection, optimization, and compensation as foundation of developmental theory. *American Psychologist* **52**, 366–380.

Barnes, D. E., Tager, I. B., Satariano, W. A., and Yaffe, K. (2004). The relationship between literacy and cognition in well-educated elders. *Journal of Gerontology: Medical Sciences* **59A**, 390–395.

Beier, M. E. and Ackerman, P. L. (2005). Age, ability, and the role of prior knowledge on the acquisition of new domain knowledge: Promising results in a real-world learning environment. *Psychology and Aging* **20**, 341–355.

Bialystok, E., Craik, F. I. M., and Freedman, M. (2007). Bilingualism as a protection against the onset of symptoms of dementia. *Neuropsychologia* **45**, 459–464.

Carstensen, L. L., Mikels, J. A., and Mather, M. (2006). Aging and the intersection of cognition, motivation, and emotion. In Birren, J. E. and Schaie, K. W. (eds.) *Handbook of the Psychology of Aging,* 6th edn., pp 343–362. New York: Academic Press.

Johnson, R. E. (2003). Aging and the remembering of text. *Developmental Review* **23**, 261–346.

Kramer, A. F., Bherer, L., Colcombe, S. J., Dong, W., and Greenough, W. T. (2004). Environmental influences on cognitive and brain plasticity during aging. *Journal of Gerontology: Medical Sciences* **59A**, 940–957.

Krampe, R. T. and Charness, N. (2006). Aging and expertise. In Ericsson, K. A., Charness, N., Feltovich, P. J., and Hoffman, R. R. (eds.) *The Cambridge Handbook of Expertise and Expert Performance*, pp 723–742. New York: Cambridge University Press.

Lachman, M. E. (2004). Development in midlife. *Annual Review of Psychology* **55**, 305–331.

Lachman, M. E. (2006). Perceived control over aging-related declines: Adaptive beliefs and behaviors. *Current Directions in Psychological Science* **15**, 282–286.

Meyer, B. J. F. and Pollard, C. K. (2006). Applied learning and aging: A closer look at reading. In Birren, J. E. and Schaie, K. W. (eds.) *Handbook of the Psychology of Aging,* 6th edn., pp 233–260. New York: Elsevier.

Riley, M. W. and Riley, J. W. Jr. (2000). Age integration: Conceptual and historical background. *Gerontologist* **40**, 266–270.

Scarmeas, N. and Stern, Y. (2003). Cognitive reserve and lifestyle. *Journal of Clinical and Experimental Neuropsychology* **25**, 625–633.

Stine-Morrow, E. A. L. (2007). The Dumbledore hypothesis of cognitive aging. *Current Directions in Psychological Science* **16**, 300–304.

Stine-Morrow, E. A. L., Miller, L. M. S., and Hertzog, C. (2006). Aging and self-regulated language processing. *Psychological Bulletin* **132**, 582–606.

Thornton, R. and Light, L. L. (2006). Language comprehension and production in normal aging. In Birren, J. E. and Schaie, K. W. (eds.) *Handbook of the Psychology of Aging,* 6th edn., pp 261–287. New York: Academic Press.

Lifelong Learning

J Field, University of Stirling, Stirling, UK

Lifelong learning has become a dominant theme of education and training polices across the advanced industrial nations. Besides a wide range of national governments, it is endorsed by a wide range of intergovernmental policy actors, including the Organisation for Economic Co-operation and Development (OECD), the European Commission (EC), the United Nations Educational, Social and Cultural Organisation (UNESCO), the World Bank and the International Labour Organisation (ILO) (Schemmann, 2007). For governments, lifelong learning is an overarching policy framework which offers solutions to a number of common economic and social challenges; globalization and competitiveness often dominate the policy discourse, but promoting lifelong learning is also seen as relevant to social cohesion, demographic change, active citizenship, migrant assimilation, and public health.

Lifelong learning therefore has broad application across a variety of policy domains. It is also widely discussed by educational professionals and by academic researchers. Some claim that lifelong learning is such a broad concept that it has virtually no practical value (Gustavsson, 1995: 92). While its meanings are many and varied, they usually emphasize learning as a ubiquitous process, which takes place throughout the lifespan, and across a variety of life contexts. The recent focus among policymakers, educationalists, and researchers on the ability to learn continuously after the phase of initial education, and across a variety of contexts of which educational institutions are one among many, distinguishes the debate over lifelong learning from more conventional policy discussions of education and training as levers across a range of economic and social policy domains.

From Social Optimism to Economic Survival?

In recent years, lifelong learning has moved steadily toward the center of the policy stage. International governmental bodies have played a particularly significant role in popularizing lifelong learning as a policy concept. While the term was in occasional use before the mid-1990s, it received huge impetus when the European Commission declared 1996 to be the European Year of Lifelong Learning, an idea first floated in the Commission's White Paper on competitiveness, employment, and growth (Commission of the European Communities, 1994). This context neatly exemplifies the way in which it is economic concerns that dominate policymakers' interest in lifelong learning. Particularly in the older industrial nations, policymakers argue that successful adjustment to a knowledge economy and society requires a highly skilled, knowledgeable, and flexible workforce as a key to sustained national and corporate competitive advantage; individuals equally need to invest continuously in their own competence in order to maintain their employability in an ever-changing labor market. This reflects and is expressed through a policy discourse that is centered on a human-capital approach to social inclusion and economic growth (Borg and Mayo, 2005; Coffield, 1999; Gustavsson, 1995).

This strong economic bias distinguishes the current debate over lifelong learning from earlier policy attempts to promote learning in adult life. Superficially, the idea of lifelong learning closely resembles notions of lifelong education, which were widely discussed in the 1970s. The idea of lifelong education was promoted particularly actively by UNESCO, who in 1972 published *Learning to Be*, a report by an international expert panel chaired by Edgar Faure, a former politician who had served in France as Minister of Education and Prime Minister (Faure, 1972). Faure's report was essentially humanistic in nature, arguing in favor of wider access to higher levels of education and greater support for and recognition of informal and non-formal learning in order to encourage personal fulfilment and development. Faure's report was enormously influential in stimulating debate, and in infusing that debate with an optimistic view of educational innovation and reform (Knoll, 1998). Its core ideas were taken up by the OECD, which developed a parallel debate over recurrent education, the aim of which was intended to provide governments with practicable means of realizing the overarching goal of lifelong education (OECD, 1973).

In practical terms, the activities undertaken by UNESCO and OECD mainly helped focus policy attention on the educational needs of those who had benefited least from the front-loaded approach to initial education. In industrial nations, this often involved developing educational entitlements for workers, with laws on paid educational leave in a number of countries. In some, there was a broad entitlement to leave for general purposes (as in Sweden, and in state-level laws on *Bildungsurlaub* in Germany); in other cases, educational leave was guaranteed for specific purposes, such as vocational training under the French law on *conge de formation* or British laws on health and safety and workplace representation. Many more countries experienced a growth of adult basic education, with particularly impressive innovations in adult literacy provision and women's basic education.

By the 1990s, a concern with personal development, or worker participation as public policy goals, had not disappeared altogether, but was found far less frequently. Much more common has been a primary concern with lifelong learning as a means of underpinning economic competitiveness and growth. In a globalized economy, where material resources are more or less ubiquitous, skills and knowledge are said to be the only sustainable sources of competitive advantage (Commission of the European Communities, 1994; Reich, 1993; Thurow, 1994). Insofar as policymakers also share an interest in equity and social cohesion, lifelong learning's importance is often valued primarily as a means of reinsertion of vulnerable individuals or inactive workers back into the labor market, leading in turn to improved income and security for individuals from disadvantaged backgrounds.

The current debate over lifelong learning is therefore distinctive in a number of ways. It is characterized by the breadth, and sometimes vagueness, with which the concept is used; it is derived more from the policy domain than from the educational field; and its dominant usage tends to be primarily economic. Yet, more positively, the concept can also be taken to emphasize and recognize the many ways in which people build up new skills and capacities throughout the lifespan and across different life spheres, including workplaces, communities, homes, and voluntary associations. It gives a central place to people's learning, as opposed to education, teaching, and institutions. To use what has become a common abbreviation, current policy concerns are with education that is lifelong, and also life-wide. For these reasons, it has often become more or less synonymous with adult learning; however, it has powerful implications for all phases of the lifespan.

Initial Education as a Platform for Learning through Life

Initial education, including early-years development, is important in its own right. From a lifelong perspective, though, it is additionally important because it provides a platform for learning later in life. A number of commentators argue that family and neighborhood influences in the early years are particularly significant in determining patterns of learning across the lifespan. From this perspective, high-quality education during the earlier years is important primarily because of its role in providing the abilities and motivation to engage effectively in learning later in life (Hargreaves, 2004; Gillies, 2005; OECD, 2004). Sociologically, many of the factors that are associated with adult well-being are already present in the early years. One

recent longitudinal analysis of adult learning in Wales demonstrated that most of the factors that affected the probabilities of participation in adult life were present by the time that the child entered primary school for the first time (Gorard et al., 1999).

Education and well-being have often been associated. The idea that education can promote individual well-being indirectly, by improving earnings and promoting social mobility, is an old one; so are notions of education helping to promote the good society by contributing to economic growth and equality of opportunity. Recent debates about the wider benefits of learning have added a new dimension to the relationship, linking education to other facets of individual and collective well-being, such as health (including mental health), security from crime, and political tolerance (Schuller et al., 2004). Through strengthening self-identity, learning is also said to help people develop a sense of authorship over their own biographies and take responsibility for their life choices (Côté, 2004).

Theoretical Perspectives

The 1970s debate over lifelong education was a broad one. While OECD's work on recurrent education was primarily concerned with the balance of resource distribution as between secondary and tertiary education, combined with an interest in worker participation in enterprise management, the work of UNESCO was profoundly influenced by the radical educational thinkers of the 1960s, along with the concerns of liberation theology and Third World development. The dominant voices in the 1990s debate, by contrast, came primarily from writers on globalization and economic change, and were almost entirely based in the economically advanced nations of the West. In a global knowledge economy, these new growth theorists argued, sustainable competitive advantage could only come from an ability to innovate continuously, and in turn this required a highly skilled and flexible workforce (e.g. Porter, 1990; Reich, 1993). Neo-Schumpeterian concerns with innovation as a basis for economic growth came to be aligned with human-capital perspectives on skills development, as well as with an interest in regional and national innovation capacities. More organizationally focused analyses have tended to emphasize the importance of organizational learning and knowledge management as strategic responses to complexity and change (Smith and Sadler-Smith, 2006).

The dominant theories of lifelong learning, then, tend to be concerned with developing workers' abilities to innovate and respond to change, and therefore contribute to sustained economic growth. Many governments, particularly those led by social democratic or Christian democratic parties, also see lifelong learning as a means of promoting equity and inclusion. Again, this is associated with a strong focus on employability as an important active measure to promote social cohesion, and equity concerns are therefore closely related to economic goals. Finally, this dominant view takes a capitalist economic order as a given; lifelong learning is not seen as a way of changing society, but at most as a way of including the least advantaged in the existing order. Particularly in its most recent phase, which may be conveniently marked by the European Commission's *Memorandum* on lifelong learning of 2000, it is a highly pragmatic concept (Schreiber-Barsch and Zeuner, 2007: 693; Commission of the European Communities, 2000). However, there are also significant critical voices, albeit from a range of differing perspectives.

Some take a broadly radical, anti-globalization stance. Thus the Maltese writers Carmel Borg and Peter Mayo suggest that the primary economic focus of dominant theories is tied to a neoliberal agenda for welfare reform (Borg and Mayo, 2005). Others have asked whether the whole concept is not associated with Western interests, and question whether, at least in its current manifestations, lifelong learning presents opportunities for or is a distraction from adult basic education as a force for development and democratization in the majority of the world (Torres, 2003). Certainly, the current policy climate tends to assume that individual workers must assume at least partial responsibility for ensuring their own employability and invest in new skills in order to maintain their labor-market value. However, this is often accompanied by incentive regimes, which seek to encourage workers to invest in new competences and improve existing skills; in some cases, workers' own organizations have promoted skills improvements as a way of protecting collective security (Payne, 2005). It is also possible to see welfare regimes as themselves bureaucratic and unresponsive to diverse needs; even in adult education, devolution and autonomy may be viewed as a form of privatization, but some will also experience it as emancipatory. In other words, there is no necessary connection between an emphasis on continuous learning and the dismantling of the welfare state, but radical perspectives do draw attention to both global and local inequalities that are material and structural, and which may be perpetuated by current lifelong learning policies.

Feminist writers have also made a significant contribution to critical debates over lifelong learning. From a feminist perspective, the radical expansion of post-compulsory education since the 1960s has brought rather ambivalent consequences. On the one hand, considerable growth in women's access to higher education has formed part of the remarkable transformation in the role of work in women's biographical trajectories (Spano, 2002). Like many radical writers, feminists tend to be sharply critical of policies and forms of provision that are driven primarily by market forces, though they go beyond the majority of radicals in identifying clear and practicable ways in which education and training might better meet the needs of women (Gouthro, 2005; Burke and Jackson, 2007).

From a feminist perspective, the invisibility of gender in a patriarchal society masks the fact that women face particular barriers to participation in learning, and much provision fails to address the diversities of women's identities; working-class women in particular are trapped in a cycle of low-paid and low-status jobs, whose skill content is barely acknowledged in public discourse about a learning society (Fenwick, 2004; Jackson, 2003). Gouthro goes rather far, suggesting that the language and ideas of lifelong learning represent a major incursion of public policy into the private sphere, as the identification of the homeplace as a site of learning is little more than a colonization of part of the lifeworld that has particular resonance for women (Gouthro, 2005).

A third alternative body of theory derives from post-structuralist and post-modernist writing. In particular, a number of writers have drawn on the thinking of Michel Foucault, the French philosopher/historian, to frame their analyses of power and knowledge and the construction of the learning citizen. Foucault's influence can be particularly seen in studies which treat knowledge as a social practice, governed by relations of power that may be expressed through various classificatory schema and their institutional manifestations. This might be seen as a relatively superficial reading of Foucault's work, and it has been supplemented more recently by studies that take Foucault's radical decentering of the human subject as their starting point. Here, instead of studying learners as agents, the focus is on studying the specific practices that constitute learning, the discourses produced by and producing these practices, and the different subject positions that are made available through these discourses and practices. These subject positions usually include the other, and discourses of nonparticipation and nonlearning are therefore analyzed as processes of othering, so that practices and discourses of lifelong learning always constitute subject positions that are excluded from the dominant framing (Fejes, 2006; Nicoll, 2006).

Finally, a number of writers have explored connections between lifelong learning and sociological theories of reflexive modernization. Ulrich Beck and Anthony Giddens both take human agency as the core of their accounts of late modernity (Beck, 1992; Giddens, 1991). There are distinct parallels between theories of reflexive modernization and core elements of the debate over lifelong learning. Beck and Giddens lead us to explore the socio-cultural forces that are shaping the demand for continuous learning, rather than seeing lifelong learning as an expression of economic forces alone. Their work also draws attention to learning and change in everyday life; people may well be confronting experiences of globalization and technological change, but they are also required to take an active approach to their own biographies, including the ways in which they negotiate intimate relationships and construct identity and social resources (Alheit, 1990; Field, 2006: 68–73).

Institutional Structures for Lifelong Learning

Lifelong learning is a highly complex area for policy, yet its current prominence is largely due to the interest of policymakers. This paradoxical position reflects the challenges that current economic, social, cultural, and political changes pose to the policy community, particularly in the Western nations, which therefore require new approaches to governance (Field, 2006: 29–43). While policymakers are still able to resort to direct intervention of the traditional kinds, the most important actors in lifelong learning are usually non-governmental – primarily enterprises and individuals, but also trade unions, families, voluntary associations, and neighborhoods. Even within government, lifelong learning policies span the interests of a range of ministries, and a variety of layers from local and regional to national and supra-national. Lifelong learning therefore poses serious challenges of coordination of a range of actors of different kinds, besides bringing risks of unintended consequences. It also poses challenges to many of the existing institutions, particularly those providing opportunities in adult learning.

Although the current debate over lifelong learning has only been underway since the mid-1990s, governments have not had to write policies on a clean sheet of paper. Rather, they have sought to modernize and systematize existing patterns of provision of adult learning, and review existing institutional structures, with a view to raising levels of participation and attainment, usually right across the lifespan but with a strong concentration on learning in and for working life. Comparative researchers have identified a number of variations in post-compulsory education and training structures, in spite of the convergent pressures of globalizing economic forces and the modernization of education systems. Particular attention has been paid to the roles of three distinct components of the lifelong learning systems:

- systems of transition between initial education and the labor market;
- higher education systems; and
- arrangements for adult education and training.

These components have attracted attention from policy analysts as well as academic researchers (see, e.g., the OECD's thematic reviews (OECD, 2005)).

The three institutional dimensions of national lifelong learning systems differ significantly from each other. The most complex, from both a policy and an analytical perspective, is the adult learning system, which involves a variety of actors and stakeholders, including a wide range of non-government organizations as well as individual citizens. Youth transition systems are only slightly less complex, as well as institutions, which may or may not be publicly funded; the key stakeholders generally include employers

and sometimes trade unions, as well as varying degrees of state provision and regulation. Some national studies note that military service may also affect youth transition processes (e.g., Tsai, 1998), and schools are also often influential actors in their own right. Initial education systems at first seem relatively unproblematic from a policy perspective; the major players are usually publicly funded schools and the state itself (though policy implementation is often influenced by teachers, particularly where the latter are able to exercise a significant degree of professional autonomy). However, initial education is often less straightforward than it first appears; particularly in early years, nongovernmental providers are often involved in nursery-level education, and families and communities exercise significant influence over children's cultural capital and social capital.

Green *et al.* (2006) identify three distinct regional models of lifelong learning and the knowledge economy. Two of these – the Anglo-Saxon, neoliberal model, and the continental European, social market model – are relatively well established, and are clearly based on conventional social policy models of welfare regimes. Green and his colleagues add a third, Nordic model, which combines high levels of social cohesion with strong support for economic competitiveness. The Nordic model has recently been subjected to particular scrutiny because of its perceived relative success in combining comparatively equal participation with high overall participation in adult learning (Tuijnman, 2003; Rubenson, 2006; Milana and Desjardins, 2007). Overall participation rates in all the Nordic countries are consistently close to or over 50% of the population of working age (OECD, 2000). Further, Nordic participation rates are high both for job-related adult education and training and for non-job-related learning (Eurobarometer, 2003).

The roots of this pattern have been traced back to the 1960s, when governments and the social partners identified adult education as a distinct and significant field of policy, linked closely to labor market policy, which itself was geared primarily to securing full employment and industrial consensus (Rubenson, 2006; Milana and Desjardins, 2007). Typically, the Nordic countries have a wide range of providing institutions, including well-established non-statutory providers (such as trade unions) and community-based providers accountable to local government. Rather than seeking to restructure the institutional system, public policy instruments since the 1960s in the Nordic nations have increasingly included targeted-funding measures aimed at engaging disadvantaged groups in the adult education system (Rubenson, 2006).

These measures have had some success in terms of overall participation. Nevertheless, despite high overall participation, and relatively high participation by disadvantaged groups, Milana and Desjardins (2007) note in a systematic review of international survey data that the same broad distribution is found in the Nordic countries as in other nations. The least likely to participate are older workers, those with lower skills levels, unemployed people, migrant workers, and those with weak initial educational qualifications. Nevertheless, on the basis of data from the International Adult Literacy Survey and a survey conducted by the EC in 2003, published by Eurobarometer, they conclude that the Nordic nations have created popular adult education systems that have led to "the attenuation of differences among these otherwise disadvantaged groups", particularly older adults of working age and less-educated workers (Milana and Desjardins, 2007: 3). They further analyze Eurobarometer data to show that although adults in the Nordic countries reported similar constraints on participation as did respondents in other European Union (EU) member states, the average incidence of the constraints was generally lower in the Nordic countries, and adults in the Nordic countries were more likely to participate even if they faced these constraints (Milana and Desjardins, 2007: 6). Interestingly, this was true for dispositional barriers as well as for more material and institutional constraints.

Milana and Desjardins conclude that public policy has been particularly significant in producing high levels of overall participation, first by maintaining a strong public adult education system, and second by adopting special targeting measures to ensure that an open and broad system of provision is not simply colonized by the already well educated (Milana and Desjardins, 2007: 14–15). In addition, Nordic economies are typically characterized by forms of organizational networking that are likely to promote informal learning. Peter Maskell and his colleagues have demonstrated that high levels of informal exchange of information, techniques, and skills are critical to the competitiveness of Nordic enterprises, particularly those who are affected by high labor costs and low levels of technological development and must therefore compete on grounds of quality and added value (Maskell et al., 1998).

Supplementing various studies of national policy, Michael Schemmann has conducted a detailed systematic analysis of the policies developed by inter and supranational government bodies such as the World Bank, UNESCO, EC, and OECD (Schemmann, 2007). Of these, the EC has been most influential in practice, since it is responsible for implementing policies directly, while UNESCO and the OECD exercise a more indirect influence. Nevertheless, Schemmann traces a number of common themes, as well as marked differences, across these four bodies; above all, he believes that they have established a global lifelong learning discourse with a number of shared reference points. In turn, of course, these common themes reflect the dominance of a neoliberal policy agenda at national level, with governments seeking similar solutions to similar problems. This includes a marked trend toward employer involvement with delivery, in order to promote responsiveness to economic demands, and the adoption of active approaches to labor-market training, particularly through welfare-to-work measures.

Schemmann also notes a pronounced tendency for international governmental bodies to seek to influence national policy by compiling comparative indicators and promoting policy borrowing and transfer, trends that he finds typical of the new governance that is being applied to complex policy areas like lifelong learning (Schemmann, 2007: 246). Both the OECD and the EC publish benchmarking data, compiled on the basis of selected indicators of educational activity; the OECD's publications usually attract high levels of media coverage. In 2003, the EC set its member states the target, by 2010, of at least 12.5% participation in learning by adults aged 25–64, though the Commission has few powers to enforce such targets other than by publicizing the results. The EC has also been charged by the European Parliament with developing a European-qualifications framework covering all areas of lifelong learning. Such developments have led some commentators to question whether there are tendencies toward an international standardization process in adult learning, particularly within the EU (Schreiber-Barsch and Zeuner, 2007: 699–700).

Conclusions

Since the mid-1990s, ideas of lifelong learning have been widely debated in policy and research circles. The idea itself rose to prominence in the mid-1990s when it was embraced by a number of international policy bodies and by several countries. While there were often exaggerated claims both for the novelty of the policies, and for the likely contributions they would make to a whole plethora of economic and social challenges, these policies did indeed mark a shift in policy focus, away from instruction toward learning and away from childhood and youth toward learning through the life span. This shift reflected policymakers' preoccupations with the consequences of globalization and rapid economic and technological change, as well as business leaders' recognition of the contribution of upskilling to competitive strategies. However, it also reflected wider sociocultural factors which were also leading to a new emphasis on continuous learning as a way of coping with the demands of everyday life in a risk society.

Conceptually, the idea of lifelong learning appears neatly to parallel influential sociological conceptions of institutionalized reflexivity and risk. The task of lifelong learning, it has been argued, is therefore to enable people to regain a degree of control over their existence, and develop a learning elective biography:

> When flexibility constitutes the crucial capacity that work organizations and the unpredictability of life demands, having a stable identity can be a disadvantage... Questions such as 'Who am I?' and 'Whom do I want to be?' can become quite haunting existential questions (Glastra et al., 2004: 294).

Others, however, view such a concern with promoting flexibility as potentially damaging and negative to the individual and community, and at worst as collusion with the excesses of globalized capitalism.

Policies for lifelong learning have tended to concentrate on learning in and for working life. Yet, particularly when compared with the innovations of the 1970s debate, most governments have notably shied away from the challenging and difficult issue of policies aimed at increasing the skills and knowledge content of jobs, especially in sectors and regions that rely on low relative labor costs as a basis for competition. Some attention has been paid to the implications for initial schooling as a preparation for learning in later life, as well as to the development of parenting skills, usually for mothers, with a view to raising their capacity for supporting their own children's learning (Gillies, 2005). Relatively little attention has so far been paid to support for learning in later life, even in countries like Scotland where population aging presents acute social and economic challenges. Patterns of participation in adult learning, even among people of working age, tend to mirror existing educational and socioeconomic inequalities. There is therefore a risk that market-led approaches to lifelong learning will simply accentuate and help to entrench the social hierarchy, as the knowledge-poor lag ever further behind in the shift to a knowledge economy. While no policy models have successfully combined uplifts in overall adult participation with a marked impact on inequality, the Nordic societies have been relatively successful in moderating the impact of existing patterns of disadvantage.

Lifelong learning is, then, a rather ambiguous concept which has been used for a range of policy purposes, mainly economic in nature. Yet, it is at heart extremely simple and – from a normative point of view – potentially rather attractive. The vision of a society where people have broad opportunities to learn across and throughout their lives is an attractive one for many educationalists – particularly those with a background in adult education. More to the point, the broad social and economic trends that have brought lifelong learning to centerstage are not short-term ones. At least in the medium term, then, the debate is likely to continue.

Bibliography

Alheit, P. (1990). *Alltag und Biographie: Studien zur gesellschaftlichen Konstitution biographischer Perspektiven*. Bremen: Universität Bremen.
Beck, U. (1992). *Risk Society*. London: Sage.
Borg, C. and Mayo, P. (2005). The EU memorandum on lifelong learning: Old wine in new bottles? *Globalisation, Societies and Education* **3**, 257–278.
Burke, P. J. and Jackson, S. (2007). *Reconceptualising Lifelong Learning: Feminist Interventions*. London: Routledge.
Coffield, F. (1999). Introduction: Lifelong learning as a new form of social control? In Coffield, F. (ed.) *Why's the Beer Always Stronger up North? Studies of Lifelong Learning in Europe*, pp 1–12. Bristol: Policy Press.
Commission of the European Communities (1994). *Competitiveness, Employment, Growth*. Luxembourg: Office for Official Publications.
Commission of the European Communities (2000). *Commission Staff Working Paper. A Memorandum on Lifelong Learning*. Brussels: Commission of the European Communities.
Côté, J. (2004). Identity capital, social capital and the wider benefits of learning. *Wider Benefits of Learning Research Centre Conference*. London, 15–16, 2004.
Faure, E. (1972). *Learning to Be: The World of Education Today and Tomorrow*. Paris: UNESCO.
Fejes, A. (2006). *Constructing the Adult Learner: A Governmentality Analysis*. Linköping: Linköpings Universitet.
Fenwick, T. (2004). What happens to the girls? Gender, work and learning in Canada's 'new economy'. *Gender and Education* **16**, 169–185.
Field, J. (2006). *Lifelong Learning and the New Educational Order*, 2nd edn. Stoke on Trent: Trentham.
Giddens, A. (1991). *Modernity and Self-Identity: Self and Society in the Late Modern Age*. Cambridge: Polity Press.
Gillies, V. (2005). Meeting parents' needs? Discourses of 'support' and 'inclusion' in family policy. *Critical Social Policy* **25**(1), 70–90.
Glastra, F., Hake, B., and Schedler, P. (2004). Lifelong learning as transitional learning. *Adult Education Quarterly* **54**(4), 291–307.
Gorard, S., Rees, G., and Fevre, R. (1999). Two dimensions of time: The changing social context of lifelong learning. *Studies in the Education of Adults* **31**(1), 35–48.
Gouthro, P. A. (2005). A critical feminist analysis of the homeplace as a learning site: Expanding the discourse of lifelong learning to consider adult women learners. *International Journal of Lifelong Education* **24**(1), 5–19.
Green, A., Preston, J., and Janmaat, J. G. (2006). *Education, Equality and Social Cohesion: A Comparative Analysis*. Basingstoke: Palgrave Macmillan.
Gustavsson, B. (1995). Lifelong learning reconsidered. In Klasson, M., Manninon, J., Tøsse, S., and Wahlgren, B. (eds.) *Social Change and Adult Education Research*, pp 89–110. Linköping: Linköping University.
Hargreaves, D. (2004). *Learning for Life: The Foundations of Lifelong Learning*. Bristol: Policy Press.
Jackson, S. (2003). Lifelong earning: Working-class women and lifelong learning. *Gender and Education* **15**, 365–376.
Knoll, J. (1998). 'Lebenslanges Lernen' und internationale Bildungspolitik – Zur Genese eines Begriffs und dessen nationale Operationalisierungen. In Brödel, R. (ed.) *Lebenslanges Lernen – Lebensbegleitende Bildung*, pp 35–50. Neuwied: Luchterhand.
Maskell, P., Eskelinen, H., Hannibalsson, I., Malmberg, A., and Vatne, E. (1998). *Competitiveness, Localised Learning and Regional Development: Specialisation and Prosperity in Small Open Economies*. London: Routledge.
Milana, M. and Desjardins, R. (2007). Enablers and constrainers to participation: Has policy in Nordic countries reached its limit for raising participation in adult learning among certain groups? *Second Nordic Conference on Adult Learning*. Linköping University, 17–19, April 2007.
Nicoll, K. (2006). *Flexibility and Lifelong Learning: Examining the Rhetoric of Education*. London: Routledge.
OECD (Organisation for Economic Co-operation and Development) (1973). *Recurrent Education: A Strategy for Lifelong Learning*. Paris: OECD.
OECD (Organisation for Economic Co-operation and Development) (2000). *Thematic Review on Adult Learning: Sweden*. Paris: OECD.
OECD (Organisation for Economic Co-operation and Development) (2004). *Completing the Foundation for Lifelong Learning: An OECD Survey of Upper Secondary Schools*. Paris: OECD.
OECD (Organisation for Economic Co-operation and Development) (2005). *Promoting Adult Learning*. Paris: OECD.
Payne, J. (2005). What progress is Norway making with lifelong learning? A study of the Norwegian competence reform. *SKOPE Research Paper 55*. Oxford and Warwick Universities.
Porter, M. (1990). *The Competitive Advantage of Nations*. New York: Free Press.
Reich, R. (1993). *The Work of Nations: Preparing Ourselves for Twenty-First Century Capitalism*. London: Simon and Schuster.

Rubenson, K. (2006). The Nordic model of lifelong learning. *Compare* **36**, 327–341.

Schemmann, M. (2007). *Internationale Weiterbildungspolitik und Globalisierung*. Bielefeld: W. Bertelsmann Verlag.

Schreiber-Barsch, S. and Zeuner, C. (2007). International–supranational–transnational? Lebenslanges Lernen im Spannungsfeld von Bildungsakteuren und Interessen. *Zeitschrift für Pädagogik* **53**, 686–703.

Schuller, T., Preston, J., Hammond, C., Bassett-Grundy, A., and Bynner, J. (2004). *The Benefits of Learning: The Impact of Education on Health, Family Life and Social Capital*. London: RoutledgeFalmer.

Smith, P. and Sadler-Smith, E. (2006). *Learning in Organizations: Complexities and Diversities*. Basingstoke: Palgrave Macmillan.

Spano, A. (2002). Female identities in late modernity. In Chamberlayne, P., Rustin, M., and Wengraf, T. (eds.) *Biography and Social Exclusion in Europe: Experiences and Life Journeys*, pp 151–173. Bristol: Policy Press.

Thurow, L. (1994). New game, new rules, new strategies. *Journal of the Royal Society of Arts* **142**, 50–53.

Torres, R. M. (2003). *Lifelong Learning: A New Momentum and a New Opportunity for Adult Basic Learning and Education (ABLE) in the South*. Bonn: Institute for International Co-operation of the German Adult Education Association.

Tsai, S. L. (1988). The transition from school to work in Taiwan. In Shavit, Y. and Müller, W. (eds.) *From School to Work*, pp 443–470. Oxford: Clarendon Press.

Tuijnman, A. C. (2003). The Nordic model of lifelong learning. *International Journal of Educational Research* **39**, 283–291.

Further Reading

Walther, A. (2006). Regimes of youth transitions. *Young* **14**, 119–139.

Classroom Discourse and Student Learning

L Hemphill, Wheelock College, Boston, MA, USA

Glossary

Academic register – The language style most commonly used in academic contexts, typically incorporating features of written language.

Authentic questions – The questions that reflect genuine openness about the sought-after response.

Code-shifting – The alternation between two or more languages or language varieties within the same discourse.

I–R–E sequence – A three-part interactional sequence beginning with a teacher initiation followed by a student response and teacher evaluation.

Decontextualized language – The language that does not rely for its interpretation on the speaker and hearer's shared context; it is often characteristic of academic and written language.

Display question – A question that requires the respondent to verbally display information that is already known to the questioner.

Elicitation sequence – A chain of teacher questions and student responses in which the teacher attempts to elicit a sought-after response.

Nonstandard dialect – A community language variety such as African-American English vernacular that displays systematic differences with the standard form of the language.

Open-ended question – A question that does not elicit only a yes–no or phrasal response.

Speech event – A routinized communication situation involving particular participants, settings, move sequences, and communicative goals.

Definition/Scope

Classroom discourse research arose in the 1970s as a special focus within the new discipline of conversation analysis and early on identified some of the distinctive formal characteristics and social purposes of talk in schools. Research has generated descriptions of the forms of talk that are specific to academic contexts, characterizations of the rules that govern teacher–student talk, and accounts of the ways in which the development of language skills can be fostered or hindered in classrooms. As analytic tools have been applied to different kinds of school settings, the field has contributed to better understanding of varied issues such as the socialization of academic language, gender roles in classrooms, and processes of second-language learning in school.

Differences with Everyday Conversation

As early research convincingly documented, teacher–student talk proceeds according to different rules and conventions than everyday conversation. These arise from the social purposes of much classroom talk, which center on the teacher's presentation of academic content and assessment of students' uptake of information. Largely absent from teacher–student communication are the phatic exchanges that are common in other forms of everyday talk: "How's it going?" Instead, teachers lecture, ask questions to check on student understanding, and provide brief evaluations of the adequacy of students' responses ("Good!" or "Anyone else?").

At the level of individual utterances, classroom talk often displays features of decontextualized language such as nominalizations (multiplication, thinking), and embedded clauses (such as that-clauses). Classroom discourse incorporates these features because teachers and students often talk about abstract concepts or entities that are physically absent from the context of conversation: carbon bonds, the Treaty of Paris, animal habitats, and the thoughts and feelings of fictional characters. In contrast to the topics of much everyday conversation outside of classrooms, the referents for classroom topics are often not visible or mutually accessible through other nonverbal channels, for example, through shared activity ("Could you hand me that?" "We can tackle it later."). The potentially supportive role of shared physical and social context is often diminished and therefore, in classroom discourse, interactants are typically obliged to use more explicit and verbally elaborated strategies for describing their conversational topics. Topical referents need to be first introduced through talk and then disambiguated and elaborated upon through verbal commentary. Repeated reference to the same topic is usually accomplished through definite reference in classroom talk (the theme of the story, the lesson, or the point) rather than through the deictic strategies more commonly used in thematic progression in everyday informal conversation (it, this, or that).

Classroom discourse is often motivated by the need to build up shared and elaborated understandings of particular topics over time, for example, across the course of a unit or academic year; thus teachers and students use a variety of strategies to mark what is jointly understood and remembered about a topic.

Asymmetric Roles

A notable characteristic of teacher–pupil talk is an asymmetry of speaking roles: teachers lecture and ask questions and students answer the questions that are posed to them. Teachers dominate and monopolize the conversational floor in classrooms at every stage of the educational system, taking longer and more frequent turns than student participants. In contrast to other types of conversation in which children and young people can take more varied roles, in classroom discourse, teachers typically reserve the right to introduce new conversational topics and to engage in most forms of questioning. Teachers control access to the conversational floor through nominating respondents to their questions ("Hands, please!") and often through limiting opportunities for side conversations or talk on student-initiated topics. In addition, different from other conversational contexts, many of the questions that teachers pose are close-ended, questions that require only minimal or fragmentary responses from students. The forms of teacher questions largely determine that syntax and degree of elaboration of student responses:

Teacher: Where do most cats live?
→ Student: Houses?
Teacher: They live in houses, right.

Many teacher questions take the form of what have been called display or known-answer questions. Unlike what have been termed authentic questions, display questions require students to present information that is already known to the teacher.

→ Teacher: So what's the title of the story that we read?
Student: The Sea Serpent.

Student responses to known-answer questions are often quite brief; the point is to demonstrate recognition of the right answer rather than to present a unique or personal perspective on the topic. Responses to known-answer questions are often only interpretable within the context of the preceding teacher talk:

Teacher: Let me see your folder first. The book report cover. Okay, what do you have here? What's that? (points)
→ Student: Title.

Teachers' open-ended questions, on the other hand, require students to construct relatively autonomous turns that often present new information about the topic:

Teacher: Do you have a prediction about that?

Student: I think if we keep rolling the dice, we'll keep getting numbers under 30. Because the dice numbers aren't that big and if you multiply them, it will be like 20 and 16 and 10 and 8 like we have been getting.

Responses to open-ended question often elicit students' most sophisticated language skills, requiring vocabulary that is specialized for particular subject areas and grammatical forms that include conditionals, subjunctives, and embedded clauses.

Three-Part Sequence

Much classroom interaction follows a three-part scheme, where the teacher first initiates a question–answer sequence, followed by a response from a student who either volunteers or is selected by the teacher to respond. A third element in what has been called an I–R–E structure is an optional teacher evaluation move, offering feedback to the student about the adequacy of his or her response. These three-part question–answer exchanges create the framework for most student contributions to talk within classrooms, typically alternating with longer stretches of teacher monolog or lecture.

Teacher: Do you know what that means, when they say water's getting rough?
Student: That the water's like getting wavier?
Teacher: Right.

Teachers use I–R–E exchanges for several social and pedagogical purposes: to assess student background knowledge before introducing a new topic or reintroducing a subject; to assess student uptake of new information, to break up monologic presentations of information; to mark transitions between topics; and to re-engage students whose attention may be flagging. Many teacher questions do not immediately elicit the desired response; thus classroom discourse often includes extended elicitation sequences in which the teacher repeats or reshapes the original question, seeking a closer approximation of a correct answer through hints, simplifications, and restatements:

Teacher: Look at the cover and tell me what you think the story will be about.
Student: It's about animals.
→ Teacher: What kind?
Student: Cats. Mice.

The teacher evaluation moves that follow partial or incorrect answers ("What kind?") provide cues to students that their expressed understanding of the topic is not yet fully adequate. A positive evaluation move by the teacher often serves to not only confirm the adequacy of an answer but can also mark the end of a particular topical focus (we're clear about this aspect of the topic now) and can set up a shift in lesson focus:

Teacher: What's a landing? If you're in a boat, what's a landing?

Student: Oh you like go to the um to the um sand?

Teacher: You go to the where?

Student: To the sand, uh the boat.

Teacher: To the sand?

Student: Where the people are, where you play.

Teacher: You mean what, you go back to. . .?

Student: Where you were.

Teacher: Where you were. What's that called? What's that called, where you were?

Student: You go back to the shore?

→ Teacher: To the shore, very good. Good word. So it's a rough landing because, why? Why was it a rough landing? What was pushing them in? They thought it was the wind, but what was it?

Student: A sea serpent?

Teacher: The sea serpent was pushing them in and it made for a rough landing.

Effects on Opportunities for Student Participation

The combined effects of several characteristics of classroom discourse: teachers' monopoly over the introduction of conversation topics and access to the floor, teacher preferences for closed questions, and the use of I–R–E sequences, all may serve to limit opportunities for extended student participation. Student turns are short in many classroom contexts because student contributions function most often to ratify, rather than expand upon topics introduced by the teacher. Although the topics of classroom talk often call for decontextualized word choices and sentence patterns, very often student turns are grammatically incomplete because they respond to closed teacher questions that require only a yes/no or phrasal response (e.g., sodium, 1815, in Philadelphia, and sad). The goal of developing student thinking and mastery of content through talk is often subordinated to the more local goal of getting the right answer on the floor.

Socialization into Academic Registers

Classrooms present opportunities not only for learning academic content but also for learning how to talk about academic topics. Children begin school with discourse histories that reflect the norms and interactional practices of their families and communities. For some children, these include an expectation of close adult attention to child-initiated topics, considerable experience with holding the conversational floor, and experience of frequent encouragement from

adults to say more, to verbally elaborate on intentions, feelings, and beliefs. Not all cultures, however, view children as entitled to set the topics and take long turns in adult–child interaction. As a result, many children begin school with greater reticence in adult-dominated conversation and with less willingness to go beyond what is minimally required in adult–child exchanges. Children also start school with varying degrees of facility with the vocabulary and syntax of academic talk, including knowledge of verbs for talking about cognition (e.g., wonder, suppose, predict, and imagine), and understanding of academic vocabulary, for example, terms commonly used in primary schooling such as add, uppercase, government, and story character. These contrasts in children's preparation for engagement in academic talk often reflect differences in family social status, parental education levels, and cultural beliefs. Parents who have experienced success through the educational system seek, often unconsciously, to reproduce that success for their children through home-socialization strategies aimed at producing verbal responsivity and fluency within some of the adult–child questioning and responding routines that are characteristic of classrooms. Children from educated families enter school with experiences from family contexts like shared book reading and mealtime talk that position them to be highly responsive and confident in classroom discourse. Other children look for cues in classroom interaction on how to participate competently, often waiting for adult guidance and prompting.

Among the tasks that children face in learning how to engage in classroom talk in the early years (and that older students face at junctures in their education as well) include acquiring the vocabulary for particular academic subjects and learning to recognize the varied forms of participation that are required in response to different types of teacher questions: "Who can tell us something about penguins?" "How did you feel when the parents couldn't find Sylvester?" "Why do we need to regroup when we're adding 15 and 6?" To be successful participants, children need to know what content is relevant to particular academic contexts and the discourse shape this content should be presented in, for example, a request for a personal response to an event in a work of literature requires the expression of emotion state words (sad, worried) followed up by specific references to details in the literary work (his mom and dad walked right next to him and couldn't tell that he was there). Some teacher questions require fragmentary answers while others signal in subtle or more marked ways that more extended student responses are required.

Classroom Speech Events

Similar to talk outside of classrooms, classroom discourse is organized into speech events or subroutines that are set off from the flow of talk by movement into particular settings: the book corner, the lab table, the rug, or by formal announcements, "It's time for morning meeting." Classroom speech events incorporate specific participants (the reading group members, lab partners, or the whole class) and specialized participant roles that children learn through participation: everyone will get a chance to speak, only one child speaks at a time, and a newsworthy contribution will merit an extended turn at speaking. Teachers use overt cues, "Let's turn on our listening ears now," and more implicit signals, for example, shifts in posture or eye gaze, to mark the initiation of specialized talk sequences. Classroom speech events typically follow a predictable sequence of moves, such as reciting names for attendance, doing a weather and calendar chart, and presenting personal news, the moves of a morning meeting speech event within many early childhood classrooms in the US. Moves within speech events also have differentiated rules governing access to speaking rights (going around the room one by one for attendance; raising hands to be selected to tell personal news) and moves have their own internal discourse structure, for example, the narrative forms required for telling personal news. The complexities of classroom speech events pose challenges to students at all stages of schooling; however, teacher talk provides support in acquiring the desired forms.

Modeling

One of the ways that teachers help children learn how to participate in classroom talk is through direct modeling of the desired response or response type. Teachers frequently answer their own questions in order to get some approximation of the sought-after response on the floor and to provide models for students of the kind of responses they are seeking. Teachers often effectively fill both slots, questioner and respondent, in the interactional sequence:

Teacher: What kind of a soup is it – how would you describe pea soup?
Student: Mmm. . . (shrugs)
Teacher: Hard to describe, huh? What does it look like?
Student: It's like it's a bunch of peas inside a pan with water.
→ Teacher: And the water's called broth and broth is real, real thick. Have you ever had it? It's a real thick – you know how some soups are almost watery?
Students: Yeah.
→ Teacher: Well this is real, real thick. And I want you to remember that cause that has something to do with why this story is called, "Pea Soup".

Modeling is especially commonplace in classrooms for students who are second-language learners or speakers of nonstandard dialects. Teacher support through modeling

is also particularly common in classrooms where students are being introduced to new topics or initiated into new classroom speech events.

Scaffolding

Teachers use a wide range of scaffolding strategies to help students articulate the desired answers to the questions they pose. These include calling on another student ("Maybe Stephen can help."), evaluating an answer as only partially correct ("Not quite."), and providing concrete strategies for arriving at a better response ("Read to the end of the sentence." "Look at the board."). Scaffolding works towards the goal of having the student arrive at the correct answer and often forestalls a negative teacher evaluation.

Teacher: Okay. Right there, what does it mean, ". . .the helicopter descended"
Student: Slowed down.
→ Teacher: Not quite.
Student: Stopped.
→ Teacher: Read to the end of the sentence.
Student: Oh, "came down".

Recasts

Teachers also offer recasts or expansions of student responses that fall short of the desired answer. Frequently, these teacher moves repeat the student's response, substituting more elaborate syntax, more precise vocabulary, or language specific to the academic subject:

Teacher: How would you get the answer?
Student: I would times it.
→ Teacher: So you times the two numbers, or multiply them to get the answer.

These moves juxtapose the learner's response with a response that expresses the same content more formally, recasts are particularly effective in promoting acquisition of the vocabulary and syntax of academic language.

Learning Specialized Academic Registers

Teacher coaching and support are often needed as students begin to participate in talk within particular academic registers. The discourse of mathematics, for example, differs in many dimensions from the ways teachers and students talk about literature, even in the early years of schooling. Mathematics talk includes generalizations about the rules governing number relations and often presents hypothetical operations upon numbers. Talk about literature, on the other hand, incorporates elements of narration (e.g., descriptions of character actions and reactions) and values direct citation from the literary text. Children learn that they are often called upon to relate a personal response or read a supporting passage during literature discussions, but virtually never are asked for these kinds of contributions during mathematics lessons.

In learning to talk in different ways during particular subject lessons, students begin to understand some of the ways of thinking that are characteristic of particular academic disciplines, for example, literary analysis' close attention to the text and mathematics' concern with the hypothetical and with logical proof and demonstration. These ways of thinking are embodied in language practices that are pervasive in classroom talk, even in the primary grades. The most successful teachers explicitly prompt students to produce discipline-specific talk and provide rich models and explanations of the language rules that operate within the disciplines.

Teacher Talk and Particular Populations

Classroom discourse research has been particularly helpful in elucidating language practices that both support and hinder the progress of particular groups of learners in schools. Second-language learners, speakers of nonstandard dialects, and girls, all face particular challenges in participating successfully in classroom talk.

Second-Language Learners

Schooling in a language of instruction that is not students' home language is common across the developing world and in communities with immigrant students in developed countries. In addition, in many countries, students from language minority communities are schooled in a national language such as English, Spanish, or Malay. Thus, many students must simultaneously acquire a new language in school and learn new academic vocabulary and discourse practices. Teachers whose students are still acquiring the language of instruction often simplify their talk and augment verbal exposition with gesture, demonstration, and illustration. Clarification sequences, where teachers use multiple interactional moves to clarify their meaning or their students' intended meaning, are commonplace in bilingual classrooms. Code-shifting and code-mixing, in which teachers and pupils alternate or mix languages within or across turns, are also common in second-language classrooms. Teachers and peers use code alternation both as a strategy for bridging or repairing communication gaps and as a social practice. Teachers who are themselves bilingual may present academic content in the national language but shift into a community language for greater clarity, for disciplinary exchanges ("¡Dámelo!"— Give it to me!), or to mark a boundary between whole class and private, off-the-record communication. Students

may read aloud in the official language but shift into the home language when offering commentary on the text. Such practices in second language classrooms are natural extensions of the complexities of language use in multilingual communities and may in fact promote more rapid acquisition of the target language.

Speakers of Nonstandard Dialects

For students who are speakers of nonstandard dialects such as African-American vernacular English, classroom talk can be a productive context for acquiring a second, standard dialect or alternatively, a context for depreciation of community language norms. Although some teachers expect standard forms in all contexts of classroom communication, many teachers, particularly those working in language minority communities, hold differentiated expectations for the appropriateness of community dialects within different classroom speech contexts. These teacher expectations often mirror community beliefs about the appropriateness of dialect or standard language forms in particular contexts. For example, children may be corrected or prompted for use of the standard dialect when reading text aloud or in recitation contexts but may be allowed to use nonstandard forms in problem-solving groups and in private teacher–student exchanges. Classroom regulation of the use of nonstandard forms begins as early as preschool, through prompts like, "No street talk, Frankie," and accelerates as school-aged children acquire skills in two dialects and develop sensitivities to the social contexts that are intertwined with dialect variation.

Children's dialect patterns often extend beyond nonstandard word choices and syntactic constructions although these sentence-level differences with the standard dialect are especially likely to be targets of teacher corrections and recasts. Particularly complex and potentially problematic in classrooms are dialect patterns that affect discourse organization and participation roles, such as preferences for overlapping turns at talking, extended silences after teacher questions, or topical chaining in narrative discourse. When teachers and students do not share discourse styles, the task of acquiring skill within academic registers is particularly difficult. Teachers may interpret students' discourse patterns as signs of defiance, academic inadequacy, or failure to understand classroom-speaking rules. If there is little teacher awareness of differences in the discourse rules between the school's language and the language of many students, classroom discourse may be experienced as a context for failure, misunderstanding, or shaming.

Gender and Participation

The participation of girls and women in classrooms has been the focus of special investigation. In gender-mixed classrooms, particularly at the secondary level, boys often volunteer to speak more readily than their female classmates and hold the floor longer when they are called on to contribute. Girls engage in more hedging in their contributions, diminishing their degree of commitment to the points they are presenting through verbal downgraders, such as "kinda," "maybe," "I think," and through question intonation when they make statements. Male students have been observed engaging in more floor competition, overlapping a classmate's turn before he or she is done speaking, and calling out answers even when the teacher is using a nomination strategy to select the next speaker turn. Although girls' language development is often in advance of male classmates', the rules of classroom engagement do not necessarily favor girls' development. In fact, boys often occupy a middle position in the classroom social hierarchy, taking on some of the roles that are reserved for teachers when they produce longer floor-holding turns, carry on side conversations, and challenge classmates for control of the conversational floor.

Conclusion/Evaluation

Classroom talk serves as a critical context for the acquisition of more sophisticated language skills and for children's socialization of academic identities. As early as preschool, children learn through contexts like classroom sharing time and morning meeting to participate in talk about physically and temporally absent topics: our family's weekend events, yesterday's weather, my pet. Different from many home contexts for extended discourse, the audience for such talk – peers and teachers – may lack first-hand knowledge of the entities that the child is talking about. Thus, classroom communication creates an essential motivation for learning to be clearer and more explicit than is typically required of children as they participate in everyday family talk.

The topics of classroom communication often draw upon children's most advanced vocabulary and cognitive skills and require that children use newly acquired metacognitive verbs and complex syntax: conditional, subjunctive, and embedded clauses. Teachers (and sometimes peers) are often demanding as communicative partners, pushing for greater clarity and elaboration, and providing models for the use of academic vocabulary and sophisticated sentence structures. For children who speak other languages or dialects at home, classroom talk provides especially rich opportunities for language learning, although these opportunities may be blunted by failure to respect and include a role for the home language or dialect in school.

Although the field of classroom discourse began with critiques of the inauthentic character of much classroom talk and was accompanied by skepticism about classrooms as environments for language learning, research of the past 15 years has demonstrated that many aspects of classroom talk support language learning and cognitive development. Teacher roles in modeling academic language and scaffolding effective contributions appear in the light of contemporary research to be much more positive than was suggested by earlier commentary. Teachers often use knowledge of the learner's current stage of development to offer prompts that press for expression of the learner's best understandings. Although the strategies teachers employ are inauthentic when compared to many adult roles in everyday conversational exchanges, teacher talk is often well adapted to the cognitive and interpersonal purposes of the classroom. Student-participation slots are often constrained and limited in classroom talk, but the simplification and orchestration of student contributions support an ability to focus on content and on precision of expression.

See also: Language and Literacy in Educational Settings.

Further Reading

Cazden, C. B. (2001). *Classroom Discourse: The Language of Learning and Teaching*, 2nd edn. Portmouth, NH: Heinemann.

Edwards, A. D. and Westgate, D. P. (1994). *Investigating Classroom Talk*. London: Falmer Press.

Edwards, D. and Mercer, N. (1987). *Common Knowledge: The Development of Understanding in the Classroom*. London: Methuen.

Lemke, J. L. (1990). *Talking Science: Language, Learning, and Values*. Norwood, NJ: Ablex.

McHoul, A. (1990). The organization of repair in classrooms. *Language in Society* **19**, 349–377.

Mehan, H. (1979). *Learning Lessons: Social Organization in a Classroom*. Cambridge, MA: Harvard University Press.

Nystrand, M. (1997). *Opening Dialogue: Understanding the Dynamics of Language and Learning in the English Classroom*. New York, NY: Teachers College Press.

O'Connor, M. C. and Michaels, S. (1993). Aligning academic task and participation status through revoicing: Analysis of a classroom discourse strategy. *Anthropology and Education Quarterly* **24**, 318–335.

Sinclair, J. M. and Coulthard, R. M. (1975). *Towards an Analysis of Discourse: The English used by Teachers and Pupils*. London: Oxford.

Snow, C. E. and Dickinson, D. K. (1991). Skills that aren't basic in a new conception of literacy. In Jennings, E. M. and Purves, A. C. (eds.) *Literate Systems and Individual Lives: Perspectives on Literacy and Schooling*, pp 179–191. Albany, NY: State University of New York Press.

Relevant Websites

http://childes.psy.cmu.edu – CHILDES: The Child Language Data Exchange System.

http://www.leaonline.com/loi/dp – Discourse Processes, Lawrence Erlbaum Associates.

http://www.societyfortextanddiscourse.org – Society for Text and Discourse.

http://talkbank.org – TalkBank.

Learning Outside of School

T Nunes, University of Oxford, Oxford, UK

Introduction

Learning is the acquisition of knowledge. Learning may be about new ideas, symbols, ways of performing (more automatically, more flexibly), or the use of something known in a new way (learning transfer). Learning happens everywhere but it is easy not to notice this because we are used to linking teaching and learning, so we tend to look for learning where there is teaching. This leads to a focus on learning in schools, colleges, and universities. In this article, the focus is on learning outside school, where much learning takes place without teaching.

This analysis is organized by a series of contrasts, which aim at making visible what is often invisible, because what we learn outside school is seen as common sense, everyday knowledge, social knowledge, professional knowledge – that is, knowledge that is taken for granted, which is part of the general culture or part of the culture of a group. "Like fish in water, we fail to 'see' culture because it is the medium within which we exist" (Cole, 1996). By contrasting learning in and out of school, a picture of the products and the processes of learning outside school are sketched. However, before we work our way through these contrasts, it must be said that looking at learning outside school is not a criticism of school learning. Schools have specific aims and functions, and one of these is to make learning an explicitly pursued venture, where the knowledge obtained can be examined critically and communicated; thus its refinement and transmission are, if not assured, made more likely, so that future generations may inherit it and build on it. Informal knowledge and learning are, by comparison, more difficult to share and their future is uncertain.

Formal and Informal Learning and Knowledge

Eraut (2000) proposed a definition of formal learning on the basis of these characteristics: (1) a prescribed learning framework; (2) an organized learning event or package; (3) the presence of a designated teacher or trainer; (4) the award of a qualification or credit; and (5) the external specification of outcomes. Not all of these are necessary to define formal learning; any one may suffice, but they tend to go together. Outside school, learning happens without explicit learning outcomes, a curriculum, or a designated teacher. The contrast between formal and informal learning also applies to knowledge: formal knowledge receives recognition and informal knowledge, though often necessary for learning formal knowledge, does not. In fact, informal knowledge is taken for granted, considered obvious, and only identified as an achievement through research.

An example from mathematics learning can help clarify the difference between informal and formal knowledge. Outside school, children are used to sharing different sorts of things: chocolate bars, sweets, turns in games, etc. They learn that these are not shared in the same way. For example, turns in games are not a matter of equal shares: one child's turn ends when a mistake is made, so you skip rope until you step on it, you play the video-game until the game is over. Turns in games are earned and regulated by the rules of the game. It is rather different when children share a chocolate bar or sweets: the assumption is that the shares will be equal, even if perfect equivalence of the shares is not attained. Children also learn through sharing that, the more people sharing, the smaller each one's share will be. This informal knowledge of fractional quantities requires an insight into the inverse relation between the divisor (i.e., the number by which something is divided) and the quotient (i.e., the result of the division). Few 5-year-olds realize this, but the majority of 7-year-olds knows it. This important insight into mathematical relations can be used to give meaning to the learning of fractions in school. However, this idea is neither taught nor receives recognition in school – it is taken for granted and not perceived as knowledge of fractions. Children are only credited with knowledge of fractions if the symbols used to represent fractions are involved in the questions that they are asked. The formal equivalent of this insight would be to know, for example, which fraction is bigger, 1/3 or 1/5. If the children can answer this, they are credited with some knowledge of fractions.

What is the difference between these two forms of knowledge, if they involve the same insight into the inverse relation between the divisor and the quotient? The comparison between 1/3 and 1/5 is a comparison of two written symbols; mastery of written symbols and their manipulations are recognized school-learning outcomes. The oral forms one-third and one-fifth are readings of these written forms, and as such they also obtain recognition in school. In contrast, when one talks about one chocolate shared among three children, and one chocolate shared among five children, this is a description of a situation, and its understanding is not given the same status as comparing two symbols that have a general meaning. Schools include in their curriculum the teaching of fractions through formal representations that can be used to designate quantities; they typically do not aim at teaching children about sharing chocolates or sweets – children should learn this at home or in preschool.

This example illustrates how some forms of knowledge are seen as aims for formal teaching and learning, whereas others are not. Two aspects of formal knowledge in this case merit further consideration – the emphasis on written versus oral forms of knowledge and the emphasis on general versus specific and situated knowledge. Each of these contrasts is discussed in turn in the context of mathematics knowledge.

Written and Oral Practices

The three R's – reading, writing, and 'rithmetic – are standard aims of Western schooling. The emphasis on written practices and their transmission is a mark of schooling; people are divided into literate and non-literate for comparative descriptions of the level of education across countries. There is no similar distinction in mathematics but the emphasis on mastering the use of written symbols is so strong in school that knowledge necessary to learn these symbols can be taken for granted and not recognized as a form of knowledge.

Analyses of written and oral arithmetic practices emerged as the interest in contrasting European and African thinking grew in anthropology and psychology. Gay and Cole (1967), Zaslavsky (1973), Reed and Lave (1981), and Lancy (1983) described mathematical thinking learned without schooling, in the market, playing games, or in the course of learning a trade. Perhaps the most systematic description of mathematics learned outside school was carried out in Brazil. The Brazilian school curriculum includes teaching children to write and read numbers and to calculate using algorithms applied to written symbols. The focus on the use of written symbols and their manipulation renders children's knowledge of mathematics developed outside school invisible. Therefore, many children fail arithmetic assessments in school when they are perfectly able to perform the same calculations outside school.

A powerful demonstration of the difference between mathematics learned in and out of school comes from a study where five young vendors working in the informal economy, selling produce at street markets and corners, were asked to solve the same set of problems as part of their commercial activities and, later, in school-like situations (Nunes *et al.*, 1993). The children were very successful when they solved problems in the course of their work in the market: 98% of their answers were correct. In contrast, when they were presented with the same numbers in the form of computation exercises, only 37% of their answers were correct. The main difference between what the children did in these two situations was that they solved the problems in the market using oral numbers – they spoke to the customers as they solved the problems – whereas they tried to solve the operations by writing them down and using the computation routines that they had been taught in school. **Figure 1(a)** shows a young vendor in his work setting, a beach in Brazil. **Table 1** presents a contrast between how one of these young people solved the same

Figure 1 (a) A young vendor selling ice-cream on the beach. (b) A young man selling hats.

Table 1   A child's answers to 35 × 4

M, a boy aged 12 years, who had 5 years of schooling, was presented with the question 35 × 4 when selling coconuts and later asked to solve the same sum.

In the informal setting:

Customer: I'm going to take four coconuts (each coconut costs 35 Cruzeiros, the Brazilian currency at the time). How much is that?

M: Three will be 105, plus 30, that's 135 . . . one coconut is 35 . . . that is. . . 140 (. . . indicates pauses where the intonation suggests that the sentence is still being continued).

Solving the computation exercise 35 × 4:

C writes down 35 × 4 in the traditional arrangement, with 35 on one line and × 4 under it, and calculates out loud: Four times five is 20, carry the two (writes 0 as a partial answer). Two plus three is five, times four is 20 (writes 20 to the left of the zero). 200.

From Nunes, T., Schliemann, A. D., and Carraher, D. W. (1993). *Street Mathematics and School Mathematics*. New York: Cambridge University Press, p 24.

arithmetic problem presented as part of a sale and later, as a computation exercise.

Brazilian young people and adults who had different occupations – fishermen, carpenters, farmers, and foremen in construction sites – and either no, or at most primary, schooling can solve many different types of problem without recourse to written symbols. Their learning outside school enables them to solve problems with any of the four basic arithmetic operations and different contents: finding out the unit price from the price for a lot, how much wood is required for building a piece of furniture, how much shrimp a fisherman has to fish if a customer wants a certain amount of shelled shrimp, how many liters of wine are needed to fill a certain number of bottles, or the size of a wall from its representation on a scale drawing. Calculating with negative numbers, simple proportions, averages, area, and volume are within the domains of what can be learned outside school. What is learned depends on the trade but the type of reasoning is not trade specific. For example, fishermen know roughly how much shelled shrimp they can get from a certain amount of untreated shrimp. They are also able to apply this proportional reasoning to agricultural products: if they are told how much cassava flour you can get from a certain amount of cassava, they can use this information to say how much cassava flour you can get from other amounts of cassava. Learning arithmetic on the job, outside school, does not only lead to job-specific knowledge, but also leads to a more general understanding of how to operate with quantities.

General versus Specific Learning

Schools are transitional places. Students are not being prepared to be students, but to go on to do something

else. Neither they nor their teachers know what they will do after they leave school. The solution to this difficult task of preparing students for doing something not yet specified is to try to teach them general knowledge, which could be used in many different occupations and settings. The expectation is that they will be able to apply this general knowledge to specific situations in which it is required. However, the application of general knowledge to specific settings is not a trivial matter. Spatial learning illustrates well the issues of general and specific knowledge. General spatial knowledge is about how to organize space: left and right, north and south, east and west can combined with measures of space and knowledge of shapes to support spatial learning. This knowledge can be used when we arrive in a new town, but it is not the same as knowing the town. We get to know the town by looking at maps, going around, recognizing landmarks, and ordering them so that we know what is farther north than what. This type of spatial learning involves the acquisition of specific knowledge, and also more general learning: when we use a map to get to know a town, we also learn about using maps in a more general way.

General spatial knowledge can be learned in school; getting to know a town requires learning outside school. When we focus on getting to know a town, we use general spatial knowledge embedded in the knowledge of the town. We may not say "going north" but say "going towards the Bronx"; this latter way of speaking often reduces the number of steps in our thinking about spatial relations. There is often a tension between the use of general knowledge, which is focused on general representations, and the use of specific knowledge, where these representations are interpreted through the meanings that they have in the situation where we learn. This contrast is explored in the next section.

Focus on Representations versus Focus on Meaning

Concept learning involves putting meanings together with their representations, which are often conventional. Learning vocabulary, for example, which starts many years before school, is about learning words – a verbal representation – and their meanings. Although representations and meanings are closely related, learning outside school influences the way we speak: we speak about the meanings rather than about the general aspects of knowledge.

A very simple example, which we encountered in our study of mathematics learned outside school, is that of a 9-year-old boy, R, solving a problem in a simulated shop situation. He used written arithmetic to solve the problem, as he would have used in school, but it was his understanding of the meaning in the situation that showed him that something had gone wrong with his calculations.

Table 2 presents an extract of his interaction with the interviewer.

A school-like argument, which a teacher could present to R, would be: if you take something away from 200, the answer cannot be 200 or greater than 200. This argument, formulated in a general way, contrasts with R's argument, which has the same sense but is presented embedded in the meaning that 200 has in this situation. He argues that he should not hand back to the customer the 200 note that the customer just gave him.

The focus on meaning when learning happens on the job was also observed by Noss *et al.* (1999), who asked nurses to read blood pressure charts and say what average blood pressure meant. Students usually learn in school a concept of average as a measure of central tendency, used to describe a population. Nurses look at blood pressure charts to see whether changes in the blood pressure of a patient are significant enough to call for medication. This gives them a different concept of average, as they add to the mathematical concept the meaning normal for the patient, which is not part of the mathematical concept. When they look at a blood pressure chart, they do not calculate the mean but consider the variation of the measurements, estimate the average to be around the most frequent value at the center of these variations, and then make a judgment about the need for medication. The meaning of average is placed in the context of their activities. When asked about the variations that are observed in the chart for a child, they think about what the child could have been doing at the time. In a statistics class, these could be treated as random variations or

Table 2 Using meaning to assess the results of a computation

Interviewer (I): Now I'm buying this, and it costs 35 Cruzeiros. I'm going to pay with a 200 note. How much will you give me back?
R: (writes 200–35 in the traditional alignment, and says): Five, to get to zero, nothing. Three, to get to zero, nothing. Two, take away nothing, two.
I: Is it right?
R: No. So you buy something from me, and it costs 35, you pay with a 200-cruzeiro note and I give it back to you?
I: Do it again, then.
R: (writes down 200–35 in the same way) Five, take away nothing, five. Three, take away zero, three. Two, take away nothing, two. Wrong again.
I: Why is it wrong again?
R: Now you buy something and it costs 35. You give me 200 and I give you 200, and 35 on top?
I: Do you know what the result is?
R: If it were to cost 30, then I'd give you one seventy.
I: But it is 35. Are you giving me a discount?
R: 165.

From Nunes, T., Schliemann, A. D., and Carraher, D. W. (1993). *Street Mathematics and School Mathematics*. New York: Cambridge University Press, p 46.

measurement error. A quote from an interview illustrates this focus on the meaning of average interpreted in situational terms.

She was... it was settled here, the early hours of the morning. ... I don't know, what with the activities of the day probably getting on top of her here, so she's probably a bit more agitated there, so you could allow for the increase [in blood pressure], or whatever. But probably in the morning she's more settled. ... Yeah, I'd like to think that she was asleep then, so she had a settled blood pressure (Noss *et al.*, 1999: 37).

Noss *et al.* (2007) further illustrate this attribution of meaning in another situation where graph reading was learned on the job. Jim, a shift leader in a large factory that makes plastic sheets, had learned, through 31 years of experience on the job, to read the complex graphs that recorded variations in tension and temperature of the materials over time and at different places in the production process. When a problem occurred in the production process, he would take the graphs and examine what was happening just before the problem occurred. Using this information, he was able to identify the location of the problem, and maintenance engineers would then be called in to check the item he had identified as the likely cause. This was not seen by the chemical engineer, who was responsible for the overall production, as a simple accomplishment: Jim had to be able to identify readings in a graph as normal, thus attributing to them a meaning that was learned in the situation. She described briefly what he had done in one instance when he thought that one straight line on the graph (which contained many different lines, including some straight ones) looked too good to be true.

By examining the "revs [revolutions] per minute" historical data and seeing that it wasn't fluctuating as Jim expected but was a constant value, he determined something was wrong with it. He alerted the maintenance engineers who found the motor on the controller had been fitted to run backward after some work done on it the previous day and so the signal it was sending for revs per minute was false. Jim doesn't know anything about motor control – he just knew that the historical data looked "wrong" (Noss *et al.*, 2007: 377).

Thus the process of learning on the job, outside school, involves going beyond the information given in the representations, by attributing to them specific meanings taken from the situation, which the representations would not convey by themselves. R's argument that it is not sensible to return to a customer the note that he just received in payment for a merchandise, the nurses reading into the blood chart that the child's blood pressure was settled while she was asleep and went up when the activities started in the ward, and Jim's identification of a specific straight line on the graph as too good to be true, all exemplify this process of going beyond the information given in the symbols by imbuing them with situation-specific meaning.

Thought versus Action

Sylvia Scribner, one of the most distinguished researchers of learning outside school, argued that models of the mind based on the metaphor of the mind as a computer fail to capture those significant aspects of learning that are based on action. In a series of works about thinking in action (Tobach *et al.*, 1997), she reasoned that learning, memory, and thinking in everyday life are not separate from what we do but part of what we do. Therefore, what we do is also part of our learning, memory, and thinking. In order to develop this argument, she drew on Luria's (1973) concept of functional systems as the basis for higher mental functions. Luria's example of how memory works helps us understand the basic notion that there is no opposition between thinking and action, or mental and manual work. When we want to remember something, we might repeat what we want to remember many times to ourselves, and be able to recall it later. However, our memory function would be greatly restricted if this were all we could do. Fortunately, we can also write down what we need to remember, and be so organized about where we write what down that we know where to look for the information when we need it. Therefore, Luria argued, memory is not an activity restricted to the brain: it can be accomplished through functional systems that maintain the task of remembering constant but accomplish it through a variety of means, including the incorporation of external objects into our memory system.

Learning outside school leads people to incorporate into their thinking systems the tools and the characteristics of the objects that are used in the environment. Scribner (in Tobach *et al.*, 1997: 338–366) analyzed how product assemblers in a dairy factory in the US incorporated the characteristics of packing into their thinking as they pre-packaged items for an order. Products were packed as different units: a case equals 4 gallons, 8 half-gallons, 16 quarts, 32 pints, or 48 half-pints. When a product assembler is putting together an order, he might have a load-out form that shows 1 – 6, that is, 1 case minus 6 units. If this order called for something that is packaged in quarts and the assembler filled it literally, he would start from a full case (which has 16 quarts) and remove six from it. However, this is not necessarily how assemblers work. If there is a half-empty case close by, the assembler is much more likely to add 2 units to it, translating the order into half-case plus 2, a solution that saves effort and time. Scribner compared product assemblers' performance with that of students,

who would be able to use the same reasoning but had not learned about assembling on the job and had limited experience of assembling products through their participation in Scribner's study. Product assemblers were about 3 times more likely to use effort-saving strategies than students, when these did not coincide with the literal solution. Learning on the job granted product assemblers greater flexibility in treating the units in cases as units of thinking: in the same way that we think easily using the decades of our number system, they had learned to use the units of packing as thinking units. Just looking at a half-full case of quarts allowed them to know that there were 8 units there, and move smoothly to the action of adding 2 units.

Scribner concluded from her different studies of thinking in action that higher-order solutions such as those illustrated above had a major effort-saving impact on the manual execution of the work: in one estimate, she concluded that literal solutions with one item assembled at a time would involve walking roughly 4 miles to complete the jobs; this contrasted with the actual solutions, which involved a little more than 2 miles. Assemblers had not learned this effort-saving from lingering over the order forms or engaging in discussions with each other. Thus, Scribner concluded, they must have learned by representing quantities and space in a way that synthesized the different forms of organizing and regulating their own actions; they learned by thinking in action.

The incorporation of cultural and cognitive tools into the learner's thinking system is not a defining characteristic of out-of-school learning. Wertsch (1998) provides a convincing example of this incorporation in his discussion of how we solve multi-digit multiplications. If we are asked to say what is 343 times 862 without using a calculator, we would write down these numbers in vertical alignment and carry out the algorithm that we learned in school. This algorithm is a cultural and cognitive tool, which we incorporate into our thinking, and without which we would not be able to solve the problem. It differs across countries slightly – for example, in some countries, when we multiply 343 by the 6 in 862, we write the product one row to the left. We are, in fact, multiplying 343 by 60, not by 6, and this is simplified by acting as if the multiplication is by 6, thereby making the multiplication routine more similar across the units, tens, and hundreds. Learners can carry out the procedure without full awareness of why a place is skipped in the process – they are, in this case, relying on a tool and downloading part of the difficulties of the process onto the paper-and-pencil record (to use Hatano's, 1997, expression).

Learning in and out of school is a process that allows people to participate in socially organized activities, so incorporating the tools that are used in these activities into our thinking is a common feature of learning in and out of school.

The Places and Processes of Learning

There are similarities between learning in and out of school. However, it is important not to forget the differences, which are related to how roles are defined for the teacher and the learner in and out of school, what is expected of each, and what is the focus of their attention as education takes place. Greenfield and Lave (1982) summarized, some years ago, the processes by which schooling and informal education seek to promote learning; the characteristics relevant to this analysis are presented in **Table 3**.

Their analysis can be complemented by a more detailed description of the implicit pedagogy that emerges from analyses of learning outside school. Rogoff (2003) analyzed how novice girl scouts become experts in selling cookies and how mothers guide their children's learning in a variety of settings outside school. She termed *guided participation* the implicit pedagogy used by adults outside school, a term that indicates that novices do not take full responsibility from the outset in learning situations, but still have some responsibility for the activities they engage in. Girl scouts are able to participate in selling cookies, even as novices, through the use of forms that they fill in, which work as tools that organize the activity, and through their interactions with peers, as they work together.

Rogoff distinguished different forms of guided participation when mothers have the role of tutors. In middle-class US families, adults organize child-centered learning events, and structure the children's learning by directing their attention, promoting their motivation, and maintaining their engagement. European and US middle-class mothers involve their children in events that are similar to school lessons in the family. Tizard and Hughes (2002) observed European mothers playing games that are aimed to prepare children for what they will learn in school (e.g., Mother: "I spy, with my little eye, something beginning with S"; child has to identify something in the room whose name begins with the letter S) and lesson-like activities in the home, where the mother writes something and the child copies it. Heath (1983) also observed, in the US, how mothers read stories to their children at bedtime and prepare them for adopting the concept of a story and for comprehension questions that are similar to those asked of children in school. In contrast, mothers from traditional societies, where tradition is a value, expect children to learn through watching and manage their own attention, motivation, and involvement. Rogoff cites examples from Japanese, Polynesian, and Mayan communities, where children are expected to learn through intent participation, being able to observe and listen in ongoing processes that were not set up for their learning. Guided participation then takes the form of encouragement of observation and responsive assistance, for example, rather than through school-like lessons enacted outside school.

Conclusion

In summary, learning outside school is learning in action, by doing something with an aim that is different from learning itself, by participation in an activity where the learner has some responsibility. Thinking in the course of these activities incorporates the representational tools and objects that are part of these activities, and does not single out, as more valuable, written over oral representations, or general over situated arguments and explanations. When using representational tools, such as number systems and graphs, people go beyond the information given in the representational tools, adding meanings from their learning in the situations where the tools are embedded. Outside school, learning is often guided, monitored, but not tested or given official recognition. There is no explicit curriculum, no designated teacher, no explicit learning outcome, and no accreditation – all of which make the learning that happens outside school invisible to some extent. The sample of studies presented here should help make out-of-school learning more visible, less taken for granted.

See also: Language and Literacy in Educational Settings; Learning in a Sociocultural Perspective; Situative View of Learning; Vygotsky and Recent Developments.

Table 3   Some of the idealized characteristics of informal and formal education

Informal education	Formal education
1. Embedded in daily-life activities	1. Set apart from the context of everyday life
2. Learner is responsible for obtaining knowledge and skill	2. Teacher is responsible for imparting knowledge and skill
3. Personal; relatives are appropriate as teachers	3. Impersonal; teachers should not be relatives
4. Little or no explicit pedagogy or curriculum	4. Explicit pedagogy and curriculum
5. Learning by observation and imitation	5. Learning by verbal interchange, questioning
6. Motivated by social contribution of novices and their participation (in real activities)	6. Less-strong social motivation

Some of the idealized characteristics of informal and formal education (adapted from Greenfield & Lave, 1982, p. 183) from the book CULTURAL PERSPECTIVES ON CHILD DEVELOPMENT ed. by D. A. Wagner and H. W. Stevenson. Copyright 1982 by W. H. Freeman. Reprinted by permission of Henry Holt and Comany, LLC.

Bibliography

Cole, M. (1996). *Cultural Psychology: A Once and Future Discipline*. Cambridge, MA: Belknap Press of Harvard University Press.

Eraut, M. (2000). Non-formal learning and tacit knowledge in professional work. *British Journal of Educational Psychology* **70**, 113–136.

Gay, J. and Cole, M. (1967). *The New Mathematics and an Old Culture. A Study of Learning among the Kpelle of Liberia*. New York: Holt, Rinehart and Winston.

Greenfield, P. and Lave, J. (1982). Cognitive aspects of informal education. In Wagner, D. A. and Stevenson, H. W. (eds.) *Cultural Perspectives on Child Development*, pp 181–207. San Francisco, CA: Freeman.

Hatano, G. (1997). Learning arithmetic with an abacus. In Nunes, T. and Bryant, P. (eds.) *Learning and Teaching Mathematics. An International Perspective*, pp 209–232. Hove: Psychology Press.

Heath, S. B. (1983). *Ways with Words: Language, Life and Work in Communities and Classrooms*. Cambridge: Cambridge University Press.

Lancy, D. F. (1983). *Cross-Cultural Studies in Cognition and Mathematics*. New York: Academic Press.

Luria, A. R. (1973). *The Working Brain. An Introduction to Neuropsychology*. Harmondsworth: Penguin.

Noss, R., Bakker, A., Hoyles, C., and Kent, P. (2007). Situating graphs as workplace knowledge. *Educational Studies in Mathematics* **65**, 367–384.

Noss, R., Pozzi, S., and Hoyles, C. (1999). Touching epistemologies: Meaning of average and variation in nursing practice. *Educational Studies in Mathematics* **40**, 25–51.

Nunes, T., Schliemann, A. D., and Carraher, D. W. (1993). *Street Mathematics and School Mathematics*. New York: Cambridge University Press.

Reed, H. J. and Lave, J. (1981). Arithmetic as a tool for investigating relations between culture and cognition. In Casson, R. W. (ed.) *Language, Culture and Cognition: Anthropological Perspectives*, pp 437–455. New York: Macmillan.

Rogoff, B. (2003). *The Cultural Nature of Human Development*. New York: Oxford University Press.

Tizard, B. and Hughes, M. (2002). *Young Children Learning*, 2nd edn. Oxford: Blackwell.

Tobach, E., Falmagne, R. J., Parlee, M. B., Martin, L. M. W., and Kapelman, A. S. (eds.) (1997). *Mind and Social Practice. Selected Writings of Sylvia Scribner*. Cambridge: Cambridge University Press.

Wertsch, J. V. (1998). *Mind as Action*. New York: Oxford University Press.

Zaslavsky, C. (1973). *Africa Counts: Number and Pattern in African Culture*. Westport, CT: Lawrence Hill.

Further Reading

Greenfield, P. M. (2004). *Weaving Generations Together. Evolving Creativity in the Maya of Chiapas*. Santa Fe, NM: School of American Research Press.

Lave, J. (1988). *Cognition in Practice*. Cambridge: Cambridge University Press.

Resnick, L. B., Levine, J. M., and Teasley, S. D. (eds.) (1991). *Perspectives on Socially Shared Cognition*, pp 349–364. Washington, DC: American Psychological Association.

Rogoff, B. and Lave, J. (1984). *Everyday Cognition*. Cambridge, MA: Harvard University Press.

Saxe, G. B. (1991). *Culture and Cognitive Development: Studies in Mathematical Understanding*. Hillsdale, NJ: Erlbaum.

Subject Index

Page numbers suffixed by t and f refer to tables and figures respectively.

Edwards Brothers Malloy
Ann Arbor MI. USA
December 21, 2016